Grand Challenges for Social Work and Society

Grand Challenges for Social Work and Society

SECOND EDITION

Richard P. Barth, Jill T. Messing, Trina R. Shanks, and James Herbert Williams

OXFORD
UNIVERSITY PRESS

Oxford University Press is a department of the University of Oxford. It furthers
the University's objective of excellence in research, scholarship, and education
by publishing worldwide. Oxford is a registered trade mark of Oxford University
Press in the UK and certain other countries.

Published in the United States of America by Oxford University Press
198 Madison Avenue, New York, NY 10016, United States of America.

© Oxford University Press 2022

All rights reserved. No part of this publication may be reproduced, stored in
a retrieval system, or transmitted, in any form or by any means, without the
prior permission in writing of Oxford University Press, or as expressly permitted
by law, by license, or under terms agreed with the appropriate reproduction
rights organization. Inquiries concerning reproduction outside the scope of the
above should be sent to the Rights Department, Oxford University Press, at the
address above.

You must not circulate this work in any other form
and you must impose this same condition on any acquirer.

Library of Congress Cataloging-in-Publication Data
Names: Barth, Richard P., 1952- editor.
Title: Grand challenges for social work and society / [edited by] Richard
P. Barth, Jill T. Messing, Trina R. Shanks, and James Herbert Williams.
Description: New York, NY : Oxford University Press, [2022] |
Earlier edition published: 2018. | Includes bibliographical references and index. |
Identifiers: LCCN 2021033431 (print) | LCCN 2021033432 (ebook) |
ISBN 9780197608043 (hardback) | ISBN 9780197608067 (epub) |
ISBN 9780197608074 (oso)
Subjects: LCSH: Social service.
Classification: LCC HV40 .G677 2022 (print) | LCC HV40 (ebook) |
DDC 361—dc23
LC record available at https://lccn.loc.gov/2021033431
LC ebook record available at https://lccn.loc.gov/2021033432

DOI: 10.1093/oso/9780197608043.001.0001

9 8 7 6 5 4 3 2

Printed by Integrated Books International, United States of America

CONTENTS

Acknowledgments ix
About the Editors xiii
About the Contributors xv

1. Introduction and Update on the Grand Challenges   1
   *Richard P. Barth, Marilyn L. Flynn, Trina R. Shanks,
   James Herbert Williams, Jill T. Messing, and Kira Silk*
   Mainstreaming Gender: Revisiting the Transformative Potential of
   Gender Mainstreaming in Social Work   8
   Kristy Kelly
2. Ensuring Healthy Development for Youth   19
   *Valerie B. Shapiro, Melissa A. Lippold, Kimberly Bender, and
   Jeffrey M. Jenson*
   Mainstreaming Gender: A Focus on Gender and Intersectionality
   Supports Healthy Youth Development   28
   Laurie M. Graham
3. Closing the Health Gap   47
   *Michael S. Spencer, Karina L. Walters, Audrey Begun, Heidi L. Allen,
   Teri Browne, Christina M. Andrews, Darrell P. Wheeler,
   Bradley J. Zebrack, Peter Maramaldi, John D. Clapp, Diana DiNitto,
   and Edwina Uehara*
   Mainstreaming Gender: Using Intersectional Gender Analysis to
   Make Visible Health (Care) Inequities   53
   Emma Carpenter and Anu Manchikanti Gómez
4. Building Healthy Relationships to End Violence   72
   *Richard P. Barth, Michelle Johnson-Motoyama, Melissa Jonson-Reid,
   Shanti J. Kulkarni, Todd I. Herrenkohl, Megan R. Holmes,
   Samuel R. Aymer, and Patricia L. Kohl*
   Mainstreaming Gender: Context Matters in Developing a Research
   Agenda to End Violence and Promote Healthy Relationships   76
   Heather L. Storer

5. Advancing Long and Productive Lives   111
   Ernest Gonzales, Christina Matz, Nancy Morrow-Howell,
   Patrick Ho Lam Lai, Cliff Whetung, Emma Zingg, Erin Keating,
   Jacquelyn B. James, and Michelle Putnam
   Mainstreaming Gender: An Analysis of Transportation among
   Older Adults   116
   Rupal Parekh and Rebecca L. Mauldin
6. Eradicating Social Isolation   145
   Suzanne Brown, Erika L. Sabbath, Robert L. Cosby, Melissa L. Bessaha,
   Michelle R. Munson, Jooyoung Kong, Sandra Edmonds Crewe,
   Elizabeth M. Tracy, and James E. Lubben
   Mainstreaming Gender: Critical Feminist Perspectives on
   Eradicating Social Isolation   147
   Karin Wachter
7. Ending Homelessness   181
   Benjamin F. Henwood, Emmy Tiderington, Amanda Aykanian,
   and Deborah K. Padgett
   Mainstreaming Gender: Inclusion of Transgender and Nonbinary
   People   183
   Jama Shelton
8. Creating Social Responses to a Changing Environment   201
   Susan P. Kemp, Lawrence A. Palinkas, Lisa Reyes Mason,
   Shanondora Billiot, Felicia M. Mitchell, and Amy Krings
   Mainstreaming Gender: Social Work's Transformative,
   Intersectional, Feminist Response to the Changing
   Environment   204
   Bonita B. Sharma
9. Harnessing Technology for Social Good   230
   Jonathan Bentley Singer, Melanie Sage, Stephanie Cosner Berzin,
   and Claudia J. Coulton
   Mainstreaming Gender: (Re)-harnessing Digital Technology for
   Social Good   235
   Megan Lindsay Brown
10. Promoting Smart Decarceration   257
    Pajarita Charles, Matthew W. Epperson, Phillipe Copeland, and
    Carrie Pettus-Davis
    Mainstreaming Gender: Understanding and Disrupting Gendered
    Social Control   261
    Gina L. Fedock
11. Reducing Extreme Economic Inequality   279
    Julia Henly, Laura Lein, Jennifer Romich, Trina R. Shanks, and
    Michael Sherraden (with contributions from Raven Jones and
    Amanda Tillotson)

Mainstreaming Gender: Structural Gender Inequities Drive Economic Inequality   281
Margaret M. C. Thomas

12. Building Financial Capability and Assets for All   310
Jin Huang, Margaret S. Sherraden, Elizabeth Johnson, Julie Birkenmaier, David Rothwell, Mathieu R. Despard, Jenny L. Jones, Christine Callahan, Joanna Doran, Jodi J. Frey, Gena G. McClendon, Terri Friedline, and Robin McKinney
Mainstreaming Gender: Inclusive Strategies for Building Financial Capability and Assets For All   317
Tina Jiwatram-Negrón

13. Achieving Equal Opportunity and Justice   341
Rocío Calvo, Jorge Delva, Sandy Magaña, and Luciana Giorgio Cosenzo
Mainstreaming Gender: Addressing Gender Inequity by Mainstreaming Intersectionality   346
Ijeoma Nwabuzor Ogbonnaya

14. Eliminating Racism   358
Martell Teasley, Susan McCarter, Bongki Woo, Laneshia R. Conner, Michael S. Spencer, and Tatyana Green
Mainstreaming Gender: Centering Intersectionality in the Challenge to Eliminate Racism: Learning from Indigenous Feminisms   364
Katie Schultz

15. Conclusions and Looking Forward   389
Richard P. Barth, Kira Silk, Marilyn L. Flynn, Eddie Uehara, Jill T. Messing, Trina R. Shanks, Michael Sherraden, and James Herbert Williams

Commentaries
Lissa Johnson, Sarah Christa Butts, Ron Manderscheid, Michael Sherraden, and Charles E. Lewis, Grand Challenges for Social Work Policy Committee   406
Mary M. McKay, President, American Academy of Social Work and Social Welfare   415
Angelo McClain, Chief Executive Officer, National Association of Social Workers   419
Darla Spence Coffey, President, Council on Social Work Education   423
Yannis Yortsos, Chair, National Academy of Engineering, NAW Grand Challenges for Engineering   425

Appendix 1: Grand Challenges Leadership Board   429
Appendix 2: Grand Challenges Network Co-Leads   432

Appendix 3: Sponsors of the Grand Challenges for Social Work   438
Appendix 4: Grand Challenges for Social Work: Vision, Mission, Domain,
    Guiding Principles, & Guideposts to Action   440
Appendix 5: Progress and Plans for the Grand Challenges   447
Index   455

ACKNOWLEDGMENTS

As with the first edition of *Grand Challenges for Social Work and Society*, this was a labor born of the love for social work, a deep commitment to a more equitable society, and an abiding commitment to strengthening society through science. Our authors deserve our deepest thanks for completing exceptionally strong chapters despite the massive demands created by COVID-19 and the very intense efforts undertaken across social work, and much of society, to address racial inequity. As editors we were often amazed to read chapter submissions that were fresh, drew on the most current research, were full of innovation, and pointed readers strategically forward. We thank all of our Grand Challenge network leads, over the last 5 years, and additional authors who joined for chapter writing, for keeping their networks strong and their work sharp.

This book, and the Grand Challenges for Social Work (GCSW) would not have been realized without the work of Rowena Fong and Jim Lubben, who coedited the first edition. Indeed, they were members of the original Grand Challenges Steering Committee, and each member of that group (listed in the first edition) deserves our great appreciation. Michael Sherraden, Marilyn Flynn, Eddie Uehara, and Mike Spencer have been among those (along with this volume's editors Richard P Barth and James Herbert Williams) who have also shouldered the responsibility for serving on the Grand Challenges Executive Committee. They have been ably assisted by an engaged and dedicated Grand Challenges Leadership Board (see Appendix 1), which has provided much guidance and many opportunities for the growth of the Grand Challenges. The emergence and realization of the Grand Challenges would have been impossible without the talents and devotion of Sarah Butts, Michelle Clark, Lissa Johnson, Miguel Vieyra, and Kira Silk. They have blended their impressive understanding of the profession, of intervention development, and of administrative structures and procedures with tenacity and relationship skills to make the Grand Challenges what they have become. Kira Silk was especially helpful in organizing this volume, which would have remained in scattered pieces without her ability to turn them into a mosaic.

We are grateful to the leadership of social work organizations and schools of social work who have embraced the Grand Challenges. Special thanks to Neil Guterman, who has chaired the St. Louis Group's Committee on the Grand Challenges, for his commitment of time and resources. We also greatly appreciate those sustaining and premier sponsors who have given in multiple years to ensure we had the support for administrative essentials (see Appendix 3). Chris Gherst and John Beilenson of Strategic Communications and Planning (SCP) have provided exemplary products, high levels of collegiality, and very favorable accounting for all the time they have put in.

Each of us—including every author—also has others to thank for giving us the time to attend to the work of the Grand Challenges and writing about them. As editors we will take the special privilege of briefly thanking some of our inspiring others.

RPB is especially thankful to Nancy Dickinson and the Barth family for many hours spent squirreled away working on Grand Challenges, and to colleagues at the University of Maryland and in the Build Healthy Relationships to End Violence network for their many ideas about how to make this work flourish. Superb scholars and professionals on the original steering committee, the Grand Challenges Executive Committee and Leadership Board, and the Grand Challenge networks have taught me vitally important content and processes, and provided me—and the field—with great benefit.

JTM is grateful to Kristy Kelly, PhD, for lending her time, expertise, and insight to the Mainstreaming Gender Inserts throughout the chapters. She is thankful for the scholars who wrote the inserts, each of whom provided a foundation for rethinking the Grand Challenges using an intersectional feminist approach. Last, she appreciates that the other editors supported the work of mainstreaming gender throughout this edition of the Grand Challenges book.

TRS is appreciative of the attention to policy relevance and educational content encouraged by the Grand Challenges movement. She is especially thankful to the support of her family, the University of Michigan, and participants in the Reduce Extreme Economic Inequality network, including leadership from Laura Lein, Jennie Romich, Dominique Crump, and Michael Sherraden.

JHW extends his gratitude to colleagues at the University of Denver Graduate School of Social Work and the Arizona State University School of Social Work for their resourcefulness and support of the various Grand Challenges programs and projects. He thanks Eddie Uehara, Marilyn Flynn, Jill Messing, Jeff Jenson, David Hawkins, Michael Sherraden, and Rick Barth for their leadership and tremendous contributions to the work of the Grand Challenges. These colleagues are important to the robustness and steadfastness of the Grand Challenges. He also gratefully acknowledges Miguel Vieyra for his support and contributions to the GCSW work at Arizona State University, and colleagues who participated in and supported the GCSW

Western Consortium. These deans, directors, and program chairs help increase the visibility of the initiative across social work programs across the western United States. The individuals mentioned here are key drivers of this initiative's efforts to bring effective change in society. JHW notes that this has been a fulfilling career experience to have worked with great colleagues on an initiative that he considers to have the potential to be a defining moment in the history of the profession.

The Grand Challenge Initiative offers a vibrant social agenda. It provides a national platform for the profession to coalesce intellectual, scientific, education, practice, and fiscal resources and political capital to solve some of the most pressing social welfare issues in our society. Across the country, educators, researchers, and practitioners have responded to the call by developing and using evidence-based approaches to reduce long-standing social problems. This initiative has generated a vast collection of publications, scientific presentations, academic roundtables, and educational/training modules, and has served as a catalyst for partnerships within and across institutions. It is our goal that this book will continue to stimulate new policies, practice innovations, and educational and scientific initiatives to support the Grand Challenge Initiative further for the upcoming quinquennial period. We also hope this book will be a valuable reference and textbook for scholars and educators.

ABOUT THE EDITORS

Richard P. Barth, PhD, MSW, is a Professor at the University of Maryland School of Social Work and Past President of the American Academy of Social Work and Social Welfare (AASWSW). Barth chairs the Executive Committee of the Grand Challenges for Social Work, and has written more than 10 books and 200 articles and chapters about children's services. Barth has twice served as a Fulbright Scholar, received a Lifetime Achievement Award from the Society for Social Work and Research (SSWR), and is a Fellow of the American Psychological Association and SSWR.

Jill T. Messing, PhD, MSW, is a Professor in the School of Social Work and Director of the Office of Gender-Based Violence at Arizona State University. Messing's research focuses on the development and testing of collaborative interventions to prevent intimate partner homicide. Messing has focused on integrating an intersectional feminist framework into the Grand Challenges, first through her leadership on the Grand Challenge to Build Healthy Relationships to End Violence, and more recently by leading an effort to mainstream gender throughout the Grand Challenges.

Trina R. Shanks, PhD, MSW, is currently a Harold R. Johnson Collegiate Professor and Director of community engagement at the University of Michigan School of Social Work. Shanks' research interests include the impact of poverty and wealth on child well-being, asset-building policy and practice across the life cycle, and community and economic development. Shanks co-leads the Grand Challenge to Reduce Extreme Economic Inequality and is the founding Director of the Center for Equitable Family & Community Well-being.

James Herbert Williams, PhD, MSW, MPA, is the Arizona Centennial Professor of Social Welfare Services at the School of Social Work at Arizona State University, member of the Grand Challenge initiative's Executive Committee and Leadership Board, and Fellow in the AASWSW and the SSWR. Williams' scholarship focuses on health equity, global practice, sustainable development, adolescent problem behaviors, positive youth development, academic achievement, Black children and families, and intimate partner violence.

ABOUT THE CONTRIBUTORS

Heidi L. Allen, PhD, MSW, is an Associate Professor at Columbia University School of Social Work. Allen's research is situated at the intersection of poverty and health, and focuses on innovative policy approaches to eliminating disparities.

Christina M. Andrews, PhD, MSW, is an Assistant Professor of social work at the University of South Carolina. Andrews' scholarship focuses on improving access to high-quality addiction treatment in the Medicaid program.

Amanda Aykanian, PhD, is an Assistant Professor of social work at the University of Texas at Arlington and has more than a decade of experience conducting community-based research and program evaluation. Aykanian's research focuses on homelessness services systems, federal policy implementation, and frontline provider perspectives.

Samuel R. Aymer, PhD, is an Associate Professor at Silberman School of Social Work, Hunter College, where he teaches the following courses: Clinical Practice and Violence Against Women. He is also the Chairperson of the School's Clinical Practice Method. Aymer's research centers on the intersection of trauma, partner violence, and sociocultural factors.

Richard P. Barth, PhD, MSW, is a Professor at the University of Maryland School of Social Work and Past President of the AASWSW. Barth chairs the Executive Committee of the Grand Challenges for Social Work, and has written more than 10 books and 200 articles and chapters about children's services. Barth has served as a Fulbright Scholar, received a Lifetime Achievement Award from the SSWR, and is a Fellow of the American Psychological Association and SSWR.

Audrey Begun, PhD, MSW, is a Professor of social work at The Ohio State University and an SSWR Fellow. Begun's recent scholarship focuses on intervening around substance misuse and preparing the professional workforce to develop and deliver evidence-supported interventions to underserved populations.

Kimberly Bender, PhD, MSW, is a Professor of social work at the Graduate School of Social Work at the University of Denver. Bender partners with young people to design, carry out, and share research about their lived experiences to improve the settings and structures that aim to support them.

Stephanie Cosner Berzin, PhD, is Dean of the College of Social Sciences, Policy, and Practice at Simmons University. Berzin has an appointment as a Professor in the School of Social Work and serves as Chair of Online Graduate Strategy for the university. Berzin joined Simmons from Boston College, where she served as Assistant Dean, Chair of Social Innovation and Leadership, and Director of the Center for Social Innovation. As a social work scholar, Berzin has published more than 70 manuscripts, including her book *Innovation from Within* (Oxford University Press, 2018).

Melissa L. Bessaha, PhD, LMSW, MA, is an Assistant Professor at the Stony Brook University School of Social Welfare where she also serves as Chair of the Families, Youth, and Transition to Adulthood Specialization in the MSW program. Bessaha's research focuses on mental health and educational disparities among youth and young adults, particularly marginalized populations and their social relationships.

Shanondora Billiot, PhD, United Houma Nation Citizen, serves as an Advisor to the National Congress of American Indians' Climate Change Taskforce and to the board of the Grand Challenge to Create Social Responses to a Changing Environment. Billiot is a Co-Principle Investigator on a National Academy of Sciences–funded grant exploring movement and climate change within an Indigenous community.

Julie Birkenmaier, PhD, LCSW, is a Professor at Saint Louis University School of Social Work, with a research focus on financial capability and financial access. Birkenmaier co-leads the Grand Challenge to Build Financial Capability and Assets for All, one of social work's 13 Grand Challenges. Birkenmaier also teaches financial capability, policy, and community practice.

Megan Lindsay Brown, MSW, PhD, is a Research Assistant Professor at Arizona State University in the Office of Gender-Based Violence. Brown's research examines how information communication technologies within intimate relationships influences trust, and especially misuse or technology-based abuse. Applied projects include online support services and help for victims of domestic violence.

Suzanne Brown, PhD, LMSW, is an Associate Professor and Chair of the interpersonal practice curriculum area in the School of Social Work at Wayne State University in Detroit, MI. Brown's scholarship focuses on clinical practice, posttraumatic stress disorder, substance misuse, attachment, and the role of social support and social networks in mitigating the effects of trauma and substance misuse on parenting among women with substance use disorders.

Teri Browne, PhD, MSW, is the Interim Dean of the University of South Carolina College of Social Work and Co-Director for interprofessional education for the health sciences at the University of South Carolina. Browne is Co-Editor of the *Handbook of Health Social Work* (3rd ed., Wiley, 2018) and an SSWR Fellow.

Sarah Christa Butts, MSW, is the Director of Public Policy at the National Association of Social Workers, responsible for leading the association's public policy, political and legislative affairs agenda. Prior to joining NASW, Sarah served as the executive director of the Grand Challenges for Social Work and was the founding administrator of the AASWSW.

Christine Callahan, PhD, LCSW-C, is a Research Associate Professor with the Financial Social Work Initiative (FSWI) at the University of Maryland School of Social Work. Callahan joined the FSWI in July 2012, and conducts research and teaches in order to grow the FSWI as a national leader in financial capability.

Rocío Calvo, PhD, is an Associate Professor and the Assistant Dean for Equity, Justice, and Inclusion at the Boston College School of Social Work. Calvo's research seeks to eliminate social service inequities for immigrants and has been funded by the Spencer Foundation and by the Russell Sage Foundation. Calvo's current work focuses on understanding older Latinx immigrants' mechanisms for effective social service navigation.

Emma Carpenter, PhD, MSW, was at the time of writing a postdoctoral research fellow at the Texas Policy Evaluation Project (University of Texas at Austin). Her research examines reproductive health, pregnancy, and family formation in LGBTQ+ communities.

Pajarita Charles, PhD, MSW, is an Assistant Professor at the University of Wisconsin-Madison Sandra Rosenbaum School of Social Work and Director of the Lab for Family Wellbeing and Justice (https://familywellbeingandjustice.com/). Charles conducts research to promote positive outcomes among families affected by incarceration and builds collaborations to foster capacity for criminal justice reform.

John D. Clapp, PhD, MSW, is a Professor and Executive Vice Dean at the Suzanne Dworak-Peck School of Social Work at the University of Southern California. Clapp's research is in the area of alcohol and drug epidemiology and prevention, and Clapp is a Fellow of the American Academy of Health Behavior.

Laneshia R. Conner, PhD, MSW, CSW, is an Assistant Professor in the College of Social Work at the University of Kentucky in Lexington, KY. As a practitioner, Conner has work experience in child welfare as well as geriatric case management, serving both communities over a span of 15 years. As an academician, since 2014, Conner has authored several publications in the fields related to HIV prevention and stigma reduction among older adults. Conner is also published and focuses on scholarship around adult learning principles, operationalizing best practices for the diverse needs of adult learners in higher education.

Phillipe Copeland, PhD, is a Clinical Assistant Professor at Boston University School of Social Work and Assistant Director of Narrative for the Boston University Center for Antiracist Research.

Robert L. Cosby, Jr., PhD, MSW, MPhil, has served as Associate Professor, Assistant Dean of Administration, and Director of the Multidisciplinary Gerontology Center at Howard University School of Social Work since 2019. Crosby's research interests and community involvement include social isolation and trauma in older adults; the impact of trauma on telomeres of older adults; racism and disparities across the life span; grandparents raising grandchildren; opioid use disorders and HIV among older adults; gentrification, technology, and older adults; and the reintegration of older offenders into the community.

Luciana Giorgio Cosenzo, MSW is a doctoral candidate at Columbia School of Social Work. Her research focuses on the effects of sociocultural stress on sleep among Latinxs. She is also interested in the influence of cultural values and gender role expectations on how individuals cope with these types of stress.

Claudia J. Coulton, PhD, is a Distinguished University Professor, Lillian F. Harris Professor and Co-Director for the Center on Urban Poverty and Community Development, Jack, Joseph and Morton Mandel School of Applied Social Sciences, Case Western Reserve University. Coulton's research focuses on structural inequality and neighborhood effects on families and children.

Sandra Edmonds Crewe, PhD, ACSW, is a Professor and Dean of social work at Howard University. Consistent with the long-standing mission of the university, Crewe is strongly committed to social justice, and addressing equity and disparities for Blacks and other historically oppressed or marginalized populations. Crewe's current scholarship relates primarily to ethnogerontology and caregiving. As the Director of the Multidisciplinary Gerontology Center, Crewe has served as Principal Investigator for professional development of aging network providers in the District of Columbia for more than 10 years.

Jorge Delva, PhD, MSW, is Dean of the Boston University School of Social Work, and Director and Paul Farmer Professor of the Center for Innovation in Social Work & Health. Delva's research seeks primarily to understand cultural variations in the etiology of substance use disorders in the United States and globally.

Mathieu R. Despard, PhD, MSW, is an Associate Professor in the Department of Social Work at the University of North Carolina-Greensboro and a Faculty Director at the Social Policy Institute at Washington University in St. Louis. Despard's research focuses on household financial security, with a focus on lower income households.

Diana DiNitto, PhD, is the Cullen Trust Centennial Professor in alcohol studies and education, Distinguished Teaching Professor at the University of Texas at Austin School of Social Work, and a Fellow of the AASWSW. DiNitto's books include *Social Welfare: Politics and Public Policy* (8th ed., Pearson, 2016) and *Chemical Dependency: A Systems Approach* (4th ed., Pearson, 2012).

Joanna Doran, PhD, is an Assistant Professor at the California State University in Los Angeles, where she teaches policy, community organizing, and master's of social work thesis. Doran is also the Founding Director of the Asset Building Clinic and Co-Chair of the Grand Challenge Work Committee to Advance Financial Capability and Asset-building through Education.

Matthew W. Epperson, PhD, MSW, is an Associate Professor at the University of Chicago Crown Family School of Social Work, Policy, and Practice, and Director of the Smart Decarceration Project (www.smartdecarceration.org). Epperson's research centers on developing, implementing, and evaluating interventions to advance decarceration and to eliminate disparities in the criminal legal system.

Gina L. Fedock, PhD, is an Assistant Professor in the Crown Family School of Social Work, Policy, and Practice at The University of Chicago. Fedock's work focuses on improving women's mental health and spans the boundaries of public health, criminal justice, law, and social work.

Marilyn L. Flynn, PhD, was Dean of the Suzanne Dworak-Peck School of Social Work at the University of Southern California from 1997 to 2018. Now retired, she is most noted for transformational leadership in graduate education and institutional building in the profession of social work.

Jodi J. Frey, PhD, LCSW-C, CEAP, is a Professor at University of Maryland, Baltimore, School of Social Work. Frey chairs the Financial Social Work Initiative, Social Work in the Workplace, and Employee Assistance Sub-specialization, and is Founder and Faculty Executive Director of the Behavioral Health and Well-Being Lab.

Terri Friedline, PhD, is an Associate Professor at the University of Michigan School of Social Work and a Faculty Affiliate with Poverty Solutions. Friedline is an Appointed Member of the Consumer Financial Protection Bureau's Academic Research Council.

Anu Manchikanti Gómez, PhD, is an Associate Professor at the School of Social Welfare and director of the Sexual Health and Reproductive Equity Program. Gómez's community-centered scholarship focuses on advancing reproductive freedom throughout the life course.

Ernest Gonzales, PhD, MSSW, is Director of the Center for Health and Aging Innovation, and Associate Professor at New York University, Silver School of Social Work.

Laurie M. Graham, PhD, MSW, is an Assistant Professor at the University of Maryland, Baltimore School of Social Work. Graham has more than a decade of experience addressing intimate partner and sexual violence prevention in community contexts. These experiences guide Graham's research, which uses an intersectional lens to developing trauma-informed, culturally responsive violence prevention strategies.

Tatyana Green, BA, is an alumna of University of North Carolina-Chapel Hill, where she studied African/Black and diaspora studies and education. After graduating, Green worked as a College Adviser for the Carolina College Advising Corps. Green is currently a master's degree of social work candidate at the University of North Carolina-Charlotte.

Julia Henly, PhD, is a Professor at the University of Chicago Crown Family School of Social Work, Policy, and Practice, where she directs the school's doctoral program and teaches courses on poverty, low-paid employment, and child care policy. Henly studies the economic and caregiving strategies of low-income families, examining how employment conditions, public benefits (especially child care assistance), and social networks interact to support and complicate family well-being.

Benjamin F. Henwood, PhD, MSW, is an Associate Professor at the University of Southern California, a National Institutes of Health–funded researcher, and a Fellow of the SSWR. Henwood is also a recognized expert in mental health and housing services research whose work connects clinical interventions with social policy.

Todd I. Herrenkohl, PhD, is a Professor and Marion Elizabeth Blue Professor of Children and Families at the University of Michigan School of Social Work. Herrenkohl's scholarship focuses on the correlates and consequences of child maltreatment, risk and resiliency, and positive youth development. Herrenkohl's funded studies and publications examine health-risk behaviors in children exposed to violence, protective factors that buffer against early risk exposure, and prevention.

Megan R. Holmes, PhD, MSW, LISW-S, is an Associate Professor and Founding Director of the Center on Trauma and Adversity at the Jack, Joseph and Morton Mandel School of Applied Social Sciences at Case Western Reserve University.

Jin Huang, PhD, MSW, is a Professor at the Saint Louis University School of Social Work. Huang co-leads the Grand Challenge to Build Financial Capability and Assets for All, one of social work's 13 Grand Challenges, and is a Research Associate Professor at the Center for Social Development, Washington University, St. Louis.

Jacquelyn B. James, PhD, is Director of the Sloan Research Network on Aging & Work at Boston College, and Research Professor in the Lynch School of Education. James is Past President of the Society for the Study of Human Development and serves on the editorial board of Work, Aging & Retirement.

Jeffrey M. Jenson, PhD, is the Philip and Eleanor Winn Endowed Professor Emeritus in the Graduate School of Social Work, University of Denver. His research focuses on the application of a public health approach to preventing child and adolescent health and behavior problems and on the evaluation of preventive interventions aimed at promoting healthy youth development.

Tina Jiwatram-Negrón, PhD, is an Assistant Professor in the School of Social Work at Arizona State University. Jiwatram-Negrón's research focuses on examining gender-based violence among socially and economically marginalized women globally, and addressing health and mental health disparities associated with gender-based violence through intervention development in partnership with community-based organizations.

Elizabeth (Lissa) Johnson, MBA, MSW, LCSW, is Associate Director of the Center for Social Development, Co-Director of the financial capability and asset-building initiative, and Adjunct Professor at Washington University in St. Louis. Johnson leads policy initiatives with the Grand Challenges for Social Work and contributes to the Grand Challenge to Build Financial Capability and Assets for All.

Michelle Johnson-Motoyama, PhD, MSW, is an Associate Professor at The Ohio State University College of Social Work and Co-Editor of *Children and Youth Services Review*. Johnson-Motoyama's scholarship examines the role of policies and programs in preventing violence and promoting child and family well-being. Her published works can be found at https://www.researchgate.net/profile/Michelle-Johnson-Motoyama.

Jenny L. Jones, PhD, MSW, ACSW, is Dean and Professor of the Whitney M. Young, Jr., School of Social Work at Clark Atlanta University. Jones has more than 23 years in higher education, with research interests that include public child welfare service systems that involve supervision and organizational culture and their impact on service delivery and child well-being, HIV/AIDS and child welfare, and financial capability and asset-building, which considers the integration of financial and economic principles and interventions in direct practice with low-income families.

Melissa Jonson-Reid, PhD, is the Ralph and Muriel Professor of Social Work at Washington University's Brown School of Social Work and Fellow of the AASWSW. Jonson-Reid's work focuses on child maltreatment prevention and cross-sector services to promote healthy outcomes following maltreatment.

Erin Keating, MSW, LCSW, graduated with an MSW from Boston College School of Social in May 2021, where she was a Spier Fellow in Aging. Her studies focused on working with older adults and families. She now works as a hospice social worker for Care Dimensions.

Kristy Kelly, PhD, is a sociologist specializing in gender and politics, politics of knowledge, gender mainstreaming, and social change in Southeast Asia. Kelly is a Faculty Member at Drexel University and is affiliated with Weatherhead East Asian Institute at Columbia University. Kelly is Co-President of the Society of Gender Professionals.

Susan P. Kemp, PhD, is Charles O. Cressey Endowed Professor Emeritus at the University of Washington School of Social Work and a Professor of social work at the University of Auckland. Kemp's scholarship focuses on place and environment, community-based social services, public child welfare, and social work history and theory.

Patricia Kohl, PhD, is an Associate Professor at the Brown School where she teaches social work policy and practice courses. Kohl's scholarship, which is informed by a decade of social work practice experience in public and nonprofit settings, is focused on understanding children's experiences within the context of families and their environment, and on adapting and implementing empirically supported interventions to improve child well-being outcomes for diverse populations within a broad range of service settings.

Jooyoung Kong, PhD, MSW, is an Assistant Professor at the Sandra Rosenbaum School of Social Work, University of Wisconsin at Madison. Kong's research focuses broadly on the effects that childhood adverse experiences have on later-life health and well-being. Kong's current research examines whether and how adults with a history of childhood maltreatment relate to their aging parent(s) who abused and/or neglected them.

Amy Krings, PhD, MSW is an Associate Professor at the Loyola University Chicago School of Social Work. The purpose of Krings' research agenda is to examine how community-based organizations use strategic campaigns to advance environmental and social justice. Krings' goal is to disseminate knowledge that reduces systemic inequalities.

Shanti Kulkarni, PhD, MSW, is a Professor of Social Work at the University of North Carolina-Charlotte. She uses community-based participatory research methods to advance knowledge about the impact of trauma, violence, and abuse on marginalized populations to develop intersectional trauma-informed prevention and intervention strategies.

Patrick Ho Lam Lai, MSW, RSW, is a doctoral student in the School of Social Work and an Affiliate in the Sloan Research Network on Aging & Work at Boston College. Lai is also a Committee Member of the Doctoral Student Committee in the Society for Social Work and Research.

Laura Lein, PhD, studies the interface between families in poverty and the institutions that serve them. Lein explores the lived experience of poverty, the impact of poverty policies, low-wage employment, the vulnerability to large-scale disasters, and access to healthcare. Lein co-leads the Grand Challenge to Reduce Extreme Economic Inequality.

Charles E. Lewis, Jr., PhD, is a political social worker, and the founder and director of the Congressional Research Institute for Social Work and Policy (CRISP), a nonprofit organization that works to engage social workers with the U.S. Congress. He is an adjunct professor at Columbia University School of Social Work and a member of the Grand Challenges for Social Work Leadership Board.

Melissa A. Lippold, PhD, MSW, MPP, is an Associate Professor in the School of Social Work, and the Prudence and Peter Meehan Early Career Distinguished

Scholar at the University of North Carolina at Chapel Hill. Lippold's research focuses on the role of parenting in preventing adolescent and young adult risky behavior and family stress processes. Lippold holds a dual master's degree in social work and public policy from the University of Chicago, and a PhD in human development and family studies from Penn State.

James E. Lubben, PhD, is Professor Emeritus at Boston College. Lubben was the Louise McMahon Ahearn Endowed Professor in social work for 15 years. Lubben is also Professor Emeritus at the University of California Los Angeles, where he taught for 20 years and was Associate Dean and Department Chair.

Sandy Magaña, PhD, MSW, holds the professorship in autism and neurodevelopmental disabilities at the Steve Hicks School of Social Work, University of Texas at Austin. Magaña's current research is focused on identifying racial and ethnic disparities among autistic children, and developing interventions to address them. Magaña's research has been funded by the National Institute of Health and the National Institute on Disability, Independent Living, and Rehabilitation Research.

Ronald Manderscheid, PhD, is Adjunct Professor at the Johns Hopkins Bloomberg School of Public Health and the University of Southern California School of Social Work. He is the former President/CEO of the National Association of County Behavioral Health & Developmental Disability Directors (NACBHDD) and National Association for Rural Mental Health (NARMH).

Peter Maramaldi, PhD, MPH, LCSW, is a Professor at the Simmons College School of Social Work, Adjunct Professor at the Harvard University T. H. Chan School of Public Health, and Instructor at the Harvard School of Dental Medicine in Oral Health Policy and Epidemiology. As a behavioral scientist, Maramaldi collaborates extensively with interprofessional teams conducting National Institutes of Health– and foundation-funded research.

Lisa Reyes Mason, PhD, MSW, is an Associate Professor at the University of Denver Graduate School of Social Work. Mason is a social worker, scholar, and advocate for climate justice. Mason also co-edited the book *People and Climate Change: Vulnerability, Adaptation, and Social Justice* (Oxford University Press, 2019).

Christina Matz, PhD, MSW, is an Associate Professor at the Boston College School of Social Work, and Director of the Center on Aging & Work. Matz's research focuses on meaningful engagement in later life and its effects on individuals, families, organizations, communities, and society at large.

Rebecca Mauldin, PhD, LMSW, is an Assistant Professor in the School of Social Work at The University of Texas at Arlington. Mauldin studies social relationships of older adults, the factors that support them in forming and maintaining positive relationships, and the ways in which their relationships affect their health and well-being.

Susan McCarter, PhD, MSW, serves as a racial and ethnic disparities scholar and forensic social work practitioner. McCarter teaches and conducts research on juvenile justice and racial equity, and helps lead the North Carolina Racial & Ethnic Disparities Subcommittee, Race Matters for Juvenile Justice, Charlotte Racial Justice Consortium, and the University of North Carolina-Charlotte's Racial Equity Skill-Building Caucus.

Angelo McClain, PhD, is Chief Executive Officer of the National Association of Social Workers (NASW) focused on leading efforts that grow and support the social work profession in the United States. Dr. McClain was Vice President and Executive Director of Value Options New Jersey where he built and oversaw administrative, clinical and quality management program infrastructures that increased access to behavioral health services for children and youth, including those in the juvenile justice system.

Gena G. McClendon, PhD, is the Director of Voter Access and Engagement and Co-Director of the Financial Capability and Asset-building initiatives at the Center for Social Development, Washington University in St. Louis. McClendon's research focuses on research and advancing policy strategies that support voting rights and asset building. McClendon earned a PhD in higher education from Jackson State University.

Mary M. McKay, PhD, is the Neidorff Family and Centene Corporation Dean of the Brown School at Washington University in St. Louis. Prior to joining the Brown School, she was the McSilver Professor of Social Work and the inaugural director of the McSilver Institute for Poverty Policy and Research at New York University's Silver School of Social Work.

Robin McKinney, MSW, is Director and Co-Founder of the Maryland CASH Campaign (Creating Assets, Savings and Hope), which promotes programs, products, and policies that increase the financial security of low-income individuals and families. The CASH network serves 30,000 residents annually through free tax preparation, financial education, and coaching. McKinney currently teaches at the University of Maryland School of Social Work.

Jill T. Messing, PhD, MSW, is a Professor in the School of Social Work and Director of the Office of Gender-Based Violence at Arizona State University. Messing's research focuses on the development and testing of collaborative interventions to prevent intimate partner homicide. Messing has focused on integrating an intersectional feminist framework into the Grand Challenges, first through her leadership on the Grand Challenge to Build Healthy

Relationships to End Violence, and more recently by leading an effort to mainstream gender throughout the Grand Challenges.

Felicia M. Mitchell, PhD, MSW, is an Assistant Professor at the School of Social Work at Arizona State University. Mitchell's primary research examines environmental change impacts related to water and their effects on Indigenous communities' health and well-being. Mitchell's other scholarship endeavors seek to dismantle anti-Black sentiments and settler–colonial standards in academia.

Nancy Morrow-Howell, PhD, MSW, holds the Bettie Bofinger Brown Distinguished Professorship at the George Warren Brown School of Social Work at Washington University. Morrow-Howell also directs the university's Harvey A. Friedman Center for Aging. Morrow-Howell is a Fellow and Past President of the Gerontological Society of America.

Michelle R. Munson, PhD, MSW, is a Professor at the New York University Silver School of Social Work. Munson's scholarship focuses on adolescent and young adult mental health services and interventions research, including the development, refinement, and empirical testing of psychosocial interventions that embed social support components such as youth mentors and peer support specialists. Munson's most recent research has been funded by the National Institute of Mental Health.

Ijeoma Nwabuzor Ogbonnaya, PhD, MSW, is an Assistant Professor of social work at Arizona State University who investigates how intimate partner violence impacts health and well-being, and how it varies across culture, race, and ethnicity. Ogbonnaya focuses on populations most vulnerable to intimate partner violence, including child welfare system-involved families and people living with HIV.

Deborah K. Padgett, PhD, has a doctorate in anthropology and is a Professor at the Silver School of Social Work at New York University. Padgett has written extensively on mental health services for underserved populations and is known for her expertise in qualitative/mixed methods and the Housing First approach to ending homelessness.

Lawrence A. Palinkas, PhD, MA, is the Albert G. and Frances Lomas Feldman Professor of social policy and health in the Suzanne Dworak-Peck School of Social Work at the University of Southern California. Palinkas also holds secondary appointments as Professor in the Departments of Anthropology and Population and Public Health Sciences at the University of Southern California.

Rupal Parekh, PhD, is an Assistant Professor in the School of Social Work at the University of Connecticut. Parekh has more than a decade of professional and practice experience working with diverse older adult populations across the continuum of care. Parekh's primary research aim is to improve outcomes for late-life immigrants.

Carrie Pettus-Davis, PhD, MSW, is an Associate Professor of Social Work at Florida State University and Founding Executive Director of the Institute for Justice Research and Development. Pettus-Davis works with community partners to develop interventions to enhance positive social support, treat trauma experiences and behavioral health disorders, and generate well-being for those impacted by criminal justice involvement.

Michelle Putnam, PhD, is a Professor and Jennifer Eckert '08SW School of Social Work Chair at Simmons University.

Jennifer Romich, PhD, studies family economic well-being, with an emphasis on low-paid workers, household budgets, and interactions with public policy. Romich co-leads the Grand Challenge to Reduce Extreme Economic Inequality and co-chairs a national research network on poverty, employment, and self-sufficiency through the U.S. Collaborative of Poverty Centers.

David Rothwell, PhD, MSW, is an Associate Professor at Oregon State University, where he studies and teaches courses on families, poverty, and social policy.

Erika L. Sabbath, ScD, is an Associate Professor at Boston College School of Social Work. Sabbath's research focuses on the ways the work environment acts as a social determinant of health. Sabbath is the Principal Investigator of the National Institute of Occupational Safety and Health–funded Boston Hospital Workers Health Study, a longitudinal cohort study of more than 20,000 nurses and nursing assistants.

Melanie Sage, PhD, MSW, is an Assistant Professor at the University at Buffalo State University of New York School of Social Work. Sage studies the intersection of technology and child welfare, and how youths in foster care use technology to support social connections. Sage is a Co-Chair of the Grand Challenge to Harness Technology for Social Good.

Katie Schultz, PhD, MSW, is an Assistant Professor in the School of Social Work at the University of Michigan. A citizen of the Choctaw Nation of Oklahoma, Schultz centers her work on Native American and Alaskan Native health equity, with a focus on violence and associated health outcomes, community and cultural connectedness, culturally grounded prevention and intervention, and community-based participatory and mixed methods research.

Trina R. Shanks, PhD, MSW, is currently a Harold R. Johnson Collegiate Professor and Director of Community Engagement at the University of

Michigan School of Social Work. Shanks' research interests include the impact of poverty and wealth on child well-being, asset-building policy and practice across the life cycle, and community and economic development. Shanks coleads the Grand Challenge to Reduce Extreme Economic Inequality and is the founding Director of the Center for Equitable Family & Community Well-being.

Valerie B. Shapiro, PhD, studies the prevention of behavioral health problems in children. Shapiro focuses on promoting the use of research evidence in community-wide and school-based prevention planning, implementing social and emotional learning initiatives, and assessing youth outcomes for continuous improvement. Shapiro is a licensed social worker and certified school social worker.

Bonita B. Sharma, PhD, MSSW, is an Assistant Professor at the University of Texas at San Antonio–Social Work. Sharma researches the impacts of social, economic, and environmental factors on women's equity, empowerment, and health in the local/global context. Sharma also studies social inclusion within the natural and built environment.

Jama Shelton, MSW, PhD, is an Assistant Professor at the Silberman School of Social Work, Hunter College. Shelton's scholarship investigates the experience of homelessness among lesbian, gay, bisexual, transgender, queer youth and young adults, and the service providers with whom they work, to drive policy and programmatic interventions to address youth homelessness in the United States and abroad.

Margaret S. Sherraden, PhD, is a Research Professor and Faculty Director at the Center for Social Development, Washington University, St. Louis; and Professor Emeritus at the University of Missouri-St. Louis. Sherraden coleads the Grand Challenge to Build Financial Capability and Assets for All, one of social work's 13 Grand Challenges. Sherraden's current research focuses on advancing household financial well-being.

Michael Sherraden, PhD, is the George Warren Brown Distinguished University Professor, Founding Director of the Center for Social Development at the Brown School of Social Work, and Director of the Next Age Institute at Washington University in St. Louis. Sherraden has defined and informed a body of applied research and policy to promote inclusion in asset-building that has influenced policies and programs in the United States and abroad. Among other awards, Sherraden has been a Fulbright Scholar and was listed by *Time Magazine* as one of the 100 most influential people in the world.

Kira Silk, MSW, is the Director of the Grand Challenges for Social Work, joining the initiative and the University of Maryland School of Social Work in 2019. Silk also supports the Institute for Innovation and Implementation's work on a federally funded state project to expedite reunification and permanency for youth in foster care. Silk's career has focused on child and family well-being.

Jonathan Bentley Singer, PhD, LCSW, is an Associate Professor of social work at Loyola University Chicago, President of the American Association of Suicidology, Co-Lead of the social work Grand Challenge to Harness Technology for Social Good, Founder and Host of the award-winning Social Work Podcast, and Coauthor of *Suicide in Schools*.

Darla Spence Coffey, PhD, MSW, is the President and Chief Executive Officer of the Council on Social Work Education (CSWE). Prior to her appointment as president, she served as professor of social work, associate provost, and dean of graduate studies at West Chester University.

Michael S. Spencer, PhD, MSSW, is the Presidential Term Professor of social work and Director of Native Hawaiian, Pacific Islander, and Oceania affairs at the Indigenous Wellness Research Institute at the University of Washington. Spencer is the Co-Lead for the Grand Challenge to Close the Health Gap and the Grand Challenge to Eliminate Racism.

Heather L. Storer, PhD, MSW, is an Associate Professor at the University of Louisville. Storer's research investigates social justice youth development approaches to preventing gender-based violence, particularly among socially excluded youth. Storer's scholarship examines gender-based violence organizations' use of digital technologies to support youth engagement, community activism, and movement building.

Martell Teasley, PhD, is Dean of the College of Social Work at the University of Utah and serves as Editor-in-Chief for the National Association of Social Workers' journal *Children & Schools*. Teasley's primary research interests include Black adolescent development, cultural diversity, social welfare policy, and Black studies. Teasley is known nationally for his research on school-age children and youth.

Margaret M. C. Thomas, PhD, MSW, is an Assistant Professor of social welfare at the University of California Los Angeles Luskin School of Public Affairs. Thomas' research focuses on material hardship, social policy, and systemic sources of marginalization and deprivation among US children and families.

Emmy Tiderington, PhD, MSW, is an Assistant Professor in the School of Social Work at Rutgers, the State University of New Jersey. Her research focuses on the implementation and effectiveness of supportive housing and other forms of homeless services. Tiderington is a recognized expert on service recipient transitions within and from homeless services.

Elizabeth M. Tracy, PhD, MSW, LISW, is the Grace Longwell Coyle Professor Emerita in social work at the Jack, Joseph and Morton Mandel School of Applied Social Sciences, Case Western Reserve University. Tracy's research and publications have focused on personal network assessment and intervention in diverse social work practice and research settings relating to child welfare and women's substance use disorders.

Edwina Uehara, PhD, is a Professor and Ballmer Endowed Dean at the University of Washington School of Social Work. Uehara's research centers on understanding the interplay of social structures and the sociocultural construction of health, illness, and healing.

Karin Wachter, PhD, MEd, is an Assistant Professor in the School of Social Work at Arizona State University. Wachter's goal is to generate applied research for local, national, and international practitioners and policymakers to alleviate the psychosocial consequences of forced migration and violence against women.

Karina L. Walters, PhD, MSW, is the William P. and Ruth Gerberding Endowed Professor at the University of Washington School of Social Work, Director of the Indigenous Wellness Research Institute, and an Enrolled Member of the Choctaw Nation in Oklahoma. She is an AASWSW and SSWR Fellow and focuses on Native American and Alaskan Native wellness.

Darrell P. Wheeler, PhD, MPH, ACSW, is the Vice Provost for public engagement at the University at Albany–The State University of New York. Wheeler is an educator and researcher on HIV prevention and intervention in the Black, gay, bisexual, and transgender communities, and uses evidence in developing innovative programs and policy initiatives.

Cliff Whetung, MSW, is a third-year doctoral student at New York University's Silver School of Social Work. He is a band member of Curve Lake First Nation, an Ojibwe reservation in Ontario, Canada. His research investigates inequities in cognitive health using longitudinal data with a focus on Indigenous populations.

James Herbert Williams, PhD, MSW, MPA, is the Arizona Centennial Professor of Social Welfare Services at the School of Social Work at Arizona State University, member of the Grand Challenges for Social Work initiative's Executive Committee and Leadership Board, Fellow in the American Academy of Social Work and Social Welfare and the Society for Social Work and Research. His scholarship focuses on health equity, global practice, sustainable development, adolescent problem behaviors, positive youth development, academic achievement, African American children and families, and intimate partner violence.

Bongki Woo, PhD, is an Assistant Professor in the College of Social Work at the University of South Carolina. Woo's work centers on the sociocultural and environmental factors that influence the mental health of racial/ethnic minorities.

Yannis C. Yortsos, PhD, MS, is the Dean of the University of Southern California Viterbi School of Engineering and the Zohrab Kaprielian Chair in Engineering, a position he holds since 2005. Prior to that he served from 2001 to 2005 as Associate Dean and then as Sr. Associate Dean for Academic Affairs. He co-founded in 2009 the Global Grand Challenges Scholars Program.

Bradley J. Zebrack, PhD, MSW, MPH, is a Professor of social work at the University of Michigan. Zebrack's research interests are in the area of health, medicine, and, in particular, the quality of healthcare service delivery to cancer patients and their families.

Emma Zingg, BA, is a master's of social work candidate at Boston College, School of Social Work.

CHAPTER 1
Introduction and Update on the Grand Challenges

RICHARD P. BARTH, MARILYN L. FLYNN,
TRINA R. SHANKS, JAMES HERBERT WILLIAMS,
JILL T. MESSING, AND KIRA SILK

Grand challenges represent a focused method of attacking the most deeply significant problems of a discipline, organization, or society itself. Since the concept was first introduced more than a century ago, more than 600 governments, foundations, and professions subsequently adopted this language and approach, often to excellent effect. In 2012, the social work profession launched its own national initiative, with aim of using science, innovation, and new forms of collaboration to accelerate progress toward critically needed social solutions. There was also strong corollary interest in changing the profession itself, introducing new forms of practice and problem-solving. The American Academy of Social Work and Social Welfare served as the first home of the Grand Challenges initiative in social work; in 2017, as the initiative grew more complex, it became an independent organization.

What Are "Grand Challenges?"

Although grand challenges have been defined by different groups throughout the years in many ways, important commonalities can be identified. As statements, grand challenges are aspirational rather than problem specific, and therefore are broadly formulated. Yet, they must be attainable, often within a decade or two. Solutions to each challenge should lie within sight, but require additional new advances in knowledge and practical development. The challenge itself must be identifiable and meaningful to most people both within and outside the group or organization. Such challenges are defined as "grand" because of their gravity and wide impact. They reflect large, transformational aims that move a field beyond its usual specialized and familiar topics, breaking old intellectual boundaries, and forming fresh patterns of learning and connection.

The Rationale for Grand Challenges

The rationale for grand challenges seems generally to have been supported over time. They have been used to powerful effect in attracting new students and scholars to a field, and in bringing talented people together in new collaborations to formulate a common understanding of the larger social aims of the work. Customary divisions between ideologies, disciplines, and organizations can be reduced with improved team effort. Last, grand challenges appear almost universally to capture the imagination of others because they are both promising and compelling for the public at large. They readily lend themselves to exciting media coverage and storylines in other narrative forms. For this reason, they have the potential for engaging communities and society as a whole in ways that traditional scientific and philanthropic communications do not.

Supporting Scientific Development in Social Work

Several trends at the beginning of the 21st century further supported the value of grand challenges organized around social issues, policy deficits, and readiness for reform. Schools of social work based in major research institutions had reached a critical juncture in their evolution. They had, for the most part, succeeded in demonstrating their value in the areas of intervention and service research, implementation science, community capacity-building, and education through the postdoctoral level. However, the pipeline for graduate programs was not satisfactory in terms of gender balance, racial equity, the breadth of prior disciplinary preparation, and—at the doctoral level—competitive volume. It was unclear how the profession could make a maximum contribution to quality of life and sustainability of an equitable society in the coming decades.

Furthermore, issues of scale (both large and small), complexity, and rapid change had altered substantially the boundaries of traditional problem-solving methods and introduced new roles for which the best schools and society at large had to be prepared. Interest in disruption and innovation was rampant in many sectors, with universities, businesses, and governments leaping on the bandwagon in search of often untested breakthroughs outside of traditional systems and practices (Uehara et al., 2015). This ferment opened some institutions to receptiveness for novel possibilities and rethinking of older conventions.

Social work as a field has never been adverse to the pursuit of broad and sweeping ideas for social change. This has been demonstrated through leadership for world peace by Jane Addams; crusades for the reduction of infant mortality and, later, the end of child abuse (through many social work leaders in the Children's Bureau); and the shaping of social programs by Harry Hopkins to end the worst consequences of the Great Depression (Barth, Gilmore, Flynn, Fraser, & Brekke, 2014; Sherraden et al., 2014). The Grand Challenges offered a 21st-century platform for expression of an expansive social vision; but, for the first time, the drive for social change would be grounded more explicitly in science.

The importance of science in social work evolved most conspicuously in the decades following the 1980s, propelled by unprecedented investment of federal resources in university research and rising academic expectations for practical scientific output from all disciplines, including the professions. As the methodological sophistication and sheer number of well-trained social workers in major research institutions grew, so did the quality of research findings and their value for improving the effectiveness of interventions at the individual, family, community, and policy levels. The first decade of the 21st century produced especially dramatic developments, as reflected in a standing ovation for Professor John Brekke from the University of Southern California at the 2010 annual meeting of the Society for Social Work and Research. Brekke proposed that "social work science" was a distinct method with its own domain, not merely an adjunct to professional practice as traditionally accepted. Today, the public is more likely than not to believe that social work is a science; this sentiment is particularly strong when assessing social work's contribution to the development and evaluation of interventions and related to public perception that science can be used to study and solve social problems (LeCroy & Kaplan, 2021).

Social Work Awakes to the Grand Challenges

In the year following Brekke's dramatic proposal, the next major evolution of the Grand Challenges was led by Edwina Uehara, Dean of Social Work, University of Washington, who connected social work science to the grand challenges concept. Speaking at a meeting of senior members of the American Academy of Social Work and Social Welfare, academic deans, and distinguished professionals, she ignited the imaginations of attendees by introducing the concept of grand challenges as a possibility for social work. Dean Uehara gave added substance to this idea by inviting the dean of engineering from her university to describe how the National Academy of Engineering had launched its own grand challenges initiative in 2008. Uehara saw the grand challenges as a strategy for focusing attention on society's most urgent problems, uniting the energies of scientists and practitioners, and overcoming traditional barriers to interdisciplinary scientific collaboration. With colleagues, Uehara and others subsequently published a keystone paper that articulated these concepts more fully, and outlined bold and historic goals for a Grand Challenges initiative (Uehara et al., 2015). After prolonged discussion, meeting participants were anxious to move forward and endorsed the American Academy of Social Work and Social Welfare to assume leadership for next steps. The American Academy of Social Work and Social Welfare Board quickly agreed to provide this leadership and to help create a collaborative, minimally sufficient infrastructure.

A 12-member committee comprised of 10 Academy members, Dean Uehara, and Dean Marilyn Flynn, of the School of Social Work at the University of Southern California, was subsequently organized and charged with bringing the grand challenge concept to life. Brekke and Rowena Fong, a chaired professor at the University of Texas-Austin, were designated as cochairs of this working group, with Rick Barth, then-President of the Academy and Dean of the University of Maryland School of Social Work, heading its executive committee. Additional members of the initial working group included James Lubben, Boston College; Michael Sherraden, Washington University, St. Louis; J. David Hawkins and Karina Walters, University of Washington; Yolanda Padilla, Diana DiNitto, and Rowena Fong, University of Texas-Austin; King Davis, Virginia Commonwealth University; James Herbert Williams and Jeffrey Jensen, University of Denver; Claudia Coulton, Case Western Reserve University; and Ronald Manderscheid, National Association of County Behavioral Health & Developmental Disability Directors. An executive director, Sarah Butts, was hired as resources became available through initial donations from the University of Southern California, Washington University, the University of Washington, and the University of Maryland. The result was a national coalescence of scientific expertise, academic leadership, and energy focused keenly on bringing the Grand Challenges to life in the social work profession.

Creating and Choosing the Grand Challenges

It was not immediately obvious how to identify and validate the most significant social challenges facing the United States in the 21st century. If social work was to play a leadership role in forming new collaborations and influencing the general public, documentation was needed to assert powerfully that this role was credible and supported by prior achievements. Underlying principles had to be stated that made clear the value base, stakeholders, and assumptions about the power of social relationships in advancing the well-being of society. A process for the working group itself had to be laid out, including time frames and desired impacts. All agreed that a strengths-based and inclusive perspective was vital.

Between 2012 and 2015, the development of two anchoring papers led by Michael Sherraden, with the support of other leading scholars, helped establish that social work could achieve grand accomplishments and that our expertise in social interventions was fundamental to strengthening society. The first foundational paper, "Grand Accomplishments of Social Work and the Grand Context of Social Work" surveyed notable social gains of the 20th century, identifying innovations and widely acknowledged examples of social impact that had been led by the social work profession (Sherraden et al., 2014). This paper sought to confirm that social work had, for nearly a century, shown its ability to seize deeply consequential ideas, put them to work, and bring them to scale. This inspirational document anchored much of the discussion in the working group in affirming tangible possibilities for addressing additional grand challenges in present times.

The second working paper, "Social Is Fundamental: Introduction and Context for the Grand Challenges for Social Work" (Sherraden et al., 2014), laid out the principle that social factors and social relationships as tools for social change have been far more influential than is commonly recognized. Because social work uses relationships as its primary lever for influencing individual and group behavior, it followed that the profession could construct and implement a major social agenda organized around this standpoint.

The process for creating the Grand Challenges moved forward at the same time the foundational papers were drafted. Multiple options were considered based on precedents set by other organizations. Ultimately, a mix of inclusive strategies for the collection of ideas was used that involved multiple contacts with students, practitioners, and faculty throughout the country. At local and national conferences and meetings, including those of the Society for Social Work and Research, the National Association of Social Workers, the Council on Social Work Education, and others, attendees were invited to offer their ideas. E-mail messages were sent to state chapter directors of the National Association of Social Workers, and a new website for the American Academy of Social Work and Social Welfare, which had the capacity to support the Grand Challenges, was opened as a backbone for communications. In this prepandemic era, conferences continued to constitute one of the most useful means of eliciting the views of academics, practitioners, and allies of the profession.

Culling of ideas was carried out by the working group that set five criteria for selection, asked for working papers for proposed ideas that met these criteria, and requested submission of additional topics seen as critical, but not among the original submissions. *The five criteria required that each grand challenge must be significant and compelling, could be completed or largely solved given current scientific evidence, would generate cross-sector or interdisciplinary collaboration, demanded real innovation, and could be addressed with meaningful and measurable progress in a decade.* The committee used a scoring system that, once applied, was identified as being weighted in favor of proposals in clinical or direct practice areas where there was an accumulation of prior scientific discovery and, in most cases, a rooted social work presence. There was concern that larger transformative ideas such as government policy at scale or social climate change were not sufficiently considered. A rewriting of the guidelines to emphasize the need for policy solutions was developed and distributed, and additional ideas were advanced. Twelve Grand Challenges were eventually chosen by the working group. Working committee members were conscious of the fact that some of the challenges appeared to lie outside generally accepted research domains in the field, whereas some iconic topics seemed to be ignored.

There was deep debate over how to respond to concept papers on gender equity, immigration, and racism; at the time, no proposals were presented that were assessed as defining interventions likely to achieve success or suggesting objective measures of progress. During the intervening years, continued and high-profile murders of Black and Brown people by law enforcement officers, the Black Lives Matter movement, and the debate within the social work profession regarding the abolition of police departments (Detlaff et al., 2020; Singer, 2020) clarified the need to address racism directly within the profession and society. In 2020, a 13th Grand Challenge to Eliminate Racism was established under the network leadership of Martell Teasley, Dean of the University of Utah; and Michael Spencer, Presidential Term Professor at the University of Washington. The addition of this Grand Challenge and steps ahead are described in Chapter 14.

The intersections of racism and sexism—examples of which can be seen in murders of Native American and Asian-American women, and the respective activism of the Murdered and Missing Indigenous Women and Stop Asian Hate movements—have foregrounded the need for movements against violence to center race and gender.

In response to feminist scholars' activism and in keeping with the agreement that "social is fundamental," a change was made to the title for Stop Family Violence in 2019 when this Grand Challenge was reconceptualized around building healthy relationships to end violence. This decision built on a lengthy discussion about how to best merge the areas of child abuse and gender-based violence. The title Grand Challenge to Stop Family Violence was one of the sparks for this vigorous debate regarding the importance of gender within the conceptualization of interpersonal violence. The original co-leads of this challenge split and created two position papers: one on gender-based violence and the other on child maltreatment. In 2019, this Grand Challenge went through a renaming process in an effort to bridge this conceptual and practical divide (Kulkarni et al., 2020). This change, and subsequent efforts to conceptualize the Grand Challenge under the revised title, Grand Challenge to Build Healthy Relationships to End Violence, are described more fully in Chapter 4. Despite a renaming process that began with the intent to address gender, the revised title does not center gender, specifically—nor does it erase it (Kulkarni, Kohl, & Edmond, 2020; Messing, 2020). Instead, it broadens the discussion to relationships—one of the ultimate forces in the creation of violence at all of society's levels.

In an effort to include an intersectional feminist approach across the Grand Challenges, Jill Messing, a professor at Arizona State University, has suggested a gender mainstreaming approach (Messing, 2020). As described later in the current chapter, gender mainstreaming was adopted as a strategy in this book in an effort to begin incorporating an intersectional feminist perspective across all of the Grand Challenges.

The Grand Challenges are not perfect, and it has been necessary to reflect and find ways of continual improvement. In particular, although some elements of an antiracist agenda and gender-equitable practice and policy were embedded in other challenges, these important matters have not been addressed sufficiently. An initial effort to demonstrate the commitment of the Grand Challenges to end racism and other injustices was written, published to the Grand Challenges website and disseminated as "Grand Challenges for Social Work: Vision, Mission, Domain, Guiding Principles, & Guideposts to Action" (Grand Challenges for Social Work, 2019). This was not bold enough. It remained imperative to establish a separate Grand Challenge to address racism and white supremacy in the United States, and to identify social work models that address racism within the social work profession.

Multiple ways to address gender inequities have now taken shape in the Grand Challenges.

In 2021, the Grand Challenges for Social Work are as follows:

Individual and Family Well-being
- Ensure healthy development for youth.
- Close the health gap.
- Build healthy relationships to end violence.
- Advance long and productive lives.

Stronger Social Fabric
- Eradicate social isolation.
- End homelessness.

- Create social response to a changing environment.
- Harness technology for social good.

Just Society
- Eliminate racism.
- Promote smart decarceration.
- Reduce extreme economic inequality.
- Build financial capacity and assets for all.
- Achieve equal opportunity and justice.

MAINSTREAMING GENDER

Revisiting the Transformative Potential of Gender Mainstreaming in Social Work

KRISTY KELLY

During the past 20 years, gender mainstreaming has become *the* strategy among the international development community and transnational feminist movements for achieving gender equality in organizations and societies around the world. Rather than conceptualizing women as a separate category needing special attention or special programs, the aim of gender mainstreaming is to integrate women and intersectional gender equity into all elements of policy design, programming, budgeting, monitoring, and evaluation. Despite its worldwide adoption, gender mainstreaming as a strategy for social transformation remains largely undertheorized and underspecified in the United States. This series of Gender Mainstreaming Inserts, curated by Jill Messing (Arizona State University), aims to fill this gap by illustrating the transformative potential of gender mainstreaming for social work.

The Grand Challenges for Social Work were imagined and constructed as gender neutral (Messing, 2020), revealing a challenge for social work in acknowledging the ways that patriarchy and racism are reproduced systematically through and by the field. The Inserts are a call to action for social work to address the institutionalized expectations, policies, and practices that continue to exclude or devalue women; Black, Indigenous, and People of Color (BIPOC); and nonbinary people of all ages. These Inserts are also a call to action for feminist scholars and social work professionals in the United States to consider gender mainstreaming as a useful strategy for social change. Together they illustrate gender mainstreaming's transformative potential to rethink binarisms; center intersectional feminisms; disentangle interpersonal identities from power structures; make global connections; situate context; connect crosscutting issues; link research, policy, and practice; and prioritize transformation.

continued

Rethink Binarisms

Gender identity shapes individual experience with all aspects of domestic and economic life, as Heather Storer (University of Louisville) notes in her contribution on the Grand Challenge to Build Healthy Relationships to End Violence. Although social work scholarship focuses on violence as a gendered phenomenon, narrow definitions of gender as binary remain entrenched in the field. Jama Shelton's (Hunter College, City University of New York) contribution on the Grand Challenge to End Homelessness illustrates how cis-normative segregated shelters require transgender and nonbinary people to alter their gender presentation to access services. Their Insert applies a gender mainstreaming framework to identify principles for redesigning systems and structures to dismantle gender binaries and create more inclusive services.

Center Intersectional Feminisms

Through an examination of the ways that racism, settler colonialism, and heteropatriarchy co-construct each other to legitimize and maintain systems of power and oppression, Katie Schultz (University of Michigan) shows how gender is experienced in racializing forms and how race is equally gendered. She uses gender mainstreaming to center Indigenous feminisms and intersectional feminists to decolonize the field of social work and eliminate racism. Ijeoma Nwabuzor Ogbonnaya (Arizona State University) calls for social work to move beyond one-axis categories of analysis such as "women" or "gender" to mainstreaming an intersectional analysis into all equity work in her contribution to the Grand Challenge to Achieve Equal Opportunity and Justice.

Disentangle Interpersonal Identities from Power Structures

As Laurie Graham (University of Maryland, Baltimore) illustrates in her Insert on the Grand Challenge to Ensure Healthy Development for Youth, gender mainstreaming must address both interpersonal and structural inequality. Failing to disentangle gendered identities from structures of power leaves underlying problems of misogyny, racism, and social inequities intact. Emma Carpenter (University of Texas at Austin) and Anu Manchikanti Gómez (University of California, Berkeley) illustrate the importance of disentangling identities from power structures in the Grand Challenge to Close the Health Gap. They focus on the example of maternal mortality to identify the ways that intersectional identities shape experiences of health and healthcare. By disentangling the interpersonal from the structural, it is easier to reframe policy problems and illuminate new areas for research and practice, according to Margaret Thomas (Columbia University). In the Grand Challenge to Reduce Extreme Economic Inequality, it is necessary

continued

to reframe the "feminization of poverty," which focuses on individuals, to "economic sexism," which focuses on structures of power.

Make Global Connections

Gender mainstreaming requires making global connections to understand how macro-level gender dynamics shape local-level policies, practices, behaviors, and beliefs. Karin Wachter's (Arizona State University) contribution to the Grand Challenge to Eradicate Social Isolation among refugee communities in the United States draws on critical feminist analysis—a tenet of gender mainstreaming—to illuminate how the problem of social isolation is itself the result of war and global displacement for refugee women. Yet, resettlement interventions focus on increasing women's individual self-reliance as if their global connections and experiences were irrelevant. By ignoring the global, social work risks further exacerbating women's experiences of isolation—or worse, renders them invisible.

Situate Context

Making global connections does not mean ignoring the specificity of local culture or historical contexts that shape experiences of gender exclusion, according to Tina Jiwatram-Negrón (Arizona State University). As she illustrates in her contribution to the Grand Challenge to Build Financial Capability and Assets for All, gender mainstreaming reveals that problems that appear global, such as lack of financial access or capital, may mean different things across diverse local contexts. For example, women's financial exclusion may be the result of underemployment in some contexts, low literacy in others, or banking hours that do not overlap with child care. Understanding gender relations as situated both globally and locally allows social work to develop and implement crosscutting policies and programs responsive to local needs and interests.

Connect Crosscutting Issues

Gender mainstreaming connects gender goals to crosscutting issues that may appear gender-neutral, but are not. Bonita Sharma (University of Texas at San Antonio) illustrates the gender–environment nexus in the Grand Challenge to Create Social Responses to a Changing Environment by demonstrating how climate change policies imagined as gender-neutral risk exacerbating environmental exposure for women and marginalized communities. In the Grand Challenge to Harness Technology for the Social Good, Megan Lindsay Brown (Arizona State University) shows how technology, when imagined as gender-neutral, can inadvertently perpetuate racist, heteropatriarchal systems of power and privilege. Likewise, in the Grand Challenge to Advance Long and Productive Lives, Rupal Parekh (University of Connecticut) and Rebecca Mauldin (University of Texas at

continued

Arlington) show how gender-blind transportation policies risk deepening social divisions between those who have access to services and those who do not, particularly immigrants, the elderly, women, and those living far from central services.

Link Research, Policy, and Practice

Intersectional feminist theory and research methods are at the core of gender mainstreaming and mandate linking research, policy, and practice to eliminate discrimination. Feminist policy analysis, gender budgeting, gender auditing, and gender monitoring and evaluation are examples of research tools that link policy and practice to center marginalized community members' needs and interests. Without systematic intersectional gender analysis, as Gina Fedock (University of Chicago) illustrates in her Insert on Smart Decarceration, social work cannot identify or address the root causes of gender inequality embedded in and impacting the Grand Challenges.

Prioritize Transformation

The goal of gender mainstreaming is gender equality. This means moving beyond gender parity—or simply counting men and women—to ensure that everyone has access to the resources and benefits they need to enjoy a full and healthy life. Gender mainstreaming is a strategy for transforming organizations and society so that all people can influence, participate in, and benefit from the Grand Challenges. The transformation of inequitable social and institutional structures into gender just structures for all people is not easy. There is always the danger that by putting the responsibility for gender equality into the mainstream, so to speak, gender mainstreaming as a strategy disappears. Because it becomes the responsibility of everyone, it risks becoming the responsibility of no one. Social work plays an essential role in preventing this erasure by calling for better data collection and gender analysis; decentering hypermasculine, white ways of knowing as "expertise"; tying research funding to gender equality priorities; establishing accountability mechanisms; and transforming the institutions where we work and train the next generation.

As evidenced collectively by the Gender Mainstreaming Inserts, social work's success at advancing the Grand Challenges is tied to gender equality. Although there is still much to learn, the intersectional feminist framework outlined in these Inserts is an important step in mainstreaming gender into the Grand Challenges, and into social work.

Reference

Messing, J. T. (2020). Mainstreaming gender: An intersectional feminist approach to the Grand Challenges for Social Work. *Social Work, 65*(4), 313–315.

IDENTIFYING AND MOTIVATING STAKEHOLDERS

Because the Grand Challenges initiative was originally nested within the American Academy of Social Work and Social Welfare, its appeal and leadership was drawn almost entirely from graduate schools of social work and academic leadership. The formal launch of the Grand Challenges in 2016 was conducted through the Society for Social Work and Research as part of a spectacular celebration. Networks of social work scholars associated with each of the Grand Challenges often included senior scholars, but also drew on the expertise of a wider array of social work scholars (and a few practitioners). This academic umbrella meant that resources from the relatively well-endowed schools in major research institutions, their master's in social work (MSW) and PhD students, and their research funding experience formed a promising base. Several special issues in professional journals showcasing the Grand Challenges were produced, including the *Journal of Policy Practice*, the *Journal of Gerontological Social Work*, the *Journal of Social Work Practice in the Addictions*, and the *Journal of Social Work Education*. Since the initiative launched, the Grand Challenges have been featured in a number of special issues, including the *Journal of the Society for Social Work and Research*, *Social Work*, the *Journal of Social Work Education*, and the *Journal of Teaching in Social Work*. Several books have also been written, including *Gerontological Social Work and the Grand Challenges: Focusing on Policy and Practice* (Sanders, Kolomer, Waites, Spellman, & Rizzo, 2019) and *Grand Challenges for Society* (Bent-Goodley, Williams, Teasley, & Gorin, 2019).

Social work professional organizations, such as the Council on Social Work Education and the National Association of Social Workers, were interested parties and became involved early in the Grand Challenges movement. To ward off insularity, academics in scientific disciplines outside of social work, as well as social work academics within the many smaller social work programs, in rural areas, and with primary commitment to service or teaching missions, were invited to join. At the outer peripheries, additional stakeholders included practicing social workers, other helping professions, sectors such as business and government, and ultimately society itself. The desire of the working group and those drawn to the initiative in its early phases was to look beyond the usual professional internal preoccupations to society itself and to push forward the most encompassing changes. Reaching new stakeholders, retaining them, and gaining legitimacy across a broad range of interested groups were critical from the beginning.

As the working group selected the Grand Challenges, the Executive Committee contracted with a firm responsible for public relations: SCP Communications (SCP's project lead, Chris Gherst, also had an MSW). SCP led the development of logos, press releases for Grand Challenges announcements, and a newsletter that was distributed quarterly, and now monthly.

SCP supported the initiative by providing ongoing strategic consultation on building tools, materials, and resources to raise awareness of and expand the reach of the Grand Challenges effort, including webinars, visuals, and advertisements for annual conference events.

As the recognition and impact of the Grand Challenges grew within social work, events and scholarship coalesced around the proffered structure for seeking social change. Conferences were themed around the Grand Challenges, and lecture and webinar series were advanced to address individual Grand Challenges or a cluster of them. *Progress and Plans for the Grand Challenges*, the 5-year impact report (Grand Challenges for Social Work, 2021), describes just a sampling of these activities. Throughout, the focus on social work as leaders in research, education, and intervention aimed at addressing social problems has remained central. The goals of impacting society as a whole and communicating outside the boundaries of social work have remained elusive.

STRUCTURES TO ENABLE ACTION

Between 2017 and 2021, greater formalization was introduced; the working committee dissolved and the Grand Challenges separated from the American Academy of Social Work and Social Welfare. Some of the most active members of the working committee moved to a newly established Distinguished Advisory Board. A formal Leadership Board was established with up to 25 members, representatives from five external social work organizations were asked to join, and an Executive Committee was created from the Leadership Board membership. After 4 years, term limits for Board officers were implemented. During the initiative's 5th year, by-laws to guide election to the Leadership Board and the Executive Committee were developed. However, no corporate identity was established and no 501(c)3 status was sought. The Grand Challenges initiative saw its strength as being able to draw on existing resources held in social work dean's and departmental offices, field departments, allies in other social work organizations, faculty, students, and practitioners.

CAMPUS AND EDUCATIONAL INITIATIVES

The Grand Challenges for Social Work aim to impact the educational pipeline of future social work professionals by offering innovation and expressing a path forward for solving society's largest problems. Since the launch of the initiative, colleges and universities have adopted the Grand Challenges in myriad ways. In 2016, under the leadership of Audrey Shillington, the Colorado State University School of Social Work revised the school's research goals to conduct impactful research responsive to the Grand Challenges for Social Work. This effort helped drive research-related decision-making to support professional development, hiring, and funding opportunities. The Suzanne Dworak-Peck School of Social Work at the University of Southern California instituted a doctorate of social work program designed entirely around the Grand Challenges. When students enter the program, they select one of the Grand Challenges as their primary focus and develop an innovative project to address their chosen challenge throughout the course of their studies, which they are expected to present and defend. By the time of graduation, they are expected to have a "shovel-ready" proposal for a pilot project that is fundable.

Courses have been developed to address the Grand Challenges, including a PhD seminar course at the National Catholic School of Social Service, designed by Joe Shields, PhD Program Chair, to bring students into the social work conversation about what the critical issues of the day are in our profession. At the University of Chicago, network lead Matt Epperson developed a course on smart decarceration that is taken by MSW-level students, as well as by students in law, public policy, and social sciences. At Arizona State University, a core group of faculty in the Office of Gender-based Violence developed an internship program, coursework, and graduate and undergraduate certificate programs to address gender-based violence across social work practice areas. In concert with the renaming of the Grand Challenge to Build Healthy Relationships to End Violence, the internship program is pivoting to providing education and interventions across the spectrum of relational health.

Bachelor's social work (BSW) education is engaged. Valerie Bryan, at the University of South Alabama, transformed her BSW macro practice class positively using problem-based learning to investigate a number of the Grand Challenges. In Spring 2018, Western Carolina University's Department of Social Work adapted their field placement curriculum to have BSW students examine ways their field agencies are working to address one or more of the challenges and share in a poster presentation to faculty, staff, and other students.

Doctoral education is gaining benefit from the Grand Challenges. At the University of Maryland School of Social Work, field placement agencies identify which of the Grand Challenge(s) their placements work to address, engaging the practice community into the educational efforts of the initiative. The School also offers a competitive dissertation award of up to $4,000 to support "Research to Advance a Grand Challenge for Social Work and Society." PhD candidates are invited to apply for this award by describing how their dissertation study addresses one of the Grand Challenges for Social Work. The University of Washington has also committed financial support to graduate student research in Grand Challenge topic areas, deepening the impact of social work innovators and scholars.

Around the country, special events have been hosted that highlight the Grand Challenges and bring together innovative minds to address these issues. The University of Illinois at Urbana-Champaign School of Social Work held a year-long lecture series designed to meet the profession's Grand Challenge to Harness Technology for Social Good, and to present innovative applications of technology powered by science to expand new opportunities and collaborations for reaching more people with greater impact on society's most vexing social problems. The Graduate School of Social Work at the University of Denver held a Social Work Grand Challenges Science for Action Series addressing all the challenges over 4 years. The New York University Silver School of Social Work held a 7-month-long, student-led competition to inspire students at both the undergraduate and graduate levels to apply the core social work values to address one or more of the pressing social issues in the Grand Challenges for Social Work initiative. The Kentucky Association of Social Work Educators 2019 conference and Wichita State University's 2020 POWER conference were themed on the Grand Challenges.

The Grand Challenges committee on education recently distributed a survey to more than 600 social work programs in the country to assess the extent Grand Challenges have been incorporated into course content in accredited social work programs. This survey was an update to one completed in 2019 that found that half the responding institutions (n = 53) had integrated the Grand Challenges into their curriculum. The reach of the Grand Challenges on campus continues to grow as new partners become involved.

NETWORKS AS THE CORNERSTONES OF THE GRAND CHALLENGES

Rather than have the Executive Committee oversee each Grand Challenge in a uniform way, a group of scholars was invited to serve as national network co-leads to implement each individual Grand Challenge. Although this was a new concept, each set of co-leads was publicly acknowledged by the American Academy of Social Work and Social Welfare, asked to generate a 2-year plan, and took on a coordination role, becoming the first point of contact for each issue. Some co-leads were recognized experts that already had a research network that could be activated and engaged easily. Others needed time to recruit collaborators and strategize to determine next steps.

Each network team was asked to incorporate research, teaching, and practice, but each Grand Challenge was allowed to develop in its own way. However, the Executive Committee offered support and made some initial requests. For example, each network generated a policy brief in late 2016 and contributed book chapters for several edited volumes. Several networks volunteered to develop webinars and offer teaching workshops on their Grand Challenge. The network leads also met regularly to provide updates, offer advice, and share successes. Over time, many Grand Challenge networks organized as special interest groups within social work and met at annual conferences to introduce plans and invite new people to join. Each network also worked with the communications team to develop messaging for the calendar month designated for each Grand Challenge.

Across the Grand Challenges for Social Work, significant progress is seen in the adoption of the initiative and the approach to changing society. There have been substantial research efforts and related publications sharing the impacts of innovative practices, including child development accounts for reducing disparities (Clancy, Beverly, Schreiner, Huang, & Sherraden, 2021) and family-centered treatment for reducing recidivism in juveniles (Bright, Farrell, Winters, Betsinger, & Lee, 2018). The policy impacts of the Grand Challenges are notable in the passage of the First Step Act on prison reform, supported by research from the Promote Smart Decarceration network, and the policy proposal report developed by the End Homelessness network in advance of the 2020 election (University of Southern California Suzanne Dworak-Peck School of Social Work & New York University Silver School of Social Work, 2019).). As evidenced in the previous pages, the Grand Challenges' largest uptake is by colleges and universities around the country that have developed curricula, events, and programming around many of the Grand Challenges to ensure students are prepared to tackle society's biggest challenges when they enter the workforce. The initiative is continuously learning of new impacts and successes throughout the nation.

MAINSTREAMING GENDER

This second edition of the *Grand Challenges for Social Work and Society* addresses a shortcoming of the first volume by giving added attention to addressing gender inequity. Gender mainstreaming is an approach to gender equity that places gender at the forefront of social problems, and thus centers gender in the interventions, policies, research, and practices intended to solve these problems. This approach emerged out of a women's movement organizing primarily in the global South and feminist activism within the United Nations, and was codified in 1995 at the Fourth World Conference for Women in Beijing (Jain, 2005). Although mainstreaming has many meanings, as a strategy, it is a response to the marginalization of women's issues and women-specific programming primarily in social development contexts (Mehra & Gupta, 2006). As the concept of gender mainstreaming is translated to social work and, specifically, to the Grand Challenges for Social Work, it is imperative that gender be approached as a nonbinary and fluid social construct that intersects with multiple marginalized identities to create and enforce social inequities (Kroehle, Shelton, Clark, & Seelman, 2020). Within an intersectional framework, multiple dimensions of oppression—sexism, racism, ableism, ageism, homophobia, transphobia, and others—are connected and cannot be addressed independently from one another (Crenshaw, 1991, 2012).

Gender mainstreaming and the Grand Challenges are both mechanisms for social change; therefore, they can and should build upon and support one another. Gender mainstreaming and the Grand Challenges both rely on a nuanced analysis of social problems and ask social workers to be leaders of social change across research, practice, and policy arenas. Rather than identifying gender inequity as a distinct challenge for social work, a gender mainstreaming approach asks social workers to use an intersectional feminist analysis to identify inequities and promote mechanisms for social change, regardless of the focus of their particular social problem. As a mechanism for mainstreaming gender throughout the Grand Challenges, social work scholars have crafted Mainstreaming Gender Inserts that are embedded within each chapter in this book. These scholars have taken various approaches based on their research and expertise, highlighting particular areas within each of the 13 individual Grand Challenges to demonstrate the importance of intersectional gender mainstreaming. As outlined in the Mainstreaming Gender Insert in this chapter, consistent themes are evidenced across the inserts, providing an agenda for transforming the Grand Challenges and the social work profession itself. The inserts provide a framework for social work scholars and practitioners to apply gender mainstreaming within their own work. For gender equity to be achieved, mainstreaming gender within the Grand Challenges must become everyone's responsibility.

REFERENCES

Barth, R. P., Gilmore, G. C., Flynn, M. S., Fraser, M. W., & Brekke, J. S. (2014). The American Academy of Social Work and Social Welfare: History and grand challenges. *Research on Social Work Practice, 24*, 495–500. doi:10.1177/1049731514527801

Bent-Goodley, T. B., Williams, J. H., Teasley, M. L., & Gorin, S. H. (Eds.). (2019). *Grand challenges for society*. Washington, DC: NASW Press.

Bright, C. L., Farrell, J., Winters, A. M., Betsinger, S., & Lee, B. R. (2018). Family centered treatment, juvenile justice, and the grand challenge of smart decarceration. *Research on Social Work Practice, 28*, 638–645. doi:10.1177/1049731517730127

Clancy, M. M., Beverly, S. G., Schreiner, M., Huang, J., & Sherraden, M. (2021). *Financial outcomes in a child development account experiment: Full inclusion, success regardless of race or income, investment growth for all*. CSD Research summary 21-06. St. Louis, MO: Washington University, Center for Social Development. doi:10.7936/fnjg-n539

Crenshaw, K. W. (1991). Mapping the margins: Intersectionality, identity politics, and violence against women of color. *Stanford Law Review, 46*, 1241–1299.

Crenshaw, K. W. (2012). From private violence to mass incarceration: Thinking intersectionally about women, race, and social control. *UCLA Law Review, 59*, 1418–1472.

Dettlaff, A. J., Weber, K., Pendleton, M., Boyd, R., Bettencourt, B., & Burton, L. (2020). It is not a broken system, it is a system that needs to be broken: the upEND movement to abolish the child welfare system. *Journal of Public Child Welfare. 14*, 1–18. 10.1080/15548732.2020.1814542.

Grand Challenges for Social Work. (2019). *Grand Challenges for Social Work: Vision, Mission, Domain, Guiding Principles, & Guideposts to Action*. https://grandchallengesforsocialwork.org/wp-content/uploads/2019/03/GCSW-Principles-2-5-19.pdf

Grand Challenges for Social Work. (2021). *Progress and Plans for the Grand Challenges: An impact report at year 5 of the 10-year initiative*. https://grandchallengesforsocialwork.org/grand-challenges-for-social-work/impact-report/

Jain, D. (2005). *Women, development and the UN: A sixty-year quest for equality and justice*. Indianapolis, IN: Indiana University Press.

Kroehle, K., Shelton, J., Clark, E., & Seelman, K. (2020). Mainstreaming dissidence: Confronting binary gender in social work's grand challenges. *Social Work* 65(4): 368–377. doi:10.1093/sw/swaa037

Kulkarni, S. J., Kohl, P. L., & Edmond, T. (2020). From "Stop Family Violence" to "Build Healthy Relationships to End Violence": The journey to reenvision a grand challenge. *Social Work, 65*(4), 401–405. doi:10.1093/sw/swaa038

LeCroy, C., & Kaplan, T. (2021). The science of social work: Public perception. *Society for Social Work & Research*. doi:10.1086/712897

Mehra, R., & Gupta, G. R. (2006). Gender mainstreaming: Making it happen. *International Center for Research on Women*. Retrieved from https://www.icrw.org/publications/gender-mainstreaming-making-it-happen/

Messing, J. T. (2020). Mainstreaming gender: An intersectional feminist approach to the grand challenges for social work. *Social Work, 65*(4). doi:10.1093/sw/swaa042.

Sanders, S., Kolomer, S. R., Spellman, W. C., & Rizzo, V. M. (Eds.) (2019). *Gerontological social work and the grand challenges focusing on policy and Practice*. Springer International Publishing. doi:10.1007/978-3-030-26334-8

Sherraden, M., Barth, R. P., Brekke, J., Fraser, M. W., Manderscheid, R., & Padgett, D. K. (2014). *Social is fundamental: Introduction and context for Grand Challenges for Social Work*. Baltimore, MD: American Academy of Social Work and Social Welfare. Retrieved from https://grandchallengesforsocialwork.org/wp-content/uploads/2015/04/FINAL-GCSW-Intro-and-Context-4-2-2015-formatted-final.pdf

Sherraden, M., Stuart, P., Barth, R. P., Kemp, S., Lubben, J., Hawkins, J. D., . . . Catalano, R. (2014). *Grand accomplishments in social work: Grand Challenges for Social Work initiative, working paper no. 2*. Baltimore, MD: American Academy of Social Work and Social Welfare. Retrieved from https://grandchallengesforsocialwork.org/wp-content/uploads/2015/10/AASWSW-GC-Accomplishments4-2-2015.pdf

Singer, J. B. (Producer). (July 19, 2020). #127—Both/And or Either/Or: Social Work and Policing [Audio Podcast]. *Social Work Podcast*. Retrieved from https://www.socialworkpodcast.com/2020/07/socialworkpolicing.html

Uehara, E. S., Barth, R. P., Catalano, R. F., Hawkins, J. D., Kemp, S. P., Nurius, P. S., . . . Sherraden, M. (2015). Identifying and tackling Grand Challenges for Social Work: Working paper no. 3. Baltimore, MD: American Academy of Social Work and Social Welfare.

University of Southern California Suzanne Dworak-Peck School of Social Work & New York University Silver School of Social Work (Eds.). (2019). *Social Work's Grand Challenge to End Homelessness Policy Proposals for the 2020 U.S. Presidential Election*. https://issuu.com/gc2eh/docs/social_work_s_grand_challenge_issuu

CHAPTER 2

Ensuring Healthy Development for Youth

Unleashing the Power of Prevention: An Update on Progress and Priorities

VALERIE B. SHAPIRO, MELISSA A. LIPPOLD,
KIMBERLY BENDER, AND JEFFREY M. JENSON

The Grand Challenge to Ensure Healthy Development for Youth centers the role of the social work profession in reducing the incidence, prevalence, and inequities of behavioral health problems experienced by children and youth. Specifically, the goal of this Grand Challenge is to reduce behavioral health problems in young people—and reduce the embedded racial and socioeconomic disparities—by 20% within a decade, by *Unleashing the Power of Prevention* (Hawkins et al., 2015). As described in a key white paper (Hawkins et al., 2015), seven key action steps are articulated to guide progress toward this goal. This chapter reviews and updates our progress to date. The majority of this chapter reviews our approach and our accomplishments over the past five years. In the first section, we describe the creation of the Coalition for the Promotion of Behavioral Health (CPBH) to provide the infrastructure needed to meet this Grand Challenge. We then review the activities and progress on each of the original seven action steps, and describe some overarching challenges to pursuing our agenda.

In the second section, we highlight the role of gender and race in this Grand Challenge. Although neither an exhaustive nor systematic review, our chapter considers efforts to target, adapt, and evaluate preventive interventions for different racial groups and gender identities. We also discuss how the infusion of new intervention components to address the experiences of sexism and racism may enhance the impact of preventive interventions and further help ensure healthy youth development.

In the final section, we outline future directions for this Grand Challenge. We describe a two-pronged strategy moving forward, in which the coalition (a) continues to use advocacy to increase awareness of the power of prevention, develop community and state infrastructure for prevention, and apply research evidence from prevention science to policy and practice to meet its goal of *reducing by 20% the overall incidence and prevalence of behavioral health problems in the population of young people from birth to age 24*; and (b) focuses more intentionally on *reducing racial, socioeconomic, and other disparities in youth behavioral health problems* by 20% through the development of a research agenda focused on prevention approaches that enhance equity.

APPROACH AND ACCOMPLISHMENTS

Our approach to ensuring healthy development for youth calls upon social work scholars, educators, and practitioners to "imagine a world where only a modest number of behavioral health problems in young people are treated, controlled, or remediated—because most are prevented from occurring in the first place" (Shapiro & Bender, 2018, p. 499). Behavioral health problems that threaten the healthy development of youth include anxiety; depression; alcohol, tobacco, and drug abuse; delinquency and violence; absenteeism and disengagement from school; risky sexual activity; and unwanted pregnancies, among other undesirable outcomes. Practice innovations and scientific validation suggest that the prevention of these behavioral health problems in youth is possible. In fact, more than 80 policies and programs have been developed, tested, and demonstrated to reduce the incidence of these behavioral health problems effectively in study samples (Jenson & Bender, 2014). Yet, the Centers for Disease Control and Prevention (2009) estimates that Americans only receive preventive healthcare at about half of the recommended rate, and the prevalence of behavioral health problems in young people remains high.

The initiative to unleash the power of prevention, as articulated in the 2015 white paper (Hawkins et al., 2015), envisions social policies and programs in every community that reduce the adversities experienced by young people and disrupt—with various protective mechanisms—the causal chain between adversity and behavioral health problems. Seven broad strategies have been envisioned for achieving these goals: (a) raising public awareness of behavioral health problems and the power of prevention; (b) increasing funding for prevention initiatives; (c) establishing criteria for preventive initiatives that are effective, sustainable, equity enhancing, and cost beneficial;

(4) increasing community capacity to assess and respond to local prevention needs; (5) increasing the infrastructure available to support the high-quality implementation of preventive initiatives; (6) increasing the number of young people receiving effective preventive interventions; and (7) training and enabling a prevention workforce.

During the past 5 years, those interested in ensuring the healthy development of youth developed the infrastructure necessary to implement these seven action steps and achieve the goals of unleashing the power of prevention. Formed as an interdisciplinary entity in 2014, the CPBH includes a growing list of more than 150 individual researchers, policymakers, practitioners, and public advocates. Its membership is diverse in nature, drawing from all levels of government, joined by prevention-oriented practitioners, and includes scholars and educators from the disciplines of social work, psychology, sociology, education, public health, and medicine. Twelve national organizations have endorsed the activities of the CPBH. The CPBH is guided by a 10-person Steering Committee and by ad hoc committees created to work on activities relative to each of the seven action steps described in *Unleashing the Power of Prevention* (Hawkins et al., 2015). A strategic plan that describes activities necessary to meet the goals of ensuring the healthy development of youth was approved by CPBH members in January 2019. This plan, and complete information about the CPBH, is available on the CPBH website (https://www.coalitionforbehavioralhealth.org/). Accomplishments and selected highlights from the CPBH's work in the past 5 years are summarized in the following sections.

Action Step #1: Develop and Increase Public Awareness of the Advances and Cost Savings of Effective Preventive Interventions that Promote Healthy Youth Development

A fundamental goal of CPBH activities is to increase public support for the vision of universal social policies and prevention programs in every community. Although public opinion surveys suggest strong support for prevention (McInturff, 2009), public support has not yet incited demand for family-, school-, and community-based prevention into a high priority for policymaking across the country at the local, state, and federal levels. To change this, CPBH members are participating in a range of activities aimed at increasing the visibility and public awareness of the benefits of implementing tested and effective prevention programs and policies. These activities include the following:

- Members of the CPBH Steering Committee have delivered more than 75 national and international presentations describing the benefits of prevention since 2017. Presentation highlights include the 2020

Stockholm Public Health Lecture by J. David Hawkins of the University of Washington, and a Science for Action event celebrating prevention accomplishments in Colorado (streamed nationally) at the University of Denver in 2018.
- The CPBH has cosponsored and participated in federal congressional briefings in coordination with the National Prevention Science Coalition to Improve Lives (NPSC) and the Collaborative on Healthy Parenting in Primary Care sponsored by the National Academies of Sciences, Engineering, and Medicine.
- A joint committee was formed by the leadership of the CPBH and the NPSC to collect and disseminate written and video accounts from young people and families that illustrate the power of prevention. These accounts are being used in advocacy efforts aimed at improving the awareness of the power of prevention among lawmakers and the public.
- Steering Committee members have published more than 100 articles and chapters since the inception of the CPBH in 2014. The CPBH publishes and disseminates an e-newsletter of its activities several times per year. Newsletters and a representative list of publications are available on the CPBH website.
- Steering Committee members coedited a special issue of the *Journal of the Society for Social Work and Research* devoted to the Grand Challenge to Ensure Healthy Development for Youth (Shapiro & Bender, 2018). This issue featured new preventive intervention and implementation research on youth aging out of foster care (Batista et al., 2018), experiencing homelessness (Rice et al., 2018), holding refugee status (Nagoshi et al., 2018), and living in impoverished, rural areas (Smokowski et al., 2018). It also featured commentaries from program developers (Haggerty & McCowan, 2018), program managers (Mason, Cogua, & Thompson, 2018), and educators (Kingston & Wilensky, 2018), and articles to advance prevention research methods (Boulton et al., 2018; Jaccard et al., 2018; Lee et al., 2018).
- CPBH members have routinely published op-eds to promote the public awareness of the benefits of prevention. Representative op-eds include recent publications in the *New York Times* by Gil Botvin (2016, https://www.nytimes.com/2016/03/04/opinion/steps-we-can-take-to-prevent-opioid-abuse.html) of Weill Cornell Medical College and National Health Promotion Associates, in the *Seattle Times* by J. David Hawkins and Kevin Haggerty (2019, https://www.seattletimes.com/opinion/invest-in-proven-prevention-programs-to-stem-addiction-epidemic/) of the University of Washington, and in the *Colorado Sun* by Jeffrey M. Jenson (2020, https://coloradosun.com/2020/05/10/colorado-coronavirus-behavioral-health-public-opinion/) of the University of Denver.

Action Step #2: Increase Funding for Tested and Effective Prevention Programs and Policies

CPBH members have contributed to recent progress in increasing funding for preventive interventions through research; consultation with local, state, and federal officials; and advocacy. Noteworthy advances include the following:

- Federal legislation in 2017 and 2018 strengthened prevention programming for children, youth, and families. The 2017 Healthy Kids Act provided a 6-year funding extension for the Children's Health Insurance Program. The 2018 Family First Prevention Services Act intended to offer preventive mental health and in-home parenting services to families at risk of entering the child welfare system. These represent important milestones in increasing funding for preventive interventions.
- Meaningful increases in state funding to support preventive interventions in Colorado, Washington, Utah, Massachusetts, and other states have occurred in recent years. See Action Steps #3 and #5 for a description of CPBH activities related to these increases.

Action Step #3: Implement Community Assessment and Capacity-Building Tools to Help Communities Prioritize Risk and Protective Factors, and Implement Effective Prevention Programs

The CPBH has worked systematically to help community and state leaders and practitioners understand the importance of using knowledge of risk and protective factors to inform the selection and implementation of preventive interventions. CPBH members have also advocated for the widespread implementation of prevention systems such as Communities That Care (CTC) (Hawkins, Catalano, & Associates, 1992) and PROmoting School–Community–University Partnerships to Enhance Resilience (PROSPER) (Spoth et al., 2004), which aim to help communities identify salient risk and protective factors, identify programs that address these factors, and implement tested and effective programs. Evidence of recent progress in meeting expanding community-wide prevention planning includes the following:

- Approximately 30 states currently use statewide surveys that include measures of risk and protective factors to understand more fully the underlying causes of localized child and adolescent behavioral health problems, and to identify and implement effective programs that target these factors.

- The widespread dissemination of program registries such as the Blueprints for Healthy Youth Development has created infrastructure for implementing tested and effective school, family, and community prevention programs in states across the country.
- The adoption and use of prevention systems has increased meaningfully during the past 5 years. The CTC system, for example, is currently being implemented in more than 250 communities across the country. An online version of the program called CTC-Plus is being used in 13 states. PROSPER is being implemented in 6 states and 60 communities.

CPBH members are also supporting efforts to increase the use of effective family-focused interventions in pediatric and healthcare settings. Recent changes within healthcare make primary care a potential home for family-focused prevention and suggest possibilities for sustainable funding of family-focused prevention programs. The CPBH is participating in efforts to scale up healthy parenting interventions in primary healthcare being led by the National Academies of Sciences, Engineering, and Medicine's Forum on Promoting Children's Cognitive, Affective, and Behavioral Health. Activities and accomplishments include the following:

- CPBH members and members of the Collaborative on Healthy Parenting in Primary Care published an article in the *American Journal of Preventive Medicine* identifying 16 family-focused prevention programs that have each been tested in controlled trials and found to be effective in reducing children's negative behavioral health outcomes, noting that few of these tested and effective programs are widely used (Leslie et al., 2016). Jenson and Hawkins (2017) published a policy action brief outlining the promise of providing family-focused interventions to children and families through primary care outlets.
- In 2016, members of the Collaborative for Healthy Parenting in Primary Care and CPBH participated in a congressional briefing on healthy parenting aimed at informing Congress of the potential for integrating family-focused preventive interventions into primary healthcare. The briefing was cosponsored by the CPBH, NPSC, American Academy of Pediatrics, the American Academy of Social Work and Social Welfare, and other national organizations.
- In 2020, the CPBH endorsed and distributed the national statement *Policy Options for Improving Children's Wellbeing by Promoting Evidence-Based Parenting Interventions in Primary Care Settings* (https://parentsforum.org/wp-content/uploads/2021/04/HPPC-PolicyOptions-9-20.pdf), supported by the American Academy of Pediatrics, Mental Health America, Trust for America's Health, Zero to Three, the NPSC, and other organizations.

Action Step #4: Establish and Implement Criteria for Preventive Interventions That Are Effective, Sustainable, Equity-enhancing, and Cost Beneficial

The criteria embedded in this action step, each important, benefit from their own consideration. For example, CPBH members, with strategic consultants, have considered ways in which we can focus more explicitly on racial and socioeconomic justice in pursuit of equity-enhancing prevention. Many of these observations, and a new discussion about the complexities of deeming an intervention *equity enhancing*, were articulated in a recent chapter situated at the intersection of the Grand Challenge to Ensure Healthy Youth Development and the Grand Challenge to Eliminate Racism (Shapiro et al., 2021). To continue this work, the CPBH will create an Equity Task Force that will be charged with developing research guidelines for examining equity-enhancing preventive interventions, catalyzing opportunities for research, and ultimately identifying and disseminating prevention-oriented strategies for reducing racial and ethnic disparities in behavioral health problems among young people. Other advances to encourage the use of rigorous program selection criteria include the following:

- At a national level, CPBH members have contributed to efforts made by the Blueprints for Healthy Youth Development initiative to encourage states and communities to select programs that meet the highest scientific standards. Members of the CPBH Steering Committee have presented the 7 Action Steps of Unleashing the Power of Prevention at annual conferences held by these and other groups in the past 5 years (e.g., Jenson & Hawkins, 2018).
- The CPBH champions the work of the Washington State Institute for Public Policy in providing rigorous benefit–cost analyses to guide prevention investments as well as the Pew-MacArthur Results First initiative to implement evidence-based decision-making systems in states.

Action Step #5: Increase Community and State Infrastructure to Support the Implementation of Preventive Interventions

CPBH members are working in selected states to enhance and promote infrastructure to deliver tested and effective preventive interventions to children, youth, and families. Activities include the following:

- The CPBH published a program brief for the Grand Challenges for Social Work initiative to illustrate its strategies for working with states to improve infrastructure support for implementing tested and effective preventive interventions (Jenson, 2020).

- CPBH members organized and conducted a series of statewide convenings of practitioners, policymakers, and researchers in Utah and Colorado between 2016 and 2020. In Utah, CPBH efforts contributed to the subsequent widespread implementation of the school-based LifeSkills Training program. In Colorado, CPBH members participated in two statewide committees and planning groups sponsored by the State Office of Behavioral Health that led to the development and adoption of a statewide prevention plan called Putting Prevention Science to Work: Colorado's Statewide Strategic Plan for Primary Prevention of Substance Abuse: 2019–2024. In 2021, the Colorado State Legislature passed a comprehensive preventive services bill that includes the creation of a university and community prevention collaborative to be administered by the State's Office of Behavioral Health. CBPH members provided an initial framework for the collaborative and gave testimony in support of the bill in legislative hearings between 2019 and 2021.
- Members of the CPBH provided testimony and consultation to a legislative commission in Massachusetts that led to a statewide plan to prevent behavioral health problems and promote healthy development in young people.

Action Step #6: Monitor and Increase Access to Effective Prevention Programs and Policies

Data surveillance systems (i.e., the gathering of population level information to understand disease burden) to monitor and increase access to tested and effective interventions are inconsistent across states and communities. There are no known indicators to monitor or track the actual implementation of preventive interventions in the nation's schools and communities. Furthermore, there is currently no database or repository of technology-assisted interventions that target behavioral health outcomes. These and other activities are currently under review by the CPBH.

Action Step #7: Create Workforce Development Strategies to Prepare Social Work Graduates and Allied Practitioners for New Roles in Promotion and Preventive Interventions

Educating and preparing practitioners to fill key roles in youth development and prevention are critical to the success of the Grand Challenge to Ensure Healthy Development for Youth. CPBH members have addressed this goal through the following activities:

- A curriculum committee of the CPBH has created four prevention training modules for use in social work and other educational programs. The modules may be used at the undergraduate and graduate levels, and include content on prevention theory, direct practice, community practice, and policy prevention. Modules may be used as stand-alone instructional tools or may be integrated in existing courses. Each module is available at no cost and may be downloaded from the CPBH website. Curriculum committee members have presented the modules at the annual conferences of the Society for Social Work and Research, Council on Social Work Education, and the Society for Prevention Research during the past several years. Jeffrey M. Jenson, Anne Williford, and Elizabeth Anthony presented a 2021 webinar explaining and disseminating these models through the Grand Challenges for Social Work initiative.

- CPBH members are also collaborating on interdisciplinary initiatives aimed at better preparing practitioners to deliver preventive interventions in behavioral health settings. These efforts include coordinating with accreditation bodies of professional degree programs, creating standardized learning objectives for prevention practice courses, identifying existing prevention training programs in allied disciplines, collating a repository of prevention course syllabi, and undertaking a study of the integration of prevention content into broader programs of study.
- Publications and presentations by CPBH members have highlighted the importance of preparing students for prevention practice (e.g., Hawkins, Shapiro, & Fagan, 2010; Jenson, 2020). Members coauthored a poster and a brief that was featured at a 2016 workshop sponsored by the National Academies of Sciences, Engineering, and Medicine titled Training the Future Child Healthcare Workforce to Improve Behavioral Health Outcomes for Children, Youth, and Families (https://sites.nationalacademies.org/cs/groups/dbassesite/documents/webpage/dbasse_177206.pdf). A co-authored paper including CPBH members has also been published as a discussion paper by the National Academy of Medicine (Boat et al., 2016). CBPH members also pursued this agenda speaking at the Inaugural Grand Challenges for Social Work Western Consortium Meeting in 2017.

CHALLENGES AND BARRIERS

Significant progress has been made in meeting the goals of the Grand Challenge to Ensure Healthy Development for Youth. The interdisciplinary CPBH has been an important mechanism for recruiting social work faculty and students who are interested in advancing the widespread implementation of preventive interventions and policies. This team is making important contributions to what is now a growing interest in prevention practice and policy in social work. Several challenges, however, remain as the CPBH strives to meet its goals fully to reduce the prevalence and disparities associated with behavioral health problems in young people.

MAINSTREAMING GENDER

A Focus on Gender and Intersectionality Supports Healthy Youth Development
LAURIE M. GRAHAM

Gender quite simply matters in the study of behavioral health concerns affecting children and adolescents. Across various areas, including but not limited to aggression, violence, and mental health issues such as anxiety and depression, research has highlighted that gender influences risk for experiencing these concerns as well as short- and long-term outcomes across physical, emotional, and social health domains. Gender also affects these issues at a macro level, shaping what we define as "healthy" and "unhealthy" behaviors as well as how to intervene with and prevent unhealthy behaviors. To address the unique and varied needs of all young people, our approaches to intervening with and preventing behavioral health concerns among children and adolescents must take up intersectional approaches that include gender as a critical consideration. Layering gender-focused analyses with attention to race, ethnicity, ability, sexual orientation, socioeconomic status, citizenship, and additional critical axes of identity and social location elucidates a more nuanced picture of social inequities and health disparities. A gender mainstreaming approach to this and all Social Work Grand Challenges has the potential to open many opportunities for and pathways to potentially effective interventions at every level of the social ecology.

Centering information on identity and social location will help interventionists with the development, implementation, and evaluation of more effective and responsive prevention strategies. Research underscores the need to attend to gender in intersectional work on understanding and addressing both the needs and resiliency of youth. Here, I briefly describe one framework to consider—a "gender transformative" (GT) approach, which offers a promising way to integrate a gender analysis into efforts to support the healthy development of young people. GT interventions intentionally offer participants space to examine critically the meaning, source, and impact of gendered expectations and norms. In doing so, these interventions seek to transform attitudes, beliefs, behaviors, and systems to be gender equitable and nonviolent (Gupta, 2000), aligning well with a gender mainstreaming approach to intractable social issues. Intersectionality should also be included as a core component of applying GT approaches. Promising GT approaches have targeted issues that impact young people detrimentally, including violence, sexually transmitted infections, and condom use (Graham, Casey, & Carlson, 2020). However, it is also important to note that additional rigorous research is needed to evaluate and improve current GT strategies as well as to develop new GT interventions. Such research should also aim to enhance our understanding of how to

continued

deliver such interventions and with whom they are most effective at the intersections of various identities, social locations, and cultural and geographic contexts.

I encourage researchers and practitioners seeking to understand more fully GT approaches and their potential relationship to their work for ensuring healthy development for all youth to review the recommendations provided next, while also examining potential limitations of such approaches. All social workers—whether they are consuming or generating knowledge, testing or implementing interventions, or creating or analyzing social policies—should seek to use an intersectional approach that centers gender as a critical axis of identity. Some steps that individuals can take include:

- examining the role of gender within your particular social problem or area of interest, including interventions that take GT approaches to prevention, and analyzing critically the ways in which that information might inform your work;
- approaching practice and research opportunities through an intersectional gender lens, designing or selecting interventions with attention to the role of gender and additional intersecting identities and social locations of potential participants;
- attempting to understand and attend to how gender is socialized and performed in contextually specific ways based on where and with whom an intervention is being developed, implemented, and/or evaluated; and
- building coalitions across siloed efforts to promote the healthy development of all youth; we're in this together.

Gender does not matter more than other forms of identity or social locations, nor is it the only axis of identity to be considered as we promote the prosocial development of young people. Yet, gender does matter, and one of the primary benefits of both gender mainstreaming and GT approaches to social inquiry and intervention is that they have the potential to reimagine the ways that people of all gender identities perform and are ultimately restricted by gender roles and expectations. If we are truly able to ensure healthy development for all youth, inclusive of young people from all social locations and with every constellation of identities, our world will be transformed for the better, and we will move closer to realizing the goals of this and other Social Work Grand Challenges.

References

Graham, L. M., Casey, E., & Carlson, J. (2020). Gender matters: Infusing a gender analysis into the healthy development of all youth Grand Challenge. *Social Work, 65*(4), 325–334. doi:10.1093/sw/swaa035

Gupta, G. R. (2000). Gender, sexuality, and HIV/AIDS: The what, the why, and the how. *Canadian HIV/AIDS Policy and Law Review, 5*, 86–93.

INTERDISCIPLINARY LEADERSHIP

A key to success for the Grand Challenge to Ensure Healthy Development for Youth—and for the other 12 Grand Challenges—may well lie in the strength of interdisciplinary leadership present at all levels of the initiative. Individual and social problems like behavioral health and youth development require the best thinking from people representing very diverse fields of study and practice. Creating a stronger interdisciplinary leadership structure in the overall Grand Challenge initiative—and in each of the 13 individual Grand Challenges—should be a priority going forward.

SOCIAL WORK ENGAGEMENT

Recruiting faculty, students, practitioners, and policymakers to engage in CPBH activities has been met with mixed results. On a positive note, and as mentioned earlier, an active curriculum committee composed of social work faculty members designed and completed four prevention modules that are now being used in schools across the country. Finding the mechanisms to involve faculty and students in policy discussions with state and federal officials, however, has been a greater challenge. One factor in recruiting participants may be attributed to the lack of funding available to support the time and travel necessary to become involved in efforts to advance prevention practices and policies in federal and state policy circles. Adequately funding the core infrastructure of the CPBH is a related and ongoing challenge to the success of ensuring healthy development for youth. Furthermore, as midcareer scholars ascend to the leadership of our coalition, we face vastly different capacities and constraints for contributing to advocacy and dissemination efforts.

Integrating individual scholarly work, teaching, and service with the goals and activities of the Grand Challenges initiative requires intentional thought and planning. For example, most faculty and doctoral students are engaged in individual or collaborative programs of research that place competing demands on their time and availability. Developing strategies to enable and recognize faculty and students for working toward the Grand Challenge objectives should be explored more fully by the leadership of the initiative and by individual schools and departments.

THE ASSUMPTION THAT THE SCIENCE IS COMPLETE

Up to this point, our challenge has aligned closely to the Grand Challenge initiative's call to use existing science to solve major social problems within a decade (Fong et al., 2017). The CPBH, to this point, has embraced this approach, having leadership that has conducted decades of rigorous research, with the platform to disseminate that evidence to inform national and state-level intervention, and a career stage well suited to doing so (Kelly, Singer, Shin, Iverson, & Williams, 2019). As we turn our attention more intentionally toward our second goal (i.e., to reduce inequities), we must recognize that the science is quite incomplete (Shapiro et al., 2021). We need to incorporate an explicit research agenda into our work.

THE ROLE OF GENDER AND RACE

In the following sections, we consider the ways in which gender and race intersect with the Grand Challenge to Ensure Healthy Development for Youth. We do so conflicted by the task. We recognize the importance of calling attention to the ways in which gender and race shape the behavioral health status of youth, the scientific literature, our social sector interventions, and our progress as a Grand Challenge, but we also recognize that our broad summary is likely to perpetuate the field's use of crude, atheoretical categorizations of people that fail to capture the complexity of the ways in which structural sexism and racism shapes the experiences and welfare of individuals. With this limitation, we review whether risk and protective factors, and preventive intervention effects have been found to differ by race and gender. We also examine the effects of (and lack of) interventions for specific genders and racial and cultural groups. Furthermore, we discuss some potential next steps (e.g., studying how interventions may be enhanced by targeting racism and discrimination more explicitly at both the individual and structural levels).

GENDER

It is important to consider gender identity in prevention research and dissemination. Gender identity may influence both the risk for and consequences of a variety of behavioral health outcomes for youth (Nolen-Hoeksema, 2004). Gender presentation may underlie exposure to specific types of violence (Graham, Casey, & Carlson, 2020). For example, although studies suggest boys and girls are both at risk for sexual harassment and violence, girls report vastly higher rates of victimization from sexual violence than boys (Graham et al., 2020). Transgender youth are also at increased risk for sexual violence (Stotzer, 2009). Gender differences are not limited to sexual violence, however. Developmental studies examining mental and behavioral health outcomes suggest there are differential risks based on gender for a host of outcomes, including greater risk of externalizing behaviors for boys (Fagan, Van Horn, Hawkins, & Arthur, 2007; Fraser, Kirby, & Smokowski, 2004; Greenberg &

Lippold, 2013), greater risk for internalizing problems for girls (Hilt & Nolen-Hoeksema, 2009), and greater risk of depression, anxiety, and suicide among transgender youth (Grossman & D'Augelli, 2007). Studies have also demonstrated different rates of protective factors by gender (e.g., Kim et al., 2015; LeBuffe et al., 2018). Understanding gender differences in profiles of risk and protection can inform the development of preventive interventions that address a particular risk factor or outcome to specific gender groups.

Gender may also be an important consideration when designing interventions. The influence or relevance of certain risk and protective factors may vary by gender (Fagan et al., 2007; Foshee et al., 2015; Greenberg & Lippold, 2013; Nolen-Hoeksema, 2004). Some studies suggest that peer relationships are more salient predictors of outcomes, especially delinquency, for boys than girls (Piquero, Gover, MacDonald, & Piquero, 2005; Weerman & Hoeve, 2012), although findings have been mixed (Fagan et al., 2007; Haynie, Doogan, & Soller, 2014). Several studies have found that family factors are stronger predictors of outcomes for girls than boys (Davies & Lindsay, 2004; Galbavy, 2003; Lippold, McHale, Davis, Almeida, & King, 2016; Lippold, Hussong, Fosco, & Ram, 2018). In addition to the inclusive findings, most studies have relied on a binary conceptualization of gender, not distinguished from biological sex, and have not gathered data on intersex, nonbinary, gender expansive, or transgender youth. This leaves a gap in the literature regarding how risk and protective factors for healthy development may be similar or different, and what specific factors may be central influences on the development of young people with specific gender identities (Horn, Kosciw, & Russell, 2009; Whitaker et al., 2016). An important future direction of prevention work is to expand our understanding of how a broad array of risk and protective factors may vary across diverse gender identities.

Very little research has examined how the effects of preventive interventions vary based on gender. The Blueprints for Healthy Youth Development registry identifies 18 model and model plus programs that have been tested through randomized trials and found to be effective in preventing adverse outcomes in young people. Upon review of the registry, all but two programs were characterized as effective for "both genders". The two exceptions were programs designed specifically for females. Digging deeper into the studies that buttress the remaining programs' evidentiary status (i.e., "Blueprints Certified Studies"), there are a variety of gender-based findings. For example, research on the effects of the Brief Alcohol Screening and Intervention for College Students (BASICS) found no gender differences in intervention effects on drinking (Marlatt et al., 1998; Turrisi et al., 2009); Treatment Foster Care Oregon (TFCO) found no gender differences in intervention effects on delinquency and violence (Gorman, 2014); and the Accelerated Study in Associate Programs (ASAP) found no gender differences on three-year nor six-year graduation rates (Weiss et al., 2019). Yet other studies did find differential effects by gender. For example, Project Towards No Drug Abuse reduced weapon carrying and victimization, but only among males (Sussman et al., 2002) and the effect of LifeSkills Training (LST) on intentions to refuse substances was stronger for females than males (Trudeau et al., 2003). Most studies did not complete gender-based subgroup or moderation analyses. In some cases, this may be because central studies had samples that were exclusively male (Forgatch & DeGarmo, 1999) or predominantly female (Rohde et al., 2014). Notably, no literature substantiating model program designations explicitly examined intervention effects for non-binary or transgendered young people. More work is needed that examines differences in preventive intervention effects by gender, including a wide range of gender identities, and makes transparent the status of gender-based evidence that qualifies an intervention as effective for all genders.

Most of the highly studied preventive interventions found in Blueprints and other repositories directly target individuals and families for change, rather than the broader societal structures that shape gender norms and cognitions as intervention targets. Youth are likely to encounter different social modeling, have different opportunities, be judged against different expectations, and receive different feedback from their peers, families, and educators based on their gender presentation (Bussey & Bandura, 1999). For example, studies suggest there are specific socialized gender cognitions for boys that may increase the risk of sexual violence perpetration (Graham et al., 2020; Tharp et al., 2013). Dominance-oriented masculinity, hostility toward women, and gender-role stress are all associated with increased risk for perpetrating sexual aggression and violence (Tharp et al., 2013). Interventions that target gender messages and the underlying implicit biases, and that promote gender equity may be critical to designing effective sexual violence prevention programs (Graham et al., 2020). Although not yet studied extensively in children and youth, there is some evidence that programs aimed at changing gender norms and beliefs are associated with reductions in sexual aggression and increased willingness to intervene when witnessing sexual aggression in others (Casey, Carlson, Two Bulls, & Yager, 2018; Miller et al., 2013; Reyes, Foshee, Niolon, Reidy, & Hall, 2016; Salazar, Vivolo-Kantor, Hardin, & Berkowitz, 2014).

Broad scale preventive interventions that shift societal or service sector norms associated with gender, and reduce discrimination and stigma will be important in shifting the context to prevent adverse outcomes, especially among gender minorities. For example, given that lesbian, gay, bisexual, transgender, questioning, intersex, and asexual (LGBTQIA+) youth may be at increased risk for experiencing bullying (Abreu & Kenny, 2018; Gower, Rider, McMorris, & Eisenberg, 2018), bullying prevention programs may be strengthened by infusing messages of gender inclusion and equity (Horn et al., 2009). Because parental acceptance has a large impact on the well-being of LGBTQ youth (Mills-Koonce, Rehder, & McCurdy, 2018; Ryan, 2008), family-based interventions may be strengthened by incorporating components on gender and sexual identity development and acceptance. Interventions aimed at increasing school connectedness and changing school climate may be enhanced by addressing school-wide gender norms (Hall, 2017; Toomey, McGuire, & Russell, 2012). Community-based interventions that provide a safe and accepting community for transgender and gender-expansive young people may buffer youth from other risks faced by targeted discrimination and oppression (Shelton, 2016). In summary, a closer examination of the role of gender in prevention is needed to assess 1) whether developmental mechanisms and intervention effects differ based on gender identity, and 2) how individual and societal level interventions to shift social norms and beliefs about gender may enhance the effectiveness of preventive interventions.

RACE

Many common risk and protective factors for behavioral health problems are found among adolescents of diverse races and ethnicities (Choi et al., 2005; Deng & Roosa, 2007; Roosa et al., 2011; Sullivan & Hirschfield, 2011; Williams et al., 1999). However, evidence suggests that experiences of microaggressions, discrimination, and racial trauma (Comas-Diaz et al., 2019) are likely to be different across racial groups and have been studied infrequently as targets of preventive interventions. We both need to help young people cope with experiences of discrimination and prevent the perpetration of discrimination and other bias-based behavior. Research has identified some universal interventions (e.g., Raising Healthy Children, Staying Connected with Your Teen) that have shown promise for narrowing disparities over time (Haggerty et al. 2007; Hawkins et al., 2008; Hill et al., 2014) and has identified some culturally specific interventions (e.g., Familias Unidas) that have shown improvements in the mental and behavioral health of marginalized young people (Perrino et al., 2014; Prado et al., 2007, Prado et al., 2012). Yet years of scientific funding to predominantly white researchers (Ginther et al., 2011) testing interventions on predominantly white samples (e.g., Rowe & Trickett, 2018) leaves much work to be done.

A review of the Blueprints for Healthy Youth Development registry of experimentally proven programs (Shapiro et al., 2021) reveals that few experimental studies adequately test for, and report on, differences by race and ethnicity. The highest rated Blueprint programs are buttressed by studies that generally describe their sample race/ethnic composition, but 31% of the time the sample is only divided into two groups (e.g., "White"/"Non-White"), inadequately capturing diversity by race and ethnicity. In addition, 61% of study samples had at least a modest (>60%) white predominance, and 33% of studies had an extreme (>80%) white predominance. Only 3% of studies had a modest Hispanic predominance and only 8% of studies had an extreme Black predominance. Ten (59%) Blueprints model programs were buttressed by studies that used race as a variable in the analysis, half of which only used race as a covariate. The remaining five programs expressed intentions to examine treatment effects by race, but for various reasons studies did not pursue, describe a method for, or display any data from such an analysis (Olds et al., 1998, Stice et al., 2006; Stice et al., 2011). Of the three remaining programs, two were assessed to be equally effective across youths of different ethnic backgrounds (Borduin et al., 1995; Brotman et al., 2011), and one had mixed findings in which it exacerbated a racial disparity on some outcomes and reduced a disparity on others (Edmunds et al., 2017; Haxton et al., 2016).

The lack of research leaves very few programs with evidentiary support for making efficacy claims for racial and ethnic marginalized populations. These findings generally comport with results users would encounter when using target group filters embedded in the Blueprints website. There is currently only one Model program (GenerationPMTO) listed as efficacious with Hispanic/Latino youth, no model programs listed as efficacious with African American youth, no programs listed as efficacious with Asian youth, and no programs listed as efficacious with American Indian/Alaskan youth. In summary, the CPBH has recognized that little information exists regarding whether rigorously tested prevention programs perpetuate, sustain, or remediate racial and ethnic disparities in behavioral healthcare and outcomes. The justification for listing GenerationPMTO as efficacious for Hispanic/Latino youth is a study (Martinez & Eddy, 2005) that is not among the "Blueprints certified studies" that officially buttress the model program designation, although it is a good example of exploring the equity-enhancing effects of an intervention. Future studies should increase sample diversity and test subgroup effects to evaluate efficacy of healthy development for all youth.

Importantly, we recognize that the sheer naming of undesirable behaviors worthy of prevention practices and policies is situated in sociocultural contexts that reflect disproportionately the worldview and priorities of the most powerful members of our society. This can lead to prevention theories and interventions that implicitly help young people cope with an unjust world rather than change the deeply rooted social structures that disrupt their healthy development. Some mechanisms and outcomes (e.g., aggression) are easier to observe than others (e.g., depression), and therefore become more frequent targets for preventive intervention. The presentation of behaviors is context and culture bound, and subject to the perceptual biases of the informant. Among the mechanisms studied most frequently, we observe that the distribution of the risk and protective factors among youth are not random; they reflect and perpetuate social inequities. It follows that different social groups—characterized by gender, race, ethnicity, citizenship, dis(ability), sexual orientation, and class—experience different levels of risk and prevalence of behavioral health problems. Furthermore, we recognize that well-intended prevention delivery systems continue to reflect and perpetuate systems of oppressions based on the ways in which prevention is differentially available, affordable, accessible, accommodable, and acceptable to diverse subpopulations of youth.

FUTURE DIRECTIONS

Much of the work accomplished by our Grand Challenge to Ensure Healthy Development for Youth in the past 5 years has focused on our first primary goal: to reduce the incidence and prevalence of behavioral health problems in the broad population of young people. To this end, and as outlined earlier in this chapter, members have made great progress on several action steps. Of note, members have engaged in important work to disseminate existing evidence-based programs through novel service sectors (i.e., healthcare) and through new state-level prevention systems. Members have also engaged in activities to advocate for prevention and to train social workers on prevention. Much of this work has been consistent with the Grand Challenges for Social Work initiative's assumptions that much of the science to address Grand Challenges is known, and we should use it to solve some of the most pressing issues through practice and policy (Fong et al., 2017). During the next 5 years, our group will continue this line of our work. As outlined in our 2019 Strategic Plan (https://www.coalitionforbehavioralhealth.org/strategic-plan), we plan to continue to advance the development of infrastructure to support community- and state-level prevention interventions, systems, and policies. Grant-writing endeavors are underway to fund and support this line of our work in additional states. We will also continue ongoing efforts to advocate for prevention at the federal and state levels and increase our emphasis on infusing more prevention content and training into the social work curriculum. Continuing and expanding our current work toward this goal is critical.

For the next 5 years, however, our Grand Challenge to Ensure Healthy Development for Youth will also focus more explicitly on our second primary goal: to reduce racial, socioeconomic, and other disparities in behavioral health problems. Shifting our work to include more explicitly and intentionally a focus on equity means we must also expand the CPBH's work from focusing primarily on advocacy and dissemination of *existing* science to focusing on advancing *new* science as well, intersecting and expanding upon what is known and understood from the research traditions of health equity and prevention. We posit that health equity depends on centering questions of relevance to the well-being of marginalized youth (Wallerstein & Duran, 2010), understanding the effects of new and previously tested programs on diverse and marginalized sociodemographic groups (Gottfredson et al., 2015), and demonstrating how a community may overcome programmatic and structural barriers to inclusive adaptation and implementation (Barerra et al., 2011).

Our focus on reducing disparities will begin with inviting new scholars to join our Grand Challenge leadership—in particular, those with a focus on equity—and engage authentically in a process of identifying ways in which racism has shaped prevention research processes and evidence (Shapiro et al., 2021). This will include understanding the National Institute of Minority Health and Health Disparities' consensus report that describes the need to study marginalized populations, regardless of the presence of disparities (Duran & Perez-Stable, 2019). Second, we have identified a need to go beyond a focus on scaling up *programs*, to also focus on scaling up the *conditions* in which programs can benefit marginalized youth. This involves advocating for poverty remediation and antidiscrimination policies, as well as eliminating other conditions that constrain the authentic choice-making upon which the success of many psychoeducational programs are predicated (Trent et al., 2019). Accordingly, we join the call of Aarons et al. (2017) for researchers to work as urgently on scaling *out* effective prevention programs (i.e., adapting to novel populations or delivery systems) as on scaling them up. Third, we hope our Grand Challenge to Ensure Healthy Development for Youth can provide a platform for developing a scientific agenda around prevention and equity, including proposing definitions, frameworks, approaches, and metrics to advance standards for equity-enhancing prevention programming. We will be further articulating specific action steps related to our goal to conduct prevention research that catalyzes a reduction in disparities and advancement of equity.

Although a scientific agenda for enhancing equity in prevention must be informed by a broad range of perspectives, and we will engage new and existing members in creating our approach, we start here with a thoughtful collection of ideas for how we may advance this agenda. First, prevention science should *examine equity as an outcome for preventive efforts*. As an initial step, more work must be done to examine subgroup differences in response to intervention, including analyzing race, gender, and socioeconomic status as moderators of intervention efficacy and effectiveness (Shapiro et al., 2021). Interventions may be accessed differentially or may have differing effects across sociodemographic subgroups that may have the unintended effect of increasing disparities. Such work will help the field understand whether our existing interventions are working the same across groups, or whether only some groups are benefitting from them. Advocacy work may be needed with journal editors to advance the publication of work that centers on marginalized groups and/or requires the reporting of subgroup effects with diverse samples.

Second, prevention science should focus more explicitly on *how intervention components and delivery systems may need to be adapted to reach disadvantaged populations*. At the program level, more studies are needed that examine the effects of intervention adaptations for specific racial, cultural, or gendered groups. The features and evaluations of adapted interventions need a peer-reviewed repository to enable evidence to accumulate about what works for whom under what conditions. Consensus standards for adaptation evaluations should be articulated such that evidence from randomized controlled trials are leveraged appropriately to "lend strength" to the adaptation (Aarons et al., 2017); however, randomized controlled trials are not required for every unique application from which we could learn (Shapiro et al., 2021). We should keep in mind that universal interventions may be more effective for high-risk populations if they are bundled with other needed supports or embedded in specific delivery systems.

Third, *engagement in more participatory research is needed to inform intervention development and adaptation for underserved populations*. Developing and adapting interventions must begin with listening to the voices of those who are intended beneficiaries. Norms, values, and preferences are not universal. Engaging in community-based research will enable the field to identify the intervention components and delivery mechanisms that will have the greatest impact and uptake for specific groups.

Last, prevention may be enhanced by *directly addressing oppressive social structures as well as the implicit biases and social norms that sustain them*. Many preventive interventions are geared toward helping young people develop individual skills (e.g., self-control). Yet, youth development often occurs within oppressive social structures. Skill development does not happen devoid of context. Indeed, behavioral health disparities will persist and widen without systemic reforms across multiple ecological levels. Young people need consistent messaging among socializing units of the importance of these skills, ample opportunities to practice these skills, and environments that recognize and reinforce a skillful performance (Haggerty & McCowan, 2018). Furthermore, trustworthy people are needed to model these skills, provide these opportunities, and celebrate successes across domains, from peer groups to family units, and from adults in educational settings to those in the broader community. The problem with a "skills only" approach to preventive interventions is well illustrated by the classic Marshmallow Experiment (Mischel, 1974), which originally revealed that a preschool child's self-control (i.e., inhibition of the urge to eat a single marshmallow immediately, predicated on the promise of getting two marshmallows if the child could delay their gratification) was predictive of important outcomes across the life course. More recently, however, follow-up studies have shown that children primed with an experience of an "unreliable adult" who failed to produce expected resources (e.g., in the study, a waiting room staffer left to get art supplies and returned with an excuse rather than supplies) would lead to a child eating the first marshmallow in far less time (Kidd et al., 2012). Therefore, life course outcomes predicated on a child's ability to wait are not only predicated on characteristics of the child, but also predicated on whether it is pragmatic and rational to wait in an environment perceived to be unreliable. This is just one piece of evidence, among many, that implores us to address disparities embedded at every ecological level. Prevention efforts should be further enhanced by examining the structural source of behavioral health outcomes and considering not just the individual, but also the broader context in which individuals develop, express, and nurture their behavioral health. Our intention is to collaborate with members of other Grand Challenge initiatives (e.g. end homelessness, reduce extreme economic inequality, eliminate racism, and achieve equal opportunity and justice) to find collaborative opportunities to build healthy environments for youth development.

SUMMARY

The Grand Challenge of Ensuring Healthy Development of Youth seeks to unleash the power of prevention to reduce behavioral health problems in young people—and reduce the embedded racial and socioeconomic disparities—by 20% within a decade (Hawkins et al., 2015). During the past 5 years, the CPBH has made measurable progress toward each of our seven action steps: (a) raising public awareness of behavioral health problems and the power of prevention; (b) increasing funding for prevention initiatives; (c) establishing criteria for preventive initiatives that are effective, sustainable, equity enhancing, and cost beneficial; (d) increasing community capacity to assess and respond to local prevention needs; (e) increasing the infrastructure available to support the high-quality implementation of preventive initiatives; (f) increasing the number of young people receiving effective preventive interventions; and (g) training and enabling a prevention workforce. During the next 5 years, we will face the challenges associated with (a) leadership transitions; (b) sustaining the engagement of our existing interdisciplinary members; (c) recruiting the participation of more social work researchers, practitioners, policymakers, and advocates; and (d) expanding our work to more explicitly and intentionally focus on prevention and equity, in which the available scientific evidence is emerging. There are meaningful gaps in what is currently understood about the role of gender and race in preventive initiatives. We intend to focus on developing a platform from which to catalyze equity research, and embedding research evidence in expanded prevention delivery systems.

Acknowledgments: We write this chapter in appreciation to the American Academy of Social Work and Social Welfare, whose leadership team gave us the grand challenge framework through which to think deeply about the potential impacts of science on society. We are indebted to all the authors of the original white paper, *Unleashing the Power of Prevention*, which articulates the steps necessary to achieve the goals for the Grand Challenge of *Ensuring Healthy Development of Youth*; founding co-leads of the Grand Challenge J. David Hawkins and Jeffrey M. Jenson; members of the Coalition for the Promotion of Behavioral Health (CPBH); the CPBH Steering Committee; CPBH graduate research assistants Erica Gleason, Miguel Trujillo, and Nehal Eldeeb; and CPBH founding chair Jeffrey M. Jenson, who have given the vision vibrant life over the past 5 years.

REFERENCES

Aarons, G. A., Sklar, M., Mustanski, B., Benbow, N., & Hendricks Brown, C. (2017). "Scaling-out" evidence-based interventions to new populations or new health care delivery systems. *Implementation Science, 12*, 111. https://doi.org/10.1186/s13012-017-0640-6

Abreu, R. L., & Kenny, M. C. (2018). Cyberbullying and LGBTQ youth: A systematic literature review and recommendations for prevention and intervention. *Journal of Child & Adolescent Trauma, 11*, 81–97.

Barrera, M., Castro, F. G., & Holleran-Steiker, L. K. (2011). A Critical Analysis of Approaches to the Development of Preventive Interventions for Subcultural Groups. *American Journal of Community Psychology, 48*, 439–454.

Batista, T., Johnson, A., & Baach Friedmann, L. (2018). The effects of youth empowerment programs on the psychological empowerment of young people aging out of foster care. *Journal of the Society for Social Work and Research*. Advance online publication. doi:10.1086/700275

Boat, T. F., Land, M. L., Leslie, L. K., Hoagwood, K. E., Hawkins-Walsh, E., McCabe, M. A., . . . Sweeney, M. (2016). Workforce Development to Enhance the Cognitive, Affective, and Behavioral Health of Children and Youth: Opportunities and Barriers in Child Health Care Training. Discussion Paper, National Academy of Medicine, Washington, DC. https://nam.edu/wp-content/uploads/2016/11/Workforce-Development-to-Enhance-the-CognitiveAffective-and-Behavioral-Health-of-Children-andYouth.pdf

Borduin, C. M., Mann, B. J., Cone, L. T., Henggeler, S. W., Fucci, B. R., Blaske, D. M., & Williams, R. A. (1995). Multisystemic treatment of serious juvenile offenders: Long-term prevention of criminality and violence. *Journal of Consulting and Clinical Psychology, 63*, 569–578.

Boulton, A. J., & Williford, A. (2018). Analyzing skewed continuous outcomes with many zeros: A tutorial for social work and youth prevention science researchers. *Journal of the Society for Social Work and Research*. Advance online publication. doi:10.1086/701235

Brotman, L. M., Calzada, E., Huang, K., Kingston, S., Dawson-McClure, S., Kamboukos, D., Rosenfelt, A., Schwab, A., & Petkova, E. (2011). Promoting effective parenting practices and preventing child behavior problems in school among ethnically diverse families from underserved, urban communities. *Child Development, 82*(1), 258–276.

Bussey, K., & Bandura, A. (1999). Social cognitive theory of gender development and differentiation. *Psychological Review, 106*(4), 676.

Casey, E. A., Carlson, J., Two Bulls, S., & Yager, A. (2018). Gender transformative approaches to engaging men in gender-based violence prevention: A review and conceptual model. Trauma, Violence, & Abuse, 19, 231–246.

Centers for Disease Control and Prevention. (2009). Preventive Health Care. http://web.archive.org/web/20190525141113/https://www.cdc.gov/healthcommunication/toolstemplates/entertainmented/tips/preventivehealth.html. Accessed June 28, 2020.

Choi, Y., Harachi, T. W., Gillmore, M. R., & Catalano, R. F. (2005). Applicability of the social development model to urban ethnic minority youth: Examining the relationship between external constraints, family socialization, and problem behaviors. Journal of Research on Adolescence, 15(4), 505–534.

Comas-Diaz, L., Hall, G. N., & Neville, H. A. (2019). Racial trauma: Theory, Research and Healing: Introduction to Special Issue. American Psychologist, 74(1), 1–5.

Davies, P. T., & Lindsay, L. L. (2004). Interparental conflict and adolescent adjustment: Why does gender moderate early adolescent vulnerability? Journal of Family Psychology, 18, 160–170.

Deng, S., & Roosa, M. W. (2007). Family Influences on Adolescent Delinquent Behaviors: Applying the Social Development Model to a Chinese Sample. American Journal of Community Psychology, 40(3-4), 333–344.

Duran, D. G., & Pérez-Stable, E. J. (2019). Novel Approaches to Advance Minority Health and Health Disparities Research. American Journal of Public Health, 109(S1), S8–S10. https://doi.org/10.2105/AJPH.2018.304931

Edmunds, J. A., Unlu, F., Glennie, E., Bernstein, L., Fesler, L., Furey, J., & Arshavsky, N. (2017). Smoothing the transition to postsecondary education: The impact of the early college model. Journal of Research on Educational Effectiveness, 10(2), 297–325.

Fagan, A. A., Van Horn, M. L., Hawkins, J. D., & Arthur, M. W. (2007). Gender similarities and differences in the association between risk and protective factors and self-reported serious delinquency. Prevention Science, 8, 115–124.

Fong, R., Lubben, J., & Barth, R. P. (Eds.). (2017). Grand challenges for social work and society. Oxford University Press.

Forgatch, M., & DeGarmo, D. (1999). Parenting Through Change: An effective prevention program for single mothers. Journal of Consulting and Clinical Psychology, 67(5), 711–724.

Foshee, V. A., Reyes, L. M., Tharp, A. T., Chang, L. Y., Ennett, S. T., Simon, T. R., . . . Suchindran, C. (2015). Shared longitudinal predictors of physical peer and dating violence. Journal of Adolescent Health, 56, 106–112.

Fraser, M. W., Kirby, L. D., & Smokowski, P. R. (2004). Risk and resilience in childhood. Risk and Resilience in Childhood: An Ecological Perspective, 2, 13–66.

Galbavy, R. J. (2003). Juvenile delinquency: Peer influences, gender differences and prevention. Journal of Prevention & Intervention in the Community, 25, 65–78.

Ginther, D. K., Schaffer, W. T., Schnell, J., Masimore, B., Liu, F., Haak, L. L., & Kington, R. (2011). Race, ethnicity, and NIH research awards. Science, 333(6045), 1015–1019.

Gorman, D. M. (2014). Is Project Towards No Drug Abuse (Project TND) an Evidence-Based Drug and Violence Prevention Program? A Review and Reappraisal of the Evaluation Studies. The Journal of Primary Prevention, 35(4), 217–232.

Gottfredson, D. C., Cook, T. D., Gardner, F. E., Gorman-Smith, D., Howe, G. W., Sandler, I. N., & Zafft, K. M. (2015). Standards of evidence for efficacy, effectiveness, and scale-up research in prevention science: Next generation. Prevention Science, 16(7), 893–926.

Gower, A. L., Rider, G. N., McMorris, B. J., & Eisenberg, M. E. (2018). Bullying victimization among LGBTQ youth: Critical issues and future directions. *Current Sexual Health Reports, 10*, 246–254.

Graham, L. M., Casey, E. A., & Carlson, J. (2020). Gender matters: Infusing a gender analysis into the "Healthy Development of All Youth" Grand Challenge. *Social Work, 65*(4), 325–334.

Greenberg, M. T., & Lippold, M. A. (2013). Promoting healthy outcomes among youth with multiple risks: Innovative approaches. *Annual Review of Public Health, 34*, 253–270.

Grossman, A. H., & D'Augelli, A. R. (2007). Transgender youth and life-threatening behaviors. *Suicide and Life-threatening Behavior, 37*, 527–537.

Haggerty, K., & McCowan, K. (2018). Using the social development strategy to unleash the power of prevention. *Journal of the Society for Social Work and Research, 9*(4), 741–763.

Haggerty, K. P., Skinner, M. L., MacKenzie, E. P., & Catalano, R. F. (2007). A randomized trial of Parents Who Care: Effects on key outcomes at 24-month follow-up. *Prevention Science, 8*, 249–260. http://dx.doi.org/10.1007/s11121-007-0077-2

Hall, W. (2017). The effectiveness of policy interventions for school bullying: A systematic review. *Journal of the Society for Social Work and Research, 8*, 45–69.

Hawkins, J. D., Catalano, R. F., Jr., & Associates. (1992). *Communities That Care: Action for Drug Abuse Prevention* (1st ed.). San Francisco, CA: Jossey-Bass.

Hawkins, J. D., Kosterman, R., Catalano, R. F., Hill, K. G., & Abbott, R. D. (2008). Effects of social development intervention in childhood 15 years later. *Archives of Pediatrics and Adolescent Medicine, 162*, 1133–1141. http://dx.doi.org/10.1001/archpedi.162.12.1133

Hawkins, J. D., Jenson, J. M., Catalano, R., Fraser, M. W., Botvin, G. J., Shapiro, V., . . . Stone, S. (2015). Unleashing the power of prevention. Discussion paper. Washington, DC: Institute of Medicine and National Research Council.

Hawkins, J. D., Shapiro, V. B., & Fagan, A. A. (2010). Disseminating effective community prevention practices: Opportunities for social work education. *Research on Social Work Practice, 20*(5), 518–527.

Haxton, C., Song, M., Zeiser, K., Berger, A., Turk-Bicakci, L., Garet, M. S., Knudson, J., & Hoshen, G. (2016). Longitudinal findings from the Early College High School Initiative Impact Study. *Educational Evaluation and Policy Analysis, 38*(2), 410–430.

Haynie, D. L., Doogan, N. J., & Soller, B. (2014). Gender, friendship networks, and delinquency: A dynamic network approach. *Criminology, 52*, 688–722.

Hill, K. G., Bailey, J. A., Hawkins, J. D., Catalano, R. F., Kosterman, R., Oesterle, S., & Abbott, R. D. (2014). The onset of STI diagnosis through Age 30: Results from the Seattle Social Development Project intervention. *Prevention Science Journal, 15*(Suppl 1), S19–S32.

Hilt, L. M., & Nolen-Hoeksema, S. (2009). The emergence of gender differences in depression in adolescence. In S. Nolen-Hoeksema & L. M. Hilt (Eds.), *Handbook of depression in adolescents* (pp. 111–135). New York: Routledge/Taylor & Francis Group. https://doi.org/10.4324/9780203809518

Horn, S. S., Kosciw, J. G., & Russell, S. T. (2009). Special issue introduction: New research on lesbian, gay, bisexual, and transgender youth: Studying lives in context. Retrieved from https://link.springer.com/article/10.1007%2Fs10964-009-9420-1

Jaccard, J., & Bo, A. (2018). Prevention science and child/youth development: Randomized explanatory trials for integrating theory, method, and analysis in program evaluation. *Journal of the Society for Social Work and Research*. Advance online publication. doi:10.1086/701388

Jenson, J. M. (2020). Improving behavioral health in young people: It is time for social work to adopt prevention. *Research on Social Work Practice, 30*, 707–711.

Jenson, J. M., & Bender, K. (2014). *Preventing child and adolescent problem behavior: Evidence-based strategies in schools, families, and communities*. New York, NY: Oxford University Press.

Jenson, J. M., & Hawkins, J. D. (2017). Provide family-focused preventive interventions to children and families through primary health care. A Policy Action Brief. Available online at Grand Challenges for Social Work. https://grandchallengesforsocialwork.org/wp-content/uploads/2017/03/PAS.1.1.pdf

Jenson, J. M., & Hawkins, J. D. (2018). Seven Ways to Unleash the Power of Prevention. Keynote presentation at the Blueprints for Healthy Youth Development Conference. Denver, CO. May 1, 2018. http://blueprintsconference.com/speakers/presentations.html

Kelly, M. S., Singer, J. B., Shin, A., Iverson, M., & Williams, D. (2019). How much social work research is in social work's grand challenges? A critical review of the evidence for the 12 challenges. *Journal of Evidence-Based Social Work, 16*, 511–523.

Kidd, C., Palmeri, H., & Aslin, R. N. (2013). Rational snacking: Young children's decision-making on the marshmallow task is moderated by beliefs about environmental reliability. *Cognition, 126*, 109–114.

Kim, B. E., Oesterle, S., Catalano, R. F., & Hawkins, J. D. (2015). Change in protective factors across adolescent development. *Journal of Applied Developmental Psychology, 40*, 26–37.

Kingston, B., & Wilensky, R. (2018). Building adult social and emotional capacity: A key ingredient for unleashing the power of prevention. *Journal of the Society for Social Work and Research*. Advance online publication. doi:10.1086/700655

LeBuffe, P. A., Shapiro, V. B., & Robitaille, J. L. (2018). The Devereux Student Strengths Assessment (DESSA) comprehensive system: Screening, assessing, planning, and monitoring. *Journal of Applied Developmental Psychology, 55*, 62–70.

Lee, J., Shapiro, V. B., Kim, B. K. E., & Yoo, J. P. (2018). Multilevel structural equation modeling for social work researchers: An introduction and application to healthy youth development. *Journal of the Society for Social Work and Research*. Advance online publication. doi:10.1086/701526

Leslie, L. K., Mehus, C. J., Hawkins, J. D., Boat, T., McCabe, M. A., Barkin, S., . . . Beardslee, W. (2016). Primary health care: potential home for family-focused preventive interventions. *American Journal of Preventive Medicine, 51*(4), S106–S118.

Letourneau, E. J., Henggeler, S. W., Borduin, C. M., Schewe, P. A., McCart, M. R., Chapman, J. E., & Saldana, L. (2009). Multisystemic therapy for juvenile sexual offenders: 1-Year results from a randomized effectiveness trial. *Journal of Family Psychology, 23*, 89–102.

Lippold, M. A., Hussong, A., Fosco, G. M., & Ram, N. (2018). Lability in the parent's hostility and warmth toward their adolescent: Linkages to youth delinquency and substance use. *Developmental Psychology, 54*, 348–361. doi:10.1037/dev0000415

Lippold, M. A, McHale, S. M., Davis, K. D., Almeida, D., & King, R. (2016). Experiences with parents and youth physical health symptoms and cortisol: A daily diary investigation. *The Journal of Research on Adolescence, 22*, 226–240.

McInturff, B. (2009, June). Prevention now for a healthier future. Alexandria, VA: Public Opinion Strategies. Retrieved from http://pos.org/prevention-now-for-a-healthier-future

Mason, W. A., Cogua, J. E., & Thompson, R. W. (2018). Turning a big ship: Unleashing the power of prevention within treatment settings. *Journal of the Society for Social Work and Research*. Advance online publication. doi:10.1086/700847

Marlatt, G. A., Baer, J. S., Kivlahan, D. R., Dimeff, L. A., Larimer, M. E., Quigley, L. A., . . . Williams, E. (1998). Screening and brief intervention for high-risk college student drinkers: Results from a 2-year follow-up assessment. *Journal of Consulting and Clinical Psychology, 66*, 604–615.

Martinez Jr, C. R., & Eddy, J. M. (2005). Effects of culturally adapted parent management training on Latino youth behavioral health outcomes. *Journal of Consulting and Clinical Psychology, 73*(5), 841.

Miller, E., Tancredi, D. J., McCauley, H. L., Decker, M. R., Virata, M. C., Anderson, H. A., et al. (2013). One-year follow-up of a coach-delivered dating violence prevention program: A cluster randomized controlled trial. *American Journal of Preventive Medicine, 45*, 108–112.

Mills-Koonce, W. R., Rehder, P. D., & McCurdy, A. L. (2018). The significance of parenting and parent–child relationships for sexual and gender minority adolescents. *Journal of Research on Adolescence, 28*, 637–649.

Mischel, W. (1974). Processes in delay of gratification. In *Advances in experimental social psychology* (Vol. 7, pp. 249–292). Academic Press.

Nagoshi, J., Nagoshi, C., Small, E., Okumu, M., Marsiglia, F. F., Dustman, P., & Than, K. (2018). Families preparing a new generation: Adaption of an adolescent substance use intervention for Burmese refugee families. *Journal of the Society for Social Work and Research*. Advance online publication. doi:10.1086/701518

Nolen-Hoeksema, S. (2004). Gender differences in risk factors and consequences for alcohol use and problems. *Clinical Psychology Review, 24*, 981–1010.

Olds, D. L., Henderson, C. R., Cole, R., Eckenrode, J., Kitzman, H., Luckey, D., Pettitt, L., Sidora, K., Morris, P., & Powers, J. (1998). Long-term effects of nurse home visitation on children's criminal and antisocial behavior: 15-year follow-up of a randomized controlled trial. *Journal of the American Medical Association, 280*(14), 1238–1244.

Perrino, T., Pantin, H., Prado, G., Huang, S., Brincks, A., Howe, G., Beardslee, W., Sandler, I., & Brown, C. H. (2014). Preventing internalizing symptoms among Hispanic adolescents: A synthesis across Familias Unidas trials. *Prevention Science, 15*(6), 917–928.

Piquero, N. L., Gover, A. R., MacDonald, J. M., & Piquero, A. R. (2005). The influence of delinquent peers on delinquency: Does gender matter? *Youth & Society, 36*, 251–275.

Prado, G., Cordova, D., Huang, S., Estrada, Y., Rosen, A., Bacio, G. A., . . . McCollister, K. (2012). The efficacy of Familias Unidas on drug and alcohol outcomes for Hispanic delinquent youth: Main effects and interaction effects by parental stress and social support. *Drug and Alcohol Dependence, 125*(Suppl 1), S18–S25.

Prado, G., Pantin, H., Briones, E., Schwartz, S. J., Feaster, D., Huang, S., . . . Szapocznik, J. (2007). A randomized controlled trial of a parent-centered intervention in preventing substance use and HIV risk behaviors in Hispanic adolescents. *Journal of Consulting and Clinical Psychology, 75*(6), 914–926.

Reyes, H. L. M., Foshee, V. A., Niolon, P. H., Reidy, D. E., & Hall, J. E. (2016). Gender role attitudes and male adolescent dating violence perpetration: Normative beliefs as moderators. *Journal of Youth and Adolescence, 45*, 350–360.

Rice, E., Yoshioka-Maxwell, A., Petering, R., Onasch-Vera, L., Craddock, J., Tambe, M., . . . Wilson, N. (2018). Piloting the use of artificial intelligence to enhance

HIV prevention interventions for youth experiencing homelessness. *Journal of the Society for Social Work and Research.* Advance online publication. doi:10.1086/701439

Rohde, P., Stice, E., Shaw, H., & Brière, F. N. (2014). Indicated cognitive behavioral group depression prevention compared to bibliotherapy and brochure control: Acute effects of an effectiveness trial with adolescents. *Journal of Consulting and Clinical Psychology, 82*(1), 65.

Roosa, M. W., Katherine H. Zeiders, George P. Knight, Nancy A. Gonzales, Jenn-Yun Tein, Delia Saenz, Megan O'Donnell, & Cady Berkel. (2011). A Test of the Social Development Model During the Transition to Junior High with Mexican American Adolescents. *Developmental Psychology, 47*(2), 527–537.

Rowe, H. L., & Trickett, E. J. (2018). Student diversity representation and reporting in universal school-based social and emotional learning programs: Implications for generalizability. *Educational Psychology Review, 30*(2), 559–583.

Ryan, S. (2008). Parent-child interaction styles between gay and lesbian parents and their adopted children. *Journal of GLBT Family Studies, 3*(2-3), 105–132.

Ryan, C., Huebner, D., Diaz, R. M., & Sanchez, J. (2009). Family rejection as a predictor of negative health outcomes in white and Latino lesbian, gay, and bisexual young adults. *Pediatrics, 123,* 346–352.

Salazar, L. F., Vivolo-Kantor, A., Hardin, J., & Berkowitz, A. (2014). A Web-based sexual violence bystander intervention for male college students: Randomized controlled trial. *Journal of Medical Internet Research, 16,* e203.

Shapiro, V. B., & Bender, K. (2018). Seven action steps to unleash the power of prevention. *Journal of the Society for Social Work and Research, 9*(4), 499–509.

Shapiro, V. B., Derr, A. S., Eldeeb, N., McCoy, H., Trujillo, M. A., & Vu, C. T. (2021). Unleashing the Power of Prevention to Ensure the Healthy Development for Youth: Expansions and Elaborations for Equity. In M. Teasley & M. Spencer (Eds.), *Social Work and the Grand Challenge to Eliminate Racism.* Oxford University Press.

Shelton, J. (2016). Reframing risk for transgender and gender-expansive young people experiencing homelessness. *Journal of Gay & Lesbian Social Services, 28,* 277–291.

Smokowski, P. R., Bacallao, M., Evans, C. B. R., Rose, R. A., Stalker, K. C., Guo, S., . . . Bower, M. (2018). The North Carolina Youth Violence Prevention Center: Using a multifaceted, ecological approach to reduce youth violence in impoverished, rural areas. *Journal of the Society for Social Work and Research.* Advance online publication. doi:10.1086/700257

Spoth, R., Greenberg, M., Bierman, K., & Redmond, C. (2004). PROSPER community-university partnership model for public education systems: Capacity-building for evidence-based, competence-building prevention. *Prevention Science, 5,* 31–39. https://doi.org/10.1023/B:PREV.0000013979.52796.8b

Stice, E., Rohde, P., Shaw, H., & Gau, J. (2011). An effectiveness trial of a selected dissonance-based eating disorder prevention program for female high school students: Long-term effects. *Journal of Consulting and Clinical Psychology, 79*(4), 500–508.

Stice, E., Shaw, H., Burton, E., & Wade, E. (2006). Dissonance and healthy weight eating disorder prevention programs: A randomized efficacy trial. *Journal of Consulting and Clinical Psychology, 74*(2), 263–275.

Stotzer, R. L. (2009). Violence against transgender people: A review of United States data. *Aggression and Violent Behavior, 14,* 170–179.

Sullivan, C. J., & Hirschfield, P. (2011). Problem Behavior in the Middle School Years: An Assessment of the Social Development Model. *Journal of Research in Crime and Delinquency, 48*(4), 566–593.

Sussman, S., Dent, C., & Stacy, A. (2002). Project Towards No Drug Abuse: A review of the findings and future directions. *American Journal of Health Behavior, 26*, 354–365.

Tharp, A. T., DeGue, S., Valle, L. A., Brookmeyer, K. A., Massetti, G. M., & Matjasko, J. L. (2013). A systematic qualitative review of risk and protective factors for sexual violence perpetration. *Trauma, Violence, & Abuse, 14*, 133–167.

Toomey, R. B., McGuire, J. K., & Russell, S. T. (2012). Heteronormativity, school climates, and perceived safety for gender nonconforming peers. *Journal of Adolescence, 35*, 187–196.

Trent, M., Dooley, D. G., & Dougé, J. (2019). The impact of racism on child and adolescent health. *Pediatrics, 144*(2), 1–14.

Trudeau, L., Spoth, R., Lillehoj, C., Redmond, C., & Wickrama, K. A. (2003). Effects of a preventive intervention on adolescent substance use initiation, expectancies, and refusal intentions. *Prevention Science, 4*(2), 109–122.

Turrisi, R., Larimer, M. E., Mallett, K. A., Kilmer, J. R., Ray, A. E., Mastroleo, N. R., . . . Montoya, H. (2009). A randomized clinical trial evaluating a combined alcohol intervention for high-risk college students. *Journal of Studies on Alcohol and Drugs, 70*, 555–567.

Wallerstein, N., & Duran, B. (2010). Community-Based Participatory Research Contributions to Intervention Research: The Intersection of Science and Practice to Improve Health Equity. *American Journal of Public Health, 100*, S40–S46.

Weerman, F. M., & Hoeve, M. (2012). Peers and delinquency among girls and boys: Are sex differences in delinquency explained by peer factors? *European Journal of Criminology, 9*, 228–244.

Weiss, M. J., Ratledge, A., Sommo, C., & Gupta, H. (2019). Supporting Community College Students from Start to Degree Completion: Long-Term Evidence from a Randomized Trial of CUNY's ASAP. *American Economic Journal: Applied Economics, 11*(3), 253–297.

Williams, J. H., Ayers, C. D., Abbott, R. D., Hawkins, J. D., & Catalano, R. F. (1999). Racial differences in risk factors for delinquency and substance use among adolescents. *Social Work Research, 23*(4), 241–256.

Whitaker, K., Shapiro, V. B., & Shields, J. P. (2016). School-based protective factors related to suicide for lesbian, gay, and bisexual adolescents. *Journal of Adolescent Health, 58*(1), 63–68.

CHAPTER 3
Closing the Health Gap

MICHAEL S. SPENCER, KARINA L. WALTERS,
AUDREY BEGUN, HEIDI L. ALLEN, TERI BROWNE,
CHRISTINA M. ANDREWS, DARRELL P. WHEELER,
BRADLEY J. ZEBRACK, PETER MARAMALDI,
JOHN D. CLAPP, DIANA DiNITTO, AND
EDWINA UEHARA

Tāne, the deity of the forest, lived with his siblings in darkness within the eternal embrace of his parents, Ranginui (sky father) and Papatūānuku (earth mother). Becoming increasingly frustrated at living in the darkness, Tāne successfully pushed the pair apart by planting his head in the earth and using his feet to lift the sky—to expose Te Ao Mārama—the world of light.

—Māori creation story

Among the Māori, the Indigenous people of Aotearoa/New Zealand, Tāne serves as a model for action in the world. His roots are in earth, and his head is in the heavens. Tāne is able to bear the weight of action to procure necessary change. Similar to Tāne, social work must assert itself, bring new light, and bear the weight of action—in collaboration with allied health professions—to achieve health equity in the next generation. Social work has already had a significant impact on health interventions in the United States—from the health-policy reform efforts of the Progressive Era to the development of innovative community-based prevention interventions in modern times. Social work's perspective is in line with approaches that go beyond population surveillance, prompting action to address health inequities and social determinants of health.

Specifically, social work has an unyielding focus on lifting the health of a nation by lifting the health of the most disenfranchised and marginalized populations. Also, the profession's historical social reform efforts have sought to procure health by addressing the conditions in which people live, work, play, learn, and age. These perspectives match the calls by the World Health Organization (2014a), the Centers for Disease Control and Prevention (Brennan Ramirez, Baker, & Metzler, 2008), and the Healthy People 2020 national strategy (US Department of Health and Human Services, Office of Disease Prevention and Health Promotion, 2000) to focus contemporary research and intervention efforts on the social conditions that produce health and health inequities. Similarly, the National Academies of Sciences, Engineering and Medicine's (2019) recent consensus study on integrating social needs care into the delivery of healthcare identifies the growing need for understanding upstream factors that impact the delivery and outcomes of healthcare among marginalized populations, including stable housing and nutritious food. In addition, the reassertion of social work into the national strategy and debate is timely, given the ongoing debate over the Patient Protection and Affordable Care Act (ACA) (2010) and the bourgeoning national effort to create culturally, linguistically, and communally grounded interventions that affect the upstream determinants of the nation's poor health. These issues have been illuminated by the devastating impact of the COVID-19 pandemic, which hit communities of color harder, and exacerbated many of the existing inequities already present in our society. For example, Native American and Alaskan Native populations experienced death from COVID-19 at 2.4 times the rate as white Americans (Centers for Disease Control and Prevention, 2021). According to the Centers for Disease Control and Prevention (2021), race and ethnicity are markers for other underlying conditions that affect health, including socioeconomic status, access to healthcare, and exposure to the virus related to occupation, such as frontline, essential, and critical infrastructure workers. We add exposure to racism and settler colonialism as an additional risk marker.

Although the United States is among the wealthiest nations in the world and spends far more per person on healthcare than any other industrialized nation, the population's health is deteriorating rapidly. During the past three decades, the US population has been dying at younger ages than those of the populations in peer nations and has endured a pervasive pattern of poorer health throughout the life course—from birth to old age (National Research Council & Institute of Medicine, 2013). Moreover, population health diminishes along a social gradient. Populations that experience high rates of social, racial, and economic exclusion bear the greatest burden of poor health and premature mortality. Although poor health follows a social gradient, deteriorating US health cannot be explained completely by the health disparities that exist among people who are uninsured or poor; in fact, even the health of relatively elite Americans—those who are white, insured, and college educated, as well as those with a high income—is worse than that of their peers in other industrialized countries (Avendano, Glymour, Banks, & Mackenbach, 2009; National Research Council & Institute of Medicine, 2013).

Health professions in the United States have become increasingly myopic, focusing on individualized healthcare rather than on population health. By prioritizing interventions that target individual behavioral change, research tends to neglect upstream opportunities to intervene on the settings and environments in which health is produced and maintained. Attention to individual and behavioral interventions is important, but alone is not sufficient to eradicate health inequities (Hood, Gennuso, Swain, & Catlin, 2016). To secure true, sustainable, population-based health changes, the health professions must unite and develop transdisciplinary approaches to examining the multilayered contributions of political, economic, and social determinants of population health inequities. Indeed, the nation's health depends on the development of this next wave of interprofessional and transdisciplinary collaboration (McGovern, Miller, & Hughes-Cromwick, 2014). Thus, if we are to truly turn the tide, health disciplines, particularly social work, must train professionals in how to invest in the social determinants of good health. We must also train professionals to develop the practice and research tools, community partnerships, and localized programs necessary to combat social and economic inequities (Hood et al., 2016; Uehara et al., 2013).

ACHIEVING HEALTH EQUITY: SOCIAL WORK ACTION PRIORITIES

We are at a critical juncture in US history. The ACA and Healthy People 2020 produced national momentum to address health inequities. However, as we have seen, changes in political leadership can sway public momentum away from this goal without active social work leadership. Although the ACA's primary focus is on expanding insurance coverage, access only does not equate to equitable systems. Thus, the ACA also invites innovations that fall within particular domains of social work expertise: the creation of equitable healthcare systems by expanding healthcare into and in collaboration with the communities in which people live and work, addressing issues of structural racism, increasing health workforce diversity, improving cultural appropriateness throughout healthcare delivery systems, fostering community-based approaches to prevention, and creating community health centers in medically underserved areas. All of these efforts are hallmarks of social work practice and history. Consistent with social work's approach and values, Healthy People 2020 advocates for an ecological, multilevel approach to examining health determinants. It focuses on building healthful social and physical environments that promote health and well-being (US Department of Health and Human Services, Office of Disease Prevention and Health Promotion, 2000) through place-based approaches. These approaches consist of "five key social determinants of health [areas]: economic stability, education, social and community context[s], health and health care, and the neighborhood and built environment (for example, buildings, bike lanes, and roads)" (Mitchell, 2015, p. e71). Although the ACA and Healthy People 2020 provide the impetus for addressing health inequities, neither offers "definitive strategies for communities and health professionals" (p. e71). Also, Mitchell notes, there remains limited evidence-based research on the fundamental determinants of health, and limited evidence of settings-based interventions that affect population health.

This chapter seeks to address these deficiencies through a "geography of science" approach that draws on diverse disciplines, community leaders, and theoretical and community-centered perspectives (Logie, Dimaras, Fortin, & Ramón-García, 2014, p. 2). The Grand Challenge to Close the Health Gap is made up of three subgroups aimed at addressing health equity in the following areas through a geography of science approach: (a) Population Health Through Community and Setting-Based Approaches, (b) Strengthening Healthcare Systems: Better Health Across America, and (3) Reducing and Preventing Alcohol Misuse and Its Consequences. In this frame, social work and the health professions can activate 10 priority areas. Although they do not address health equity comprehensively in its entirety, these priorities are proposed as the first steps in initiating community and scientific conversations, and launching broad, multisectoral, and interprofessional collaboration. The following are the 10 priority areas:

Population Health through Community and Setting-based Approaches
1. Focus on settings to improve the conditions of daily life.
2. Advance community empowerment for sustainable health.
3. Generate research on social determinants of health inequities.
4. Stimulate multisectoral advocacy to promote health equity policies.

Strengthening Healthcare Systems: Better Health Across America
5. Cultivate innovation in primary care.
6. Promote full access to healthcare.
7. Foster development of an interprofessional health workforce.

Reducing and Preventing Alcohol Misuse and Its Consequences
8. Develop research and scholarship in alcohol misuse and its consequences.
9. Develop interdisciplinary, multisectoral, and sustainable collaborations.
10. Develop the workforce in social work to address alcohol misuse.

COMING TO TERMS: SOCIAL DETERMINANTS AND HEALTH EQUITY

In assessing population health, research has typically considered such indicators as mortality, life expectancy, morbidity, health status (physical and mental), functional limitations, disability, and quality of life (Hood et al., 2016; McGovern et al., 2014). Health determinants, also known as *social determinants of health*, refer to the economic and "social conditions into which people are born, grow, live, work, play, and age"—the conditions that "influence health" (Newman, Baum, Javanparast, O'Rourke, & Carlon, 2015, p. ii127). In the United States, these conditions are shaped by the specific social structures that differentiate access to and distribution of money, wealth, power, knowledge, prestige, resources, and social connectedness (Link & Phelan, 1995; McGovern et al., 2014). Health inequalities are the persistent, systematic differences in the health of social groups within a nation—differences resulting from unequal exposure to and distributions of the social determinants of health (Farrer, Marinetti, Cavaco, & Costongs, 2015). Quite often, impoverished conditions attend populations that have endured significant legacies of discrimination based on their racial, ethnic, class, gender identity, or sexuality. Such conditions include unequal distribution of resources—such as quality education, culturally relevant medical care, and housing—that are typically tied to good health (Mitchell, 2015).

Racial and ethnic minorities bear the greatest burden from conditions that give rise to poor health and premature mortality. These conditions have structural components as well as social ones (Agency for Healthcare Research and Quality, 2013; Mitchell, 2015; Smedley, Stith, & Nelson, 2003). Social determinants of health inequities are conditions of social stratification. These conditions "create . . . differences in health status between population groups that are socially produced, systematic in their distribution across the population and avoidable and unfair" (Dahlgren & Whitehead, 1992, as cited in Newman et al., 2015, p. ii127). Social determinants give rise to a common soil in which health disparities grow; health inequalities take root; and inequities become reproduced at distal, intermediate, and proximal levels.

Health equity refers to a state characterized by the "absence of systematic inequalities in health" (Farrer et al., 2015, p. 394). A large body of research has established the strong links between socioeconomic disadvantage and poor health outcomes across the life span (Braveman & Gottlieb, 2014; Commission on Social Determinants of Health, 2008; Kaplan, Shema, & Leite, 2008; Marmot & Bell, 2012). Although lack of access to health insurance and health services contributes to poor health outcomes, disparities in access to coverage and services also stem from significant social, economic, and environmental deprivation (i.e., social disadvantage) grounded in race- and culture-based discrimination. Those disparities often produce cumulative, intergenerational disadvantages that affect health profoundly (Braveman & Gottlieb, 2014). Such disadvantages correlate positively to levels of debilitating chronic disease (Gordon-Larsen, Nelson, Page, & Popkin, 2006) and rates of premature mortality (Commission on Social Determinants of Health, 2008). Environmental disadvantage, a manifestation of this stratification and the underlying determinants, is a condition tied to residing in communities with concentrated poverty, food deserts, and high rates of trauma and violence.

For populations of color, racism at the structural and interpersonal levels also constitutes an important social determinant of health. Racism is systemic, structural, and institutional, and is enacted through racist policies and racist ideas that perpetuate racial inequity (Kendi, 2019). It exists globally and locally. At a societal–cultural level, racism, white supremacy, and settler colonialism have been sources of both historical trauma and contemporary trauma experienced by communities of color (Fieland, Walters, & Simoni, 2007; Comas-Diaz, 2016). For most communities, US imperialism and settler colonialism continues to mean loss of lives, family, identity, land/nation, language, spirituality, livelihood, values, practices, and norms. Settler colonialism distinctively drives health inequities for Indigenous Peoples through historically-related traumatic events that function to disrupt Indigenous thoughtways (i.e., epistemicide), lifeways (i.e., ethnocide), and healthful ties to land and territories (i.e., ecocide) (Walters, Johnson-Jennings, Stroud, et al., 2020). At an institutional level, racist policies and systems such as housing segregation, other forms of social segregation, immigration policies, and the criminal justice system interact with one another to perpetuate poor health outcomes for communities of color (Gee & Ford, 2011; Williams & Mohammed, 2013; Krieger, 2014). At an interpersonal level, stress and coping models suggest that instances of interpersonal racism such as racial discrimination and microaggressions act as psychological stressors that have a negative impact on communities of color's health and well-being (e.g., Dressler, Oths, & Gravlee, 2005; Ho-Lastimosa et al., 2019; Kaholokula et al., 2012; Krieger, 2014).

Meeting the grand challenge of health equity and eliminating health inequities require dealing with "root causes"—focusing on what can be seen as upstream interventions and primary prevention, and addressing "unequal distribution of power, income, goods and services" (World Health Organizaiton, 2014a, p. 2; see also, Gehlert, Mininger, Sohmer, & Berg, 2008a). This challenge entails an explicit commitment to eliminating health disparities at individual and population levels. Meeting the challenge also involves eliminating social determinants that function as precursors to adverse health conditions and outcomes. Social work's pursuit of health equity as a grand challenge means the profession strives to ensure the highest possible standard of health and wellness for all people while prioritizing upstream interventions and primary prevention efforts among those who are at greatest risk for poor health—those who, because of social, racial, and economic disadvantages, experience the extremes of health inequalities. To be healthy, people require access to quality, culturally resonant care as well as to socioeconomic conditions that promote well-being in community, family, school, workplace, recreation, and environmental systems.

MAINSTREAMING GENDER

Using Intersectional Gender Analysis to Make Visible Health (Care) Inequities

EMMA CARPENTER AND ANU MANCHIKANTI GÓMEZ

Gender and its intersections with other systems of oppression have tremendous implications for health and health equity. Current medical knowledge relies primarily on how individuals assigned male at birth present and respond to health conditions and treatments, coloring our collective understanding of what illness looks like and how to treat it, and perpetuating health inequities. Using an intersectional gender lens to inform strategies to close the health gap requires attending to the disparities between (presumed cisgender) women and men, and related shifts in funding, research, and clinical practice. However, this analysis calls for more than dividing the world into cisgender women and men—and therefore highlighting "women's" health—and instead requires us to attend to the needs of individuals of all genders. Structurally gendered care such as "women's" healthcare (e.g., pregnancy-related care, abortion, gynecological care) presents barriers for those existing outside the binary, and leads to worse health outcomes, undergirding persistent disparities for nonbinary and gender expansive people. Furthermore, even within the conventional realm of "women's" health, it is clear that some women's health and lives are valued more highly than others, which explains persistent disparities related to intersections of oppression.

One critical example of what is lost without an intersectional gender analysis on closing the health gap is maternal mortality, long understood to be a litmus test for a society's health and well-being (United Nations, 1996). Here, we see both how women's lives are devalued broadly, as well as the privileging of some women (namely, those who are white and have a higher income) depending on their social statuses. The United States has the highest rate of maternal mortality among high-income countries. Unconscionable inequities persist in pregnancy-related deaths (those that occur within 1 year of pregnancy), with Black and Indigenous women experiencing rates that are nearly triple and double, respectively, those of white women (Petersen et al., 2019). These disparities are a result of

continued

structural racism, as well as institutional and interpersonal racism within the healthcare system, as opposed to individual behavior or genetics. An intersectional gender analysis not only highlights the significance of racial inequities in maternal mortality, but also foregrounds the role of intergenerational trauma and structural inequity in this health gap, tracing its origins through the United States's history of reproductive oppression since the time of enslavement. Although expanded Medicaid access through the Affordable Care Act has contributed to important declines in maternal mortality and reduced disparities experienced by Black women, the states least likely to expand Medicaid are those with the greatest inequities in maternal mortality (Eliason, 2020), demonstrating the need to include an intersectional analysis in policy efforts to address persistent health gaps adequately.

Without a gender lens, social work scholars may fall into the analytic gap where marginalized women and gender expansive people who face health inequities are held responsible for their own health improvement, leaving underlying misogyny, racism, and social inequities unaddressed. Scholarship that attempts to understand the sources of inequity must center marginalized experiences and voices. In addition, scholarship focused on social determinants of health must use intersectional feminist frameworks, such as reproductive justice, to center how gender structures health inequities and shapes social experiences of health. Last, our investigations must also focus on upstream causes and solutions, including a critical examination of social work's role in perpetuating racial and gender inequities that exist in and out of the health system. In shifting how we conduct our research and by using a gender lens, we can produce knowledge that centers the margins and promotes solutions that will fully address health inequities.

References

Eliason, E. L. (2020). Adoption of Medicaid expansion is associated with lower maternal mortality. *Women's Health Issues*, 30, 147–152. doi:10.1016/j.whi.2020.01.005

Petersen, E. E., Davis, N. L., Goodman, D., Cox, S., Syverson, C., Seed, K., . . . , & Barfield, W. (2019). Racial/ethnic disparities in pregnancy-related deaths: United States, 2007–2016. *MMWR Morbidity and Mortality Weekly Report*, 68, 762–765. doi:10.15585/mmwr.mm6835a3

United Nations. (1996). Maternal mortality figures substantially underestimated, new WHO/UN ICEF study says. Retrieved from un.org/press/en/1996/19960205.h2896.html

ACHIEVING POPULATION HEALTH: MOVING BEYOND THE INDIVIDUAL/CLINICAL TO THE COMMUNITY AND SOCIAL DETERMINANTS

Priority 1: Focus on Settings to Improve the Conditions of Daily Life

Combating the distal-level influence of racial and socioeconomic inequality on health and the intermediate-level consequences in a community's institutions (e.g., inadequate schools, unsafe streets, food deserts, families with an incarcerated member) requires a sphere of interventions centered on changing the community environment to elevate the health prospects of a local population. Although large-scale social and economic (distal-level) policy changes may be the ultimate instrument for resolving the nation's health crisis, an accessible starting point for social work is to build the community-enhanced evidence base for change from the bottom up (National Research Council & Institute of Medicine, 2013).

Highly promising components of community-based research and practice for addressing social determinants of health inequities are found in the "places" and "social contexts where people engage in daily activities, in which environmental, organizational and personal factors interact to affect health and well-being, and where people actively use and shape the environment, thus creating or solving health problems" (Newman et al., 2015, p. ii127). Such settings include, but are not limited to, geographic places (e.g., cities), physical spaces where people congregate (e.g., religious centers), workplaces, green spaces (e.g., community gardens or playgrounds), and virtual worlds (e.g., social websites) (Newman et al., 2015). It is critical for social work to be particularly present in settings that target and include young people—from birth to young adulthood—to address the cycle of intergenerational disadvantage.

The importance of addressing the social determinants of health inequities within settings has been highlighted by the Commission on Social Determinants of Health (2008) as well as by social determinant researchers (Marmot, 2005; Marmot & Bell, 2012). Newman et al. (2015) note that in addressing the social determinants of health within settings, there is room to "integrate individual behavior approaches with approaches at structural" or distal levels (p. ii135). Moreover, they note that settings approaches require cross-sectoral collaboration, committed leadership, genuine involvement of stakeholders, and strong research.

Priority 2: Advance Community Empowerment for Sustainable Health

A community organized for health improvement may work on either or both of two goals: representation in governance of the healthcare delivery system and interventions that create sustainable community changes. Representation in the governance of disadvantaged communities is critical for (a) efforts to ensure the enrollment in healthcare of as many community residents as possible and (b) active participation in evaluating services and resolving deficiencies to the community's benefit. Maximizing healthcare enrollment, especially among children and youth, ensures that they are counted in the assessment of efforts to improve the health of a vulnerable community. Representation in the governance of the health system may be accomplished through community organizing that strives to improve health equity. The particular task of securing representation over the long term calls for continued commitment to face-to-face, community-level education on the issues (Horton, Freire, Bell, Gaventa, & Peters, 1990). It also calls for engagement with all the organic social/cultural threads and groups in the community (e.g., religious and spiritual institutions) (Stout, 2010). Community health coalitions and local learning communities can also play critical roles in developing local capacity for representation, monitoring progress, training volunteers, and demonstrating local options if reform implementations break down. By focusing on the community as the center of efforts to advance health—efforts that complement those of the health service sector—activists build community-based interventions that are not only culturally grounded, but also sustainable.

In parallel to practice-based research networks, community-oriented research networks can be developed to identify common measures and themes as well as lead in the design and development of culturally grounded health promotion interventions. Last, social work can also partner with existing organizations, such as the National Community Building Network, the US Department of Housing and Urban Development's Office of University Partnerships, and the Alliance for Children and Families, to identify common interests and strategies for community-engaged research and action (Johnson, 2004).

Priority 3: Generate Research on Social Determinants of Health Inequities

Research on social determinants of health is essential for analyzing how environmental and traumatic stressors and racism (and other -isms) harm health, and how these determinants become embodied over time, generations, and political–historical contexts. There are many social and cultural pathways by which discrimination harms health, including "economic and social deprivation; excess exposure to toxins, hazards, and pathogens; social trauma; health-harming responses to discrimination; targeted marketing of harmful commodities; and ecosystem degradation" (Krieger, 2012, p. 937). In particular, stress in response to these determinants may be an underdeveloped mechanism influencing how people respond to upstream and downstream determinants (McGovern et al., 2014).

Many emerging models of social determinants of health equity require testing. Moreover, there is quite often a gap between what is known through health equity research and what is actually taken up within communities. Davison, Ndumbe-Eyoh, and Clement (2015) identified six health equity models that bridge research and practice, but require further testing: the Knowledge Brokering Framework (Oldham & McLean, 1997), the Framework for Research Transfer (Nieva et al., 2005), the Joint Venture Model of Knowledge Utilization (Edgar et al., 2006), the Translational Research Framework to Address Health Disparities (Fleming et al., 2008), the Model of Knowledge Translation and Exchange with Northern Aboriginal Communities (Jardine & Furgal, 2010), and the Ecohealth Model applied to knowledge translation (Arredondo & Orozco, 2012). The models have many strengths. They value the direct participation of community stakeholders; prioritize multisectoral engagement; recognize the importance of environmental and contextual determinants; have a proactive, collaborative, problem-solving approach; and support an inclusive conceptualization of knowledge (community and traditional, culture-based knowledge, as well as qualitative and quantitative forms).

Priority 4: Stimulate Multisectoral Advocacy to Promote Health Equity Policies

Social work's disciplinary competencies related to the person-in-environment perspective and applied ecological theory offer unique opportunities to forge broad alliances capable of advocating for a more comprehensive, multisectoral view of health determinants as well as for practices and policies to address the racial and economic injustices that form the bedrock for health inequities. Part of the strategy to close the gaps in health among subgroups is "'leveling up' the health of less advantaged groups" (Farrer et al., 2015, p. 394). The World Health Organization has demonstrated the utility of multisectoral approaches to leveling-up conditions for vulnerable and marginalized populations. Government, healthcare, public health, and university entities have been the traditional participants in efforts to eliminate health disparities, but many settings within communities could be used in advocacy and change efforts. According to Williams and Wyatt (2015, p. 556): "Multilevel policies . . . in homes, schools, neighborhoods, workplaces, and religious organizations can help remove barriers to healthy living and create opportunities to usher in a new culture of health in which the healthy choice is the easy choice."

Multisectoral approaches have translated research effectively into action through networks of individuals, communities, government entities, health providers, institutions, businesses, and industries, but more innovation is needed. The urgency of the need to make rapid progress in the health of poor communities and communities of color calls for national collaboration both to advance the science for breaking the cycle of intergenerational disadvantage and to translate that science into action.

STRENGTHENING HEALTHCARE SYSTEMS: BETTER HEALTH ACROSS AMERICA

Priority 5: Cultivate Innovation in Primary Care

Improving the health of those suffering lifelong and even intergenerational disadvantages, especially those previously without regular primary healthcare, requires innovation in primary and other care. An exemplar of the viability of innovation in primary care is the emergence of accountable care organizations (ACOs) in which groups of providers agree to improve the overall healthcare experience of a defined patient population through efficiency of care delivery that reduces costs and improves quality of healthcare and health (DeVore & Champion, 2011). In fact, the first ACOs were targeting what might be considered disadvantaged populations through the Centers for Medicare and Medicaid Services' Medicare Shared Savings Program (Fisher, Shortell, Kreindler, Van Citters, & Larson, 2012). ACOs have demonstrated the need for more integrated approaches in primary care. A more widely adopted and far-reaching innovation is the Substance Abuse and Mental Health Services Administration's screening, brief intervention, and referral to treatment (SBIRT) initiative to address substance abuse issues in primary care (Babor, Del Boca, & Bray, 2017; Campbell et al., 2020). Given that one third of all healthcare resources in the United States are spent on individuals with behavioral health needs associated with persistent medical illness (Kathol, Patel, Sacks, Sargent, & Melek, 2015), ACOs and SBIRT are timely innovations that promote health equity and benefit society.

Even in the worst of times, such as the year 2020, we have seen evidence of innovation. The necessity of quarantining during the COVID-19 pandemic has also led to an increased use of telehealth as a means of accessing healthcare in ways never seen before. The promise of telehealth is significant for health equity because it puts social workers in a position to extend the reach of social work practice in addressing issues of social care as well as reduce structural barriers that restrict access.

In addition, as members of practice-based research networks, social workers now cooperate with other groups in identifying successful social innovations for medical, hospital, community, and mental health settings. Social workers examine healthcare processes and care of patients, designing and developing culturally grounded health interventions. Last, social workers provide an organizational structure for surveillance and research.

Priority 6: Promote Full Access to Healthcare

We can think of access in healthcare as receiving the right care, at the right time, and in the right place, for the best health and mental health outcomes. This is a lot to unpack, and there is a tremendous and ever-evolving body of research on identifying what constitutes the best treatments or prevention strategies for any given health condition; when is the right time to receive preventive, diagnostic, or medical interventions; and what settings are the most effective and efficient places for care to be received. In the United States, access barriers remain a significant source of health disparities.

By far the greatest barrier to accessing healthcare is cost. Few Americans possess the wealth necessarily to move through life paying for their healthcare out-of-pocket. This means essential screenings and treatments are harmfully delayed, foregone, or provided in settings that are not designed to provide follow-up (such as emergency departments). The purpose of health insurance is to remove affordability barriers to healthcare by pooling participants' money and redistributing the resources from the well to the sick. In the United States, we have implemented a piecemeal system of financing healthcare bit by bit and population by population, over the decades spanning modern medicine. Most people receive health insurance through their employer, which varies in generosity of coverage. Very large public programs have been created during the past 50 years to provide health insurance for those older than 65 years (Medicare), low-income women and children (State Children's Health Insurance Program), and low-income adults in general (Medicaid). Some populations, such as Native Americans and veterans, have health insurance connected with a specific healthcare delivery system. Despite significant public (tax-payer) investments in all of these forms of coverage, millions of Americans are still uninsured and rely entirely on the healthcare safety net, which often has robust primary care but not equivalent access to specialists, hospitals, intensive treatments such as surgeries, or many prescriptions (Makaroun, et al., 2017). In the United States, people live sicker and die prematurely from cost-related access barriers to healthcare (Chokshi, 2018). They also go bankrupt or spend money on healthcare that is desperately needed elsewhere, such as for housing or food.

During roughly the past decade, there have been several significant steps forward in addressing financial access barriers to healthcare. In 2010, the ACA passed Congress, which offered unparalleled opportunities to reduce inequality in healthcare access and health. First, the ACA created several new avenues for health insurance coverage. It expanded Medicaid to adults who were not previously eligible and it created a federal marketplace for health insurance, where middle-income people who file taxes could receive federal subsidies for the cost of premiums. After these expansions went into full effect in 2014, more than 23 million US residents gained health insurance (Carman, Eibner, & Paddock, 2015). However, challenges remained. The ACA was not successful in obtaining universal access to insurance coverage. A 2012 Supreme Court decision allowed states to opt out of Medicaid expansion; subsequently, 12 states still have not expanded. This decision left millions in a "coverage gap" without access to Medicaid and too poor to be eligible for the subsidized private marketplaces (Andrews, 2014; Andrews et al., 2015; Garfield, Damico, Cox, Claxton, & Levitt, 2016). Some states expanding Medicaid while others don't is a classic example of structural racism. Blacks, Native Americans, and Alaskan Natives are more likely to reside in states that have not expanded Medicaid, and although insurance disparities have decreased overall, they have decreased significantly less in Medicaid nonexpansion states (Chaudry, Jackson, & Glied, 2019). The ACA also did not provide an avenue for undocumented immigrants to gain coverage, even without receiving government support (Joseph, 2016). It has not been surprising that the ACA has been effective in narrowing, but not closing, national racial and ethnic gaps in insurance coverage (Buchmueller, Levinson, Levy, & Wolfe, 2016).

In the context of a global pandemic and a weakened national economy, Congress and the Biden administration significantly, if temporarily, upgraded the ACA by passing the American Rescue Plan Act of 2021. This Act provides strong incentives for Medicaid holdout states to expand (Musumeci, 2021), something for which social workers in these states should be strongly advocating, and increases the subsidies for buying coverage in the federal marketplace (Pollitz, 2021), which research suggested was still unaffordable for many (Sommers, 2020).

Priority 7: Foster Development of an Interprofessional Health Workforce

According to the Bureau of Labor Statistics (2021), between 2019 and 2029, employment of healthcare social workers is projected to grow by 14%, and employment of mental health and substance abuse social workers is projected to grow by 17%. Because of these occupational trends, social work can create integrated pathways to health careers in social intervention. Social work can lead integrated initiatives for evidence-based workforce development by reviewing practitioner preparation for transdisciplinary social interventions, defining a core curriculum for such initiatives, establishing training standards for advanced practice in specialized areas, and identifying new competence areas for the emerging health system (e.g., prevention science, place- and settings-based research, community engagement, improvement science, health–data analytics, team methods for collaborative behavioral and physical healthcare). In addition, we should develop an integrated public health social work curriculum across master's of social work programs that goes beyond the master's of social work–master's of public health dual-degree programs.

REDUCING AND PREVENTING ALCOHOL MISUSE AND ITS CONSEQUENCES

Alcohol misuse is a compelling problem for the social work profession, encountered in almost every practice setting and related directly or indirectly to every domain of well-being about which the profession is concerned. The biopsychosocial and multisectoral nature of the social work profession makes it uniquely suited to lead a transdisciplinary effort for reducing and preventing the wide range of consequences associated with alcohol misuse. Alcohol issues intersect with multiple other Grand Challenges for Social Work. Among the priority areas that emerged in the Reducing and Preventing Alcohol Misuse and Its Consequences workgroup (Begun, Clapp, & The Alcohol Misuse Grand Challenge Collective, 2016) are (a) develop research and scholarship; (b) develop interdisciplinary, multisectoral, and sustainable collaborations; and (c) focus on workforce development.

Priority 8: Develop Research and Scholarship in Alcohol Misuse and Its Consequences

In both the United States and throughout the world, alcohol misuse is associated with high rates of morbidity, mortality, and co-occurring physical, mental health, and social problems. Harmful alcohol use causes an array of acute and chronic health problems, accounting globally for 3 million deaths annually: "The harmful use of alcohol ranks among the top five risk factors for disease, disability and death throughout the world" (World Health Organization, 2014b, p. 2). Alcohol misuse is among the leading risk factors for both infectious and noncommunicable diseases, as well as threats to maternal and child health, mental health, and injury risk (World Health Organization, 2018). In addition to these health consequences, alcohol misuse often accompanies the misuse of other substances, significant cognitive impairments, multiple forms of mental disorder, physical disability, and a host of social problems: intimate partner violence; child maltreatment; human trafficking; sexual assault; problem gambling; school failure; criminal justice system involvement; and insecurity around employment, housing, and safety.

Alcoholic beverages are by far the most commonly used and abused psychoactive substances (Dawson, Goldstein, Saha, & Grant, 2015). In the United States, almost 140 million individuals age 12 years and older were estimated to have used alcohol during the past month in 2019, more than 65 million engaged in binge drinking, and 16 million engaged in heavy drinking (Substance Abuse and Mental Health Services Administration, 2020). More than 12 million persons in this age group met criteria for an alcohol use disorder during the past year, with an additional 2.4 million experiencing substance use disorders involving both alcohol and other substances (Substance Abuse and Mental Health Services Administration, 2020). There exists a considerable healthcare gap in the United States between the many millions of individuals potentially needing treatment for an alcohol use disorder and the estimated 2.5 million receiving specialized alcohol treatment (Substance Abuse and Mental Health Services Administration, 2020). In the United States, the cost estimate associated with excessive alcohol use was $249 billion in 2010, which translates to $807 per person or $2.05 per drink (Centers for Disease Control and Prevention, 2019).

Once depicted as entrenched, unalterable problems, decades of research have proved that evidence-informed strategies can address alcohol misuse and its consequences successfully (Begun & Murray, 2020; Warren & Hewitt, 2010). Alcohol researchers use varied methods and designs, and include variables ranging from the microlevel (e.g., neuroscience, genomics, epigenetics, proteomics, metabolomics) to the macro level (e.g., population-based epidemiology; "big data, small n" studies; econometrics; health–human services; policy at local, state, regional, national, and global levels). Contemporary and emerging research approaches to studying alcohol misuse are among many that social work scholars use and around which we should continue to develop mastery. Social work scholars need to highlight their alcohol research contributions both within the profession and in transdisciplinary ways.

Priority 9: Develop Interdisciplinary, Multisectoral, and Sustainable Collaborations

Partnerships working across disciplines and across the various service delivery sectors that serve individuals, families, communities, and larger social systems can "bring the pieces together" to reduce the impact of alcohol-related problems. Scientific collaboration between social work, computer sciences, and engineering researchers on system dynamic approaches to address alcohol problems such as event-level drinking behavior, driving under the influence, sexual assault, and violence behavior (Clapp, 2018; Clapp et al., 2018). At the community level, participatory approaches currently being used in environmental design, such as collaborative modeling, can be used to link scientists and citizens both to understand alcohol problems and to develop community-designed solutions to them (Richardson, Olabisi, Waldman, Sakana, & Brugnone, 2020).

Priority 10: Develop the Workforce in Social Work to Address Alcohol Misuse

Social work and interprofessional curricula tap into the evidence base related to alcohol misuse to prepare individuals to intervene in ways that reduce or prevent alcohol misuse and its consequences. For example, curricula are available to train practitioners to deliver evidence-based SBIRT for alcohol misuse, and the Council on Social Work Education has developed curricular resources and a Substance Abuse and Mental Health Services Administration–funded practitioner education project to promote evidence-informed social work education about alcohol and other substance misuse (Council on Social Work Education, 2020). The advent of open-source online training mechanisms offers innovative opportunities for both preservice and in-service/continuing education related to meeting workforce demands associated with the AGC.

SOCIAL WORK'S ROLES IN LEADING A HEALTH EQUITY GRAND CHALLENGE

Social work is uniquely positioned for a leadership role in addressing health inequities because, as indicated in Jane Addams' speech at the 1930 National Conference of Social Work, "social work's special genius is its closeness to the people it serves" (as quoted in Johnson, 2004, p. 319). Social work's historical social justice mission as well as its commitment to serve the most disenfranchised and health-burdened populations affirm the profession's ability to provide leadership in association with allied health professions. The attributes also speak to the profession's ability to design and develop community-based approaches to eradicate health inequities.

Several factors demonstrate why social work should lead a grand challenge to achieve health equity. First, social workers understand the complex pathways from disadvantages to health risks and outcomes. These pathways run through the vulnerable communities in which social workers routinely operate. In addition, health risks and outcomes among disadvantaged populations correlate to structural and sociodemographic disadvantages (e.g., poverty, low levels of education, substandard housing, poor access to services) as well as to high rates of co-occurring physical health problems (e.g., alcohol misuse, diabetes, cardiovascular disease). Also, trauma and violence exposure (including intergenerational and historical trauma exposures) are associated with co-occurring psychopathology (e.g., posttraumatic stress disorder and depression) (Brand et al., 2010; Matthews & Phillips, 2010; Walters et al., 2011). Addressing these associations require multitasking across multiple levels of intervention, and such a broad deployment of effort is a hallmark of social work practice. Stated simply, health is not created in a clinic, and we cannot rely on traditional health services alone to heal the wrongs of history and persistent inequality.

Second, social work's leadership is needed to elucidate problems and test solutions. Despite the glaring health disparities, there is a paucity of culturally relevant research on some of the most vulnerable populations. Because of this, the health fields have few data on important risk factors, coping behaviors, and health outcomes. Without a larger body of evidence, it will be difficult to identify the strategies and develop the programs necessary to reduce health inequalities and improve health equity in the United States. Many social work researchers are already at the forefront of research on health disparities and prevention needs among vulnerable populations, particularly among racial and ethnic minorities as well as lesbian, gay, bisexual, and transgender populations (Evans-Campbell, Lincoln, & Takeuchi, 2007; Fredriksen-Goldsen et al., 2014; Marsiglia, Kulis, Yabiku, Nieri, & Coleman, 2011; Wheeler, 2003). Moreover, social work researchers have advanced innovative, community-based, participatory research approaches as well as conceptual models that include multilevel influences on health (Gehlert & Coleman, 2010; Gehlert et al., 2008b; Spencer et al., 2011; Walters & Simoni, 2002; Walters et al., 2012). Since the beginning of the Grand Challenge to Close the Health Gap, there has been an exponential growth in the number of researchers in social work conducting research in health equity, as evidenced by publication and federal grants. As we emerge from the pandemic, we expect this number to grow.

Social work's long-standing commitment to a diverse workforce with full representation of all stakeholders is a third reason for the profession to lead the health equity grand challenge. The ACA and recent national reports, including one from the National Institutes of Health, call for more inclusion of underrepresented ethnic and racial minorities among funded investigators and community-based researchers (Shavers et al., 2005; Sopher et al., 2015). Despite these calls, a very limited number of underrepresented ethnic and racial minorities have served as principal investigators for awards by the National Institutes of Health. Moreover, racial and ethnic minorities remain significantly underrepresented in higher education. In the United States, they account for only 12% of all people with doctorates and less than 3% of medical school professors (Sopher et al., 2015). A broad and dense network of highly trained and productive health science scholars, a network that includes underrepresented ethnic and racial minorities and is dedicated to culturally grounded research, is needed to ameliorate health disparities.

Finally, as suggested previously, the legacy of social work and the roles historically played by social workers should spur the profession to lead the grand challenge of health equity. Throughout history, social workers have played pivotal roles in efforts to increase critical consciousness within competing systems, link key health system stakeholders, and lead efforts to incorporate social and ecological realities into assessment and treatment. This distinctive legacy enables social work to provide leadership at a time when the ACA is driving the promotion of community involvement (Andrews et al., 2013). The legacy also provides paradigms for creative solutions to problems that extend across systems.

The social work profession is also positioned to facilitate interdisciplinary efforts among applied social and behavioral scientists, educators, and practitioners. As members of interprofessional teams, social workers already contribute in the movement toward patient-centered care. They also are engaged in the implementation of integrated care models to address more fully physical, mental, and behavioral health issues (e.g., alcohol and substance abuse) (Saunders-Adams et al., 2020). The next decade offers an opportunity to develop a strategy for leveraging the momentum of healthcare reform efforts to create a social determinants-focused agenda for research, practice, and action. Such a strategy would enable social workers to set measurable targets and time frames for alleviating the deep and persistent health inequities in the United States.

Social work is poised and primed to bring our research, education, policy, and practice skills together to adapt and apply what we know for use in national efforts to reduce health disparities; to improve mental and physical health outcomes, particularly among society's most vulnerable and marginalized; and ultimately to promote health equity and well-being for our society as a whole. As our science and profession have matured, we have grown in readiness to tackle the "scale, complexity, and interrelatedness of societal problems—from poverty and dramatic inequality to the sustainability of health and human service infrastructures across the globe—[and to] demand problem-solving skill and collaboration at levels perhaps unprecedented in our history" (Uehara et al., 2013, p. 165). The health of future generations depends on the actions we take in our current generation. Let us be remembered not only for our science and practice but also for our resolve to harness our collective will and intelligence to transform the health of the nation.

REFERENCES

Agency for Healthcare Research and Quality (2013). *Environmental Scan of Patient Safety Education and Training Programs.* https://www.ahrq.gov/research/findings/final-reports/environmental-scan-programs/index.html

Andrews, C. M. (2014). Unintended consequences: Medicaid expansion and racial inequality in access to health insurance. *Health & Social Work, 39,* 131–133. doi:10.1093/hsw/hlu024

Andrews, C. M., Darnell, J. S., McBride, T. D., & Gehlert, S. (2013). Social work and implementation of the Affordable Care Act. *Health & Social Work, 38,* 67–71. doi:10.1093/hsw/hlt002

Andrews, C. M., Guerrero, E. G., Wooten, N. R., & Legnick-Hall, R. (2015). The Medicaid expansion gap and racial and ethnic minorities with substance use disorders. *American Journal of Public Health, 105,* S452–S454. doi:10.2105/AJPH.2015.302560

Arredondo, A., & Orozco, E. (2012). Application of the Ecohealth model to translate knowledge into action in the health sciences. *Environmental Health Perspectives, 120,* A104–A105. doi:10.1289/ehp.1104847

Avendano, M., Glymour, M. M., Banks, J., & Mackenbach, J. P. (2009). Health disadvantage in US adults aged 50 to 74 years: A comparison of the health of rich and poor Americans with that of Europeans. *American Journal of Public Health, 99,* 540–548. doi:10.2105/AJPH.2008.139469

Babor, T. F., Del Boca, F., & Bray, J. W. (2017). Screening, brief intervention and referral to treatment: Implications of SAMHSA's SBIRT initiative for substance abuse policy and practice. *Addiction, 112,* 110–117.

Begun, A. L., Clapp, J. D., & The Alcohol Misuse Grand Challenge Collective. (2016). *Reducing and preventing alcohol misuse and its consequences: A grand challenge for social work.* Grand Challenges for Social Work Initiative working paper no. 17. Cleveland, OH: American Academy of Social Work and Social Welfare. Retrieved from http://aaswsw.org/wp-content/uploads/2015/12/WP14-with-cover.pdf

Begun, A. L., & Murray, M. M. (Eds.). (2020). *The Routledge handbook of social work and addictive behaviors.* New York, NY: Routledge.

Brand, S. R., Brennan, P. A., Newport, D. J., Smith, A. K., Weiss, T., & Stowe, Z. N. (2010). The impact of maternal childhood abuse on maternal and infant HPA axis function in the postpartum period. *Psychoneuroendocrinology, 35,* 686–693. doi:10.1016/j.psyneuen.2009.10.009

Braveman, P., & Gottlieb, L. (2014). The social determinants of health: It's time to consider the causes of the causes. *Public Health Reports, 129,* 19–31.

Brennan Ramirez, L. K., Baker, E. A., & Metzler, M. (2008). *Promoting health equity: A resource to help communities address social determinants of health.* Atlanta, GA: US Department of Health and Human Services, Centers for Disease Control and Prevention.

Buchmueller, T. C., Levinson, Z. M., Levy, H. G., & Wolfe, B. L. (2016). Effect of the Affordable Care Act on racial and ethnic disparities in health insurance coverage. *American Journal of Public Health, 106,* 1416–1421.

Bureau of Labor Statistics, U.S. Department of Labor (2020). *Occupational Outlook Handbook,* Social Workers, at https://www.bls.gov/ooh/community-and-social-service/social-workers.htm

Campbell, C., Smith, D., Clary, K. L., & Egizio, L. (2020). Screening, brief intervention, and referral to treatment (SBIRT) in the substance use system of care. In A. L. Begun & M. M. Murray (Eds.), *Routledge handbook of social work and addictive behaviors* (pp. 343–354). New York, NY: Routledge.

Carman, K. G., Eibner, C., & Paddock, S. M. (2015). Trends in health insurance enrollment, 2013–15. *Health Affairs, 34,* 6. doi:10.1377/hlthaff.2015.0266

Centers for Disease Control and Prevention. (2019). Excessive drinking is draining the U.S. economy. Retrieved from https://www.cdc.gov/alcohol/features/excessive-drinking.html

Centers for Disease Control and Prevention. (2021). Risk for COVID-19 infection, hospitalization, and death by race/ethnicity. Retrieved from https://www.cdc.gov/coronavirus/2019-ncov/covid-data/investigations-discovery/hospitalization-death-by-race-ethnicity.html

Chaudry, A., Jackson, A., & Glied, S. A. Did the Affordable Care Act reduce racial and ethnic disparities in health insurance coverage? doi:10.26099/d8hs-cm53

Chokshi, D. A. (2018). Income, poverty, and health inequality. *Journal of the American Medical Association, 319*, 1312–1313. doi:10.1001/jama.2018.2521

Clapp, J. D. (2018). The promise of systems science in health behavior research: The example of drinking events. *Health Behavior Research, 1*.

Clapp, J. D., Madden, D. R., Gonzalez Villasanti, H. J., Giraldo, L. F., Passino, K. M., Reed, M. B., & Fernandez Puentes, I. (2018). A system dynamics model of drinking events: Multi-level ecological approach. *Systems Research and Behavioral Science, 35*, 265–281.

Comas-Díaz, L. (2016). Racial trauma recovery: A race-informed therapeutic approach to racial wounds. In A. N. Alvarez, C. T. H. Liang, & H. A. Neville (Eds.), The cost of racism for people of color: Contextualizing experiences of discrimination (pp. 249–272). American Psychological Association. https://doi.org/10.1037/14852-012

Commission on Social Determinants of Health. (2008). Closing the gap in a generation: Health equity through action on the social determinants of health. Final report. Retrieved from http://whqlibdoc.who.int/publications/2008/978924 156 3703_eng.pdf

Council on Social Work Education. (2020). *Specialized practice curricular guide for substance use social work practice.* Alexandria, VA: Council on Social Work Education.

Dahlgren, G., & Whitehead, M. (1992). *Policies and strategies to promote equity in health.* Copenhagen, Denmark: World Health Organization Regional Office for Europe.

Davison, C. M., Ndumbe-Eyoh, S., & Clement, C. (2015). Critical examination of knowledge to action models and implications for promoting health equity. *International Journal for Equity in Health, 14*. doi:10.1186/s12939-015-0178-7

Dawson, D. A., Goldstein, R. B., Saha, T. D., & Grant, B. F. (2015). Changes in alcohol consumption: United States 2001–2002 to 2012–2013. *Drug and Alcohol Dependence, 148*, 56–61.

DeVore, S., & Champion, R. W. (2011). Driving population health through accountable care organizations. *Health Affairs, 30*, 41–50.

Dressler, W. W., Oths, K. S., & Gravlee, C. C. (2005). Race and Ethnicity in Public Health Research: Models to Explain Health Disparities. *Annual Review of Anthropology, 34*(1), 231–252. doi:https://doi.org/10.13016/itea-fj2c

Edgar, L., Herbert, R., Lambert, S., MacDonald, J.-A., Dubois, S., & Latimer, M. (2006). The joint venture model of knowledge utilization: A guide for change in nursing. *Nursing Leadership, 19*, 41–55. doi:10.12927/cjnl.2006.18172

Evans-Campbell, T., Lincoln, K. D., & Takeuchi, D. T. (2007). Race and mental health: Past debates, new opportunities. In W. R. Avison, J. D. McLeod, & B. A. Pescosolido (Eds.), *Mental health, social mirror* (pp. 169–189). New York, NY: Springer.

Farrer, L., Marinetti, C., Cavaco, Y. K., & Costongs, C. (2015). Advocacy for health equity: A synthesis review. *Milbank Quarterly, 93*, 392–437. doi:10.1111/1468-0009.12112

Fieland, K. C., Walters, K. L., & Simoni, J. M. (2007). Determinants of health among two-spirit American Indians and Alaska Natives. In I. H. Meyer & M. E. Northridge (Eds.), *The health of sexual minorities: Public health perspectives on lesbian, gay, bisexual, and transgender populations* (pp. 268–300). Springer Science + Business Media. https://doi.org/10.1007/978-0-387-31334-4_11

Fisher, E. S., Shortell, S. M., Kreindler, S. A., Van Citters, A. D., & Larson, B. K. (2012). A framework for evaluating the formation, implementation, and performance of accountable care organizations. *Health Affairs, 31*, 2368–2378. doi:10.1377/hlthaff.2012.0544

Fleming, E. S., Perkins, J., Easa, D., Conde, J. G., Baker, R. S., Southerland, W. M., … Norris, K. C. (2008). The role of translational research in addressing health disparities: A conceptual framework. *Ethnicity & Disease, 18*, S2-155–S2-160.

Fredriksen-Goldsen, K. I., Simoni, J. M., Kim, H.-J., Lehavot, K., Walters, K. L., Yang, J., … Muraco, A. (2014). The Health Equity Promotion Model: Reconceptualization of lesbian, gay, bisexual, and transgender (LGBT) health disparities. *American Journal of Orthopsychiatry, 84*, 653–663. doi:10.1037/ort0000030

Garfield, R., Damico, A., Cox, C., Claxton, G., & Levitt, L. (2016). New estimates of eligibility for ACA coverage among the uninsured. Retrieved from http://files.kff.org/attachment/data-note-new-estimates-of-eligibility-for-aca-coverage-among-the-uninsured

Gee, G. C., & Ford, C. L. (2011). Structural Racism and Health Inequities: Old Issues, New Directions. *Du Bois Review: Social Science Research on Race, 8*(1), 115–132. https://doi.org/10.1017/S1742058X11000130

Gehlert, S., & Coleman, R. (2010). Using community-based participatory research to ameliorate cancer disparities. *Health & Social Work, 35*, 302–309. doi:10.1093/hsw/35.4.302

Gehlert, S., Mininger, C., Sohmer, D., & Berg, K. (2008a). (Not so) gently down the stream: Choosing targets to ameliorate health disparities. *Health & Social Work, 33*, 163–167. doi:10.1093/hsw/33.3.163

Gehlert, S., Sohmer, D., Sacks, T., Mininger, C., McClintock, M., & Olopade, O. (2008b). Targeting health disparities: A model linking upstream determinants to downstream interventions. *Health Affairs, 27*, 339–349. doi:10.1377/hlthaff.27.2.339

Gordon-Larsen, P., Nelson, M. C., Page, P., & Popkin, B. M. (2006). Inequality in the built environment underlies key health disparities in physical activity and obesity. *Pediatrics, 117*, 417–424. doi:10.1542/peds.2005-0058

Ho-Lastimosa, I., Chung-Do, J. J., Hwang, P. W., Radovich, T., Rogerson, I., Ho, K., Keaulana, S., Keaweʻaimoku Kaholokula, J., & Spencer, M. S. (2019). Integrating Native Hawaiian tradition with the modern technology of aquaponics. *Global Health Promotion, 26*(3_suppl), 87–92. https://doi.org/10.1177/1757975919831241

Hood, C. M., Gennuso, K. P., Swain, G. R., & Catlin, B. B. (2016). County health rankings: Relationships between determinant factors and health outcomes. *American Journal of Preventive Medicine, 50*, 129–135. doi:10.1016/j.amepre.2015.08.024

Horton, M., Freire, P., Bell, B., Gaventa, J., & Peters, J. (Eds.). (1990). *We make the road by walking: Conversations on education and social change*. Philadelphia, PA: Temple University Press.

Jardine, C., & Furgal, C. (2010). Knowledge translation with northern aboriginal communities: A case study. *Canadian Journal of Nursing Research, 42*, 119–127.

Johnson, A. K. (2004). Social work is standing on the legacy of Jane Addams: But are we sitting on the sidelines? *Social Work, 49*, 319–322. doi:10.1093/sw/49.2.319

Joseph, T. D. (2016). What health care reform means for immigrants: Comparing the Affordable Care Act and Massachusetts health reforms. *Journal of Health Politics, Policy and Law, 41*, 101–116.

Kaholokula, J. K., Grandinetti, A., Keller, S., Nacapoy, A. H., Kingi, T. K., & Mau, M. K. (2012). Association between perceived racism and physiological stress indices in Native Hawaiians. *Journal of Behavioral Medicine, 35*, 27–37. https://doi.org/10.1007/s10865-011-9330-z

Kaplan, G. A., Shema, S. J., & Leite, C. M. A. (2008). Socioeconomic determinants of psychological well-being: The role of income, income change, and income sources during the course of 29 years. *Annals of Epidemiology, 18*, 531–537. doi:10.1016/j.annepidem.2008.03.006

Kathol, R. G., Patel, K., Sacks, L., Sargent, S., & Melek, S. P. (2015). The role of behavioral health services in accountable care organizations. *American Journal of Managed Care, 21*, e95–e98.

Kendi, I. X. (2019). *How to be an antiracist*. One World.

Krieger, N. (2012). Methods for the scientific study of discrimination and health: An ecosocial approach. *American Journal of Public Health, 102*, 936–945. doi:10.2105/AJPH.2011.300544

Krieger, N. (2014). Discrimination and Health Inequities. *International Journal of Health Services, 44*(4), 643–710. https://doi.org/10.2190/HS.44.4.b

Link, B. G., & Phelan, J. C. (1995). Social conditions as fundamental causes of disease. *Journal of Health and Social Behavior, 35*, 80–94. doi:10.2307/2626958

Logie, C., Dimaras, H., Fortin, A., & Ramón-García, S. (2014). Challenges faced by multidisciplinary new investigators on addressing grand challenges in global health. *Globalization and Health, 10*. doi:10.1186/1744-8603-10-27

Makaroun, L. K., Bowman, C., Duan, K., Handley, N., Wheeler, D. J., . . . Chen, A. H. (2017). Specialty care access in the safety net: The role of public hospitals and health systems. *Journal of Health Care for the Poor and Underserved, 28*, 566–581. doi:10.1353/hpu.2017.0040

Marmot, M. (2005). Social determinants of health inequalities. *Lancet, 365*, 1099–1104. doi:10.1016/S0140-6736(05)71146-6

Marmot, M., & Bell, R. (2012). Fair society, healthy lives. *Public Health, 126*, S4–S10. doi:10.1016/j.puhe.2012.05.014

Marsiglia, F. F., Kulis, S., Yabiku, S. T., Nieri, T. A., & Coleman, E. (2011). When to intervene: Elementary school, middle school or both? Effects of Keepin' It REAL on substance use trajectories of Mexican heritage youth. *Prevention Science, 12*, 48–62. doi:10.1007/s11121-010-0189-y

Matthews, S. G., & Phillips, D. I. W. (2010). Minireview: Transgenerational inheritance of the stress response: A new frontier in stress research. *Endocrinology, 151*, 7–13. doi:10.1210/en.2009-0916

McGovern, L., Miller, G., & Hughes-Cromwick, P. (2014). The relative contribution of multiple determinants to health outcomes. Health policy brief. Retrieved from http://www.healthaffairs.org/healthpolicybriefs/brief.php?brief_id=123

Mitchell, F. M. (2015). Racial and ethnic health disparities in an era of health care reform. *Health and Social Work, 40*, e66–e74. doi:10.1093/hsw/hlv038

Musumeci, M. (2021). Medicaid provisions from the American Rescue Plan Act. Kaiser Family Foundation issues brief. Retrieved from https://www.kff.org/medicaid/issue-brief/medicaid-provisions-in-the-american-rescue-plan-act/ on May 9, 2021.

National Academies of Sciences, Engineering, and Medicine. (2019). *Integrating social care into the delivery of health care: Moving upstream to improve the nation's health*. Washington, DC: The National Academies Press. https://doi.org/10.17226/25467.

National Research Council & Institute of Medicine. (2013). *U.S. health in international perspective: Shorter lives, poorer health*. Institute of Medicine report brief. Washington, DC: National Academies Press.

Newman, L., Baum, F., Javanparast, S., O'Rourke, K., & Carlon, L. (2015). Addressing social determinants of health inequities through settings: A rapid review. *Health Promotion International, 30,* ii126–ii143. doi:10.1093/heapro/dav054

Nieva, V. F., Murphy, R., Ridley, N., Donaldson, N., Combes, J., Mitchell, P., ... Carpenter, D. (2005). From science to service: A framework for the transfer of patient safety research into practice. In K. Henriksen, J. B. Battles, E. S. Marks, & D. I. Lewin (Eds.), *Advances in patient safety: From research to implementation: Vol. 2. Concepts, and methodology* (pp. 441–453). Rockville, MD: Agency for Healthcare Research and Quality.

Oldham, G., & McLean, R. (1997). Approaches to knowledge-brokering. Retrieved from https://www.iisd.org/pdf/2001/networks_knowledge_brokering.pdf

Patient Protection and Affordable Care Act, 42 U.S.C. § 18001 (2010).

Pollitz, K. (2021). How the American Rescue Plan will improve the affordability of private health coverage. Kaiser Family Foundation issues brief. Retrieved from https://www.kff.org/health-reform/issue-brief/how-the-american-rescue-plan-will-improve-affordability-of-private-health-coverage/

Richardson, R. B., Olabisi, L. S., Waldman, K. B., Sakana, N., & Brugnone, N. G. (2020). Using participatory systems dynamics modeling of agricultural–environmental systems in a developing country context. In L. S. Olabisi, M. McNall, W. Porter, & J. Zhao (Eds.), *Innovations in collaborative modeling* (pp. 125–160). MI: Michigan State University Press, East Lansing, MI.

Saunders-Adams, S., Hechmer, C., Peck, A., & Murray, M. M. (2020). Integrated care: Identifying and intervening with substance misuse in primary care. In A. L. Begun & M. M. Murray (Eds.), *Routledge handbook of social work and addictive behaviors* (pp. 436–452). New York, NY: Routledge.

Shavers, V. L., Fagan, P., Lawrence D., McCaskill-Stevens, W., McDonald, P., Browne, D., ... Trimble, E. (2005). Barriers to racial/ethnic minority application and competition for NIH research funding. *Journal of the National Medical Association,* 971063–1077.

Smedley, B. D., Stith, A. Y., & Nelson, A. R. (Eds.). (2003). *Unequal treatment: Confronting racial and ethnic disparities in health care*. Washington, DC: National Academies Press.

Sommers, B.D. (2020). Health insurance coverage: What comes after the ADA. *Health Affairs, 39,* 502–508. doi:10.1377/hlthaff.2019.01416

Sopher, C. J., Adamson, B. J. S., Andrasik, M. P., Flood, D. M., Wakefield, S. F., Stoff, D. M., ... Fuchs, J. D. (2015). Enhancing diversity in the public health research workforce: The research and mentorship program for future HIV vaccine scientists. *American Journal of Public Health, 105,* 823–830. doi:10.2105/AJPH.2014.302076

Spencer, M. S., Rosland, A.- M., Kieffer, E. C., Sinco, B. R., Valerio, M., Palmisano, G., ... Heisler, M. E. (2011). Effectiveness of a community health worker intervention among African American and Latino adults with type 2 diabetes: A randomized controlled trial. *American Journal of Public Health, 101,* 2253–2260. doi:10.2105/AJPH.2010.300106

Stout, J. (2010). *Blessed are the organized: Grassroots democracy in America*. Princeton, NJ: Princeton University Press.

Substance Abuse and Mental Health Services Administration. (2020). National Survey of Drug Use and Health (NSDUH) detailed tables for 2019. Retrieved from https://www.samhsa.gov/data/report/2019-nsduh-detailed-tables

Uehara, E., Flynn, M., Fong, R., Brekke, J., Barth, R. P., Coulton, C., . . . Walters, K. (2013). Grand challenges for social work. *Journal of the Society for Social Work and Research*, 4, 165–170. doi:10.5243/jsswr.2013.11

US Department of Health and Human Services, Office of Disease Prevention and Health Promotion. (2000). Healthy People 2020. Retrieved from https://www.healthypeople.gov

Walters, K. L., Johnson-Jennings, M., Stroud, S., Rasmus, S., Charles, B., John, S., . . . Boulafentis, J. (2020). Growing from Our Roots: Strategies for Developing Culturally Grounded Health Promotion Interventions in American Indian, Alaska Native, and Native Hawaiian Communities. *Prevention Science: the Official Journal of the Society for Prevention Research*, 21(Suppl 1), 54–64. https://doi.org/10.1007/s11121-018-0952-z

Walters, K. L., LaMarr, J., Levy, R. L., Pearson, C., Maresca, T., Mohammed, S. A., . . . Jobe, J. B. (2012). Project həli? dxw/Healthy Hearts Across Generations: Development and evaluation design of a tribally based cardiovascular disease prevention intervention for American Indian families. *Journal of Primary Prevention*, 33, 197–207. doi:10.1007/s10935-012-0274-z

Walters, K. L., Mohammed, S. A., Evans-Campbell, T., Beltrán, R. E., Chae, D. H., & Duran, B. (2011). Bodies don't just tell stories, they tell histories: Embodiment of historical trauma among American Indians and Alaska Natives. *Dubois Review*, 8, 179–189. doi:10.1017/S1742058X1100018X

Walters, K. L., & Simoni, J. M. (2002). Reconceptualizing native women's health: An "indigenist" stress-coping model. *American Journal of Public Health*, 92, 520–524. doi:10.2105/AJPH.92.4.520

Warren, K. R., & Hewitt, B. G. (2010). NIAAA: Advancing alcohol research for 40 years. *Alcohol Research & Health*, 33, 5–17.

Wheeler, D. P. (2003). Methodological issues in conducting community-based health and social services research among urban Black and African American LGBT populations. *Journal of Gay & Lesbian Social Services*, 15, 65–78. doi:10.1300/J041v15n01_05

Williams, D. R., & Mohammed, S. A. (2013). Racism and Health I: Pathways and Scientific Evidence. *American Behavioral Scientist*, 57(8), 1152–1173. https://doi.org/10.1177/0002764213487340

Williams, D. R., & Wyatt, R. (2015). Racial bias in health care and health challenges and opportunities. *Journal of the American Medical Association*, 314, 555–556. doi:10.1001/jama.2015.9260

World Health Organization. (2014a). Global status report on alcohol and health. Retrieved from http://www.who.int/substance_abuse/publications/global_alcohol_report/en

World Health Organization. (2014b). Promoting health and reducing health inequities by addressing the social determinants of health. Retrieved from http://www.euro.who.int/__data/assets/pdf_file/0016/141226/Brochure_promoting_health.pdf

World Health Organization. (2018). *Global status report on alcohol and health 2018*. Geneva, Switzerland: World Health Organization.

CHAPTER 4

Building Healthy Relationships to End Violence

Broadening the Vision of the Grand Challenge to Stop Family Violence

RICHARD P. BARTH, MICHELLE JOHNSON-MOTOYAMA,
MELISSA JONSON-REID, SHANTI J. KULKARNI,
TODD I. HERRENKOHL, MEGAN R. HOLMES,
SAMUEL R. AYMER, AND PATRICIA L. KOHL

Violence continues to be a pervasive and costly social problem in the United States. The societal response is largely reactive and oriented toward criminal justice for those who engage in violence, with little or no attention to the breakdown in social and intimate relationships that often underlie violence. Scientific developments offer an alternative foundation for designing innovative, effective, and culturally relevant solutions. Social work has long recognized that social relationships are fundamental to growth, problem-solving, well-being, and the cultivation of human potential (Sherraden et al., 2014). As a field concerned with social relationships and dedicated to science, social work is poised to lead, develop, and implement solutions that prevent and reduce violence. In this chapter, we provide a review of the transition from the original Grand Challenge to Stop Family Violence over to the current framing of the Grand Challenge to Build Healthy Relationships to End Violence. We then describe a conceptual model that calls out adverse structural factors contributing to violence, relational risk and protective factors that help explain violence, and outcomes that could be derived from greater attention and intervention development for building healthy relationships. We describe promising social work interventions that could reduce violence.

DEFINING VIOLENCE

Violence is defined in varying ways for various purposes. For the purposes of the Grand Challenge to Build Healthy Relationships to End Violence, we have adopted the World Health Organization (WHO) definition of violence: "The intentional use of physical force or power, threatened or actual, against oneself, another person, or against a group or community, that either results in or has a high likelihood of resulting in injury, death, psychological harm, maldevelopment or deprivation" (Krug et al., 2002, p. 4). The definition encompasses multiple acts of violence, threats as well as actual acts, and a range of consequences of violence that affect individuals, families and communities. The WHO (Krug et al., 2002) categorizes violence according to who engages in the violent behavior: individuals toward themselves (self-directed violence), individuals and smaller groups toward others (interpersonal violence), and collective entities such as nations and terrorist organizations toward other individuals and groups (collective violence). Figure 4.1 includes the nature of the violence committed (physical, sexual, psychological, or involving deprivation or neglect), and broad categories of violence are defined further by the relationships between those who commit violent acts and those who are victims of violence.

In Figure 4.1, self-directed violence is categorized further into suicidal behavior and other forms of self-harm. Interpersonal violence includes the acts that take place between family members and partners, such as child maltreatment, intimate partner violence (IPV), and elder abuse. Community violence typically occurs between acquaintances and strangers who are unrelated, and includes but is not limited to gender-based and sexual violence, youth violence, violence in institutional settings, and violence that occurs at random.

Collective violence occurs when individuals affiliated with a group commit violence against other individuals or other groups to achieve goals defined by their social, political, or economic character. A few examples include domestic and international terrorism, organized violent crime, armed conflict, genocide, state-sanctioned violence, hate crimes, and other human rights abuses.

Although the WHO violence definition is broad, various manifestations of violence are strongly interconnected because they tend to co-occur and reinforce each other (Ahmadabadi et al., 2018; Chan, 2014; Turner, Shattuck, Finkelhor, & Hamby, 2016; Wilkins, Tsao, Hertz, Davis, & Klevens, 2014). We believe that violence prevention and intervention strategies at all levels can be scaffolded by building healthy relationships. The values and environmental conditions that undergird these relationships are fundamental to supporting and sustaining these preventive and interventive efforts. The work of this grand challenge has, so far, focused primarily on interpersonal violence—also

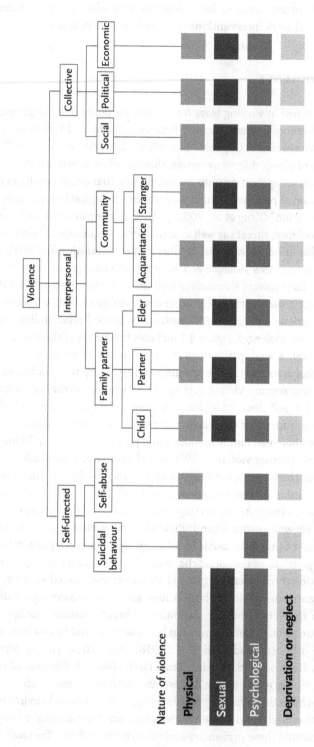

Figure 4.1 The World Health Organization's typology of violence (WHO, 2002)

the focus of this chapter. Our expectation is that a focus on interpersonal violence represents a first step, and that future efforts may be expanded within this effort or in coordination with other Grand Challenges (e.g., see Chapter 2 on ensuring healthy development for youth).

The priority of addressing interpersonal violence in the United States was reflected in the U.S. DHHS's Healthy People 2020 Goals (U.S. DHHS, n.d.) and the CDC's corresponding efforts to clarify programs, policies, and practices to prevent intimate partner violence (Niolon et al., 2017). Of note, the actual prevalence and trends in various forms of interpersonal violence do vary by source, although all sources indicate relatively small gains and point to the serious nature of the work ahead. For instance, although there was a decline in officially reported child maltreatment from the mid-1990s through 2006, annual rates of substantiated physical abuse (slightly more than 30 per 10,000) and sexual abuse (approximately 25 per 10,000) have remained relatively stable in the past decade except for a troubling uptick in child maltreatment deaths (approximately 2.4 per 100,000) of 4% from 2018 to 2019 (Finkelhor, Seito, & Jones, 2021). Lifetime prevalence from official substantiated reports and repeated national self-report surveys ranges from 12.5% to more than 25% of US children (Finkelhor, Shattuck, Turner, & Hamby, 2014; Wildeman et al., 2014). Although homicides fell to a low of 5.1 per 100,000 in 2014, they increased to 6.2 per 100,000 by 2017. Firearms-related deaths, nonfatal firearm-related injuries, and nonfatal physical assault injuries have also increased exponentially. Although bullying behaviors among youth appear to have remained relatively constant, we have some evidence of a reduction in fighting among adolescents, which dropped from 35.5 per 100,000 in 2007 to 23.6 per 100,000 in 2017.

Unlike mortality or maltreatment, there is no one national reporting system or database that captures IPV, sexual violence, stalking, and psychological abuse by former and current intimate partners. Incidence and prevalence numbers are typically drawn from either criminal justice records or the National Intimate Partner and Sexual Violence Survey and tend to lag several years behind sources for other forms of violence mentioned earlier. Although annual rates of IPV had followed a decreasing trend similar to maltreatment, this changed in 2015, when IPV rates increased by 46%. The lifetime prevalence for rape, physical violence, or stalking has remained stable at one in three for 2010 and 2015 in the National Intimate Partner and Sexual Violence Survey data (Breiding, Chen, & Black Cheng, 2014). The lack of consistent and rigorously collected data for these indicators signals the need for investments to support epidemiological and etiologic research.

Overall, personal crime in the United States cost almost $2.6 trillion in 2017 (approximately $2,000 for every person in the United States), according to a recent cost–benefit analysis (Miller et al., 2021). *Rape* and *other sexual assault* have long been major sources of the total cost of crime. Two principle new contributors of the cost per crime that derives from loss of quality of life are IPV and child maltreatment.

MAINSTREAMING GENDER

Context Matters in Developing a Research Agenda to End Violence and Promote Healthy Relationships

HEATHER L. STORER

Multifaceted and intersecting social issues such as gender-based violence (GBV), child maltreatment, and sexual assault are inherently context bound. To develop a substantive research agenda to address these issues, the field of social work must start with elevating people's intersecting identities. Gender identity has a powerful influence on individuals lived experiences—especially within the realms of domestic and economic life. Gender identity significantly affects GBV survivors' willingness to seek help from service providers, and contributes to feelings of fear, shame, and stigma. Thus, efforts to prevent violence and promote healthy relationships start with the foundational premise that intersectional notions of gender identity *matter*. As long as women-identified individuals are murdered by their intimate partners at three times the rate of male-identified individuals, we must foreground the understanding that a socially constructed marker of identity is influential in people's lives (and deaths).

Historically, movements to prevent GBV have relied on theoretical frameworks that have privileged male dominance as a root cause of abuse. Although problematizing gender inequality across the ecosystem is essential for eradicating violence, when the concept of gender is not applied intersectionally, it can reinforce socially constructed binaries, erase the experiences of nonbinary and gender-queer people, and exacerbate inequality for Black, Indigenous, and People of Color (BIPOC)-identified survivors. Because people who identify as gender nonconforming; BIPOC; and Lesbian, Gay, Bisexual, Transgender, Queer or Questioning, Intersex, Asexual, and Pansexual + (LGBTQIA+) endure disproportionately high rates of abuse, any efforts to mainstream gender must take on an antioppression lens that accounts for the diversity of survivors' lived experiences. The GBV field must call attention to adverse outcomes while *also* actively working to dismantle the root causes of these inequities.

This Grand Challenge's focus of Building Healthy Relationships to End Violence is a strategy with implications for primary and secondary prevention. Mainstreaming gender in primary prevention approaches requires a focus on the myriad ways that gender has influenced upstream social scripts, commonplace narratives, and social norms. Thus, social work scholars and practitioners must center the ways in which societal constructions of gender influence youths' conceptualizations of relationships and, in particular, intimate relationships. Throughout their social development, young people are exposed to hypermasculine, patriarchal, and heteronormative constructions of gender; these are replicated in their attitudes and

continued

behaviors in dating relationships. Thus, by middle school, young people have internalized antiquated societal expectations regarding how their gender identities dictate their interactions. In my practice work with young people in school-based settings, youth shared rigid binary understandings of expected behaviors of "boys" and "girls." Female-identified youth faced harsh social consequences when their behaviors were perceived to violate these social norms. Therefore, a gender mainstreaming approach to primary prevention programs needs to acknowledge and unpack the upstream messaging that contributes to these belief systems while also helping young people reimagine equity in their romantic and peer relationships.

"Flipping the script" on gender norms within relationships has long been a feature of evidence-informed dating violence interventions such as SafeDates, given the critical ways that gender contextualizes this social issue. In the future, we—as a field—should consider integrating a more intersectional gender lens into the development of community-based primary prevention interventions. For example, within the context of bystander intervention programs now ubiquitous in the arsenal of evidence-informed prevention-based programming, we should consider how intersectional notions of gender influence youths' ability to act as bystanders. In my work, I have found that a lack of attention to racial context and exposure to community violence exacerbates bystanders' perceived risks and likelihood to intervene (Storer, McCleary, & Hamby, 2020). Thus, we must consider how social contexts, including gender identity, influence bystanders' perceptions of risk, potential impacts on their well-being, and the unintended consequences of these interventions. For many female and BIPOC-identified young people, these barriers are insurmountable.

Research informs how and what we teach and, therefore, what the next generation of social workers does in the field. Efforts to center gender identity in solutions to end violence also involve a philosophical shift in social work education to thinking *both* clinically and structurally. Thus, we must support social work students in identifying the gendered assumptions inherent in seemingly neutral social policies and organizational practices that drive gender, economic, and racial inequality, rather than leaning on well-worn social scripts that attribute social problems to individual-level deficits and behaviors. Developing contextualized solutions to these issues and strategies to support abuse survivors involves both calling attention to the structural factors that perpetuate multiple forms of oppression, including gender inequity, while also honoring female-identified, BIPOC, and nonbinary individuals' voices of strength, fortitude, and resistance.

Reference

Storer, H. L., McCleary, J., & Hamby, S. (2020). When it's safer to walk away: Urban, low opportunity emerging adults' willingness to use bystander behaviors in response to community and dating violence. *Children and Youth Services Review, 121*, 105833. doi:10.1016/j.childyouth.2020.105833

BROADENING THE VISION: BUILDING HEALTHY RELATIONSHIPS TO END VIOLENCE

In the first edition of *Grand Challenges for Social Work and Society*, the Grand Challenge to Stop Family Violence described its vision and direction. In the years following, the leadership of that network has used an array of organizational tools to generate an exceptionally innovative and inclusive new direction and new title: Building Healthy Relationships to End Violence. The commentary by Kulkarni, Kohl, and Edmond (2020) describes the efforts of the Grand Challenge to Stop Family Violence leadership to resolve internal philosophical and theoretical differences arising from efforts to integrate the various theories, language, and traditions at work in the grand challenge.

Using community-based systems dynamics, the leadership endeavored to create a shared language and understanding of interconnections across child maltreatment, IPV, and gender-based violence. Participants of a 2-day workshop engaged in structured activities (a) to describe trends, (b) to map underlying systems, and (c) to identify common risk and protective factors across the spectrum of violence. The visual diagrams produced illustrated complex influences of poverty, patriarchy, marginalization, and trauma on child maltreatment, IPV, and gender-based violence (Figure 4.2).

Workshop participants achieved consensus with a framework focused on building healthy relationships to end violence. The reconceptualized Grand Challenge to Build Healthy Relationships to End Violence broadly embraces scholarship relating to violence, oppression, prevention, intervention, relationships, and health across a range of theoretical perspectives, developmental stages, social contexts, funding mechanisms, and service systems. The newly named grand challenge offers many advantages, including a more nuanced treatment of gender, expanded prevention opportunities, and reduce stigma through a strengths-based configuration.

Whatever the name, stopping violence has been a goal of social work even before social work became a formal profession (Gordon, 1988). Efforts to achieve this goal have taken many directions and have evolved over time into family therapy intervention, child maltreatment prevention, youth violence and dating violence prevention/intervention, programs to prevent and lessen harm associated with intimate partner abuse, and more. Social work has also added its own great interest and expertise in responding to gender-based violence, which has focused both on reducing violence, and increasing survivor empowerment and choice. The work of this grand challenge focuses on developing models of practice that are effective and congruent with the values we espouse as social workers.

The Grand Challenge to Stop Family Violence recognized the overlap between child maltreatment, IPV, and gender-based violence. Therefore, the Grand Challenge to Build Healthy Relationships to End Violence has accepted

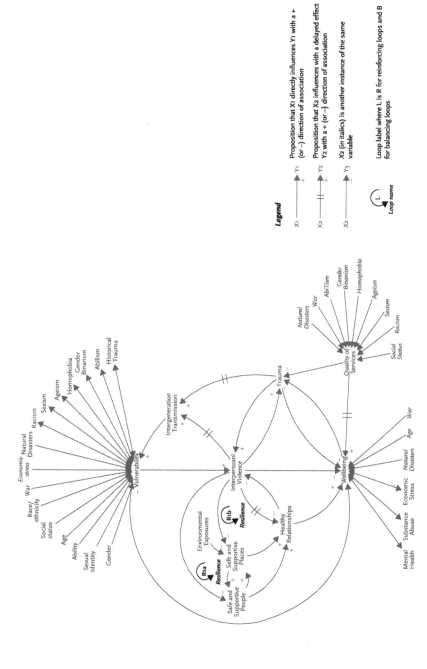

Figure 4.2 CDC VETO Violence website showing Violence Types within the Social-Ecological Model

an even broader challenge: to understand and address violence of different forms, both within and outside the family. This broadening is consistent with the "Connecting-the-Dots" framework of the Centers for Disease Control and Prevention (CDC) (Wilkins et al., 2014), which has diligently documented the common risk and protective factors related to various interrelated forms of violence, including child maltreatment, bullying, youth violence, IPV, and elder maltreatment. Indeed, the risk and protective factors and exposure to types of many kinds of violence are nested and interconnected, as displayed beautifully on the CDC's VetoViolence website (https://vetoviolence.cdc.gov/apps/connecting-the-dots/) (Figure 4.3). Although this chapter cannot reprise the research that underlies this graphic, we can emphasize the importance of thinking about violence prevention and intervention as being most likely to succeed when multiple levels of intervention are engaged. The focus of this chapter is on the relationship level of contributors to violence, but we want to underscore the importance of policy- and community-level interventions—often requiring policy change—to reduce violence.

The establishment of a new focus for the grand challenge required additional work to create a coherent conceptual framework (see Figure 4.4 for a pictorial of the path that this Grand Challenge has followed). We are a substantial way through this process and will continue the work over the coming months.

Conceptual Framework for Building Healthy Relationships to End Violence

Work on our conceptual framework began after the workshop and was intended to bring forward the connections between prevention and intervention strategies that work across levels of the social ecology to reduce violence. The model centers the role of healthy relationships in strengths-based models of practice designed to mitigate risks and enhance protection from violence, as well as to narrow service gaps for survivors and those at risk for violence.

Consistent with the Connecting-the-Dots Framework, we adopted a holistic and developmental perspective that explores how violence within the family extends beyond the family, and how violence exposure and perpetration are linked developmentally. In this work, we acknowledge the importance of developing, implementing, and scaling prevention and intervention programs that address micro, meso, and macro risk and protective factors comprehensively, while also appreciating that efforts to address root causes of violence have been located primarily at the individual and interpersonal levels (Figure 4.5). The model shown in Figure 4.3 draws attention to the importance of locating interventions to strengthen relationships and end violence at all levels of the social ecology.

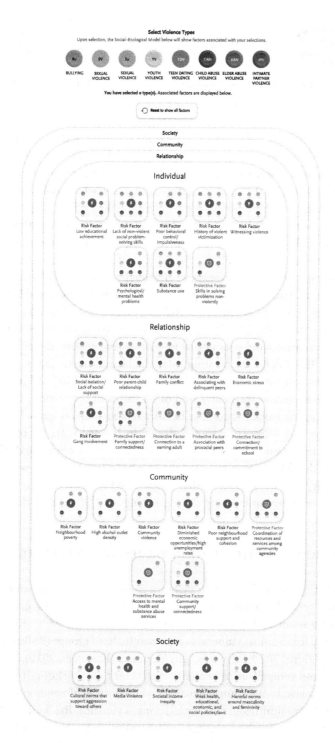

Figure 4.3 The CDC's *Veto Violence* Framework to Build on *Connecting the Dots*, vetoviolence.cdc.gov

Figure 4.4 Pathway to New Conceptual framework for the Grand Challenge to Build Healthy Relationships to End Violence

The conceptual model draws on ideas from a number of theories and frameworks. For example, we rely on the public model of violence prevention to identify common risk and protective factors for different forms of violence (e.g., Wilkins et al., 2014), and to capture the ways in which violence is embedded in ecological and relational contexts and is linked across stages of the life course (Herrenkohl et al., 2020). We also rely on various practice theories and systems models to emphasize a set of core values and guiding principles to support primary and secondary prevention efforts, and to narrow service gaps and improve outcomes for those affected by violence (Kulkarni, 2019).

Practices and policies consistent with our framework are based in theories of resilience and empowerment, as well as perspectives on gender and racial (in)equality (Messing, 2020). Each deepens our commitment to strengths-based interventions and policy-level initiatives that seek to identify and mitigate risks for violence by creating safe, stable, and nurturing relationships (Centers for Disease Control and Prevention, n.d.), and by working actively to end racism, gender inequality, and other forms of oppression. In research and practice, our work to promote healthy relationships is guided by an understanding that violence is rooted deeply in learned patterns of behavior stemming from family of origin and society, as well as norms and practices of society that place some in positions of power and others in positions of vulnerability. The interventions that follow build on these principles and on promising relationship-building strategies long used by social workers.

PREVENTION AND INTERVENTION VALUES AND KEY TENETS

Although funding and access to violence prevention and intervention programs has greatly expanded during the past three decades, the gap between community needs and available services and resources is wide and persists, particularly for the most vulnerable and marginalized groups (Kulkarni, 2019; Lakind & Atkins, 2018; Reynolds, Ou, Mondi, & Giovanelli, 2019). This gap is troubling and compels us to examine our current approaches critically to be more responsive to the comprehensive and wide array of needs expressed by people and communities affected by all forms of violence. The "building healthy relationships" approach encourages collaborative engagement rooted in empirical research, intersectional feminist theory, trauma-informed principles, and social work values. From an intersectional trauma-informed perspective,

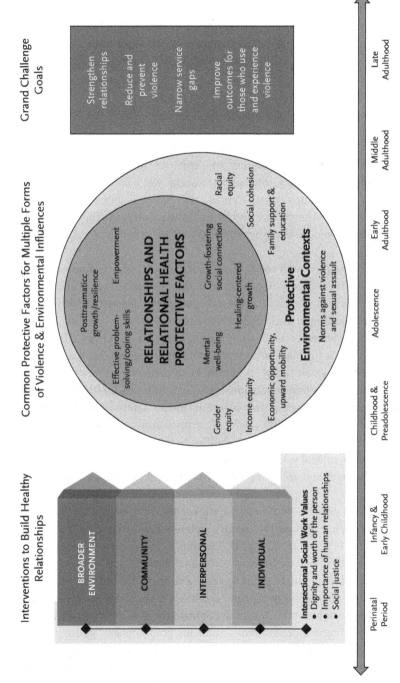

Figure 4.5 Conceptual framework for the Grand Challenge to Build Healthy Relationships to End Violence

these include power-sharing, authenticity, individualized services, and systems advocacy. These frameworks support relational health by embedding and modeling healthy relationships in program development, implementation, and evaluation. Similarly, policy initiatives are essential for ensuring the environmental context and access to resources necessary for relationships to thrive. Last, it is critical that both preventive and interventive approaches be grounded in the best available evidence for effectiveness and implementation across diverse populations.

In developing the framework, our group agreed about the need to shift from a deficit frame in theory, practice, and policy to one based on core social work values and on science. These core values include the importance of human relationships, the dignity and worth of the person, and social justice. Human relationships are central to social work because our goal is to strengthen relationships to enhance the well-being of individuals and communities. Social workers value and respect the dignity, worth, and diversity of every person, and we challenge social injustices on behalf of vulnerable and oppressed people.

Theories that align with social work values are critical in framing our work. Relational–cultural theory is grounded in the idea that healthy and optimal development across the life course is a product of the degree to which one participates in meaningful and supportive relationships with others. Such relationships are referred to as *growth-fostering connections* (Jordan, 2008; Lenz, 2016). Growth-fostering connections are framed within mutual empathy (attunement, responsiveness, commitment to the relational connection, and the capacity to impact one's relational partner), authenticity (the ability to express oneself honestly and openly in a relationship, safety within the relationship, and the feeling of being validated), empowerment (feelings of personal strength and believing in personal abilities to take action and effect change), and the ability to deal with difference or conflict (the process of expressing, working through, and accepting differences in background, perspective, and feeling).

Strong and positive relationships are consistently associated with many forms of resilience in ways that reduce violence and mitigate against its negative effects (Wilkins et al., 2014). Programs that focus on strengthening relationships and building networks of support are critical to preventing violence and reducing outcomes of violence exposure for children and adults. In addition, evidence suggests that systemic racism and white supremacy, poverty, and socioeconomic insecurity contribute to environmental contexts in which violence is more endemic, and thus programs and policies focused on lessening disparities in income and employment are also important for preventing violence. We believe that more integrative work is needed to connect disparate lines of violence research to broaden the focus from specific etiologic and ecological domains to common risk and protective factors; and patterns of behavior that cut across social, psychological, and ecological contexts and developmental life stages. We also believe it essential to conceptualize interventions at the intersection of policy and practice so that levers of change are positioned at the macro, meso, and micro levels. We understand that building healthy relationships also requires access to the resources and supports necessary to meet basic material and health needs foundational to positive growth. In the sections that follow, we provide a brief overview of empirical research related to strategies to building healthy relationships, and reducing and preventing violence at the societal, community, and individual levels (Noltemeyer, Bush, Patton, & Bergen, 2012; Goodman, Smyth, Borges, & Singer, 2009).

SOCIETAL STRATEGIES TO STRENGTHEN RELATIONSHIPS

The Grand Challenges endeavor to expand the availability and impact of interventions that address some of society's greatest problems. Studies have demonstrated the relationship of weak health and social policies to multiple forms of violence such as child maltreatment, IPV, and sexual violence (Wilkins et al., 2014). We also have an increasingly clear understanding that child maltreatment and IPV are related to financial problems or stressors, legal problems with the justice system, housing instability, and other adverse circumstances that strain interpersonal relationships (Conger, Conger, & Martin, 2010; Masarik & Conger, 2017).

A small but growing body of research suggests that income support policies such as Temporary Assistance to Needy Families, the Supplemental Nutrition Assistance Program, and the earned income tax credit (EITC) are associated with child maltreatment (Maguire-Jack, Johnson-Motoyama, & Parmenter, 2021) and foster care entries (Johnson-Motoyama & Ginther, 2019; Rostad, Klevens, Ports, & Ford, 2020). A key observation is that even small amounts of money may reduce child maltreatment risk for families with limited resources (Cancian, Yang, & Slack, 2013). Refundable EITC programs have also demonstrated protective effects against multiple forms of IPV (Spencer et al., 2020). As such, we understand that what might be the most significant way to strengthen relationships to end violence is to reduce economic stressors and support families. The grand challenge also presents us with the opportunity to imagine how we might better address basic human needs through strategies that replace means-tested programs that are costly to administer and result in low take-up rates resulting from stigma. We refer readers to the chapters in this volume on Reducing Extreme Economic Inequality (Chapter 11), and Achieving Equal Opportunity and Justice (Chapter 13).

In the United States, federal policy often provides the broad mandates for state responses to various forms of interpersonal violence. The Child Abuse

Prevention and Treatment Act, the Adoption and Safe Families Act, and the Violence Against Women Act (VAWA) are three cornerstone laws that have shaped the national response, funding, and accountability for reducing child maltreatment and IPV. The CDC's Domestic Violence Prevention Enhancement and Leadership Through Alliances program funds state domestic violence coalitions and calls expressly for developing the capacity of organizations to improve relationship dynamics and individual well-being by improving communication, conflict management, and emotional regulation skills (Centers for Disease Control and Prevention, 2019). This program is controversial and not often used for funding relationship-building interventions. When it is, it is largely only to work with engaged couples or new parents and rarely—if at all—to work with couples already engaged in low-frequency or low-intensity violence.

In addition, there are a number of other policies that guide income, housing, food, home-visiting, and health supports for families and partners—such as the Affordable Care Act, the EITC, SNAP, and TANF—that may provide the ecological context needed for healthy relationships to thrive, although state implementation of these policies varies in regard to the relative ease of access and generosity of the benefits (Brown et al., 2019; Dauber, Hogue, Henderson, Nugent, & Hernandez, 2019; Johnston, Strahan, Joski, Dunlop, & Adams, 2018; Spencer & Komro, 2017). There is no federal law that supports relationship-building or -strengthening to end violence per se, although home visitation for parents of infants and toddlers could be conceptualized this way. There are, however, more localized policies at the community or school levels that may relate more directly to relationship-building.

COMMUNITY INTERVENTIONS TO STRENGTHEN RELATIONSHIPS

The CDC has identified an array of community risk factors associated with violence, including neighborhood poverty, high alcohol outlet density, community violence, diminished economic opportunities, high unemployment, and low neighborhood support and cohesion. There are also relationship-building interventions that operate at the community level. Although violence interventions have traditionally targeted individuals, changes to the built environment in places where violence occurs show promise as practical, sustainable, and high-impact preventive measures. Some evidence suggests that reducing alcohol availability, improving street connectivity, and providing green housing environments can reduce violent crimes (Kondo, Andreyeva, South, MacDonald, & Branas, 2018). Although we lack clear evidence regarding the extent to which these violence prevention strategies are mediated by changes in healthy relationships, we believe that this is likely to be part of the causal explanation.

Home visitation for parents of young children has as one of its foci supporting parent–child relationships. The Maternal, Infant, and Early Childhood Home Visiting Program provides funds to state and Tribal entities funding to support the implementation of evidence-based home visitation, although not all qualifying programs are widely offered (Condon, 2019; Peterson et al., 2018). One of the primary foci of these programs is the support of the parent–child relationship as well as the relationship between the parent and the home visitor (Peterson et al., 2018). These programs also seek to connect families with resources that meet other needs, such as those described in the previous section (West, Duggan, Gruss, & Minkovitz, 2020). Results related to preventing maltreatment are inconsistent, but current work is focused on understanding the relative benefit of specific regional approaches that may hold the most promise (Goodman, Dodge, Bai, O'Donnell, & Murphy, 2019; Lee, Kirkland, Miranda-Julian, & Greene, 2018).

Mediation has a long history of success (at least since the 1960s) in resolving conflicting relationships between community members. Neighborhood Justice Centers, later renamed Community Mediation Centers, were established to reduce underlying levels of intergroup and interpersonal conflict. More than 400 Community Mediation Centers now exist across the United States—each handling an average of 1,000 disputes a year. The extent to which these programs reduce violence between mediation participants is not known, although we do have some evidence that conflict resolution and restorative justice programs may reduce recidivism for those previously involved with crimes (Harmon-Darrow, 2020). Chicago's CeaseFire is the best known and has experienced many replications. A replication in Phoenix has also been successful, resulting in a significant decrease in overall levels of violence by more than 16 incidents on average per month and a decrease of 16 assaults on average per month, and resulted in a significant increase of 3.2 shootings on average per month, controlling for comparison areas and violence trends (Fox, Katz, Choate, & Hedberg, 2015).

Baltimore has replicated Chicago's violence interrupter project and, along with Chicago colleagues, examined what the successful practice looks like (Whitehill, Webster, Frattaroli, & Parker, 2014). These community conflict mediations have relationship-building as a component. Staff, known as *violence interrupters*, spend time trying to develop relationships with high-violence prospects and introducing them to other violence interrupters who may have a relationship with some of their antagonists. The optimal outcome is a signed agreement to let violence cease; thousands of these have been signed. These are certainly prototyping of other forms of relationship contracts that have been used with other parties experiencing persistent and powerful conflicts. Much more development and testing of these methods are needed (Hall, 2017) especially given the finding that initially positive outcomes may diminish over time (Buggs, Webster, & Crifasi, 2020).

There are also other examples of more localized approaches to interpersonal violence. Bullying prevention policies are typically enacted at the school level (Hall, 2017). The Olweus Bullying Prevention program is one of the best-known prevention programs that, in part, works on building an emotional connection with bullied peers (Limber, Olweus, Wang, Masiello, & Breivik, 2018). Similarly, bystander approaches seek to build relationships with the potential victim and/or the individual that may be at risk of committing violence, and tend to be enacted by educational or other community-based organizations. Although developed largely in response to sexual violence, the approach is being translated to child maltreatment (Mujal, Taylor, Fry, Gochez-Kerr, & Weaver, 2019; Weaver, Taylor, Weaver, & Kutz, 2020).

RELATIONSHIP-STRENGTHENING VIA SOCIAL WORK INTERVENTIONS

Relationship-strengthening has long been a signature characteristic and central goal of social work interventions. Social workers were essential to the development of family therapy, which was created—in great part—to repair highly strained relationships between parents and children who were "beyond parental control," had run away, or were in juvenile detention (Satir, 1964). These relationships were often characterized by abuse of power by parents, lack of honest communication, mistrust, physical confrontations, and escalating conflict and self-harm. Social work remains the only profession that routinely teaches courses in family and couples therapy to nearly every clinical student. Nevertheless, during the past few decades, clinical interventions such as these are often not seen as appropriate for relationships that have included violence. This view may be changing as a response to the broad reexamination of carceral methods for responding to violence. At least some states (e.g., Utah, Oklahoma) now support the use of couples counseling after completion of standard batterer's intervention programs. The development and testing of these methods have largely been conducted in university communities and need to be steered by affected populations and communities.

The significant reluctance to use relationship-strengthening methods with couples using violence (in some states this is prohibited by regulation) may, in part, be true because relationship-strengthening interventions such as family and couples counseling have often lacked sufficiently detailed protocols or training in the necessity of assessing the risk of violence in relationships. Without establishing the ability to determine reasonably whether the separation of violence-involved couples is feasible, relationship-strengthening interventions are not seen as meeting a basic "safety-first" criteria of social work. Any significant expansion of this work must be built on closer ties to the emerging work on harm and lethality assessment [see, for example, Graham et al. (2021) and Messing, (2019)]. Close collaboration between researchers and practitioners is essential and squarely within the bailiwick of the Grand Challenges.

Also, social workers have contended that couples in which there is a clear victim and perpetrator have such unequal power dynamics that there cannot be effective communication and treatment. This concern about the need to address power dynamics before couples can be supported in strengthening their relationships has also led to concerns about, and restrictions on, the use of mediation with couples using violence. Concern about custody mediators overlooking IPV has also been a limiter on its use (see, for example, Johnson, Saccuzzo, & Koen, 2005). Concerns about any intervention that might compromise safety of victims of IPV also characterizes the field's relationship to restorative practices, although the use of this practice (and related research) seems to be on the rise (Center for Court Innovation, 2019). Relationship strengthening interventions must meet the test of being used safely. Relationship-strengthening interventions must also meet the test of alignment with core social work values.

Nonetheless, the field continues to search for alternatives to conventional criminal justice interventions that involve police involvement and referral to single-gender batterer's intervention programs (BIPs) that emphasize changing power and control behavior of the participants. This reconsideration of how we work with violence-involved families is also consistent with our recognition that criminal justice interventions are in misalignment with our values and in recognition of the intended or unintended harms that are produced, especially around the support of the punitive tools of white supremacy. This view finds alignment with critical race theory, which raises skepticism about the lack of equity and justice for people of color seeking assistance from police interventions.

The current array of interventions is also narrow and not very productive. Rigorous research designs, including quasi-experimental studies and randomized controlled trials, of conventional BIPs have shown mixed or no results in decreasing recidivism or reassault rates that follow the use of this approach (Aaron & Beaulaurier, 2017). One part of the critique is that BIPs do not work with couples on their relationships; instead, they separate batterers from victims and focus on changing batterer power and control dynamics. Some promising innovations are to improve BIPs by combining features of BIPs and restorative justice (Mills, Barocas, Butters, & Ariel, 2019). Others are maintaining the structure of BIPs [treating perpetrators alone but also including cognitive behavior therapy (CBT) or mindfulness] and are showing promise in reducing physical, psychological, or sexual violence even when partners are not treated together (Nesset, Bjørngaard, Whittington, & Palmstierna, 2020).

We observe that the tide is turning away from one-size-fits-all batterer intervention strategies toward approaches that are more trauma-informed, culturally responsive, and empowerment focused (Barocas, Emery, & Mills, 2016; Kulkarni, 2019; Voith, Logan-Greene, Strodthoff, & Bender, 2018). These approaches need to be evaluated and disseminated in ways that increase survivor choice and social equity.

Progress in ending violence through relationship-strengthening depends on changing the broad array of factors from the federal legal framework to state and local program administration to the expansion of the service array available to those who experience violence and those who use it. Our current conceptual model recognizes that the predominant framework for responding to violence emphasizes a narrow, legalistic, and carceral strategy that is not sufficiently responsive to the expressed needs of victims of violence (Jacobs et al., 2021). This approach is also not based empirically with regard to changing the behavior of those who use violence, and is almost certainly exacerbating the national problem of overincarceration. Traditional approaches that focus almost entirely on family separation and punishment are also not often seen as empowering of what women want, which is very often to maintain their relationship with partners but to stop the violence. These approaches are increasingly understood to be insensitive to the differing needs of Black and Asian women at least (Kim & Schmuhl, 2020; Moment of Truth, 2020; Ritchie, 2012). We next describe several areas of intervention that focus on relationship-strengthening and could add to the service array that social work and allied professions bring to bear to end violence. For Black women, issues of race, gender, and community are intertwined and cannot be divorced from the experiences they have with their partners and with the society at large. When the narrative of Black people in America is understood in the context of their lived experiences, the serious limitations of our current helping and carceral systems will be recognized as in need of change (Lawrence, Matusda, Delgado, & Crenshaw, 1993).

As an example of frameworks that are emerging to respond to this change, Hamel (2020) has proposed a general framework for evidence-based treatment that encourages front-line providers to find common ground across theoretical perspectives and to meet client needs by combining clinical experience and client preferences with established empirical research findings. This approach addresses risk factors common to all offenders, with an emphasis on some factors over others, depending on the client population (e.g., misogyny and gender roles for patriarchal men, and poor impulse control and inadequate relationship skills for clients whose violence is mostly expressive or situational). Preliminary efforts (e.g., in Colorado) to assess the extent of violence risk and assign services accordingly are underway, although few couples are identified as low risk.

Positive parent–child interactions are also at the core of evidence-based parenting interventions. Home visitation approaches were mentioned earlier, but there is also a growing number of parenting interventions that focus on older children and their parents. A review by Chen and Chan (2016) found that parenting interventions did show effectiveness in preventing maltreatment. A number of evidence-based parenting interventions have shown effectiveness across diverse populations (Garcia et al., 2019). Access to effective and culturally appropriate intervention remains a challenge, but there is promise in current efforts to draw on technological enhancements and community engagement to enhance access and participation (Lakind & Atkins, 2018). At least one review suggests that some parenting interventions hold promise more broadly for violence prevention in addition to child maltreatment (Altafin & Linhares, 2016). These interventions may be mounted in a number of settings, including child welfare, schools, and community-based agencies.

Childhood maltreatment and/or exposure to IPV is also related to later risk of involvement as both victim and perpetrator of later forms of interpersonal violence (Godbout et al., 2017; Herrenkohl et al., 2020; Madigan et al., 2019; Mass, Herrenkohl, & Sousa, 2008; Millett, Kohl, Jonson-Reid, Drake, & Petra, 2013; Morris, Mrug, & Windle, 2015). Prevention of child maltreatment and/or exposure to IPV in childhood, therefore, may have important longer term impacts on reduction of violence in other areas. Longer term follow-up for maltreatment and IPV prevention is warranted to understand more fully the longer term benefits across forms of interpersonal violence.

STRENGTHENING THE INTERPERSONAL SKILLS OF THOSE WHO USE AND EXPERIENCE VIOLENCE

Social workers and providers of women's legal services have long recognized that many victims of violence do not want to leave the relationships they are in because those relationships often include many other important qualities (Mills, 2009). Yet, recognition of the potential lethality of IPV has generated major concerns about the risks of endorsing, in any way, the continuity of relationships that have been violent. Part of this concern arises from a construal of the general risks of IPV inevitably getting worse per the well-known "cycle of violence" in which violence—in some couples—continues to accelerate in frequency and harm until it is lethal or is ended by the separation of the victim and perpetrator. Yet, we also know that many couples do not have accelerating, worsening violence (Goodmark, 2021). They may have some low-level concerns that it might worsen, but want to take the chance, nevertheless, that they can achieve a much lower level of violence so that they can continue their relationship safely. They often do not want to separate from their partner because of close relational ties, the impact on their own well-being, economic circumstances, their housing, and the related impact on their children. Evidence is accumulating from a range of countries and settings that couples that use situational violence can learn to stop doing so within a carefully managed treatment paradigm that includes a violence risk assessment and consideration of whether the couple's power dynamics will allow them to have a positive treatment experience (Bennett et al., 2020).

Although we know from our practitioners that many couples who sometimes use violence are being treated by social work professionals, we identified fewer than a dozen studies of dyadic treatment with low-violence couples. These studies have rarely been completed by social workers. Most of them were conducted in university settings. All couples had to engage voluntarily. Although each program or study differed in their intervention techniques and subsequent outcomes, a majority of the studies used similar screening tools and assessments, and had clear restrictions about who they treated (e.g., older than 18 years, had to be in a relationship with their significant other for at least 1 year) [the study by Fals-Stewart and Clinton-Sherrod (2009) study required 1 year of marriage]. Couples were often excluded if they had ongoing substance abuse, psychotic disorders or antisocial disorders, prior conviction, asymmetrical violence within the relationship (i.e., power dynamics, control), serious violence within a specific span of time as related to the time of treatment, and if partners had ever sought medical care in relation to their IPV. These qualifications help to show that perhaps the most significant thread of commonality among all the studies is that they focused on (in their terms) psychological IPV, low-level IPV, and situational violence. This appears to represent about one third of all IPV cases (Breiding et al., 2014), but is certainly the large preponderance of cases treated with counseling. The situational violence that has been treated in relationship-strengthening interventions such as couples counseling can be understood to occur when one or both partners try to manage clashes with violence (Blackburn Center, 2015). Situational violence may more often be mutual and occur with less frequency within a relationship than other types of domestic violence. Situational violence does not form a primary pattern of interacting across time and types of conflict, and has not, previously, escalated over time. Last, the term *situational* (or *low-level*) *violence* is used broadly to describe types of violence that have not ever resulted in serious injury or hospitalization. Although we would agree with those that argue that no level of violence between partners should be condoned, we also recognize that many relationships contain violence and are, nonetheless, judged by their participants as worthy of continuing.

Although additional work is emerging to match violence subtypes to the best social interventions (e.g., Rossi, Holtzworth-Munroe, Applegate, & Beck, 2020) and to test the sensitivity of different screening approaches (Babcock et al., 2019; Rossi et al., 2015), this work needs to be solidified to understand more completely who is most likely to succeed in work with violent couples to ensure that safety is not unduly compromised (many couples do not expect there will be zero risk of new violence). Communication to survivors about what is going on with abuser interventions is, at least, viewed as a very helpful component for helping survivors determine their options (Nnawulezi & Murphy, 2019).

Most of the interventions that have been studied for work with couples using low levels of violence range in length from 8 to 32 weekly sessions, often mixing some individual sessions with the preponderance of couple sessions or group-based conjoint therapy. A majority of the interventions had a duration of 1 to 2 hours and was subsequently led by trained clinicians—with occasional gender-specific therapeutic roles. The interventions varied in their techniques, with an emphasis on CBT, mindfulness, skill building, psychoeducation, active listening, stress reduction, solution orientation, reflection, conflict de-escalation, attachment framework, and emotional regulation (Bradley, Drummey, Gottman, & Gottman, 2014).

The outcomes of these couples' interventions are, in general, modestly positive and result in significant reductions in aggressive verbal interactions and reductions of violent cognitions and the expression of psychological violence; few incidents of serious injuries are reported by participants (Bennett et al., 2020). Some have also measured physiological and psychological changes, such as the reduction of emotional distress, anxiety, depression, and overall dissatisfaction (O'Leary, Heyman, & Neidig, 1999). Stith and McCollum (2011) found that couples completing treatment were more likely to remain in their relationship.

We recognize the importance of expanding the choices of couples who experience violence—for a relatively narrow band (but not a small number) of violence-involved couples—on the reduction of IPV, as well as other reported factors of marital satisfaction, communication, aggression, depression, likeliness to stay together, and so on. More specifically, conjoint treatments for couples, group treatments, gender-specific treatments, and individual treatments were all successful in decreasing IPV; however, conjoint therapy or multigroup therapy seemed to be more effective. Last, most studies have had short posttreatment follow-ups 1 year or 2 years later, with a primary maintenance of original results. It is important to note that each study did not eliminate or eradicate all instances of IPV. Thus, it is imperative that additional and more comprehensive research be completed to undertake the treatment of IPV completely.

Mediation

Another emerging method for working with violent couples is mediation. Couples and family mediation has developed as a practice, largely within the framework of divorce resolution, which is where most research is sited. Warnings against using mediation with couples involved with IPV go back at least 40 years (e.g., Rowe, 1984), primarily because of the assumption that successful mediation requires equal power among parties. As a result, screening for IPV is included increasingly as part of this practice (Olson, 2013), although this may require multiple methods, including surveys, having parents in separate rooms, or having parents come in on separate days. Despite the availability of additional (and standardized) procedures, the specificity, sensitivity, and universality of screening remain in doubt (Bingham, Beldin, & Dendinger, 2014; Cleak & Bickerdike, 2016). A recent randomized clinical trial comparing two approaches to mediation for divorce-related disputes reporting high levels of IPV showed that parents felt safer in mediation than in traditional litigation (Holtzworth-Munroe et al., 2020). The findings confirm that when strong safety protocols are in place and the intervention is carried out in a protected environment by well-trained professionals, mediation may be an appropriate alternative to court—even with IPV-involved couples.

Restorative Practices

Restorative practice programs were recently surveyed and visited to understand their intentions, procedures, priorities, and barriers (Pennell et al., 2020). The programs primarily served victims of IPV, but half also served victims of sexual assault. These entirely voluntary programs use a variety of formats, including peacemaking circles (39%), support circles (27%), family group conferencing (21%), and educational programming (18%). Programs generally prioritized ending violence, promoting safety and empowerment, and changing social norms. Programs gave lower priority to providing an alternative to, or promoting confidence in, the justice system. Few endeavored to provide economic services. Some programs do leverage legal pressures (e.g., as part of a plea agreement) to enhance the appeal of voluntary program participation. Beyond the persons harmed and those causing harm, others who commonly participate in the programs include program staff, community members, family members and friends, neutral facilitators, and staff from other programs.

The programs work closely with other agencies. About two thirds of the programs reported making referrals to external social service agencies to the person causing harm or the harmed person. Referrals reflect a wide variety of needs, including counseling, housing, medical, mental health and substance use treatment, vocational, and access to benefits. Program self-assessments included an emphasis on participants' strengths rather than deficits; an ability to provide all members of the family with a voice; incorporation of participants' larger communities into the process; and the expertise of dedicated, flexible staff. Program representatives found four major challenges: resistance to restorative approaches, unmotivated participants, participants' unmet needs beyond the program scope, and insufficient program resources.

The emergence of restorative practices as a reliable intervention for IPV should not be oversold. A systematic review of the literature on restorative justice interventions to address IPV found that about half of all articles found interventions to be inadequate at responding to IPV effectively (Barocas, Avieli, & Shimizu, 2020). Such results can exacerbate hopelessness and disempower those who seek to end violence, especially when no other approach is considered appropriate.

Nonetheless, there is growing recognition of mediation, restorative practices, and counseling as contributors to the service array to prevent and respond safely to IPV (Davis, Frederick, & Ver Steegh, 2019; Pennell, Burford, Sasson, Packer, & Smith, 2020; Wagers, 2020). Funding for research on these approaches—and others that rely on strengthening relationships to reduce violence—is critically needed to clarify their effectiveness and the long anticipated possibility of adverse outcomes. Additional research on risk assessment is also needed, as well as research into alternatives to current interventions that do not compromise safety but enhance and empower women's opportunities to stop violence and maintain important family relationships. These research efforts should specify resources for understanding the needs of women of color, whose concerns have not been recognized adequately.

At the same time, we recognize the concerns of those (e.g., Kim, 2020) who support the concept of restorative justice practices but resist the current tendency of the restorative justice field to underplay or ignore the role of law enforcement involvement in what is otherwise characterized as a promising resolution to the carceral crisis. Social work's involvement with the police must be consistent with social work values and intensely attentive to the concerns of those we serve. In general, the potential for couples counseling, mediation, and restorative practices for helping situationally violent couples is promising. The demand exists from families and some providers, but will not be maximized until there is more work done to understand types of IPV, levels and recency of IPV, and the array of intervention components that might fit the safety and relationship needs of couples. The supply of these programs deserves a boost.

Although evidence-based parenting interventions exist, most were initially developed and tested to treat child disruptive behavioral disorders and not to prevent or treat child maltreatment. The testing of such approaches within the population of families identified as maltreating has lagged behind (Horwitz, Chamberlain, Landsverk, & Mullican, 2010). There are increasing numbers of interventions identified as promising or effective with child welfare–involved families (Barth & Liggett-Creel, 2014 Silovsky et al., 2011; Storer, Barkan, Sherman, Haggerty, & Mattos, 2012). Such programs have shown promise in reducing recurrent child welfare system involvement (Batzer, Berg, Godinet, & Stotzer, 2018; Chaffin, Funderburk, Bard, Valle, & Gurwitch, 2011). Work is also being done to understand how and when to adapt such interventions to specific populations (e.g.,

Bigfoot & Funderbunk, 2018). Work on parenting intervention in the context of IPV is nascent (Austin, Shanahan, Barrios, & Macy, 2019).

STRENGTHENING INDIVIDUAL SKILLS TO BUILD HEALTHY RELATIONSHIPS

Individual interventions that are expressed in better, safer relationships are also relatively new and untested, but are developing as part of the relationship-strengthening ecology. Although violence stems ultimately from breakdowns in relationships, there is some reason to believe that individual interventions may reduce this likelihood. CBT and motivational interviewing are two of the individual interventions gaining greater use with people involved with IPV. A recent study of professionals delivering Duluth-oriented (BIP) programs and CBT-oriented programs shows growing awareness of the importance of research-supported practices, including the potential of CBT and motivational interviewing—strategies found to be effective in the treatment of IPV by extant research (Hamel, Cannon, Buttell, & Ferreira, 2020). There appears to have been an evolution among practitioners toward more eclecticism, and an acknowledgment that programs should be research supported. This understanding and openness to eclecticism is also beginning, very slowly, to be absorbed by practitioners, program managers, and licensing boards.

At the individual level, clinical interventions that promote healthy relationships could be expected to have a common focus by building relational skills to lessen conflict, promote nurturing and safe parenting, or provide access to substance use and mental health treatment. For example, Kids' Club and Pre Kids' Club are 10-session programs developed for school-age children and preschool-age children, respectively, who have been exposed to domestic violence (Graham-Berman, Miller-Graff, Howell, & Grogan-Kaylor, 2015). These interventions address the cognitive, social, and emotional needs of children exposed to domestic violence by helping children express a range of feelings about violence, helping children understand they are not responsible for violence between their caregivers, and fostering the development of healthy relational and coping skills to promote healing (Graham-Bermann, 2011). Mothers participate in a concurrent support group that promotes the strengths and resources of mothers, discusses safety planning for the family, and provides psychoeducation about the effects of domestic violence exposure on children (Graham-Bermann et al., 2015).

TEEN DATING VIOLENCE

Teen dating violence prevention programs typically focus on developing healthy relationship skills and conflict resolution strategies (Jaffe, Wolfe,

& Campbell, 2012). The Youth Relationships Project, for example, strives to prevent later domestic violence perpetration and victimization among adolescents who experience various forms of violence. This 18-session program provides psychoeducation, healthy relationship and coping skills development, and involvement in community antiviolence activities. A study among maltreated and domestic violence–exposed adolescents found a greater reduction in existing posttraumatic stress disorder symptoms, and violence victimization and perpetration among participants in the Youth Relationships Project compared with their peers (Wolfe et al., 2003). Much remains left to be done to develop culturally responsive clinical-, family-, school-, and judicial-level interventions to assist children who have experienced violence not to repeat their learned experiences in future relationships (Berg et al., 2020).

Trauma-informed approaches to interventions with children who have been exposed to maltreatment or IPV may also hold promise to prevent later victimization or perpetration of interpersonal violence, and to promote adaptive coping (Aymer, 2008). Evidence for the effectiveness of trauma-informed practices for children of varying ages is emerging and, to a lesser extent, trauma-informed system approaches (Auslander et al., 2020; Bartlett et al., 2018; Zettler, 2021). However, most studies have only examined impacts on immediate trauma symptoms or behaviors compared to longer term risk of violence. Longer term studies are needed to understand the effect sizes as well as downstream impacts on forms of violence.

THIS GRAND CHALLENGE IS HIGHLY INTERDISCIPLINARY

The Grand Challenge to Build Healthy Relationships to End Violence should be highly interdisciplinary. The work in this field builds on the research and practice of social workers, certainly, but also of sociologists, feminist study scholars, criminologists, pediatricians, and other health professionals, health educators, nurses, and community health workers, to name a few. Engagement with professions outside the social sciences, collaboration with new disciplines, and broad public engagement of a kind that may be largely unfamiliar to social work should all be invoked in the most compelling Grand Challenges.

The field already draws on public health, criminology, women's studies, K–12 education and higher education, nursing, sociology, and psychology. These efforts can also draw on a wide array of intervention and research methodologists, including leaders in community-based participatory research, survey research, and implementation science. Broader conversations with nearly every other grand challenge network are also critical to the success of this work. We have mentioned clear areas of overlap related to social equity and economic inequality, but we also know that interpersonal violence is affected by climate, social isolation, social and emotional regulation, racism, and many other factors that the Grand Challenges are addressing.

LOOKING FORWARD: THE BUILDING HEALTHY RELATIONSHIPS TO END VIOLENCE 5-YEAR STRATEGIC PLAN

The Grand Challenge to Build Healthy Relationships to End Violence adopts a strengths-based approach to preventing and eradicating violence that centers on an anti-oppressive, life course framework in which interconnected influences of poverty, patriarchy, marginalization, and trauma are identified and addressed by deepening knowledge, and advancing programs and services for victims and perpetrators that are nonstigmatizing (Kulkarni et al., 2020). Although funding and access to violence intervention and prevention programs has greatly expanded during the past three decades, the gap between community needs and available services and resources is wide and persists, particularly for the most vulnerable and marginalized groups (Kulkarni, Kohl, & Edmond, 2021). This gap is troubling and compels us to examine critically our current approaches to be more responsive to the comprehensive and wide array of needs expressed by people and communities that are affected by all forms of violence. The building healthy relationships approach encourages collaborative engagement rooted in intersectional feminist theory, trauma-informed principles, and social work values. From an intersectional trauma-informed perspective, these include power-sharing, authenticity, individualized services, and systems advocacy. These frameworks support relational health by embedding and modeling healthy relationships in program development, implementation, and evaluation. Similarly, policy initiatives are essential for ensuring the environmental context and access to resources necessary for relationships to thrive.

Goals reflected in a 5-year strategic plan are intended to strengthen efforts at collaborative scholarship, policy advocacy, and workforce development that reflect broad and synergistic thinking grounded in a racial equity perspective (Andrews, Parekh, & Peckoo, 2019). In research and practice, this perspective focuses on acknowledging and attending to the ways in which racism and disparities based on race and ethnicity contribute to the proliferation of violence. We commit to ongoing efforts that deepen our understanding of racism in the context of violence, as well as support the development of an antiracist workforce where racism is understood to be a major factor in all intersectional issues (e.g., gender, race) and is a part of all social work training content. Evaluating these initiatives through an understanding of institutional racism permits us to understand how the confluence of race, racism, and denial of justice affect Black and Brown communities.

To organize this effort more effectively, we envision five cores. In the scientific leadership core, members lead in the development of products that ground the Grand Challenge to Build Healthy Relationships to End Violence to inform future research such as conceptual papers and systematic reviews of the literature related to relational health. The mentorship core leads in mentoring and doctoral student training to support the development of a pipeline of healthy relationship researchers. The research translation and curricular core leads in the development of products for researchers and practitioners, including courses, learning objectives, and practice competencies for addressing violence and promoting healthy relationships. The development core leads to identifying potential funders and funding opportunities. The communications and dissemination core leads the research dissemination and communications strategy for the Grand Challenge to Build Healthy Relationships to End Violence (https://grandchallengesforsocialwork.org/wp-content/uploads/2021/10/BHREV-Five-Year-Plan-3.21.pdf). We encourage those who are engaged as network partners to post their reviews and critiques regarding this Grand Challenge.

Our greatest accomplishment has been to develop a conceptual understanding of interpersonal violence that centers social relationships and social interventions. The following are two specific examples of demonstrable progress we expect to make based on this work and the 5-year plan. We hope this conceptualization is sufficiently transformative to become a permanent element of violence prevention and response.

1. By promoting healthy, violence-free relationships, we seek to bring about a 10% reduction in interpersonal violence, such as child maltreatment and gender-based violence, elder mistreatment, and community violence across the life span within the next decade.
2. Increase the availability and accessibility of relationship-strengthening services by 10% to prevent and interrupt interpersonal violence.

A POLICY DIRECTION TO BUILDING HEALTHY RELATIONSHIPS

The risks and protective factors for child maltreatment, youth violence, IPV, sexual violence, suicide, and elder abuse are significantly shared and have origins in the stressors of daily life, the impact of adverse environments and childhood experiences, power norms and differentials between dominant and nondominant groups, and interpersonal relationships that mediate these challenges toward a safe, or violent, resolution (Wilkins et al., 2014). Violence too often leads to more violence because we lack the resources and array of interventions to intervene.

We envision a policy future in which national leaders address the need to strengthen relationships to end violence, and the intervention and implementation research needed to advance this work. This work begins with understanding of the Connecting-the-Dots Framework, and the fundamental protective and restorative impact of social relationships. This should all build on policy work that reduces economic strains on families and provides children's development accounts, greater earned income support, and continued evaluation of programs that provide a minimum family allowance. (See Chapter 12, in this volume, on financial capability for all for more details on such programs.) These programs deserve more rigorous evaluation that recognizes in a longitudinal perspective the interplay between social equity, social relationships, and violence. First, and at a minimum, we need consistent and accurate tracking of incidence and prevalence supported. Second, because any federal policy is likely to vary in regard to state and regional implementation, it will be important to track variations across places and population groups to identify an array of programming options that best advances healthy relationships and ultimately reduces violence.

Our understanding of the role that violence against children plays in creating future violence calls for policies that support intensive, coordinated, and longitudinal care (National Academies of Sciences, Engineering, and Medicine, 2016). Interrupting future violence requires more than a one-time, one-form approach. Taken together, the accumulating information on the risks of subsequent child maltreatment among those who have ever been reported to child welfare services and have ever been involved with child welfare services requires developing an approach that is less episodic and more focused on engaging families in ways that reduce the risks that arise when violent strategies for solving relationship challenges become violent (Jones-Harden, Simons, Johnson-Motoyama, & Barth, 2020).

This also speaks to the ongoing need for linked data and collaboration across multiple programs for multiple purposes, including surveillance, evaluation of existing and new policies, planning and implementation of community-level violence prevention and interventions, child maltreatment prevention strategies, IPV prevention and intervention, and evaluation of services. The CDC could certainly better leverage funding to states for the accumulation of birth records—under the National Vital Records Program—by asking states to link those data to child welfare services data to generate intervention opportunities to assist child welfare services–involved families who are having newborns (Shaw, Barth, Mattingly, Ayer, & Berry, 2013). We could also learn much more about service needs, usual care in child welfare, and preventive services through investments in cross-systems data exchanges such as the Comprehensive Child Welfare Information System, and to support research, administration, practice, and client data needs. For children in the United States, policy at the state and federal levels requires a marked shift from the reactive responses of the child welfare system to a set of prevention strategies that crosses disciplines, service sectors, policies, and funding streams to build the safe, stable, and supportive environments that all children deserve.

Policy advances would also include revising the VAWA to eliminate barriers to providing women with services that are trauma-informed, empowering, survivor informed, and research informed. The VAWA should be modified to support such research as part of the Office of Violence Against Women grant program. To maximize the benefit of a relationship-strengthening approach, intervention research should be supported by the US Department of Health and Human Services, National Institutes of Health, the CDC, and the Agency for Children and Families. We also need to reframe the idea of public safety to promote practices that resist abuse and oppression, encourage the empowerment of women, and support safety and accountability. These include decriminalizing victim survival by addressing such policies as mandatory arrest and failure to protect (see Chapter 10 in this volume for a discussion of smart decarceration strategies); investing in research studying safe alternatives to incarceration for the perpetrators of violence such as mediation, restorative practices, and counseling; and identifying alternatives to current interventions, especially for women of color.

We hope that states will support the emergence of relationship-strengthening efforts in concert with their current and conventional methods for reducing violence. We see a growing openness to combining measures of accountability with the opportunity—for those genuinely seeking it—to build stronger and safer relationships and families. New systems of care that offer relationship-strengthening opportunities, before and after violence, may emerge from local innovation—an innovation that will be shaped by those most disadvantaged by current approaches.

REFERENCES

Aaron, S. M., & Beaulaurier, R. L. (2017). The need for new emphasis on batterers intervention programs. *Trauma, Violence, & Abuse, 18*, 425–432. doi:10.1177/1524838015622440

Ahmadabadi, Z., Najman, J. M., Williams, G. M., Clavarino, A. M., d'Abbs, P., & Abajobir, A. A. (2018). Maternal intimate partner violence victimization and child maltreatment. *Child Abuse & Neglect, 82*, 23–33.

Altafim, E. R. P., & Linhares, M. B. M. (2016). Universal violence and child maltreatment prevention programs for parents: A systematic review. *Psychosocial Intervention, 25*, 27–38.

Andrews, K., Parekh, J., & Peckoo, S. (2019). How to embed a racial equity perspective in research. Washington, DC: Child Trends. Retrieved from https://www.childtrends.org/wp-content/uploads/2019/09/RacialEthnicEquityPerspective_ChildTrends_October2019.pdf

Auslander, W., Edmond, T., Foster, A., Smith, P., McGinnis, H., Gerke, D., . . . Jonson-Reid, M. (2020). Cognitive behavioral intervention for trauma in adolescent girls in child welfare: A randomized controlled trial. *Children and Youth Services Review*, *119*, 105602.

Austin, A. E., Shanahan, M. E., Barrios, Y. V., & Macy, R. J. (2019). A systematic review of interventions for women parenting in the context of intimate partner violence. *Trauma, Violence, & Abuse*, *20*, 498–519.

Aymer, S. R. (2008). Exposure: Adolescents male's coping responses to domestic violence: A qualitative study. *Children & Youth Services Review*, *30*, 654–664.

Babcock, J. C., Snead, A. L., Bennett, V. E., & Armenti, N. A. (2019). Distinguishing subtypes of mutual violence in the context of self-defense: Classifying types of partner violent couples using a modified Conflict Tactics Scale. *Journal of Family Violence*, *34*(7), 687–696. doi:10.1007/s10896-018-0012-2.

Barocas, B., Avieli, H., & Shimizu, R. (2020). Restorative justice approaches to intimate partner violence: A review of interventions. *Partner Abuse*, *11*(3), 318–349. doi:10.1891/PA-2020-0010.

Barocas, B., Emery, D., & Mills, L. G. (2016). Changing the domestic violence narrative: Aligning definitions and standards. *Journal of Family Violence*, *31*, 941–947. doi:10.1007/s10896-016-9885-0

Barth, R. P., Berrick, J. D., Garcia, A., Drake, B., Jonson-Reid, M., Greeson, J., & Gyourko, J. (in press). Misconceptions that should be addressed as part of CWS redesign. *Research on Social Work Practice*.

Barth, R. P., Jonson-Reid, M., Greeson, J. K. P., Drake, B., Berrick, J. D., Garcia, A. R., . . . Gyourko, J. R. (2020). Outcomes following child welfare services: What are they and do they differ for black children? *Journal of Public Child Welfare*, *14*, 477–499. doi:10.1080/15548732.2020.1814541

Barth, R. P., & Liggett-Creel, K. (2014). Common components of parenting programs for children birth to eight years of age involved with child welfare services. *Children and Youth Services Review*, *40*, 6–12.

Bartlett, J. D., Griffin, J. L., Spinazzola, J., Fraser, J. G., Noroña, C. R., Bodian, R., . . . Barto, B. (2018). The impact of a statewide trauma-informed care initiative in child welfare on the well-being of children and youth with complex trauma. *Children and Youth Services Review*, *84*, 110–117.

Batzer, S., Berg, T., Godinet, M. T., & Stotzer, R. L. (2018). Efficacy or chaos? Parent-child interaction therapy in maltreating populations: A review of research. *Trauma, Violence, & Abuse*, *19*, 3–19.

Bennett, V. E., Godfrey, D. A., Snead, A. L., Kehoe, C. M., Bastardas-Albero, A., & Babcock, J. C. (2020). Couples and family interventions for intimate partner aggression: A comprehensive review. *Partner Abuse*, *11*, 292–317. doi:10.1891/PA-2020-0011

Berg, K. A., Bender, A. E., Evans, K. E., Holmes, M. R., Davis, A. P., Scaggs, A. L., & King, J. A. (2020). Service needs of children exposed to domestic violence: Qualitative findings from a statewide survey of domestic violence agencies. *Children and Youth Services Review*, *118*, 1–10. doi:10.1016/j.childyouth.2020.105414.

Bigfoot, D. S., & Funderburk, B. (2018). Cultural enhancement of PCIT for American Indian families: Honoring children, making relatives. In *Handbook of Parent-Child Interaction Therapy: Innovations and Applications for Research and Practice* (pp. 235–251).

Bingham, S. G., Beldin, K. L., & Dendinger, L. (2014). Mediator and survivor perspectives on screening for intimate partner abuse. *Conflict Resolution Quarterly*, *31*, 305–330. doi:10.1002/crq.21090

Blackburn Center. (November 4, 2015). Situational violence versus domestic violence. Retrieved from https://www.blackburncenter.org/post/2015/11/04/situational-violence-versus-domestic-violence#:~:text=In contrast, situational violence not escalate over time

Bradley, R. P. C., Drummey, K., Gottman, J. M., & Gottman, J. S. (2014). Treating couples who mutually exhibit violence or aggression: Reducing behaviors that show a susceptibility for violence. *Journal of Family Violence, 29,* 549–558.

Breiding, M. J., Chen, J., & Black, M. C. (2014). Intimate partner violence in the United States—2010. Atlanta, GA: National Center for Injury Prevention and Control, Centers for Disease Control and Prevention.

Brown, E. C. B., Garrison, M. M., Bao, H., Qu, P., Jenny, C., & Rowhani-Rahbar, A. (2019). Assessment of rates of child maltreatment in states with Medicaid expansion vs states without Medicaid expansion. *JAMA Network Open 2,* e195529.

Buggs, S. A., Webster, D. W., & Crifasi, C. K. (2020). Using synthetic control methodology to estimate effects of a Cure Violence intervention in Baltimore, Maryland. *Injury Prevention.* injuryprev-2020-044056; doi:10.1136/injuryprev-2020-044056

Cancian, M., Yang, M. Y., & Slack, K. S. (2013). The effect of additional child support income on the risk of child maltreatment. *Social Service Review, 87,* 417–437.

Cannon, C., Hamel, J., Buttell, F., & Ferreira, R. J. (2020). The pursuit of research-supported treatment in batterer intervention: The role of professional licensure and theoretical orientation for Duluth and CBT programs. *Journal of Evidence-Based Social Work (United States), 17,* 469–485. doi:10.1080/26408066.2020.1775744

Center for Court Innovation. (2019). A national portrait of restorative approaches to intimate partner violence: Pathways to safety accountability, healing, and well-being. New York, NY: Author.

Centers for Disease Control and Prevention. (2019). About DELTA impact. Retrieved from https://www.cdc.gov/violenceprevention/intimatepartnerviolence/delta/impact/index.html

Centers for Disease Control and Prevention. (n.d.). Essentials for childhood: Creating safe, stable, and nurturing relationships and environments for all children. https://www.cdc.gov/violenceprevention/pdf/essentials-for-childhood-framework508.pdf

Chaffin, M., Funderburk, B., Bard, D., Valle, L. A., & Gurwitch, R. (2011). A combined motivation and parent–child interaction therapy package reduces child welfare recidivism in a randomized dismantling field trial. *Journal of Consulting and Clinical Psychology, 79,* 84–89.

Chan, K. L. (2014). Child victims and poly-victims in China: Are they more at-risk of family violence? *Child Abuse & Neglect, 38,* 1832–1839.

Chen, M., & Chan, K. L. (2016). Effects of parenting programs on child maltreatment prevention: A meta-analysis. *Trauma, Violence, & Abuse, 17,* 88–104.

Cleak, H., & Bickerdike, A. (2016). One way or many ways: Screening for family violence in family mediation. *Family Matters, 98,* 16–25.

Clemants, E., & Gross, A. (2007). "Why aren't we screening?" A survey examining domestic violence screening procedures and training protocol in community mediation centers. *Conflict Resolution Quarterly, 24,* 413–431. doi:10.1002/crq.182

Condon, E. M. (2019). Maternal, infant, and early childhood home visiting: A call for a paradigm shift in states' approaches to funding. *Policy, Politics, & Nursing Practice, 20,* 28–40.

Conger, R. D., Conger, K. J., & Martin, M. J. (2010). Socioeconomic status, family processes, and individual development. *Journal of Marriage and Family, 72,* 685–704.

Dauber, S., Hogue, A., Henderson, C. E., Nugent, J., & Hernandez, G. (2019). Addressing maternal depression, substance use, and intimate partner violence in home visiting: A quasi-experimental pilot test of a screen-and-refer approach. *Prevention Science, 20,* 1233–1243.

Davis, G., Frederick, L., & Ver Steegh, N. (2019). Intimate partner violence and mediation. Washington, DC. American Bar Association, https://www.americanbar.org/groups/dispute_resolution/publications/dispute_resolution_magazine/2019/spring-2019-family-matters/11-davis-et-al-safer/

Dettlaff, A. J., Weber, K., Pendleton, M., Boyd, R., Bettencourt, B., & Burton, L. (2020). It is not a broken system, it is a system that needs to be broken: The upEND movement to abolish the child welfare system. *Journal of Public Child Welfare, 14,* 500–517. doi:10.1080/15548732.2020.1814542

Dokkedahl, S., Kok, R. N., Murphy, S., Kristensen, T. R., Bech-Hansen, D., & Elklit, A. (2019). The psychological subtype of intimate partner violence and its effect on mental health: Protocol for a systematic review and meta-analysis. *Systematic Reviews, 8,* 198.

Fals-Stewart, W., & Clinton-Sherrod, M. (2009). Treating intimate partner violence among substance-abusing dyads: The effect of couples therapy. *Professional Psychology: Research and Practice, 40,* 257–263.

Finkelhor, D., Seito, K., & Jones, L. (2021) Updated trends in child maltreatment 2019. Crimes Against Children Research Center. Retrieved from http://www.unh.edu/ccrc/pdf/CV203%20-%20Updated%20trends%202019_ks_df.pdf

Finkelhor, D., Shattuck, A., Turner, H. A., & Hamby, S. L. (2014). Trends in children's exposure to violence, 2003 to 2011. *JAMA Pediatrics, 168,* 540–546.

Fox, A. M., Katz, C. M., Choate, D. E., & Hedberg, E. C. (2015). Evaluation of the Phoenix TRUCE Project: A replication of Chicago CeaseFire. *Justice Quarterly, 32,* 85–115. doi:10.1080/07418825.2014.902092.

Garcia, A. R., DeNard, C., Morones, S. M., & Eldeeb, N. (2019). Mitigating barriers to implementing evidence-based interventions in child welfare: Lessons learned from scholars and agency directors. *Children and Youth Services Review, 100,* 313–331. doi:https://doi.org/10.1016/j.childyouth.2019.03.005.

Godbout, N., Daspe, M. È., Lussier, Y., Sabourin, S., Dutton, D., & Hébert, M. (2017). Early exposure to violence, relationship violence, and relationship satisfaction in adolescents and emerging adults: The role of romantic attachment. *Psychological Trauma: Theory, Research, Practice, and Policy, 9,* 127–132.

Goodman, W. B., Dodge, K. A., Bai, Y., O'Donnell, K. J., & Murphy, R. A. (2019). Randomized controlled trial of Family Connects: Effects on child emergency medical care from birth to 24 months. *Development and Psychopathology, 31,* 1863–1968.

Goodman, L. A., Smyth, K. F., Borges, A. M., & Singer, R. (2009). When crises collide: How intimate partner violence and poverty intersect to shape women's mental health and coping. *Trauma, Violence, & Abuse, 10,* 306–329.

Goodmark, L. (2021). Reimagining VAWA: Why criminalization is a failed policy and what a non-carceral VAWA could look like. *Violence Against Women, 27,* 84–101. doi:10.1177/1077801220949686

Gordon, L. (1988). *Heroes of their own lives: The politics and history of family violence.* New York, NY: Viking Press.

Graham, L. M., Sahay, K. M., Rizo, C. F., Messing, J. T., & Macy, R. J. (2021). The validity and reliability of available intimate partner homicide and reassault risk assessment tools: A systematic review. *Trauma, Violence, & Abuse, 22*, 18–40. doi:10.1177/1524838018821952

Graham-Bermann S. (2011). Evidence-based practices for school-age children exposed to intimate partner violence and evaluation of the Kids' Club program. In S. A. Graham-Bermann & A. A. Levendosky (Eds.), How intimate partner violence affects children: Developmental research, case studies, and evidence-based interventions (pp. 179–205). Washington, DC: American Psychological Association.

Graham-Bermann, S., Miller-Graff, L., Howell, K. H., & Grogan-Kaylor, A. (2015). An efficacy trial of an intervention program for children exposed to intimate partner violence. *Child Psychiatry and Human Development, 46*, 928–939.

Hall, W. (2017). The effectiveness of policy interventions for school bullying: A systematic review. *Journal of the Society for Social Work and Research, 8*, 45–69.

Hamel, J. (2020). Beyond gender: Finding common ground in evidence-based batterer intervention. In B. Russell (Ed.), *Intimate partner violence and the LGBT+ community: Understanding power dynamics* (pp. 195–223). Cham Switzerland, Springer.

Hamel, J., Cannon, C., Buttell, F., & Ferreira, R. (2020). A survey of IPV perpetrator treatment providers: Ready for evidence-based practice? *Partner Abuse, 11*, 387–414. doi:10.1891/PA-2020-0024

Harmon-Darrow, C. (2020). Conflict resolution interventions and tertiary violence prevention among urban nonintimate adults: A review of the literature. *Trauma, Violence, & Abuse, 21*, 1–17, doi:10.1177/1524838020918672

Herrenkohl, T. I., Fedina, L., Roberto, K. A., Raquet, K. L., Hu, R. X., Rousson, A. N., & Mason, W. A. (in press). Child maltreatment, youth violence, intimate partner violence, and elder mistreatment: A review and theoretical analysis of research on violence across the life course. *Trauma, Violence, & Abuse*.

Holtzworth-Munroe, A. (2011). Controversies in divorce mediation and intimate partner violence: A focus on the children. *Aggression and Violent Behavior, 16*, 319–324. doi:10.1016/j.avb.2011.04.009.

Holtzworth-Munroe, A., Beck, C. J., Applegate, A. G., Adams, J. M., Rossi, F. S., Jiang, L. J., ... Hale, D. F. (2020). Intimate Partner Violence (IPV) and Family Dispute Resolution: A Randomized Controlled Trial Comparing Shuttle Mediation, Videoconferencing Mediation, and Litigation. *Psychology, Public Policy, and Law*. doi:10.1037/law0000278.

Horwitz, S. M., Chamberlain, P., Landsverk, J., & Mullican, C. (2010). Improving the mental health of children in child welfare through the implementation of evidence-based parenting interventions. *Administration and Policy in Mental Health and Mental Health Services Research, 37*, 27–39.

Jacobs, L. A., Kim, M. E., Whitfield, D. L., Gartner, R. E., Panichelli, M., Kattari, S. K., ... Mountz, S. E. (2021). Defund the police: Moving towards an anti-carceral social work. *Journal of Progressive Human Services, 32*, 37–62. doi:10.1080/10428232.2020.1852865

Jaffe, P., Wolfe, D. A., & Campbell, M. (2012). Growing up with domestic violence: Assessment, intervention, and prevention strategies for children and adolescents. Vol. 23. Cambridge, MA: Hogrefe Publishing.

Johnson, N. E., Saccuzzo, D. P., & Koen, W. J. (2005). Child custody mediation in cases of domestic violence: Empirical evidence of a failure to protect. *Violence Against Women, 11*, 1022–1053. doi:10.1177/1077801205278043

Johnson-Motoyama, M., & Ginther, D. (2019, April). *Changes to the U.S. social safety net are causally related to child maltreatment: Policy is a strategy for prevention*. Paper or poster session presented at the 21st National Conference on Child Abuse and Neglect (NCCAN), Washington, DC.

Maguire-Jack, K., Johnson-Motoyama, M., & Parmenter, S. (2021). A scoping review of economic supports for working parents: The relationship of TANF, child care subsidy, SNAP, and EITC to child maltreatment. *Aggression and Violent Behavior*, 101639.

Johnston, E. M., Strahan, A. E., Joski, P., Dunlop, A. L., & Adams, E. K. (2018). Impacts of the Affordable Care Act's Medicaid expansion on women of reproductive age: Differences by parental status and state policies. *Women's Health Issues*, 28, 122–129.

Jones-Harden, B., Simons, C., Johnson-Motoyama, M., & Barth, R. (2020). The child maltreatment prevention landscape: Where are we now, and where should we go? *The Annals of the American Academy of Political and Social Science*, 692, 97–118. doi:10.1177/0002716220978361

Jordan, J. V. (2008). Recent developments in relational-cultural theory. *Women and Therapy*, 31(2-4), 1–4. doi:10.1080/02703140802145540

Kim, C., & Schmuhl, M. (2020). Understanding intimate partner violence in the Asian communities in America: A systematic review. *Trauma, Violence, & Abuse*, 21, 779–787.

Kim, M. E. (2020). Anti-carceral feminism: The contradictions of progress and the possibilities of counter-hegemonic struggle. *Affilia-Journal of Women and Social Work*, 35(3), 309–326. doi:10.1177/0886109919878276

Kondo, M. C., Andreyeva, E., South, E. C., MacDonald, J. M., & Branas, C. C. (2018). Neighborhood interventions to reduce violence. *Annual Review of Public Health*, 39, 253–271. doi:10.1146/annurev-publhealth-040617-014600O1

Krug, E. G., et al. (Eds.) (2002). *World report on violence and health*. Geneva, World Health Organization.

Kulkarni, S. (2019). Intersectional trauma-informed intimate partner violence (IPV) services: Narrowing the gap between IPV service delivery and survivor needs. *Journal of Family Violence*, 34, 55–64. doi:10.1007/s10896-018-0001-5.

Kulkarni, S. J., Kohl, P. L., & Edmond, T. (2020). From "Stop Family Violence" to "Build Healthy Relationships to End Violence": The journey to reenvision a grand challenge. *Social Work*, 65, 401–405. doi:10.1093/sw/swaa038

Lakind, D., & Atkins, M. S. (2018). Promoting positive parenting for families in poverty: New directions for improved reach and engagement. *Children and Youth Services Review*, 89, 34–42.

Lawrence, C., Matusda, M., Delgado, R., & Crenshaw, K. (1993). Introduction. In M. Matsuda, C. Lawrence, R. Delgado, & K. Crenshaw (Eds.), *Words that would: Critical race theory, assaultive speech, and the First Amendment* (pp. 6–8). Boulder, CO: Westview Press.

Lee, E., Kirkland, K., Miranda-Julian, C., & Greene, R. (2018). Reducing maltreatment recurrence through home visitation: A promising intervention for child welfare involved families. *Child Abuse & Neglect*, 86, 55–66.

Lenz, A. S. (2016). Relational–cultural theory: Fostering the growth of a paradigm through empirical research. *Journal of Counseling & Development*, 94, 415–428.

Limber, S. P., Olweus, D., Wang, W., Masiello, M., & Breivik, K. (2018). Evaluation of the Olweus Bullying Prevention Program: A large scale study of US students in grades 3–11. *Journal of School Psychology*, 69, 56–72.

Maas, C., Herrenkohl, T. I., & Sousa, C. (2008). Review of research on child maltreatment and violence in youth. *Trauma, Violence, & Abuse, 9*, 56–67.

Madigan, S., Cyr, C., Eirich, R., Fearon, R. P., Ly, A., Rash, C., . . . Alink, L. R. (2019). Testing the cycle of maltreatment hypothesis: Meta-analytic evidence of the intergenerational transmission of child maltreatment. *Development and Psychopathology, 31*, 23–51.

Maguire-Jack, K., Johnson-Motoyama, M., & Parmenter, S. (2021). A scoping review of economic supports for working parents: The relationship of TANF, child care subsidy, SNAP, and EITC to child maltreatment. *Aggression and Violent Behavior*, 101639.

Masarik, A. S., & Conger, R. D. (2017). Stress and child development: A review of the Family Stress Model. *Current Opinion in Psychology, 13*, 85–90.

Messing, J. T. (2019). Risk-informed intervention: Using intimate partner violence risk assessment within an evidence-based practice framework. *Social Work (United States), 64*, 103–111. doi:10.1093/sw/swz009

Messing, J. T. (2020). Mainstreaming gender: An intersectional feminist approach to the Grand Challenges for Social Work. *Social Work, 65*, 313–315.

Miller, T., Cohen, M., Swedler, D., Ali, B., & Hendrie, D. (2021). Incidence and Costs of Personal and Property Crimes in the USA, 2017. *Journal of Benefit-Cost Analysis, 12*(1), 24–54. doi:10.1017/bca.2020.36

Millett, L. S., Kohl, P. L., Jonson-Reid, M., Drake, B., & Petra, M. (2013). Child maltreatment victimization and subsequent perpetration of young adult intimate partner violence: An exploration of mediating factors. *Child Maltreatment, 18*, 71–84.

Mills, L. G. (2009). *Insult to injury: Rethinking our responses to intimate abuse*. Princeton, NJ: Princeton University Press.

Mills, L. G., Barocas, B., Butters, R. P., & Ariel, B. (2019). A randomized controlled trial of restorative justice-informed treatment for domestic violence crimes. *Nature Human Behaviour, 3*), 1284–1294. doi:10.1038/s41562-019-0724-1

Moment of Truth Letter. (June, 2020). Retrieved from https://www.violencefreecolorado.org/wp-content/uploads/2020/07/Moment-of-Truth.pdf

Morris, A. M., Mrug, S., & Windle, M. (2015). From family violence to dating violence: Testing a dual pathway model. *Journal of Youth and Adolescence, 44*, 1819–1835.

Mujal, G. N., Taylor, M. E., Fry, J. L., Gochez-Kerr, T. H., & Weaver, N. L. (2019). A systematic review of bystander interventions for the prevention of sexual violence. *Trauma, Violence, & Abuse, 22*, 381–396.

National Academies of Sciences, Engineering, and Medicine. (2016). *Parenting matters: Supporting parents of children ages 0–8*. Washington, DC: The National Academies Press.

Nesset, M. B., Bjørngaard, J. H., Whittington, R., & Palmstierna, T. (2020). Does cognitive behavioural therapy or mindfulness-based therapy improve mental health and emotion regulation among men who perpetrate intimate partner violence? A randomized controlled trial. *International Journal of Nursing Studies*, 113–119.

Niolon, P. H., Kearns, M., Dills, J., Rambo, K., Irving, S., Armstead, T., & Gilbert, L. (2017). *Preventing Intimate Partner Violence Across the Lifespan: A Technical Package of Programs, Policies, and Practices*. Atlanta, GA: National Center for Injury Prevention and Control, Centers for Disease Control and Prevention.

Nnawulezi, N., & Murphy, C. (2019). Understanding formal help-seeking among women whose partners are in abuser treatment programs. *Psychology of Violence, 9,* 383–391.

Noltemeyer, A., Bush, K., Patton, J., & Bergen, D. (2012). The relationship among deficiency needs and growth needs: An empirical investigation of Maslow's theory. *Children and Youth Services Review, 34,* 1862–1867.

O'Leary, K. D., Heyman, R. E., & Neidig, P. H. (1999). Treatment of wife abuse: A comparison of gender-specific and conjoint approaches. *Behavior Therapy, 30,* 475–505. doi:10.1016/S0005-7894(99)80021-5

Olson, K. B. (2013). Screening for intimate partner violence in mediation. *Dispute Resolution Magazine, 20,* 25.

Pennell, J., Burford, G., Sasson, E., Packer, H., & Smith, E. L. (2020). Family and community approaches to intimate partner violence: Restorative programs in the United States. *Violence Against Women, 27,* 1608–1629, doi:10.1177/1077801220945030

Peterson, C. A., Hughes-Belding, K., Rowe, N., Fan, L., Walter, M., Dooley, L., . . . Steffensmeier, C. (2018). Triadic interactions in MIECHV: Relations to home visit quality. *Maternal and Child Health Journal, 22,* 3–12.

Reynolds, A. J., Ou, S. R., Mondi, C. F., & Giovanelli, A. (2019). Reducing poverty and inequality through preschool-to-third-grade prevention services. *American Psychologist, 74,* 653–660.

Ritchie, B.E. (2012). *Arrested justice: Black women, violence, and America's prison nation.* New York, NY: NYU Press.

Rossi, F. S., Holtzworth-Munroe, A., Applegate, A. G., & Beck, C. J. (2020). Subtypes of violent separating or divorcing couples seeking family mediation and their association with personality and criminality characteristics. *Psychology of Violence, 10,* 390–399. doi:10.1037/vio0000271.10.1037/vio0000271.supp

Rossi, F. S., Holtzworth-Munroe, A., Applegate, A. G., Beck, C. J. A., Adams, J. M., & Hale, D. F. (2015). Detection of intimate partner violence and recommendation for joint family mediation: A randomized controlled trial of two screening measures. *Psychology, Public Policy, and Law, 21,* 239–251. doi:10.1037/law0000043

Rostad, W. L., Klevens, J., Ports, K. A., & Ford, D. C. (2020). Impact of the United States federal child tax credit on childhood injuries and behavior problems. *Children and Youth Services Review, 109,* 104718, doi:10.1016/j.childyouth.2019.104718

Rowe, K. (1984). The limits of the neighborhood justice center: Why domestic violence cases should not be mediated. *Emory Law Journal, 34,* 885–923.

Satir, V. (1964). *Conjoint family therapy.* Palo Alto, CA: Science and Behavior Books.

Shaw, T. V., Barth, R. P., Mattingly, J., Ayer, D., & Berry, S. (2013). Child welfare birth match: The timely use of child welfare administrative data to protect newborns. *Journal of Public Child Welfare, 7,* 217–234.

Sherraden, M., Barth, R. P., Brekke, J., Fraser, M. W., Manderscheid, R., & Padgett, D. K. (2014). *Social is fundamental: Introduction and context for Grand Challenges for Social Work.* Baltimore, MD: American Academy of Social Work and Social Welfare. Retrieved from https://grandchallengesforsocialwork.org/wp-content/uploads/2015/04/FINAL-GCSW-Intro-and-Context-4-2-2015-formatted-final.pdf

Silovsky, J. F., Bard, D., Chaffin, M., Hecht, D., Burris, L., Owora, A., . . . Lutzker, J. (2011). Prevention of child maltreatment in high-risk rural families: A randomized clinical trial with child welfare outcomes. *Children and Youth Services Review, 33,* 1435–1444.

Spencer, R. A., & Komro, K. A. (2017). Family economic security policies and child and family health. *Clinical Child and Family Psychology Review, 20*, 45–63.

Spencer, R. A., Livingston, M. D., Woods-Jaeger, B., Rentmeester, S. T., Sroczynski, N., & Komro, K. A. (2020). The impact of temporary assistance for needy families, minimum wage, and earned income tax credit on women's well-being and intimate partner violence victimization. *Social Science & Medicine, 266*, 269.

Stith, S. M., & McCollum, E. E. (2011). Conjoint treatment of couples who have experienced intimate partner violence. *Aggression and Violent Behavior, 16*(4), 312–318. doi:10.1016/j.avb.2011.04.012.

Stith, S. M., Spencer, C. M., Ripoll-Núñez, K. J., Jaramillo-Sierra, A. L., Khodadadi-Andariyeh, F., Nikparvar, F., . . . Metelinen, J. (2020). International adaptation of a treatment program for situational couple violence. *Journal of Marital and Family Therapy, 46*, 272–288.

Storer, H. L., Barkan, S. E., Sherman, E. L., Haggerty, K. P., & Mattos, L. M. (2012). Promoting relationship building and connection: Adapting an evidence-based parenting program for families involved in the child welfare system. *Children and Youth Services Review, 34*, 1853–1861.

Turner, H. A., Shattuck, A., Finkelhor, D., & Hamby, S. (2016). Polyvictimization and youth violence exposure across contexts. *Journal of Adolescent Health, 58*, 208–214.

U.S. DHHS. (n.d.). Healthy people 2020 framework: The vision, mission, and goals of healthy people 2020, https://www.healthypeople.gov/sites/default/files/HP2020Framework.pdf

Voith, L. A., Logan-Greene, P., Strodthoff, T., & Bender, A. E. (2018). A paradigm shift in batterer intervention programming: A need to address unresolved trauma. *Trauma, Violence, & Abuse, 21*, 691–705, doi:10.1177/1524838018791268

Wagers, S. (2020). Domestic violence growing in wake of coronavirus outbreak. The Conversation. Retrieved on 10th April, 2020 from: https://theconversation.com/domestic-violence-growing-in-wake-of-coronavirus-outbreak-135598

Weaver, N. L., Taylor, M. E., Weaver, T. L., & Kutz, T. J. (2020). Support Over Silence for KIDS: A bystander training program to address public child maltreatment. *Children and Youth Services Review, 118*, 124.

West, A., Duggan, A. K., Gruss, K., & Minkovitz, C. S. (2020). The role of state context in promoting service coordination in maternal, infant, and early childhood home visiting programs. *Journal of Public Health Management and Practice, 26*, E9–E18.

Whitehill, J. M., Webster, D. W., Frattaroli, S., & Parker, E. M. (2014). Interrupting violence: How the CeaseFire program prevents imminent gun violence through conflict mediation. *Journal of Urban Health, 91*, 84–95. doi:10.1007/s11524-013-9796-9

Wildeman, C., Emanuel, N., Leventhal, J. M., Putnam-Hornstein, E., Waldfogel, J., & Lee, H. (2014). The prevalence of confirmed maltreatment among US children, 2004 to 2011. *JAMA Pediatrics, 168*, 706–713.

Wilkins, N., Tsao, B., Hertz, M., Davis, R., & Klevens, J. (2014). *Connecting the dots: An overview of the links among multiple forms of violence*. Atlanta, GA: National Center for Injury Prevention and Control, Centers for Disease Control and Prevention.

Wolfe, D. A., Wekerle, C., Scott, K., Straatman, A., Grasley, C., & Reitzel-Jaffe, D. (2003). Dating violence prevention with at-risk youth: A controlled outcome evaluation. *Journal of Consulting and Clinical Psychology, 71*, 279–291.

World Health Organization. (2002). *World report on violence and health: A summary.* Geneva, Switzerland: Author.

Zettler, H. R. (2021). Much to do about trauma: A systematic review of existing trauma-informed treatments on youth violence and recidivism. *Youth Violence and Juvenile Justice, 19,* 113–134.

CHAPTER 5

Advancing Long and Productive Lives

ERNEST GONZALES, CHRISTINA MATZ,
NANCY MORROW-HOWELL, PATRICK HO LAM LAI,
CLIFF WHETUNG, EMMA ZINGG, ERIN KEATING,
JACQUELYN B. JAMES, AND MICHELLE PUTNAM

THE CHALLENGE

The age distribution of societies throughout the world is changing rapidly. In the United States and most other countries with advanced economies, lower birth rates and increasing life expectancy are shifting populations toward "top-heavy" societies, in which there are more people older than age 60 years than there are people younger than age 15 years (He, Goodkind, & Kowal, 2016). In the United States, the population older than age 65 years increased from 36.6 million in 2005 to 47.8 million in 2015 (a 30% increase), and it is projected to more than double to 98 million by 2060 (Administration on Aging, 2016). Throughout the world, 8% of the population was age 65 years or older in 2010, and this will increase to 16% by 2050 (National Institute on Aging, 2011). The growing number and proportion of older adults in these nations present aging-related challenges to families, communities, and countries as a whole—challenges that are unprecedented because never before in human history have so many people lived into the eighth and ninth decades of life. The success of this new longevity has often been overshadowed in public discourse by the daunting issues of economic security and healthcare, especially long-term care, in these extended years of life.

The press of these challenges has made it more difficult to focus on the opportunities that come with population aging. Of principal note is the reality that as the health, education, and economic security of older adults have become better over time, so too has the interest of individuals to initiate and continue productive activities longer into the life course, as evidenced by greater numbers of older adults engaging in paid work, volunteering, caregiving, and other activities. Thus, another challenge that nations face is increased demand for older adults to continue in and/or take on these roles. Provision of more productive aging opportunities requires a social development response to shape social policies and programs to engage the growing experiences, talents, skills, and professional and personal goals of older adults, and to ensure the inclusion of all segments, especially among those who are more likely to be excluded. In short, productive aging asserts the fundamental view that aging societies will do better when they make better use of older adults' capacity to make economic contributions through employment, volunteering, and caregiving (Gonzales, Matz-Costa, & Morrow-Howell, 2015; Morrow-Howell & Greenfield, 2015).

Multiple positive societal outcomes can be achieved through optimizing the productive engagement of older adults. First, the paid labor force has the potential to benefit from the infusion of experienced workers at the same time as the supply of younger workers shrinks, and longer working lives can extend the time that people rely on earned income rather than public pensions and savings (Street & Tompkins, 2017). Second, public and nonprofit agencies would greatly benefit from higher levels of volunteering by older adults (Bridgeland, McNaught, Reed, & Dunkelman, 2009), particularly those with relevant technical and professional skills, and also by those with lesser skills and great enthusiasm. Third, there will be an increasing demand for caregivers as the number of people older than age 85 years increases. This demand for caregivers (National Alliance for Caregiving & AARP, 2020) can be met—at least in part—by the growing number of older adults with the time, energy, and ability to provide care for those in their families and social networks who need assistance.

Productive engagement can benefit individuals as well. As societies age, living 25 years beyond the normal retirement age of 65 years will be common. Maintaining economic security, social ties, health, and a sense of purpose in later life have been shown to be important for quality of life (James, Matz-Costa, & Smyer, 2016). At the individual level, productive engagement can contribute to these important outcomes. Thus, national attention to advancing productive engagement opportunities for older adults at both the society level and the individual level is a crucial investment in maximizing positive outcomes for aging societies.

ANALYSIS OF THE PROBLEM AND OPPORTUNITY FOR IMPROVEMENT

Although societal aging is often viewed as a "problem," the trends toward lower birth rates and longer life expectancy have resulted from significant positive economic and social developments in the United States and other advanced economies (Morrow-Howell, Hinterlong, & Sherraden, 2001; Sherraden et al., 2014). However, as noted previously, these demographic shifts put pressure on various sectors of societies, ranging from publicly funded social welfare programs to private family budgets, from employment markets to individual business owners in search of skilled labor, and from demands for formal long-term care services from nonprofit and public service sectors to demands for informal care from families and friends. Part of the problem is that although we have known for many decades that the population is aging, we have done little to prepare for it. Our institutions, infrastructures, and policies and programs were designed when human lives were much shorter and roles were more singular and sequential rather than multiple and less age specific. For example, we created pathways that were segmented by age—young people go to school, adults work and raise families, and older adults step back and engage in leisure for their retirement years. Arguably, this pathway was never universal, but with much larger numbers of people living 20 to 30 years past their 60th birthday, the lack of fit of this presumed life course pattern becomes much more obvious, as have the barriers for productive engagement.

It is not just our physical and social infrastructures that are out of step with the current demographic shifts; our expectations and attitudes about later life and older adults also limit the potential of a productive aging society. Stereotypes of the frail, cognitively impaired elder ignore the demographic reality, highlighting how pervasive ageism still is in our society. The COVID-19 pandemic has laid bare these underlying attitudes and inequalities like never before, with older adults being portrayed as a weak and vulnerable, and a monolithic group.

Institutional and societal barriers to productive engagement among older adults must be confronted and changed. In part, this can be done by working to shift public discourse away from the idea that population aging is a social problem, and toward the view that the growing number of older adults represents a new resource for families, communities, and society at large. Creating more productive engagement opportunities will require institutional change, which is difficult but possible. Specifically, we must improve work environments and employment policies to enable *all* people (regardless of race, gender, socioeconomic status, disability, sexual orientation, gender identity, immigration status, etc.) to obtain and maintain good, quality work across the life span, to work longer if needed or desired, and to enjoy a comfortable retirement. We must improve the way we support caregiving and other forms of care work across the life span—and in later life particularly—so that individuals and families have increased control and choice, and reduced stress. We must create more diverse opportunities for older adults to give back to others and their communities, and to engage socially while helping organizations use this talent pool more fully. And we must restructure educational institutions to be accessible and inclusive so that individuals can develop new knowledge and skills across the life course.

Robert Butler, a pioneer in the field of gerontology who coined the term *productive aging* in 1983, warned that society cannot afford to dismiss the human capital of the older population. Butler described older adults' productive engagement as a necessity, not a luxury (Butler, 1997). However, we must view this societal necessity within a paradigm that optimizes choice to engage in productive activities rather than a mandate to do so (Morrow-Howell et al., 2001). Not all individuals have achieved the same longevity gains, nor do all have the ability to perform or interest in activities such as paid work, volunteering, and caregiving compared to other activity choices or responsibilities. In addition, we must address larger social and structural factors, such as racism, sexism, gender discrimination, and disability discrimination, that shape life opportunities for individuals to participate in their communities.

As we seek to transform societal norms, programs, and policies to facilitate productive engagement, we must be guided by principles of choice, opportunity, and inclusion instead of by coercion, obligation, or elitism. Gutman and Spencer (2010) and Holstein and Minkler (2007) express concern that certain older adults will be marginalized, or continue to be marginalized, if certain expectations for productive engagement are not met. Therefore, we propose that efforts to advance productive engagement include the following: (a) ample opportunities for continued engagement for those older adults who choose this route, (b) identification and removal of barriers that reduce productive engagement artificially by older adults, and (c) support for caregivers to participate in and/or transition to other forms of productive engagement, and for those engaged in work and volunteering to transition to caregiving roles. The grand challenge is to reimagine a lifetime filled with opportunities to acquire new knowledge and skills, and to use talents and resources in a variety of paid and unpaid roles that foster economic security, provide purpose in life, and enrich families and communities. The trend of societal aging presents an open window for moving a productive engagement agenda forward as a means of meeting the challenge of an aging society and improving health, social, and economic outcomes for older individuals.

POTENTIAL OUTCOMES OF PRODUCTIVE ENGAGEMENT

Productive engagement is a potentially powerful mechanism that influences numerous well-being outcomes. Scholars have conceptualized the effects of engagement in productive roles at the level of the individual, the family, the organization, the community, and society as a whole. Box 5.1 lists the outcomes that are achievable.

Box 5.1 POTENTIAL OUTCOMES OF THE PRODUCTIVE ENGAGEMENT OF OLDER ADULTS

Individual
- Physical health and function

Mental health
- Self-efficacy
- Purpose in life
- Economic well-being

Family
- Engaged grandparents and caregivers
- Transfer of income and assets from older to younger
- Healthier, happier older relatives

Organizations and Community
- Experienced workers and volunteers
- Loyal and dependable workers and volunteers
- Age and generational diversity
- Mentors for younger workers

Society
- Less reliance on public pensions and savings
- More intergenerational exchange
- Less demand for long-term care resulting from postponement of disability

The physical, psychological, and financial effects of productive engagement on the individual have received the most scholarly attention because there are straightforward methods to estimate them. Evidence suggests that working can increase economic security while also leading to decreased mortality and better mental health and cognitive function (Calvo, 2006; Rohwedder & Willis, 2010). Volunteering has also been associated with positive health and psychological outcomes, as well as greater odds of employment (Gonzales & Nowell, 2017; Gonzales, Suntai, & Abrams, 2019; Hong & Morrow-Howell, 2010; Kim & Ferraro, 2013; Spera, Ghertner, Nerino, & DiTommaso, 2013). Reduced mortality as well as caregiver report of benefits have been associated with caregiving (Roth, Fredman, & Haley, 2015). However, outcomes are not always positive. Working longer in certain employment conditions can reduce health and mental health (Magnusson Hanson et al., 2018). In addition, the negative effects of caregiving on older adults are widely documented (Coughlin, 2010; Feinberg, Reinhard, Houser, & Choula, 2011).

Assessing the societal outcomes of the productive engagement of older adults may be more challenging than measuring its impact at the individual level. Theoretically, the increased productive engagement of older adults could lead to less reliance on public and private postretirement income support programs, stronger civic society through increased involvement in volunteering and political engagement, increased intergenerational reciprocity, and higher levels of health among the older population. Indeed, Alvor Svanborg (2001) suggested that the major dividend of productive engagement would come at the society level, from postponing decline associated with aging.

The rates and levels of participation of older adults as workers, volunteers, and caregivers have been captured, and we can continue to track these metrics over time. These benchmarks can be attained from several large nationally representative data sets that track older adults and their engagement in productive activities longitudinally. Furthermore, dollar values of these time commitments can be assigned. Reinhard, Feinberg, Houser, Choula, and Evans (2019) estimate 41 million caregivers in the United States who devote 34 billion hours of care to individuals with limitations in daily activities, with an estimated economic value of $470 billion. In 2015, adults age 55 years and older contributed more than 3.3 billion hours of civic service, which is valued at $77 billion annually. Emerging evidence also suggests older workers contribute to a large portion of the US gross domestic product (Cohen, 2014).

MAINSTREAMING GENDER

An Analysis of Transportation among Older Adults

RUPAL PAREKH AND REBECCA L. MAULDIN

Several low-density, automobile-dependent metropolitan areas such as Dallas/Fort Worth, TX, are experiencing growing numbers of older immigrant women—a trend that poses transportation challenges. We recently conducted a study that examined transportation use and needs among 95 older Vietnamese immigrants in Dallas/Fort Worth, TX (Mauldin, Mattingly, & Parekh, 2019). We found that although women and men had equal rates of household automobile ownership, only 40% of women drove compared to 72% of men. In fact, almost 1.8 times as many women than men relied on someone else to give them rides, leaving them dependent on others for productive aging activities. Although equal portions of women and men (approximately one fourth) had missed an activity in the previous month because

continued

they did not have transportation, there were differences in the types of activities each group had to forego. Women were more likely to have missed trips to the senior center or religious services, which provide opportunities for volunteering and social support. They were also more likely to miss trips to the grocery store or healthcare appointments. Men were more likely to have missed recreational or social activities (e.g., eating out, going to the movies). The study results highlight transportation-related gender differences in access to opportunities. Focusing on the example of gender inequities in transportation places a spotlight on the need for centering gender across all areas of aging policy, practice, and research to support productive aging.

Transportation equity is important because convenient, accessible, and affordable transportation options are necessary for older adults to engage fully in work, volunteering, and caregiving. However, accessing transportation can be a major challenge for many older adults who have experienced changes to their physical, cognitive, or financial circumstances. The findings of our study of older Vietnamese immigrants reflect a more general pattern in the United States in which a wide range of transportation barriers experienced by older women can affect their social participation negatively, thereby threatening quality of life, health, and well-being. Patterns of daily mobility such as transport model choice, travel frequency, and duration of trips are highly gendered. Although, on average, Americans outlive their ability to drive by 7 to 10 years, older women are more likely than older men to give up their driver's license proactively as they age. Older women and immigrants, predominantly low-income older women, tend to be more dependent on public transportation, getting rides from friends and family, and walking to meet their daily transportation needs. This can affect their ability to work, volunteer, or provide care by making them rely on individuals and systems for their mobility. It can also place them in vulnerable positions in potentially unsafe environments, such as ride-hailing with strangers or waiting at dangerous bus stops or on sidewalks. Older immigrants face transportation barriers similar to native-born older adults, but their challenges can be exacerbated by language and cultural barriers, increased risk of disability, and economic insecurity. More research is needed to understand more fully how the intersection of age, immigration status, and gender relates to transportation and productive aging. However, it seems likely that transportation barriers stymie the productive potential of older immigrant women, even as they experience productive aging by remaining active in the workforce, providing substantial contributions to family caregiving, and supporting their communities formally and informally.

As the US population ages and becomes more diverse, an intersectional gendered lens is necessary to advance policies, practices, and research that affect older adults. As illustrated in this insert, transportation is one social space where a gendered perspective is necessary to facilitate equitable opportunities for productive engagement. Examining how gender and social policy contexts intersect to influence political, cultural, and

continued

socioeconomic inequalities—and their relationship to productive aging—is necessary to position gender at the forefront and work toward social change. With a focus on ecological systems, environmental fit, and social justice, social workers are well positioned to advocate for equitable, gender-focused policies; research; and practice. This advocacy can support the Grand Challenges for Social Work to advance long, healthy, and productive lives from a gendered intersectional lens.

Reference

Mauldin, R. L., Mattingly, S., & Parekh, R. (2019). Using social network analysis to optimize access to culturally responsive and affordable transportation for older (im)migrants. National Institute for Transportation and Communities. Retrieved from https://nitc.trec.pdx.edu/research/project/1302

CURRENT REALITIES AND INNOVATIONS

Working

The number of people 65 years or older who remain in the US workforce is growing as the average age of retirement has risen in the past two decades (US Department of Labor, Bureau of Labor Statistics, 2016a). According to a 2014 survey by the American Association of Retired Persons, a clear majority of workers older than age 50 years plan to work past the age of 65 years, including a sizable 18% who indicate that they never intend to retire (Skufca, 2014). There are several noteworthy elements in this overall trend toward working longer. First, more women are working in their later years than ever before. The labor force participation rates of women age 55 to 65 years increased from 53.2% in 2000 to 59.2% in 2015 (Brown, Rhee, Saad-Lessler, & Oakley, 2016). The number of working women older than 65 years also increased from 17% in 1990 to 27% in 2010—a trend that is expected to continue for some time (Poterba, 2014). Although labor force participation rates for older women have risen, women older than 65 years are 80% more likely than men to live in poverty. Many of these women like their work and want to continue (Kerman & Keenan, 2017); however, many older women need to work to make ends meet.

A second later life trend is toward more full-time work than part-time work (i.e., fewer than 35 hours/week). Since 2000, the number of adults older than 65 years working full-time rather than part-time more than doubled from approximately 4 million people (approximately 13%) to 9 million (approximately 20%) (DeSilver, 2016). An important factor in this trend may be the recent evidence that increasingly fewer people are "very confident" that they have enough money for a comfortable retirement—only 18% of respondents in a recent survey (Greenwald, Copeland, & VanDerhei, 2017). Whites are more likely to have access to employer-sponsored pension plans and accumulate wealth from mid-to-later life when compared to racial and ethnic minorities, which offers some support to the life cycle hypothesis and critical race theory (Brown, 2016). As a result of inequitable access to pension plans and other saving vehicles, women—and especially women of color—have very little savings for retirement (Brown, 2012; Dushi & Iams, 2009). Last, there is a trend toward self-employment in later life (Halvorsen & Morrow-Howell, 2016). According to the US Department of Labor, Bureau of Labor Statistics data, the rate of self-employment among workers older than 65 years was the highest (at 15.5%) of any age group (Hipple & Hammond, 2016). Indeed, analyses of the Health and Retirement Study reveal that 1 in 10 career wage and salary workers transition into self-employment before full retirement (Cahill, Giandrea, & Kovacs, 2014).

When viewed from an intersectional lens, work in later life becomes far more complex (Figure 5.1). We analyzed data from the latest waves in the Health and Retirement Study, a representative sample of older adults in the United States (Figure 5.1). Women are more likely to work part-time compared to men. Surprisingly, men report higher levels of major lifetime discrimination, such as being fired or not hired, compared to women, but Blacks report greater incidences of discrimination compared to whites and Latinx. Women of color tend to have jobs that are more physically demanding when compared to white women. And women of color are also more likely to experience disability and be forced into retirement when compared to white women. Latinas report the highest levels of forced retirement across gender, racial, ethnic groups. Although these cross-sectional statistics are basic, they nonetheless support aspects of critical race and Black feminist standpoint theories (Bowleg, 2012; Brown, 2012; Crenshaw, 1991), in that women do not all have

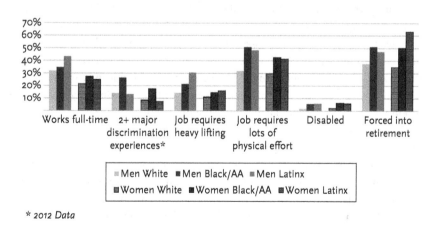

* *2012 Data*

Figure 5.1 Occupational Status by Gender, Race and Ethnicity.

the same position in society, and women of color are marginalized further in society compared to white women.

Social stratification and inequity are contexts that shape choices and opportunities to work. Providing care to family, for example, often results in more time off of work to provide care and to transition from full- to part-time work, forced retirement, and a decreased likelihood of returning to work after retirement (Gonzales, Lee, & Brown, 2017; Smith, Cawley, Williams, & mustard, 2020a). Women who provide unpaid care tend to have a weak relationship with the formal labor force across their adult lives resulting from a lack of institutional support, such as flexible work and respite care. Consequently, they are at risk of poverty in later life (Greenfield, 2013; Lee, Tang, Kim, & Albert, 2015; Wakabayashi & Donato, 2006). The recent COVID-19 pandemic has highlighted how age, race, ethnicity, and gender intersect in complex ways that heighten the risk for economic insecurity (Halvorsen & Yulikova, 2020a). Older workers' labor force participation declined significantly during the first quarter of 2020 (Papadopoulous, Fisher, Ghilarducci, & Radpour, 2020). Approximately 4 of 10 older workers did not have paid sick leave (Ghilarducci & Farmand, 2020), many of whom are frontline workers in healthcare settings, grocery and retail stores, and transportation. Racial and ethnic minorities are often in jobs with very little flexibility or paid sick leave; thus, they are more likely to contract and die from COVID-19 (Gonzales, Gordon, Whetung, Connaught, Collazo, & Hilton, 2020; Selden & Berdahl, 2020). Further research is needed to understand the full and long-term effects of COVID-19 on work and retirement pathways across gender, race, ethnicity, and socioeconomic status.

Clearly, federal and state work policies influence tenure in the workforce, as exemplified by raising the full retirement age from 65 to 67 years for Social Security benefits and eliminating the earnings test for workers older than the normal retirement age (Coile & Gruber, 2003; Olshansky, Goldman, & Rowe, 2015). Organizational policies also play a major role in retirement decisions. Specifically, the need for increased flexible work options has been well documented for employees of all ages. More than 90% of nonretirees who plan to work during retirement would like some kind of reduced work arrangement. However, in the face of this demand, only approximately one third of employed retirees have such arrangements (Bankers Center for a Secure Retirement, 2015). McGuire, Kenney, and Brashler (2010) report that flexible work options include flexibility in the scheduling of hours worked (e.g., compressed work weeks), the number of hours worked (e.g., part-time and/or job-sharing), and the place of work (e.g., working offsite or at home) (Cahill, James, & Pitt-Catsouphes, 2015). Although many employers indicate that such options are established policies, few employees take advantage of them for a host of reasons, the most important of which is lack of managerial support and encouragement (Sweet, Pitt-Catsouphes, & James, 2017).

There are innovative employment programs, including career counseling and job search websites, geared toward older adults, yet the effectiveness of these programs is unclear. Private and nonprofit organizations have supported programming at community colleges to guide older workers in career decision-making and training curricula (Halvorsen & Emerman, 2013–2014). The federal investment in workforce development for older adults remains low, but for more than 55 years, Title V of the Older American's Act has supported a job training program for low-income older workers (Carolan, Gonzales, Lee, & Harootyan, 2018; Gonzales, Lee, & Harootyan, 2019; Halvorsen & Yulikova, 2020b; Halvorsen, Werner, & McColloch, 2020). A nonprofit organization, Senior Entrepreneurship Works, provides training and support to individuals age 50 years or older to start new businesses.

In summary, there has been program and policy attention at the employer level to support older workers. Employers have been slow to innovate while age discrimination, informal caregiving, job insecurity, and changing technology continue to affect the employment options of older adults (Roscigno, 2010). Women, and women of color, continue to be marginalized in the world of work, and more intervention and basic research are necessary to identify effective workplace policies and practices, as well as to trace heterogeneous pathways of work and retirement.

Volunteering

Approximately one fourth of the US population 65 years and older volunteers (US Department of Labor, Bureau of Labor Statistics, 2016b)—a rate less than that of younger adults. The fact is that retired older adults volunteer less than working adults, despite an increase in discretionary time. Decreases in rates of volunteering can be explained by disconnection from work and educational organizations, the major avenues through which people are asked to volunteer (Opportunity Nation, 2014). There is evidence that older adults are more likely to volunteer when asked (US Census Bureau, 2010–2015, 2017) and contribute more hours per year than younger adults (90 hours per year vs. 32 hours per year, respectively) (Turner, Klein, & Sorrentino, 2020). Furthermore, older adults provide informal volunteer hours assisting neighbors and friends that are not captured in volunteer metrics (Taniguchi, 2012).

To elucidate more fully the issues of intersectionality and volunteer behavior, data from the 2010 to 2015 and the 2017 Volunteer Supplement in the Current Population Survey, which includes a representative sample of people 65 years or older in the United States (Figure 5.2), were analyzed. Men were less likely to spend any time in volunteer activities; this gender difference remained similar between racial and ethnic groups (Lee, Johnson, & Lyu, 2018). White older adults tended to have higher volunteer rates than

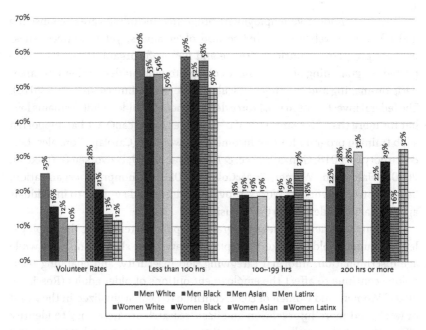

Figure 5.2 Volunteer rates and volunteer hours by gender, race, and ethnicity. Data from the database are weighted automatically, which accounts for supplement nonresponse. Data only include samples for those older than 65 years. Volunteer rates (measured as a percentage) refer to the ratio of samples spent any time doing volunteering activities for any organization in the past year over all samples. Latinx, persons of Hispanic/Spanish/Latino origins.
Source: Volunteering Supplement to the Current Population Survey, 2010–2015, 2017.

older adults of color. Latinx older adults showed the lowest proportion of engaging in volunteering in the United States compared to other groups. There is an interesting pattern among older Asian adults, with Asian women having more volunteer hours than whites in the 100- to 200-hours-per-year category. In contrast, Asian men had similar volunteer hours as other men of color, which is consistent with the results from a previous study (Miranda, 2011). These data suggest that older adults of color (perhaps with the exception of Asian women) may not be experiencing the full benefits associated with volunteering, given that it is documented that health and well-being outcomes increased in the first 100 hours per year and increased slightly between 100 and 200 hours. Further research is needed to understand volunteer behaviors across gender, race, and ethnicity, and to elucidate effects on differential outcomes.

The gap between the actual and potential volunteer time among older adults has increased interest in encouraging greater civic involvement among the older population. Service programs geared toward engaging older volunteers have received attention in the past decade. Examples include intergenerational tutoring programs (e.g., OASIS Intergenerational Tutoring, Experience Corps), coaching/mentoring programs (e.g., Wisdom of Age–National Mentoring Partnership), and friendly visitor programs (e.g., Village model's Neighbors Helping Neighbors). Federal programs, including Senior Companion Program, Foster Grandparents, and the Retired and Senior Volunteer Program (RSVP), continue to place older adults in service roles in their local communities. Online websites have reached out to older adults to match them with community needs (see http://comingofage.org and https://www.volunteermatch.org). The Serve America Act of 2009 recognized the potential of late-life volunteering and prompted AmeriCorps to increase the number of older adults involved in this national service program.

The COVID-19 pandemic affected formal volunteer roles in major ways. First, many in-person service positions were suspended, such as serving meals in congregate settings or in-person mentoring, and these important roles provided engagement and purpose for many older adults. These role losses may have contributed to the increased social isolation that many experienced during the pandemic (Smith, Steinman, & Casey, 2020b). On the other hand, some volunteer roles continued as person-power was needed to deliver food and medicine or provide rides to essential doctor appointments. Older volunteers expressed anxiety about exposure to the virus created by fulfilling these services, and some stopped whereas others continued despite their fears (Galucia, Morrow-Howell, Sun, Meyer, & Li, 2020). Last, the pandemic led to some volunteer services going virtual. Before the pandemic, there had been a movement toward virtual volunteering, with the hopes of including older adults who had mobility issues or geographic constraints (Cravens & Ellis, 2014). The pandemic required a rapid switch to online formats. As an example, the national OASIS Intergenerational Tutoring program, in which older adults work with elementary school children, had to go virtual if volunteers were going to continue to tutor. Tutors expressed concerns about developing relationships with the children online as well as having the digital competence to conduct tutoring sessions remotely. In fact, only 60% of the tutors expressed willingness to engage in the virtual program, and this varied by education and comfort with technology (Sun, Morrow-Howell, Pawloski, & Helbach, 2020).

It must be noted that informal volunteering and acts of neighboring have been spotlighted in the media during the pandemic, as people of all ages reached out to make and distribute masks, to contact isolated neighbors, and to pick up groceries. Retired healthcare professionals returned to work to help with growing demands on the healthcare system, and people stepped in to help parents with online schooling (Halpern, 2020; Van Buren, 2020). Hopefully, this "invisible" volunteering will continue to flourish, along with other positive outcomes of the pandemic (Turner et al., 2020). Organizations and older adults have learned a great deal about the potential of online connections that can increase inclusivity of volunteer programs. Yet, the digital divide within the older population has been exposed more clearly during the pandemic; and although some remedies are being sought through the distribution of digital devices and increased training to use software programs, many low-resource older people will not be able to take advantage (Sun et al., 2020).

In summary, programs and policies have acknowledged the growing number of older adults and facilitated involvement in volunteering. However, efforts have not been commensurate with the growing potential of the aging population, and recovering from the COVID-19 pandemic poses new challenges and opportunities.

Caregiving

Growing numbers of older adults are providing various forms of unpaid care to family and friends, yet the wide spectrum of different types of caregiving and the intensity of some forms of caregiving, even under the most privileged of circumstances, are often underestimated. In 2020, an estimated 21.3% of individuals in the United States were caregivers, up from 18.2% in 2015 (American Association of Retired Persons, 2020). The majority (54%) of all caregivers in the United States are 50 years of age or older (35% are 50–64 years old, 12% are 65–74 years old, and 7% are older than 75 years), and caregivers age 50 to 64 tend to care for loved ones for longer periods of time than their counterparts age 18 to 49 (5.6 years vs. 3.4 years, respectively) (American Association of Retired Persons, 2020).

Caregiving comes in a variety of forms. Some grandparent caregivers raise grandchildren on their own (skipped generation or custodial grandparenting), while others live with their adult child and grandchildren (co-parenting); collectively, it is estimated that 3 million middle-aged and older grandparent caregivers care for nearly 6 million children (Hayslip, Fruhauf, & Dolbin-MacNab, 2019). Approximately 16.6% of people nationwide provide care to an adult child, sibling, spouse, or other family member who may have been ill or disabled from birth or has become ill or disabled through accident or disease (Family Caregiver Alliance, 2019). When we look at developmental disabilities (e.g., cerebral palsy, Down syndrome, epilepsy) alone, we see that about 76% of individuals with developmental disabilities reside at home and, in 25% of these homes, the family caregiver is older than 60 years of age, whereas the average age of the care recipient is 38 years (Family Caregiver Alliance, 2019).

Eldercare is defined by the Bureau of Labor Statistics as providing "unpaid care to someone age 65 or older who needs help because of a condition related to aging" (Bureau of Labor Statistics, 2019, p. 1). Fifty-eight percent of all eldercare providers are women and 42% are 55 years or older (Bureau of Labor

Statistics, 2019). One study found that, among US workers, more than 40% have provided care for an aging relative or friend during the past 5 years, and almost half anticipate doing so within the next 5 years (Aumann, Galinsky, Sakai, Brown, & Bond, 2010). And last, approximately 12% of the US population is "sandwiched" between multiple forms of caregiving (e.g., care for children and parents simultaneously) (Livingston, 2018). Eighty-two percent of eldercare providers who are parents are employed and 69% are employed full time (Bureau of Labor Statistics, 2019).

Those providing unpaid family care often struggle to manage demands from work and other life roles while simultaneously confronting their own age-related changes—often with inadequate support from healthcare and social service systems. For those who are working and caregiving, securing accommodations or flexibility because of care responsibilities of a loved one can be very challenging, especially for those who work hourly, low-wage jobs that provide minimal benefits (Jacobs & Padavic, 2015). Those forced into reducing their hours or exiting the workplace permanently because of care responsibilities are, disproportionately, women, racial and ethnic minorities, and immigrant workers, and are at greater risk of poverty in later life as a result of reduced earnings, lower Social Security benefits, and loss of employer-sponsored health insurance (Feinberg & Choula, 2012; Lahaie, Earle & Heymann, 2013).

Lesbian, gay, bisexual, transgender, and queer (LGBTQ) caregivers may face several additional barriers, including legal recognition of families of choice, access to services, and burnout and isolation from lack of support (Stewart & Kent, 2017). Furthermore, a greater percentage of LGBTQ caregivers report more financial strain (27%) compared to those not identifying as such (18%) (American Association of Retired Persons, 2020).

The COVID-19 pandemic has made family care work even more challenging by adding uncertainty and stress, limiting access to care, and complicating service delivery. When caregivers cannot access the typical social supports of friends and neighbors on whom they rely for social interactions and care, or the home-based and congregate supports on which they rely (e.g., respite, home health aides, adult day centers), social isolation and burnout can escalate quickly (Roman & Snyder, 2020). Lack of access to or comfort with technology may provide further barriers, and severe financial hardships are possible as caregivers are faced with reduced work hours, are unemployed as a result of the pandemic, or are unable to work because of the fear of exposing a high-risk loved one to the virus (Roman & Snyder, 2020).

Nonprofit and public agencies have offered psychoeducational support programs and respite programs for caregivers for many years, and a large number of evidence-based interventions aimed at supporting caregiving have been developed. For example, the Rosslyn Carter Institute lists more than 70 evidence-based programs, such as REACH, New York University's Caregiving Counseling and Support Intervention, and Skills2Care. Furthermore, to promote the implementation of the strongest programs, the Institute sorts the interventions into two levels of evidence: those tested in randomized controlled trials, demonstrating positive outcomes for caregivers and published in peer-reviewed journals, and those without these characteristics. There is also an indication of whether the intervention is "implementation ready," in that there are adequate materials for training.

The current challenge is that most caregivers are not reached by these programs. Dissemination and implementation of these programs is limited, and resources are not available within aging network services (Gitlin & Czaja, 2012). Online resources and support groups are being developed to eliminate access barriers. Some of these efforts are directed toward subpopulations of caregivers, such as custodial grandparents and parents of adult children with developmental disabilities. Financial support for caregivers is being made possible by public consumer-directed care programs in which relatives and friends can be paid to provide assistance (Mahoney, Simon-Rusinowitz, Simone, & Zgoda, 2006).

In summary, there are promising practices and interesting innovations to support older caregivers, but reach is limited. Research must acknowledge the plentitude of forms of caregiving and the ways in which they constrain or expand choice in later life, especially for lower-income individuals. There is also a need for narratives that uphold the value of the work that unpaid caregivers do; that highlight and celebrate the racial, ethnic, and cultural contexts that shape caregiving; and that seek to understand the ways in which caregiving can be both excruciating and rich in meaning simultaneously (Burch, Dugan, & Barnes-Farrell, 2018).

NEXT STEPS

As reviewed previously, research and demonstrations have supported the development of interventions to facilitate the productive engagement of older adults as workers, volunteers, and caregivers. Despite this promise, efforts are not widespread enough, not institutionalized enough, and not commensurate with the current demographic revolution. There are immediate next steps to be taken.

Increase Financial Support to Caregivers

Most caregivers are employed, and the challenges of working and caregiving concurrently can cause significant financial strains and conflict (Rainville, Skufca, & Mehegan, 2016). Current policies reinforce existing health and economic Inequalities experienced by historically oppressed groups such as women; Black, Indigenous, and people of color; and those with low levels of education (Feinberg, 2014; Gonzales, Lee, & Brown, 2017). The United States is the only developed country without paid sick and family leave for all workers. Although federal law allows workers to take up to 6 weeks of leave to take care of a relative, this time is typically unpaid. Nearly half of caregivers who take time away from work to fulfill their eldercare responsibilities report losing income (Aumann et al., 2010). Of this group, more than half stated they had to leave their job because their employers did not allow the flexibility needed to work and provide eldercare (Matos, 2014). The Family and Medical Leave Act of 1993 does not guarantee access for all workers to unpaid leave. Employees with low levels of education, low-wage workers, and working women are often not covered by the act (Chen 2016). The average caregiver older than 50 years who leaves the workforce to care for a parent loses more than $300,000 in wages and retirement income (MetLife Mature Market Institute, 2011). There is legislation under consideration to address the impact of unpaid caregiving. The FAMILY Act of 2020 would provide paid leave when caregivers must leave the workforce temporarily to care for family members.

Evidence from the implementation of paid leave policies at the state level reveals that families benefit and that productivity is not affected negatively (National Partnership for Women and Families, 2016). The Society for Human Resource Management, one of the chief opponents of paid family leave in California, issued a report finding that the law had created "relatively few" new burdens for employers and that employers' concerns about the program "have so far not been realized" (Redmond & Fkiaras, 2010). Similarly, a survey of New Jersey employers found that a majority did not experience negative effects on profitability or increased paperwork, and no employer was aware of a single instance of the program being abused (Lerner & Appelbaum, 2014).

We can also expand participant-directed programs within the long-term service and support system, particularly those funded through Medicaid that permit beneficiaries to pay caregivers of their choice, including family members. Evidence from participant direction programs, such as the Cash and Counseling randomized control trial, has demonstrated that consumers and caregivers have high rates of satisfaction and low rates of unmet needs, and that this type of service delivery model offers flexibility that cannot be achieved through traditional case management (Mahoney et al., 2006). This flexibility permits both individuals and caregivers to exercise choice and preference that supports them in better meeting their care needs (San Antonio et al., 2010) and in adapting to change over time (Harry et al., 2016).

Expand Federal Recognition and Local Support for Older Adults Who Volunteer

The Corporation for National and Community Service operates several model programs under SeniorCorps, including RSVP, the Foster Grandparents program, and the Senior Companion Program, which together link more than 243,000 older adults to service opportunities annually (Corporation for National and Community Service, 2017). However, SeniorCorps is currently threatened by federal budget cuts or elimination altogether, despite its success in engaging low-income adults in stipendiary service aimed at children or older adults who need assistance (Tan et al., 2016). Instead of cutting or eliminating funding to these programs, there are compelling arguments for expansion. Not only do these national service programs have a history of broad bipartisan support, but also the entire Corporation for National and Community Service budget represents only 0.03% of federal spending (Mulhere, 2017, p. 91). SeniorCorps programs provided almost 75 million hours of national service in fiscal year 2017, and more than 1.2 million elderly, children, and veterans in need were served (Corporation for National and Community Service, 2017). According to Belfield (2013), the social benefits are almost four times as large as the costs of these programs, and the taxpayer benefits are twice the taxpayer costs. Wacker and Roberto (2013) estimate a 26.1-fold return on the federal dollar for RSVP in 2011. However, these programs are currently only able to reach a small portion of the older adults who could benefit from them because most older adults do not know about these programs, and racial and ethnic minorities, immigrants, low-income older adults, noncollege-educated individuals, and the disabled continue to be underrepresented in these programs and service programs in general (Wacker & Roberto, 2013).

Similarly, the promise of the Edward M. Kennedy Serve America Act of 2009 has yet to be fully realized in its potential as a tool for promoting productive engagement. This Act is significant in that it includes several provisions specifically targeting older adults, and contains language that promotes service for older adults of all socioeconomic backgrounds by stipulating that organizations specifically target, recruit, and leverage the resources of seniors (Cutler, Hendricks, & O'Neill, 2011). However, the authorized ramp-up of AmeriCorps positions from 75,000 to 250,000 by 2017—10% of which were for those age 55 years or older—has not yet occurred because funding levels have not kept pace.

Last, we can develop innovative ways to incentivize volunteering at the local level. Many municipalities throughout the country offer property tax work-off programs. For example, the town of Littleton, MA, offers property owners older than 60 years the opportunity to provide volunteer services to the town in exchange for a reduction of up to $1,000 on the amount paid on their property taxes via a minimum wage hourly rate (Town of Littleton, Massachusetts, n.d.). Some local communities have implemented programs that facilitate the exchange of noncash incentives (e.g., "time-banking"). In Montpelier, VT, the Administration on Aging has invested in a form of time banks called "Carebanks," in which older adults can get informal care and support if they or their families pay regular premiums—in "time dollars"—which are earned helping to build community or helping other seniors in various ways (Cahn, 2011).

Encourage Employers to Support Older Workers

Federal and state governments and research institutions can be more active in influencing employing organizations to support longer working lives. According to a recent survey (Transamerica Center for Retirement Studies, 2021), almost 80% of employers agree that they are supportive of their employees working past age 65 years. However, workers are less likely to assess that their employers are indeed supportive (Collinson, 2016). There needs to be more research and dissemination of evidence that older workers and flexible arrangements create positive outcomes for all involved. In a randomized controlled trial, Cahill et al. (2015) found that older workers who perceived increased organizational support for flexible work options (the intervention) increased their expected retirement age over the course of 2 years. A second analysis of these same data revealed that having a greater sense of schedule control makes a difference for employee satisfaction with work–family balance, even under conditions of high work-unit pressure (James, Pitt-Catsouphes, McNamara, Snow, & Johnson, 2015).

There needs to be more education and advice for employers about options for recruiting and supporting older workers. Practices such as adding age diversity to the interviewing team, publicizing an "age-friendly" image, partnering with external organizations that connect employers with older job seekers, and implementing such innovations as "returnships" (an unpaid internship for a specified time) might help employers move beyond the current status quo with regard to hiring practices (Boston College Center on Aging & Work & AARP, 2015).

In addition to support from employers, there are policy options that can enhance the productive engagement of older adults. Berkman, Boersch-Supan, and Avendano (2015) suggest policies that invest in human capital throughout individuals' lives that enable them to work longer, including early childhood education, poverty reduction, and healthcare access. Similarly, the government can offer incentives for reinvesting in skill development, especially for blue-collar workers (Zissimopoulos, Goldman, Olshansky, Rother, & Rowe, 2015). The government can invest in research evaluating and strengthening current government programs, such as the Senior Community Service Employment Program, that support low-income workers specifically. The government can also protect individuals from hostile work environments. The Fair Employment Protection Act of 2019 protects individuals from discrimination on various characteristics and identities including age, race, ethnicity, gender, gender and sexual identities, and disability.

Support Transitions among Working, Volunteering, and Caregiving

Research confirms that older adults who volunteer while still employed are more likely to volunteer after retirement (Tang, 2016). Furthermore, retirement planning can lay the foundation for later-life volunteering. As such, it would be useful for organizations to develop employee volunteer programs geared toward offering continuity after retirement. For example, Intel's Encore Fellows program places retiring employees at a local nonprofit for an assignment that typically lasts 6 to 12 months, half or full time, and involves a commitment to work (on average) 1,000 hours; Fellows are paid a set annual stipend of $25,000 (Encore.org, n.d.). Such an experience can facilitate the transition from the private sector to the nonprofit sector in either paid or unpaid work.

We can support caregivers financially who transition in and out of caregiving and the workforce by acknowledging this important work via the Social Security system. Legislation has been proposed that would not jeopardize caregivers' future retirement income from Social Security. This legislation, the Social Security Caregiver Credit Act of 2014, counts time dedicated to caregiving toward employment history, with a formula assigning a paid wage to Social Security work history records during each month in which a caregiver provides at least 80 hours of assistance without financial compensation.

Transform Physical and Social Environments to Promote Productive Engagement

Aging-friendly community initiatives show promise to improve physical and social environments to support productive engagement. Many local governments and community organizations are focusing on ways to reduce barriers and facilitate participation of older adults, improve the possibilities to age in place, and increase age inclusiveness [e.g., see the AARP's and the World Health Organization's (2007) age-friendly community initiatives]. These efforts include increasing walkability and accessibility, improving public transportation, providing affordable housing options, promoting respect and inclusion, and ensuring essential health and social services. Although working, volunteering, and caregiving are all supported through any of these transformations in community infrastructures, many initiatives have specific goals in regard to these productive activities. For example, Age-Friendly NYC (2009) calls for action include the following: provide job training and search assistance to older New Yorkers, increase the number of paid job opportunities for older New Yorkers, promote intergenerational volunteering and learning through partnerships with schools and nonprofit organizations, provide new volunteer opportunities, provide counseling and support services to grandparents raising grandchildren, expand educational materials and supports available to family caregivers, explore policies that would allow more New Yorkers to take family leave when needed, conduct outreach and workshops on long-term care and caregiving resources for employers in New York City, and expand training opportunities and other supports for paid caregivers.

New York City has since started to answer this call to action, expanding their Paid Sick Leave Law in 2014 by including grandparents, siblings, and grandchildren in the definition of family members that workers can take time off to care for. The city also enacted legislation requiring the Department for the Aging to survey unpaid caregivers to inform future legislation addressing their needs (NYC Department for the Aging, 2017).

Last, the COVID-19 pandemic has highlighted the challenges older adults face accessing resources in their communities. The pandemic has prompted temporary expansions of Medicare coverage for telehealth visits. The Centers for Medicare and Medicaid Services have already made some of these telehealth coverages permanent (Centers for Medicare and Medicaid Services, 2020). Passing the Protecting Access to Post-COVID-19 Telehealth Act of 2020 would further expand permanent Medicare telehealth coverage. This is an important step in eliminating barriers that older adults face in accessing healthcare. However, it is also important for policymakers to consider that telehealth still is not accessible to all older adults. Recent research found that 26.3% of Medicare beneficiaries do not have digital access at home (Roberts & Mehrotra, 2020). Therefore, supporting older adult's access to in-person healthcare services remains centrally important.

End Discrimination and Bias

The negative effects of discrimination and bias in any form and at any age have been documented. The aging population is very diverse, and there is evidence linking perceived discrimination on basic features of an individual—age, gender, race, ethnicity, sexual orientation, physical ability, weight, and appearance—with deleterious physical, cognitive, and emotional health, as well as negative economic outcomes (Allen, 2016; Marchiondo, Gonzales, & Ran, 2016; Sutin, Stephen, Carretta, & Terracciano, 2015). Individuals who perceive discrimination within the workplace are at a greater risk of turnover and early retirement (Brooke & Taylor, 2005; Lim, Cortina, & Magley, 2008). Older adults with multiple vulnerable identities are susceptible to ageism and other biases (Sutin et al., 2015), which underscores the importance of social workers to advocate for populations that have been historically discriminated at any age for any reason. The research on structural or institutional discrimination based on race is quite sophisticated (Delgado & Stephancic, 2012; Miller & Garran, 2008), and more can be done to link it with age discrimination, health, and productive engagement. We must see beyond stereotypes, negative or positive, and match the capacity of individuals with the employment, volunteering, or caregiving role—as opposed to current stereotypes of incompetent, useless, and "greedy geezers" (Gendron, Welleford, Inker, & White, 2016).

Future research is needed to identify the prevalence and consequences of discrimination in various contexts (e.g., workplace, volunteer and community settings, and home), as well as the individual and institutional protective mechanisms that buffer health and social engagement across the life span. Greater understanding is also needed regarding the effects of the pandemic on age discrimination. Clearly, the pandemic has exposed the widespread ageism in our society: the threat of the virus was deemed "not that great" because it only killed old people (Barnes, 2020), there have been discussions of diverting medical resources to younger people in the face of shortages (Ault, 2020), and it was suggested that targeted lockdown of "seniors" could help reopen the economy (Acemoglu, Chernozhukov, Werning, & Whinston, 2020). The extent of job loss has been substantial among older workers, and previous experience from the 2008 recession suggests that reentering the workforce will be challenged by age discrimination (Bui, Button, & Picciotti, 2020). There has been concerned expressed that we have been set back in efforts to promote a productive aging perspective (Morrow-Howell & Gonzales, 2020).

Current legislation seeks to strengthen protection against age discrimination. The Protect Older Workers Against Discrimination Act will reinstate Congress' original intent for age to be a factor in an age discrimination claim, as opposed to the primary factor. The Fair Employment Protection Act of 2014 will also protect employees from covert discriminatory practices based on age and other vulnerable identities. Employers and volunteer sites that foster inclusion can also benefit financially with a healthier workforce and stronger commitment of diverse employees.

Calls for Innovation

Several specific issues warrant innovative, indeed transformative, solutions. First, there are not many examples of interventions to change attitudes and social expectations about later life or to confront ageism. Perhaps these changes will emerge as programs and policies further re-create the social roles of older adults. However, there may be interventions to accelerate these changes. It is necessary to seek creative solutions to reduce the widespread age discrimination and stereotyping that currently exist, and that limit fundamentally the participation of older adults in productive roles.

Second, solutions that directly address gender, ethnic, and racial diversity are essential, especially given society's history of discrimination in the educational and employment sector. For example, older racial minorities are underrepresented and underrecognized in the paid and volunteer labor forces, and women provide the bulk of unpaid caregiving. American society has a long history of paid and unpaid roles that are tied to gender and race, and Butler (1980) drew parallels between ageism, racism, and sexism. Intervention development to facilitate productive engagement in later life will require innovative solutions that confront the exclusion of less-advantaged older adults; otherwise, disparities in later life could increase.

Third, solutions must be developed from a life course perspective. Early- and midlife health, education, work, volunteering, and caregiving experiences shape subsequent abilities to engage successfully in paid and unpaid work in later life (Hirshorn & Settersten, 2013). Attitudes and motivations for involvement in family and community are not formed when one reaches older adulthood, but rather are shaped over decades. Significant innovation will be necessary for solutions that address how attitudes, expectations, programs, and policies can be shaped across the life course to ensure a productive old age.

Charge to the Social Work Profession

Social work education traditionally includes curricula on older adults, aging policies, and aging network services. However, the topic of the productive engagement of older adults requires a new perspective for social work because we have largely focused on human problems. Indeed, the roots of gerontological social work are helping with the inability to take care of oneself financially or because of disability or dementia. We must confront our own professional expectations and practices because social workers are as vulnerable to age bias and age stereotyping as anyone else. In fact, social work's important commitment to individuals who face challenging psychosocial life situations makes us more vulnerable to distorted views of the aging population. That is, we focus on problems older adults face, including dementia, disabling health conditions, mental disorder, isolation, and neglect, rather than focusing on the whole person and the strengths of each older adult. It is easy to forget that most older adults are living well, and those who face challenges still may be quite interested and capable of participating in productive activities—and often are—despite our misperceptions.

Correspondingly, our educational curricula skew toward the problems commonly experienced in later life and fail to capture adequately the reality of normal human development throughout the life course. We use language, examples, and experiences that support age stereotyping. For example, discussions of later life in foundation social work courses are often relegated to a single class or reading, whereas discussion of issues related to youth and middle adulthood are well represented throughout curricula. Furthermore, these discussions often conflate older adulthood with disability, with little focus on an assets-based orientation in later life, intergenerational equity approaches, or understanding that disability does not preclude engagement.

Clearly, these are critical topics for social workers, and all social workers need to be equipped to mediate the great social transformation signaled by the growing proportion of older adults in society. Yet, we fail to include content that portrays the reality of the capacity, desire, and strength of older adults, and the potential to improve their lives and the lives of others via productive engagement. These issues could be incorporated into curricula in innovative and seamless ways, ranging from an exercise in which students are asked to reflect on maintaining or creating meaningful roles and identities across the life span, and particularly in later life, to staging a debate focused on intergenerational tensions/equity/fairness in different contexts and how these issues might be resolved with the goal of an age-inclusive society.

Infusion of productive aging perspectives into social work curricula is facilitated by the reality that the productive aging framework is highly compatible with social work's person–environment fit perspective. The productive aging perspective focuses on programs, policies, and social contexts to leverage the growing capital of the older population. Interventions to promote working, volunteering, and caregiving focus on supports and opportunities, not on changing the individual older adults themselves. This person–environment fit approach positions social work to lead initiatives and partner with many disciplines to work toward maximizing the productive engagement of older adults. Colleagues from medical and allied professions, psychology, sociology, economics, architecture, business, and public health must be involved to make significant progress toward achieving an aging society that can be characterized, in part, by older adults' productive activity. Social work scholars are also leaders of research that examines productive engagement in later life, with particular attention paid to issues concerning social and economic justice. The Productive Aging Interest Group, associated with the Hartford Geriatric Social Work Leadership Initiative and the Gerontological Society of America, is further evidence of social work's leadership on productive aging within gerontology as a whole.

CONCLUSION

Population aging is transforming societies throughout the world. The demographic shift is creating significant challenges but also presents great opportunity. To complement long-standing problem-oriented approaches, such as fixing Social Security and reforming healthcare, we must take a more strengths-based perspective by focusing on increasing the productive engagement of a growing natural human resource: the older population (Freedman, 2011, p. 97). To do this requires applied research and innovations in policy and programs across multiple disciplines, and changes in assumptions about older adults and aging populations. Social work can help lead the productive engagement agenda with an emphasis on creating equity in opportunity for all older adults who desire to participate in productive activities.

NOTE

1. Data are analyzed from the 2016 wave, with the exception of discrimination measures that come from 2012.

REFERENCES

AARP (May, 2020). Caregiving in the U.S. Research Report. Retrieved on October 26, 2021 from https://www.aarp.org/content/dam/aarp/ppi/2020/05/full-report-caregiving-in-the-united-states.doi.10.26419-2Fppi.00103.001.pdf

Acemoglu, D., Chernozhukov, V., Werning, I., & Whinston, M. (2020). The road to recovery: How targeted lockdowns for seniors can help the U.S. reopen. Time Magazine. Retrieved from https://time.com/5840194/targeted-lockdowns-coronavirus/Administration on Aging & Administration on Community Living

Administration on Aging. (2016). *Profile of older Americans: 2016*. Washington, DC: Administration on Aging, Administration for Community Living, US Department of Health and Human Service. Retrieved from https://www.acl.gov/sites/default/files/Aging%20and%20Disability%20in%20America/2016-Profile.pdf

Age-Friendly NYC. (2009). Enhancing our city's livability for older New Yorkers. Retrieved from http://www.nyc.gov/html/dfta/downloads/pdf/age_friendly/agefriendlynyc.pdf

Allen, J. O. (2016). Ageism as a risk factor for chronic disease. *The Gerontologist*, 56, 610–614. doi:10.1093/geront/gnu158

Ault, A. (2020). Alabama alters COVID-19 vent policy after discrimination complaints. Medscape. Retrieved from https://www.medscape.com/viewarticle/928524?nlid=134997_3901&src=wnl_newsalrt_200412_MSCPEDIT&uac=324770DY&impID=2344371&faf=1

Aumann, K., Galinsky, E., Sakai, K., Brown, M., & Bond, J. T. (2010). The elder care study: Everyday realities and wishes for change. Retrieved from http://familiesandwork.org/site/research/reports/elder_care.pdf

Bankers Center for a Secure Retirement. (2015). *New expectations, new rewards: Work in retirement for middle-income boomers*. Chicago, IL: Bankers Life. Retrieved from http://www.centerforasecureretirement.com/media/65648/work-in-retirement-report-may-2015.pdf

Barnes, P. (2020). Did U.S. response to COVID-19 lag due to age discrimination? Forbes. Retrieved from https://www.forbes.com/sites/patriciagbarnes/2020/03/13/did-us-response-to-covid-19-lag-due-to-age-discrimination/#3d79c1491784

Belfield, C. (2013). *The economic value of national service*. New York, NY: Center for Benefit–Cost Studies in Education. Retrieved from http://voicesforservice.org/wp-content/uploads/2016/03/Sep19_Econ_Value_National_Service-2.pdf

Berkman, L. F., Boersch-Supan, A., & Avendano, M. (2015). Labor-force participation, policies, & practices in an aging America: Adaptation essential for a healthy & resilient population. *Dædalus, 144*, 41–54. doi:10.1162/DAED_a_00329

Boston College Center on Aging & Work & AARP. (2015). Workforce benchmarking tool. Retrieved from http://virgo.bc.edu/employerbenchmarking

Bowleg, L. (2012). The problem with the phrase women and minorities: Intersectionality—An important theoretical framework for public health. *American Journal of Public Health, 102*, 1267–1273. doi:10.2105/AJPH.2012.300750

Bridgeland, J. M., McNaught, M., Reed, B., & Dunkelman, M. (2009). The quiet crisis: The impact of the economic downturn on the nonprofit sector. *Civic Enterprises*, Democratic Leadership Council. WK Kellogg Foundation. https://files.eric.ed.gov/fulltext/ED513451.pdf.

Brooke, L., & Taylor, P. (2005). Older workers and employment: Managing age relations. *Ageing and Society, 25*, 415–429.

Brown, T. (2012). The intersection and accumulation of racial and gender inequality: Black women's wealth trajectories. *The Review of Black Political Economy, 39*, 239–258. doi:10.1007/s12114-011-9100-8

Brown, T. H. (2016). Diverging fortunes: Racial/ethnic inequality in wealth trajectories in middle and late life. *Race Social Problems, 8*, 29–41. doi:10.1007/s12552-016-9160-2

Brown, J. E., Rhee, N., Saad-Lessler, J., & Oakley, D. (2016). *Shortchanges in retirement: Continuing challenges to women's financial future*. Washington, DC: National Institute on Retirement. Retrieved from http://laborcenter.berkeley.edu/pdf/2016/NIRS-Women-In-Retirement.pdf

Bui, T., Button, P., & Picciotti, E. (2020). Early evidence on the impact of coronavirus disease 2019 (COVID-19) and the recession on older workers. *Public Policy & Aging Report, 30*, 154–159. doi:10.1093/ppar/praa029

Burch, K. A., Dugan, A. G., Barnes-Farrell, J. L. (2018). Understanding what eldercare means for employees and organizations: A review and recommendations for future research. *Work, Aging and Retirement, 5*(1), 44–72.

Butler, R. N. (1980). Ageism: A foreword. *Journal of Social Issues, 36*, 8–11. doi:10.1111/j.1540-4560.1980.tb02018.x

Butler, R. N. (1997). Living longer, contributing longer. *Journal of the American Medical Association, 278*, 1372–1374. doi:10.1001/jama.1997.03550160092044

Cahill, K. E., Giandrea, M. D., & Kovacs, G. J. (2014). Self-employment: The answer for an aging workforce and a sluggish economy? Retrieved from http://agingandwork.bc.edu/blog/self-employment-the-answer-for-an-aging-workforce-and-a-sluggish-economy

Cahill, K. E., James, J. B., & Pitt-Catsouphes, M. (2015). The impact of a randomly assigned time and place management initiative on work and retirement expectations. *Work, Aging and Retirement, 1*, 350–368. doi:10.1093/workar/wav012

Cahn, E. (2011). Time banking: An idea whose time has come? *Yes! Magazine*. Retrieved from http://www.yesmagazine.org/new-economy/time-banking-an-idea-whose-time-has-come

Calvo, E. (2006). *Does working longer make people healthier and happier?* Work Opportunities for Older Americans Brief, Series 2. Chestnut Hill, MA: Center for Retirement Research, Boston College.

Carolan, K., Gonzales, E., Lee, K., & Harootyan, B. (2020). Institutional and Individual Factors Affecting Health and Employment among Low-Income Women with Chronic Health Conditions. *Journals of Gerontology: Social Sciences, 75*(5), 1062–1071. doi:10.1093/geronb/gby149

Centers for Medicare and Medicaid Services. (2020). Trump administration finalizes permanent expansion of Medicare telehealth services and improved payment for time doctors spend with patients. [Press release]. Retrieved from https://www.cms.gov/newsroom/press-releases/trump-administration-finalizes-permanent-expansion-medicare-telehealth-services-and-improved-payment

Chen, M.-L. (2016). The growing costs and burden of family caregiving of older adults: A review of paid sick leave and family leave policies. *Gerontologist, 56*, 391–396. doi:10.1093/geront/gnu093

Cohen, N. (2014). Rise in number of older workers set to drive UK economy. *Financial Times*. Retrieved from http://www.ft.com/cms/s/0/c562a032-881f-11e3-a926-00144feab7de.html#axzz362YhGvxr

Coile, C. C., & Gruber, J. (2003). Fiscal effects of social security reform in the United States. Retrieved from http://crr.bc.edu/working-papers/fiscal-effects-of-social-security-reform-in-the-united-states

Collinson, S. (2016). *The current state of 401(k)s: The employer's perspective: 16th Annual Transamerica retirement survey*. Los Angeles, CA: Transamerica Center for Retirement Studies. Retrieved from https://www.transamericacenter.org/docs/default-source/employer-research/tcrs2016_sr_the_current_state_of_401ks_the_employer_perspective.pdf

Corporation for National and Community Service. (2017). Corporation for National and Community Service fact sheet: SeniorCorps. Retrieved from https://www.nationalservice.gov/sites/default/files/documents/CNCS-Fact-Sheet-2017-SeniorCorps_0.pdf

Coughlin, J. (2010). Estimating the impact of caregiving and employment on well-being. *Outcomes & Insights in Health Management, 2*, 1–7.

Cravens, J., & Ellis, S. J. (2014). *The last virtual volunteering guidebook: Fully integrating online service into volunteer involvement*. Philadelphia, PA: Energize, Inc.

Crenshaw, K.W. (1991). Mapping the margins: Intersectionality, identity politics, and violence against women of color. *Stanford Law Review, 43*, 1241–1299.

Cutler, S. J., Hendricks, J., & O'Neill, G. (2011). Civic engagement and aging. In B. H. Binstock & L. George (Eds.), *Handbook of aging & the social sciences* (7th ed., pp. 221-233). New York, NY: Academic Press.

Delgado, R., & Stephancic, C. (2012). *Critical race theory: An introduction* (2nd ed.). New York, NY: New York University Press.

DeSilver, D. (2016). *More older Americans are working than in recent years.* Washington, DC: Pew Research Center. Retrieved from http://www.pewresearch.org/fact-tank/2016/06/20/more-older-americans-are-working-and-working-more-than-they-used-to

Dushi, I., & Iams, H. (2009). Cohort Differences in Wealth and Pension Participation of Near-Retirees. *Social Security Bulletin, 68*(3), 45–66, 2008, Available at SSRN: https://ssrn.com/abstract=1359321

Encore.org. (n.d.). Intel Encore Fellows: A pathway to a new stage of work and contribution. Retrieved from http://encore.org/fellowships/intel

Family Caregiver Alliance. (2019). Caregiver Statistics: Demographics. Retrieved on October 26, 2021 from https://www.caregiver.org/resource/caregiver-statistics-demographics/

Feinberg, L. F. (2014). Recognizing and supporting family caregivers: The time has come. *Public Policy and Aging Report, 24,* 65–69. doi:10.1093/ppar/pru007

Feinberg, L., & Choula, R. (2012). Understanding the Impact of Family Caregiving on Work. Fact Sheet. AARP Public Policy Institute. Retrieved on October 26, 2021 from https://www.aarp.org/content/dam/aarp/research/public_policy_institute/ltc/2012/understanding-impact-family-caregiving-work-AARP-ppi-ltc.pdf

Feinberg, L., Reinhard, S. C., Houser, A., & Choula, R. (2011). Valuing the invaluable: 2011 Update, the growing contributions and costs of family caregiving. Retrieved from https://assets.aarp.org/rgcenter/ppi/ltc/i51-caregiving.pdf

Freedman, M. (2011). *The big shift: Navigating midlife and beyond.* New York, NY: Perseus.

Galucia, N., Morrow-Howell, N., Sun, P., Meyer, T., & Li, Y. (2020). *The impact of COVID-19 on villages: Results from a national survey.* Working paper. St. Louis, MO: Washington University.

Gendron, T. L., Welleford, A., Inker, J., & White, J. T. (2016). The language of ageism: Why we need to use words carefully. *The Gerontologist, 56,* 997–1006. doi:10.1093/geront/gnv066

Ghilarducci, T., & Farmand, A., (2020). Older workers on the COVID-19 frontlines without paid sick leave. *Journal of Aging & Social Policy, 32*(4-5), 471–476, doi:10.1080/08959420.2020.1765685

Gitlin, L. N., & Czaja, S. (2012, November). Pre-conference workshop: Current and future challenges in designing behavioral interventions: From randomized trials to community implementations. Paper presented at the annual conference of the Gerontological Society of America, San Diego, CA.

Gonzales, E., Gordon, S., Whetung, C., Connaught, G., Collazo, J., & Hilton, J. (2021). Acknowledging systemic discrimination in the context of a pandemic: Advancing an anti-racist and anti-ageist movement. *Journal of Gerontological Social Work.* doi:10.1080/01634372.2020.1870604

Gonzales, E., Lee, Y., & Brown, C. (2017). Back to work? Not everyone: Examining the longitudinal relationships between informal caregiving and paid-work after formal retirement. *The Journals of Gerontology, Series B: Psychological Sciences and Social Sciences, 72*(3), 532–539. doi:10.1093/geronb/gbv095.

Gonzales, E., Lee, K., & Harootyan, B. (2019). Voices from the field: Ecological factors that promote employment and health among low-income older adults with implications for direct social work practice. *Clinical Social Work Journal,* 211–222. doi: 10.1007/s10615-019-00719-x.

Gonzales, E., Matz-Costa, C., & Morrow-Howell, N. (2015). White House Conference on Aging 2015. Increasing Opportunities for the Productive Engagement of Older Adults: A Response to Population Aging. *The Gerontologist, 55*(2), 252–261. Special Issue for the Policy Forum. doi:10.1093/geront/gnu176

Gonzales, E., & Nowell, W. B. (2017). Social Capital and Unretirement: Exploring the Bonding, Bridging, and Linking Aspects of Social Relationships. *Research on Aging, 39*(10), 1100–1117, doi:10.1177/0164027516664569

Gonzales, E., Suntai, Z., & Abrams, J. (2019). Volunteering and Health Outcomes Among Older Adults. In D. Gu & M. Dupre (Eds.), *Encyclopedia of Gerontology and Population Aging*. Springer, Cham. https://doi.org/10.1007/978-3-319-69892-2_649-1

Greenfield, J. C. (2018). The Long-Term Costs of Caring: How Caring for an Aging Parent Impacts Wealth Trajectories of Caregivers (2013). All Theses and Dissertations (ETDs). 1108. https://openscholarship.wustl.edu/etd/1108

Greenwald, L., Copeland, C., & VanDerhei, J. (2017). *The 2017 retirement confidence survey: Many workers lack retirement confidence and feel stressed about retirement preparations*. Issue Brief, no. 431. Washington, DC: Employee Benefit Research Institute.

Gutman, G., & Spencer, C. (2010). *Aging, ageism and abuse*. Burlington, MA: Elsevier, Inc. doi:10.1016/C2009-0-63985-4

Halpern, J. (2020). Introducing the "grandparents academy." *The New York Times*. Retrieved from https://www.nytimes.com/2020/03/26/opinion/covid-home-school-grandparents.html

Halvorsen, C., & Emerman, J. (2013–2014). The encore movement: Baby boomers and older adults building community. *Generations, 37*, 33–39.

Halvorsen, C., & Morrow-Howell, N. (2016). A conceptual framework on self-employment in later life: Toward a research agenda. *Work, Aging and Retirement, 3*(4), 313–324. doi:10.1093/workar/waw031

Halvorsen, C. J., Werner, K., & McColloch, E. (2020). The Senior Community Service Employment Program: Its influence on participant well-being—and recommendations to strengthen it. Center on Aging & Work and the Center for Social Innovation at Boston College. Retrieved from https://www.bc.edu/content/dam/files/research_sites/agingandwork/pdf/publications/scsepreport.pdf

Halvorsen, C. J., & Yulikova, O. (2020a). Job training and so much more for low-income older adults: The Senior Community Service Employment Program. *Clinical Social Work Journal, 48*, 223–229. doi:10.1007/s10615-019-00734-y

Halvorsen, C. J., & Yulikova, O., (2020b) Older workers in the time of COVID-19: The Senior Community Service Employment Program and implications for social work. *Journal of Gerontological Social Work, 63*, 530–541, doi:10.1080/01634372.2020.1774832

Harry, M. L., Kong, J., MacDonald, L. M., McLuckie, A., Battista, C., & Mahoney, K. J. (2016). The long-term effects of participant direction of supports and services for people with disabilities. *Care Management Journals, 17*, 2–12. doi:10.1891/1521-0987.17.1.2

Hayslip, B., Jr, Fruhauf, C., & Dolbin-MacNab, M. (2019). Grandparents raising grandchildren: *The Gerontologist, 59*, e152–e163, https://doi.org/10.1093/geront/gnx106

He, W., Goodkind, D., & Kowal, P. (2016). *U.S. Census Bureau, international population reports P95/16-1: An aging world: 2015*. Washington, DC: US Government Publishing Office.

Hipple, S. F., & Hammond, L. A. (2016). Self-employment in the United States: Spotlight on statistics (p. 5). Washington, DC: Bureau of Labor Statistics. Retrieved from http://www.bls.gov/spotlight/2016/self-employment-in-the-united-states/home.htm

Hirshorn, B. A., & Settersten, R. A., Jr. (2013). Civic involvement across the life course: Moving beyond age-based assumptions. *Advances in Life Course Research*, *18*, 199–211. doi:10.1016/j.alcr.2013.05.001

Holstein, M. B., & Minkler, M. (2007). Critical gerontology: Reflections for the 21st century. In M. Bernard & T. Scharf (Eds.), *Critical perspectives on ageing societies* (pp. 12–26). Buckingham, UK: Open University Press.

Hong, S. I., & Morrow-Howell, N. (2010). Health outcomes of Experience Corps: A high-commitment volunteer program. *Social Science & Medicine*, *71*, 414–420. doi:10.1016/j.socscimed.2010.04.009

Jacobs, A. W., & Padavic, I. (2015). Hours, scheduling and flexibility for women in the US low-wage labour force. *Gender, Work and Organization*, *22*, 67–86.

James, J. B., Matz-Costa, C., & Smyer, M. (2016). Retirement security: It's not just about the money. *American Psychologist*, *7*, 334–344. doi:10.1037/ a0040220

James, J. B., Pitt-Catsouphes, M., McNamara, T. K., Snow, D. L., & Johnson, P. (2015). The relationship of work unit pressure to satisfaction with work–family balance: A new twist on negative spillover? In S. Ammons & E. Kelly (Eds.), *Research in the sociology of work: Work and family in the new economy* (pp. 219–247). Bingley, UK: Emerald Group. doi:10.1108/S0277-283320150000026015

Kerman, S. C., & Keenan, T. A. (2017). *The multi-generational labor force: Perceptions of jobs among Millennials, Gen-xers, and Boomers*. Washington, DC: American Association of Retired Persons. Retrieved from http://www.aarp.org/content/dam/aarp/research/surveys_statistics/econ/2016/multi-gen-labor-force-report-res-econ.pdf

Kim, S., & Ferraro, K. F. (2013). Do productive activities reduce inflammation in later life? Multiple roles, frequency of activities, and C-reactive protein. *The Gerontologist*, *54*, 830–839. doi:10.1093/geront/gnt090

Lahaie, C., Earle, A., & Heymann, J. (2013). An uneven burden: Social disparities in adult caregiving responsibilities, working conditions, and caregiver outcomes. *Research on Aging*, *35*(3), 243–274.

Lee, S. H., Johnson, K. J., & Lyu, J. (2018). Volunteering among first-generation Asian ethnic groups residing in California. *Journal of Cross-cultural Gerontology*, *33*, 369–385.

Lee, Y., Tang, F., Kim, K. H., & Albert, S. M. (2015). The vicious cycle of parental caregiving and financial well-being: A longitudinal study of women. *The Journals of Gerontology, Series B: Psychological Sciences and Social Sciences*, *70*, 425–431. doi:10.1093/geronb/gbu001

Lerner, S., & Appelbaum, E. (2014). Business as usual: New Jersey employers' experiences with family leave insurance. Retrieved from http:// www.cepr.net/documents/nj-fli-2014-06.pdf

Lim, S., Cortina, L. M., & Magley, V. J. (2008). Personal and workgroup incivility: Impact on work and health outcomes. *Journal of Applied Psychology*, *9*, 95–107.

Livingston, G. (November, 2018). More than one-in-ten U.S. parents also caring for an adult. Pew Research Center. Retrieved on October 26, 2021 from https://www.pewresearch.org/fact-tank/2018/11/29/more-than-one-in-ten-u-s-parents-are-also-caring-for-an-adult/

Magnusson Hanson, L. L., Westerlund, H., Chungkham, H. S., Vahtera, J., Rod, N. H., Alexanderson, K., Goldberg, M., Kivimäki, M., Stenholm, S., Platts, L. G., Zins, M., & Head, J. (2018). Job strain and loss of healthy life years between ages 50 and 75 by sex and occupational position: Analyses of 64,934 individuals from four prospective cohort studies. *Occupational and Environmental Medicine, 75*, 486–493. https://doi.org/10.1136/oemed-2017-104644

Mahoney, K. J., Simon-Rusinowitz, L., Simone, K., & Zgoda, K. (2006). Cash and counseling: A promising option for consumer direction of home- and community-based services and supports. *Care Management Journals, 7*, 199–204.

Marchiondo, L., Gonzales, E., & Ran, S. (2016). Development and validation of the Workplace Age Discrimination Scale (WADS). *Journal of Business and Psychology, 31*, 493–513. doi:10.1007/s10869-015-9425-6

Matos, K. (2014). *Highlights from the 2014 older adult caregiver study*. Retrieved from http://www.familiesandwork.org/downloads/2014-Older-Adult-Caregiver-Study.pdf

McGuire, J. F., Kenney, K., & Brashler, P. (2010). Flexible work arrangements: The fact sheet. Washington, DC: *Workplace Flexibility 2010*, 1–10. https://scholarship.law.georgetown.edu/legal/13.

MetLife Mature Market Institute. (2011). *The MetLife study of caregiving costs to working caregivers: Double jeopardy for baby boomers caring for their parents*. Retrieved from https://www.metlife.com/assets/cao/mmi/publications/studies/2011/Caregiving-Costs-to-Working-Caregivers.pdf

Miller, J., & Garran, A. M. (2008). *Racism in the United States: Implications for the helping professions*. Belmont, CA: Brooks/Cole.

Miranda, V. (2011). Cooking, caring and volunteering: Unpaid work around the world, OECD Social, Employment and Migration Working Papers, No. 116, OECD Publishing. doi: 10.1787/5kghrjm8s142-en.

Morrow-Howell, N., & Gonzales, E. (2020). *Recovering from Covid-19: Resisting ageism and recommitting to a productive aging perspective*. Public policy and aging report. Washington, DC: Gerontological Society of America.

Morrow-Howell, N., & Greenfield, E. (2015). Productive engagement in later life. In L. George & K. Ferraro (Eds.), *Handbook of aging and the social sciences* (8th ed., pp. 293–314). London, UK: Elsevier.

Morrow-Howell, N., Hinterlong, J., & Sherraden, M. (2001). *Productive aging: Concepts and challenges*. Baltimore, MD: Johns Hopkins University Press.

Mulhere, K. (2017). Trump's budget would kill the beloved volunteer program AmeriCorps. *Money*. Retrieved from http://time.com/money/4703924/trump-budget-americorps-college-funding-cut

National Alliance for Caregiving & AARP. (2020). Caregiving in the U.S. 2020. Retrieved from https://www.caregiving.org/caregiving-in-the-us-2020/

National Institute on Aging. (2011). *Global health and aging*. NIH publication no. 11-7737. Washington, DC: National Institutes of Health.

National Partnership for Women and Families. (2016). Paid leave works in California, New Jersey and Rhode Island. Retrieved from http://www.nationalpartnership.org/research-library/work-family/paid-leave/paid-leave-works-in-california-new-jersey-and-rhode-island.pdf

NYC Department for the Aging. Age-friendly NYC: New commitments for a city for all ages. (2017) Retrieved from https://www.aarp.org/content/dam/aarp/livable-communities/age-friendly-network/2017/AgeFriendlyNYC2017.pdf

Olshansky, S. J., Goldman, D. P., & Rowe, J. W. (2015). Resetting Social Security. *Dædalus, 144*, 68–79. doi:10.1162/DAED_a_00331

Opportunity Nation. (2014). Connecting youth and strengthening communities: The data behind civic engagement and economic opportunity. Retrieved from http://www.pointsoflight.org/sites/default/files/resources/files/opportunity_nation_civic_engagement_report_2014.pdf

Papadopoulous, M., Fisher, B., Ghilarducci, T., & Radpour, S. (August, 2020). Status of Older Workers. The New School Retirement Equity Lab. Retrieved on October 26, 2021 from https://www.economicpolicyresearch.org/images/INET_docs/Status_of_older_workers_reports/Q1_2020_OWAG_V12.pdf

Poterba, J. M. (2014). Retirement security in an aging population. *American Economic Review, 104*, 1–30. doi:10.1257/aer.104.5.1

Rainville, C., Skufca, L., & Mehegan, L. (2016). *Family caregiving and out-of-pocket costs: 2016 Report*. Washington, DC: American Association of Retired Persons. Retrieved from http://www.aarp.org/content/dam/aarp/research/surveys_statistics/ltc/2016/family-caregiving-cost-survey-res-ltc.pdf

Redmond, J., & Fkiaras, E. (2010). Legal report: California's Paid Family Leave Act is less onerous than predicted. Retrieved from https://www.sheppardmullin.com/media/article/809_CA%20Paid%20Family%20Leave%20Act%20Is%20Less%20Onerous%20Than%20Predicted

Reinhard, S. C., Feinberg, L. F., Houser, A., Choula, R., & Evans, M. (2019). *Valuing the invaluable: 2019 Update: Charting a path forward*. Washington, DC: AARP Public Policy Institute. doi:10.26419/ppi.00082.001

Roman, C. & Snyder, R. (2020, June 2). Supporting Family Caregivers in the Time of COVID-19: State Strategies. Hamilton, NJ: Center for Healthcare Strategies. https://www.chcs.org/supporting-family-caregivers-in-the-time-of-covid-19-state-strategies/

Roberts, E. T., & Mehrotra, A. (2020). Assessment of disparities in digital access among Medicare beneficiaries and implications for telemedicine. *JAMA Internal Medicine, 180*, 1386–1389. doi:10.1001/jamainternmed.2020.2666

Rohwedder, S., & Willis, R. J. (2010). Mental retirement. *Journal of Economic Perspectives, 24*, 119–138. doi:10.1257/jep.24.1.119

Roscigno, V. (2010). Ageism in the American workplace. *Contexts, 9*, 16–21.

Roth, D., Fredman, L., & Haley, W. (2015). Informal caregiving and its impact on health: A reappraisal from population-based studies. *The Gerontologist, 55*, 309–319. doi:10.1093/geront/gnu177

San Antonio, P., Simon-Rusinowitz, L., Loughlin, D., Eckert, J. K., Mahoney, K. J., & Ruben, K. A. D. (2010). Lessons from the Arkansas Cash and Counseling Program: How the experiences of diverse older consumers and their caregivers address family policy concerns. *Journal of Aging & Social Policy, 22*, 1–17.

Selden, T. M., & Berdahl, T. A. (2021). Risk of Severe COVID-19 Among Workers and Their Household Members. *JAMA Internal Medicine, 181*(1), 120–122. doi:10.1001/jamainternmed.2020.6249

Sherraden, M., Stuart, P., Barth, R. P., Kemp, S., Lubben, J., Hawkins, J. D., ... Catalano, R. (2014). *Grand accomplishments in social work*. Grand Challenges for Social Work Initiative working paper no. 2. Baltimore, MD: American Academy of Social Work and Social Welfare.

Skufca, L. (2014). *Planning for health care costs in retirement: A 2014 survey of 50 + workers*. Washington, DC: American Association of Retired Persons. Retrieved from http://www.aarp.org/content/dam/aarp/research/surveys_statistics/econ/2014/Planning-for-Health-Care-Costs-in-Retirement-A-2014-Survey-of-50-Plus-Workers-AARP-econ.pdf

Smith, P. M., Cawley, C., Williams, A., & Mustard, C. (2020a). Male/female differences in the impact of caring for elderly relatives on labor market attachment and hours of work: 1997–2015. *The Journals of Gerontology: Series B, 75*, 694–704. doi:10.1093/geronb/gbz026

Smith, M., Steinman, L., & Casey, E. (2020b). Combatting social isolation among older adults in the time of physical distancing. *Frontiers in Public Health, 8*(403). doi:10.3389/fpubh.2020.00403

Spera, C., Ghertner, R., Nerino, A., & DiTommaso, A. (2013). *Volunteering as a pathway to employment: Does volunteering increase odds of finding a job for the out of work?* Washington, DC: Corporation for National & Community Service, Office of Research & Evaluation. Retrieved from https://www.nationalservice.gov/sites/default/files/upload/ employment_research_report.pdf

Stewart, D. B., & Kent, A. (2017). Caregiving in the LGBT Community: A Guide to Engaging and Supporting LGBT Caregivers through Programming. Retrieved September 29, 2019, from https://www.lgbtagingcenter.org/resources/resource.cfm?r=883

Street, D., & Tompkins, J. (2017). Is 70 the new 60? Extending American women's and men's working lives. In D. Street, Á. Léime, S. Vickerstaff, C. Krekula, & W. Loretto (Eds.), *Gender, ageing and extended working life: Cross-national perspectives* (pp. 193–216). Bristol, UK: Bristol University Press. doi:10.2307/j.ctt1t897cs.17

Sun, P., Morrow-Howell, N., Pawloski, E., & Helbach, A. (2020). *Older adults' attitudes toward virtual volunteering during the COVID-19 pandemic.* Working paper. St. Louis, MO. Washington University.

Sutin, A. R., Stephen, Y., Carretta, H., & Terracciano, A. (2015). Perceived discrimination and physical, cognitive, and emotional health in older adulthood. *American Journal of Geriatric Psychiatry, 23*, 171–179. doi:10.1016/j.jagp.2014.03.007

Svanborg, A. (2001). Biomedical perspectives on productive aging. In N. Morrow-Howell, J. Hinterlong, & M. Sherraden (Eds.), *Productive aging: Concepts and challenges* (pp. 81–101). Baltimore, MD: Johns Hopkins University Press.

Sweet, S., Pitt-Catsouphes, M., & James, J. (2017). Manager attitudes concerning flexible work arrangements: Fixed or changeable? *Community, Work & Family, 20*, 50–71. doi:10.1080/13668803.2016.1271311

Tan, E. J., Georges, A., Gabbard, S. M., Pratt, D. J., Nerino, A., Roberts, A. S., . . . Hyde, M. (2016). The 2013–2014 SeniorCorps study: Foster grandparents and senior companions. *Public Policy & Aging Report, 26*, 88–95. doi:10.1093/ppar/prw016

Tang, F. (2016). Retirement patterns and their relationship to volunteering. *Nonprofit and Voluntary Sector Quarterly, 45*, 910–930. doi:10.1177/0899764015602128

Taniguchi, H. (2012). The determinants of formal and informal volunteering: Evidence from the American Time Use Survey. *Voluntas, 23*, 920–939. doi:10.1007/s11266-011-9236-y

Town of Littleton, Massachusetts. (n.d.). Senior citizen property tax work-off program. Retrieved from http://www.littletonma.org/filestorage/ 19479/28346/20201/20312/Senior_Tax Work-off_Program.pdf

Transamerica Center for Retirement Studies. (August, 2021). Living in the COVID-19 Pandemic: The Health, Finances, and Retirement Prospects of Four Generations. Retrieved on October 26, 2021 from https://transamericacenter.org/docs/default-source/retirement-survey-of-workers/tcrs2021_sr_four-generations-living-in-a-pandemic.pdf

Turner, J., Klein, B. & Sorrentino, C. (2020) *Making volunteer work visible: Supplementary measures of work in labor force statistics.* Washington, DC: Monthly labor review. US Bureau of Labor Statistics. doi:10.21916/mlr.2020.15

U.S. Bureau of Labor Statistics (2019). Unpaid Eldercare in the United States—2017–2018 Summary. Retrieved on October 26, 2021 from https://www.bls.gov/news.release/elcare.nr0.htm

US Census Bureau. (2010–2015, 2017). Current population survey. Retrieved from https://cps.ipums.org/cps-action/variables/group

US Department of Labor, Bureau of Labor Statistics. (2016a). Household data annual averages: Employment status of the civilian noninstitutional population by age, sex, and race. Retrieved from https://www.bls.gov/cps/cpsaat03.pdf

US Department of Labor, Bureau of Labor Statistics. (2016b). Volunteering in the United States—2015. Retrieved from https://www.bls.gov/news.release/pdf/volun.pdf

Van Buren, E. (2020). Coronavirus: FDOH's retired nursing project offers support during pandemic. *The Daytona Beach News-Journal*. Retrieved from https://www.news-journalonline.com/news/20200602/coronavirus-fdohrsquos-retired-nursingproject-offers-support-during-pandemic

Wacker, R. R., & Roberto, K. A. (2013). *Community resources for older adults: Programs and services in an era of change* (4th ed.). Thousand Oaks, CA: Sage.

Wakabayashi, C., & Donato, K. M. (2006). Does caregiving increase poverty among women in later life? Evidence from the Health and Retirement Survey. *Journal of Health and Social Behavior, 47*, 258–274. doi:10.1177/002214650604700305

World Health Organization. (2007). Global Age-Friendly Cities: A Guide. Retrieved on October 26, 2021 from https://www.who.int/ageing/publications/Global_age_friendly_cities_Guide_English.pdf

Zissimopoulos, J., Goldman, D., Olshansky, S., Rother, J., & Rowe, J. (2015). Individual & social strategies to mitigate the risks & expand opportunities of an aging America. *Dædalus, 144*, 93–102. doi:10.1162/DAED_a_00333

CHAPTER 6
Eradicating Social Isolation

SUZANNE BROWN, ERIKA L. SABBATH,
ROBERT L. COSBY, MELISSA L. BESSAHA,
MICHELLE R. MUNSON, JOOYOUNG KONG,
SANDRA EDMONDS CREWE, ELIZABETH M. TRACY,
AND JAMES E. LUBBEN

Social isolation and its consequences are a critical challenge facing the social work profession in the 21st century (Lubben, 2017). Economic insecurity, immigration, increased mobility, as well as the COVID-19 pandemic have implications for social isolation among individuals and entire communities, bringing this issue to the forefront of social work practice, policy, and research. Public health experts (House, 2001; Pantell et al., 2013) posit that the association between social isolation and health is as strong as the epidemiological evidence that linked smoking and health (House, 2001; Pantell et al., 2013). Some health researchers report that social isolation is as detrimental to one's health as smoking 15 cigarettes a day (Holt-Lunstad, Smith, Baker, Harris, & Stephenson, 2015; Holt-Lunstad, Smith, & Layton, 2010).

The risks of social isolation are often studied in older adults, but isolation can also damage physical health, mental health, and well-being for young people and those in midlife. Thus, it is appropriate for social work to address the challenge of social isolation strategically across the life span (Cigna, 2018). Working in tandem with other key professions, social workers possess unique expertise to partner in working to reduce the risk and consequences of social isolation for people at all ages.

Americans may be more socially isolated now than ever before. McPherson, Smith-Lovin, and Brashears (2006) compared personal network structures from 1985 to those of 2004 and found that the number of people in the study who reported not having anyone with whom to discuss important matters nearly tripled, indicating that Americans were far less tightly connected than before. The mean network size decreased from an average of 2.94 to 2.08 people per person, and individuals reported fewer contacts with network members that existed through voluntary associations and neighborhoods (McPherson et al., 2006). In addition, approximately 10% of elementary school-age children, a developmental period typically expected to be characterized by peer friendships, report perceived social isolation (or loneliness) some or all of the time (Asher & Paquette, 2003). Developmental changes of autonomy and individuation during adolescence may tend to increase the risk of and pose special vulnerabilities for social isolation during this developmental period (Laursen & Hartl, 2013) that may lead to other challenges. Indeed, with the advent of numerous social media platforms, studies are reporting increases in cyberbullying and what pediatricians and researchers alike are calling "Facebook depression," the experience of feeling unpopular in comparison to others, which is especially problematic for children whose self-esteem is already low (O'Keeffe, Clarke-Pearson, & Council on Communications and Media, 2011).

Among both young and older adult populations, social isolation has been linked to a wide array of health problems, ranging from susceptibility to the common cold (Cohen, 2001) to the ability to survive a natural disaster (Pekovic, Seff, & Rothman, 2007; Semenza et al., 1996). A number of health researchers have demonstrated that limited social support networks are associated with increases in both morbidity and mortality (Berkman, 1986; Bosworth & Schaie, 1997; Ceria et al., 2001; Holt-Lunstad, 2017; Holt-Lunstad et al., 2010). Other scholars have reported a significant association between limited social ties and poor overall health and well-being (Cacioppo & Cacioppo, 2014; Chappell, 1991; Krause, Herzog, & Baker, 1992; Lubben, Weiler, & Chi, 1989; Stuck et al., 1999). Still others have documented a connection between social support networks and adherence to desired health practices (Pescosolido, 2011; Pescosolido, Gardner, & Lubell, 1998; Umberson & Montez, 2010). Social isolation has been associated with increased symptoms of psychological distress or loneliness, which may be risk factors for future disease and disability (Lin, Ye, & Ensel, 1999; Thoits, 1995; Wenger, Davies, Shahtahmasebi, & Scott, 1996). Chronic isolation in childhood has been associated with dropping out of school, depression, substance use, and medical problems (Asher & Paquette, 2003). Among marginalized youth and young adults, research has documented that the presence of a supportive adult, such as a mentor, natural mentor, or extended relative, can improve psychological and social outcomes (Thompson, Greeson, & Brunsink, 2016).

Isolation is also associated with an array of social problems. Stigmatization and labeling are linked to social isolation across the life span (Crewe & Guyot-Diagnone, 2016; Kranke, Floersch, Kranke, & Munson, 2011). Victor, Scambler, Bond, and Bowling (2000) note that loneliness itself is a stigma.

Race, class, and neighborhood effects have been associated with increased isolation, thereby constraining social resources (Tigges, Browne, & Green, 1998; Wang et al., 2018b). Social marginalization resulting from racism, transphobia, and heterosexism (among others) may limit access to social resources and opportunities for social connection for entire groups of individuals (Krieger, 2020). Among youth, obesity and stigma associated with weight may intensify isolation (Puhl & Lessard, 2020). Furthermore, people with disabilities are more vulnerable to discrimination, stigmatization, marginalization, and ostracization, and therefore are more likely to report higher perceived loneliness and social isolation than people without disabilities (Emerson, Fortune, Llewellyn, & Stancliffe, 2021; Hall 2009; Paul, Ayis, & Ebrahim, 2006).

The COVID-19 pandemic continues as of Spring 2021 to impact catastrophically social relationships and opportunities for social interaction (Twenge & Joiner, 2020). These effects continue to influence people differentially across the developmental spectrum, with elders and children being most affected by social-distancing protocols (Iqbal & Tayyab, 2021; Kotwal et al., 2021). The effects of COVID-related social isolation on children includes health effects; children are eating more unhealthy foods and spending more time being sedentary than they were during the prepandemic period (Teixeira et al., 2021). Among adults over the age of 22, thoughts of suicide have increased, and social support appears to moderate the influence of COVID-related isolation on thoughts of suicide (Elbogen, Lanier, Blakey, Wagner, & Tsai, 2021). Among elders with dementia, postquarantine orientation to time and day decreased significantly during COVID-19 quarantine compared to nonsocial distanced controls (Voccia, Kruczek, & Kettren, 2020). Illustrating the protective effects of social contact, Ingram, Hand, and Maciejewski (2021) found that cognitive performance improved among elders when opportunities for social contact increased.

MAINSTREAMING GENDER

Critical Feminist Perspectives on Eradicating Social Isolation
KARIN WACHTER

A confluence of intersecting social positions, life trajectories, and contextual factors shape lived experiences of social isolation, and needs for interpersonal connections, belonging, and social support. Burgeoning research provides robust evidence of the varied adverse outcomes associated with social isolation across the life span among diverse groups. When conceptualized as a symptom of broader marginalizations, social isolation offers important insights into the health and well-being of individuals, families, communities, and societies.

continued

Critical feminist perspectives (e.g., see Wahab, Anderson-Nathe, & Gringeri, 2015) compel us to understand the social, economic, and political scaffolding that allows social isolation to flourish. In contrast, framing social isolation as an individual or family issue depoliticizes the causes and effects of isolation, and negates the imperative for structural and political solutions (Breheny & Severinsen, 2018). Efforts to eradicate social isolation must therefore conceptualize and study macro-level dynamics and inequities that foster social isolation, with far-reaching implications across the social ecology.

We must strive to answer and address big-picture questions that lend themselves to macro-level solutions. What political, legal, economic, and social systems—embedded in global and local hierarchies—foster social isolation? How are manifestations of isolation shaped by intersecting gendered and racialized social locations, access to economic and social resources, and power? Whose isolation is worthy of study and intervention? Whose disconnections matter?

In addition to broadening our scope of study and levels of intervention, our work must also go deep to elucidate and honor complex processes and nuanced lived experiences. The internalized and less visible effects of prolonged social isolation have profound implications for understanding and relating to oneself, as well as to others and the broader environment. Indeed, as many have queried from time immemorial, how do we know who we are if not through meaningful and authentic connections and interactions? Although at its core, the study of social isolation seeks to understand systemic and sustained disconnections—from family, peers, community, nature, resources, and opportunities—with explicit and subtle implications for well-being, we must also strive to build knowledge of the ways in which connections flourish.

A challenge for social work is envisioning research, policy, and practice that mitigate systemic disconnections in people's lives and strengthen social connectedness. For example, research has highlighted the isolating effects of war and forced migration that systematically disconnect women from vital social support networks and interdependent ways of life (Wachter & Gulbas, 2018). Women resettling as refugees from central African contexts to the United States, for example, face distinctly separate and closed-off ways of life, and may be alone for the first time. Over time, women may learn to "stand alone" but not without internal and relational consequences. Yet, mainstream American values of self-reliance and independence render the isolation women experience invisible, and US refugee resettlement policy and practice overlook, and thereby exacerbate, gendered and contextual needs for social connectedness and support (Wachter & Gulbas, 2018). This is just one example of the importance of centering lived experiences of disconnection and social isolation in examining and informing social policies.

The growing shift from closed to open domestic violence shelters in the US context offers another poignant example. Long-standing policies

continued

of domestic violence shelters have isolated survivors from their support networks (Goodman et al., 2020). Open shelters have begun to pivot from these policies by revealing their locations and allowing visitors. These shelters report important shifts, including improved relationships between shelter residents and advocates, improved access to services, enhanced community life in the shelters, deepened relationships between survivors and their support networks (i.e., family and friends), and decreased shame (Goodman et al., 2020). Interventions that seek to strengthen social connections challenge us to situate and challenge the supremacy of formal services within a broader spectrum of relational needs.

Critical feminist approaches to social work research and practice boldly envision interventions that promote meaningful connections at all levels of the social ecology, grounded in intersectional and antiracist perspectives. Eradicating social isolation demands forging strong relationships with communities and collaborative efforts across disciplines, social services, and government agencies (e.g., transportation, city planning, healthcare) to mitigate the structural forces that sow seeds of marginalization and disconnection. It requires that we reconsider policies and practices at macro, mezzo, and micro levels, incorporating global as well as local perspectives, as illustrated in the previous examples. Political action, resources, and public support are necessary to challenge the institutions that perpetuate and normalize social isolation (Breheny & Severinsen, 2018), such as the US prison system (and state-sanctioned policies of solitary confinement); healthcare, housing, and education systems; immigration policies; and myriad social, economic, and racial injustices.

As social work researchers and practitioners, it is vital that we center social connections in all aspects of our work and interpersonal lives as a means of resisting and healing disconnections fostered by entrenched hierarchies. This work begins by envisioning, designing, and engaging in research and practice that intentionally promote and strengthen authentic, meaningful, and equitable connections within our direct spheres of influence and beyond.

References

Breheny, M., & Severinsen, C. (2018). Is social isolation a public health issue? A media analysis in Aotearoa/New Zealand. *Critical Public Health, 28,* 484–493. doi:10.1080/09581596.2017.1400162

Goodman, L. A., Epstein, D., Hailes, H. P., Slocum, A., Wolff, J., Coyne, K., & McCraney, A. (2020). From isolation to connection: The practices and promise of open domestic violence shelters. *Journal of Interpersonal Violence.* doi:10.1177/0886260520969233

Wachter, K., & Gulbas, L. (2018). Social support under siege: An analysis of forced migration among women from the Democratic Republic of the Congo. *Social Science and Medicine, 208,* 107–116. doi:10.1016/j.socscimed.2018.04.056

Wahab, S., Anderson-Nathe, B., & Gringeri, C. (Eds.). (2015). *Feminisms in social work research.* New York, NY: Routledge.

EVIDENCE INDICATES THAT SOCIAL ISOLATION CAN BE REDUCED

As a result of the overwhelming body of evidence, a special committee at the National Institutes of Health (National Research Council, 2001) issued a report in 2001 that identifies a domain of behavioral and social sciences research questions; their resolution could lead to major improvements in the health of the US population. The National Research Council report lists *personal ties* as one of the top-10 priority areas for research investment that could lead to major health improvements. It summarizes a growing body of epidemiological findings that link social relationships with mental and physical health outcomes, including mortality. Furthermore, the report explores how disruption of personal ties, loneliness, and conflictual interactions produce stress, and discusses how supportive social ties are vital sources of emotional well-being.

Since the publication of the National Research Council (2001) report, evidence regarding the impact of social isolation on various measures of morbidity and mortality has grown even stronger (Berkman, 2009; Eng, Rimm, Fitzmaurice, & Kawachi, 2002; Giles, Glonek, Luszcz, & Andres, 2005; Holt-Lunstad et al., 2010; Laugesen et al., 2018; Lubben et al., 2006; Pantell et al., 2013; Schnittger, Wherton, Prendergast, & Lawlor, 2012; Zhang, Norris, Gregg, & Beckles, 2007). Similarly, researchers have further documented the negative consequences of social isolation on mental health (Adams, Sanders, & Auth, 2004; Alspach, 2013; Esgalhado, Reis, Pereira, & Afonso, 2010; Loades et al., 2020). There has also been increased evidence of the impact of social isolation on self-reported health and well-being (Chan, Malhotra, Malhotra, & Ostbye, 2011; Kimura, Yamazaki, Haga, & Yasumura, 2013; McHugh & Lawlor, 2012; Schnittger et al., 2012; Thompson, Rodebaugh, Bessaha, & Sabbath, 2020; Wang, Mann, Lloyd-Evans, Ma, & Johnson, 2018a).

Increasingly, interventions are being developed and tested to determine their effectiveness in reducing isolation and loneliness for a broad range of populations, including parents and caregivers, individuals with mental illness, people with disabilities, those with chronic illnesses, military members, and refugees and immigrants (Bessaha et al., 2020). For example, Barlott, Adams, Díaz, & Molina (2015) used an SMS text-messaging intervention for caregivers of individuals with disabilities and found that the intervention broadened caregivers' social support networks and made them feel less alone. Similarly, for those with chronic illnesses, intervention programs containing a group support component were effective at reducing loneliness among women with breast cancer (Cleary & Stanton, 2015; Fukui, Koike, Ooba, & Uchitomi, 2003; Tabrizi, Radfar, & Taei, 2016). The use of group interventions may help individuals increase their number of social contacts, thereby increasing the size of their social networks, increasing their sense of belonging, and even mediating stress responses. Regardless of the mechanisms through which interventions are effective, a growing body of evidence supports the effectiveness of interventions in reducing isolation and loneliness for many groups across the life span (Brown & Munson, 2020).

Social Isolation in Children and Youth

Attachment and social functioning formed early in life have profound impacts on the ways individuals interface with the social world throughout their lives, and inform one's ability to form and maintain strong relationships (Bowlby, 1969). Research suggests that a sensitive period during which social connections benefit health and well-being is infancy and early childhood (Berkman, 2009). Furthermore, more recent research has shown that attachments throughout the life cycle can influence health and well-being (Chopik, Edelstein, & Grimm, 2019). For example, strong social support networks and close relationships are particularly important to mental health and the prevention of behavioral health problems throughout the life span (McPherson et al., 2014).

Social connections can also help parents cope with stress and influence parent–child relationships, and have direct and indirect effects on child development (Goosby, Bellatorre, Walsemann, & Cheadle, 2013; Thompson et al., 2020). Caregivers who know people on whom they can rely for child-care advice and assistance have been found to be more sensitive to their infant's needs and are able to have higher quality interactions with their infants. Their infants, in turn, are less avoidant of interactions (Green, Furrer, & McAllister, 2007). Research on parenting during the COVID-19 pandemic found that parents with greater social support reported having more positive experiences with their children than parents with less social support (Gambin et al., 2020). In addition, support for parenting increases parental self-regulation, with resultant benefits to child self-regulation (Sanders, Turner, & Metzler, 2019).

In particular, social isolation has been associated with increased risk of depressive symptoms, suicide attempts, and low self-esteem in young people (Endo et al., 2017; Hall-Lande, Eisenberg, Christenson, & Neumark-Sztainer, 2007). In fact, the Centers for Disease Control and Prevention has focused on increasing "connectedness" among youth as an orienting framework because of its fundamental understanding about the importance of social relationships on overall health and well-being, including decreasing suicide (Whitlock, Wyman, & Moore, 2014). Social isolation in younger people may also threaten the safety and well-being of others when negative emotions are externalized. This has been documented in the cases of many adolescent mass murderers who were described retrospectively as socially isolated or ostracized from peers (Levin & Madfis, 2009).

In a large national child development study in the United Kingdom, researchers found that social isolation in childhood was associated with greater levels of C-reactive protein (an indicator of coronary heart disease) in midlife (Lacey, Jumari, & Bartley, 2014). Furthermore, a longitudinal cohort study monitoring children over 20 years, found that social isolation experienced during childhood and adolescence led to significantly poorer health outcomes in adulthood (Caspi, Harrington, Moffitt, Milne, & Poulton, 2006). Health consequences of loneliness in the early life course is also associated with experiencing adult depression, metabolic risk factors related to cardiovascular disease, and poor self-rated health. Lonely adolescent females are most vulnerable to being overweight or obese in adulthood—a risk for cardiovascular disease (Goosby et al., 2013). There are many groups of children who are at heightened risk for social isolation during critical periods of their development. Overweight adolescents, for example, are more likely to be isolated socially and on the periphery of social networks (Strauss & Pollack, 2003). Research has documented the degree to which youth with an autism spectrum disorder are vulnerable both to social isolation and to bullying (Bauminger, Shulman, & Agam, 2003; Rowley et al., 2012). Research on the friendship patterns of children with autism spectrum disorders also reveals the intersection of race, disability, and grade; one study of friendship patterns among children with autism spectrum disorder found that children who were Black and Latino received the fewest friendship nominations; also, Latino children in upper grades were at the greatest risk for social isolation (Azad, Locke, Kasari, & Mandell, 2017).

The estimated 5.5 million children and adolescents raised by undocumented immigrants are at increased risk of social isolation because fear of detainment, and socioeconomic and environmental barriers lead families not to take advantage of social services (Hurtado-de-Mendoza, Gonzales, Serrano, & Kaltman, 2014; Simmons, Menjívar, & Valdez, 2020), and sometimes they do not encourage or allow their children to be involved with after-school or community activities (Chavez, Lopez, Englebrecht, & Viramontez Anguiano, 2012). US immigration policies have long resulted in the separation of families (Ojeda, Magana, Burgos, & Vargas-Ojeda, 2020), and the recent policies of the Trump administration, which are focused on separating migrant children from their families at the border, has only intensified these concerns (Barajas-Gonzalez, Ayon, & Torres, 2018). These policies have often led to negative outcomes for citizen children and deported parents, such as less access to resources, mental health difficulties, and, among parents, the frustration of not being able to provide love and support for their children (i.e., Gulbas & Zayas, 2017; Gulbas et al., 2016; Ojeda et al., 2020).

Regarding social isolation, in one Canadian study, 1 in 10 immigrant children were socially isolated (Oxman-Martinez et al., 2012), and this social isolation combined with ethnic discrimination was associated with children's self-esteem, sense of academic competence, and actual academic performance. Many immigrant parents are not aware that their US-born children are eligible for benefits (Yoshikawa & Kalil, 2011). The result is that the one in five American children who have a foreign-born parent have restricted access to contexts that support development: child care, preschool, school, work, and so on (Suarez-Orozco, Yoshikawa, Teranishi, & Suarez-Orozco, 2011). Another group of children and youth at risk of social isolation resulting from discrimination and social exclusion are lesbian, gay, bisexual, and transgender (LGBT) youth. Johnson and Amella (2014) identified the following dimensions of social isolation common among LGBT youth: emotional isolation, cognitive isolation, concealment of identity, and recognition of self as different. Transgender youth may be particularly isolated from family support because of transphobic attitudes within social networks that lead to less social support availability (Mizock & Lewis, 2008).

Young people who are considered "marginalized" and who are involved in the child welfare system are also at tremendous risk for high levels of social isolation and disconnection (Sapiro & Ward, 2020), which can be a result of the realities of removal from home and experiences of high levels of transience during their child and adolescent years. Initial loss, complicated by repeated losses that can cause trauma and challenges with emotion regulation, can create challenges for these young people in forming and sustaining healthy relationships (Cummings & Cicchetti, 1990).

Social Isolation in Midlife

Although much public attention has focused on the risks of social isolation in young people and in older adults, a growing body of evidence suggests that midlife (between 18 years and 65 years) can be a period of profound isolation and loneliness (Nersesian et al., 2018). Midlife shifts in family structure, roles, and responsibilities can cut off relationships that previously provided companionship and support (Gray, Azizoddin, & Neresian, 2020). Among working adults, workplace exposures, experiences, and organizational structures may lead to or may exacerbate social isolation (Scott, 2018). Experiences of isolation in midlife may be heightened among those who are part of racial and ethnic minority groups, and those who are immigrants (Lee, Hong, Zhou, & Robles, 2020; Taylor, Taylor, Nyguyen, & Chatters, 2020). These trends have likely been amplified during the physical isolation imposed by the COVID-19 pandemic (Usher, Bhullar, & Jackson, 2020). Furthermore, midlife may be a crucial etiologic period for the development of social isolation and its health consequences in older adults (Berkman, 2009; Morris, 2019).

Midlife may also be a sensitive period for interventions that reduce loneliness and its consequences. A recent review found that several interventions, particularly those involving technology and support groups, reduced loneliness significantly (Bessaha et al., 2020). Approximately 87% of the 59 studies reviewed included a group component in the intervention design, such as online support, individual peer mentoring, and group psychosocial support, proposing that group involvement may be an important strategy in reducing loneliness in midlife. Moreover, interventions involving technology that target loneliness (e.g., online adaptation of a friendship enrichment program, virtual self-help group) may also reduce loneliness during midlife (Bessaha et al., 2020).

In addition, a large, recent national online survey of more than 20,000 American adults 18 years and older found generational differences in perceived feelings of loneliness (Cigna, 2018). Findings from the survey revealed that Generation Z (adults ages 18-22) and Millennials (adults ages 23–37 years) were lonelier and reported poorer health than older generations. Social media use alone was not a predictor of loneliness, and students reported higher loneliness scores than retirees. The survey results highlight certain traits that less lonely individuals tend to have frequent, meaningful in-person interactions; report good overall physical and mental health; are employed; and have a balance of daily activities (Cigna, 2018). Interestingly, there was no major difference between men and women or among races when examining average reported loneliness scores (Cigna, 2018). Gender differences in loneliness among the general population are difficult to pin down. In a few studies, males were more likely than females to report lower perceived loneliness (Arber & Ginn, 1994; Koenig & Abrams, 1999; Nicolaisen & Thorsen, 2014; Pinquart & Sörensen, 2001); yet other studies found opposite results (Qualter & Munn, 2002; Vanhalst et al., 2012) or no differences (Cacioppo, Hawkley, & Thisted, 2010). These findings suggest that loneliness is likely to be experienced at some period across the life span and by individuals of all genders.

Social Isolation in Older Adults

Social isolation among older adults is becoming increasingly recognized as a critical issue worthy of more attention. The American Association of Retired Persons (AARP) Foundation (2016) reported that social isolation is a growing epidemic in America, affecting more than 8 million older adults. The National Academies of Sciences, Engineering and Medicine (2020) recently published a consensus study report regarding social isolation and loneliness among older adults.

Social isolation is a significant risk factor for cognitive impairment and dementia (Crooks, Lubben, Petitti, Little, & Chiu, 2008; Ertel, Glymour, & Berkman, 2008; Maki et al., 2012; Seeman, Lusignolo, Albert, & Berkman, 2001). Acierno et al. (2010) found that low social support increased the likelihood of elder mistreatment, most often resulting from neglect. In addition to physical, emotional, or mental abuse, socially isolated older adults are also highly vulnerable to financial scams and manipulation. Other types of mistreatment linked to social isolation and dementia include physical, emotional, and financial abuse, and financial exploitation. The most common form of elder mistreatment is financial exploitation, but it is the least studied, according to Peterson et al. (2014). The National Council on Aging (2021) along with the National Center on Elder Abuse (2020) estimate financial loss resulting from social isolation of older adults, including those with dementia such as Alzheimer's disease, ranges from $2.8 billion to $36.5 billion annually (National Center on Elder Abuse, 2020). Human costs of such abuse carry financial costs of approximately $12 million annually (Dong & Simon, 2011).

Two specific isolating factors tied to the increasing risk of elder mistreatment are loss of friends and perceived social alienation from the community (Von Heydrich, Schiamberg, & Chee, 2012). For some vulnerable older adults, living with a caregiver, particularly with a spouse, is also associated with an increased risk of abuse (Beach et al. 2005; Beach, Schulz, Castle, & Rosen, 2010; Cooney, Howard, & Lawlor, 2006; DeLiema & Conrad, 2017; Paveza et al., 1992). This suggests that social alienation may create vulnerability to abuse within isolated dyads. Without a larger support structure, older adults are at increased risk for being either the victim or the potential perpetrator of mistreatment.

An AARP report synthesized research findings about social isolation in older populations (AARP Foundation, 2012). The 2012 report identified key risk factors for social isolation: physical or functional impairments, particularly for older adults who lack instrumental support (e.g., transportation); low socioeconomic status; and poor mental health status (e.g., depression, cognitive impairments). Since this report, these factors remain areas of concern. One recommendation from the report led to stimulating intervention research and the development of the AARP campaign Connect2Affect in 2016. In this campaign, AARP identified best practices from across the globe designed to reduce social isolation. One such example showcased an easy-to-use tandem telephone and simple screen computer that works with an app similar to Zoom. The device is very intuitive and easy to use by older adults. The telephone/computer app provides an inexpensive way for families to stay in touch with older family members without smartphones. Many older adults thought highly of the devices because they could connect with grandchildren and other family members, also creating ways to have telehealth visits, receive reminders, and so on.

More recently, an AARP Foundation–funded report by Smith, Steinman, and Casey (2020) indicated what has been known for some time: there is a "complex interconnectedness" when speaking about social isolation, loneliness, and depression, particularly with older adults. What is new is that the complexities of the COVID-19 pandemic have created what Smith et al. (2020) refer to as a paradox in public health whereby older adults are being separated at hospitals, nursing homes, and assisted living homes at a time when they are most in need of attention, social interaction, and connectedness.

The COVID-19 pandemic in 2020 and 2021 has affected older adults and communities of color disproportionately, particularly Black and Brown persons. The result has been uncovering more social isolation in addition to disparities and inequities across communities in housing, income, and health disparities. Trying to identify workable solutions to address these challenges has created a watershed period for generating ideas for connecting with older adults who otherwise have been dying from COVID-19-related illnesses, but also dying from emotional loss of social connectedness and so on (Smith, Steinman, & Casey, 2020). For example, one potential solution is being used in Washington, DC. A historic safety net, faith-based nonprofit group, the Leadership Council for Healthy Communities, has collaborated and partnered with several groups, including the Black Coalition Against COVID-19, to address some of the health inequalities and to access concerns by launching a virtual health ministry to demonstrate how healthcare can be provided to older adults who may be shut in and at risk for social isolation and COVID-19. This outreach was being done by the Leadership Council for Healthy Communities to help educate, promote, and inspire healthy behaviors. The pilot project leaders have partnered with four churches in Washington, DC—in the northwest, northeast, and southeast—and with the Howard University School of Social Work (a historic Black college/university) to identify older adults at risk for social isolation at a time when government agencies were completely closed and then opened incrementally. In addition to checking for social isolation, representatives identify other community persons in need. The group of stakeholders is expanding as health providers, social workers, and other community groups and businesses have been asked to contribute. One key aspect of reducing or eliminating social isolation is identifying appropriate sources of social support.

Historical Progress of Research on Social Isolation

Research on social isolation has made remarkable progress since the seminal article by Berkman and Syme (1979) in the *American Journal of Epidemiology*. Their research examined the connection between social networks and mortality among a general adult population. They constructed the Berkman–Syme Social Network Index (SNI) for this research by summing up whether a respondent was (a) married, (b) belonged to a church or temple, (c) participated in clubs or organized groups, or (d) had social contact with family or friends. Remarkably, this relatively simple SNI measure correlated significantly with mortality rates in this 9-year follow-up epidemiological study.

Soon thereafter, health researchers across the board scrambled to replicate these results using various proxies for social networks. Some of the selected proxies (e.g., marital status and living alone) failed to capture important nuances of social connections, so health researchers spent the 1980s and 1990s refining measures for social networks and supports. The central goal of this process was to determine which aspects of an individual's social connections should be measured, and which dimensions or perceptions of those relationships are particularly relevant for predicting subsequent morbidity and mortality. Identifying ways of minimizing or eradicating social isolation, particularly for older adults, remain important goals and will become more important as more baby boomers reach retirement age in the coming years.

One distinction elucidated by recent research is related to identifying the types and sources of social support. *Primary social groups* (e.g., family, friends, and neighbors) are the foundation of social ties across the life span, particularly in youth and old age. Family is generally considered the most central primary group to which an individual belongs. However, close or intimate friends can also be as vital as family ties, especially when family relations are geographically unavailable, strained, or deficient for other reasons. Alternative family arrangements and the formation of unmarried couples—especially as social norms and practices of family formation change—impart new complexity to quantifying social connections. *Secondary social groups* include membership organizations such as recreational or culture clubs, professional societies, and various political and religious organizations. The workplace is an important forum for social relationships, and for individuals who are otherwise isolated, it can serve as a regular form of social contact and connection. There is evidence that those who maintain contact with colleagues from their workplace after retirement are less depressed (Shiba, Kondo, Kondo, & Kawachi, 2017).

The distinction between primary and secondary social groups is relevant to understand major approaches to measuring social isolation. For example, many social researchers tend to examine social networks through a lens that measures participation in social activities and organizations, whereas clinical researchers have largely focused on primary social groups. The SNI (Berkman & Syme, 1979; Pantell et al., 2013), which remains a common instrument in public health research, is a classic example of a measure that emphasizes secondary social groups. The Lubben Social Network Scale (Lubben, 1988; Lubben & Gironda, 2003; Lubben et al., 2006; Rubenstein, Lubben, & Mintzer, 1994) is an example of a measure of social isolation that focuses on primary group membership, so it has particularly found favor with social workers, health practitioners, and clinical researchers.

Although there are differences in focus, researchers can now draw from a wide array of social network measures with excellent psychometric properties

(Berkman, Kawachi, & Glymour, 2014). A number of sociometric surveys are used to study social isolation in children by mapping peer interactions as well as peer acceptance in social settings, such as in the classroom. There is also a growing body of social network analysis techniques to study the composition, functioning, and structure of social networks (Rice & Yoshioka-Maxwell, 2015; Rice et al., 2018; Tracy & Brown, 2011; Tracy & Whittaker, 2015). Remarkably, the connection between social isolation and health remains quite consistent despite the lack of consistency in measuring both social support networks and health outcomes. Such diversity of studies adds significance to the convergence of their findings.

Within the past 5 years scholars have produced a wealth of research examining social isolation and interventions to reduce isolation or increase social support across the life span, and with a range of populations. Consistent with social work's person-in-environment perspective, social work scholars in this area are considering factors that span micro, mezzo, and macro levels in research on social isolation, loneliness, and social support. For example, Storer, McCleary, Pepin, & Stallings (2020) identified the usefulness of isolation as a survival strategy for marginalized youth, keeping them safe from bullying and violence. Azhar, Gandham, Vaudrey, Oruganti, & Samuel (2020) examined the role of stigma, disease, and isolation among women with HIV in India, and Lee et al. (2020) identified the importance of social support in building resilience among Latinx immigrants to the United States. Recent research has begun to define more specifically the common constructs used in research on social isolation and refine the distinctions between them. For example, Taylor (2020) distinguished between social isolation (the absence of tangible network connections) and loneliness (the feeling of social isolation), and examined the relationship between the two. Similarly, Nguyen, Taylor, Taylor, and Chatters (2020) considered the relationship between objective social isolation and the subjective experience of isolation among Black adults with psychiatric problems.

Research Efforts to Overcome Social Isolation

House (2001) concluded that social isolation kills, but how and why it does damage remained very much unknown. The developmental period in which isolation may affect later disease risk disproportionately was also very much unknown. In addition, the reversibility of social isolation's health effects, if isolation is reduced successfully, remained unidentified (House, 2001). Testing interventions to *reduce* loneliness and isolation, not just identify its negative effects, is a key component of the charge of the Grand Challenges.

Since 2001, researchers have made progress in understanding these basic questions. Nicholson (2012) reported a systematic review of 70 studies that examined the negative impact of isolation on a wide array of outcome measures. He concluded that social isolation is an important but underassessed condition in and of itself, as well as a risk factor for other physical and mental health conditions.

Berkman et al. (Berkman, Glass, Brissette, & Seeman, 2000; Berkman et al., 2014) proposed four key pathways to explain apparent links between social isolation and health: (a) provision of social support, (b) social influence, (c) social engagement and attachment, and (d) access to resources. For example, social networks may provide essential support needed during times of illness, thereby contributing to better adaptation and quicker recovery time. Social ties can be instrumental in adherence to good health practices and the cessation of bad ones (Umberson & Montez, 2010). The role of social networks in helping persons with substance use disorders maintain sobriety has been well documented (Brown, Tracy, Jun, Park, & Min, 2015; Stone, Jason, Light, & Stevens, 2016). Strong social bonds may offer a stress-buffering effect that reduces the susceptibility of an individual to stress-related illnesses (Cassel, 1976; Cobb, 1976; Krause et al., 1992; Thoits, 1995). Social connections might also provide improved access to important resources such as relevant health knowledge, timely care, or transportation to and from healthcare appointments. Relatively recent research explored possible biological effects of social ties on human physiology, perhaps by stimulating the immune system to ward off illnesses more effectively (Seeman, Singer, Ryff, Dienberg Love, & Levy-Storms, 2002). There is also evidence from neuroimaging studies that social exclusion "hurts" in a similar way in the brain as physical pain (Eisenberger, 2012; Eisenberger, Lieberman, & Williams, 2003).

Recently, systematic reviews of social isolation and loneliness interventions across the life span have shown potential for reducing isolation and loneliness among participants. These intervention studies have identified positive results for children and youth, midlife adults, older adults, refugees, those with chronic illnesses, individuals with disabilities, LGBT elders, and individuals with mental illness (Barlott et al., 2015; Bessaha et al., 2020; Cleary & Stanton, 2015; Fukui et al., 2003; Perone, Ingersoll-Dayton, & Watkins-Dukhie, 2020; Tabrizi et al., 2016). Although there is increasing evidence to support the effectiveness of interventions to reduce isolation and loneliness across the life span, evidence about whether that reduction precipitates downstream health and well-being outcomes is limited. Future research should focus on the longitudinal effects of interventions to reduce isolation and loneliness to determine their ability to influence a range of variables across the life course, such as physical health, mental health, quality of life, morbidity, and mortality.

Social Isolation in Practice Settings

Although extensive evidence links social ties to health and well-being, this body of research is only beginning to change social work practice (Gironda & Lubben, 2002). In healthcare settings, minimal attention has historically been given to social health status compared to that given to other attributes people present when seeking care. Specifically, the healthcare system shows much more regard for the physical and mental health dimensions of patients while giving only minor attention to the social health dimensions of patients. During the COVID-19 pandemic, that dynamic was amplified by public health concerns with allowing ill and dying patients to be surrounded by loved ones (Andrist, Clarke, & Harding, 2020). However, watching patients die without their loved ones nearby also highlighted the extent to which healthcare staff experienced distress and moral injury when asked to prioritize patients' physical health over their social health (Wakam, Montgomery, Biesterveld, & Brown, 2020). In addition, the pandemic highlighted the high level of baseline social isolation experienced by older adults (Berg-Weger & Morley, 2020).

Among Organization for Economic Co-operation and Development countries, social expenditures exceed health expenditure by a ratio of 2:1; however, it is only 0.8:1 in the United States, indicating that health spending is crowding out social and educational spending (Kaplan, 2013; Sherradan et al., 2015). This marginal concern for social health is demonstrated in many healthcare encounters. For example, geriatric assessment has been called the "heart and soul" of geriatric practice (Solomon, 2000, p. ix). However, geriatric assessment instruments seldom deal with social health matters, suggesting they are not perceived to be central to geriatric practice. Although healthcare providers have made great strides in getting patients to understand that their mental health is as important as their physical health, health professionals have yet to devote sufficient attention to getting people to value the importance of their social health.

Therefore, indicators of a person's social health should be a part of geriatric assessment protocols along with mental and physical health markers (Lubben & Gironda, 2003; Pantell et al., 2013). In an era that stresses community-based delivery of healthcare, members of a person's social support network are often more responsible for successful execution of treatment plans than members of the formal healthcare team. For isolated older adults, social supports often end up being the in-home care managers who monitor compliance with treatment regimens and provide early detection of new problems that require intervention. Accordingly, in-depth quality assistance from close supportive relationships should be facilitated and encouraged throughout the healthcare process.

Increased sensitivity to the importance of social support networks might help identify those individuals in need of a more comprehensive assessment and intervention from a social worker or other health or mental healthcare practitioner (Hagan, 2020). As community health nurses are being urged to screen home health clients and assisted living residents for social isolation (Tremethick, 2001), other practitioners should be encouraged to adopt such practice protocols similarly for both screening and intervention. A practitioner's focus on the importance of social connections can also increase the patient's or client's attention to his or her own social health. Similarly, those working with families can assess the extent to which the family has supports and resources for parenting and other related family issues.

MEANINGFUL AND MEASURABLE PROGRESS TO ADDRESS SOCIAL ISOLATION CAN BE MADE IN THE NEXT DECADE

The coming decade provides an opportunity to develop and test specific interventions that rebuild the fabric of frayed social connections in both older adults and younger people. With a Grand Challenge focus on social isolation, social workers could better consolidate the existing knowledge about social isolation and initiate a paradigm shift in the practice community. The possibilities of such a concerted effort are suggested in a website launched by the AARP that provides practical hints regarding what can be done to address social isolation (AARP Foundation, 2012). Another approach for aging populations can be found in the World Health Organization Age-Friendly Cities and Communities movement (World Health Organization, 2018). In the United States, the Village models of age-friendly communities attempt to fabricate new social ties to replace those lost or frayed among older adults wishing to remain in their long-term communities as they age (Scharlach, Davitt, Lehning, Greenfield, & Graham, 2014).

Another example is a community-based intervention called Eliciting Change in At-Risk Elders (or ECARE), which is aimed at building resilience in response to extreme stressors and lowering the risk of elder abuse. This program assists suspected victims of elder abuse and self-neglect with building connections with family members and support services in their communities (Mariam, McClure, Robinson, & Yang, 2015). In an evaluation of the program, results showed that risk factors of elder abuse, including isolation, decreased over the course of the intervention.

Further examples of efforts to modify social work practice can be gleaned from an open-access social isolation module developed by the Institute on Aging at Boston College (2017) in conjunction with the Hartford Center of

Excellence at the Boston College School of Social Work. This online module includes YouTube videos and links to other references that inform both lay- and professional people about the importance of addressing social isolation, and it offers suggestions for interventions. The online module has been used by local and national health and social agencies to train their staff, and it is available to the general public.

Examples of innovative approaches to address isolation among younger populations also exist. Social isolation in children and youth differs from that in adults because children and youth have certain mandates for social participation—namely, enrollment in educational programs that offer some degree of social inclusion. Young people differ from adults in terms of how and where they develop social connections (Morgan, 2010). Strong school connectedness has been shown to reduce the risk of depressive symptoms, suicide attempts, and low self-esteem among youth (Hall-Lande et al., 2007). Building connections to enable all students to feel less isolated through school-based universal support programs has also been proposed as one way to address bullying in school (Newman, Holden, & Delville, 2005). Furthermore, youth mentoring, both formal and informal, is an approach that is increasingly illustrating efficacy among varying groups of youth in improving health outcomes and psychosocial outcomes (Ahrens, DuBois, Richardson, Fan, & Lozano, 2008; Keller, Perry, & Spencer, 2020; Munson & McMillen, 2009; Thompson et al., 2016).

Researchers have also demonstrated a link between childhood trauma and health effects of social isolation in later life. In a study that examined whether perceived social isolation moderates the relationship between early trauma and pulse pressure (a marker for cardiovascular health), it was found that those with higher levels of perceived social isolation showed a significant positive association between childhood trauma and pulse pressure (Norman, Hawkley, Ball, Berntson, & Cacioppo, 2013). Accordingly, more attention is required to assess for social isolation among survivors of child abuse and neglect. Violence, including bullying among children and youth, also has a social isolation component. Murthy and Murthy (2020), in speaking about loneliness (and related social isolation), stated that Cacioppo and Cacioppo (2018), Anderson and Thayer (2018), and others have shown that loneliness can be a marker in our genetic makeup related to how we behave when we feel unconnected at a very deep level. This may say a great deal about how we interact with each other in social connectedness as humans. We understand only a small amount of what is actually going on inside of us with loneliness and social isolation, but deep underneath, where we cannot see, at the cellular, phylogenetic level there is much more to understand. Additional research has begun to break down some of this genetic-level understanding (Romano et al., 2013). Stein et al. (2018) and Hanson and

Gluckman (2015) have shown that long-term psychopathology trajectories for telomere (the end of the DNA strand) length has shown that environmental stresses disrupt telomere-length homeostasis. This shortening takes place every time cells divide, and the blueprint for future cell division or biological embedding affect these genetic markers or the related protein development. Together, this may show physical signs of social isolation creating stress on the body. Shrira (2020), Vaiserman and Koliada (2017), and others indicate that telomeres are biomarkers of cellular aging. Telomeres may hold valuable information, based on their shortening in length, about premature cellular aging for disadvantaged groups from childhood to older adulthood resulting from trauma such as posttraumatic stress disorder (Kang et al., 2020). The decreasing length of our telomeres may hold information about why social isolation can be so devastating for some persons. Furthermore, additional research may show links to our historical ability to overcome trauma and those cellular markers in our physical bodies. These biological and gene-related markers may be passed down physically in our psyche for generations. This neuropsychiatric research may provide some evidence to researchers looking at reasons for great variance in life expectancy among racial and ethnic groups, based in part on disadvantaged group experiences, such as discrimination and racial bias. Some epigenomic research points to the possibility that the reaction to trauma (neuropsychiatric responses) from childhood or trauma associated with events decades ago may be triggered by modern-day events. Together, this multidisciplinary research in biological neuroscience linked with social work, and behavioral and other physical sciences can direct efforts to understand more fully the responses to past epigenomic markers of prior generations. Social workers see the impact of loneliness and social isolation in present-day triggered events, in persons across the life span from children through older adults. Perhaps the case could be made that psychic pain identified in humans of all ages may have been further triggered by events and survival passed down in generations, such as from the Holocaust, or slavery in the United States. Whether with ancestors or with individual pain associated with social isolation in present-day distancing, the results point to negative outcomes that must be explored further, and better hypotheses and solutions to combating social isolation offered.

The Centers for Disease Control and Prevention launched a program to reduce youth violence that includes a component that attempts to build positive relationships between youths and adults and peers (David-Ferdon & Simon, 2012). Peer support is also increasingly being integrated into psychosocial interventions for youths who are often socially marginalized, such as youths with serious mental health challenges (Gopalan, Lee, Harris, Acri, & Munson, 2017) and those aging out of foster care (Geenen et al., 2013).

MEETING THE CHALLENGE OF SOCIAL ISOLATION WILL REQUIRE INTERDISCIPLINARY AND CROSS-SECTOR COLLABORATION

The approach to solve social isolation needs to be more inclusive and incorporate diverse populations. Studies of social isolation tend to focus on older populations, but social isolation is an important issue for all ages. The impact of "otherness" and stigma are important considerations when addressing social isolation. In addition, researchers should pay more attention to socially marginalized groups, especially those exposed to generational poverty. This will require an interdisciplinary, multisystem approach that considers social isolation not only at the individual level, but also at the familial, community, and societal levels. For example, enhancing social inclusion for older adults has to be a part of creating aging-friendly community environments, which will provide more sustainable and comprehensive solutions for the population (Scharlach et al., 2014).

Similarly, there will need to be more interdisciplinary cooperation to address the complexity of social isolation. Much of the scholarship to date has been conducted in disciplinary silos, but cross-sector and interdisciplinary approaches are crucial for moving to the next level of understanding. A preliminary taxonomy of these disciplinary silos includes (a) epidemiologists focused on identifying at-risk populations and subpopulations, (b) health service researchers focused on "controlling for" social isolation in their models rather than seeking to understand the phenomena, (c) biologists and neuroscientists examining biological pathways that account for the link between isolation and health consequences, and (d) clinical researchers focused on developing and testing interventions with limited capacity to digest all of the new information from the other disciplinary silos. Adopting social isolation as a Grand Challenge will motivate and empower social workers to take the lead on this enterprise and to break down these disciplinary barriers to improve the flow of knowledge and innovation across groups.

The Role of Social Work

Social work is well positioned for interdisciplinary research on social isolation. Most schools of social work are housed at universities with easy access to other disciplines and professions. Close proximity and shared goals related to reducing social isolation increase the potential for cross-disciplinary collaboration. Social work is poised to lead on scholarship related to social isolation, given the profession's long-standing grounding in community-based practice orientations, and research and scholarship developed in partnership with families and communities. Social workers have a long history of doing community-based and person-centered research. These "client"-centered research frameworks have now become mandatory in clinical effectiveness research funded by the Patient-Centered Outcomes Research Institute through the Patient Protection and Affordable Care Act of 2010. Specifically, key users of study information (e.g., patients, caregivers, clinicians, community members, policymakers) are now expected to be active members of the research "team" (Selby, Beal, & Frank, 2012), putting social workers in a pivotal role of bringing key stakeholders to the table.

Although this may be a new approach for some disciplines, social work researchers have a long history of community-based participatory research with an interdisciplinary approach. Sabir et al. (2009) suggested that community-based research on transportation barriers, psychiatric disabilities, varying types of communities, and multicomponent and person-centered interventions could further advance the field of social isolation. More recently, social work scholars have conducted research on interventions to reduce social isolation using community-engaged methods. For example, Peron et al. (2020) engaged older LGBT adults in a pilot-friendly caller program to reduce isolation; Weiler, Scafe, Spencer, and Cavell (2020) partnered with foster parents to create a caregiver-initiated mentoring intervention for use by social workers and other helping professionals. Recommended future research priority areas include (a) the need to understand use of service (or, more to the point, nonuse), (b) measures to identify isolated adults during a community crisis (e.g., disaster relief), (c) evaluation of direct or indirect contact interventions, (d) efficacy of multicomponent interventions, and (e) research that reflects respect for continuing self-determination in older adulthood. These are all areas of research in which social work has been involved that can accommodate an interdisciplinary focus and move forward the Grand Challenge to Eradicate Social Isolation.

OVERCOMING SOCIAL ISOLATION REQUIRES SIGNIFICANT INNOVATION

Reducing the incidence of social isolation will require innovation to develop and test individual- and societal-level interventions. For example, social workers can explore new social media technologies to test innovative interventions that reweave frayed networks and provide lifelines to vulnerable isolated individuals. As stated in the work by Sherraden et al. (2015, p. 5), "It is not overstating to say that we live in a time of emergence of new social worlds of social media, social networks, and other social engagements via internet technology."

In addition, there is a critical need for innovative approaches that make use of new mobile technologies. For example, a Pew Research Center 2012 survey reported that fully 85% of adults in the United States own a cell phone. Of those, 53% own smartphones. Approximately one third of cell phone owners (31%) have used their phones to search for health information, which is almost double the rate (17%) reported in a Pew survey conducted just 2 years earlier. Every major demographic group experienced significant year-to-year growth in smartphone ownership. This changing means of communication and information-seeking requires new approaches to reducing isolation that are nimble to our quickly evolving technological landscape.

Currently, there is a multitude of mobile device health apps created for a variety of health issues. The challenge is to understand how information technology can be used to enhance social connections among vulnerable populations. The use of newer information and communication technologies (e.g., Internet social networking services) can be particularly beneficial for some groups to address social isolation. For example, several studies have found that adults with physical and functional health decline combat loneliness and increase a sense of connectedness by using computers (Gatto & Tak, 2008; Sayago & Blat, 2010; Smith et al., 2020). In a review of the literature that examines the potential for social networks and support to enhance telehealth interventions for people with a diagnosis of schizophrenia, most studies focused on improving medical adherence, providing medical information, and monitoring symptoms. However, the benefits of technology for mobilizing resources for self-management and peer support were evident but more peripheral (Daker-White & Rogers, 2013). In a meta-analysis of the effect of Internet group support for family caregivers, 10 peer-reviewed studies were identified showing that Internet support groups have a positive effect on social support and self-efficacy (Oliver et al., 2017). Technology-based interventions may be especially of interest to youth. For example, a pilot study testing a digital smartphone application called "+Connect," which delivers content on positive psychology to adolescents with and without a mental illness, identified positive outcomes for those with social anxiety (Lim et al., 2019).

Social isolation is linked inextricably to social and environmental justice. Conditions that breed poverty and economic insecurity also contribute to social isolation. Interventions aimed at eradicating social isolation should be mindful of how to address social stigmas such as mental health, HIV/AIDS, poverty, and otherness, which can result in social isolation. Accordingly, strategies to eradicate social isolation must also include advocacy to address a range of social justice issues, including poverty and racism, that present barriers to access to services. The Grand Challenges for Social Work aimed at eliminating racism, reducing extreme economic insecurity, achieving equal opportunity and justice, and ending homelessness offer additional valuable context for addressing critically important structural dimensions associated with social isolation.

CONCLUSION

In 1979, the World Health Organization noted that social isolation needed to be addressed as a major health risk factor. Twenty-two years later, the World Health Organization reaffirmed the importance of addressing social isolation in a report on active aging (World Health Organization, 2002), and it did so again in its Age-Friendly Cities and Communities initiative (World Health Organization, 2018). The importance of social ties—the inverse of social isolation—has been affirmed as a top-10 area for future National Institutes of Health research investment (National Research Council, 2001), and recent National Institutes of Health program announcements have focused specifically on the biopsychosocial factors of social connectedness and isolation on health and well-being (Department of Health and Human Services, 2019). The AARP includes it as one of its top-five new initiatives (AARP Foundation, 2012, 2020). The National Academies of Sciences, Engineering and Medicine's (2020) recent consensus report offered an extensive set of recommendations to address social isolation and loneliness among older populations, but also added that isolation and loneliness are critical issues across the life span. It is fitting and timely for social work to adopt social isolation as one of its greatest challenges. Social work has the unique capacity to work with complex systems and generate research that can bridge disciplinary silos that currently impede a complete understanding of social isolation.

The inclusion of social isolation as a grand challenge will undoubtedly elevate this domain between practitioners and their clients and patients. Indeed, the social element of social work is essential for solving the Grand Challenge to Eradicate Social Isolation among all populations.

ACKNOWLEDGMENTS

The authors thank both Melanie Gironda and Carrie Johnson, who contributed to the first edition of this chapter.

REFERENCES

AARP Foundation. (2012). Framework for isolation in adults over 50. Retrieved from http://www.aarp.org/content/dam/aarp/aarp_foundation/2012_PDFs/AARP-Foundation-Isolation-Framework-Report.pdf

AARP Foundation. (2016). Connect2Affect campaign. Retrieved from https://www.aarp.org/about-aarp/press-center/info-12-2016/aarp-foundation-draws-attention-social-isolation-with-launch-connect2affect.html and https://connect2affect.org

AARP Foundation. (2020). Two-thirds of adults are suffering from social isolation: The pandemic effect. Retrieved from https://press.aarp.org/2020-10-7-Foundation-Social-Isolation.

Acierno, R., Hernandez, M. A., Amstadter, A. B., Resnick, H. S., Steve, K., Muzzy, W., & Kilpatrick, D. G. (2010). Prevalence and correlates of emotional, physical, sexual, and financial abuse and potential neglect in the United States: The National Elder Mistreatment Study. *American Journal of Public Health, 100,* 292–297. doi:10.2105/AJPH.2009.163089

Adams, K., Sanders, S., & Auth, E. (2004). Loneliness and depression in independent living retirement communities: Risk and resilience factors. *Aging & Mental Health, 8,* 475–485.

Ahrens, K. R., DuBois, D. L., Richardson, L. P., Fan, M. Y., & Lozano, P. (2008). Youth in foster care with adult mentors during adolescence have improved adult outcomes. *Pediatrics, 121,* e246–e252.

Alspach, J. (2013). Loneliness and social isolation: Risk factors long overdue for surveillance. *Critical Care Nurse, 33,* 8–13. doi:10.4037/ccn2013377

Anderson, G. O., & Thayer, C. E. (2018). Loneliness and social connections: A national survey of adults 45 and older. *Washington, DC: AARP Foundation.*

Andrist, E., Clarke, R. G., & Harding, M. (2020). Paved with good intentions: Hospital visitation Restrictions in the age of coronavirus disease 2019. *Pediatric Critical Care Medicine, 21,* e924–e926.

Arber, S., & Ginn, J. (1994). Women and aging. *Reviews in Clinical Gerontology, 4,* 349–358.

Asher, S. R., & Paquette, J. A. (2003). Loneliness and peer relations in childhood. *Current Directions in Psychological Science, 12,* 75–78. doi:10.1111/1467-8721.01233

Azhar, S., Gandham, S., Vaudrey, J., Oruganti, G., & Samuel, R. S. (2020). "They kept away": Social isolation of cisgender women living with HIV in Hyderabad, India. *Clinical Social Work Journal, 48,* 64–76.

Azad, G. F., Locke, J., Kasari, C., & Mandell, D. S. (2017). Race, disability, and grade: Social relationships in children with autism spectrum disorders. *Autism, 21,* 92–99. doi:10.1177/1362361315627792

Barajas-Gonzalez, R. G., Ayón, C., & Torres, F. (2018). Applying a community violence framework to understand the impact of immigration enforcement threat on Latino children. *Social Policy Report, 31*(3), 1–24.

Barlott, T., Adams, K., Díaz, F. R., & Molina, M. M. (2015). Using SMS as a tool to reduce exclusions experienced by caregivers of people with disabilities in a resource-limited Colombian community. *Disability & Rehabilitation: Assistive Technology, 10,* 347–354.

Bauminger, N., Shulman, C., & Agam, G. (2003). Peer interaction and loneliness in high-functioning children with autism. *Journal of Autism and Developmental Disorders, 33,* 489–507. doi:10.1023/A:1025827427901

Beach, S. R., Schulz, R., Castle, N. G., & Rosen, J. (2010). Financial exploitation and psychological mistreatment among older adults: Differences between African Americans and non-African Americans in a population-based survey. *The Gerontologist, 50,* 744–757.

Beach, S. R., Schulz, R., Williamson, G. M., Miller, L. S., Weiner, M. F., & Lance, C. E. (2005). Risk factors for potentially harmful informal caregiver behavior. *Journal of the American Geriatrics Society, 53*, 255–261. doi:10.1111/j.1532-5415.2005.53111.x

Berg-Weger, M., & Morley, J. E. (2020). Editorial: Loneliness and social isolation in older adults during the COVID-19 pandemic: Implications for gerontological social work. *The Journal of Nutrition, Health & Aging, 24*, 456–458.

Berkman, L. F. (1986). Social networks, support and health: Taking the next step forward. *American Journal of Epidemiology, 123*, 559–562.

Berkman, L. F. (2009). Social epidemiology: Social determinants of health in the United States: Are we losing ground? *Annual Review of Public Health, 30*, 27–41.

Berkman, L. F., Glass, T., Brissette, I., & Seeman, T. E. (2000). From social integration to health: Durkheim in the new millennium. *Social Science and Medicine, 51*, 843–857.

Berkman, L. F., Kawachi, I., & Glymour, M. (2014). *Social epidemiology* (2nd ed.). New York, NY: Oxford University Press.

Berkman, L. F., & Syme, S. L. (1979). Social networks, host resistance, and mortality: A nine-year follow-up study of Alameda County residents. *American Journal of Epidemiology, 109*, 186–204.

Bessaha, M. L., Sabbath, E. L., Morris, Z., Malik, S., Scheinfeld, L., & Saragossi, J. (2020). A systematic review of loneliness interventions among non-elderly adults. *Clinical Social Work Journal, 48*, 110–125.

Bessaha, M., Reed, R., Donlon, A. J., Mathews, W., Bell, A. C., & Merolla, D. (2020). Creating a more inclusive environment for students with disabilities: Findings from participatory action research. *Disability Studies Quarterly, 40*(3).

Bosworth, H. B., & Schaie, K. W. (1997). The relationship of social environment, social networks, and health outcomes in the Seattle Longitudinal Study: Two analytical approaches. *Journal of Gerontology: Psychological Sciences, 52B*, P197–P205.

Bowlby, J. (1969). *Attachment and loss volume 1: Attachment.* London, UK: Hogarth.

Brown, S., & Munson, M. R. (2020). Introduction to the special issue on social isolation across the lifespan. *Clinical Social Work Journal, 48*, 1–5.

Brown, S., Tracy, E. M., Jun, M. K., Park, H., & Min, M. O. (2015). Personal network recovery enablers and relapse risks. *Qualitative Health Research, 25*, 371–385.

Cacioppo, J. T., & Cacioppo, S. (2014). Social relationships and health: The toxic effects of perceived social isolation. *Social and Personality Psychology Compass, 8*, 58–72.

Cacioppo, J. T., & Cacioppo, S. (2018). Loneliness in the modern age: an evolutionary theory of loneliness (ETL). In *Advances in experimental social psychology* (Vol. 58, pp. 127–197). Academic Press.

Cacioppo, J. T., Hawkley, L. C., & Thisted, R. A. (2010). Perceived social isolation makes me sad: 5-Year cross-lagged analyses of loneliness and depressive symptomatology in the Chicago Health, Aging, and Social Relations Study. *Psychology and Aging, 25*, 453–463.

Caspi, A., Harrington, H., Moffitt, T. E., Milne, B. J., & Poulton, R. (2006). Socially isolated children 20 years later: Risk of cardiovascular disease. *Archives of Pediatrics and Adolescent Medicine, 160*, 805–811.

Cassel, J. (1976). The contribution of the social environment to host resistance. *American Journal of Epidemiology, 104*, 107–123.

Ceria, C. D., Masaki, K. H., Rodriguez, B. L., Chen, R., Yano, K., & Curb, J. D. (2001). The relationship of psychosocial factors to total mortality among older Japanese American men: The Honolulu Heart Program. *Journal of the American Geriatrics Society, 49*, 725–731.

Chan, A., Malhotra, C., Malhotra, R., & Ostbye, T. (2011). Living arrangements, social networks and depressive symptoms among older men and women in Singapore. *International Journal of Geriatric Psychiatry, 26*, 630–639. doi:10.1002/gps.2574

Chappell, N. L. (1991). Living arrangements and sources of caregiving. *Journal of Gerontology: Social Sciences, 46*, S1–S8.

Chavez, J. M., Lopez, A., Englebrecht, C. M., & Viramontez Anguiano, R. P. (2012). Sufren los niños: Exploring the impact of unauthorized immigration status on children's well-being. *Family Court Review, 50*, 638–649. doi:10.1111/j.1744-1617.2012.01482.x

Cleary, E. H., & Stanton, A. L. (2015). Mediators of an Internet-based psychosocial intervention for women with breast cancer. *Health Psychology, 34*, 477–485. doi:10.1037/hea0000170

Chopik, W. J., Edelstein, R. S., & Grimm, K. J. (2019). Longitudinal changes in attachment orientation over a 59-year period. *Journal of Personality and Social Psychology, 116*, 598–611.

Cigna. (2018). Cigna U.S. loneliness index. Retrieved from https://www.multivu.com/players/English/8294451-cigna-us-loneliness-survey/docs/Index Report_15240 69371598-173525450.pdf

Cobb, S. (1976). Social support as a moderator of life stress. *Psychosomatic Medicine, 38*, 300–313.

Cohen, S. (2001). Social relationships and susceptibility to the common cold. In C. D. Ryff & B. S. Singer (Eds.), *Emotion, social relationships and health* (pp. 221–232). New York, NY: Oxford University Press.

Cooney, C., Howard, R., & Lawlor, B. (2006). Abuse of vulnerable people with dementia by their carers: Can we identify those most at risk? *International Journal of Geriatric Psychiatry, 21*, 564–571. doi:10.1002/gps.1525

Crewe, S. E., & Guyot-Diagnone, J. (2016). Stigmatization and labelling. In *Encyclopedia of social work*. Washington, DC/New York, NY: National Association of Social Workers Press/Oxford University Press. doi:10.1093/acrefore/9780199975839.013.1043

Crooks, V., Lubben, J., Petitti, D., Little, D., & Chiu, V. (2008). Social network, cognitive function, and dementia incidence among elderly women. *American Journal of Public Health, 98*, 1221–1227. doi:10.2105/AJPH.2007.115923

Cummings, E. M., & Cicchetti, D. (1990). Toward a transactional model of relations between attachment and depression. In M. T. Greenberg, D. Cicchetti, & E. M. Cummings (Eds.), *Attachment in the preschool years* (pp. 339–374). Chicago, IL: University of Chicago.

Daker-White, G., & Rogers, A. (2013). What is the potential for social networks and support to enhance future telehealth interventions for people with a diagnosis of schizophrenia: A critical interpretive synthesis. *BMC Psychiatry, 13*, 1–12.

David-Ferdon, C., & Simon, T. R. (2012). *Striving to Reduce Youth Violence Everywhere (STRYVE): The Centers for Disease Control and Prevention's national initiative to prevent youth violence foundational resource*. Atlanta, GA: Centers for Disease Control and Prevention.

DeLiema, M., & Conrad, K. J. (2017). Financial exploitation of older adults. In Xinqi Dong (ed.), *Elder abuse: Research, Practice and Policy* (pp. 141–157). U.K.: Springer.

Department of Health and Human Services. (2019). Research on biopsychosocial factors of social connectedness and isolation on health, wellbeing, illness, and recovery. Retrieved from https://grants.nih.gov/grants/guide/pa-files/PAR-19-373.html.

Dong, X. Q., & Simon, M. A. (2011). Enhancing national policy and programs to address elder abuse. *Journal of the American Medical Association, 305*, 2460–2461.

Eisenberger, N. I. (2012). The neural bases of social pain: Evidence for shared representations with physical pain. *Psychosomatic Medicine, 74*, 126–135.

Eisenberger, N. I., Lieberman, M. D., & Williams, K. D. (2003). Does rejection hurt? An fMRI study of social exclusion. *Science, 302*, 290–292. doi:10.1126/science.1089134

Elbogen, E. B., Lanier, M., Blakey, S. M., Wagner, H. R., & Tsai, J. (2021). Suicidal ideation and thoughts of self-harm during the COVID-19 pandemic: The role of COVID-19-related stress, social isolation, and financial strain. *Depression and Anxiety, 38*, 739–748.

Emerson, E., Fortune, N., Llewellyn, G., & Stancliffe, R. (2021). Loneliness, social support, social isolation and wellbeing among working age adults with and without disability: Cross sectional study. *Disability and Health Journal, 14*, 1–7. doi:10.1016/j.dhjo.2020.100965.

Endo, K., Ando, S., Shimodera, S., Yamasaki, S., Usami, S., Okazaki, Y., . . . Nishida, A. (2017). Preference for solitude, social isolation, suicidal ideation, and self-harm in adolescents. *Journal of Adolescent Health, 61*(2), 187–191.

Eng, P., Rimm, E., Fitzmaurice, G., & Kawachi, I. (2002). Social ties and change in social ties in relation to subsequent total and cause-specific mortality and coronary heart disease incidence in men. *American Journal of Epidemiology, 155*, 700–709.

Ertel, K. A., Glymour, M. M., & Berkman, L. F. (2008). Effects of social integration on preserving memory function in a nationally representative US elderly population. *American Journal of Public Health, 98*, 1215–1220. doi:10.2105/AJPH.2007.113654

Esgalhado, M., Reis, M., Pereira, H., & Afonso, R. (2010). Influence of social support on the psychological well-being and mental health of older adults living in assisted-living residences. *International Journal of Developmental and Educational Psychology, 1*, 267–278.

Fukui, S., Koike, M., Ooba, A., & Uchitomi, Y. (2003). The effect of a psychosocial group intervention on loneliness and social support for Japanese women with primary breast cancer. *Oncology Nursing Forum, 30*, 823–830. doi:10.1188/03.ONF.823-830

Gambin, M., Woźniak-Prus, M., Sekowski, M., Cudo, A., Pisula, E., Kiepura, E., . . . Kmita, G. (2020). Factors related to positive experiences in parent–child relationship during the COVID-19 lockdown: The role of empathy, emotion regulation, parenting self-efficacy and social support, 1–35.

Gatto, S. L., & Tak, S. H. (2008). Computer, Internet, and e-mail use among older adults: Benefits and barriers. *Educational Gerontology, 34*, 800–811.

Geenen, S., Powers, L. E., Powers, J., Cunningham, M., McMahon, L., Nelson, M., . . . Fullerton, A. (2013). Experimental study of a self-determination intervention for youth in foster care. *Career Development and Transition for Exceptional Individuals, 36*, 84–95.

Giles, L., Glonek, G., Luszcz, M., & Andres, G. (2005). Effect of social networks on 10-year survival in very old Australians: The Australian Longitudinal Study of Aging. *Journal of Epidemiology & Community Health, 59*, 574–579.

Gironda, M., & Lubben, J. (2002). Preventing loneliness and isolation in older adulthood. In T. Gullotta & M. Bloom (Eds.), *Encyclopedia of primary prevention and health promotion* (pp. 20–34). New York, NY: Kluwer /Plenum.

Goosby, B., Bellatorre, A., Walsemann, K., & Cheadle, J. (2013). Adolescent loneliness and health in early adulthood. *Sociological Inquiry, 83*, 505–536. doi:10.1111/soin.12018

Gopalan, G., Lee, S. J., Harris R., Acri, M. C., & Munson, M. R. (2017). Utilization of peers in services for youth with emotional and behavioral challenges: A scoping review. *Journal of Adolescence, 55*, 88–115.

Gray, T., Azizoddin, D., & Nersesian, P. (2020). Loneliness among cancer caregivers: A narrative review. *Palliative and Supportive Care, 18*, 359–367. doi:10.1017/S14789515190000804

Green, B. L., Furrer, C., & McAllister, C. (2007). How do relationships support parenting? Effects of attachment style and social support on parenting behavior in an at-risk population. *American Journal of Community Psychology, 40*, 96–108. doi:10.1007/s10464-007-9127-y

Gulbas, L. E., Zayas, L. H., Yoon, H., Szlyk, H., Aguilar-Gaxiola, S., & Natera, G. (2016). Deportation experiences and depression among US citizen-children with undocumented Mexican parents. *Child: Care, Health and Development, 42*(2), 220–230.

Gulbas, L. E., & Zayas, L. H. (2017). Exploring the effects of US immigration enforcement on the well-being of citizen children in Mexican immigrant families. *RSF: The Russell Sage Foundation Journal of the Social Sciences, 3*(4), 53–69.

Hagan, R. (2020). Loneliness, older people and a proposed social work response. *Journal of Social Work, 21*, 1084–1104.

Hall, S. A. (2009). The social inclusion of people with disabilities: A qualitative meta-analysis. *Journal of Ethnographic & Qualitative Research, 3*, 162–173.

Hall-Lande, J. A., Eisenberg, M. E., Christenson, L. S., & Neumark-Sztainer, D. (2007). Social isolation, psychological health, and protective factors in adolescence. *Adolescence, 42*, 265–286.

Hanson, M. A., & Gluckman, P. D. (2015). Developmental origins of health and disease: Global public health implications. *Best Practice & Research: Clinical Obstetrics Gynaecology, 29*, 24–31.

Holt-Lunstad, J. (2017). The potential public health relevance of social isolation and loneliness: Prevalence, epidemiology, and risk factors. *Public Policy & Aging Report, 27*, 127–130. doi:10.1093/ppar/prx030

Holt-Lunstad, J., Smith, T., Baker, M., Harris, T., & Stephenson, D. (2015). Loneliness and social isolation as risk factors for mortality: A meta-analytic review. *Perspectives on Psychological Science, 10*, 227–237. doi:10.1177/1745691614568352

Holt-Lunstad, J., Smith, T., & Layton, B. (2010). Social relationships and mortality risk: A meta-analytic review. *PLOS Medicine, 7*, e1000316. doi:10.1371/journal.pmed.1000316

House, J. S. (2001). Social isolation kills, but how and why? *Psychosomatic Medicine, 63*, 273–274.

Hurtado-de-Mendoza, A., Gonzales, F. A., Serrano, A., & Kaltman, S. (2014). Social isolation and perceived barriers to establishing social networks among Latina immigrants. *American Journal of Community Psychology, 53*, 73–82.

Ingram, J., Hand, C. J., & Maciejewski, G. (2021). Social isolation during COVID-19 lockdown impairs cognitive function. *Applied Cognitive Psychology, 35*, 935–947 doi:10.1002/acp.3821

Institute on Aging at Boston College. (2017). Module 1: Social isolation. Retrieved from http://www.bc.edu/centers/ioa/videos/social-isolation.html

Iqbal, S. A., & Tayyab, N. (2021). COVID-19 and children: The mental and physical reverberations of the pandemic. *Child Care Health and Development, 47,* 136–139. doi:10.1111/cch.12822

Johnson, M. J., & Amella, E. J. (2014). Isolation of lesbian, gay, bisexual and transgender youth: A dimensional concept analysis. *Journal of Advanced Nursing, 70,* 523–532. doi:10.1111/jan.12212

Kang, J. I., Mueller, S. G., Wu, G. W., Lin, J., Ng, P., Yehuda, R., & PTSD Systems Biology Consortium. (2020). Effect of combat exposure and posttraumatic stress disorder on telomere length and amygdala volume. *Biological Psychiatry: Cognitive Neuroscience and Neuroimaging, 5,* 678–687.

Kaplan, R. (2013, January). *Stimulating the science of social work thinking.* Paper presented at the annual conference of the Society for Social Work and Research, San Diego, CA.

Keller, T. E., Perry, M., & Spencer, R. (2020). Reducing social isolation through formal youth mentoring: Opportunities and potential pitfalls. *Clinical Social Work Journal, 48,* 35–45.

Kimura, M., Yamazaki, S., Haga, H., & Yasumura, S. (2013). The prevalence of social engagement in the disabled elderly and related factors. *ISRN Geriatrics, 2013,* 1–8. doi:10.1155/2013/709823

Koenig, L. J., & Abrams, R. F. (1999). Adolescent loneliness and adjustment: A focus on gender differences. In K. J. Rotenberg & S. Hymel (Eds.), *Loneliness in childhood and adolescence* (pp. 296–322). Cambridge, UK: Cambridge University Press.

Kotwal, A. A., Holt-Lunstad, J., Newmark, R. L., Cenzer, I., Smith, A.K., Covinsky, K. E., . . . Perissinotto, C. M. (2021). Social isolation and loneliness among San Francisco Bay area older adults during the COVID-19 shelter-in-place orders. *Journal of the American Geriatrics Society, 69,* 20–29. doi:10.1111/jgs.16865

Kranke, D., Floersch, J. E., Kranke, B., & Munson, M. R. (2011). A qualitative investigation of self-stigma among adolescents taking psychiatric medications. *Psychiatric Services, 62,* 893–899.

Krieger, N. (2020). Measures of racism, sexism, heterosexism, and gender binarism for health equity research: From structural injustice to embodied harm-an ecosocial analysis. *Annual Review of Public Health, 41,* 37–62. doi.10.1146/annurevpubhealth-040119-094017

Krause, N., Herzog, A. R., & Baker, E. (1992). Providing support to others and well-being in later life. *Journal of Gerontology: Psychological Sciences, 47,* P300–P311.

Lacey, R. E., Jumari, M., & Bartley M. (2014). Social isolation in childhood and adult inflammation: Evidence from the National Child Development Study. *Psychoneuroendocrinology, 50,* 85–94.

Laugesen, K., Baggesen, L. M., Schmidt, S. A. J., Glymour, M. M., Lasgaard, M., Milstein, A., . . . Ehrenstein, V. (2018). Social isolation and all-cause mortality: a population-based cohort study in Denmark. *Scientific Reports, 8*(1), 1–8.

Laursen, B., & Hartl, A. (2013). Understanding loneliness during adolescence: Developmental changes that increase the risk of perceived social isolation. *Journal of Adolescence, 36,* 1261–1268. doi:10.1016/j.adolescence.2013.06.003

Lee, J., Hong, J., Zhou, Y., & Robles, G. (2020). The relationships between loneliness, social support, and resilience among Latinx immigrants in the United States. *Clinical Social Work Journal, 48,* 99–109.

Levin, J., & Madfis, E. (2009). Mass murder at school and cumulative strain: A sequential model. *American Behavioral Scientist, 52*, 1227–1245.

Lim, M. H., Rodebaugh, T. L., Eres, R., Long, K. M., Penn, D. L., & Gleeson, J. F. (2019). A pilot digital intervention targeting loneliness in youth mental health. *Frontiers in Psychiatry, 10*, 1–13.

Lin, N., Ye, X., & Ensel, W. (1999). Social support and depressed mood: A structural analysis. *Journal of Health and Social Behavior, 40*, 344–359.

Loades, M. E., Chatburn, E., Higson-Sweeney, N., Reynolds, S., Shafran, R., Brigden, A., . . . Crawley, E. (2020). Rapid systematic review: the impact of social isolation and loneliness on the mental health of children and adolescents in the context of COVID-19. *Journal of the American Academy of Child & Adolescent Psychiatry, 59*(11), 1218–1239. doi.10.1016/j.jaac.2020.05.009

Lubben, J. E. (1988). Assessing social networks among elderly populations. *Family and Community Health, 11*, 42–52.

Lubben, J. (2017). Addressing social isolation as a potent killer! *Public Policy & Aging Report, 27*, 136–138. doi:10.1093/ppar/prx026

Lubben, J. E., Blozik, E., Gillmann, G., Iliffe, S., von Renteln Kruse, W., Beck, J., & Stuck, A. (2006). Performance of an abbreviated version of the Lubben Social Network Scale among three European community-dwelling older adult populations. *The Gerontologist, 46*, 503–513. doi.org/10.1093/geront/46.4.503

Lubben, J. E., & Gironda, M. (2003). Centrality of social ties to the health and well-being of older adults. In B. Berkman & L. K. Harooytoan (Eds.), *Social work and health care in an aging world* (pp. 319–350). New York, NY: Springer.

Lubben, J. E., Weiler, P. G., & Chi, I. (1989). Health practices of the elderly poor. *American Journal of Public Health, 79*, 731–734. doi:10.2105/AJPH.79.6.731

Maki, Y., Ura, C., Yamaguchi, T., Murai, T., Isahai, M., Kaiho, A., & Yamaguchi, H. (2012). Effects of intervention using a community-based walking program for prevention of mental decline: A randomized controlled trial. *Journal of the American Geriatrics Society, 60*, 505–510. doi:10.1111/j.1532-5415.2011.03838.x

Mariam, L. M., McClure, R., Robinson, J. B., & Yang, J. A. (2015). Eliciting Change in At-Risk Elders (ECARE): Evaluation of an elder abuse intervention program. *Journal of Elder Abuse and Neglect, 27*, 19–33. doi:10.1080/08946566.2013.86724

McHugh, J., & Lawlor, B. (2012). Social support differentially moderates the impact of neuroticism and extraversion on mental well-being among community-dwelling older adults. *Journal of Mental Health, 21*, 448–458. doi:10.3109/09638237.2012.689436

McPherson, K. E., Kerr, S., McGee, E., Morgan, A., Cheater, F. M., Mclean J., & Egan J. (2014). The association between social capital and mental health and behavioral problems in children and adolescents: An integrative systematic review. *BMC Psychology, 2*, 1–16. doi:10.1186/2050-7283-2-7

McPherson, M., Smith-Lovin, L., & Brashears, M. E. (2006). Social isolation in America: Changes in core discussion networks over two decades. *American Sociological Review, 71*, 353–375.

Mizock, L., & Lewis, T. K. (2008). Trauma in transgender populations: Risk, resilience, and clinical care. *Journal of Emotional Abuse, 8*, 335–354. doi:10.1080/10926790802262523

Morgan, A. (2010). Social capital as a health asset for young people's health and wellbeing. *Journal of Child and Adolescent Psychology, S2*, 19–42.

Morris, Z. A. (2019). Loneliness as a predictor of work disability onset among non-disabled, working older adults in 14 countries. *Journal of Aging and Health, 32*, 554–563.

Munson, M. R., & McMillen, J. C. (2009). Natural mentoring and psychosocial outcomes among older youth transitioning from foster care. *Children and Youth Services Review, 31*.

Murthy, V. H., & Murthy, V. H. (2020). *Together*. Harper Collins Publishers.

National Academies of Sciences, Engineering and Medicine. (2020). *Social isolation and loneliness in older adults: Opportunities for the health care system*. Washington, DC: National Academies Press. doi:10.17226/25663

National Center on Elder Abuse. (2020). Research, statistics and data. Retrieved from https://ncea.acl.gov/What-We-Do/Research/Statistics-and-Data.aspx

National Council on Aging. (2021). Get the facts on elder abuse. Retrieved from https://www.ncoa.org/public-policy-action/elder-justice/elder-abuse-facts/#:~:text=While%20likely%20under%2Dreported%2C%20estimates,and%20sexual%20abuse%20or%20neglect

National Research Council. (2001). *New horizons in health: An integrative approach*. Washington, DC: National Academies Press.

Nersesian, P. V., Han, H.- R., Yenokyan, G., Blumenthal, R. S., Nolan, M. T., Hladek, M. D., & Szanton, S. L. (2018). Loneliness in middle age and biomarkers of systemic inflammation: Findings from midlife in the United States. *Social Science and Medicine, 209*, 174–181.

Newman, M. L., Holden, G. W., & Delville, Y. (2005). Isolation and the stress of being bullied. *Journal of Adolescence, 28*, 343–357. doi:10.1016/j.adolescence.2004.08.002

Nguyen, A. W., Taylor, R. J., Taylor, H. O., & Chatters, L. M. (2020). Objective and subjective social isolation and psychiatric disorders among African Americans. *Clinical Social Work Journal, 48*, 87–98.

Nicholson, N. R., Jr. (2012). A review of social isolation: An important but underassessed condition in older adults. *Journal of Primary Prevention, 33*, 137–152.

Nicolaisen, M., & Thorsen, K. (2014). Who are lonely? Loneliness in different age groups (18–81 years old), using two measures of loneliness. *The International Journal of Aging and Human Development, 78*, 229–257.

Norman, G. J., Hawkley, L., Ball, A., Berntson, G. G., & Cacioppo, J. T. (2013). Perceived social isolation moderates the relationship between early childhood trauma and pulse pressure in older adults. *International Journal of Psychophysiology, 88*, 334–338.

Ojeda, V. D., Magana, C., Burgos, J. L., & Vargas-Ojeda, A. C. (2020). Deported Men's and Father's Perspective: The Impacts of Family Separation on Children and Families in the U.S. *Frontiers in Psychiatry, 11*, 148. https://doi.org/10.3389/fpsyt.2020.00148

O'Keeffe, G. S., Clarke-Pearson, K., & Council on Communications and Media (2011). The impact of social media on children, adolescents, and families. *Pediatrics, 127*, 800–804.

Oliver, P. D., Patil, S., Benson, J. J., Gage, A., Washington, K., Kruse, R. L., & Demiris, G. (2017). The effect of Internet group support for caregivers on social support, self-efficacy, and caregiver burden: A meta-analysis. *Telemed Journal of Electronic Health, 23*, 621–629. doi:10.1089/tmj.2016.0183

Oxman-Martinez, J., Rummens, A. J., Moreau, J., Choi, Y. R., Beiser, M., Ogilvie, L., & Armstrong, R. (2012). Perceived ethnic discrimination and social exclusion: Newcomer immigrant children in Canada. *American Journal of Orthopsychiatry, 82*, 376–388. doi:10.1111/j.1939-0025.2012.01161.x

Pantell, M., Rehkopf, D., Jutte, D., Syme, S. L., Balmes, J., & Adler, N. (2013). Social isolation: A predictor of mortality comparable to traditional clinical risk factors. *American Journal of Public Health, 103,* 2056–2062. doi:10.2105/AJPH.2013.301261

Paul, C., Ayis, S., & Ebrahim, S. (2006). Psychological distress, loneliness and disability in old age. *Psychology, Health & Medicine, 11,* 221–232.

Paveza, G. J., Cohen, D., Eisdorfer, C., Freels, S., Semla, T., Ashford, J. W., . . . Levy, P. (1992). Severe family violence and Alzheimer's disease: Prevalence and risk factors. *Gerontologist, 32,* 493–497.

Pekovic, V., Seff, L., & Rothman, M. D. (2007). Planning for and responding to special needs of elders in natural disasters. *Generations, 31,* 37–41.

Perone, A. K., Ingersoll-Dayton, B., & Watkins-Dukhie, K. (2020). Social isolation loneliness among LGBT older adults: Lessons learned from a pilot friendly caller program. *Clinical Social Work Journal, 48,* 126–139.

Pescosolido, B. A. (2011). Organizing the sociological landscape for the next decades of health and health care research: The network episode model III-R as cartographic subfield guide. In B. A. Pescosolido, J. K. Martin, J. D. McLeod, & A. Rogers (Eds.), *Handbook of the sociology of health, illness, and healing* (pp. 39–66). New York, NY: Springer.

Pescosolido, B. A., Gardner, C. B., & Lubell, K. M. (1998). How people get into mental health services: Stories of choice, coercion and "muddling through" from "first-timers." *Social Science and Medicine, 46,* 275–286.

Peterson, J. C., Burnes, D. P., Caccamise, P. L., Mason, A., Henderson, C. R., Wells, M. T., . . . Lachs, M. S. (2014). Financial exploitation of older adults: A population-based prevalence study. *Journal of General Internal Medicine, 29,* 1615–1623.

Pew Research Center. (2012). Mobile health 2012. Retrieved from http://pewresearch.org/internet/2012/11/08/mobile-health-2012/

Pew Research Center. (2010). Mobile health 2010. Retrieved from http://pewresearch.org/internet/2010/10/19/mobile-health-2010/

Pinquart, M., & Sörensen, S. (2001). Gender differences in self-concept and psychological well-being in old age: A meta-analysis. *The Journals of Gerontology Series B: Psychological Sciences and Social Sciences, 56,* P195–P213.

Puhl, R. M., & Lessard, L. M. (2020). Weight stigma in youth: Prevalence, consequences, and considerations for clinical practice. *Current Obesity Reports, 9,* 402–411. doi:10.1007/s13679-020-00408-8.

Qualter, P., & Munn, P. (2002). The separateness of social and emotional loneliness in childhood. *Journal of Child Psychology and Psychiatry, 43,* 233–244.

Rice, E., et. al. (2018). Piloting the use of artificial intelligence to enhance HIV prevention interventions for youth experiencing homelessness. *Journal of the Society for Social Work and Research, 9,* 551–573. doi:10.1086/701439

Rice, E., & Yoshioka-Maxwell, A. (2015). Social network analysis as a toolkit for the science of social work. *Journal of the Society for Social Work and Research, 6,* 369–383. doi:10.1086/682723

Romano, G. H., Harari, Y., Yehuda, T., Podhorzer, A., Rubinstein, L., Shamir, R., . . . Kupiec, M. (2013). Environmental stresses disrupt telomere length homeostasis. *PLoS Genetics, 9,* e1003721.

Rowley, E., Chandler, S., Baird, G., Simonoff, E., Pickles, A., Loucas, T., & Charman, T. (2012). The experience of friendship, victimization and bullying in children with an autism spectrum disorder: Associations with child characteristics and school placement. *Research in Autism Spectrum Disorders, 6,* 1126–1134. doi:10.1016/j.rasd.2012.03.00

Rubenstein, R. L., Lubben, J. E., & Mintzer, J. E. (1994). Social isolation and social support: An applied perspective. *Journal of Applied Gerontology, 13*, 58–72.

Sabir, M., Wethington, E., Breckman, R., Meador, R., Reid, M. C., & Pillemer, K. A. (2009). Community-based participatory critique of social isolation intervention research for community-dwelling older adults. *Journal of Applied Gerontology, 28*, 218–234.

Sanders, M. R., Turner, K. M., & Metzler, C. W. (2019). Applying self-regulation principles in the delivery of parenting interventions. *Clinical Child and Family Psychology Review, 22*, 24–42.

Sapiro, B., & Ward, A. (2020). Marginalized youth, mental health, and connection with others: a review of the literature. *Child and Adolescent Social Work Journal, 37*(4), 343–357.

Sayago, S., & Blat, J. (2010). Telling the story of older people e-mailing: An ethnographical study. *International Journal of Human–Computer Studies, 68*, 105–120. doi:10.1016/j.ijhcs.2009.10.004

Scharlach, J. K., Davitt, A. J., Lehning, E. A., Greenfield, C. L., & Graham, C. L. (2014). Does the Village model help to foster age-friendly communities? *Journal of Aging & Social Policy, 26*, 181–196. doi:10.1080/08959420.2014.854664

Schnittger, R., Wherton, J., Prendergast, D., & Lawlor, B. (2012). Risk factors and mediating pathways of loneliness and social support in community-dwelling older adults. *Aging & Mental Health, 16*, 335–346. doi:10.1080/13607863.2011.629092

Scott, H. S. (2018). Extending the Duluth model to workplace bullying: A modification and adaptation of the workplace power–control wheel. *Workplace Health & Safety, 66*, 444–452.

Seeman, T. E., Lusignolo, T. M., Albert, M., & Berkman, L. (2001). Social relationships, social support, and patterns of cognitive aging in healthy, high-functioning older adults: MacArthur studies of successful aging. *Health Psychology, 20*, 243–255.

Seeman, T. E., Singer, B. H., Ryff, C. D., Dienberg Love, G., & Levy-Storms, L. (2002). Social relationships, gender, and allostatic load across two age cohorts. *Psychosomatic Medicine, 64*, 395–406.

Selby, J. V., Beal, A. C., & Frank, L. (2012). The Patient-Centered Outcomes Research Institute (PCORI) national priorities for research and initial research agenda. *Journal of the American Medical Association, 307*(15), 1583–1584.

Semenza, J. C., Rubin, C. H., Falter, K. H., Selanikio, J. D., Flanders, W. D., Howe, H. L., & Wilhelm, J. L. (1996). Heat-related deaths during the July 1995 heat wave in Chicago. *New England Journal of Medicine, 335*, 84–90.

Sherraden, M., Barth, R. P., Brekke, J., Fraser, M., Madershied, R., & Padgett, D. (2015). *Social is fundamental: Introduction and context for Grand Challenges for Social Work.* Grand Challenges for Social Work Initiative, working paper no. 1. Baltimore, MD: American Academy of Social Work and Social Welfare.

Shiba, K., Kondo, N., Kondo, K., & Kawachi, I. (2017). Retirement and mental health: Does social participation mitigate the association? A fixed-effects longitudinal analysis. *BMC Public Health, 17*, 1–10.

Shrira, A. (2020). Parental Holocaust exposure, related PTSD symptoms and subjective aging across the generations. *The Journals of Gerontology: Series B, 75*, 30–41.

Simmons, W. P., Menjívar, C., & Valdez, E. S. (2020). The gendered effects of local immigration enforcement: Latinas' social isolation in Chicago, Houston, Los Angeles, and Phoenix. *International Migration Review, 55*, 108–134.

Smith, M. L., Steinman, L. E., & Casey, E. A. (2020). Combatting social isolation among older adults in a time of physical distancing: The COVID-19 social connectivity paradox. *Frontiers in Public Health, 8*, 403–411.

Solomon, D. H. (2000). Foreword. In D. Osterweil, K. Brummel-Smith, & J. C. Beck (Eds.), *Comprehensive geriatric assessment* (pp. ix–xii). New York, NY: McGraw-Hill.

Stein, J. Y., Levin, Y., Lahav, Y., Uziel, O., Abumock, H., & Solomon, Z. (2018). Perceived social support, loneliness, and later life telomere length following wartime captivity. *Health Psychology, 37*(11), 1067.

Stone, A., Jason, L. A., Light, J. M., & Stevens, E. B. (2016). The role of ego networks in studies of substance use disorder recovery. *Alcoholism Treatment Quarterly, 34*, 315–328.

Storer, H. L., McCleary, J. S., Pepin, E., & Stallings, A. (2020). "That's Why I Stay to Myself": Marginalized youths' meaning making processes of social disconnectedness. *Clinical Social Work Journal, 48*, 25–34.

Strauss, R. S., & Pollack, H. A. (2003). Social marginalization of overweight children. *Archives of Pediatrics & Adolescent Medicine, 157*, 746–752.

Stuck, A. E., Walthert, J. M., Nikolaus, T., Bula, C. J., Hohmann, C., & Beck, J. C. (1999). Risk factors for functional status decline in community-living elderly people: A systematic literature review. *Social Science and Medicine, 48*, 445–469.

Suarez-Orozco, C., Yoshikawa, H., Teranishi, R., & Suarez-Orozco, M. (2011). Growing up in the shadows: The developmental implications of unauthorized status. *Harvard Educational Review, 81*, 438–472.

Tabrizi, F. M., Radfar, M., & Taei, Z. (2016). Effects of supportive-expressive discussion groups on loneliness, hope and quality of life in breast cancer survivors: A randomized control trial. *Psycho-Oncology, 25*, 1057–1063. doi:10.1002/pon.4169

Taylor, H. O. (2020). Social isolation's influence on loneliness among older adults. *Clinical Social Work Journal, 48*, 140–151.

Taylor, R. J., Taylor, H. O., Nguyen, A. W., & Chatters, L. M. (2020). Social isolation from family and friends and mental health among African Americans and Black Caribbeans. *American Journal of Orthopsychiatry, 90*, 468–478.

Teixeira, M. T., Vitorino, R. S., da Silva, J. H., Raposo, L. M., Aquino, L. A., & Ribas, S. A. (2021). Eating habits of children and adolescents during the COVID-19 pandemic: The impact of social isolation. *Journal of Human Nutrition and Dietetics. 34*, 670–678. doi:10.1111/jhn.12901

Thoits, P. A. (1995). Stress, coping and social support processes: Where are we? What next? *Journal of Health and Social Behavior, 35*, 53–79.

Thompson, A. E., Greeson, J. K. P., & Brunsink, A. M. (2016). Natural mentoring among older youth in and aging out of foster care: A systematic review. *Children and Youth Services Review, 61*, 40–50.

Thompson, T., Rodebaugh, T. L., Bessaha, M. L., & Sabbath, E. L. (2020). The association between social isolation and health: An analysis of parent–adolescent dyads from the family life, activity, sun, health, and eating study. *Clinical Social Work Journal, 48*, 18–24.

Tigges, L. M., Browne, I., & Green, G. P. (1998). Social isolation of the urban poor: Race, class and neighborhood effects on social resources. *Sociological Quarterly, 39*, 53–77.

Tracy, E. M., & Brown, S. (2011). Social networks and social work practice. In F. Turner (Ed.), *Social work treatment* (5th ed., pp. 447–459). New York, NY: Oxford University Press.

Tracy, E. M., & Whittaker, J. K. (2015). Commentary: Social network analysis and the social work profession. *Journal of the Society for Social Work and Research, 6,* 643–654.

Tremethick, M. J. (2001). Alone in a crowd: A study of social networks in home health and assisted living. *Journal of Gerontological Nursing, 27,* 42–47.

Twenge, J. M., & Joiner, T. E. (2020). Mental distress among U.S. adults during the COVID-19 pandemic. *Journal of Clinical Psychology, 76,* 2170–2182. doi:10.1002/jclp.23064

Umberson, D., & Montez, J. K. (2010). Social relationships and health: A flashpoint for health policy. *Journal of Health and Social Behavior, 51,* S54–S66.

Usher, K., Bhullar, N., & Jackson, D. (2020). Life in the pandemic: Social isolation and mental health. *Journal of Clinical Nursing, 29,* 2756–2757.

Vaiserman, A. M., & Koliada, A. K. (2017). Early-life adversity and long-term neurobehavioral outcomes: Epigenome as a bridge? *Human Genomics, 11,* 1–15.

Vanhalst, J., Klimstra, T. A., Luyckx, K., Scholte, R. H., Engels, R. C., & Goossens, L. (2012). The interplay of loneliness and depressive symptoms across adolescence: Exploring the role of personality traits. *Journal of Youth and Adolescence, 41*(6), 776–787.

Victor, C. R., Scambler, S. J., Bond, J., & Bowling, A. (2000). Being alone in later life: Loneliness, isolation and living alone in later life. *Reviews in Clinical Gerontology, 10,* 407–417. doi:10.1017/S0959259800104101

Voccia, P., Kruczek, K., & Kettren, J. (2020). A look at possible effects of mandated COVID-19 social isolation on orientation scores for research participants reporting mild memory concerns. *Alzheimer's & Dementia, 16.* e47604 doi:10.1002/alz.047604

Von Heydrich, L., Schiamberg, L. B., & Chee, G. (2012). Social-relational risk factors for predicting elder physical abuse: An ecological bi-focal model. *International Journal of Aging & Human Development, 75,* 71–94. doi:10.2190/Ag.75.1.F

Wakam, G. K., Montgomery, J. R., Biesterveld, B. E., & Brown, C. S. (2020). Not dying alone: Modern compassionate care in the Covid-19 pandemic. *New England Journal of Medicine, 382,* e88.

Wang, J., Mann, F., Lloyd-Evans, B., Ma, R., & Johnson, S. (2018a). Associations between loneliness and perceived social support and outcomes of mental health problems: A systematic review. *BMC Psychiatry, 18*(156), 1–16.

Wang, Q., Phillips, N. E., Small, M. L., & Sampson, R. J. (2018b). Urban mobility and neighborhood isolation in America's 50 largest cities. *Proceedings of the National Academy of Sciences of the United States of America, 115,* 7735–7740. doi:10.1073/pnas.1802537115

Weiler, L. M., Scafe, M., Spencer, R., & Cavell, T. A. (2020). Caregiver-initiated mentoring: Developing a working model to mitigate social isolation. *Clinical Social Work Journal, 48,* 6–17.

Wenger, C., Davies, R., Shahtahmasebi, S., & Scott, A. (1996). Social isolation and loneliness in old age: Review and model refinement. *Ageing & Society, 16,* 333–358.

Whitlock, J., Wyman, P. A., & Moore, S. R. (2014). Connectedness and suicide prevention in adolescents: Pathways and implications. *Suicide and Life-threatening Behavior, 44,* 246–272.

World Health Organization. (1979). *Psychogeriatric care in the community: Public health in Europe.* No. 10. Copenhagen, Denmark: World Health Organization Regional Office for Europe.

World Health Organization. (2002). *Active ageing: A policy framework*. Geneva, Switzerland: Author. Retrieved from http://whqlibdoc.who.int/hq/2002/WHO_NMH_NPH_02.8.pdf?ua=1

World Health Organization. (2018). *The global network for age-friendly cities and communities: Looking back over the last decade, looking forward to the next*. Geneva, Switzerland: Author. Retrieved from https://www.who.int/ageing/publications/gnafcc-report-2018.

Yoshikawa, H., & Kalil, A. (2011). The effects of parental undocumented status on the developmental contexts of young children in immigrant families: Undocumented status in immigrant families. *Child Development Perspectives, 5*, 291–297. doi:10.1111/j.1750-8606.2011.00204.x

Zhang, X., Norris, S., Gregg, E., & Beckles, G. (2007). Social support and mortality among older persons with diabetes. *The Diabetes Educator, 33*, 273–281.

CHAPTER 7

Ending Homelessness

Progress on a Major and Compelling Challenge

BENJAMIN F. HENWOOD, EMMY TIDERINGTON,
AMANDA AYKANIAN, AND DEBORAH K. PADGETT

Starting in 2015, we made the case for ending homelessness as one of the major and compelling challenges that constituted a bold agenda for the social work profession (Henwood et al., 2015b; Padgett & Henwood, 2018). As part of a national Grand Challenge initiative, the Grand Challenge to End Homelessness (GC2EH) was presented as a call to action to the profession. The original call contained what can best be described as signposts or markers of progress rather than a specific roadmap for how the GC2EH could be achieved. As such, it included recommendations such as a) scaling up evidence-based practices for specific target populations, such as Housing First for individuals experiencing chronic homelessness; b) establishing an evidence base for how best to intervene with understudied subpopulations, such as transition-age youth; and c) promoting interdisciplinary training and collaboration to foster innovation in methods for ending homelessness (Henwood et al., 2015b). Since then, schools of social work have taken up the GC2EH through educational innovations, research collaborations, and university–community partnerships (Henwood & Aykanian, 2020; Larkin et al., 2016; Padgett & Henwood, 2020).

Our work remains unfinished. Despite decreases in some parts of the United States, the number of people experiencing homelessness has increased in recent years, especially in large cities such as New York and Los Angeles. Thus, a decade-long downward trend since 2007 was reversed. In the most recently published point-in-time count, there were an estimated 568,000 people experiencing homelessness on a single night in January (Henry, Watt, Mahathey, Ouellette, & Sitler, 2020).

In this chapter, we take stock of the GC2EH in terms of accomplishments achieved thus far. In the first half of the chapter, we review a number of major initiatives or advances in workforce development and research that have been implemented by schools of social work across the United States. Most were organized by a major partner with the GC2EH—the National Center for Excellence in Homeless Services (NCEHS), which is headquartered at the University at Albany (2017) and was funded by the New York Community Trust from 2015 to 2019. The NCEHS represents a number of cooperating schools of social work across the country that have taken up the GC2EH. Another major achievement of the GC2EH was the publication of a series of policy recommendations in the lead-up to the 2020 US presidential election that featured leading national experts in homelessness (University of Southern California Suzanne Dworak-Peck School of Social Work & New York University Silver School of Social Work, 2019).

In the second half of the chapter, we review ongoing and persistent institutional and structural factors, including systemic racism and income/wealth inequality, that perpetuate or exacerbate the problem of homelessness. We also address the impact of the COVID-19 pandemic that poses dire consequences for America's homeless populations, especially for those riding out the pandemic in crowded congregate living situations or living unhoused on the streets. We conclude the chapter by arguing that much of the work that has been accomplished during the first 5 years of the GC2EH lays the groundwork for progress over the next 5 years, but only if there are major structural changes in how homelessness is addressed.

APPROACH AND ACCOMPLISHMENTS

A main focus of the original GC2EH working paper was to scale up evidence-based practices, such as Housing First (Padgett, Henwood, & Tsemberis, 2016) and Critical Time Intervention (Herman, Conover, Felix, Nakagawa, & Mills, 2007). This goal remains critical. However, a prevention framework put forth as a necessary part of the GC2EH (Nicholas & Henwood, 2018; Padgett & Henwood, 2018) shows that although there remains a need to bring to scale effective downstream interventions that are able to address the current scope of the problem, upstream factors must also be addressed to stem the inflow into homelessness.

To address both upstream and downstream factors, the GC2EH recognizes the need for additional work and is actively pursuing several key areas, including the need for workforce development, expanded research, increased collaboration, and policy advocacy, especially for expanded funding for affordable housing. Next we highlight some of the ways these key areas have been addressed over the past 5 years. We also note that because the GC2EH was originally formulated as a call to action more than a strategic initiative, it is possible there are projects inspired by the GC2EH that have not been tracked systematically and therefore are omitted unintentionally from this report.

MAINSTREAMING GENDER

Inclusion of Transgender and Nonbinary People
JAMA SHELTON

People of color, nonbinary people, transgender women, and cisgender women who experience homelessness also face higher rates of violence, victimization and negative health outcomes. Mainstreaming gender in the Grand Challenge to End Homelessness thus requires that we stop prioritizing white cisgender women as the starting point for gender analysis and equity, and include all expressions of gender and gender identities subject to racialized and cis/heteronormative oppression.

Homelessness among transgender and nonbinary (TNB) people is, at least in part, a manifestation of the oppressive structural dynamics of racism and cisgenderism. Although it is imperative that those working with people experiencing homelessness are able to provide safe and affirming care to TNB people, that alone is not sufficient. A holistic approach to addressing homelessness for any population, and particularly for TNB people, requires a conceptual shift from the idea of housing as a privilege to be earned to housing as a human right, as well as a commitment to addressing the structural inequities that produce and maintain the marginalization of TNB people (Shelton & Pucci-Garcon, 2020).

Because homelessness, particularly unsheltered homelessness, is reportedly on the rise for TNB populations, it is imperative that the field respond by centering the experiences of TNB people in efforts to end homelessness. This approach extends beyond simply adding TNB people to the list of populations in need of individualized care and intervention. It places those most marginalized by current systems and structures at the forefront of intervention development, such that systems are redesigned with the explicit goal of equitable access for all. Placing TNB people, particularly transgender women of color, at the center of research, policy, and systems change efforts will not only benefit TNB people, but also will create more effective and equitable solutions for all. For instance, ensuring that TNB people have equitable access to facilities by providing single bathrooms affords *all* people safe and private access. At the core of centering TNB people is an obligation to dismantle the binary gender system and the ways in which it reinforces gender disparities and injustice. The following are three ways social workers can include TNB people intentionally in efforts to address homelessness.

continued

Enact universal employment protections that are inclusive of gender identity and expression. TNB people are more likely to live in poverty and be underemployed, and are less likely to own homes than the general population, all of which make TNB people more vulnerable to homelessness. Employment discrimination undoubtedly contributes to the high poverty levels among TNB people. Their unemployment rate is three times that of the general population (James et al., 2016). Without universal employment protections inclusive of gender identity and expression, TNB people may face unsurmountable challenges to obtaining an income adequate enough to maintain housing. As such, ending homelessness must also be linked to advocacy efforts aimed at nondiscrimination protections that are inclusive of TNB people.

Redesign systems to eliminate cis-normative assumptions. Identifying within the gender binary is a requirement for entrance into and acceptance within many public institutions. Using a binary classification of gender as a way to organize society creates functional challenges for TNB individuals within homelessness systems. Cis-normative assumptions are evident in intake and documentation procedures, the design of binary sex/gender-segregated programs, determinations about an individual's basic needs, and case planning activities that fail to take into account the societal barriers unique to TNB people (such as a lack of inclusive nondiscrimination protections in employment, housing, and public accommodations).

Abolish congregate shelters. Congregate shelter settings are often sites of violence for TNB people who, despite the current Equal Access Rule, continue to face discrimination and victimization in large congregate shelters. TNB people have reported being denied access to shelter, needing to alter their gender presentation (in ways that may make them physically safer but simultaneously impact their mental health) to access shelter, and lacking the privacy needed to prepare oneself for the day (Shelton, 2015). With the COVID-19 crisis, many homelessness systems have had to identify alternative ways to house people to minimize the spread of the virus. This has undoubtedly been a difficult task. Yet, in some instances, communities have used temporary housing placements effectively to reduce the size of the shelter population and maintain social-distancing requirements. This provides a unique opportunity to reexamine the congregate model of shelter.

To address homelessness adequately requires the intentional inclusion of TNB people in policy and programmatic interventions. Social workers must not only focus on individual-level interventions, but must also address the structural inequities that lead to disproportionate rates of homelessness among multiply marginalized populations.

References

James, S. E., Herman, J. L., Rankin, S., Keisling, M., Mottet, L., & Anafi, M. (2016). *The report of the 2015 U.S. transgender survey.* Washington, DC: National Center for Transgender Equality.

continued

> Shelton, J. (2015). Transgender youth homelessness: Understanding programmatic barriers through the lens of cisgenderism. *Children and Youth Services Review*, 59, 10–18.
> Shelton, J. & Pucci-Garcon, T. (2020). Homelessness among transgender and non-binary individuals. In S.K. Kattari, N.E. Walls, L. Kattari, & M.K. Kinney (Eds.), *Social work and health care with transgender/non-binary individuals and communities*. New York, NY: Routledge Press.

Workforce Development

Despite the existence of evidence-based housing and homelessness prevention interventions, their adoption by homeless service systems has not been widespread, or (as in the case of Housing First) they have been adopted more in name than in practice. Bridging the gap between evidence and implementation requires a well-trained workforce, including social workers. Over the past 5 years, there have been several efforts to improve social work education and provide a new generation of social work practitioners and leaders in homelessness services. For example, in 2019, the Council on Social Work Education, in partnership with the NCEHS, produced a series of webinars and a curricular guide for addressing homelessness that provided examples of readings and activities for teaching about homelessness across each of Council on Social Work Education's nine educational competencies. The curricular guide was developed by an advisory committee of 10 faculty members from NCEHS partner schools. The NCEHS also published a coedited textbook that featured chapters written by faculty and students from schools of social work across the United States (Larkin, Aykanian, & Streeter, 2020).

Other efforts from across schools of social work were captured in a special edition of the *Journal of Social Work Education* dedicated to the GC2EH (Henwood & Aykanian, 2020). Some of the articles in the special edition addressed existing gaps in social work classroom curricula (Cronley, Murphy, & Petrovich, 2020; Smith-Maddox, Brown, Kratz, & Newmyer, 2020). Other articles emphasized the advantage of developing interdisciplinary curricular approaches that incorporate fields beyond social work (Bender, Wilson, Adelman, DeChants, & Rutherford, 2020; Petrovitch & Navarro, 2020; Siegel, Smith, & Melluci, 2020). Two articles addressed the need to develop innovative field placement programs that focus on homelessness (Aykanian et al., 2020; Gallup et al., 2020). One described the establishment of a collective workgroup across all schools of social work in the Los Angeles area, home to the largest unsheltered population in the country. Students in this program are provided a stipend and are introduced to the GC2EH with the goal of developing future leaders given local workforce shortages (Gallup et al., 2020).

The greatest number of articles from the special edition of the *Journal of Social Work Education* focused on the importance of university–community partnerships in addressing homelessness (Burns, Kwan, & Walsh, 2020; Charlesworth and Metzger, 2020; Jacob, Tauati, & Brown, 2020; Lery, Miller Haight, & Roscoe, 2020; Plitt Donaldson et al., 2020). This included work done by the NCEHS, which used its collaborative model to advocate for effective policy by engaging federal government agencies, including the Department of Veterans Affairs and the Substance Abuse and Mental Health Services Administration. One particularly promising collaboration is with Substance Abuse and Mental Health Services Administration's SSI/SSDI (Social Security income/Social Security disability insurance) Outreach, Access, and Recovery (SOAR) Technical Assistance Center. SOAR is a federal program designed to increase access to Social Security income/Social Security disability insurance benefits for homeless individuals with complex physical, mental, or behavioral health needs. The SOAR model involves training providers to assist individuals experiencing homelessness with completing benefit applications, which is a skill that is valuable for social workers entering positions in community-based services. Recognizing this, multiple schools of social work have begun integrating SOAR training into coursework or field training with SOAR-related university–community partnerships located at California State University at Long Beach, the University at Albany, Catholic University of America, and the University of Texas at Austin (Plitt Donaldson et al., 2020).

Collectively, the special edition demonstrated how schools of social work can strengthen curricula, enhance field placements, and train future practitioners, scholars, advocates, and policymakers to address the GC2EH. The larger impact of this work remains to be seen, and will require time and monitoring, but we are hopeful these efforts have increased the overall capacity of the field.

Expanded Research

During the past 5 years, considerable research has been undertaken by social work scholars and others related to the GC2EH. This research portfolio is best understood through the comprehensive prevention-centered framework mentioned earlier (Nicholas & Henwood, 2018; Padgett & Henwood, 2018), in that it has developed evidence on both downstream services that address homelessness and upstream points of intervention to prevent homelessness. Research collaboratives created by and/or including social work scholars are actively working to produce and disseminate this body of knowledge. An example of social work–influenced collaborative efforts is the inclusion of social work faculty members on the Research Council of the National Alliance to End Homelessness (NAEH). The NAEH has produced several key reports intended to inform policymakers, providers, and the public. These include the "State of Homelessness: 2020 Edition," which is the tenth in a series of reports charting progress in ending homelessness in the United States (National

Alliance to End Homelessness, 2020b), and "A Research Agenda for Ending Homelessness," which was developed to inform government agencies, philanthropic organizations, and other funders about research questions on homeless populations and interventions designed to end homelessness (National Alliance to End Homelessness, 2020a).

Social workers also have a significant presence as part of the Homelessness Policy Research Institute at the University of Southern California. This group aims to accelerate local solutions to end homelessness in Los Angeles County (Sol Price Center for Social Innovation, 2020). In addition, during the past 5 years there have been two research centers developed within schools of social work, including the Center for Homelessness, Housing, and Health Equity Research at the University of Southern California (USC Suzanne Dworak-Peck School of Social Work, n.d.) and the Center for Housing and Homelessness Research at the University of Denver (Graduate School of Social Work, 2020).

Social work scholars from these collaborative groups and others have expanded GC2EH-related research in several key areas. In recognition of the need for downstream improvements within homeless services, researchers have sought to identify the unique needs of particular subgroups within the general homeless population and examine the ways in which one-size-fits-all services can be better adapted to meet the needs of these subgroups. Of particular concern, the number of older homeless adults has been increasing disproportionately relative to other groups, and elder homelessness (the aging baby boom generation) is expected to triple in the United States during the next 10 years (Culhane et al., 2019). In response to this changing demographic, researchers have worked to describe more completely their pressing health needs, including cognitive decline, chronic illness, and palliative care needs (Henwood, Lahey, Rhoades, Winetrobe, & Wenzel, 2018; Henwood et al., 2020). Additional research has focused on how formerly homeless older adults view their life priorities (Padgett, Bond, Gurdak, & Henwood, 2020), the need to develop best practices for "aging in place" (Henwood, Katz, & Gilmer, 2015a), and how to propose policy responses to support elders within homeless services (Culhane et al., 2019).

Recent research has also focused on groups who are represented disproportionately among the homeless in the United States, such as youths; students; lesbian, gay, bisexual, transgender, queer (LGBTQ) individuals; and certain groups of color, including Black, Indigenous, multiracial, and Hispanic/Latinx. Homeless adults are predominantly male, comprising 60% of all people experiencing homelessness (National Alliance to End Homelessness, 2020d). However, homeless women experience greater rates of intimate partner violence and sexual assault than homeless men, and therefore require special attention and services to meet those needs. The Grand Challenges for Social Work, including the GC2EH, recognize the need to center gender (Messing, 2020). As such, the GC2EH acknowledges the unique needs of homeless women, and further research in this area is warranted. Recent research includes examinations of child abuse victimization, depression, and substance use among homeless women (Song, Wenzel, & Cho, 2019); women's health and social support when entering permanent supportive housing (Winetrobe et al., 2017); and community integration experiences of women with problematic substance use in Housing First (Bassi, Sylvestre, & Kerman, 2020).

In addition to addressing the unique needs of homeless women, centering gender requires an inclusive approach that recognizes the expansiveness of gender identity and attends to the differential experiences of subgroups within the larger LGBTQ+ population (Kroehle, Shelton, Clark, & Seelamn, 2020). The available data indicate that homelessness among transgender and nonbinary individuals is increasing, and this group faces higher rates of health problems and victimization than cisgender groups (Fraser, Pierse, Chisolm, & Cook, 2019; Henry et al., 2020; National Alliance to End Homelessness, 2020d). Because homeless service settings are traditionally designed with a binary view of gender (e.g., male/female divisions in shelters or shelter beds), access barriers exist for transgender and nonbinary individuals, including being denied shelter and experiencing harassment in shelters (Fraser et al., 2019; James et al., 2016; Shelton, 2015). Perhaps as a result of this, transgender and gender nonconforming individuals experience unsheltered homelessness at a greater rate (67%) than cisgender individuals (37%) (Henry et al., 2020), and being unsheltered results in more health problems and safety risks for this group (National Alliance to End Homelessness, 2020d). In response to these disparities, there is a growing body of social work research addressing the need to make homeless services more gender responsive, which includes improving intake assessments, creating safe physical spaces, training staff to be gender affirming, and addressing discrimination in shelter and housing (Begun & Kattari, 2016; Kattari, Whitfield, Walls, Langenderfer-Magruder, & Ramos, 2016; Maccio & Ferguson, 2016).

Homeless youth, including LGBTQ youth and youth aging out of foster care, are also groups that have been the focus of recent research related to the GC2EH. This work includes studies of risk behaviors and risk-related outcomes of homeless youth (Alessi, Greenfield, Manning, & Dank, 2020; Barman-Adhikari, Hsu, Begun, Portillo, & Rice, 2017; Harris, Rice, Rhoades, Winetrobe, & Wenzel, 2017; Narendorf et al., 2020; Srivastava et al., 2019), as well as research on protective factors and interventions that can be used to address these risks (Chassman et al., 2020; Hsu et al., 2019; Yadav et al., 2018; Yoshioka-Maxwell & Rice, 2020; Young, Mayaud, Suen, Tambe, & Rice, 2020). Students experiencing and at risk for homelessness are another special population that has recently received attention from social work researchers (Crutchfield, 2018; Crutchfield, Chambers, Carpena, & McCloyn, 2020; Crutchfield & Meyer-Adams, 2019; Hallett & Crutchfield, 2018; Huang, Fernandez, Rhoden, & Joseph, 2018).

Veterans continue to be a population of special interest in their prioritization for services within the US homeless service system. Among the most successful initiatives to end homelessness in the past decade has been the US Department of Housing and Urban Development (HUD)–Veterans Affairs Supportive Housing program, with its Housing First–focused package of services, including aggressive outreach combined with rental assistance vouchers and intensive support services (Evans, Kroeger, Palmer, & Pohl, 2019). Reducing and even eliminating veterans' homelessness in many cities, the HUD–Veterans Affairs Supportive Housing program has generated a large body of research highlighting its successes and challenges (Kertesz et al., 2017). More recent work includes a focus on homeless veterans who use opioids (Midboe et al., 2019), those who are registered sex offenders (Byrne et al., 2020a), and those living in rural areas (Byrne, Cusack, True, Montgomery, & Smith, 2020b).

Transitions within and from services is a recent topic of interest for social work scholars working to end homelessness, as there remains a need to "right-size" homeless services to fit individual needs, to increase service system capacity, and to promote independent living beyond supportive housing (Tiderington, Petering, Huang, Harris, & Tsai, 2020c). Thus far, this research has primarily focused on describing implementation and outcomes of Moving On initiatives (MOIs), programs that assist permanent supportive housing residents who are no longer in need of intensive supports, with the transition to mainstream housing. Research in this area has described challenges associated with the implementation of MOIs (Tiderington, Ikeda, & Lovell, 2020b), various individual-level outcomes of MOIs (Gurdak, Tiderington, & Stefancic, 2020; Tiderington, Aykanian, Huang, &Tsai, 2020a), and individual transition experiences (Tiderington, 2020a).

Upstream causal factors of homelessness such as income inequality, systemic racism, and inequities within US systems and institutions have also been interrogated by social work researchers during the first phase of the GC2EH. Prompted in part by structural shifts that occurred after 2016, including the changing policy priorities of the Trump administration, social movements such as Black Lives Matter, and the COVID-19 global pandemic, interest in homelessness was extended to understand and address its root causes more fully. Research on upstream efforts to predict and prevent homelessness has been undertaken by investigators examining predictive factors associated with housing instability (McCollum, Fargo, Byrne, & Montgomery, 2020) and the risk of eviction (Desmond, 2016).

Groups such as the California Policy Lab and the University of Chicago Poverty Lab (Evans, Sullivan, & Wallskog, 2016; Von Wachter, Bertrand, Pollack, Rountree, & Blackwell, 2019) have sought to identify people at high risk for homelessness, and to design and test prevention strategies based on these predictive risk factors. In perhaps what is the most rigorously empirical response to date on the question of income inequality and homelessness,

GC2EH-related work has found that income inequality is a significant driver of homelessness at the local level, which suggests that broader policy efforts to reduce income inequality are likely to have the collateral effect of reducing homelessness (Byrne, Henwood, & Orlando, 2020). The focus on upstream factors has also resulted in a call to develop a more comprehensive measure of housing insecurity in which homelessness can be considered an extreme outcome (Cox, Henwood, Rodnyansky, Rice, & Wenzel, 2019).

Last, it is important to highlight the increasing attention to the role of racism in contributing to homelessness (Wenzel, Rhoades, LaMotte-Kerr, & Duan, 2019), including the recent addition of a new Grand Challenge to Eliminate Racism, and the GC2EH's response describing the historic and ongoing role of racism in the US homelessness crisis (Padgett, Henwood, & Petrovich, in press).

Policy Advocacy

For most of the past 4 years, federal policies to address homelessness have either languished from inattention or been the subject of direct hostility. Congressional oversight ensured that budgetary outlays from HUD were not severely cut, but the Trump administration took action where its purview was ensured—the US Interagency Council on Homelessness. A leader in advancing the cause of ending homelessness through Housing First policies dating back to the Bush administration–era of the early 2000s, the US Interagency Council on Homelessness underwent a drastic change in leadership in 2020 with the appointment of a director whose reputation was made through rejecting Housing First in favor of an antiquated "bootstraps" approach wherein homeless persons were responsible for their fate (National Low Income Housing Coalition, 2019).

Undaunted and further galvanized into action by these policy changes, national organizations such as the NAEH and the National Low Income Housing Coalition led advocacy efforts intended to counter this disturbing trend. A link between the GC2EH and these organizations was forged with the GC2EH-sponsored publication and distribution of a set of policy recommendations for the 2020 presidential election that featured proposals from NAEH Executive Director Nan Roman and National Low Income Housing Coalition Director Diane Yentel, among other national experts. Social work scholars also featured in the policy briefs included Dennis Culhane, Daniel Treglia, and Beth Horowitz, along with the editors Deborah Padgett and Benjamin Henwood (University of Southern California Suzanne Dworak-Peck School of Social Work & New York University Silver School of Social Work, 2019).

Meanwhile, states and localities mounted funding initiatives on their own, all of which reached crisis levels with the onset of the COVID-19 pandemic in early 2020 as congregate shelters were highly susceptible to contagion. At the local level, the GC2EH officially endorsed two ballot measures in Los Angeles passed by voters in 2016 and 2017 (United Way of Greater Los Angeles, 2020). Together, these measures are expected to generate more than $2 billion over 10 years to fund key aspects of Los Angeles' plan to end homelessness. Work related to the GC2EH also helped change policy so that unaccompanied women were designated as a unique subpopulation for the first time in two large counties in California. This designation brings with it greater attention and more dedicated funding to a subpopulation that has at times been overlooked.

Other efforts to advance the GC2EH have occurred through the judicial system, with the American Civil Liberties Union and pro bono law firms enlisting the co-leads of the GC2EH to serve as expert witnesses for court cases in Miami, Los Angeles, and Washington, DC, to assert the rights of homeless persons. Op-eds in national and local news outlets have also been used to advocate homelessness policy, including those written to advocate for an increase in affordable housing (Tiderington, 2020b), changes in HUD policies (HUD's Making Affordable Housing Work Act: Dangerous policy in a time of crisis, May, 2018), favoring permanent housing over shelter expansions (Padgett, 2019), and leveraging opportunities brought about the COVID-19 pandemic (Byrne, Henwood, & Orlando, 2021).

As mentioned earlier, efforts to advance the GC2EH began to focus on the 2020 US presidential election, resulting in the set of essay policy recommendations made by national experts. Topics ranged from the crisis of the aging homeless population to the special needs of homeless youth and families to systemic racism in homelessness. All the essays ended with recommendations intended to influence policymakers and the 2020 presidential candidates, including calls for increasing the stock of affordable housing, instituting a universal basic income, expanding access to rental assistance, and changing taxation policies. The essays were compiled into a readable short document and were distributed to policymakers, including members of Congress and their staff. They also served as the basis for a webinar hosted by the NAEH to help bring attention to the importance of homelessness and housing during the election season (National Alliance to End Homelessness, 2020c).

In 2020, policy advocacy to advance the GC2EH also focused on the COVID-19 pandemic and its impact on homelessness. A report authored by faculty from multiple schools of social work analyzed the potential impact that COVID-19 infection would have on the homeless population and healthcare system, and estimated the resources that would be needed to mitigate this risk (Culhane, Treglia, Steif, Kuhn, & Byrne, 2020). This report supported the inclusion of $4 billion for COVID-19 risk mitigation within homeless service systems as part of the $2 trillion emergency Coronavirus Aid, Relief, and Economic Security Act and deployed across the nation in mid-2020.

FUTURE DIRECTIONS

As the GC2EH approaches its next phase, the election of Joseph Biden as President and Senator Kamala Harris as Vice President offers a measure of hope for long overdue funding increases and policy changes that will assist Americans who are homeless and housing insecure. (Indeed, several of the Democratic candidates' campaign platforms brought unprecedented attention to this issue.) It is heartening to see housing become a national priority along with other economic and existential problems, such as unemployment and climate change. The incoming Biden administration's proposals include zoning reform, legal assistance for tenants facing eviction, increasing the housing stock, and expanding the federal rental voucher program, with a proposed budget of $640 billion over the next decade (Mojadad, 2020). Although the reality of congressional approval for such an expansive housing program is surely open to question, even the existence of such a detailed plan represents a welcome change from previous federal policies that favored emergency shelters over rental assistance and expanding the stock of affordable housing. In this context, the GC2EH and its partners can envision a new era of possibilities.

One of these new possibilities was entirely unanticipated and stems from the COVID-19 pandemic that besieged the nation through 2020 and continues as of this writing. As the virus rapidly spread during the early months of 2020, the presence of thousands of crowded congregate living facilities presented an immediate public health hazard of contagion and immense human suffering. The particular vulnerability of homeless persons who experience premature aging and comorbid medical problems further heightened the urgency of this crisis (Culhane et al., 2020).

The coincident existence of empty hotels (as travel and tourism fell to record lows) presented an opportunity hardly considered imaginable before—moving homeless shelter residents and street homeless persons into private hotel rooms to protect them (and the general public) from the spread of COVID-19. Congressional passage of the Coronavirus Aid, Relief, and Economic Security Act in April 2020 allocated emergency federal funding to cover these hotel costs, and a number of cities took advantage of this windfall of new (albeit temporary) revenue. A national eviction moratorium was also mandated at the federal level to prevent already-high levels of homelessness from increasing because of the massive loss of jobs attributable to the pandemic. This moratorium was extended until the end of 2020. But, without renewal in the New Year, tenants will be expected to pay rent moving forward and cover past-due rental arrears, which could trigger a new crisis of evictions and homelessness (National Low Income Housing Coalition, 2016).

With the hotel transitions made possible on a wide scale, advocates for homeless persons—not to mention those most affected—witnessed a revelatory event: a homeless person stuck in a crowded, unsafe shelter or sleeping on a subway is "suddenly" offered a private hotel room complete with bathroom, clean linens, and microwave and/or small refrigerator for food storage. Hotel staff—grateful to have jobs—adjusted to their new guests who were finally able to observe social distancing and reside in their own private space. And, with the exception of some isolated but at times fierce "not in my backyard" reactions (Smith, Dillon, & Oreskes, 2020), most of the hotel guests found a welcome, if temporary, home that was far superior to what they had left behind. Preliminary research on their experiences showed substantial benefits, including the tangible (eased access to entitlements such as food stamps and Medicaid enrollment) and the intangible (the deeply satisfying experience of a restful night's sleep; feelings of safety, autonomy, and improved nutrition, not to mention protection from COVID exposure). That such an experience was temporary gave pause to residents who feared a return to the shelters, but its short-term benefits were consequential. In a University of Washington study in Seattle's repurposed hotels, reduced numbers of 911 calls and interpersonal conflicts were cited alongside improvements in health and faster exits to permanent housing (Colburn, Fyall, Thompson, & Dean, 2020).

Preliminary reports of successful transitions raised the larger question of novel opportunities for more permanent housing; many of these hotels would not recover their former tourist clientele given the pandemic's longevity. Perhaps such hotels could be bought (or leased) and retrofitted to be semipermanent living quarters? Advocates argued that such conversions—although often complicated by zoning restrictions and conversion costs—could eventually save money through reduced reliance on shelters, hospital visits, and so on (Levin, 2020). Some localities moved to increase local revenues rather than wait for federal funds to jump-start new housing initiatives. For example, King County in Washington passed a 1% increase in the local sales tax that would generate $70 million annually devoted to housing chronically homeless persons (Markovich, 2020).

Social workers play a key (and too-often invisible) role in helping shelter and street homeless persons' transition to housing, whether temporary or permanent. The GC2EH could be instrumental in forging partnerships with national organizations such as the NAEH and local entities in heavily affected cities such as New York and Los Angeles. Three areas (in ranked order) come to mind: a) *local advocacy* (join campaigns to lengthen hotel stays until the pandemic is over and simultaneously begin the repurposing of hotels into semipermanent living quarters), b) *rapid research assessments* of client needs and satisfaction as well as "hard" outcomes (e.g., reduced costs of hospital visits, fewer 911 calls, and more access to job training, housing rental vouchers, and permanent housing), and c) *partnering with national advocacy organizations* in the broader (and heavier) "lift" of making affordable housing more readily available through increased federal funding for rental assistance, rapid rehousing, and low-interest loans for first-time home buyers (especially Black individuals and families who have suffered historical discrimination). A more detailed description of the historic and ongoing impact of systemic racism in creating and sustaining disproportionate rates of homelessness among Blacks can be found in a chapter authored by GC2EH leads (Padgett et al., in press) as part of an edited book featuring the newest Grand Challenge to Eliminate Racism (Teasley & Spencer, in press). The insidious role of racism is central to understanding the varied contributors to the rise of homelessness during the 1980s.

CONCLUSION

Although much has been accomplished under the aegis of the GC2EH, there is much more left to do to achieve the goal of ending homelessness. Since the start of the GC2EH, social work scholars have worked actively to scale up evidence-based practices and establish an evidence base for intervening with understudied subpopulations. Interdisciplinary training and collaboration between key stakeholders have been used to foster innovation and new methods for ending homelessness.

However, to meet this challenge fully and address both the upstream and downstream factors that have led to high current rates of homelessness in the United States, additional workforce development, expanded research, increased collaboration, and policy advocacy will be necessary going forward. With a new presidential administration taking the reins at the federal level, there is reason for cautious optimism even in the face of a foreboding public health crisis.

However, without major structural changes in housing policies and funding allotments, the GC2EH's ultimate goal remains elusive. It is difficult to overestimate the interlocking factors that undergird the current status quo—ranging from zoning ordinances that forbid multifamily dwellings to tax benefits for homeowners and developers to a multibillion-dollar "industry" designed to manage rather than end homelessness. The Grand Challenge to End Homelessness has much work to do.

REFERENCES

Alessi, E. J., Greenfield, B., Manning, D., & Dank, M. (2020). Victimization and resilience among sexual and gender minority homeless youth engaging in survival sex. *Journal of Interpersonal Violence*. Advanced online publication. doi:10.1177/0886260519898434

Aykanian, A., Morton, P., Trawver, K., Victorson, L., Preskitt, S., & Street, K. (2020). Library-based field placements: Meeting the diverse needs of patrons, including those experiencing homelessness. *Journal of Social Work Education*, 56, S72–S80.

Barman-Adhikari, A., Hsu, H. T., Begun, S., Portillo, A. P., & Rice, E. (2017). Condomless sex among homeless youth: The role of multidimensional social norms and gender. *AIDS and Behavior, 21*, 688–702.

Bassi, A., Sylvestre, J., & Kerman, N. (2020). Finding home: Community integration experiences of formerly homeless women with problematic substance use in Housing First. *Journal of Community Psychology, 48*, 2375–2390.

Begun, S., & Kattari, S. K. (2016). Conforming for survival: Associations between transgender visual conformity/passing and homelessness experiences. *Journal of Gay and Lesbian Social Services, 28*, 54–66.

Bender, K., Wilson, J., Adelman, E., DeChants, J., & Rutherford, M. (2020). A human-centered design approach to interdisciplinary training on homelessness. *Journal of Social Work Education, 56*, S28–S45.

Burns, V., Kwan, C., & Walsh, C. A. (2020). Co-producing knowledge through documentary film: A community-based participatory study with older adults with homeless histories. *Journal of Social Work Education, 56*, S119–S130.

Byrne, T., Cashy, J., Metraux, S., Blosnich, J. R., Cusack, M., Culhane, D. P., . . . Montgomery, A. E. (2020a). Association between registered sex offender status and risk of housing instability and homelessness among veterans. *Journal of Interpersonal Violence*. Online ahead of print. doi:10.1177/0886260520959646

Byrne, T., Cusack, M., True, G., Montgomery, A. E., & Smith, M. (2020b). "You don't see them on the streets of your town": Challenges and strategies for serving unstably housed veterans in rural areas. *Housing Policy Debate, 30*, 409–430.

Byrne, T. H., Henwood, B. F., & Orlando, A. W. (2021). A rising tide drowns unstable boats: How inequality creates homelessness. *The Annals of the American Academy of Political and Social Science, 693*, 28–45.

Charlesworth, L. W., & Metzger, J. (2020). Scaffolding student learning: The Project Homeless Connect Model. *Journal of Social Work Education, 56*, S142–S149.

Chassman, S., Littman, D. M., Bender, K., Santa Maria, D., Shelton, J., Ferguson, K. M., . . . Petering, R. (2020). Educational attainment among young adults experiencing homelessness in seven cities across the United States. *Children and Youth Services Review, 119*, https://doi.org/10.1016/j.childyouth.2020.105676

Colburn, G., Fyall, R., Thompson, S., & Dean, T. (2020). Impact of hotels as non-congregate emergency shelters. Retrieved from https://depts.washington.edu/urbanuw/news/final-report-impact-of-hotels-as-non-congregate-emergency-shelters/

Council on Social Work Education. (2019). Curricular guide for addressing homelessness. Retrieved from https://cswe.org/getattachment/Education-Resources/2015-Curricular-Guides/6623_cswe_2015EPAS_Homelessness_WEB144_rev1.pdf.aspx

Cox, R., Henwood, B., Rodnyansky, S., Rice, E., & Wenzel, S. (2019). Road map to a unified measure of housing insecurity. *Cityscape, 21*, 93–128.

Cronley, C., Murphy, E. R., & Petrovich, J. C. (2020). Homelessness from a holistic paradigm: Bridging gaps in curriculum through supplemental education opportunities. *Journal of Social Work Education, 56*, S16–S27.

Crutchfield, R. M. (2018). Under a temporary roof and in the classroom: Service agencies for youth who are homeless while enrolled in community college. *Child & Youth Services, 39*, 117–136.

Crutchfield, R. M., Chambers, R. M., Carpena, A., & McCloyn, T. N. (2020). Getting help: An exploration of student experiences with a campus program addressing basic needs insecurity. *Journal of Social Distress and Homelessness, 29*, 16–24.

Crutchfield, R. M., & Meyer-Adams, N. (2019). "If I don't fight for it, I have nothing": Supporting students who experience homelessness while enrolled in higher education. In H. Larkin, A. Aykanian, & C. L. Streeter (Eds.), *Homelessness prevention and intervention in social work: Policies, programs, and practices* (pp. 359–377). New York, NY: Springer.

Culhane, D., Doran, K., Schretzman, M., Johns, E., Treglia, D., Byrne, T., . . . & Kuhn, R. (2019). The emerging crisis of aged homelessness in the US: Could cost avoidance in health care fund housing solutions? *International Journal of Population Data Science, 4,* 24. doi:10.23889/ijpds.v4i3.1185

Culhane, D. P., Treglia, D., Steif, K., Kuhn, R., & Byrne, T. (2020). Estimated emergency and observational/quarantine capacity need for the US homeless population related to COVID-19 exposure by county: Projected hospitalizations, intensive care units and mortality. Retrieved from http://works.bepress.com/dennis_culhane/237/

Desmond, M. (2016). *Evicted: Poverty and profit in the American city.* New York, NY: Crown.

Evans, W. N., Kroeger, S., Palmer, C., & Pohl, E. (2019). Housing and Urban Development–Veterans Affairs Supportive Housing vouchers and veterans' homelessness, 2007–2017. *American Journal of Public Health, 109,* 1440–1445.

Evans, W. N., Sullivan, J. X., & Wallskog, M. (2016). The impact of homelessness prevention programs on homelessness. *Science, 353,* 694–699.

Fraser, B., Pierse, N., Chisolm, E., & Cook, H. (2019). LGBTIQ+ homelessness: A review of the literature. *International Journal of Environmental Research and Public Health, 16,* 2677–2690.

Gallup, D., Briglio, J., Devaney, E., Samario, D., Veldman, D., Cianni, A., & Papel, D. (2020). Addressing a homeless services workforce deficit through collaborative social work field placements. *Journal of Social Work Education, 56,* S81–S98.

Graduate School of Social Work. (2020). Center for housing and homelessness research. Retrieved from https://socialwork.du.edu/chhr

Gurdak, K., Tiderington, E., & Stefancic, A. (2020). Community integration when moving on from permanent supportive housing. *Journal of Community Psychology, 48,* 1913–1928. doi:10.1002/jcop.22389

Hallett, R. E., & Crutchfield, R. (2018). *Homelessness and housing insecurity in higher education: A trauma-informed approach to research, policy, and practice.* ASHE higher education report. John Wiley & Sons, Hoboken, New Jersey.

Harris, T., Rice, E., Rhoades, H., Winetrobe, H., & Wenzel, S. (2017). Gender differences in the path from sexual victimization to HIV risk behavior among homeless youth. *Journal of Child Sexual Abuse, 26,* 334–351.

Henry, M., Watt, R., Mahathey, A., Ouellette, J., & Sitler, A. (2020). The 2019 annual homelessness assessment report (AHAR) to Congress. Retrieved from https://www.hudexchange.info/resource/5948/2019-ahar-part-1-pit-estimates-of-homelessness-in-the-us/

Henwood, B. F., & Aykanian, A. (2020). Advancing social work education to meet the grand challenge of ending homelessness. *Journal of Social Work Education, 56),* S1–S3.

Henwood, B. F., Katz, M. L., & Gilmer, T. P. (2015a). Aging in place within permanent supportive housing. *International Journal of Geriatric Psychiatry, 30,* 80–87.

Henwood, B. F., Lahey, J., Rhoades, H., Winetrobe, H., & Wenzel, S. L. (2018). Examining the health status of homeless adults entering permanent supportive housing. *Journal of Public Health, 40,* 415–418.

Henwood, B. F., Rhoades, H., Lahey, J., Pynoos, J., Pitts, D. B., & Brown, R. T. (2020). Examining fall risk among formerly homeless older adults living in permanent supportive housing. *Health & Social Care in the Community, 28,* 842–849.

Henwood, B. F., Wenzel, S. L., Mangano, P. F., Hombs, M., Padgett, D. K., Byrne, T., . . . Uretsky, M. C. (2015b). The grand challenge of ending homelessness. Grand Challenges for Social Work Initiative working paper no. 9. American Academy of Social Work and Social Welfare.

Herman, D., Conover, S., Felix, A., Nakagawa, A., & Mills, D. (2007). Critical time intervention: An empirically supported model for preventing homelessness in high risk groups. *Journal of Primary Prevention*, 28, 295–312. doi:10.1007/s10935-007-0099-3

Hsu, H. T., Rice, E., Wilson, J., Semborski, S., Vayanos, P., & Morton, M. (2019). Understanding wait times in rapid re-housing among homeless youth: A competing risk survival analysis. *The Journal of Primary Prevention*, 40, 529–544.

Huang, H., Fernandez, S., Rhoden, M. A., & Joseph, R. (2018). Serving former foster youth and homeless students in college. *Journal of Social Service Research*, 44, 209–222.

HUD's Making Affordable Housing Work Act: Dangerous policy in a time of crisis. (May, 2018) Retrieved from https://www.gc2eh.org/post/ hud-s-making-affordable-housing-work-act- dangerous-policy-in-a-time-of-crisis

Jacob, A., Tauati, A., & Brown, A. (2020). Applied response to homelessness: Model for Service learning across the micro–macro social work practice continuum. *Journal of Social Work Education*, 56, S131–S141.

James, S. E., Herman, J. L., Rankin, S., Keisling, M., Mottet, L., & Anafi, M. (2016). *The report of the 2015 U.S. transgender survey*. National Center for Transgender Equality.

Kattari, S. K., Whitfield, D. L., Walls, E., Langenderfer-Magruder, L., & Ramos, D. (2016). Policing gender through housing and employment discrimination: Comparison of discrimination experiences of transgender and cisgender LGBQ individuals. *Journal of the Society for Social Work Research*, 7, 427–447.

Kertesz, S. G., Austin, E. L., Holmes, S. K., DeRussy, A. J., Van Deusen Lukas, C., & Pollio, D. E. (2017). Housing First on a large scale: Fidelity strengths and challenges in the VA's HUD-VASH program. *Psychological Services*, 14, 118–128.

Kroehle, K., Shelton, J., Clark, E., & Seelamn, K. (2020). Mainstreaming dissidence: Confronting binary gender in social work's grand challenges. *Social Work*, 65(4), 368–377. doi:10.1093/sw/swaa037

Larkin, H., Aykanian, A., & Streeter, C. (Eds.). (2020). *Homelessness prevention and intervention in social work: Policies, programs, and practices*. New York, NY: Springer Nature.

Larkin, H., Henwood, B., Fogel, S. J., Aykanian, A., Briar-Lawson, K. H., Donaldson, L. P., . . . Streeter, C. L. (2016). Responding to the Grand Challenge to End Homelessness: The National Homelessness Social Work Initiative. *Families in Society*, 97, 153–159.

Lery, B., Miller Haight, J., & Roscoe, J. N. (2020). Skills for collaboration: Training graduate students in using evidence to evaluate a homelessness program. *Journal of Social Work Education*, 56, S111–S118.

Levin, M. (2020, November 9). Converting a motel to homeless housing step by step. Retrieved from https://calmatters.org/housing/2020/06/motel-conversion-homeless-housing-california/

Maccio, E. M., & Ferguson, K. M. (2016). Services to LGBTQ runaway and homeless youth: Gaps and recommendations. *Children and Youth Services Review*, 63, 47–57.

Markovich, M. (2020, October 13). King County raises sales tax in effort to help house the chronic homeless population. Retrieved from https://komonews.com/news/

project-seattle/king-county-raises-sales-tax-in-effort-to-help-the-areas-chronic-homeless-population

McCollum, C., Fargo, J. D., Byrne, T., & Montgomery, A. E. (2020). Working upstream: Risk factors for homelessness and opportunities for prevention. In *APHA's 2020 VIRTUAL Annual Meeting and Expo (Oct. 24–28)*. San Francisco, CA: Conference Poster presentation.

Messing, J. T. (2020). Mainstreaming gender: An intersectional feminist approach to the Grand Challenges for Social Work. *Social Work, 65*(4), 313–315. doi:10.1093/sw/swaa042

Midboe, A. M., Byrne, T., Smelson, D., Jasuja, G., McInnes, K., & Troszak, L. K. (2019). The opioid epidemic in veterans who were homeless or unstably housed. *Health Affairs, 38*, 1289–1297.

Mojadad, I. (2020, November 15). Biden administration will bring new focus on housing—and possibly new funding as well. Retrieved from https://www.sfexaminer.com/news/biden-administration-will-bring-new-focus-on-housing-and-possibly-new-funding-as-well/

Narendorf, S. C., Brydon, D. M., Santa Maria, D., Bender, K., Ferguson, K. M., Hsu, H.-T., . . . Petering, R. (2020). System involvement among young adults experiencing homelessness: Characteristics of four system-involved subgroups and relationship to risk outcomes. *Children and Youth Services Review, 108*, 104609.

National Alliance to End Homelessness. (2020a). A research agenda for ending homelessness. Retrieved from https://endhomelessness.org/resource/a-research-agenda-for-ending-homelessness1/

National Alliance to End Homelessness. (2020b). State of homelessness: 2020 edition. Retrieved from https://endhomelessness.org/homelessness-in-america/homelessness-statistics/state-of-homelessness-2020/

National Alliance to End Homelessness. (2020c). The Grand Challenge to End Homelessness: A broad view of the challenges and solutions. YouTube. [video]. Retrieved from https://www.youtube.com/watch?v=rqzGPhUDjAY

National Alliance to End Homelessness. (2020d). Transgender homeless adults and unsheltered homelessness: What the data tell us. Retrieved from https://endhomelessness.org/resource/transgender-homeless-adults-unsheltered-homelessness-what-the-data-tell-us/

National Low Income Housing Coalition. (2016). Out of reach 2016. Retrieved from http://nlihc.org/oor

National Low Income Housing Coalition. (2019). Robert Marbut confirmed as head of U.S. Interagency Council on Homelessness. Retrieved from https://nlihc.org/resource/robert-marbut-confirmed-head-us-interagency-council-homelessness

Nicholas, W. C., & Henwood, B. F. (2018). Applying a prevention framework to address homelessness as a population health issue. *Journal of Public Health Policy, 39*, 283–293.

Padgett, D. K. (2019, December 17). Why California should not adopt New York's 'right to shelter.' *OZY*. Retrieved from https://www.ozy.com/news-and-politics/why-california-should-not-adopt-new-yorks-right-to-shelter/254818/

Padgett, D. K., Bond, L., Gurdak, K., & Henwood, B. F. (2020). Eliciting life priorities of older adults living in permanent supportive housing. *The Gerontologist, 60*, 60–68.

Padgett, D. K., & Henwood, B. F. (2018). End homelessness. In R. Fong, J. Lubben, & R. P. Barth (Eds.), *Grand challenges for social work and society* (pp. 124–139). New York, NY: Oxford University Press.

Padgett, D. K., & Henwood, B. F. (2020). Social work's Grand Challenge to End Homelessness: Policy proposals for the 2020 U.S. presidential election. Retrieved from https://a82940b1-6726-4847-84f4-80859ccc329e.filesusr.com/ugd/2a8466_37f1e1e18c694f44b112d41d04272cfa.pdf

Padgett, D. K., Henwood, B. F., & Petrovich, J. (in press). Race and racism in the homelessness crisis in the United States: Historic antecedents, current best practices and recommendations to end racial disparities in housing and homelessness. In M. Teasley & M. Spencer (Eds.), *Eliminating racism grand challenge*. New York, NY: Oxford University Press.

Padgett, D. K., Henwood, B. F., & Tsemberis, S. J. (2016). *Housing First: Ending homelessness,* transforming systems, and *changing lives.* New York, NY: Oxford University Press.

Petrovich, J. C., & Navarro, C. (2020). A breath of fresh air: Social work IPE with people experiencing homelessness. *Journal of Social Work Education, 56,* S46–S58.

Plitt Donaldson, L., Streeter, C. L., Larkin, H., Briar-Lawson, K., Meyer-Adams, N., Lupfer, K., . . . Grimshaw, A. (2020). The SOAR model as an effective mechanism for university–community partnerships to end homelessness. *Journal of Social Work Education, 56,* S99–S110.

Shelton, J. (2015). Transgender youth homelessness: Understanding programmatic barriers through the lens of cisgenderism. *Children and Youth Services Review, 59,* 10–18.

Siegel, D. H., Smith, M. C., & Melucci, S. C. (2020). Teaching social work students about homelessness: An interdisciplinary interinstitutional approach. *Journal of Social Work Education, 56,* S59–S71.

Smith, D., Dillon, L., & Oreskes, B. (2020, April 23). 'We aren't the dumping ground': Homeless people fleeing coronavirus meet NIMBY resistance. *Los Angeles Times.* Retrieved from https://www.latimes.com/homeless-housing/story/2020-04-23/coronavirus-homeless-housing-shelter-hotel-nimby-cities-california

Smith-Maddox, R., Brown, L. E., Kratz, S., & Newmyer, R. (2020). Developing a policy advocacy practice for preventing and ending homelessness. *Journal of Social Work Education, 56,* S4–S15.

Sol Price Center for Social Innovation. (2020). Homeless Policy Research Institute. Retrieved from https://socialinnovation.usc.edu/special-initiatives/homelessness-policy-research-institute/

Song, A., Wenzel, S. L., & Cho, Y. (2019). Child abuse victimization, depression, and substance use among homeless women: Application of general strain theory. *Journal of Interpersonal Violence, 36*(17-18), 8852–8873. doi:10.1177/0886260519853410

Srivastava, A., Rusow, J. A., Holguin, M., Semborski, S., Onasch-Vera, L., Wilson, N., & Rice, E. (2019). Exchange and survival sex, dating apps, gender identity, and sexual orientation among homeless youth in Los Angeles. *The Journal of Primary Prevention, 40,* 561–568.

Teasley, M. & Spencer M. (Eds.). (in press). *Eliminating racism grand challenge.* New York, NY: Oxford University Press.

Tiderington, E. (2020a). "I achieved being an adult": A qualitative exploration of voluntary transitions from permanent supportive housing. *Administration and Policy in Mental Health and Mental Health Services Research, 48,* 9–22.

Tiderington, E. (2020b, February 4). Jersey City Council wants to make housing more affordable, but for whom? Retrieved from https://www.nj.com/hudson/2020/02/jersey-city-council-wants-to-make-housing-more-affordable-but-for-whom-opinion.html

Tiderington, E., Aykanian, A., Huang, B., & Tsai, J. (2020a). Change in housing environment and residential satisfaction following the move from permanent supportive housing. *Journal of Community Psychology, 49*(2), 305–320. doi:10.1002/jcop.22458

Tiderington, E., Ikeda, J., & Lovell, A. (2020b). Stakeholder perspectives on implementation challenges and strategies for moving on initiatives in permanent supportive housing. *Journal of Behavioral Health Services & Research, 47*, 346–364. doi:10.1007/s11414-019-09680-6

Tiderington, E., Petering, R., Huang, M., Harris, T., & Tsai, J. (2020c). Expert perspectives on service user transitions within and from homeless service programs. *Housing Policy Debate*, 1–11. doi:10.1080/10511482.2020.1825012

United Way of Greater Los Angeles. (2020). Measure H and Prop. HHH. Retrieved from https://everyoneinla.org/basecamp/measure-h-and-prop-hhh/

University at Albany. (2017). National Center for Excellence in Homeless Services. Retrieved from http://www.albany.edu/excellencehomelessservices

University of Southern California Suzanne Dworak- Peck School of Social Work & New York University Silver School of Social Work (Eds.). (2019). *Social Work's Grand Challenge to End Homelessness Policy Proposals for the 2020 U.S. Presidential Election*. https://issuu.com/gc2eh/docs/social_work_s_ grand_challenge_issuu

USC Suzanne Dworak-Peck School of Social Work. (n.d.). Center for Homelessness, Housing and Health Equity Research. Retrieved from https://sites.usc.edu/h3eresearch/

Von Wachter, T., Bertrand, M., Pollack, H., Rountree, J., & Blackwell, B. (2019). Predicting and preventing homelessness in Los Angeles. California Policy Lab. Retrieved from https://www.capolicylab.org/wp-content/uploads/2019/12/Predicting_and_Preventing_Homelessness_in_Los_Angeles.pdf

Wenzel, S. L., Rhoades, H., LaMotte-Kerr, W., & Duan, L. (2019). Everyday discrimination among formerly homeless persons in permanent supportive housing. *Journal of Social Distress and the Homeless, 28*, 169–175.

Winetrobe, H., Wenzel, S., Rhoades, H., Henwood, B., Rice, E., & Harris, T. (2017). Differences in health and social support between homeless men and women entering permanent supportive housing. *Women's Health Issues, 27*, 286–293.

Yadav, A., Wilder, B., Rice, E., Petering, R., Craddock, J., Yoshioka-Maxwell, A., . . . Woo, D. (2018). Bridging the gap between theory and practice in influence maximization: Raising awareness about HIV among homeless youth. In J. Lang (Ed.), *Proceedings of the Twenty-seventh International Joint Conference on Artificial Intelligence Best Sister Conferences* (pp. 5399–5403). Stockholm, Sweden: International Joint Conference on Artificial Intelligence.

Yoshioka-Maxwell, A., & Rice, E. (2020). Exploring the relationship between foster care experiences and social network engagement among a sample of homeless former foster youth. *Children and Youth Services Review, 116*, 105132.

Young, L. E., Mayaud, J., Suen, S. C., Tambe, M., & Rice, E. (2020). Modeling the dynamism of HIV information diffusion in multiplex networks of homeless youth. *Social Networks, 63*, 112–121.

CHAPTER 8

Creating Social Responses to a Changing Environment

SUSAN P. KEMP, LAWRENCE A. PALINKAS,
LISA REYES MASON, SHANONDORA BILLIOT,
FELICIA M. MITCHELL, AND AMY KRINGS

Enhancing the field's socioenvironmental impact is central to creating social responses to a changing environment—truly a global Grand Challenge for Social Work. Worldwide, communities face unprecedented environmental degradation. Human activity has caused unsustainable trends in environmental problems such as air pollution (World Health Organization, 2016), water shortages (UNESCO, 2019), and climate change (Intergovernmental Panel on Climate Change, 2018), threatening the health, well-being, and survival of people and entire ecosystems.

Although the challenge of solving these environmental challenges is in large part *technical*, requiring knowledge from across the biological, physical, engineering, and computational sciences, it is also inherently *social*. To ensure an environmentally sustainable and healthy world for all, solutions are urgently needed that are socially and culturally responsive, ethical, and equitable. Environmental change is fundamentally a social justice issue: climate change and other forms of environmental degradation affect marginalized populations disproportionately (Mason & Rigg, 2019). Impacted groups are many and diverse, including ethnic and racial minorities, women, children, gender and sexual minorities, older adults, people in rural and urban poverty, individuals with a history of mental or behavioral health problems, and people with disabilities, as well as low-income, geographically vulnerable communities and nations. Disproportionate impacts include climate-related morbidity and mortality, disruptions in employment and income, escalating food and

Susan P. Kemp, Lawrence A. Palinkas, Lisa Reyes Mason, Shanondora Billiot, Felicia M. Mitchell, and Amy Krings,
Creating Social Responses to a Changing Environment In: *Grand Challenges for Social Work and Society*. Second Edition.
Edited by: Richard P. Barth, Jill T. Messing, Trina R. Shanks, and James Herbert Williams, Oxford University Press.
© Oxford University Press 2022. DOI: 10.1093/oso/9780197608043.003.0008

water insecurity, heightened risks of gendered violence, and the devastating effect of extreme weather events on the ecologically vulnerable locations where people in poverty often live.

At the heart of the Grand Challenge to Create Social Response to a Changing Environment is the belief that the social work profession is "uniquely positioned to catalyze, facilitate, and propel social innovation at the human-environment nexus, promoting justice, equity, and human and social development through person-in-environment oriented policies and practices" (Kemp et al., 2016, p. 1). If successful, it will lead to social responses that strengthen individual, collective, and community capacities for anticipating and adapting to environmental changes, reduce patterned inequities in exposure to environmental risks, and enhance socioenvironmental well-being for all.

Although social work has frequently focused more on people than on challenges in their physical environments (Kemp, 2011), the contemporary profession has a growing body of scholarship, teaching, and practice focusing centrally on the environmental dimensions of human well-being. Building on a series of conceptual and call-to-action papers, empirical social work research in this area has increased significantly since 2010 (Krings, Victor, Mathias, & Perron, 2020; Mason, Shires, Arwood, & Borst, 2017c). The Global Agenda for Social Work and Social Development endorses "promoting sustainable communities and environmentally sensitive development" as one of its key pillars (Truell & Jones, 2012, p. 7). The US Council on Social Work Education has incorporated environmental justice into its educational competencies for social work program accreditation (Council on Social Work Education, 2015). The Grand Challenge to Create Social Responses to a Changing Environment thus aligns with, but also aims to amplify, growing national and international awareness that the profession has a critical role to play in crafting social responses to escalating environmental crises and injustices.

Climate change and related environmental impacts are key drivers of shifts in contemporary social workers' environmental consciousness. However, the COVID-19 pandemic has further underlined the urgent need for equity-oriented environmental action. Both the pandemic and climate change are risk multipliers, affecting marginalized groups disproportionately and deepening existing social and spatial inequities. Around the globe, low-income workers and racial and ethnic minorities—who frequently have limited job flexibility, rely on public transportation, and live in dense, environmentally marginal neighborhoods, often in crowded and substandard housing—are at greater risk of infection and death (Cole et al., 2020). Furthermore, evidence suggests that climate change, environmental degradation, and habitat loss create conditions favorable to infectious diseases (Wu et al., 2016). In other words, environmental changes and the risk of devastating pandemics go hand in hand, underscoring the critical importance of bringing a focus on environmental issues to the center of social work research, practice, and teaching.

GOALS OF THE GRAND CHALLENGE

Current focal goals of the Grand Challenge to Create Social Response to a Changing Environment are to

- Adopt and implement an evidence-based approach to disaster preparedness and response;
- Develop policies and practices targeting environmentally induced migration and population displacement;
- Strengthen equity-oriented urban resilience policies and practices, and engage marginalized communities proactively in adaptation planning; and
- Engage with individuals, groups, and communities in learning about and crafting responses to the local impacts of global changes.

Each of these goals and sets of recommendations for their achievement are detailed next.

Disaster Risk Reduction

Not only was 2020 tied for the hottest year on record (National Aeronautics and Space Administration, 2021) but extreme weather events such as floods, storms, tornados, heatwaves, droughts, and wildfires are expected to increase in both severity and number (US Environmental Protection Agency, 2016). Between 1995 and 2015, climate-related disasters affected an average of 205 million people per year globally, a figure that is likely to rise as weather-related events escalate (Centre for Research on the Epidemiology of Disasters, 2015).

Adequate preparation for and response to extreme weather events and other natural hazards requires initiatives in five key areas, framed within critical awareness that the impacts of disasters fall disproportionately on minority and marginalized groups and communities. First, an evidence-based approach to disaster risk reduction should be adopted and implemented, targeting three categories or tiers of disaster impact: biopsychosocial, interpersonal, and intrapersonal or behavioral health (Palinkas, 2015). Second, in all three tiers, evidence-based and evidence-informed interventions should become the standard in preparing for and responding to disaster impacts. Priority should be given to developing, evaluating, and scaling up interventions designed to build community resilience, address human insecurity, and manage social conflict before and after disasters. Third, social workers should be trained in the use of these evidence-based interventions and skilled in adapting to place and local community knowledge and needs. For instance, funding should be made available to create and deliver trauma-informed programs for training disaster-relief and recovery personnel in such interventions as Psychological First Aid (Forbes et al., 2011), Skills for Psychological Recovery (Berkowitz et al., 2010), and Cognitive–Behavioral Intervention for Trauma in Schools (Jaycox, 2004). Fourth, in tandem with ensuring that content on the physical environment is incorporated into all courses (Council on Social Work Education, 2015, 2020), all master's-level social work curricula in the United States should include content in disaster preparedness and response (Dominelli, 2013; Pyles, 2017), including evidence-based interventions targeting posttraumatic stress. Fifth, specially trained social workers should be added to interdisciplinary teams and programs for disaster management and response at local, state, and national levels.

MAINSTREAMING GENDER

Social Work's Transformative, Intersectional, Feminist Response to the Changing Environment

BONITA B. SHARMA

Intersectional gender analysis draws attention to disproportionate outcomes for women; girls; Lesbian Gay Bisexual Transgender Questioning Queer Intersex Asexual Pansexual + (LGBTQIA+) individuals; and other vulnerable groups at various intersections of race, ethnicity, age, ability, class, and nationality. No policies are gender-neutral, and treating them as if they are can grossly overlook the specific needs of diverse populations, exacerbating inequities during times of environmental challenges. Within the gender-and-environment nexus in social work, it is imperative to recognize that people are affected differentially by the intersections of identity *and* that we all have important roles to play in enabling environmental justice and sustainability. The realization of human rights and inclusive environmental justice requires that we use a gender-responsive framework that embeds accountability, equity, and effective participation of all in making a sustainable change.

Social workers can draw from the tenets of gender mainstreaming, focusing on its transformative and feminist approaches in addressing current environmental challenges. Feminist approaches challenge the patriarchy and other oppressive forces, whereas transformational work requires ongoing and collaborative efforts to create change. To apply gender mainstreaming successfully, social workers both need to dismantle inequitable power dynamics collectively within our profession and to integrate analyses of power structures individually in our work. To achieve this, I suggest the following gender-responsive research, policy, practice framework.

Social work research, policy, and practices should apply a gendered lens to address environmental changes; this can occur through primary, secondary, and tertiary pathways, as shown in Figure 8.1. Within the

continued

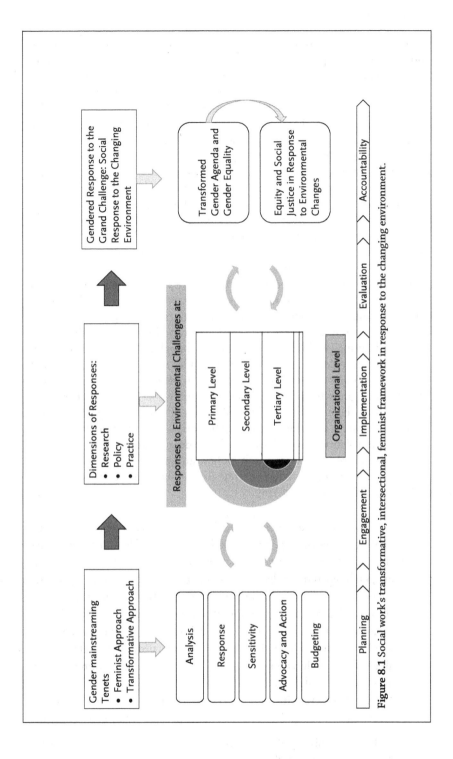

Figure 8.1 Social work's transformative, intersectional, feminist framework in response to the changing environment.

changing environmental context, such as in times of disasters, primary effects include disparities generated through direct impacts. Although all groups may be impacted by environmental exposures, those who are the most vulnerable, such as women and the aging, tend to be affected more. For example, they are more likely to be in the flood zone and lose access to resources such as electricity, water, sanitation, and hygiene. Secondary impacts are associated with the primary context that further exacerbates the conditions for vulnerable groups. This may be through a greater likelihood of being sexually violated, harassed, or denied services as a result of gender identity; or prolonged water and food insecurity may lead to unmet nutritional needs that are particularly dangerous for pregnant mothers or caregivers of very young children. Tertiary impacts are felt disproportionately by vulnerable populations as a result of the lack of inclusion and representation in long-term community rebuilding projects, policies, and programs that further exacerbate their conditions. For instance, gender-based criteria and environment-related displacements are not included in the United Nations' 1951 Convention Relating to the Status of Refugee definition of refugee.[1] During its inception, the plenipotentiaries who signed the original treaty were mainly men from the global north and focused on settling those displaced during World War II in Europe. Although a protocol was added to include other regions around the world, gender-related and environmental context continues to be missing. Within each of these primary, secondary, and tertiary contexts, applying gender-responsive policies and practices after assessing the distinct needs and vulnerabilities of women and gender-diverse individuals can be transformative—particularly when this process identifies and uses the distinct strengths and skills of these groups.

The gender-responsive research, policy, and practice approach to environment must integrate five key strategies: analysis, response, sensitivity, advocacy/action, and budgeting.

- *Gender analysis* should include any data collection and analyses carried out with intersectional gender considerations to understand the impact of the changing environment, such as assessing, gathering, and developing gendered and sex-disaggregated data on environmental disasters.
- *Gender response* requires the implementation of the findings of gendered analyses and considering the potential contributions of all genders to mitigate and adapt to change. It is crucial that we ensure representation of gender minorities in environmental policies, programs, and practices at all levels, from decision-making to creating a plan of action to implementation and evaluation.
- *Gender sensitivity* requires gender equity-oriented perspectives in the relief, rebuilding, and policy reformulation process by directly engaging

1. UNHCR. Convention and protocol relating to the Status of Refugees. https://www.unhcr.org/en-us/3b66c2aa10

continued

marginalized communities in adaptation planning. When adapting a context-specific response, consider the ways that patriarchal cultures have direct or indirect impacts on recovery. Tap into resiliency by using community knowledge and resources to promote sustainability.
- *Gender advocacy and action* should consider specific ways to transform the agenda. Create feedback loops in assessment, intervention, monitoring, and evaluation with intersections of gender representations; create space for community dialogue; and disseminate knowledge in accessible ways so communities can empower themselves in the case of future disaster.
- *Gender budgeting* requires considerations that environmental impacts and costs are not distributed evenly across populations. Create budgets attending specifically to addressing the unique needs of marginalized people.

The gender-responsive research, policy, and practice approach provides a framework for mainstreaming transformative feminist approaches systematically in our own organizational structures, policies, and processes to address environmental change. This allows social workers to promote and ensure inclusion, diversity, and equity in creating a socially just response to environmental challenges. We must create space continuously to reimagine the experiences and interests of all those who are at various intersections of gender, race, age, ability, institution, and nationality, while challenging the existing social power structures and norms within these Grand Challenges and across the profession. We can do this in several ways, including providing support to those who are underrepresented and creating opportunities through funding, collaboration, and promotion. The research, policy, and practice approach reflects the social justice and equity in social work's Grand Challenge to Create Social Responses to the Changing Environment and includes a transformational gender agenda for gender equity.

Environmentally Displaced Populations

Increasing numbers of migrants are displaced by climate-related environmental factors such as sea-level rise, prolonged drought, agricultural disruption, and food shortages (Palinkas, 2020; Rechkemmer et al., 2016). Human-driven factors, including man-made disasters, political conflict (e.g., in South Sudan and Syria), and infrastructure neglect and failure (as with Hurricane Katrina), frequently interact with environmental events to increase human vulnerability significantly, particularly for already marginalized populations (Palinkas, 2020). During the COVID-19 pandemic, closed borders and severe restrictions on international travel, refugee quotas, and migrant intakes deepened these vulnerabilities by curtailing people's ability to flee unsustainable and unsafe environmental conditions significantly (IOM Migration, Environment and Climate Change Division, n.d.).

The profession's long experience with serving immigrants and refugees, and its commitment to human rights and social justice position it for leadership in crafting policy and practice responses to the growing numbers of environmentally displaced persons (Drolet, Sampson, Jebaraj, & Richard, 2014). Social workers can mobilize efforts (a) to raise awareness of the numerous challenges posed by global environmental migration; (b) advocate at all governance levels for new and enhanced policies to protect environmentally displaced persons (Sears, Kemp, & Palinkas, 2017); (c) push policymakers to negotiate an amendment to the 1951 Geneva Convention, granting refugee status to environmental migrants, and requiring receiving nations to grant adequate legal status in the meantime; (d) reduce vulnerability to displacement, decrease unplanned displacement, and strengthen community resilience (e.g., through investments to reduce dependence on climate-dependent livelihoods); (e) develop strategies for planned, long-term relocation of environmental migrants; and (f) engage affected communities in planning and decision-making (Palinkas, 2020).

Urban Adaptation and Resilience to Environmental Change

The growing urbanization of the world's population increases environmental risks such as air and water pollution and heat concentration; places enormous strains on infrastructure, service systems, and urban ecologies; and deepens social and economic inequities (United Nations, Department of Economic and Social Affairs, Population Division, 2019; United Nations Human Settlements Programme, 2016). Recognizing that in urban contexts climate change amplifies existing threats significantly, the 2015 United Nations Sustainable Development Goals (United Nations, 2015) stress the importance of action to develop inclusive, resilient, and sustainable cities (goal no. 11) in concert with efforts to strengthen adaptive capacity to climate-related hazards and natural disasters (goal no. 13).

Emerging emphases on urban community adaptation align closely with social work expertise in research and interventions aimed at strengthening community resilience and reducing disparities (Appleby, Bell, & Boetto, 2017). Yet, mainstream adaptation-oriented policies and initiatives frequently overlook sociostructural factors—such as housing affordability, access to employment, and historical and contemporary patterns of racism, discrimination, and exploitation—that compound the vulnerability of marginalized groups, particularly in the context of rising social and economic inequality (Krings & Copic, 2020; Shi et al., 2016). Social workers should therefore (a) ensure that policies and interventions aimed at fostering urban resilience routinely focus on the social equity and environmental justice implications of adaptation efforts (e.g., equitable land and water use; safe, secure, and affordable housing; nontoxic built and natural environments; and equitable access to services, resources, and jobs); (b) broaden engagement with marginalized and vulnerable communities, and local knowledges in resilience and adaptation planning; (c) strengthen policy and planning attention to the social dimensions of climate change adaptation; and (d) advocate for the inclusion of social agencies, social workers, and community development practitioners in adaptation planning teams.

Community Engagement for Local Responses and Action

A growing number of social workers are centering environmental change and ecological justice in their practice and are becoming actively engaged in community and policy change efforts (Gray, Coates, & Hetherington, 2012). Social work practice in this arena spans a range of environmental change issues, including contamination and pollution related to land-use decisions (Krings, Spencer, & Jimenez, 2013), food justice and the availability of fresh food and community gardens (Shephard, 2013), and access to affordable, sufficient, and safe water (Case, 2017; Mitchell, 2019b; Willett, 2015b).

Bottom-up approaches, grounded in local knowledge and partnerships, are an essential component of effective and responsive environmental change efforts (Appleby, Bell, & Boetto, 2017; Bell, Dennis, & Krings, 2019; Krings & Schusler, 2020). Social workers can contribute to these efforts by (a) asking critical questions to ensure participation and development processes are clear, transparent, and accessible; (b) conducting assessments to prioritize community concerns; (c) using a diverse suite of community practice methodologies and skills; (d) integrating community knowledge into solutions; (e) challenging policies and practices that create sacrifice zones; (f) advancing visions of development that include paradigms of sustainability and equity; (g) developing new interventions and building community capacity, leadership, and civic engagement; (h) thinking creatively with communities about where points of disruption may lie; (i) partnering across disciplines and sectors; (j) decolonizing implementation of adaptation and mitigation policies; and (k) partnering with local groups and pressing for change on the root causes of environmental problems: fighting for racial equity, developing institutions accountable to marginalized communities, and improving public participation in environmental policymaking (Billiot, Beltran, Brown, Mitchell, & Fernandez, 2019a; Krings & Thomas, 2018; Matthies, Peeters, Hirvilammi, & Stamm, 2020; Teixeira & Krings, 2015; Teixeira, Mathias, & Krings, 2019).

CRITERIA FOR A GRAND CHALLENGE

Big, Important, and Compelling

Over the first 5 years of the Grand Challenge to Create Social Response to a Changing Environment, it has become increasingly clear that the environmental challenges facing contemporary societies globally pose significant and growing risks to human health and well-being, particularly for marginalized communities. At the same time, social and behavioral interventions—to strengthen individual, family, and community resilience, build adaptive and sustainable socioecological systems, enhance disaster preparedness and responses, and reduce social and economic inequities—are increasingly recognized as central to the capacity to respond and adapt to current and forthcoming challenges (Hackmann, Moser, & St. Clair, 2014; Palinkas, 2020; Palinkas, O'Donnell, Lau, & Wong, 2020).

Amenability to Analysis, Assessment, and Demonstrable Progress

Developing metrics for assessing measurable progress toward creating social responses to a changing environment faces several obstacles. Early in the Grand Challenges initiative, these included skepticism by the public in general and social workers in particular of the need to prioritize environmental action. Five years later, attitudes are changing. Polls conducted in 2020 by the Pew Research Center found that 60% of American adults believed climate change to be a serious problem, and more than two thirds believed the federal government was doing too little to reduce the effects of global climate change (Funk & Kennedy, 2020). Social workers likewise are increasingly aware of environmental issues and the importance of moving them to the center of the profession's work (Mason et al., 2017c). Nonetheless, relative to other domains, environmental practice and research are still relatively emergent, fragmented areas of focus for the profession, creating challenges in capturing outcomes.

We propose to assess progress in achieving our priority areas—disaster risk reduction, environmentally displaced populations, and community adaptation and resilience to environmental change (Kemp, Mason, Palinkas, Rechkemmer, & Teixeira, 2016), in addition to the critical areas of prevention and mitigation of environmental harms—using the reach, efficacy/effectiveness, adoption, implementation, and maintenance, or RE-AIM, framework (http://re-aim.org), which is often used to understand and monitor the feasibility and success of intervention effectiveness, dissemination, and implementation in real-life settings. *Reach* refers to the absolute number, proportion, and representativeness of individuals who are willing to participate in a given initiative, intervention, or program. With respect to the Grand Challenge to Create Social Response to a Changing Environment, these might include a master's level course in ecosocial work, a certificate program in social justice and environmental change, a training program for first responders, an evidence-based intervention for treatment of mental health problems in survivors of climate-related disasters, or community-academic partnerships to address environmental racism. *Effectiveness* refers to the impact of an intervention on important outcomes, such an improved quality of life or indicators of social, economic, and environmental equity and sustainability. *Adoption* refers to the absolute number, proportion, and representativeness of settings (community and academic) and service providers willing to initiate a program. *Implementation* refers to intervention agents' fidelity to the various elements of an intervention's protocol, including consistency of delivery as intended (e.g., application of an evidence-based protocol for delivery of mental health services), the time and cost of the intervention at the setting level (e.g., health and social services), and clients' use of the intervention strategies (e.g., course syllabi, cognitive–behavioral therapy) at the individual level. *Maintenance* refers to the extent to which a program or policy becomes part of the routine organizational practices and policies of an institution (e.g., master's in social work program, community clinic).

Demonstrable Progress in a Decade

In addition to assessing the reach, effectiveness, adoption, implementation, and maintenance of new and innovative programs and interventions sponsored by the Grand Challenge to Create Social Responses to a Changing Environment, we plan to assess (a) the number of network members; (b) numbers of interdisciplinary collaborations involving network members; (c) numbers of social work doctoral degrees awarded to students engaged in research on social responses to changing physical environments; (d) the number of faculty in schools of social work in the United States with expertise in ecosocial work, environmental justice, climate change, social sustainability, and climate-related mental health services; (e) the degree to which content on environmental justice and environmental practice is incorporated into the curricula of social work education programs; and (f) the nature of this content (e.g., the extent to which it incorporates a racial or gender equity lens).

Interdisciplinary Collaboration

Engaging socioenvironmental challenges in innovative, equitable ways necessarily involves social work scholars and practitioners in collaborations with a diverse array of partners. Broad-based collaborations spanning diverse disciplines and tapping the valuable knowledge and expertise of key stakeholders are common in global environmental change efforts (Intergovernmental Panel on Climate Change, 2014). Increasingly, as the contributions detailed in the following paragraphs demonstrate, participation in broadly collaborative environmental research and environmental change efforts is normative for environmental social work researchers and practitioners.

Significant Innovation

Transformational social responses to pressing environmental issues require significant innovation in social work research, practice, and education. Investments in building the profession's socioenvironmental research capacity are particularly critical to achieving the multidimensional agenda envisioned by the Grand Challenge to Create Social Responses to a Changing Environment (Kemp & Palinkas, 2015). Shifts are needed (a) to bring socioenvironmental issues to the foreground of social work's research agenda and (b) to strengthen the capacity of social work researchers to engage in socioenvironmental and sustainability research. Investments in social work's emerging and early-career scholars are particularly important to ensure that, going forward, they can participate in and contribute confidently to innovative, cross-sector socioenvironmental research programs (Gehlert, Hall, & Palinkas, 2017). In addition to exposure to a broadened base of methodological skills, training in the skill sets required for collaborative transdisciplinary and translational research is also essential (Matthies, Krings, & Stamm, 2020; Moore, Martinson, Nurius, & Kemp, 2018; Nurius, Kemp, Köngeter, & Gehlert, 2017; Palinkas & Soydan, 2012).

Preparing current and future social workers for effective engagement in environmental practice also requires innovation in the profession's educational paradigms and practices (Miller & Hayward, 2014), including shifts in curriculum content and foci, a willingness to embrace community- and place-based pedagogies, and investments in involving social work professional-degree students in broadly inclusive interdisciplinary learning (Chalise, Erickson, & Lee, 2020).

INTERSECTIONS WITH RACE AND GENDER EQUITY

Questions of racial and gender justice are central to the Grand Challenge to Create Social Responses to a Changing Environment and the social and environmental challenges it addresses. Globally, racial and ethnic minorities are affected disproportionately by environmental threats and challenges, from massive fast-onset dislocations caused by disasters and extreme weather events to the "slow violence" of climate change and environmental degradation. Communities of color are more likely to live in marginalized geographic locations, with inadequate infrastructure and services, limited resources, and high levels of pollution and other environmental toxins. In consequence, they experience disproportionately high levels of environmentally related diseases and are at elevated risk of dislocation, harm, and death (see, for example, Wilson, Bullard, Patterson, & Thomas [2020] on racism, environmental justice, and COVID-19 as interlocking pandemics).

These inequities are exacerbated for Indigenous communities and peoples. Climate change and environmental degradation threaten traditional environmental practices and cultural and spiritual transmission of knowledge, damage ancestral lands and environmental resources, and create food and water insecurity (Billiot et al., 2019a; Billiot, Kwon, & Burnette, 2019b; Mitchell, 2019a). Environmental threats—and the histories of settler–colonial subjugation, exploitation, and trauma that underpin and sustain them—affect directly and indirectly Indigenous peoples' traditional lifeways and livelihood strategies, local knowledge, and physical and mental health (Walters, Beltran, Huh, & Evans-Campbell, 2011).

At the same time, paradoxically, the environmental wisdom and knowledge of Indigenous peoples are increasingly recognized as vital resources in the context of contemporary environmental threats. Over generations, Indigenous peoples have closely observed and lived in harmony with changing local ecologies; in the current global environmental crisis, their environmental insights and practices are acquiring new relevance. Traditional ecological knowledge thus offers important opportunities for improvements in environmental research, management, and education (Pierotti & Wildcat, 2000). However, a significant risk in the resurgent interest in Indigenous knowledges and practices is that they will be engaged in ways that replicate ongoing colonial processes of extraction and exploitation, rather than from within critical decolonial approaches that center Indigenous sovereignty and rights (Hiller & Carlson, 2018).

In their article engaging the Grand Challenge to Create Social Responses to a Changing Environment from an Indigenous perspective, Billiot et al. (2019a) identify several pathways for bringing traditional ecological knowledge to the center of social work's environmental research and practice, including the identification of new paradigms to understand more fully the natural world and our relation to it; movement away from a reliance on western science toward holistic, integrative paradigms; and practical, productive collaborations with Indigenous and marginalized communities. Related activities include (a) incorporating Indigenous and local knowledge into social work education, (b) mobilizing communities through coordination and reciprocity, (c) recognizing interventions as opportunities for healing, and (d) decolonizing approaches to adaptation and mitigation policies (Billiot et al., 2019a, p. 303).

Globally, the impacts of environmental injustice, climate change, disasters, and extreme weather events also fall more heavily on women and gender and sexual minorities. Interdisciplinary research evidence, including foundational work by social work scholar Margaret Alston, highlights a range of areas in which environmental challenges impact women and girls negatively, including an increased risk of physical and sexual violence, threats to their physical and reproductive health and employment, added burdens of work and labor, and poverty (Alston, 2013, 2020; Epstein, Bendavid, Nash, Charlebois, & Weiser, 2020; Pearse, 2017). Recent social work scholarship adds to this body of knowledge by underscoring women's equally important contributions to environmental leadership and action (Dennis & Bell, 2020; Nyahunda, Makhubele, Mabvurira, & Matlakala, 2020), and arguing for the relevance of holistic feminist frameworks in environmental practice and research (Klemmer & McNamara, 2020).

Most of the emphasis on gender inequities in the context of environmental challenges and injustices has focused on women. Although a small but growing body of interdisciplinary scholarship highlights the heightened vulnerability of sexual and gender minorities in the context of environmental threats such as disasters, including lack of access to resources and services, discriminatory responses from service providers, and increased risk of violence (Gaillard, Gorman-Murray, & Fordham, 2017), gender and sexual minorities are largely invisible in global, national, and local disaster response policies and practices (Gaillard et al., 2017). This invisibility is mirrored in the mainstream research literature (Rushton, Gray, Canty, & Blanchard, 2019). As Kroehle, Shelton, Clark, and Seelman (2020) have rightly pointed out, social work's environmental literature, including publications pertaining to the Grand Challenge to Create Social Response to a Changing Environment, is no different: it frequently conflates a concern with gender with a focus on women, perpetuates binary male/female gender constructions, and in general overlooks the particular challenges confronting gender and sexual minorities.

Taken as a whole, these bodies of work underline the vital importance of more forthrightly centering racial and gender justice in social work's environmental research, practice, and education efforts. In concert, they also highlight three analytic and conceptual moves at the heart of moving this work forward. First, intersectional analyses and approaches are critical to addressing the multiple, interconnecting inequalities that shape differential experiences and outcomes in response to environmental threats (Messing, 2020). Second, addressing complex, intersectional socioenvironmental challenges requires holistic frameworks that transcend reductionist and marginalizing binaries (Billiot et al., 2019a; Klemmer & McNamara, 2020; Kroehle et al., 2020). Third, and perhaps most importantly given the extent to which experiences of colonization, displacement, and racism underpin experiences of environmental injustice, decolonial approaches are vital (Billiot et al., 2019a; Pyles, 2017), including recognition of the central importance of land and place to Indigenous peoples and many other racial and ethnic minorities (Sousa, Kemp, & El-Zuhairi, 2019; Tuck & McKenzie, 2014).

APPROACH AND ACCOMPLISHMENTS

Relative to several others, the Grand Challenge to Create Social Responses to a Changing Environment draws from a smaller and "younger" scholarly and practice base. Thus, in the first 5 years of the initiative (2015–2020), we prioritized growing and disseminating environmental research and scholarship, and supporting efforts to strengthen environmental content in social work education and practice. To advance these goals we have supported new research projects (especially those involving doctoral students and early-career scholars), convened research sessions on topics related to this Grand Challenge, disseminated work publicly, and collaborated with other social work associations to create curricular resources for training future social workers. In this section, we summarize progress in this area, as well as challenges experienced to date.

Grand Challenge Organization

The co-leads of the Grand Challenge to Create Social Responses to a Changing Environment are Susan Kemp, Lawrence Palinkas, and Lisa Reyes Mason. Several other faculty lead or co-lead working groups in the following areas: advancing research, influencing policy, social work and professional education, and network communications and membership. The team created a public website for the Grand Challenge (http://envchange.org/), including a rotating spotlight on a scholar engaged in research for environmental change, blog posts on a range of climate and environmental justice topics, and a database for searching for others connected to the grand challenge with similar interests.

An advisory council was launched in 2020. In form and function, the council is intended to be a collaborative, creative, and forward-looking group, generating ideas for practical action with members volunteering for short-term leadership of or involvement with concrete actions as they are able. Now that the pipeline of scholars engaged with the Grand Challenge to Create Social Responses to a Changing Environment has grown and continues to increase, a particular interest of the council is to bring the Grand Challenge closer to change-oriented environmental social work practice, including by building robust crosswalks with the Grand Challenge to Close the Health Gap and the Grand Challenge to Eliminate Racism.

Early-career scholars and doctoral students have brought creative energy, exciting new research, and an expansion of the Grand Challenge to Create Social Responses to a Changing Environment into broader conversation with other disciplines and partners. At the same time, an understandable challenge for many has been the tensions entailed in balancing their desire to advance the Grand Challenge with other academic commitments, particularly in light of what kinds of work are typically more "rewarded" by the academy (i.e., by institutions of higher education). Supporting these early-career scholars thus continues to be an important priority.

Research Projects and Initiatives

Scholars involved with the Grand Challenge to Create Social Responses to a Changing Environment have invested steadily in moving it forward, producing journal articles and book chapters (Gehlert, Hall, & Palinkas, 2017; Kemp & Palinkas, 2017; Kemp, Palinkas, & Mason, 2018; Palinkas & Wong, 2019; Palinkas et al., 2020), providing background for articles produced by our universities and by the National Association of Social Workers (NASW) (2017), and consulting on institution-level efforts to bring the Grand Challenge to the center of social work curricula and research programs.

Key research contributions include

- *Disaster preparedness and response.* Marleen Wong and Vivien Villaverde trained teachers and first responders in the Philippines and South Korea using the three-tiered framework developed by Palinkas (2015). Wong and Villaverde are also developing trauma-informed schools as a tool for coping with inner-city violence and responding to natural disasters. Lisa Reyes Mason collaborated with engineers, geographers, and urban planners in examining socially responsible storm water management in the face of climate change uncertainty, tornado warning responses in Tennessee, and flood management in the US Midwest. Andreas Rechkemmer explored fear-related behaviors related to environmental disasters and emerging infectious diseases such as Ebola.
- *Food and water insecurity.* Michelle Kaiser has examined food insecurity, social worker roles in community food strategies, and use of food pantries (Kaiser, 2017; Kaiser & Hermsen, 2015; Kaiser, Usher, & Spees, 2015). Water insecurity and injustice has been studied in the Philippines by Lisa

Reyes Mason (2015); in Kenya by Jennifer Willett (2015b); in Flint, MI, by Amy Krings (Krings, Kornberg, & Lane, 2018); and among American Indian communities by Felicia Mitchell (2019b).

- *Older adults.* Tam Perry has conducted research on older adults' experiences and understandings of the Flint, MI, water crisis as part of a larger effort to identify the problems that environmental degradation and climate change can yield for older adults and families, and to develop research that can strengthen multisystemic responses to prevent and mitigate such negative effects.
- *Low- and middle-income countries.* Jennifer Willett conducted research on experiences of environmental degradation in poor communities in Kenya, including the occurrence of micro disasters, formal aid responses, and community support through social networks (Willett, 2015a, 2015b, 2019). Andreas Rechkemmer examined the social, political, and legal ramifications of climate-related forced migration in low- and middle-income countries. Praveen Kumar has conducted intervention research in India on energy poverty, air pollution, and clean energy alternatives (Kumar et al., 2020; Pandey et al., 2021).
- *Indigenous communities.* Shanondora Billiot, Felicia Mitchell, and Angela Fernandez are among a growing group of Indigenous early-career researchers focusing on the intersections among environmental changes, historical inequities, and the health and well-being of Indigenous peoples (Billiot et al., 2019a; Mitchell, 2019a/b).
- *Urbanization and climate.* In collaboration with colleagues from the fields of geography and engineering, Lisa Reyes Mason has examined spatiotemporal variability of urban heat islands and its impact on quality of life for low-income neighborhoods (Mason, Ellis, & Hathaway, 2017a; Mason, Hathaway, Ellis, & Harrison, 2017b). Susan Kemp has played a leadership role in the Urban@UW Initiative at the University of Washington (https://depts.washington.edu/urbanuw/). In collaboration with colleagues from the fields of engineering and preventive medicine, Lawrence Palinkas is examining mental health outcomes associated with heatwaves in Southern California. His chapter with Marleen Wong on the mental health impacts of climate change (Palinkas & Wong, 2020) has been recognized with an Elsevier Atlas Award for research that can significantly impact people's lives around the world (https://www.elsevier.com/connect/atlas/climate-change-causes-mental-health-issues-and-we-need-to-address-them).
- *Youth.* Samantha Teixeira focuses on engaging youth in creating solutions to environmental problems in their communities (Teixeira & Zuberi, 2016). In an article recognized as Paper of the Year by the *Journal of Community Practice*, Amy Krings and colleagues explored opportunities for engaging actively youth in ecosocial work (Schusler, Krings, & Hernández, 2019).

Convening Research Sessions

The Grand Challenge to Create Social Response to a Changing Environment advocated successfully for the development of a new research cluster within the Society for Social Work and Research—Sustainable Development, Urbanization, and Environmental Justice—and a special interest group that meets at the annual conference. These venues have provided new ways for scholars interested in this area to "find" each other, including those in other areas of social work research who seek out the cluster and the special interest group because of potential overlapping interests and synergies from new collaborations.

The Grand Challenge to Create Social Responses to a Changing Environment has also convened international and interdisciplinary symposia. Lisa Reyes Mason co-convened an interdisciplinary symposium titled "People and Climate Change: Vulnerability, Adaptation, Social Justice" at Washington University in St. Louis. At the University of Washington in Seattle, Susan Kemp collaborated with colleagues to convene a symposium on "Urban Environmental Justice in a Time of Climate Change." Grand Challenge scholars have also presented on the initiative at international conferences in Singapore, the Philippines, Portugal, Denmark, Australia, and Taiwan, among others.

Public Dissemination

During the past 5 years, network members have published several books, book chapters, and journal articles, and edited special issues of journals on topics such as social work and sustainable development (Chong & Chi, 2019), Indigenous perspectives on global environmental change (Billiot et al., 2019a), population displacement (Palinkas, 2020; Rechkemmer et al., 2016; Shultz, Rechkemmer, Rai, & McManus, 2019), disaster preparedness (Sandifer et al., 2020) and recovery (Enrile, Aquino, & Villaverde, 2019; Powell & Black, 2019), social and environmental justice (Mason, 2020a; Mason & Rigg, 2019; Powers, Willett, Mathias, & Hayward, 2018; Teixeira & Krings, 2015), and mental health (Palinkas & Wong, 2019; Palinkas et al., 2020). The Grand Challenge to Create Social Responses to a Changing Environment has also been represented in policy briefs (Kemp et al., 2016; Krings, Kornberg, & Lee, 2019; Sears et al., 2017) and editorials (Mason, 2020b; Palinkas, 2019). Although federal policy action to address environmental challenges was stymied during the Trump administration (2016–2020), network members continued to advocate for social work advocacy in this area [e.g., Rao and Teixeira's (2020) discussion of social work and a Green New Deal], and through providing invited policy consultation for the NASW on these issues.

Co-leads and advisory council members have been interviewed as guest speakers on the inSocialWork podcast from the University of Buffalo. Lawrence Palinkas discussed the translation and implementation of evidence-based practices, Lisa Reyes Mason discussed an expanded concept of person-in-environment and the urgency of social work taking action to respond to global environmental change, and Amy Krings explored the connection between austerity politics and local impacts, including environmental injustices.

Curriculum Development

Several affiliated faculty and their university programs have led or been part of efforts to develop curriculum content related to the Grand Challenge to Create Social Responses to a Changing Environment. Network members have served on Council on Social Work Education's Environmental Justice Curricular Guide (Council on Social Work Education, 2020) task force, contributed entries to the International Federation of Social Workers' open-access sustainability workbooks (e.g., Rinkel & Powers, 2017), and authored an entry on "Social Responses to a Changing Environment" for the forthcoming, online *Macro Encyclopedia of Social Work*. At the program level, the Grand Challenges are foundational to the University of Southern California's doctoral degree in social work program, with several students completing capstone projects linked to the Grand Challenge to Create Social Responses to a Changing Environment. Faculty members Marleen Wong and Vivien Villaverde have also developed and implemented postdisaster mental health curricula for first responders and teachers in the Philippines and South Korea. The University of Denver is revising its master's in social work concentration in sustainable development and global practice to focus on ecological justice. The Adelphi School of Social Work now offers a postgraduate certificate in environmental justice and social work. There is also increasing investment, across a range of master's and bachelor's degree programs in social work, in offering stand-alone courses focused on environmental social work. Given growing student interest, we are hopeful that social work doctoral programs will likewise make space for curricular content relevant to environmentally focused social work research.

FUTURE DIRECTIONS: THE NEXT 5 YEARS

Capitalizing on these accomplishments, the Grand Challenge to Create Social Responses to a Changing Environment will devote its efforts to the following tasks during the next 5 years:

1. Refining and updating the goals of the Grand Challenge and the associated actions required to achieve them
2. Increasing training and mentoring supports for doctoral students and earlier-stage researchers
3. Developing strategic partnerships with other Grand Challenges, including Closing the Health Gap and Eliminating Racism
4. Generating new partnerships with social work practitioners, those already engaged in environmental change work and those who may not yet see or work at the intersection of this with their own practice (e.g., partnerships with NASW state/local chapters)
5. Pursuing opportunities to effect policy at all levels—local, state, and national
6. Increasing involvement in local community development efforts
7. Establishing stronger connections between social workers, environmental justice advocates, and community coalitions engaged in racial and environmental justice efforts
8. Continuing to advocate for their policy recommendations by adopting and implementing evidence-based approaches to prevention and treatment of climate-related social and mental health problems, strengthening equity-oriented urban resilience policies and engaging marginalized communities proactively in adaptation planning, and developing policies targeting environmentally induced migration and population displacement (e.g., amending the Stafford Act)
9. Advancing a social justice perspective in creating sustainable communities

CONCLUSION

Given the significant complexities inherent in addressing "wicked" problems, moving Grand Challenge initiatives to full implementation requires careful attention to the mechanisms necessary to "link strategy and action to achieve specific grand challenges goals" (Uehara, Barth, Coffey, Padilla, & McClain, 2017, p. 77). A range of such mechanisms are needed to further the influence of the Grand Challenge to Create Social Responses to a Changing Environment, many of which we have referred to in this chapter. In closing, we summarize two that we view as key.

The first includes *visibility and outreach*. If social work is to be viewed as a value-added contributor in interdisciplinary socioenvironmental research and policymaking, it is essential that we raise the profession's profile and reach. In addition to cross-disciplinary and transdisciplinary partnerships, robust networks within the profession—nationally and cross-nationally—are critical to elevating social work's environmental research capacity and reach. Some key connective mechanisms are already in place, notably the Green-EcoSocial

Work Network listserve (Green-EcoSocial-Work-Network-l@uncg.edu) and the newly developed Institute for Social and Environmental Justice at the Adelphi University School of Social Work (https://www.iswej.org/). The Grand Challenge to Create Social Responses to a Changing Environment complements and extends these by supporting environmentally focused conferences and webinars, including (in 2021) a three-part environmental and racial justice series with webinars on practice and partnership, social work education, and policy change. It also provides a platform for a more intentional focus on the development of research-oriented environmental social work collaborations, from research clusters organized around topical issues to broader national and cross-national networks focused on shaping and coordinating social work's socioenvironmental research agenda, strengthening the profession's environmental research capacity, solidifying connections with scholars in other disciplines, and elevating social work's access to national and cross-national funding opportunities. The Grand Challenge to Create Social Responses to a Changing Environment network likewise provides an opportunity to inventory and build on the various connections that individual social work scholars and practitioners have forged with local, national, and global sustainability efforts.

The second key mechanism is *policy advocacy and action*. The NASW's *2021 Blueprint of Federal Policy Priorities*, which highlights key issues for policy attention by the Biden administration across the 13 individual Grand Challenges, is an important example of a strategic, collaboratively developed mechanism for communicating beyond the profession about socioenvironmental justice and equity issues that social work identifies as critical (https://www.socialworkers.org/LinkClick.aspx?fileticket=KPdZqqY60t4%3d&portalid=0). In a range of ways, social workers associated with the Grand Challenge to Create Social Responses to a Changing Environment are also beginning to communicate to wider audiences what social work brings to the table in these areas. For instance, Lawrence Palinkas has given presentations to physicians and psychologists in Norway, and to legal and global health experts in the United States on climate-related factors that have precipitated mass migrations of poor, traumatized, and malnourished immigrants from Africa and the Middle East to Europe, and from Latin America to the US–Mexico border. Lisa Reyes Mason was selected for the city of Denver's Sustainability Advisory Council and co-chairs its Science and Research Committee. Also, an infographic series that helps "connect the dots" across intersecting issues such as health insurance, financial capability, access to mental health services, social isolation and support, and climate and environmental justice is planned.

As these various efforts ramp up, and as social work's environmental scholars increasingly work in broadly transdisciplinary research teams, publish in interdisciplinary journals, present at interdisciplinary conferences, and communicate outward via widely accessible mechanisms such as blogs and podcasts, the profession is incrementally building stronger, more ramified connections in wider environmental and sustainability circles.

The first 5 years of the Grand Challenge to Create Social Responses to a Changing Environment has taught us that addressing social and racial inequities created and/or amplified by a changing environment requires the active involvement of social workers at all levels—and in all areas—of policy and practice. Although social work has lagged behind sister disciplines (such as public health and psychology) in recognizing the importance of focusing on climate change and related environmental challenges, we believe the profession is on the cusp of significant change in this regard: new generations of social work students, practitioners, and scholars are increasingly motivated to bring environmental issues to the center of their work, and to do so from an environmental justice lens that is cognizant of race and gender inequities. Our task now is to support social workers in leading specific efforts to address the growing social problems associated with changing environments. At the same time, the Grand Challenge to Create Social Responses to a Changing Environment will continue its commitments to preparing social workers for collaborative action to address environmental challenges and injustices, educating social workers in understanding the impacts of environmental changes on other aspects of social work policy and practice, and building—and looking outward—to create a robust, research-informed knowledge base on the social problems and inequities created by environmental threats and injustice, and the contributions policy and practice can make to addressing them.

REFERENCES

Appleby, K., Bell, K., & Boetto, H. (2017). Climate change adaptation: Community action, disadvantaged groups and practice implications for social work. *Australian Social Work, 70*, 78–91.

Alston, M. (2013). Environmental social work: Accounting for gender in climate disasters. *Australian Social Work, 66*, 218–233.

Alston, M. (2020). Gendered vulnerabilities and adaptation to climate change. In Routledge *handbook of gender and agriculture* (pp. 137–148).

Bell, F., Dennis, M. K., & Krings, A. (2019). Collective survival strategies and anti-colonial practice in ecosocial work. *Journal of Community Practice, 27*, 279–295.

Berkowitz, S., Bryant, R., Brymer, M., Hamblen, J., Jacobs, A., Layne, C., . . . Watson, P. (2010). Skills for psychological recovery: Field operations guide. Retrieved from https://www.ptsd.va.gov/professional/treat/type/SPR/SPR_Manual.pdf

Billiot, S., Beltran, R., Brown, D., Mitchell, F. M., & Fernandez, A. (2019a). Indigenous perspectives for strengthening social responses to global environmental changes: A response to the social work grand challenge on environmental change. *Journal of Community Practice, 27*, 296–216.

Billiot, S., Kwon, S., & Burnette, C. E. (2019b). Repeated disasters and chronic environmental changes impede generational transmission of indigenous knowledge. *Journal of Family Strengths, 19*, 11. Available at: https://digitalcommons.library.tmc.edu/jfs/vol19/iss1/11

Burton, L. M., Kemp, S. P., Leung, M., Matthews, S. A., & Takeuchi, D. T. (Eds.). (2011). *Communities, neighborhoods, and health: expanding the boundaries of place* (Vol. 1). Springer Science & Business Media.

Case, R. A. (2017). Eco-social work and community resilience: Insights from water activism in Canada. *Journal of Social Work, 17*, 391–412.

Centre for Research on the Epidemiology of Disasters. (2015). The human cost of weather-related disasters, 1995–2015. United Nations Office for Disaster Risk Reduction. Retrieved from https://www.unisdr.org/we/inform/publications/46796

Chalise, N., Erickson, C., & Lee, N. (2020). Teaching note: Handmaidens to environmentalists? Claiming social work's expertise in environmental justice. *Journal of Social Work Education*, 1–8. doi:10.1080/10437797.2020.1798313

Chong, A. M. L., & Chi, I. (Eds.). (2019). *Social work and sustainability in Asia and the Pacific Rim: Facing the challenges of global environmental changes*. London, UK: Routledge.

Cole, H. V., Anguelovski, I., Baró, F., García-Lamarca, M., Kotsila, P., Pérez del Pulgar, C., ... Triguero-Mas, M. (2020). The COVID-19 pandemic: Power and privilege, gentrification, and urban environmental justice in the global north. *Cities & Health*, 1–5. doi:10.1080/23748834.2020.178517

Council on Social Work Education. (2015). *2015 Educational policy and accreditation standards for baccalaureate and master's social work programs*. Alexandria, VA: Author.

Council on Social Work Education. (2020). *Curricular guide for environmental justice*. Alexandria, VA: Author.

Dennis, M. K., & Bell, F. M. (2020). Indigenous women, water protectors, and reciprocal responsibilities. *Social Work, 65*, 378–386.

Dominelli, L. (2013). Social work education for disaster relief work. In M. Gray, J. Coates, & T. Hetherington (Eds.), *Environmental social work* (pp. 280–298). London, UK: Routledge.

Drolet, J., Sampson, T., Jebaraj, D. P., & Richard, L. (2014). Social work and environmentally induced displacement: A commentary. *Refuge: Canada's Journal on Refugees, 29*, 55–62.

Enrile, A. D., Aquino, G., & Villaverde, V. (2019). In the typhoon corridor: Rebuilding communities in the Philippines through empowerment and innovation. In: A. M. L. Chong & I. Chi (Eds.), *Social work and sustainability in Asia and the Pacific Rim: Facing the challenges of global environmental changes* (pp. 119–136). London, UK: Routledge.

Epstein, A., Bendavid, E., Nash, D., Charlebois, E. D., & Weiser, S. D. (2020). Drought and intimate partner violence towards women in 19 countries in sub-Saharan Africa during 2011–2018: A population-based study. *PLoS Medicine, 17*, e1003064. doi:10.1371/journal. pmed.1003064

Forbes, D., Lewis, V., Varker, T., Phelps, A., O'Donnell, M., Wade, D. J., . . . Creamer, M. (2011). Psychological first aid following trauma: Implementation and evaluation framework for high-risk organizations. *Psychiatry, 74*, 224–239. doi:10.1521/psyc.2011.74.3.224

Funk, C., & Kennedy, B. (2020). How Americans see climate change and the environment in 7 charts. Pew Research Center Fact Tank. https://www.pewresearch.org/fact-tank/2020/04/21/how-americans-see-climate-change-and-the-environment-in-7-charts/

Gaillard, J. C., Gorman-Murray, A., & Fordham, M. (2017). Sexual and gender minorities in disaster. *Gender, Place & Culture, 24,* 18–26. doi:10.1080/0966369X.2016.1263438

Gehlert, S., Hall, K. I., & Palinkas, L. A. (2017). Preparing our next-generation scientific workforce to address the grand challenges for social work. *Journal of the Society for Social Work and Research, 8,* 119–136.

Gray, M., Coates, J., & Hetherington, T. (Eds.). (2012). *Environmental social work.* London: Routledge.

Hackmann, H., Moser, S. C., & St. Clair, A. L. (2014). The social heart of global environmental change. *Nature Climate Change, 4,* 653–655.

Hiller, C., & Carlson, E. (2018). THESE ARE INDIGENOUS LANDS: Foregrounding settler colonialism and indigenous sovereignty as primary contexts for Canadian environmental social work. *Canadian Social Work Review, 35,* 45–70.

Intergovernmental Panel on Climate Change. (2014). *Climate change 2014: Impacts, adaptation, and vulnerability part A: Global and sectoral aspects.* New York, NY: Cambridge University Press. Retrieved from http://ipcc-wg2.gov/AR5/images/uploads/WGIIAR5-PartA_FINAL.pdf

Intergovernmental Panel on Climate Change. (2018). Global warming of 1.5° Celsius: Summary for policymakers. Retrieved from https://report.ipcc.ch/sr15/pdf/sr15_spm_final.pdf

IOM Migration, Environment and Climate Change Division. (n.d.). The COVID-19 pandemic, migration and the environment. Retrieved from https://environmentalmigration.iom.int/covid-19-pandemic-migration-and-environment

Jaycox, L. (2004). *Cognitive behavioral intervention for trauma in schools (CBITS).* Longmont, CO: Lopris West.

Kaiser, M. L. (2017). Redefining food security in a community context: An exploration of community food security indicators and social worker roles in community food strategies. *Journal of Community Practice, 25,* 213–234.

Kaiser, M. L., & Hermsen, J. (2015). Food acquisition strategies, food security, and health status among families with children using food pantries. *Families in Society: The Journal of Contemporary Social Services, 96,* 83–90. doi:10.1606/1044-3894.2015.96.16

Kaiser, M. L., Usher, K., & Spees, C. K. (2015). Community food security strategies: An exploratory study of their potential for food insecure households with children. *Journal of Applied Research on Children: Informing Policy for Children at Risk, 6.* Retrieved from http://digitalcommons.library.tmc.edu/childrenatrisk/vol6/iss2/2/

Kemp, S. P. (2011). Recentring environment in social work practice: Necessity, opportunity, challenge. *British Journal of Social Work, 41,* 1198–1210.

Kemp, S. P., Mason, L. R., Palinkas, L. A., Rechkemmer, A., & Teixeira, S. (2016). Policy recommendations for meeting the Grand Challenge to Create Social Responses to a Changing Environment. Grand Challenges for Social Work: Policy brief no.7, September 2016. Retrieved from https://csd.wustl.edu/Publications/Documents/PB7.pdf

Kemp, S. P., & Palinkas, L. A. (2015). Create social responses to the human impacts of environmental change. Retrieved from http://aaswsw.org/grand-challenges-initiative/12-challenges/create-social-responses-to-a-changing-environment/

Kemp, S. P., & Palinkas, L. A. (2017). Responding to global environmental change: A grand challenge for social work. In A. L. Palaez & E. R. Diez (Eds.), *Social work research and practice: Contributing to a science of social work* (pp. 167–190). London, UK: Thomson Reuters.

Kemp, S. P., Palinkas, L. A., & Mason, L. R. (2018). Create social responses to a changing environment. In R. Fong, J. E. Lubben, & R. P. Barth (Eds.), *Grand challenges for social work and society* (pp. 140–160). New York, NY: Oxford University Press.

Klemmer, C. L., & McNamara, K. A. (2020). Deep ecology and ecofeminism: Social work to address global environmental crisis. *Affilia, 35*, 503–515.

Krings, A., & Copic, C. (2020). Environmental justice organizing in a gentrifying community: Navigating dilemmas of representation, issue selection, and recruitment. *Families in Society, 102*(2), 154–166.

Krings, A., Kornberg, D., & Lane, E. (2018). Organizing under austerity: How residents' concerns became the Flint water crisis. *Critical Sociology, 45*, 583–597. doi:10.1177/0896920518757053

Krings, A., Kornberg, D., & Lee, S. (2019). *Lessons and policy implications from the Flint water crisis*. CSD policy brief no. 19-41. St. Louis, MO: Washington University, Center for Social Development.

Krings, A., & Schusler, T. M. (2020). Equity in sustainable development: Community responses to environmental gentrification. *International Journal of Social Welfare, 29*, 321–334.

Krings, A., Spencer, M. S., & Jimenez, K. (2013). Organizing for environmental justice: From bridges to taro patches. In S. Dutta & C. Ramanathan (Eds.), *Governance, development, and social work* (pp. 186–200). London, UK: Routledge.

Krings, A., & Thomas, H. (2018). Integrating green social work and the U.S. environmental justice movement: An introduction to community benefits agreements. In L. Dominelli (Ed.), *The Routledge handbook of green social work* (pp. 397–406). London, UK: Routledge. doi:10.4324/9781315183213

Krings, A., Victor, B. G., Mathias, J., & Perron, B. E. (2020). Environmental social work in the disciplinary literature, 1991–2015. *International Social Work, 63*, 275–290.

Kroehle, K., Shelton, J., Clark, E., & Seelman, K. (2020). Mainstreaming dissidence: Confronting binary gender in social work's grand challenges. *Social Work, 65*, 368–377.

Kumar, P., Dover, R. E., Díaz-Valdés Iriarte, A., Rao, S., Garakani, R., Hadingham, S., . . . Yadama, G. N. (2020). Affordability, accessibility, and awareness in the adoption of liquefied petroleum gas: A case–control study in rural India. *Sustainability, 12*, 4790. doi:10.3390/su12114790

Mason, L. R. (2015). Beyond improved access: Seasonal and multidimensional water security in urban Philippines. *Global Social Welfare, 2*, 119–128.

Mason, L. R. (2020a). Achieving environmental justice. In M. R. Rank (Ed.), *Towards a livable life: A 21st century agenda for social work* (pp. 232–252). New York, NY: Oxford University Press.

Mason, L. R. (2020b). The urgency of public-impact scholarship: Inside higher ed, conditionally accepted. Retrieved from https://www.insidehighered.com/advice/2020/03/20/more-faculty-should-share-their-research-expertise-help-address-crucial-public#.XnS261ZB5mc.twitter

Mason, L. R., Ellis, K. N., & Hathaway, J. M. (2017a). Experiences of urban environmental conditions in socially and economically diverse neighborhoods. *Journal of Community Practice, 25*, 48–67.

Mason, L. R., Hathaway, J. M., Ellis, K. N., & Harrison, T. (2017b). Public interest in microclimate data in Knoxville, Tennessee, USA. *Sustainability*, 9, 23. doi: 10.3390/su9010023

Mason, L. R., & Rigg, J. (2019). Climate change, social justice: Making the case for community inclusion. In L. R. Mason & J. Rigg (Eds)., *People and climate change: Vulnerability, adaptation, and social justice* (pp. 3–19). New York, NY: Oxford University Press.

Mason, L. R., Shires, M. K., Arwood, C., & Borst, A. (2017c). Social work research and global environmental change. *Journal of the Society for Social Work and Research*, 8, 645–672.

Matthies, A.-L., Krings, A., & Stamm, I. (2020). Research-based knowledge about social work and sustainability. *International Journal of Social Welfare*, 4, 297–299.

Matthies, A.-L., Peeters, J., Hirvilammi, T., & Stamm, I. (2020). Ecosocial innovations enabling social work to promote new forms of sustainable economy. *International Journal of Social Welfare*, 29, 378–389. doi:10.1111/ijsw.12423

Messing, J. T. (2020). Mainstreaming gender: An intersectional feminist approach to the Grand Challenges for Social Work. *Social Work*, 65(4), 313–315. doi:10.1093/sw/swaa042

Miller, S. E., & Hayward, R. A. (2014). Social work education's role in addressing people and a planet at risk. *Social Work Education*, 33, 280–295.

Mitchell, F. M. (2019a). Water (in)security and American Indian health: Social and environmental justice implications for policy, practice, and research. *Public Health*, 176, 98–105. doi:10.1016/j.puhe.2018.10.010

Mitchell, F. M. (2019b). "Water Is Life": Using photovoice to document American Indian perspectives of water and health. *Social Work Research*. https://doi.org/10.1093/swr/svy025

Moore, M., Martinson, M. I., Nurius, P. S., & Kemp, S. P. (2018). Transdisciplinarity in research: Perspectives of early career faculty. *Research on Social Work Practice*, 28, 254–264.

National Aeronautics and Space Administration. (2021). 2020 Tied for warmest year on record, NASA analysis shows. NASA Global Climate Change, January 14, 2021. Retrieved from https://climate.nasa.gov/news/3061/2020-tied-for-warmest-year-on-record-nasa-analysis-shows/

National Association of Social Workers. (2017). Climate change, natural disasters affect well-being. *NASW News*, 62. Retrieved from http://www.socialworkers.org/pubs/news/2017/2/Climate%20change.asp

National Association of Social Workers. (2021). *2021 Blueprint of Federal Social Policy Priorities*. National Association of Social Workers. https://www.socialworkers.org/LinkClick.aspx?fileticket=KPdZqqY60t4%3d&portalid=0

Nurius, P. S., Kemp, S. P., Köngeter, S., & Gehlert, S. (2017). Next generation social work research education: Fostering transdisciplinary readiness. *European Journal of Social Work*, 20, 907–920.

Nyahunda, L., Makhubele, J. C., Mabvurira, V., & Matlakala, F. K. (2020). Vulnerabilities and inequalities experienced by women in the climate change discourse in South Africa's rural communities: Implications for social work. *The British Journal of Social Work*. doi:10.1093/bjsw/bcaa118

Palinkas, L. A. (2015). Behavioral health and disasters: Looking to the future. *The Journal of Behavioral Health Services & Research*, 42, 86–95.

Palinkas, L. A. (2019). One of the most overlooked consequences of climate change? Our mental health. *Environmental Health News*. December 2, 2019, 1–7. https://www.ehn.org/how-climate-change-affects-mental-health-2641458829.html

Palinkas, L. A. (2020). *Global climate change, population displacement and public health: The next wave of migration.* New York, NY: Springer.

Palinkas, L. A., O'Donnell, M. L., Lau, W., & Wong, M. (2020). Strategies for delivering mental health services in response to global climate change: A narrative review. *International Journal of Environmental Research and Public Health, 17,* 8562. doi:10.3390/ijerph17228562

Palinkas, L. A., & Soydan, H. (2012). *Translation and implementation of evidence-based practice.* New York, NY: Oxford University Press.

Palinkas, L. A., & Wong, M. (2019). Social sustainability and global climate change: A new challenge for social work. In A, Chong & I. Chi (Eds.), *Social work and sustainability in Asia and the Pacific Rim: Facing the challenges of global environmental changes* (pp. 33–47). London, UK: Routledge.

Palinkas, L. A., & Wong M. (2020). Global climate change and mental health. *Current Opinion in Psychology, 32,* 12–16. doi:10.1016/j.copsyc.2019.06.023

Pandey, A., Brauer, M., Cropper, M. L., Balakrishnan, K., Mathur, P., Dey, S., . . . Dandona, L. (2021). Health and economic impact of air pollution in the states of India: The Global Burden of Disease Study 2019. *The Lancet Planetary Health, 5,* e25–e38.

Pearse, R. (2017). Gender and climate change. *Wiley Interdisciplinary Reviews: Climate Change, 8,* e451.

Pierotti, R., & Wildcat, D. (2000). Traditional ecological knowledge: The third alternative. *Ecological Applications, 10,* 1333–1340. [commentary].

Powell, T., & Black, J. (2019). Humanitarian response after a complex environmental disaster: A case study of Typhoon Haiyan. In A. Chong & I. Chi (Eds.), *Social work and sustainability in Asia and the Pacific Rim: Facing the challenges of global environmental changes* (pp. 109–118). London, UK: Routledge.

Powers, M., Willett, J., Mathias, J., & Hayward, A. (2018). Green social work for environmental justice: Implications for international social workers. In L. Dominelli, B. R. Nikku, & H. B. Ku (Eds.), *The Routledge handbook of green social work* (pp. 74–84). London, UK: Routledge.

Pyles, L. (2017). Decolonising disaster social work: Environmental justice and community participation. *British Journal of Social Work, 47,* 630–647.

Rao, S., & Teixeira, S. (2020). The Green New Deal: Social work's role in environmental justice policy. *Social Work, 65,* 197–200.

Rechkemmer, A., O'Connor, A., Rai, A., Decker Sparks, J. L., Mudliar, P., & Shultz, J. M. (2016). A complex social–ecological disaster: Environmentally induced forced migration. *Disaster Health, 3,* 112–120.

Rinkel, M., & Powers, M. (2017). *Social work promoting community and environmental sustainability: A workbook for global social workers and educators.* Berne, Switzerland: International Federation of Social Workers.

Rushton, A., Gray, L., Canty, J., & Blanchard, K. (2019). Beyond binary: (Re) defining "gender" for 21st century disaster risk reduction research, policy, and practice. *International Journal of Environmental Research and Public Health, 16,* 3984. doi:10.3390/ijerph16203984

Sandifer, P., Knapp, L., Lichtveld, M., Manley, R., Abramson, D., Caffey, R., . . . Singer, B. (2020). Framework for a community health observing system for the Gulf of Mexico region: Preparing for future disasters. *Frontiers of Public Health, 8.* doi:10.3389/fpubh.2020.578463

Sachs, C. E., Jensen, L., Castellanos, P., & Sexsmith, K. (Eds.). (2020). *Routledge Handbook of Gender and Agriculture.* New York: Routledge.

Schusler, T., Krings, A., & Hernández, M. (2019). Integrating youth participation and ecosocial work: New possibilities to advance environmental and social justice. *Journal of Community Practice, 27*, 460–475.

Sears, J., Kemp, S. P., & Palinkas, L. A. (2017). Develop policies targeting environmentally induced displacement in the United States. Retrieved from http://aaswsw.org/wp-content/uploads/2017/03/PAS.7.1.pdf

Shepard, B. (2013). Community gardens, creative community organizing, and environmental activism. In M. Gray, J. Coates, & T. Hetherington (Eds.), *Environmental social work* (pp. 121–134). New York, NY: Routledge.

Shi, L., Chu, E. M., Anguelovski, I., Aylett, A., Debats, J., Goh, K., . . . & Van Deveer, S. D. (2016). Roadmap towards justice in urban climate adaptation research. *Nature Climate Change, 6*, 131–137.

Shultz, J. M., Rechkemmer, A., Rai, A., & McManus, K. T. (2019). Public health and mental health implications of environmentally induced forced migration. *Disaster Medicine and Public Health Preparedness 13*, 116–122. doi:10.1017/dmp.2018.27

Sousa, C. A., Kemp, S. P., & El-Zuhairi, M. (2019). Place as a social determinant of health: Narratives of trauma and homeland among Palestinian women. *The British Journal of Social Work, 49*, 963–982.

Teixeira, S., & Krings, A. (2015). Sustainable social work: An environmental justice framework for social work education. *Social Work Education, 35*, 513–527.

Teixeira, S., Mathias, J. & Krings, A. (2019). The future of environmental social work: Looking to community initiatives for models of prevention. *Journal of Community Practice, 27*, 414–429. doi:10.1080/10705422.2019.1648350

Teixeira, S., & Zuberi, A. (2016). Mapping the racial inequality in place: Using youth perceptions to identify unequal exposure to neighborhood environmental hazards. *International Journal of Environmental Research and Public Health, 13*, 844. doi:10.3390/ijerph13090844

Truell, R., & Jones, D. N. (2012). *The global agenda for social work and social development: Extending the influence of social work*. Rheinfelden, Switzerland: International Federation of Social Workers. Retrieved from http://cdn.ifsw.org/assets/ifsw_24848-10.pdf

Tuck, E., & McKenzie, M. (2014). *Place in research: Theory, methodology, and methods*. New York, NY: Routledge.

Uehara, E. S., Barth, R. P., Coffey, D., Padilla, Y., & McClain, A. (2017). An introduction to the special section on Grand Challenges for Social Work. *Journal of the Society for Social Work and Research, 8*, 75–85.

UNESCO. (2019). *Leaving no one behind: Executive summary*. Paris: Author.

United Nations. (2015). Sustainable development goals. Retrieved from http://www.un.org/sustainabledevelopment/sustainable-development-goals/

United Nations (2019). World Urbanisation Prospects 2018: Highlights (ST/ESA/SER.A/421). New York: United Nations. Retrieved from: https://population.un.org/wup/Publications/

United Nations Human Settlements Programme. (2016). World cities report: 2016: Urbanization and development. Retrieved from http://wcr.unhabitat.org/main-report/

US Environmental Protection Agency. (2016). U.S. national climate assessment: Extreme weather. Retrieved from http://nca2014.globalchange.gov/highlights/report-findings/extreme-weather

Walters, K. L., Beltran, R., Huh, D., & Evans-Campbell, T. (2011). Dis-placement and dis-ease: Land, place, and health among American Indians and Alaska Natives. In *Communities, neighborhoods, and health* (pp. 163–199). New York, NY: Springer.

Willett, J. (2015a). Exploring the intersection of environmental degradation and poverty: Environmental injustice in Nairobi, Kenya. *Social Work Education, 35*, 558–572.

Willett, J. (2015b). The slow violence of climate change in poor rural Kenyan communities: "Water is life. Water is everything." *Contemporary Rural Social Work, 7*, 39–55.

Willett, J. (2019). Micro disasters: Expanding the social work conceptualization of disasters. *International Social Work, 62*, 133–145. https://doi.org/10.1177/0020872817712565

Wilson, S. M., Bullard, R., Patterson, J., & Thomas, S. B. (2020). Roundtable on the pandemics of racism, environmental injustice, and COVID-19 in America. *Environmental Justice, 13*, 56–64.

World Health Organization. (2016). *Ambient air pollution: A global assessment of exposure and burden of disease.* Geneva, Switzerland: Author.

Wu, X., Lu, Y., Zhou, S., Chen, L., & Xu, B. (2016). Impact of climate change on human infectious diseases: Empirical evidence and human adaptation. *Environment international, 86*, 14–23.

CHAPTER 9

Harnessing Technology for Social Good

JONATHAN BENTLEY SINGER, MELANIE SAGE,
STEPHANIE COSNER BERZIN, AND
CLAUDIA J. COULTON

The Grand Challenge to Harness Technology for Social Good is unique among the Grand Challenges in that it sets out not to address a specific issue or problem, but to transform the field of social work fundamentally with respect to its relationship to technology. Specifically, it aims to harness big data and to deploy information and communication technology to improve the efficacy of social programs, accelerate the pace of social discovery, and reduce inequalities.

The COVID-19 pandemic accelerated the adoption of technology by social workers at a pace inconceivable just a few years earlier. In the first edition of this chapter, Berzin and Coulton (2018, p. 161) noted that "social work has been slow to adopt technology.... [L]imited resources, ethical and legal considerations, lack of training, and social work's historical reliance on face-to-face communications have prevented significant progress in the field." Many of these barriers were eliminated temporarily in the weeks following the March 13, 2020, shut down of the United States. Public and private insurance companies lifted restrictions on telehealth reimbursement; legislators at the federal and state levels suspended language that prohibited the use of telephones and webcams for psychotherapy. Schools of social work and private providers jumped into providing online education and educating providers about best practices for providing telehealth. The desire to minimize contagion and flatten the curve of infections and hospitalizations flipped the

Jonathan Bentley Singer, Melanie Sage, Stephanie Cosner Berzin, and Claudia J. Coulton, *Harnessing Technology for Social Good* In: *Grand Challenges for Social Work and Society*. Second Edition. Edited by: Richard P. Barth, Jill T. Messing, Trina R. Shanks, and James Herbert Williams, Oxford University Press. © Oxford University Press 2022.
DOI: 10.1093/oso/9780197608043.003.0009

long-standing question "Is it ethical to provide telehealth services" to "Is it ethical to provide face-to-face services?" The COVID-19 pandemic accelerated the pace of technology adoption, social workers' familiarity with technology terms and concepts, and consumer use of technologies. Even before George Floyd's murder sparked the Black Lives Matter protests of 2020, the racial and economic disparities in COVID infection rates raised questions about historical disparities in health and healthcare access for Blacks, Indigenous people, and people of color. Conversations that were once niche about the role of technology in addressing or reinforcing racial and economic disparities became headline news (Benjamin, 2019). The era of technology was upon us.

Despite all these changes, many of the foundational concepts related to social work and technology remain. Information and communication technology (ICT) is transformational in its power to connect, create access to, and embolden new opportunities to rethink social work practice. Social workers have an ethical obligation to make sure that technologies are used to dismantle, not reinforce, oppressive systems. Although selected examples of practice and policy innovation through digital technologies have been documented (Berzin & Coulton, 2018), there are few social work practitioners or scholars who provide leadership in technology. Two of the chapter authors (M. S. and J. B. S.) posted a request on Twitter to identify social workers who are in (leadership) positions related to technology (e.g., advisors or consultants at tech start-ups or board members for tech-related organizations) (https://twitter.com/socworkpodcast/status/1357704746811981826). The crowdsourced list included several social workers who address race/ethnicity, including Desmond Patton, Fallon Wilson, and Tianca Crocker, and others who work for startup companies that develop technology and provide services or training for direct practice, such as Melissa McCool, Meredith Ferguson, Samantha Nadler, Elizabeth Rhodes, and Renee Daly.

Despite existing troves of data and promising analytic technology, the social and human services sector lags in using data-driven strategies in designing programs and policies. Although social workers have a lot to say about what is good and bad about technology, they have been largely absent from the emerging field of tech ethics. We live in a digital society in which people produce vast quantities of data, but social workers and human service organizations are rarely involved in designing or harnessing these data for social good. As we move into the post-COVID-19 pandemic world, a grand challenge for the social work profession is to continue to recognize, participate in, invest in, and harness technological and digital advancements for social good.

Marginalized communities have arguably faced barriers to accessing information and analytic tools that could advance their quality of life and economic opportunities individually or collectively. Although currently there is great unevenness on the part of government agencies in providing open access to public data, technology used well could provide diverse communities information they can use to better their own circumstances (Goldsmith & Crawford, 2014).

If social work does not invest in building the capacity to make full use of technology to benefit society—and vulnerable groups and communities in particular—the promise of these innovations will not be achieved universally. Innovative technologies, if made affordable and available, can connect populations previously marginalized by geography, disability, or economics. The power of previously isolated groups using technology to join forces and dismantle oppressive structures is a terrifying prospect to those who currently control the resources. Without social works' involvement, however, the risks and burdens emanating from technological advances may fall disproportionately on those who are not equipped to engage with them.

The compelling nature of this challenge stems from not only the magnitude of use, but also from the possibility of solutions. Digital and technology-based solutions have the power to create massive change and radical transformation in who is served and how. Technology has shifted fundamentally the way humans communicate with each other and their environment (Mishna, Milne, Bobo, &Pereira, 2020), made disruptive shifts in philanthropy (Arrillaga-Andreessen, 2015), and created transformational opportunities for new interventions in social work education (Huttar & BrintzenhofeSzoc, 2020) and practice (Barak & Grohol, 2011; Chan & Holosko, 2016).

Meeting this challenge would result in a broader and more equitable distribution of the benefits of technology in society. Enhanced by innovative integration of ICT into practice, social work would expand its reach and impact. Social services would be available to people who traditionally have been excluded because of structural racism, geography, transportation, and scheduling barriers. Powerful data analytics would enable more customized, timelier, and better targeted services. Technology would support the design of more effective assessment tools, intervention modalities, and real-time feedback mechanisms. Populations currently victimized by the digital divide would be able to participate on an equal footing.

OPPORTUNITIES FOR IMPROVEMENT

Failure to incorporate technological advances into social work and social welfare means that large portions of the population fail to benefit fully, and scarce resources are not deployed optimally. Progress on many fronts will be hindered if promising technologies are not incorporated into social work interventions, service delivery systems, organizational decision-making, program and policy evaluation, and social innovation. Opportunities exist for integration of technology using social media, mobile technology, wearable technology and sensors, robotics and artificial intelligence, gaming, geospatial technology, big data, and data analytics.

Although this robust set of opportunities for technology integration exists, several limitations prevent the intentional use of technology into practice (Mishna, Fantus, & McInroy, 2017). Limited education and training prevent many practitioners from knowing how to incorporate technology effectively (Mishna, Bogo, & Sawyer, 2015). Limited exposure to innovative applications of technology to therapeutic work creates misperceptions that also prevent their widespread adoption. A 2016 systematic review of social work interventions using technology, for instance, found that of 17 studies that met criteria for good validity and high intervention fidelity, only three evaluated the role that technology played in the intervention (Chan & Holosko, 2016).

The implication is that there are very few social work interventions that use ICT, and there is even less empirical information about the role that technology plays in the interventions. Limited financial resources hinder the adoption and testing of technologies in the field. Although the availability of mobile technology, wireless services, and low-cost apps has removed several barriers, social workers are adapting and modifying technologies developed for nonsocial work purposes instead of being part of technology development. In addition, although many sectors are developing technologies that will improve the emotional, behavioral, and cognitive well-being of people, the promise of innovating and integrating technology into social work practice has yet to be realized.

At the policy and systems levels, human service delivery systems are not learning about, analyzing critically, or developing ethical tools to use technological advances in data science and analytics. Massive amounts of valuable social data remain locked up in legacy data systems and agency silos, where the data cannot be used readily to improve performance or respond optimally to changing needs. Shrinking resources for social programs make leveraging data to drive programming even more vital. Although there is a growing demand to prove what works, human service systems often lack the data management and analysis infrastructure necessary to evaluate programs efficiently. Moreover, such systems lack interoperability and standardization, making it challenging to integrate data across sectors to examine the long-term costs and benefits of social programs. Last, much debate exists about ethical ways to integrate the use of big data, especially for predicting service delivery needs (Eubanks, 2019).

At the same time, nonprofit organizations and foundation funders are expecting social service systems to use a variety of data analytic tools and predictive analytics to precisely inform sound decisions. Agency executives and managers are now expected to have data at the ready to support their operational decisions and long-term strategies. They are increasingly required to provide metrics to show what is working and to ensure that quality standards and outcomes are meeting the mark. They expect data to drive innovation and agency practice.

In addition, the general public is beginning to call for more civic engagement with socially relevant data. Open government and civic hacking movements provide vehicles for mining data and generating information for communal use. The term *open data* describes the idea that certain kinds of data should be disseminated freely so they can be reused, analyzed, published, and transformed into new and useful products (Bertot, Gorham, Jaeger, Sarin, & Choi, 2014). Furthermore, community coalitions that work to improve outcomes for target populations (e.g., vulnerable youth, homeless veterans, children growing up in deep poverty) require access to cross-system data to keep all the partners on track and working toward common goals (Wolff et al., 2017). Yet, open data are tricky in public systems, where several data points may make an individual subject identifiable and where regulations may apply regarding how data are reshared (Tai, 2021).

Despite the push toward data applications, the social sector needs to address numerous obstacles to benefit from its data resources. Data security breaches and privacy are a central concern, especially with respect to human service, educational, and health records (Jacquemard, Doherty, & Fitzsimons, 2020; Strang & Sun, 2020). Although the law permits many of these records to be used for research, evaluation, and quality improvement purposes, agencies are often reluctant to share the records for analysis. Moreover, the social sector must consider the ethical matter of using digital material for purposes of which individuals may not have been aware when providing personal information. Social work cannot endorse or design technology solutions intentionally or unintentionally that perpetuate racial injustice in the form of a new Jim Code (Benjamin, 2019). A related difficulty concerns data ownership and control, especially when data from various sources are combined to create applications beyond the scope of the original intent. Although such mash-ups often yield information of very high value, exemplifying the power of big data, they require agencies to cede individual control to achieve a larger societal benefit. Such agreements often encounter legal and practical complications.

Curation of big data is another significant challenge because the data are a byproduct of numerous processes, not generated specifically for the purpose to which they are eventually applied. Understanding how these processes shape the data is crucial to producing valid information and correct interpretation. The data require careful cleaning and validation by specialists with a deep understanding of data-generating processes. A related issue is determining how to allow other analysts to replicate the results from big data. Unlike the fixed data sets associated with traditional research projects, big data platforms are typically refreshed by a continuous flow of new information. It may be difficult to reproduce results exactly if the data have shifted between the original analysis and the validation analysis. Before fully adopting big data applications, social work professionals need to develop, vet, and document rigorous quality assurance, versioning, and archiving techniques, and ensure awareness of the factors that affect the data-generating process (Lazer, Kennedy, King, & Vespignani, 2014).

> ## MAINSTREAMING GENDER
>
> ### (Re)-harnessing Digital Technology for Social Good
> MEGAN LINDSAY BROWN
>
> Information technology offers intelligence without integrity. It takes on whatever rules or moral standards its designers and controllers choose.
> —Glastonbury, LaMendola, and Sharpley (1988)
>
> Technology is not a neutral tool; it is used to support and extend an individualistic, patriarchal, and white supremacist value system. The social work profession has an opportunity to reshape technology for positive human benefit, but this requires social workers to incorporate our professional values actively—in particular, the values of human dignity and social justice—into technological spaces. Social workers have historical knowledge of how harm manifests for those occupying a multiplicity of disenfranchised positions, allowing us to recognize the ways in which technology harms women, nonbinary and gender fluid individuals, and Black, Indigenous, People of Color (BIPOC). Akin to rectifying the social work profession itself, Harnessing Technology for Social Good requires that we reckon with past harms, identify inequitable systems, and actively seek to reverse technology that serves to maintain and expand disproportionate power structures.
>
> The Grand Challenge to Harness Technology for Social Good must approach technology from a gendered and intersectional framework to invert social structures of power and privilege. Individuals and ideologies that have been excluded from the design process must be the driving forces for better technology and a better society. Social work's way of understanding the world allows us the perspective to say that technology is harmful *and* helpful. But, rather than simply accepting that some benefit and some are harmed, an intersectional feminist perspective requires that we go further in evaluating technological innovations by asking, "*Who* is benefitting?" and "*Who* could be harmed?" The answer (more often than not) is that those who benefit are men and white people; those who are harmed are women and BIPOC, and, in particular, people who sit at the intersection of these identities.
>
> This duality of benefits and harms can be seen across multiple contemporary examples of technological innovation. In Summer 2020, as the United
>
> *continued*

States roiled over the murders of Black people by police, the American Civil Liberties Union was suing the Chicago Police Department over their pursuit of contracts with Clearview to use facial recognition algorithms. These algorithms are fatally flawed because the images used for coding are disproportionately white and male (D'Iganazio & Klein, 2020). Benefits of this technological innovation to the criminal legal system (i.e., faster suspect identification) do not outweigh the potential harms of mistaken identity and unnecessary exposure that fall disproportionately upon Latino and Black men who are already at risk of police violence. Consider, as an alternative, the development of an algorithm to identify police officers likely to abuse their power. Police violence is a social problem, but the development of such a resource within the current technological structure is unlikely. At the crux of the technology landscape is the patriarchal and white supremacist power hierarchy that determines who is protected for acts of violence. This example demonstrates how the production and use of data is a social act, is often a companion to social control, and replicates the racism, sexism, classism, and ableism within society.

This pattern of maintaining and reinforcing the existing power structure is evident across technological innovations. Amazon is using surveillance technology (e.g., heat sensors, wearables to track movement) to monitor workers, leaving them feeling dehumanized and degraded. The information technology firm MindGeek allowed, and arguably encouraged, nonconsensual sharing of explicit images and videos, including sexual content containing minors on the site PornHub. Victims were expected to remove the images themselves, and many women endured stalking and harassment from strangers who repeatedly uploaded the images or e-mailed them to employers and others close to the victim after initial removal. At the same time, strides toward social justice are being made, led by BIPOC and women who are standing up to large tech firms. Amazon workers, led primarily by Black women, organized to create the first Amazon Union in Bessemer, Alabama. A class action lawsuit against MindGeek led to the internal decision to verify users and removal of 80% of the total content on PornHub because it came from unverified sources. And there are examples of technology being used proactively to benefit oppressed people. Leaders of the Navajo Nation and Apache Tribe used surveillance technology from Google maps to identify and organize potential voters in the northwest corner of Arizona. This surveillance was used with the express purpose of empowering Indigenous people who have been disenfranchised to participate in the democratic process. The myPlan app is an online safety planning tool for survivors of intimate partner violence that uses technology to make evidence-based, expert knowledge freely available to people who may not have otherwise sought help.

Examples of the beneficial use of technology foreground gender, race/ethnicity, and socioeconomic status in their design and implementation. To Harness Technology for Social Good, social workers must begin to participate actively in the social shaping of technology to ensure these tools

continued

are in service of a more equitable society, and not just a more efficient, uniform, and accelerated version of the already discriminatory and inequitable social structure. Mainstreaming an intersectional gender approach to technological innovation includes recognizing the harms that have come from technology and working actively to dismantle the racist and sexist systems that perpetuate these harms in the technological space.

References

D'Iganazio, C., & Klein, L. F. (2020). Data feminism. Cambridge, MA: MIT Press.

Glastonbury, B., LaMendola, W., & Sharpley, R. (1988). The integrity of intelligence: A bill of rights for the information age. London: Palgrave Macmillan.

INNOVATIONS AND THEIR IMPORTANCE

Recent accomplishments across a range of technologies suggest they can be applied successfully in social work and social welfare. Action can be taken in a number of areas during the next decade to ensure that available technology is applied effectively in social work and social welfare to maximize attainment of social good.

Considering the range of ICT services, ample opportunities exist for expanding social work practice by geography, availability, access to providers, and lower cost. Populations that have had difficulty accessing traditional face-to-face services found opportunities for engagement in social work services through technology during the COVID-19 pandemic (Craig, Iacono, Pascoe, & Austin, 2021). Services provided across a range of Internet and technology-enabled platforms transformed access for those with disabilities, those who lacked transportation, those who were homebound, or those who needed specific communication strategies. More broadly, ICT enhances the speed and flexibility of services, and it provides the ability for individual pacing (Song et al., 2021). Data mining tools and integrated data systems (IDSs) provide the potential for directing policy and programs more effectively. In the area of technology, there has been a huge range of innovations and demonstrated effectiveness (Stoll, Müller, & Trachsel, 2020). Specific innovations are discussed next.

SOCIAL MEDIA AND THE INTERNET

Internet and social media have been applied to social work clinical and macro practice through online help-seeking, advocacy, peer support, and self-care, and health promotion and education (Berzin & Coulton, 2018). In addition, data applications include the use of social media to identify emerging social movements (Tinati, Halford, Carr, & Pope, 2014) and to track trends related to social issues (Stephens-Davidowitz, 2013). Social media platforms increasingly allow ad-buyers to use specific user targeting, which allows those recruiting research study participants to draw from new potential crowds of audiences that may not otherwise know about the work (Jones, Walters, & Brown, 2020). On the other hand, social media and the Internet also create a new target for interventions resulting from problems such as bullying or sex trafficking online, and social workers and others need to stay abreast of these problems and the technology-mediated interventions that may address these issues (Espelage & Hong, 2017). Innovators such as Desmond Patton have combined machine learning and qualitative analysis to gain insights into the lives of gang involved youth from social media data (Patton, Eschmann, Elsaesser, & Bocanegra, 2016; Patton et al., 2019; Patton, MacBeth, Schoenebeck, Shear, & McKeown, 2018).

MOBILE TECHNOLOGY

The promise of mobile technology allows for accessing information and services where and when they are needed. According to the Pew Research Center, 97% of Americans own a cellphone and 85% own a smartphone (Pew Research Center: Internet, Science & Tech, 2021). Used in the healthcare field, mobile technology allows for the delivery of interventions with access to information, tracking, and monitoring on a constant basis (Christensen, 2018; Marcolino et al., 2018). In social work practice, this might include access to intervention components, model fidelity checks, real-time assessment, and connection to mental health professionals. Supplementing with global positioning systems and sensors allows for more specified tracking and notification systems. Cognitive interventions making use of these technologies (Christensen, 2018; Lorenzo-Luaces, Peipert, De Jesús Romero, Rutter, & Rodriguez-Quintana, 2021) have obtained positive outcomes related to services delivered in real time. Mobile technology that provides ongoing information and support has also been shown to improve practice (Lee & Walsh, 2015). Mobile technologies increasingly close access gaps. Social work research found that homeless youth with access to mobile technologies, for instance, were more likely to have access to other resources such as shelter and food (Rice & Barman-Adhikari, 2014). Thus, it is important that social workers continue to consider ways that mobile technology interventions might reach the most vulnerable.

WEARABLE TECHNOLOGY AND SENSORS

Although mobile technology provides some access to ongoing data collection and real-time intervention, wearable technology and sensors provide another avenue for monitoring [see Sheikh, Qassem and Kyriacou (2021) for a review]. Wearables can be combined with self-report measures or used alone. There are wrist devices that monitor skin valence; glasses that track eye movements; a t-shirt with embedded sensors to monitor electrocardiogram–heart rate variability, respiration activity, and activity recognition in the treatment of patients with serious mental illness; and other sensors to track noise, body metrics, ingestion, and location as a supplement to existing data (Goldkind & Wolf, 2015).

Physiological tracking allows self-report and retrospective data to be supplemented with real-time and continuous data. Social work assessment and intervention can make use of these new sources of data to create more personalized feedback (Sheikh et al., 2021) and enhance client self-management (Craig & Calleja Lorenzo, 2014). Feedback that goes directly to clinicians can also help direct treatment and support clinical decision-making (Lanata, Valenza, Nardelli, Gentili, & Scilingo, 2015). In addition, self-monitoring via sensor technology may increase self-awareness and thereby supplement social work interventions (Til, McInnis, & Cochran, 2020).

ROBOTICS AND ARTIFICIAL INTELLIGENCE

Another innovation that supports real-time assessment, intervention, and feedback derives from the promise of robotics and artificial intelligence (Kumar et al., 2013). Integrating artificial intelligence into screening and intake might support detection of particular response patterns or support clinical decision-making. Artificial intelligence includes a wide swath of technology-mediated activities that use reasoning to learn from their own behavior and improve their interaction with a user over time. This may include the use of algorithms, chat bots, or other devices, such as Amazon's Alexa. The social work profession can consider the ways in which these tools might serve the most vulnerable and support the lowest level of interventions so that people can live with autonomy and self-determination (Tambe & Rice, 2018). Many methods of artificial intelligence that can enhance self-efficacy are tools called the *Internet of Things*, in which the Internet is built in to an in-home device. Examples include fall detection devices that send a signal to chosen people when the sensor detects a fall (Yacchirema, de Puga, Palau, & Esteve, 2019). As another example, passive mood detection algorithms identify the frequency of phone use or movement and notice atypical patterns that might indicate a depressive or manic episode and can cue the user or provider to check in about a patient's mental health (Garcia-Ceja et al., 2018).

GAMING AND GAMIFICATION

Although not directly an ICT, gaming and gamification represent avenues of innovation that come out of the ICT landscape. Video games have become ubiquitous in modern life, and exploiting them and their mechanisms has potential for social work practice. Gamification, which includes the use of game like mechanisms in nongaming environments, such as badging and recognition systems, supports learning specific behaviors (Langlois, 2013). Early applications addressed the treatment of depression (Rao, 2013), anxiety (Dennis & O'Toole, 2014), substance abuse, and violence prevention (Schoech, Boyas, Black, & Elias-Lambert, 2013). Gamification is currently used to support physical activity, such as in the case of FitBit badges; biofeedback games that help users practice calm brain states; and cognitive training games, for example in which participants practice and model coping skills (Fleming et al., 2017). These types of serious games appear to increase engagement and motivation, which are important components of treatment persistence.

Related to gamification, gaming uses actual games in the intervention. The prevalence of technology-based gaming has led video games to be incorporated in the treatment of posttraumatic stress disorder (Holmes, James, Coode-Bate, & Deeprose, 2009) and schizophrenia (Välimäki et al., 2021), and to address suicide risk in military veterans (Colder Carras, Bergendahl, & Labrique, 2021).

Virtual reality has been shown to be effective in therapeutic treatment (Morina, Ijntema, Meyerbroker, & Emmelkamp, 2015). Virtual reality games have the benefit of including immersive video, audio, and other stimuli. Home-use headsets offer rapidly growing accessibility for these types of interventions, but price points and disability considerations still limit who might be able to benefit from these devices (Trahan, Smith, & Talbot, 2019). Virtual reality has been used as a tool to augment social worker training; for instance, social work students who interacted with virtual patients increased their self-efficacy in interviewing skills (Atuel & Kintzle, 2021). Social workers who have used virtual reality in treatment have found that they can reduce significantly the length of sessions for posttraumatic stress disorder in returning soldiers, for instance, when compared to treatment as usual (Peskin, Mello, Cukor, Olden, & Difede, 2019). Emerging opportunities for virtual reality include innovations in which participants can have an immersive visit for group or individual therapy in a simulated setting (Dilgul, Hickling, Antonie, Priebe, & Bird, 2021).

GEOSPATIAL TECHNOLOGY

Geographically referenced information is now ubiquitous coming from global positioning system-enabled devices, sensors, images, geocoded records, and other sources. Geographic information systems (GISs) integrate spatial data and information, and also incorporate tools that enable displays, mapping, visualization, and spatial analysis. Geospatial technology is already being incorporated into social work practice and research, but it has the potential to be more valuable in a very broad range of applications (Mandayam & Joosten, 2016). One area in which it has found immediate relevance is in community practice. For example, youth have been engaged in exploring their community and the issues that affect them using spatial data and mapping tools (Teixeira & Zuberi, 2016). Also, these technologies are used extensively in planning the locations and needs for services, evaluating service accessibility, and identifying clusters of social need or risk (Daley et al., 2016; Freisthler & Weiss, 2008; Thurston et al., 2017). For instance, participants recruited in a homeless shelter wore GIS devices to help researchers map the movements of people who were homeless to assess more comprehensively their service delivery needs (North et al., 2017). On an individual intervention level, GIS technology may alert a provider if a person enters or exits a GIS-indicated (or "fenced") area; for instance, a treatment provider could be notified if a person wearing a GIS device enters a drinking establishment (Clapp et al., 2018).

BIG DATA AND IDSS

There is a growing interest in how to take advantage of big data in social work. Social agencies are the holders of massive data systems that can be turned into generators of actionable information. Agencies are beginning to automate performance metrics, progress dashboards, and assessment tools that support practice and policy.

Another significant development using big data is the movement to build and maintain multiagency IDSs as a permanent utility for the social sector. In most IDSs, administrative records from many agencies are retrieved on an ongoing basis, linked at the individual level, cleaned and organized, and made available for analysis. Although these systems are under development, they have great potential to deliver high-quality big data with almost unlimited possibilities to yield vital information to transform social policy and practice. For example, such systems are already making it possible to estimate the scope of multiple-system use, patient trajectories through these systems, and the associated costs, suggesting starting points for overall improvements in the social service sector (Barrett & Katsiyannis, 2017). They are also foundational for data-driven social innovations such as community-wide, collaborative impact projects (Tudor, Gomez, & Denby, 2017) and social impact financing (Butler, Bloom, & Rudd, 2013; Stoesz, 2014). A series of case studies of selected IDSs affirms the technical and practical feasibility of building these systems and generating actionable information for policy (Fantuzzo & Culhane, 2015), while acknowledging the challenges of global–local (aka *glocal*) eco-social justice (Izlar, 2019).

Social services IDSs are not the only innovative type of integrated data platform emerging in the social sector. Community revitalization work is benefiting from mash-ups of property, housing, and neighborhood data using GIS technology (Kingsley, Coulton, & Pettit, 2014). For example, community partners in some cities have been enabled to fight blight and disinvestment using open data portals that link numerous transactional records (e.g., foreclosure filings, deed transfers, evictions, complaints) in real time and make them available through a user-friendly interface for action on the ground (Nelson, 2014). This has been used to fight predatory lending with data-based evidence (Coulton, Schramm, & Hirsh, 2010), and to understand the effects of evictions on children and their families (Richter, Coulton, Urban, & Steh, 2021).

ADVANCED DATA ANALYTICS

To get the most out of massive amounts of social data, it is necessary to move beyond standard statistical models (Hindman, 2015). Big data allow many more variables to be considered in predicting what interventions will work for individuals with a unique social profile or in evaluating risk potential within populations. For example, predictive analytics have been applied to linked birth and child welfare records to identify young children at high risk of child maltreatment (Chouldechova, Benavides-Prado, Fialko, & Vaithianathan, 2018), households that are highly likely to become homeless (Greer, Shinn, Kwan, & Zuiderveen, 2016), and veteran suicide after psychiatric hospitalization (Kessler et al., 2019, 2020). Validation with holdout samples and various calibration techniques enable these prediction models to be refined so they can be incorporated into practice and evaluated further for their impact.

Machine learning algorithms are increasingly being applied in efforts to enhance the accuracy of predictions and improve decisions. For example, risk-scoring algorithms derived from machine learning have been used to assess risk of flight and crime among pretrial defendants (Kleinberg, Lakkaraju, Leskovec, Ludwig, & Mullainathan, 2017). Text mining methods are evolving rapidly and are now being applied to unstructured notes to gain a more complete picture of behaviors—for example, in child welfare cases—that could not be ascertained simply by tabulating structured data fields (Goerge, Ozik, & Collier, 2012). Similarly, the application of a hybrid text mining approach to massive numbers of text records in the Veterans Administration's data warehouse yielded an innovative method to calibrate suicide risk in that population (Hammond & Laundry, 2014). An emerging use of these kinds of algorithms is in the use of personalized medicine, in which treatments are matched specifically to the characteristics of the client (Lorenzo-Luaces et al., 2021).

Microsimulation models are also proving useful for evaluating how policy or practice changes might play out over entire human service systems

(Goldhaber-Fiebert et al., 2012). In addition, applying predictive analytics from numerous digital touch points to detailed data on individuals and their social settings might eventually lead to policy or practice interventions that could modify elements of behavior (Moore, Sacks, Manlove, & Sawhill, 2014). Such types of analyses consider the sequential nature of the elements and the potential for nonlinear and reciprocal relationships, and the complex system dynamics that may evolve over various layers of social organization. Therefore, they hold great promise for eventually customizing social interventions with precision. Such discoveries could ultimately be the basis for social interventions that are fine-tuned to the person in the situation—interventions that will work with relatively greater levels of certainty.

Randomized controlled trials can be implemented frequently and at low cost when they are embedded in a data-rich environment and are carried out with the help of automated systems. Just like the for-profit sector that engages experiment-driven innovation (Manzi, 2012), human service organizations can use randomized controlled trials fruitfully to test the impact of changes in practices or procedures and observe results through data in their automated systems. With the advent of IDSs described earlier, they can also look beyond their own programs to track longer term effects of innovative practices through rigorous designs. If outcomes for experimental and control subjects can be tracked through IDSs, findings can be produced more quickly and at a lower cost compared to those obtained from conventional experiments, which require expensive follow-up studies (Coalition for Evidence-Based Policy, 2012). For example, a randomized trial of a new case management model with disabled Medicaid beneficiaries relied on linked individual records from several social service agencies to show the positive impact on emergency hospital readmissions, homelessness, and receipt of substance abuse treatment but no discernable cost savings (Bell et al., 2015). This type of information can be directly pertinent to government decisions.

INTERSECTIONS WITH RACE AND GENDER EQUITY

Social workers are especially interested in how technological innovations affect those who are most marginalized. In some instances, fast-moving innovations disenfranchise people who already experience bias. For instance, facial recognition software algorithms are often trained using white faces, which may underidentify Black faces, leading to wrongful arrests when facial recognition is used for crime analysis (Williams, 2020). Similarly, algorithms that rely on past data to predict future risk or success can make predictions that underrepresent people who are already underrepresented, such as in the case of Amazon's employment recommender algorithm that predicted that men would make better executive employees (Tambe, Cappelli, & Yakubovich,

2019). In fact, in all the promising interventions outlined here, there is also the potential that existing and future innovations may further bias who benefits and experiences risk when encountering human services systems. For these reasons, it is even more important that social workers (a) understand how technology works and (b) are involved in the development of tools that impact marginalized populations (Hossain & Ahmed, 2021). For instance, social work program directors may be tasked with implementing algorithms in human services systems. If they do not understand where the data come from and how the algorithm might introduce bias, the algorithm could contribute to disparate outcomes for clients. Many argue that this is the case in the Alleghany County child welfare system, in which linked public service databases inform risk scores for children referred for assessment of neglect or abuse (Keddell, 2019; Turner Lee, 2018). Because the data draw primarily on public service users who are more already racialized and affected by poverty, the use of these data for surveillance further tracks the behavior of these groups and leads to a loop in which they are more likely to be involved with public systems.

APPROACH AND ACCOMPLISHMENTS

The innovations discussed thus far, although not exhaustive, represent some of the most promising avenues for social work research, policy, and practice. Moving forward in these areas will take coordinated efforts and investment. In addition, it will be crucial to guard against potential negative consequences of technology, such as disproportionate impacts on disadvantaged groups, violations of privacy and human rights, and cyber victimization. Table 9.1 summarizes some of the outcomes that we anticipate can be accomplished and steps that are needed to achieve measurable progress. Although developing specific metrics is difficult because of the evolving nature of technology, we expect considerable progress in these areas during the next 5 years.

OPPORTUNITIES FOR NEW INITIATIVES IN INTERDISCIPLINARY AND CROSS-SECTOR INVOLVEMENT

As indicated at many points in Table 9.1, leveraging the promise of technology toward social good requires not only the investment of social work, but also the collaboration of social work with other disciplines. Together with computer science, engineering, statistics, social science, and business, we must create interdisciplinary partnerships to support this work. Working with computer scientists, technologists, and software engineers, we can build the technology that will support social service delivery (Aguirre, McCoy, &

Table 9.1 TECHNOLOGY INNOVATION FOR SOCIAL WORK: PROMISE AND PROGRESS

Technology	Promise	Moving Forward
Social media	1. Social media will provide immediate access to personalized services. 2. Social media will be a protective tool to help people at risk (e.g., for people having indicated risk for suicide, send message or connect to a suicide helpline). 3. Social media will enable social work to leverage the collective crowd to engage in problem-solving. 4. Blogs will enhance treatment fidelity through standardized instructions and algorithms. 5. Social media (e.g., Twitter) will identify emerging social movements and issues.	1. Partner with social media companies to leverage potential. 2. Train social workers to use social media effectively.
Mobile devices	1. Mobile apps will enable people to get the services they need at their pace and when they want them. 2. Combining GPS technology, mobile apps will allow behavior tracking when people are in a no-go zone (e.g., bar, casino). 3. Interventions, particularly cognitive–behavioral interventions, with mobile devices including GPS and self-paced Internet modules will create positive outcomes and increase effectiveness.	1. Understand when, where, and how to work with self-paced mobile technologies to improve outcomes for people. 2. Collaborate with computer software engineers to develop mobile apps with consideration for social justice.
Wearable technology and sensors	1. Using wearable sensors will enable clients to gather constant data for assessment and intervention. 2. Real-time tracking will enhance opportunities for client self-management.	1. Partner with companies developing wearable technology. 2. Research examining the connection between physiological indicators and mental health outcomes. 3. Train social workers in integrating physiological markers with other sources of data.

(continued)

Table 9.1 CONTINUED

Technology	Promise	Moving Forward
Robotics and artificial intelligence	1. Robotics will provide alternatives to human interaction for assessment, monitoring, and intervention. 2. Integrating artificial intelligence into intake phone calls will improve client satisfaction and client–therapist match by using algorithms to detect optimal response patterns.	1. Collaborate with engineers and computer scientists to develop appropriate social robots. 2. Train to prepare social workers for integration with this new technology. 3. Increase efficiency and effectiveness by increasing automation of service delivery.
Gamification and gaming	1. Gamification will promote positive in-game behaviors to be used in other environments. 2. The use of gaming will reduce clients' symptoms and improve functioning, for example, through simulation or role-playing (e.g., using video games to treat posttraumatic stress disorder).	1. Promote development and responsible games that support mental health. 2. Train social workers with skills to integrate gaming and gamification into practice.
Geospatial technology	1. GIS-enabled applications allow location-based work, monitoring, and community engagement.	1. Train social workers in geospatial technology. 2. Enable GIS mobile record and data collection systems. 3. Improve geographic accessibility using programs and resources.
IDSs	1. IDSs will deliver high-quality big data to yield vital information to transform social policy and practice, considering the scope of multiple systems and costs. 2. IDSs will enable data-driven social innovations such as community-wide, collaborative impact projects. 3. IDSs will allow many more variables to be taken into account in predicting what interventions will work for individuals with unique social profiles. 4. Open data portals will enhance IDSs, making a user-friendly interface for action on the ground.	1. Standardize policies and practices to expand data access and use. 2. Form and maintain relationships with numerous data providers to access big data beyond open data portals. 3. Implement advanced data management, security, and analysis. 4. Prepare data-savvy social workers by providing advanced curricula. 5. Promote data-driven social policy and practice.

Table 9.1 CONTINUED

Technology	Promise	Moving Forward
Advanced data analytics	1. Predictive models inform prevention or early intervention. 2. Machine learning supports decision-making. 3. Text mining and visualization reveals previously hidden patterns. 4. Rapid experimentation improves service design.	1. Train social workers in data science. 2. Refine and evaluate predictive analytics. 3. Build visualization tools and data mining in electronic records systems. 4. Train social workers to incorporate analytics into practice and program operations.
Digital privacy, ethics, and equity	1. Security and privacy tools are uniform and effective. 2. Disadvantaged groups have full digital access. 3. Ethical applications of digital capability.	1. Develop standards and best practices for data security and privacy. 2. Achieve equity in high-speed Internet access and digital literacy. 3. Develop methods for tracking adverse events and potential harms to individuals and groups from technology.

IDS, integrated data system; GIS, geographic information system; GPS, global positioning system.

Roan, 2013). Transforming big data into useful information for social work requires computational science and data expertise. Teams of specialists that blend substantive knowledge with analytic and technological expertise allow us to realize the promise of ICT innovations. In addition, collaboration with government supports access to data that can be used in the social sector and application of technology in government-run or government-funded programs. Because technology has significant commercial applications, the business sector is another potential partner. National social work organizations have an opportunity to play a role in facilitating the connections between technology companies and social workers. A joint technology institute of the National Association of Social Workers and the Council on Social Work Education could provide technology companies with access to social work students, practitioners, and scholars, and provide social workers with access to emerging technologies intended for human consumption.

Technology has the power to transform our response to social problems and the structures of the social sector. Disruptive paradigms that marry new partners, blend scholarship across disciplines, and create integrated training models will be required to realize this potential. The field of social work requires significant investment and restructuring to leverage new discoveries and new technologies as they emerge. Social workers with a new understanding of and enhanced appreciation for technologies and the promise of big data will advance the field at a pace that allows us to realize the benefits of this progress. As the sector becomes more adept at integrating these advances, our ability to respond to novel problems becomes enhanced. Shifting social work to respond to these challenges and lead these conversations is imperative for our continued ability to meet the demands of complex social problems.

FUTURE DIRECTIONS AND CONCLUSION

Harnessing technology for social good calls for the field's engagement with existing technologies and readiness for new technologies that emerge. Technology changes at a rapid pace, with new developments occurring on a constant basis. Full involvement is required to ensure that the fruits of technology are distributed equitably, and that social programs and services reach optimal effectiveness. To realize these aims and make significant progress requires transformations in social work education, research programs, and human services systems.

Social work education programs require shifts in pedagogy and curricula to support the adoption of technology innovations (Craig & Calleja Lorenzo, 2014; Hitchcock & Battista, 2013; Huttar & BrintzenhofeSzoc, 2020). The Council on Social Work Education is considering technology competencies for the 2022 Educational Policies and Accreditation Standards and has recently established a technology advisory group. Further progress will be achieved only with significant changes to social work training and pedagogy that supports technology infusion across courses and across schools (Hitchcock, Sage, & Smyth, 2019; Huttar & BrintzenhofeSzoc, 2020). It will be important that the field develop measures to evaluate the development of digital literacy among social work students and practitioners (Young, McLeod, & Brady, 2018; Zgoda & Shane, 2018). Development of an accessible repository of technology-related assignments, syllabi, and teaching materials that meet accreditation standards, and freely accessible webinars and podcasts for social work faculty on current trends in technology and practice would help accelerate the pace of incorporation of technology into the overall curriculum (Singer, 2019).

In addition to a focus on technology for practice, the field needs to attract, train, and retain a generation of social workers who are passionate about data and able to work in teams to manage, curate, analyze, interpret, and apply big data for social good. Some social workers will choose to specialize, but it will also be important to prepare all social workers to appreciate their role in data generation and become adept at applying data in their practice (Naccarato,

2010; Shaw, Lee, & Wulczyn, 2012). These individuals need to have skills in working with large and complex data sets, and they need to become trained in data science (López Peláez, Pérez García, Aguilar-Tablada Massó, 2018). More schools of social work should consider developing joint programs with computer science departments to train some social workers in both fields. Columbia University has taken on this challenge, pairing their Data Science Institute and School of Social Work. This is more common in selected public policy and social science departments, suggesting that social work can also move in this direction. Such programs would attract a new type of student to the field and give those already committed to social work an opportunity to use technology and data science in their practice, analysis, and research. The availability of such opportunities, when widely promoted, will bring in a number of talented individuals who want to be part of the digital revolution but who are also interested in having an impact in their communities.

Investment in research around social work practice and technology is critical to harnessing this potential. The field of social work has the opportunity to develop, test, and refine interventions that use technology. A lack of empirical research on technology-based interventions has inhibited practitioners (Ceranoglu, 2010). Funding significant research in this area and testing its use would remove this barrier to full implementation. Research on the integration of technology into practice will shed light on which technologies are best incorporated in social work. A research agenda should be built that includes evaluating existing programs, developing technology-based interventions while collecting empirical data on the impact of the technology (Chan & Holosko, 2016), and researching technology-assisted and hybrid interventions (Eack, 2012). In addition, research that makes use of large administrative data sets (Putnam-Hornstein & King, 2014; Wulczyn, Chen, & Hislop, 2007) helps us realize the potential uses of technology to support social work outcomes.

Technology raises or brings into focus various ethical and human rights issues that must be addressed. Although principles of protecting confidentiality, privacy, and self-determination are not new to social work, technology raises the risk of such breaches that are immeasurably greater. The amount of information amassed on unsuspecting individuals is growing and could disadvantage them. Issues around social worker–client boundaries, client safety, and cross-jurisdictional practice arise with the inclusion of technology in social work practice (Barsky, 2017). Social workers must join with other professions to evaluate the potential harms and risks that will emerge as technologies are used increasingly.

As we consider potential progress, we must remain steadfast in our commitment to the value of social justice. Technological innovation alters continuously the landscape of human possibility, but it does not guarantee the momentum toward this value. Social work is both uniquely positioned and ethically obligated to ensure that the drive of technological evolution is a project open to all, that it does not replicate or amplify existing inequalities, and that negative effects of technology on individuals and groups are minimized as much as possible (Goldkind & Wolf, 2015). As we measure progress, this remains a most important consideration.

REFERENCES

Aguirre, R. T. P., McCoy, M. K., & Roan, M. (2013). Development guidelines from a study of suicide prevention mobile applications (apps). *Journal of Technology in Human Services, 31*, 269–293. doi:10.1080/15228835.2013.814750

Arrillaga-Andreessen, L. (2015). Disruption for good. *Stanford Social Innovation Review*, Spring, 34–39.

Atuel, H. R., & Kintzle, S. (2021). Comparing the training effectiveness of virtual reality and role play among future mental health providers. *Psychological Trauma: Theory, Research, Practice, and Policy*. Advance online publication. https://doi.org/10.1037/tra0000997

Barak, A., & Grohol, J. A. (2011). Current and future trends in Internet-supported mental health interventions. *Journal of Technology in Human Services, 29*, 155–196.

Barrett, D. E., & Katsiyannis, A. (2017). The Clemson Juvenile Delinquency Project: Major findings from a multi-agency study. *Journal of Child and Family Studies, 26*, 2050–2058. doi:10.1007/s10826-017-0714-8

Barsky, A. E. (2017). Social work practice and technology: Ethical issues and policy responses. *Journal of Technology in Human Services, 1*, 8–29.

Bell, J. F., Krupski, A., Joesch, J. M., West, I. I., Atkins, D. C., Court, B., & Roy-Byrne, P. (2015). A randomized controlled trial of intensive care management for disabled Medicaid beneficiaries with high health care costs. *Health Services Research, 50*, 663–689. doi:10.1111/1475-6773.12258

Benjamin, R. (2019). *Race after technology: Abolitionist tools for the new Jim Code* (1st ed.). Medford, MA: Polity.

Bertot, J. C., Gorham, U., Jaeger, P. T., Sarin, L. C., & Choi, H. (2014). Big data, open government and e-government: Issues, policies and recommendations. *Information Polity, 19*, 5–16.

Berzin, S. C., & Coulton, C. J. (2018). Harness technology for social good. In R. Fong, J. Lubben, & R. P. Barth (Eds.), *Grand Challenges for Social Work and Society* (1st ed., pp. 161–180). New York, NY: Oxford University Press.

Butler, D., Bloom, D., & Rudd, T. (2013). Using social impact bonds to spur innovation, knowledge-building, and accountability. *Community development investment review, 9*(1), 57–62. San Francisco, CA: Federal Reserve Bank of San Francisco.

Ceranoglu, T. A. (2010). Video games in psychotherapy. *Review of General Psychology, 14*, 141–146.

Chan, C., & Holosko, M. J. (2016). A review of information and communication technology enhanced social work interventions. *Research on Social Work Practice, 26*, 88–100. doi:10.1177/1049731515578884

Chouldechova, A., Benavides-Prado, D., Fialko, O., & Vaithianathan, R. (2018). A case study of algorithm-assisted decision making in child maltreatment hotline screening decisions. *Proceedings of the 1st Conference on Fairness, Accountability and Transparency,* in *Proceedings of Machine Learning Research, 81,* 134–148. Available from https://proceedings.mlr.press/v81/chouldechova18a.html

Christensen, J. K. B. (2018). The emergence and unfolding of telemonitoring practices in different healthcare organizations. *International Journal of Environmental Research and Public Health, 15,* 1–16. doi:10.3390/ijerph15010061

Clapp, J. D., Madden, D. R., Villasanti, H. G., Giraldo, L. F., Passino, K. M., Reed, M. B., & Puentes, I. F. (2018). A system dynamic model of drinking events: Multi-level ecological approach. *Systems Research and Behavioral Science, 35,* 265–281. doi:10.1002/sres.2478

Coalition for Evidence-Based Policy. (2012). *Rigorous program evaluations on a budget: How low-cost randomized controlled trials are possible in many areas of social policy.* Washington, DC: Author.

Colder Carras, M., Bergendahl, M., & Labrique, A. B. (2021). Community case study: Stack Up's Overwatch Program, an online suicide prevention and peer support program for video gamers. *Frontiers in Psychology, 12,* 1–11. doi:10.3389/fpsyg.2021.575224

Coulton, C. J., Schramm, M., & Hirsh, A. (2010). REO and beyond: The aftermath of the foreclosure crisis in Cuyahoga County, Ohio. In E. Rosengren & S. Pianalto (Eds.), *REO & vacant properties: Strategies for neighborhood stabilization* (pp. 47–54). Boston, MA: Federal Reserve Banks of Boston and Cleveland.

Craig, S. L., & Calleja Lorenzo, M. V. (2014). Can information and communication technologies support patient engagement? A review of opportunities and challenges in health social work. *Social Work in Health Care, 53,* 845–864. doi:10.1080/00981389.2014.936991

Craig, S. L., Iacono, G., Pascoe, R., & Austin, A. (2021). Adapting clinical skills to telehealth: Applications of affirmative cognitive–behavioral therapy with LGBTQ+ youth. *Clinical Social Work Journal,* 1–11. doi:10.1007/s10615-021-00796-x

Daley, D., Bachmann, M., Bachmann, B. A., Pedigo, C., Bui, M. T., & Coffman, J. (2016). Risk terrain modeling predicts child maltreatment. *Child Abuse & Neglect, 62,* 29–38.

Dennis, T. A., & O'Toole, L. J. (2014). Mental health on the go: Effects of a gamified attention-bias modification mobile application in trait-anxious adults. *Clinical Psychological Science, 2,* 576–590. doi:10.1177/2167702614522228

Dilgul, M., Hickling, L. M., Antonie, D., Priebe, S., & Bird, V. J. (2021). Virtual reality group therapy for the treatment of depression: A qualitative study on stakeholder perspectives. *Frontiers in Virtual Reality, 1,* 42. https://doi.org/10.3389/frvir.2020.609545

Eack, S. M. (2012). Cognitive remediation: A new generation of psychosocial interventions for people with schizophrenia. *Social Work, 57,* 235–246.

Espelage, D. L., & Hong, J. S. (2017). Cyberbullying prevention and intervention efforts: Current knowledge and future directions. *The Canadian Journal of Psychiatry, 62,* 374–380. doi:10.1177/0706743716684793

Eubanks, V. (2019). *Automating inequality: How high-tech tools profile, police, and punish the poor* (reprint ed.). New York, NY: Picador.

Fantuzzo, J., & Culhane, D. (2015). *Actionable intelligence: Using integrated data systems to achieve more effective and efficient government.* New York, NY: Palgrave/MacMillan.

Fleming, T. M., Bavin, L., Stasiak, K., Hermansson-Webb, E., Merry, S. N., Cheek, C., . . . Hetrick, S. (2017). Serious games and gamification for mental health: Current status and promising directions. *Frontiers in Psychiatry, 7,* article 215, 1–7. doi:10.3389/fpsyt.2016.00215

Freisthler, B., & Weiss, R. E. (2008). Using Bayesian space–time models to understand the substance use environment and risk for being referred to Child Protective Services. *Substance Use & Misuse Special Issue, 43,* 239–251.

Garcia-Ceja, E., Riegler, M., Nordgreen, T., Jakobsen, P., Oedegaard, K. J., & Tørresen, J. (2018). Mental health monitoring with multimodal sensing and machine learning: A survey. *Pervasive and Mobile Computing, 51,* 1–26. doi:10.1016/j.pmcj.2018.09.003

Goerge, R., Ozik, J., & Collier, N. (2012). *Bringing big data into public policy research: Text mining to acquire richer data on program participants, their behavior and services.* Paper presented at the Association of Public Policy and Management, Baltimore, MD. Retrieved from http://www.appam.org/assets/1/7/Goerge_20text_20mining_20final_2012_20pt.pdf

Goldhaber-Fiebert, J. D., Bailey, S. L., Hurlburt, M. S., Zhang, J., Snowden, L. R., Wulczyn, F., & Horwitz, S. M. (2012). Evaluating child welfare policies with decision-analytic simulation models. *Administration and Policy in Mental Health and Mental Health Services Research, 39,* 466–477.

Goldkind, L., & Wolf, L. (2015). A digital environment approach: Four technologies that will disrupt social work practice. *Social Work, 60,* 85–87. doi:10.1093/sw/swu045

Goldsmith, S., & Crawford, S. (2014). *The responsive city: Engaging communities through data-smart governance.* Hoboken, NJ: Wiley.

Greer, A. L., Shinn, M., Kwon, J., & Zuiderveen, S. (2016). Targeting services to individuals most likely to enter shelter: Evaluating the efficiency of homelessness prevention. *Social Service Review, 90,* 130–155.

Hammond, K. W., & Laundry, R. J. (2014, January). *Application of a hybrid text mining approach to the study of suicidal behavior in a large population.* Paper presented at System Sciences (HICSS) 2014 47th Hawaii International Conference, Waikoloa, HI.

Hindman, M. (2015). Building better models: Prediction, replication, and machine learning in the social sciences. *Annals of the American Academy of Political and Social Science, 659,* 48–62.

Hitchcock, L. I., & Battista, A. (2013). Social media for professional practice: Integrating Twitter with social work pedagogy. *Journal of Baccalaureate Social Work, 18,* 43–54.

Hitchcock, L. I., Sage, M., & Smyth, N. J. (2019). *Teaching social work with digital technology.* Alexandria, VA: CSWE Press.

Holmes, E. A., James, E. L., Coode-Bate, T., & Deeprose, C. (2009). Can playing the computer game "Tetris" reduce the build-up of flashbacks for trauma? A proposal from cognitive science. *PLoS One, 4,* e415.

Hossain, S., & Ahmed, S. I. (2021). Towards a new participatory approach for designing artificial intelligence and data-driven technologies. https://arxiv.org/ftp/arxiv/papers/2104/2104.04072.pdf

Huttar, C. M., & BrintzenhofeSzoc, K. (2020). Virtual reality and computer simulation in social work education: A systematic review. *Journal of Social Work Education, 56,* 131–141. doi:10.1080/10437797.2019.1648221

Izlar, J. (2019). Local–global linkages: Challenges in organizing functional communities for ecosocial justice. *Journal of Community Practice, 27,* 369–387. doi:10.1080/10705422.2019.1657536

Jacquemard, T., Doherty, C. P., & Fitzsimons, M. B. (2020). Examination and diagnosis of electronic patient records and their associated ethics: A scoping literature review. *BMC Medical Ethics, 21,* 1–13. doi:10.1186/s12910-020-00514-1

Jones, A., Walters, J., & Brown, A. (2020). Participant recruitment in social work: A social media approach. *Social Work Research, 44*, 247–255. doi:10.1093/swr/svaa017

Keddell, E. (2019). Algorithmic justice in child protection: Statistical fairness, social justice and the implications for practice. *Social Sciences, 8*, 1–22. doi:10.3390/socsci8100281

Kessler, R. C., Bauer, M. S., Bishop, T. M., Demler, O. V., Dobscha, S. K., Gildea, S. M., . . . Bossarte, R. M. (2020). Using administrative data to predict suicide after psychiatric hospitalization in the Veterans Health Administration System. *Frontiers in Psychiatry, 11*, 1–19. doi:10.3389/fpsyt.2020.00390

Kessler, R. C., Bernecker, S. L., Bossarte, R. M., Luedtke, A. R., McCarthy, J. F., Nock, M. K., . . . Zaslavsky, A. M. (2019). The role of big data analytics in predicting suicide. In I. C. Passos, B. Mwangi, & F. Kapczinski (Eds.), *Personalized psychiatry: Big data analytics in mental health* (pp. 77–98). Switzerland: Springer International Publishing. doi:10.1007/978-3-030-03553-2_5

Kingsley, G. T., Coulton, C. J., & Pettit, K. L. (2014). *Strengthening communities with neighborhood data*. Washington, DC: Urban Institute.

Kleinberg, J., Lakkaraju, H., Leskovec, J., Ludwig, J., & Mullainathan, S. (2017). Human decisions and machine predictions. No. w23180). National Bureau of Economic Research. Retrieved from http://www.nber.org/papers/w23180

Kumar, S., Nilsen, W. J., Abernethy, A., Atienza, A., Patrick, K., Pavel, M., . . . Swendeman, D. (2013). Mobile health technology evaluation: The mHealth evidence workshop. *American Journal of Preventive Medicine, 45*, 228–236. doi:10.1016/j.amepre.2013.03.017

Lanata, A., Valenza, G., Nardelli, M., Gentili, C., & Scilingo, E. P. (2015). Complexity index from a personalized wearable monitoring system for assessing remission in mental health. *IEEE Journal of Biomedical and Health Informatics, 19*, 132–139. doi:10.1109/JBHI.2014.2360711

Langlois, M. (2013). *Reset: Video games & psychotherapy* (2nd ed.). Cambridge, MA: Online Therapy Institute.

Lazer, D. M., Kennedy, R., King, G., & Vespignani, A. (2014). The parable of Google flu: Traps in big data analysis. *Science, 343*, 1203–1205.

Lee, S. J., & Walsh, T. B. (2015). Using technology in social work practice: The mDad (Mobile Device Assisted Dad) case study. *Advances in Social Work, 16*, 107–124.

López Peláez, A., Pérez García, R., & Aguilar-Tablada Massó, M. V. (2018). e-Social work: Building a new field of specialization in social work? *European Journal of Social Work, 21*, 804–823.

Lorenzo-Luaces, L., Peipert, A., De Jesús Romero, R., Rutter, L. A., & Rodriguez-Quintana, N. (2021). Personalized medicine and cognitive behavioral therapies for depression: Small effects, big problems, and bigger data. *International Journal of Cognitive Therapy, 14*, 59–85. doi:10.1007/s41811-020-00094-3

Mandayam, G., & Joosten, D. (2016). Understanding client communities spatially for developing effective interventions: Application of geographic information systems (GIS) technology for program planning in health and human services agencies. *Journal of Technology in Human Services, 34*, 171–182.

Manzi, J. (2012). *Uncontrolled: The surprising payoff of trial and error for business, politics, and society*. New York, NY: Basic Books.

Marcolino, M. S., Oliveira, J. A. Q., D'Agostino, M., Ribeiro, A. L., Alkmim, M. B. M., & Novillo-Ortiz, D. (2018). The impact of mHealth interventions: Systematic review of systematic reviews. *JMIR MHealth and UHealth, 6*, e23. doi:10.2196/mhealth.8873

Mishna, F., Bogo, M., & Sawyer, J.- L. (2015). Cyber counseling: Illuminating benefits and challenges. *Clinical Social Work Journal, 43*, 169–178.

Mishna, F., Fantus, S., & McInroy, L. B. (2017). Informal use of information and communication technology: Adjunct to traditional face-to-face social work practice. *Clinical Social Work Journal, 45*, 49–55.

Mishna, F., Milne, E., Bogo, M., & Pereira, L. F. (2020). Responding to COVID-19: New trends in social workers' use of information and communication technology. *Clinical Social Work Journal*, 1–11. doi:10.1007/s10615-020-00780-x

Moore, K. A., Sacks, V. H., Manlove, J., & Sawhill, I. (2014). *"What if" you earned a diploma and delayed parenthood?* Research brief publication no. 2014-27. Bethesda, MD: Child Trends.

Morina, N., Ijntema, H., Meyerbroker, K., & Emmelkamp, P. M. G. (2015). Can virtual reality exposure therapy gains be generalized to real-life? A meta-analysis of studies applying behavioral assessments. *Behaviour Research and Therapy, 74*, 18–24. doi:10.1016/j.brat.2015.08.010

Naccarato, T. (2010). Child welfare informatics: A proposed subspecialty for social work. *Children and Youth Services Review, 32*, 1729–1734.

Nelson, L. (2014). Cutting through the fog. In G. T. Kingsley, C. J. Coulton, & K. L. Pettit (Eds.), *Strengthening communities with neighborhood data* (pp. 205–218). Washington, DC: Urban Institute.

North, C. S., Wohlford, S. E., Dean, D. J., Black, M., Balfour, M. E., Petrovich, J. C., . . . Pollio, D. E. (2017). A pilot study using mixed GPS/narrative interview methods to understand geospatial behavior in homeless populations. *Community Mental Health Journal, 53*, 661–671. doi:10.1007/s10597-016-0057-8

Patton, D. U., Eschmann, R. D., Elsaesser, C., & Bocanegra, E. (2016). Sticks, stones and Facebook accounts: What violence outreach workers know about social media and urban-based gang violence in Chicago. *Computers in Human Behavior, 65*, 591–600.

Patton, D. U., Leonard, P., Elaesser, C., Eschmann, R. D., Patel, S., & Crosby, S. (2019). What's a threat on social media? How Black and Latino Chicago young men define and navigate threats online. *Youth & Society, 51*, 756–772.

Patton, D. U., MacBeth, J., Schoenebeck, S., Shear, K., & McKeown, K. (2018). Accommodating grief on Twitter: An analysis of expressions of grief among gang involved youth on Twitter using qualitative analysis and natural language processing. *Biomedical Informatics Insights, 10*, 1–9. doi:10.1177/1178222618763155

Peskin, M., Mello, B., Cukor, J., Olden, M., & Difede, J. (2019). Virtual reality applications to treat posttraumatic stress disorder. In A. "Skip" Rizzo & S. Bouchard (Eds.), *Virtual reality for psychological and neurocognitive interventions* (pp. 85–102). Springer. doi:10.1007/978-1-4939-9482-3_4

Pew Research Center: Internet, Science & Tech. (2021, April 7). Demographics of mobile device ownership and adoption in the United States. Mobile fact sheet. Retrieved from https://www.pewresearch.org/internet/fact-sheet/mobile/

Putnam-Hornstein, E., & King, B. (2014). Cumulative teen birth rates among girls in foster care at age 17: An analysis of linked birth and child protection records from California. *Child Abuse & Neglect, 38*, 698–705.

Rao, V. (2013). Challenges of implementing gamification for behavior change: Lessons learned from the design of Blues Buddies. In *Proceedings of CHI 2013 workshop "Designing Gamification"* (pp. 61–64). Alpha, NJ: Sheridan Communications.

Rice, E., & Barman-Adhikari, A. (2014). Internet and social media use as a resource among homeless youth. *Journal of Computer-Mediated Communication, 19*, 232–247. doi:10.1111/jcc4.12038

Richter, F. G.-C., Coulton, C., Urban, A., & Steh, S. (2021). An integrated data system lens into evictions and their effects. *Housing Policy Debate*, *31*(3-5), 762–778. doi:10.1080/10511482.2021.1879201

Schoech, D., Boyas, J. F., Black, B. M., & Elias-Lambert, N. (2013). Gamification for behavior change: Lessons from developing a social, multiuser, Web-tablet based prevention game for youths. *Journal of Technology in Human Services*, *31*, 197–217.

Shaw, T. V., Lee, B. R., & Wulczyn, F. (2012). "I thought I hated data": Preparing MSW students for data-driven practice. *Journal of Teaching in Social Work*, *32*, 78–89.

Sheikh, M., Qassem, M., & Kyriacou, P. A. (2021). Wearable, environmental, and smartphone-based passive sensing for mental health monitoring. *Frontiers in Digital Health*, *3*, 1–20. doi:10.3389/fdgth.2021.662811

Singer, J. B. (2019). Podcasting as social scholarship: A tool to increase the public impact of scholarship and research. *Journal of the Society for Social Work and Research*, *10*, 571–590. doi:10.1086/706600

Song, J., Jiang, R., Chen, N., Qu, W., Liu, D., Zhang, M., . . . Tan, S. (2021). Self-help cognitive behavioral therapy application for COVID-19-related mental health problems: A longitudinal trial. *Asian Journal of Psychiatry*, *60*, 1–5. doi:10.1016/j.ajp.2021.102656

Stephens-Davidowitz, S. (2013). *Unreported victims of an economic downtown*. Retrieved from http://static1.squarespace.com/static/51d894bee4b01caf-88ccb4f3/t/51e22f38e4b0502fe211fab7/1373777720363/childabusepaper13.pdf

Stoesz, D. (2014). Evidence-based policy reorganizing social services through accountable care organizations and social impact bonds. *Research on Social Work Practice*, *24*, 181–185.

Stoll, J., Müller, J. A., & Trachsel, M. (2020). Ethical issues in online psychotherapy: A narrative review. *Frontiers in Psychiatry*, *10*, 1–16. doi:10.3389/fpsyt.2019.00993

Strang, K. D., & Sun, Z. (2020). Hidden big data analytics issues in the healthcare industry. *Health Informatics Journal*, *26*, 981–998. doi:10.1177/1460458219854603

Tai, K.-T. (2021). Open government research over a decade: A systematic review. *Government Information Quarterly*, *38*, 1–15. doi:10.1016/j.giq.2021.101566

Tambe, M., & Rice, E. (2018). *Artificial intelligence and social work*. New York, NY: Cambridge University Press.

Tambe, P., Cappelli, P., & Yakubovich, V. (2019). Artificial intelligence in human resources management: Challenges and a path forward. *California Management Review*, *61*, 15–42. doi:10.1177/0008125619867910

Teixeira, S., & Zuberi, A. (2016). Mapping the racial inequality in place: Using youth perceptions to identify unequal exposure to neighborhood environmental hazards. *International Journal of Environmental Research and Public Health*, *13*, 1–15. doi:10.3390/ijerph13090844

Thurston, H., Freisthler, B., Bell, J., Tancredi, D., Romano, P., Miyamoto, S., & Joseph, J. G. (2017). The temporal–spatial distribution of seriously maltreated children. *Spatial and Spatio-temporal Epidemiology*, *20*, 1–8.

Til, K. V., McInnis, M. G., & Cochran, A. (2020). A comparative study of engagement in mobile and wearable health monitoring for bipolar disorder. *Bipolar Disorders*, *22*, 182–190. doi:10.1111/bdi.12849

Tinati, R., Halford, S., Carr, L., & Pope, C. (2014). Big data: Methodological challenges and approaches for sociological analysis. *Sociology*, *48*, 663–681.

Trahan, M. H., Smith, K. S., & Talbot, T. B. (2019). Past, present, and future: Editorial on virtual reality applications to human services. *Journal of Technology in Human Services, 37*, 1–12. doi:10.1080/15228835.2019.1587334

Tudor, J., Gomez, E., & Denby, R. W. (2017). Public child welfare and a multi-agency collaborative: Lessons learned from the DREAMR Project. *The Lincy Institute Issue Brief Social Services Series* (4), 1–15. https://digitalscholarship.unlv.edu/lincy_publications/37

Turner Lee, N. (2018). Detecting racial bias in algorithms and machine learning. *Journal of Information, Communication and Ethics in Society, 16*, 252–260. doi:10.1108/JICES-06-2018-0056

Välimäki, M., Yang, M., Lam, Y. T. J., Lantta, T., Palva, M., Palva, S., . . . Bressington, D. (2021). The impact of video gaming on cognitive functioning of people with schizophrenia (GAME-S): Study protocol of a randomised controlled trial. *BMC Psychiatry, 21*, 1–12. doi:10.1186/s12888-020-03031-y

Williams, D. P. (2020). Fitting the description: Historical and sociotechnical elements of facial recognition and anti-Black surveillance. *Journal of Responsible Innovation, 7*, 74–83. doi:10.1080/23299460.2020.1831365

Wolff, T., Minkler, M., Wolfe, S., Berkowitz, B., Bowen, L., Butterfoss, F., . . . Lee, K. (2016). Collaborating for equity and justice: Moving beyond collective impact. *Nonprofit Quarterly*, Winter (1).

Wulczyn, F., Chen, L., & Hislop, K. B. (2007). *Foster care dynamics, 2000–2005: A report from the Multistate Foster Care Data Archive*. Chicago, IL: Chapin Hall Center for Children at the University of Chicago.

Yacchirema, D., de Puga, J. S., Palau, C., & Esteve, M. (2019). Fall detection system for elderly people using IoT and ensemble machine learning algorithm. *Personal and Ubiquitous Computing, 23*, 801–817. doi:10.1007/s00779-018-01196-8

Young, J. A., McLeod, D. A., & Brady, S. R. (2018). The ethics challenge: 21st Century social work education, social media, and digital literacies. *Journal of Social Work Values & Ethics, 15*, 1–13.

Zgoda, K., & Shane, K. (2018). Digital literacy in social work education: A case study incorporating technology and social media within the social work curriculum. *Journal of Nonprofit Education and Leadership, 8*, 32–40. doi:10.18666/JNEL-2018-V8-I1-8350

CHAPTER 10

Promoting Smart Decarceration

PAJARITA CHARLES, MATTHEW W. EPPERSON,
PHILLIPE COPELAND, AND CARRIE PETTUS-DAVIS

It has been more than 5 years since the launch of the Grand Challenge to Promote Smart Decarceration—a period of advancement in knowledge and strategies to reform the criminal legal system.[1] Smart decarceration emerged during a time of growing recognition of the unjust and ineffective nature of incarceration in the United States. Today, the call to end mass incarceration continues at a time marked by the confluence of racial unrest and a global pandemic. It is within this context that we have seen police violence and COVID-19 affect particular groups disproportionately in society, similar to the impact of the criminal legal system on those in marginalized groups.

On any given day, nearly 1.4 million individuals reside in state or federal prisons, and more than 734,500 people are confined in local jails (Carson, 2020; Zeng & Minton, 2021). Although incarceration is the cause of widespread negative consequences for most people, what stands out is the toll on those incarcerated not solely for engaging in criminalized behaviors, but because of inequitable policies.

The United States has hit a tipping point: it no longer has the ability to continue mass incarceration. In fact, a growing number of political leaders are pushing for reforms (Obama, 2017; Rosenberg, 2017; Zorn, 2015). Moreover, incarceration rates have been declining modestly for a decade (Ghandnoosh,

---

1. We recognize the variety of terms used to reference the criminal legal system (e.g., criminal justice system, carceral state). We are choosing to use the term *criminal legal* in lieu of *criminal justice* as an acknowledgment that justice is not often actualized in the system.

2020). This shift is encouraging, but no other developed country has grappled with decarceration efforts of such magnitude. As a result, the United States is faced with a grand social challenge that has few guideposts to reference, but requires decarceration through comprehensive, evidence-driven, and unprecedented strategies. This includes efforts that must balance justice and rehabilitation approaches with significant increases in investments that move scientifically based treatments and supports into communities, and result in reduced reliance on incarceration.

Several complex histories led to mass incarceration; therefore, the smart decarceration approach must not use quick and simplistic methods to cut incarceration rates (Epperson & Pettus-Davis, 2015b). There must also be an intentional effort to assess whether and how emerging decarceration policies improve or exacerbate the disparities of the criminal legal system as it currently exists [see, for example, Gottlieb, Charles, McLeod, Kjellstrand, and Bonsu, (2020)]. Reductions in racial, economic, and behavioral health disparities should be the cornerstone of federal, state, and local smart decarceration policies. As such, we define *smart decarceration* as effective, sustainable, and socially just decarceration with three simultaneous outcomes: (a) the incarcerated population in US jails and prisons is decreased substantially, (b) existing racial and economic disparities in the criminal legal system are redressed, and (c) community safety and public well-being are maximized. Ultimately, smart decarceration aims to build social capacity through robust and community-driven responses to local issues that do not resort to the default incarceration approach. Local jails, and state and federal prisons, must no longer be used to address society's greatest problems, which include limited access to behavioral and mental health services, inadequate education and employment opportunities, and lack of affordable housing and healthcare.

Although the broad goals of the original smart decarceration framework remain the same, we have expanded the perspective in several ways in this updated chapter. First, we discuss more explicitly groups such as lesbian, gay, bisexual, transgender, or queer (LGBTQ+) populations and incarcerated women who have historically been underrepresented in incarceration research and criminal legal innovations. Second, we bring renewed emphasis to the importance of "front-end" criminal legal system changes to mitigate and prevent more harmful involvement further down the incarceration pipeline (e.g., police practices, diversion, sentencing). Third, we have made more explicit the histories of racism and oppression embedded in mass incarceration, and call for decarceration strategies that are antiracist and inclusive of a wider array of approaches (e.g., restorative justice, abolitionist, family systems).

What follows is a brief overview of mass incarceration and description of the smart decarceration framework, including any changes that reflect our renewed perspective about criminal legal reform efforts. We highlight activities and accomplishments during the past 5 years and conclude with a discussion about future directions for decarceration efforts and strategies to reduce the footprint of the criminal legal system.

MASS INCARCERATION AND THE CRIMINAL LEGAL SYSTEM

Overview

Mass incarceration in the United States began in the 1970s and extended into the early 21st century, resulting in a nearly sevenfold increase in incarceration rates. The United States has the largest incarcerated population in the world and, despite a recent decline leading to its lowest level of incarceration in 20 years, still incarcerates a larger portion of its population than any other country in the world (Gramlich, 2018; Human Rights Watch, 2021). Approximately 2.1 million people are incarcerated (Maruschak & Minton, 2020) and an estimated 10.3 million people are jailed annually (Zeng & Minton, 2021). The reach of the criminal legal system exists beyond the confines of prison and jail, with more than 4 million people on probation or parole in communities around the United States (Maruschak & Minton, 2020).

Although we have seen a rise in bipartisan support for criminal legal reform to address mass incarceration, it has emerged in the absence of significant change to the underlying structure of the criminal legal system that today still produces massive inequities and negative outcomes—particularly for the 56% of the incarcerated population that is Black or Hispanic (Carson, 2020). In 2018, for instance, the First Step Act was signed into law, one of the most significant pieces of federal-level criminal legal reform seen in years (James, 2019). Its main purpose was to limit sentences for nonviolent offenses, reduce retroactively overly long sentences, and expand rehabilitation programs inside federal prisons. Although meaningful, it is limited in reach and fraught with implementation problems (Skeem & Monahan, 2020; Subramanian et al., 2020). Indeed, much work remains to be done not only in the federal prison system, but in state prisons, local county jails, and communities seeking transformation with a focus on advancing police reform, reducing life-long collateral consequences, and addressing racial and ethnic disparities that permeate throughout the criminal legal system.

Disparities in the Criminal Legal System

Race and Ethnicity

Mass incarceration and the criminal legal system is problematic both because of the sheer volume of individuals incarcerated and because of the overall number of people involved in the system. It also bears the consequence of having a disproportionate effect on individuals in poverty and people of color. Disparities by race, age, and gender, for instance, have led to exorbitant rates of incarceration among young Black men (Western & Pettit, 2010). Blacks are more than five times as likely to be incarcerated than a white person, whereas Hispanics are 2.5 times as likely (Carson, 2020). However, people of color and individuals who identify as white engage in illegal behavior at relatively comparable rates (Brame, Bushway, Paternoster, & Turner, 2014). Despite similar behaviors, people of color—particularly Blacks—are much more likely to come into contact with law enforcement (Nellis, 2016; Rojek, Rosenfeld, & Decker, 2012) and are significantly more likely to be charged with a crime (Wooldredge, Frank, Goulette, & Travis, 2015). Once charged, they are sentenced more harshly (Johnson, 2003); once sentenced, they are at greater risk of a subsequent incarceration (Berg & Huebner, 2011). Meaningful reform to the criminal legal system cannot be accomplished without acknowledgment of the fundamental role of racism in shaping disparities, and focused attention on its elimination (Sered, 2017).

Poverty and racial disparities permeate the entire criminal legal system, impacting people at every turn, including police interactions, arrests, pretrial detention, sentencing, and reentry (The Sentencing Project, 2018). One striking example is the cash bail and pretrial detention system that criminalizes poverty by mandating people presumed innocent to stay in jail unless they can afford to pay while they await trial. Research shows that incarceration stays like this are likely to increase someone's chances of pleading guilty, being convicted, receiving a harsher sentence, and committing future crimes (Digard & Swavola, 2019; Heaton, Mayson, & Stevenson, 2017). Among the worst examples of racial disparities is the manifestation of racial profiling and lethal force by police on communities of color. In 2020, the killings of George Floyd, Breonna Taylor, Daniel Prude, and Rayshard Brooks sparked widespread protests in response to the lack of police accountability. The elimination of disparities must lead criminal legal reform efforts in order for the effects of transformation to be truly realized by communities of color.

Substance Use and Mental Health

Mass incarceration affects people with substance use and mental health disorders disproportionately. Nearly 1.5 million people incarcerated in prisons and jails meet the criteria for a substance use disorder, and more than 375,000 people with serious mental illnesses are incarcerated on any given day (Clear, 2007; National Center on Addiction and Substance Abuse at Columbia University, 2010; Roberts, 2004; Sampson & Loeffler, 2010). Defunded community systems of care and the criminalization of public health issues have led to jails and prisons becoming de facto treatment locations for those with behavioral health impairments. Rates of mental illness are three to six times greater among the incarcerated population compared to the general population (Fazel & Danesh, 2002; Steadman, Osher, Robbins, Case, & Samuels, 2009). More than two thirds of incarcerated persons have histories of substance use disorders, many with co-occurring mental health issues, and less than 10% receive evidence-based treatments (National Center on Addiction and Substance Abuse, 2010; Taxman, Perdoni, & Harrison, 2007).

MAINSTREAMING GENDER

Understanding and Disrupting Gendered Social Control

GINA L. FEDOCK

Gender inequity and gendered social control contribute to and occur within mass incarceration. To Promote Smart Decarceration, the field of social work must not only recognize gender differences in engagement in criminalized behaviors, arrest, and incarceration, but also must examine and disrupt the power dynamics that contribute to forms of harmful gendered social control. The criminal legal system makes decisions and responds to individuals based on their perceived gender, which is evident in gender differences in what is considered criminalized behaviors, differences in experiences while incarcerated, and differences while under forms of community-based correctional supervision.

The juvenile and criminal legal systems respond differently to girls and women in comparison to boys and men. For example, women and girls face harsher arrest and sentencing for less-severe types of behaviors (e.g., status and drug-related offenses) than men and boys. Furthermore, teachers and school-based professionals label and react to Black girls' behaviors more punitively than the same behavior by white girls, resulting in a greater risk of involving Black girls in the juvenile and criminal legal systems, and fostering a distinct school-to-prison pipeline. Gendered and racialized definitions of criminalization are bounded within and are distinct mechanisms of gendered and racialized social control leading to harsher sentencing, more imprisonment, and the social problem of mass incarceration. Mainstreaming an intersectional gender approach is crucial for illuminating and addressing these interconnected forms of social control.

Pathways to criminal legal system involvement for girls and women are commonly shaped by the multiple impacts of interpersonal violence, institutional and organizational neglect toward women because of their social position, extensive experiences of sexual exploitation and trauma, pervasive poverty, and the dynamics of addiction. Forms of harm include state-sanctioned violence (such as sexual violence perpetrated by police and

continued

other state actors disproportionately against women of color) and those connected to identity (such as transgender-based exclusion, violence, and misogynoir). Often, survival strategies in the face of adversities are criminalized, as women commonly experience restricted forms of social capital and social power related to gender-based and interlocking forms of oppression. Adversities framed and defined as individual-level risk factors are devoid of context, depoliticized, and relegated solely to individual responsibility. Criminal legal-based models that frame individuals as "risky" embody an ethic of risk that perpetuates forms of racism, sexism, and additional systems of oppression. The field of social work has sustained and legitimized these models to varying degrees, and needs to name the forms of power operating as well as craft strategies to disrupt and prevent harm. Smart decarceration requires social work moving from this risk-based individual focus to tackling the ways that criminal, legal, and surveillance systems create risk for people, specifically and in exacerbated forms for those already marginalized. In addition, social workers can work to reverse the focus on punishment and surveillance, and instead invest resources in building more economic, social, and political capital for populations and communities.

Gender is one of the first triage points in the criminal legal system; jails and prisons are often designated for women or for men, operating on a binary understanding of gender. In the United States, prison design and programming reflect differences in gender socialization and forms of gendered social control. For example, prisons for women have historically offered programming and employment to further the skills of domestic labor, such as sewing, cleaning, and cooking, whereas prisons for men have focused on manual labor applicable to the public employment sphere. Goals for women's rehabilitation are based on racialized and gendered ideas of deviance, womanhood, and legitimate, legal behaviors. Prisons have focused on restoring certain women to standards of femininity and enforced gender roles of homemakers and mothers. White, middle-class women have been viewed as capable of a moral rehabilitation to a particular form of womanhood within prisons; in contrast, prisons have served as sites of racialized state violence, dehumanization, forced labor, and degradation for Black women. The field of social work plays a role in creating, implementing, and testing forms of programming within prisons related to a range of concerns, such as substance use, trauma, employment training, and parenting, and needs to be more active in critiquing forms of harm occurring within the discourse of rehabilitation. For example, principles of gender responsivity are commonly used within criminal justice to add programs, but these principles can be used to advocate and push for decarceration as a safety need for women and for uplifting women's socioeconomic status as a priority action. In addition, social work can stress decarceration with an investment in community-based programming, training, and treatment that does not replicate oppressive conditions and expectations, particularly for women.

continued

As another form of gendered control, women have higher rates of receiving misconduct tickets while incarcerated, but their tickets are often for nonviolent acts, such as actions considered by correctional staff as verbally or attitudinally disrespectful and emotional. Higher rates of institutional misconducts lead to consequences in prisons, such as loss of jobs, restricted visiting "privileges," placement in segregated housing/solitary confinement, and extended stays in prison. Forms of gendered social control contribute to the persistence of human rights violations within correctional settings, as exemplified by the disproportionately high rates of sexual victimization perpetrated by correctional staff against incarcerated women and the forms of gendered invalidation that occur related to this victimization, contributing to a lack of prevention and intervention by the criminal legal system and the field of social work.

While under forms of community-based correctional system supervision (such as probation or parole), women face myriad stressors and concerns, such as seeking safe housing, obtaining employment, preventing homelessness, reuniting with children and family members, and connecting with needed forms of treatment—all while also meeting the goals of supervision. They commonly face a range of permanent punishments (e.g., sanctions, stigma) that create barriers to stability. Too many women experience intensified poverty, worsening health, further abuse within relationships and from community correctional officers, and other major issues. The field of social work needs to play a key role in centering women's well-being and stability beyond a criminal legal perspective of only preventing recidivism. In addition, by prioritizing the well-being of previously incarcerated women, social work can interrupt policies and practices that create restrictions and, instead, bolster resource provision (e.g., safe, quality housing; economic support) and women's thriving.

At the center of mainstreaming gender in the Grand Challenge to Promote Smart Decarceration is the need to bring attention to improving the social, economic, and political status of women and girls involved in the criminal legal system and to consider the ways that forms of gendered social control exist and are sustained, from rates of arrest to rates of misconduct tickets, and in the conceptualization of key terminology, including risk, rehabilitation, deviance, and criminalization. In addition, we have to steer away from using gender stereotypes that promote gendered social control and instead provide explicit context to the historical and current sociopolitical dynamics that contribute to mass incarceration. We have to perceive gender differences in rates of incarceration, sentencing, incarceration experiences, and reentry needs through a lens of multiple forms of gendered social control. Most importantly, our work to contribute to disrupting the harm that occurs as a result of mass incarceration goes beyond a single program or policy change. Social workers must focus on improving the lives of women and girls in ways that resist punitive dynamics substantively; provide real, direct resources; and transform power dynamics.

LGBTQ+ Populations

Those who identify as LGBTQ+ represent another group impacted disproportionately by the criminal legal system. Research about the LGBTQ+ community in the criminal legal system is underdeveloped, but what is known suggests heightened risk of contact and involvement. The 2011–2012 National Inmate Survey found that 7.6% of jail and prison inmates identified as lesbian, gay, or bisexual (Beck, Berzofsky, Caspar, & Krebs, 2016)—a notably larger proportion of LGBTQ+ persons than is represented in the general population (4.5% in 2017) (Newport, 2018). Moreover, LGBTQ+ persons, and especially LGBTQ+ people of color, face higher rates of not only incarceration, but discrimination, stigmatization, abuse, and unequal treatment at all points in the criminal legal system (Movement Advancement Project and Center for American Progress, 2016).

Gender

All told, the growth in women's incarceration has been more than double that of men for the past 40 years (Sawyer, 2018). Although women make up 7% of the population in state and federal prisons (Carson, 2020), their rate of incarceration increased by more than 700% between 1980 and 2019 (The Sentencing Project, 2020). The rise of women in local jails is particularly striking, with more women being held in local jails than in state prisons (Kajstura, 2019). Women of color are incarcerated disproportionately, with rates of imprisonment for Black women 1.7 and 1.3 times that of white and Hispanic women, respectively (Carson, 2020). The increase in incarceration among women is considered especially problematic because the majority (more than 60%) are mothers of minor children (Glaze & Maruschak, 2010) and they are likely to have been the child's primary caregiver prior to incarceration (Mumola, 2000).

Incarcerated women have distinct psychological and health-, trauma-, and family-related needs that often go unmet (Dallaire & Shlafer, 2017), including having children who face an array of negative consequences. The pathways of women that lead to incarceration also tend to differ from those of men and include higher rates of sexual, physical, and emotional abuse (Messina, Grella, Burdon, & Prendergast, 2007), and increased risk of criminal legal involvement when faced with economic abuse by an intimate partner (Gottlieb & Mahabir, 2019). Incarcerated women also suffer from pervasive problems related to safety and lack of access to healthcare treatment and information, including shackling during birth, despite regulations that theoretically limit their use during pregnancy or the postpartum period (Goshin, Sissoko, Neumann, Sufrin, & Byrnes, 2019; Thomas & Lanterman, 2019).

SMART DECARCERATION FRAMEWORK

Social Capacity

A central concept of smart decarceration is the building of *social capacity*—that is, a community's ability to work together to build and sustain its own set of solutions rather than relying on a set of external actors (e.g., the criminal legal system). We define community as individuals, families, formal and informal institutions, and public- and private-sector actors grouped locally and interacting within larger structures. As applied to the Grand Challenge to Promote Smart Decarceration, building social capacity calls for investment in behavioral and mental health services, public education, employment opportunities, housing infrastructure, and other community supports that prioritize diverse, equitable, and inclusive approaches. Investments in high-incarceration communities must be prioritized, as there has been an excessive investment in incarcerating members of these communities, but not in building community supports. Building social capacity also calls for alternatives to and early exit points from the criminal legal system to reduce undue harm from legal system contact and to promote well-being with minimal disruption to community connections and ongoing participation in civic activities.

Solutions that reduce police contact and address harmful and unjust policing practices are examples of early-exit or "front-end" approaches that aim to reduce short- and longer-term criminal legal system involvement. Shifts in police practices, for instance, have the potential to reduce racist practices and decrease pretrial incarcerations. This in turn reduces government expenses, freeing up resources to be diverted and reinvested in communities, and leading to social capacity-building (Wilson & Wilson, 2020). Front-end frameworks that include deflection and diversion are also drawing increased attention, with several models emerging as promising local and national examples (Kopak & Frost, 2017; Neusteter, O'Toole, & Khogali, 2018). Communities are working to institute alternatives that reduce criminal legal involvement and divert people to services when substance abuse, mental health issues, trauma, and other problems exist. For example, Seattle's Law Enforcement Assisted Diversion, or LEAD, prearrest diversion program redirects people to case management and support services instead of jail and prosecution, and has been shown to reduce the likelihood of arrests and felony charges after program participation (Collins, Lonczak, & Clifasefi, 2017). The Sequential Intercept Model is another example that was developed to address the criminalization of individuals with behavioral and mental health disorders that refers people to services (e.g., crisis care) at different points to prevent further criminal legal system involvement (Abreu, Parker, Noether, Steadman, & Case, 2017; Munetz & Griffin, 2006).

The growing number of alternative sentencing models differ in their characteristics and purpose, and more evidence is needed to determine their effectiveness. However, the use of alternatives to arrest and incarceration has the potential to shift resources away from corrections within local communities to enact community-driven solutions that meet individuals' needs, limit interactions with law enforcement, and decrease police misconduct. In turn, such efforts have the potential to contribute to social capacity-building in the short-run, and a reduction in mass incarceration in the long-run.

Smart Decarceration Guiding Concepts

Smart decarceration requires recognizing that altering the overreliance on incarceration and other forms of social control (e.g., community corrections) is a multifaceted endeavor. Although there is increasing attention to the problem of mass incarceration and steps are being made toward the building of social capacity to reduce the use of the criminal legal system, guiding concepts are needed to help inform practice, research, and policy actions as the field moves forward in this area. Consequently, we offer three guiding concepts: (a) changing the narrative on incarceration and the incarcerated, (b) making criminal legal system-wide innovations, and (c) implementing transdisciplinary policy and practice interventions using evidence-driven strategies (Epperson & Pettus-Davis, 2015b).

Changing the Narrative on Incarceration

Incarceration is the default response to criminalized behaviors in the United States. However, there is little evidence that incarceration achieves greater safety, and the majority of individuals incarcerated in US jails and prisons do not pose an imminent risk to public safety (Minton & Zeng, 2015; Snyder, 2012; Subramanian, Delaney, Roberts, Fishman, & McGarry, 2015). In addition, incarceration does not reduce future offending for most, and in many cases it increases the risk for recidivism (Durose, Cooper, & Snyder, 2014; Lowenkamp, VanNostrand, & Holsinger, 2013). As such, the first strategy for changing the narrative on incarceration involves altering the default response that uses incarceration to address all forms of offending. Instead, we must offer alternatives and address the underlying conditions that led to the behavior, because incarceration is not effective at decreasing criminal legal involvement for most people.

The second strategy on changing the narrative is to promote leadership and meaningful involvement among directly affected individuals, including formerly incarcerated people and their family members. Often, however, these individuals are disenfranchised systematically from efforts to reform the criminal legal system. A key component of building social capacity is to prioritize the social and financial investment in individuals and communities most affected by incarceration. People with histories of incarceration and their loved ones have expert knowledge about the factors that contribute to criminal legal involvement and the conditions needed to prevent future recidivism. These individuals are well-positioned to bring a much-needed perspective to the table (Epperson & Pettus-Davis, 2015a).

Changing narratives on incarceration and the incarcerated can be accomplished through multiple means, including public awareness campaigns in which the realities of incarceration and its ineffectiveness are made clear. These sober appraisals of incarceration must be incorporated into an array of criminal legal policies, particularly sentencing policies. Decarceration-driven policymaking should include legislative provisions with the input of individuals, families, and communities most affected by incarceration. Policies will be shaped by asking the following difficult questions: What would the use of incarceration look like if it were used strictly as a last-resort option? What if incarceration was *not* an option for a range of offenses? Public forums at the local, state, and national levels are needed to develop critical dialogues and construct new narratives. In many settings, these conversations are taking place and should include formerly incarcerated leaders as key planners and facilitators. Formerly incarcerated individuals could also be incorporated as peer mentors in interventions targeting people with criminal records (Pettus-Davis, Epperson, & Grier, 2017).

Making Criminal Legal System-wide and Community Innovations

Although the physical structures of incarceration—namely, jails and prisons—are central to decarceration efforts, each sector of the criminal legal system (e.g., law enforcement, courts, jails, prisons, community supervision) must be engaged to achieve smart decarceration. In developing innovations across the criminal legal system, priority should be given to efforts that prevent entry into the system to begin with, and then create or expand exit points from incarceration and the broader system altogether. When paired with building social capacity, expanding exit points from the criminal legal system creates an environment in which local communities are better resourced and empowered to respond to local issues without excessive and ineffective use of incarceration or other mechanisms of social control.

Examples of potential innovations to achieve smart decarceration abound (Epperson & Pettus-Davis, 2017). One strategy is to shift the scope of policing responsibilities to restrict their role and reduce their presence while increasing investments concomitantly in communities to produce the safety and social outcomes that are most desirable. Prosecutorial innovations, such as deferred prosecution, have tremendous potential to create new exit points from criminal legal entrenchment and incarceration (Boggess & McGregor, 2013; Campana,

2013; Dembo et al., 2008; George et al., 2015). Problem-solving courts, such as drug courts, mental health courts, veterans' treatment courts, and community restorative courts, represent court-based alternatives to incarceration, with promising effects on reducing recidivism (Rossman et al., 2011; Sarteschi, Vaughn, & Kim, 2011). A range of behavioral interventions have been developed to reduce future offending among people involved in the criminal legal system, and these interventions could be deployed beyond prison and jail settings to nonincarceration efforts (Aos, Miller, & Drake, 2006; Lipsey & Cullen, 2007). Also, evidence-based community supervision that emphasizes prosocial supports and services, combined with expanded social capacity, can help create community-based interventions that will reduce the use of incarceration.

Implementing Transdisciplinary Interventions Using Evidence-driven Strategies

The policies and practices that fueled mass incarceration were accompanied by very few coherent and effective interventions to address the needs of the expanding incarcerated population or to prevent incarceration. To build a field of smart decarceration means incorporating the perspectives of experts from multiple disciplines and sectors, both within and outside the criminal legal system. It also requires linked service delivery systems that provide comprehensive supports but are not duplicative across the criminal legal system. For example, services offered to someone in prison should not be required again upon reentry merely because the prison and community corrections systems are without standardized protocols for treatment and mechanisms to communicate about programming needs. Moreover, drawing from the lessons of deinstitutionalization of people with serious mental illness in the latter half of the 20th century, community resources and capacity-building are needed to support effective decarceration efforts. Cross-sector innovations and the use of evidence-driven strategies are central to avoid replicating the turbulent history of deinstitutionalization.

Much of what led to mass incarceration was the proliferation of policies and practices based on political ideology, reactive impulses, and immediate, ungrounded attempts at solutions. Many of these policies and practices were implemented without evaluation, and their expansion often occurred despite any meaningful evidence on effectiveness or, worse, decades of poor outcomes. By contrast, the Grand Challenge to Promote Smart Decarceration must use an evaluative and evidence-driven approach—one that assesses the effects of interventions continuously at multiple levels and responds to emerging evidence. Gaps in knowledge must be addressed through research on the drivers of incarceration, including social determinants, and how decarceration innovations can have an impact on the social and individual drivers of crime (Pettus-Davis et al., 2017).

SMART DECARCERATION GOALS

The three key outcomes identified previously, and their advancement, will mark sustained progress toward meeting the Grand Challenge to Promote Smart Decarceration. In this section, we further describe each goal and offer suggestions on how progress for each could be measured.

Reduce Substantially the Incarcerated Population in Jails and Prisons

A major indicator of successful decarceration is the number of people being held in both jails and prisons (Epperson & Pettus-Davis, 2017). Building on the small but meaningful declines since 2009, smart decarceration approaches have the potential to reduce the prison and jail population by 25% or more during the next 10 years. Doing so requires cohesive strategies that reduce the flow of individuals into the front end of the system and also reduce lengths of stay for those who are incarcerated (Jacobson, 2005; Subramanian et al., 2015). Connecticut's recent success at reducing incarceration by 50% for people who violate probation provides evidence that even relatively minor structural interventions can lead to dramatic reductions in the incarcerated population (Clement, Schwarzfeld, & Thompson, 2011).

A key question to ponder in smart decarceration is: what are the exact metrics to determine if the goal of decarceration has been met? For example, one potential target for long-term decarceration efforts could be a return to the previous mass incarceration rate of roughly fewer than 200 per 100,000 people, a reduction in the total incarcerated population by 1 million individuals. However, it must be carefully considered whether 200 per 100,000 people incarcerated is an acceptable rate or whether it is possible to downsize incarceration even further with the appropriately based supports in place. In addition, the spirit of smart decarceration will not be met if incarceration is used less, but other forms of social control and punishment (e.g., electronic monitoring, house arrest) are increased. How would we think differently about smart decarceration efforts if the ultimate goal was to reduce (and even eliminate) multiple forms of carcerality? If smart decarceration efforts contribute to the building of social capacity, we should expect to shrink the overall footprint of the criminal legal system and the carceral state as a whole.

Redress Existing Social Disparities in the Criminal Legal System

As discussed previously, the phenomenon of mass incarceration has affected unevenly people of color; people with various forms of social disadvantages, including those with marginalized identities such as LGBTQ+ persons; and people with behavioral health disorders. The overrepresentation of social disparities in the criminal legal system stems from numerous causes, including systemic bias in court case processing (Kingsnorth, MacIntosh, & Sutherland, 2002), uneven policing in poor minority neighborhoods (Brunson & Miller, 2006), irregular sentencing practices (Bushway & Piehl, 2001), and, for some crimes, differential offending patterns (Sampson, Morenoff, & Raudenbush, 2005). In a postdecarceration era, the way in which a person experiences the criminal legal system will not depend on the color of one's skin, on how much money a person can access, or their sexual orientation, gender identity, or gender expression. Nor should people be more likely to be incarcerated because they suffer from drug or alcohol dependence or a mental illness. Reaching this state requires a sober acknowledgment of the role of racism, systemic oppression, and various forms of inequality on how incarceration operates. Building social capacity as a means to counteract oppression and reduce disparities is critical to ensuring that decarceration is achieved in a way that is socially just while maximizing community safety and well-being.

Maximize Community Safety and Well-being

Although there is considerable political and social will to undo mass incarceration, decarceration efforts must continue to uphold community safety. Reductions in the overall number of incarcerated people, as well as reduced racial, gender, and behavioral health disparities in incarceration, will especially benefit communities hardest hit by the past four decades of mass incarceration. Reversing the ripple effects of mass incarceration on individuals and communities will ultimately improve community well-being by reducing the likelihood that individuals' and families' lives will be disrupted by incarceration. In those cases in which a person does become involved in the criminal legal system, evidence-driven and effective exit strategies will assist with reinstating access to prosocial life, and will ensure the likelihood of social participation and social mobility for a large segment of society. A focus on investments in the types of programs and practices that research demonstrates matters for postincarceration success—housing, social support, food security, family connections, and mental and behavioral health—is central to achieving the kind of community capacity-building needed to achieve health and well-being among formerly incarcerated individuals and their family members (Taxman, 2020).

ACCOMPLISHMENTS IN THE FIRST 5 YEARS OF THE GRAND CHALLENGE TO PROMOTE SMART DECARCERATION

Although systemic and significant disparities still exist, progress has been made in numerous ways since the Grand Challenge to Promote Smart Decarceration was launched. We have seen an explosion of media coverage with print articles, social media communications, news reports, and interviews on decarceration and criminal legal reform issues. During the past 5 years, the term *decarceration* has moved from relative obscurity to common language inside and outside the criminal legal system. Alongside the increased visibility and recognition of the need for decarceration, engagement in and support for decarceration work has blossomed. There has been vigorous interest in funding and supporting decarceration-focused research, policy, and practice, at multiple levels of government, as well as from private foundations and other forms of philanthropy. We have also witnessed an upsurge of advocacy organizations in local communities and on a national scale working to implement reform efforts that will advance decarceration. Significant changes in state policies and practices related to COVID-19 prison releases, sentencing reductions, authorizations to vote despite incarceration with a felony conviction, and approvals to challenge sentences to demonstrate evidence of racial discrimination have all been observed. Topics pertinent to the criminal legal system, including policing, sentencing, incarceration, and building sustainable and effective community pathways to avoid criminal legal system involvement, have become a more common thread in national discourse than ever seen before.

The national momentum toward decarceration has certainly aligned with efforts from members of the Promote Smart Decarceration Network. Although it is impossible to identify every accomplishment from the more than 100 social work scholars and practitioners involved in this grand challenge, several areas of progress should be noted. Numerous multisector convenings have been organized, including two national conferences, legislative briefings at the national and state levels, and numerous presentations on principles of smart decarceration in university, criminal legal, and community settings. Social work education initiatives have launched, including the development of a guide to incorporate smart decarceration practice behaviors in curricula, and the development of numerous decarceration-relevant courses and training programs at schools of social work, including inside/out courses and new concentrations and specializations in criminal legal work (Copeland et al., 2018). Countless research projects have been launched that are informed by the goals and guiding concepts of smart decarceration, and this scholarship is being disseminated to both academic and community audiences. In the year 2019 alone, Promote Smart Decarceration Network members published more than 30 manuscripts and provided 20 conference presentations, podcasts, and public talks on decarceration topics. And in 2020, the Promote Smart Decarceration Network added to its network leadership and reenergized network engagement with the development of six new workgroups focusing on the following topics: abolition, antiracism, behavioral health, policing, reentry, and the social work profession. In these and many other ways, the grand challenge has helped to mobilize social work's engagement and leadership in change-oriented criminal legal efforts.

We have also seen a significant increase and broadening of research activities that go beyond problem description, with attention to solutions and systemic changes needed to alter the criminal legal system permanently. This research is being conducted in an unprecedented way because of the variety of disciplines involved, including medicine, education, psychology, nursing, public health, and social work. Traditional disciplines such as sociology and criminal justice have continued their work in this area, but are now joined by a growing group of scholars that complement their work, bringing renewed perspectives and approaches.

FUTURE DIRECTIONS FOR SMART DECARCERATION

Because decarceration is a nascent field that is growing to include a broader range of social work practitioners, scholars, and formerly incarcerated leaders, its scope and breadth remain fluid and evolving. With this in mind, we offer examples of ways in which social workers can pursue research, practice, and policy change in this area. These future directions for smart decarceration are certainly not exhaustive, as many voices and perspectives should shape the direction of social work's role in promoting smart decarceration.

A critical and timely issue that must be grappled with is how to engage in social work practice, policy, research, and teaching in ways that do not uphold the status quo of the criminal legal system, but instead prioritize socially just change on multiple levels. Centering issues of race, gender and sexuality, class, and structural oppression are essential to advancing antiracism at all levels of social work practice and scholarship. Restorative and transformative justice orientations are useful to undergird an approach to social work that pursues direct engagement with criminal legal institutions and actors without becoming complicit in policies and practices that create harm to individuals, families, and communities (Kim, 2018; Sered, 2019). Similarly, incorporating an abolitionist vision and anticarceral framework to decarceration work will center a focus on root causes of mass incarceration and structural analyses, and provide an emphasis on reducing not only brick-and-mortar forms of incarceration, but the larger carceral state (Davis, 2003; Hereth & Bouris, 2020; Jacobs et al., 2020).

Last, increased emphasis and engagement of those most affected by incarceration is necessary for smart decarceration to realize its full potential. Although individuals with incarceration histories have been acknowledged as key leaders in decarceration, numerous structural barriers, including those within social work educational institutions, limit the pathways for people with lived experience to enter and lead the social work profession (Epperson, McHarris, Ulrich, & Sawh, 2021; Smith & Kinzel, 2020). Although the consequences of incarceration for families have been well documented in previous work (Turney & Wildeman, 2013; Wakefield & Wildeman, 2013), a family systems decarceration approach is needed that takes into account the entirety of the impact of incarceration on parents, children, and extended kin, and informs research to advance practices and policies that mitigate the harm done to current and future generations (Charles, Frankham, Garthe, Visher, & Kay, 2021). And building on the existing concept of social capacity, communities most affected by incarceration must be centered in research and practice efforts so that community-driven approaches can replace the criminalization of social and health issues and emphasize the ability to thrive and the well-being of individuals and communities that have been harmed. By pursuing these and other goals, social work can develop its leadership, advance smart decarceration, and promote socially just change.

REFERENCES

Abreu, D., Parker, T. W., Noether, C. D., Steadman, H. J., & Case, B. (2017). Revising the paradigm for jail diversion for people with mental and substance use disorders: Intercept 0. *Behavioral Sciences & the Law, 35*, 380–395.

Aos, S., Miller, M. G., & Drake, E. (2006). Evidence-based adult corrections programs: What works and what does not. Retrieved from http://www.wsipp.wa.gov/ReportFile/924

Beck, A. J., Berzofsky, M., Caspar, R., & Krebs, C. (2016). Sexual victimization in prisons and jails reported by inmates, 2011–12. US Department of Justice, Office of Justice Programs, Bureau of Justice Statistics. Retrieved from https://www.bjs.gov/content/pub/pdf/svpjri1112.pdf

Berg, M. T., & Huebner, B. M. (2011). Reentry and the ties that bind: An examination of social ties, employment, and recidivism. *Justice Quarterly, 28*, 382–410.

Boggess, P., & McGregor, C. (2013). Tarrant County's deferred prosecution program. *The Prosecutor, 43*. Retrieved from https://www.tdcaa.com/journal/tarrant-countys-deferred-prosecution-program-dpp/

Brame, R., Bushway, S. D., Paternoster, R., & Turner, M. G. (2014). Demographic patterns of cumulative arrest prevalence by ages 18 and 23. *Crime & Delinquency, 60*, 471–486.

Brunson, R. K., & Miller, J. (2006). Young Black men and urban policing in the United States. *British Journal of Criminology, 46*, 613–640.

Bushway, S. D., & Piehl, A. M. (2001). Judging judicial discretion: Legal factors and racial discrimination in sentencing. *Law and Society Review, 35*(4), 733–764.

Campana, D. (2013, May 13). Kane "second chance" program gets high marks. Chicago Tribune. Retrieved from http://www.chicagotribune.com/suburbs/aurora-beacon-news/news/ct-abn-kane-states-st-0506-20150505-story.html

Carson, A. E. (2020). Prisoners in 2019 (NCJ 255115). US Department of Justice, Office of Justice Programs, Bureau of Justice Statistics. Retrieved from https://www.bjs.gov/content/pub/pdf/p19.pdf

Charles, P., Frankham, E., Garthe, R., Visher, C., & Kay, A. (2021). Father involvement in the first year after prison: Considerations for social work intervention research. *Research on Social Work Practice,* online first, 1–17.

Clear, T. R. (2007). *Imprisoning communities: How mass incarceration makes disadvantaged neighborhoods worse.* New York, NY: Oxford University Press.

Clement, M., Schwarzfeld, M., & Thompson, M. (2011). The National Summit on Justice Reinvestment and Public Safety: Addressing recidivism, crime, and corrections spending. The Council of State Governments Justice Center. Retrieved from https://bja.ojp.gov/sites/g/files/xyckuh186/files/Publications/CSG_JusticeReinvestmentSummitReport.pdf

Collins, S. E., Lonczak, H. S., & Clifasefi, S. L. (2017). Seattle's Law Enforcement Assisted Diversion (LEAD): Program effects on recidivism outcomes. *Evaluation and Program Planning, 64,* 49–56.

Copeland, P., Jacob, D., Young, D., Grier, A., Kennedy, S., & Tripodi, S. (2018). *Smart decarceration practice behaviors for social work competencies: A guide for educators and learners.* Tallahassee, FL: Florida State University College of Social Work, Institute for Justice Research and Development. Retrieved from https://csd.wustl.edu/18-63/

Dallaire, D. H., & Shlafer, R. J. (2017). Programs for currently and formerly incarcerated mothers. In C. Wildeman, A. R. Haskins, & J. Poehlmann-Tynan (Eds.), *When parents are incarcerated: Interdisciplinary research and interventions to support children* (pp. 83–107). Washington, DC: American Psychological Association.

Davis, A. (2003). *Are Prisons Obsolete?* New York, NY: Seven Stories Press.

Dembo, R., Walters, W., Wareham, J., Burgos, C., Schmeidler, J., Hoge, R., & Underwood, L. (2008). Evaluation of an innovative post-arrest diversion program: 12-Month recidivism analysis. *Journal of Offender Rehabilitation, 47,* 356–384.

Digard, L., & Swavola, E. (2019). Justice denied: The harmful and lasting effects of pretrial detention. Vera Evidence Brief. New York, NY: Vera Institute of Justice. Retrieved from https://www.vera.org/downloads/publications/Justice-Denied-Evidence-Brief.pdf

Durose, M. R., Cooper, A. D., & Snyder, H. N. (2014). Recidivism of prisoners released in 30 states in 2005: Patterns from 2005 to 2010. Bureau of Justice Statistics. Retrieved from https://www.bjs.gov/content/pub/pdf/rprts05p0510.pdf

Epperson, M. W., McHarris, M., Ulrich, B., & Sawh, L. (2021). The box in social work education: Prevalence and correlates of criminal history questions on MSW applications. *Journal of the Society for Social Work and Research.* https://www.journals.uchicago.edu/doi/pdf/10.1086/713476

Epperson, M. W., & Pettus-Davis, C. (2015a). Formerly incarcerated individuals are a crucial element in building a decarceration movement. Retrieved from https://safetyandjusticechallenge.org/blog/formerly-incarcerated-individuals-are-a-crucial-element-in-building-a-decarceration-movement/

Epperson, M. W., & Pettus-Davis, C. (2015b). *Smart decarceration: Guiding concepts for an era of criminal justice transformation.* CSD working paper no. 15-53. Center for

Social Development, George Warren Brown School of Social Work, Washington University in St. Louis. Retrieved from https://csd.wustl.edu/15-53/

Epperson, M. W., & Pettus-Davis, C. (Eds.). (2017). *Smart decarceration: Achieving criminal justice transformation in the 21st Century*. New York, NY: Oxford University Press.

Fazel, S., & Danesh, J. (2002). Serious mental disorder in 23,000 prisoners: A systematic review of 62 surveys. *Lancet, 359*, 545–550.

George, C., Orwat, J., Stemen, D., Cossyleon, J., Hilvers, J., & Chong, E. (2015). An evaluation of the Cook County State's Attorney's Office deferred prosecution program. Retrieved from http://www.icjia.state.il.us/assets/pdf/ResearchReports/Cook_County_Deferred_Prosecution_Evaluation_0715.pdf

Ghandnoosh, N. (2020). U.S. prison decline: Insufficient to undo mass incarceration. Policy brief. The Sentencing Project. Retrieved from https://www.sentencingproject.org/publications/u-s-prison-decline-insufficient-undo-mass-incarceration/

Glaze, L., & Maruchak, L. (2010). Parents in prison and their minor children. US Department of Justice Office of Justice Programs, Bureau of Justice Statistics. Retrieved from https://www.bjs.gov/content/pub/pdf/pptmc.pdf

Goshin, L. S., Sissoko, D. G., Neumann, G., Sufrin, C., & Byrnes, L. (2019). Perinatal nurses' experiences with and knowledge of the care of incarcerated women during pregnancy and the postpartum period. *Journal of Obstetric, Gynecologic & Neonatal Nursing, 48*, 27–36.

Gottlieb, A., Charles, P., McLeod, B., Kjellstrand, J., & Bonsu, J. (2020). Were California's decarceration efforts smart? A quasi-experimental examination of racial, ethnic, and gender disparities. *Criminal Justice and Behavior, 48*, 116–134.

Gottlieb, A., & Mahabir, M. (2019). The effect of multiple types of intimate partner violence on maternal criminal justice involvement. *Journal of Interpersonal Violence, 36*(13-14), 6797–6820. doi:10.1177/0886260518820705

Gramlich, J. (2018). America's incarceration rate is at a two-decade low. FACTANK: News in the Numbers. Pew Research Center. Retrieved from https://www.pewresearch.org/fact-tank/2018/05/02/americas-incarceration-rate-is-at-a-two-decade-low/

Heaton, P., Mayson, S., & Stevenson, M. (2017). The downstream consequences of misdemeanor pretrial detention. *Stanford Law Review, 69*, 711–794.

Hereth, J., & Bouris, A. (2020). Queering smart decarceration: Centering the experiences of LGBTQ+ young people to imagine a world without prisons. *Affilia: Journal of Women and Social Work, 35*, 358–375.

Human Rights Watch. (2021). World report 2021: Events of 2020. Retrieved from https://www.hrw.org/sites/default/files/media_2021/01/2021_hrw_world_report.pdf

Jacobs, L. A., Kim, M. E., Whitfield, D. L., Gartner, R. E., Panichelli, M., & Kattari, S. K. (2020). Defund the police: Moving towards an anti-carceral social work. *Journal of Progressive Human Services, 32*, 37–62. doi:10.1080/10428232.2020.1852865

Jacobson, M. (2005). *Downsizing prisons: How to reduce crime and end mass incarceration*. New York, NY: NYU Press.

James, N. (2019). The First Step Act of 2018: An overview. Congressional Research Service. Retrieved from https://fas.org/sgp/crs/misc/R45558.pdf

Johnson, B. (2003). Racial and ethnic disparities in sentencing departures across modes of conviction. *Criminology, 41*, 449–490.

Kajstura, A. (2019). Women's mass incarceration: The whole pie 2019. Prison Policy Initiative. Retrieved from https://www.prisonpolicy.org/reports/pie2019women.html

Kim, M. E. (2018). From carceral feminism to transformative justice: Women-of-color feminism and alternatives to incarceration. *Journal of Ethnic & Cultural Diversity in Social Work, 27*, 219–233.

Kingsnorth, R. F., MacIntosh, R. C., & Sutherland, S. (2002). Criminal charge or probation violation? Prosecutorial discretion and implications for research in criminal court processing. *Criminology, 40,* 553–578.

Kopak, A. M., & Frost, G. A. (2017). Correlates of program success and recidivism among participants in an adult pre-arrest diversion program. *American Journal of Criminal Justice, 42,* 727–745.

Lipsey, M. W., & Cullen, F. T. (2007). The effectiveness of correctional rehabilitation: A review of systematic reviews. *Annual Review of Law and Social Science, 3,* 297–320.

Lowenkamp, C. T., VanNostrand, M., & Holsinger, A. M. (2013). The hidden costs of pretrial detention. The Arnold Foundation. Retrieved from http://www.arnoldfoundation.org/wp-content/uploads/2014/02/LJAF_Report_hidden-costs_FNL.pdf

Maruschak, L., & Minton, T. (2020). Correctional populations in the United States, 2017–2018. NCJ 252157. US Department of Justice, Office of Justice Programs, Bureau of Justice Statistics. Retrieved from https://www.bjs.gov/content/pub/pdf/cpus1718.pdf

Messina, N., Grella, C., Burdon, W., & Prendergast, M. (2007). Childhood adverse events and current traumatic distress: A comparison of men and women drug-dependent prisoners. *Criminal Justice and Behavior, 34,* 1385–1401.

Minton, T. D., & Zeng, Z. (2015). Jail inmates at midyear 2014. Bureau of Justice Statistics. Retrieved from https://www.bjs.gov/content/pub/pdf/jim14.pdf

Movement Advancement Project and Center for American Progress. (2016). Unjust: How the broken criminal justice system fails LGBT people. Retrieved from https://www.lgbtmap.org/lgbt-criminal-justice

Mumola, C. J. (2000). Special report: Incarcerated parents and their children. US Department of Justice, Bureau of Justice Statistics. Retrieved from https://www.bjs.gov/content/pub/pdf/iptc.pdf

Munetz, M., & Griffin, P. A. (2006). Use of the Sequential Intercept Model as an approach to decriminalization of people with serious mental illness. *Psychiatric Services, 57,* 544–549.

National Center on Addiction and Substance Abuse at Columbia University. (2010). *Behind bars II: Substance abuse and America's prison population.* New York, NY: Author.

Nellis, A. (2016). The color of justice: Racial and ethnic disparity in state prisons. The Sentencing Project. Retrieved from http://www.sentencingproject.org/publications/color-of-justice-racial-and-ethnic-disparity-in-state-prisons

Neusteter, R., O'Toole, M., & Khogali, M. (2018). *Emerging issues in American policing* (Vol. 3, special ed.). New York, NY: Vera Institute of Justice. Retrieved from https://www.vera.org/publications/emerging-issues-in-american-policing-digest/volume-3/digest-3

Newport, F. (2018). In U.S., estimate of LGBT population rises to 4.5%. Gallup. Retrieved from https://news.gallup.com/poll/234863/estimate-lgbt-population-rises.aspx

Obama, B. (2017). The president's role in advancing criminal justice reform. *Harvard Law Review, 130,* 811–866.

Pettus-Davis, C., Epperson, M. W., & Grier, A. (2017). *Guideposts for the era of smart decarceration: Smart decarceration strategies for practitioners, advocates, reformers, and researchers.* St. Louis, MO: Center for Social Development, Washington University. Retrieved from https://ijrd.csw.fsu.edu/sites/g/files/upcbnu1766/files/Publications/Guideposts_SmartDecarceration.pdf

Roberts, D. E. (2004). The social and moral costs of mass incarceration in African American communities. *Stanford Law Review*, *56*, 1271–1305.

Rojek, J., Rosenfeld, R., & Decker, S. (2012). Policing race: The racial stratification of searchers in police traffic stops. *Criminology*, *50*, 993–1024.

Rosenberg, T. (2017). Even in Texas, mass imprisonment is going out of style. *The New York Times*. Retrieved from https://www.nytimes.com/2017/02/14/opinion/even-in-texas-mass-imprisonment-is-going-out-of-style.html

Rossman, S. B., Zweig, J. M., Kralstein, D., Henry, K., Downey, P. M., & Lindquist, C. (2011). *The multi-site adult drug court evaluation: The drug court experience: Volume 3*. Washington, DC: Urban Institute. Retrieved from https://www.ojp.gov/pdffiles1/nij/grants/237111.pdf

Sampson, R. J., & Loeffler, C. (2010). Punishment's place: The local concentration of mass incarceration. *Daedalus*, *139*, 20–31.

Sampson, R. J., Morenoff, J. D., & Raudenbush, S. (2005). Social anatomy of racial and ethnic disparities in violence. *American Journal of Public Health*, *95*, 224–232.

Sarteschi, C. M., Vaughn, M. G., & Kim, K. (2011). Assessing the effectiveness of mental health courts: A quantitative review. *Journal of Criminal Justice*, *39*, 12–20.

Sawyer, W. (2018). The gender divide: Tracking women's state prison growth. Prison Policy Initiative. Retrieved from https://www.prisonpolicy.org/reports/women_overtime.html

Sered, D. (2017). Accounting for violence: How to increase safety and break our failed reliance on mass incarceration. New York, NY: Vera Institute of Justice. Retrieved from https://storage.googleapis.com/vera-web-assets/downloads/Publications/accounting-for-violence/legacy_downloads/accounting-for-violence.pdf

Sered, D. (2019). *Until we reckon: Violence, mass incarceration, and a road to repair*. New York, NY: The New Press.

Skeem, J., & Monahan, J. (2020). Lost in translation: "Risks," "needs," and "evidence" in implementing the First Step Act. *Behavioral Sciences & the Law*, *38*, 287–297.

Smith, J. M., & Kinzel, A. (2020). Carceral citizenship as strength: Formerly incarcerated activists, civic engagement and criminal justice transformation. *Critical Criminology*, *29*, 93–110.

Snyder, H. (2012). Arrests in the United States, 1990 to 2010. US Department of Justice, Office of Justice Programs, Bureau of Justice Statistics. Retrieved from https://www.bjs.gov/content/pub/pdf/aus9010.pdf

Steadman, H. J., Osher, F. C., Robbins, P. C., Case, B., & Samuels, S. (2009). Prevalence of serious mental illness among jail inmates. *Psychiatric Services*, *60*, 761–765.

Subramanian, R., Delaney, R., Roberts, S., Fishman, N., & McGarry, P. (2015). *Incarceration's front door: The misuse of jails in America*. New York, NY: Vera Institute of Justice. Retrieved from https://www.vera.org/publications/incarcerations-front-door-the-misuse-of-jails-in-america

Subramanian, R., Eisen, L. B., Merkl, T., Arzy, L., Stroud, H., King, T., . . . Nahra, A. (2020). Transition 2020-2021: Federal agenda for criminal justice reform. Brennan Center for Justice. Retrieved from https://www.brennancenter.org/sites/default/files/2020-12/FederalAgendaCriminalJustice.pdf

Taxman, F. S. (2020). Community capacity-building and implementation advances to addressing the RNR framework. In A. Leverentz, E. Chen, & J. Christian (Eds.), *Beyond recidivism: New approaches to research on prisoner reentry and reintegration* (pp. 39–56). New York, NY: NYU Press.

Taxman, F. S., Perdoni, M. L., & Harrison, L. D. (2007). Drug treatment services for adult offenders: The state of the state. *Journal of Substance Abuse Treatment, 32,* 239–254.

The Sentencing Project. (2018). Report of the Sentencing Project to the United Nations Special Rapporteur on contemporary forms of racism, racial discrimination, xenophobia, and related intolerance regarding racial disparities in the United States criminal justice system. Retrieved from https://www.sentencingproject.org/publications/un-report-on-racial-disparities/

The Sentencing Project. (2020). Fact sheet: Incarcerated women and girls. Retrieved from https://www.sentencingproject.org/publications/incarcerated-women-and-girls/

Thomas, S. Y., & Lanterman, J. L. (2019). A national analysis of shackling laws and policies as they relate to pregnant incarcerated women. *Feminist Criminology, 14,* 263–284.

Turney, K., & Wildeman, C. (2013). Redefining relationships: Explaining the countervailing consequences of paternal incarceration for parenting. *American Sociological Review, 78,* 949–979.

Wakefield, S., & Wildeman, C. (2013). *Children of the prison boom: Mass incarceration and the future of American inequality.* New York, NY: Oxford University Press.

Western, B., & Pettit, B. (2010). *Collateral costs: Incarceration's effect on economic mobility.* Washington, DC: The Pew Charitable Trusts. Retrieved from http://www.pewtrusts.org/~/media/legacy/uploadedfiles/pcs_assets/2010/collateralcosts1pdf.pdf

Wilson, A, & Wilson, M. (2020). Reimagining policing: Strategies for community reinvestment pre-arrest diversion; and innovative approaches to 911 emergency responses. Social Justice Brief, National Association of Social Workers. Retrieved from https://www.socialworkers.org/LinkClick.aspx?fileticket=GjXJr6rDzss%3d&portalid=0

Wooldredge, J., Frank, J., Goulette, N., & Travis, L. (2015). Is the impact of cumulative disadvantage on sentencing greater for Black defendants? *Criminology & Public Policy, 14,* 187–223.

Zeng, Z., & Minton, T. D. (2021). Jail inmates in 2019 (NCJ 255608). US Department of Justice, Office of Justice Programs, Bureau of Justice Statistics. Retrieved from https://www.bjs.gov/content/pub/pdf/ji19.pdf

Zorn, E. (2015). Rauner takes aim at high prison population. *The Chicago Tribune.* Retrieved from http://www.chicagotribune.com/news/opinion/zorn/ct-bruce-rauner-prison-taxes-perspec-0215-20150213-column.html

CHAPTER 11
Reducing Extreme Economic Inequality

JULIA HENLY, LAURA LEIN, JENNIFER ROMICH,
TRINA R. SHANKS, AND MICHAEL SHERRADEN
(WITH CONTRIBUTIONS FROM RAVEN JONES
AND AMANDA TILLOTSON)

ADDRESSING EXTREME ECONOMIC INEQUALITY: THE NATURE OF THE PROBLEM

Our grand challenge continues to address the growing economic inequality that faces the United States. The COVID-19 pandemic, the ever-more-visible evidence of racial and ethnic inequality in the United States, and the economic recession combine to cast a vivid spotlight on differences in income and assets, financial security, and material and other hardships. The impact of the pandemic itself has been more pronounced in communities of color (Miller, 2020). The harsh economic fallout from the pandemic, as well as the particularly pronounced trauma experienced in communities of color has spotlighted the continuing economic, racial, and gender inequalities in our society. The Grand Challenge to Reduce Extreme Economic Inequality works to identify and describe the nature of the problem, and to engage with the design and implementation of policies and practices to lessen economic inequality.

The relatively high rates of poverty in the United States—compared to other "mature economies" (Grusky, Mattingly, & Varner, 2016)—contribute to economic inequality; however, economic inequality is the focus of our work. In the United States, compared to other developed countries, income and wealth are consolidated among the highest income and wealthiest segment of the population. Not only is the gap between rich and poor increasing, but also the gaps in both wealth (Asante-Mohammed, Collins, Hoxie, & Nieves, 2016) and income (Akee, Jones, & Porter, 2019; Economic Policy Institute,

2017a) are increasing by race and ethnicity, and also by gender. The Great Recession widened income and wealth inequality, and exacerbated racial gaps in earnings and wealth (Hamilton, Darity, Price, Sridharan, & Tippett, 2015), and the confluence of public health, economic, and political events in 2020 seems likely to do the same.

Changing labor market conditions during the past 4 years, such as deunionization, rising levels of precarious employment conditions, stagnating income, and deteriorating worker protections, have contributed to the growing economic inequality that increasingly characterizes the United States (Howell & Kalleberg, 2019; Kalleberg, 2011; Weil, 2019; Henly, Lambert, & Dresser, 2021). Although wage growth has been used to track productivity growth, since 1979 the two statistics have diverged. Cumulative productivity increased almost 70% between 1979 and 2018; however, overall hourly pay increased by only 11.6 percentage points (Economic Policy Institute, 2019). The wages of the bottom 50% of workers have stagnated whereas wages of the top earners have risen steadily during this period (Howell & Kalleberg, 2019). Furthermore, the wages of workers of color continue to lag behind those of white workers (Elsby, Hobijn, & Şahin, 2013; Karabarbounis & Neiman, 2013). Even as wages have increased overall during the past 5 years, gaps among racial and ethnic groups have persisted and grown in size (Wilson, 2020). Furthermore, inequality is more pronounced in the United States than in other economically developed countries. Approximately one fourth of US workers have low pay, as judged by the international comparative standard (less than two thirds of the median wage). This share of US workers receiving low pay is greater than all other countries in the Organization for Economic Co-operation and Development (2014). The United States is also less likely than other Organization for Economic Co-operation and Development countries to lift families out of poverty through government policies and programs (Smeeding, 2005).

In the United States, the highest 1% of wealthy people own more than three times as much wealth as the lowest 80%. This consolidation of wealth became increasingly pronounced during the Great Recession, despite some rebounds in median wealth (Wolff, 2021). Furthermore, Native American, Black, Latino, and many Asian American households hold only a fraction of the wealth on average that accrues in white households (Lui, Robles, Leondar-Wright, Brewer, & Adamson, 2006). And, women hold only a fraction of the wealth held by men (Chang, 2015). These trends mark the United States as an outlier among developed economies in terms of the magnitude of inequality that it tolerates (Grusky et al., 2016). In this chapter, we examine the problems of inequality in employment and income, as well as in wealth and investment. By doing so, we see even more starkly the relationship of these ongoing trends in income and wealth by race and ethnicity. We then explore some policy alternatives to these continuing trends, and their potential advantages and disadvantages.

This chapter examines the mechanisms and outcomes of inequality in employment and income on the one hand, and wealth and assets on the other hand. It then highlights a number of policy and practice developments in which social workers are deeply involved. It concludes by recognizing the need for ongoing efforts in the development of these efforts.

MAINSTREAMING GENDER

Structural Gender Inequities Drive Economic Inequality
MARGARET M. C. THOMAS

In the 1970s, sociologist Diana Pearce described the "feminization of poverty." This phrase is far more familiar to many people than any more nuanced analysis of the labor market, public assistance, and family structure developments that drive the "feminization" of poverty. Critically, without such explanations, the phrase on its own conveys that the experience of poverty is fundamentally gendered.

This language has consequences for our conceptualization of poverty. Consider different constructions of the same issue. In contrast to the "feminization of poverty," we could describe the "patriarchy of social policy," the "essential inequity of capitalism," the "gendering of occupation," or "economic sexism." Any one of these phrases describes central aspects of the forces that have been identified as "feminizing" poverty. But instead of suggesting a relationship between gender and inequitable outcomes, these constructions focus our attention on the systemic causes of the ultimate economic inequities across gender. Poverty is not gendered; rather, systems are patriarchal, sexist, and marginalizing.

Extreme economic inequality exists along numerous intersecting lines: between those with wealth and those without; between low- and high-resource countries; across racialized groups; between different communities within the United States, from states and regions down to neighborhoods and blocks. Economic inequality exists related to gender too, with aggregate inequalities among groups across the gender spectrum. Feminist work addresses structural causes of economic inequality across gender. Yet, a critical shift in our more routine conversations, particularly in many foundational social work policy and practice courses, should reframe the fundamental nature of what links economic inequality and gender: political, economic, and social systems are patriarchal, marginalizing women, transgender, and gender-expansive people. Without consistently underscoring the structural causes of marginalization, we passively reinforce that harm and unjustly attribute responsibility for marginalization to those who experience it.

Likewise, when we report quantitative research findings that indicate gender is associated with income poverty, we are capturing the

continued

consequences of a proximate measure—gender—of a much more complex, distal predictor of income poverty: gendered marginalization. This is not a technical, methodological problem. Our students, colleagues, and community partners routinely encounter evidence that suggests gender and poverty are inexorably related. This is despite strong extant research that identifies systemic causes of economic inequality by gender, highlighting factors such as occupational segregation and attendant wage inequality. Such examples are an essential first step toward shifting responsibility for gender-based economic inequality away from the marginalized. A critical next step is to nest this structural analysis in the hierarchy of constructs that shape this inequality. Why does occupational segregation produce economic inequality across gender? Because political, economic, and social expressions of patriarchy decree that cisgender men's work merits premium pay. Whether we label this sexism a "value" or the "framing of an issue," it is a socially constructed, politically reinforced reality. The power and privileges of those benefiting from gendered wage inequality cause economic inequality by gender. It is a self-interested, society-level choice that high-skill, majority female occupations, such as social work, teaching, and nursing, are lower paid than high-skill, majority male occupations, such as engineering, finance, and computer science.

To meet the Grand Challenge to Reduce Extreme Economic Inequality, we have to situate our examination of vital, person-level inequities in the complex and intangible systems in which people's real lives take place. For instance, in research, this includes seeking out sources of contextual data capturing systemic forces, grounding our work in the expertise of community members, and interpreting our findings through structural, social justice perspectives. Ending economic inequality requires identifying and eliminating fundamental causes of inequity. We have to acknowledge and then change the ways we enact core tenets of US social, political, and economic reality—among others: ableism, ageism, classism, colonialism, heteronormativity, neurotypicality, racism, sexism, and xenophobia. Striving to attribute inequities consistently to their structural causes rather than associate inequities with the marginalized people and groups they harm is a central step toward justice.

INEQUALITY IN EMPLOYMENT AND INCOME

Labor market forces and institutions create and reinforce economic inequality. One theme of our grand challenge is that the market for labor is not a "free" market governed only by supply and demand. Rather, employer practices, labor laws, social policies, and the relative power of institutions and workers shape the distribution of income. Formed in 2015, the Grand Challenge to Reduce Extreme Economic Inequality took shape as new evidence was coming forth about the extent to which years of change in market institutions had reduced worker power and concentrated the gains of the market to the highest earners and owners of capital. In the 5 years since our founding, further changes in the market have both accelerated and sought to change that trend. As of this writing—more than a year into the COVID-19 pandemic and well into the first term of the Biden administration—some signs indicate movement in policy directions that may reduce extreme income inequality.

A Brief View Backward

Since the 1970s, structural changes in the labor market coupled with a loosening of labor standards and changing employer practices have affected the economic well-being of US workers negatively, especially those earning the least (Hacker, 2006; Howell & Kalleberg, 2019; Henly, Lambert, & Dresser, 2021; Lambert, Haley-Lock, & Henly, 2012; Lambert & Henly, 2012; Weil, 2019). A growing proportion of US workers are in precarious employment arrangements such as contingent work, temporary jobs, and "gig" jobs. These arrangements exist across pay scales, but nonstandard employment frequently delivers low and unstable earnings, limited security, and few if any worker protections and benefits (Henly et al., 2021; Howell & Kalleberg, 2019). Moreover, employment settings have become increasingly bifurcated, with jobs at the very top of the labor market often requiring long hours, but nevertheless providing generous compensation and benefits. Jobs at the bottom half of the labor market have become more precarious, characterized by low wages, scarce and erratic work hours, few if any employer-sponsored benefits, and high turnover (Howell & Kalleberg, 2019; Kalleberg, 2011; Lambert, Henly, & Kim, 2019). These changes have been accompanied by a "hollowing out" (Autor, 2010) of the traditional middle of the labor market. That is, jobs that require limited educational requirements but provide middle-class incomes are increasingly scarce, although skill-based technological changes are insufficient to explain the rise in wage inequality (Schmitt, Shierholz, & Mishel, 2013).

Through the growth of the service sector, opportunities for job seekers with limited educational backgrounds still exist, but without the promise of stability in hours, earnings, and benefits. Indeed, earnings growth is concentrated among workers with graduate degrees; stagnation and decline characterize the earnings of workers with a bachelor's degree or less (Holzer, 2015). Although parents can do their best to earn an adequate living and provide a safe, stimulating, and warm environment for their children, it is difficult to succeed without the security of stable, adequate earnings and flexibility that allows employees to respond to family needs while retaining the status of a responsible employee.

Wages

The majority of all wage and salaried workers (58.1%) are paid an hourly rate (US Bureau of Labor Statistics, 2020a). For workers paid by the hour, their earnings are a product of hourly wages and work hours. Thus, differences in wage levels are one important source of economic inequality. For the past several decades, wages have grown for top earners, but have stagnated for median and lower earners. Since 1989, top earners have seen wages increase by more than 30%, after adjusting for inflation, whereas earners at the bottom of pay scales saw decreases (Nunn & Shambaugh, 2020). Furthermore, wage gains have been most prominent among white and male earners. At the bottom of the pay scale are those that pay at or just above the minimum wage (and jobs in the irregular economy that can pay less than minimum wage). For most families, these jobs do not provide sustainable earnings. In 2020, the pretax minimum living wage required for a family with two full-time working adults and two children in the United States was estimated to be $16.54 per hour for each employed adult. At the current federal minimum wage of $7.25 per hour, however, each wage earner would need to work 75 hours per week to meet this goal (Nadeau, 2020). Given the growth of part-time jobs with low pay, workers are frequently burdened by both low wages and too few hours of work (Golden, 2016; Lambert et al., 2012; Valletta, Bengali, & van der List, 2020).

The minimum wage varies among states. As of 2021, 29 states and the District of Columbia had minimum wages greater than those set by the federal government, although minimum wages even in these states are not sufficient to provide a living wage for families working full time (National Conference of State Legislatures, 2021). For a two-adult, two-child family, the percentage of the living wage provided by the minimum wage ranges from a high of 73.1% in the District of Columbia to a low of 41.1% in Virginia (Nadeau, 2020). Evidence suggests state minimum wages decrease income inequality; higher state minimum wages are associated with faster wage growth at the bottom of the income scale (Gould, 2016).

Local jurisdictions throughout the United States sometimes establish minimum wage levels higher than state and federal minimums. Some have also passed living wage legislation that establishes higher minimum wages for employees in specific sectors. As of January 2021, 45 cities or counties had wages higher than their state minimums (Economic Policy Institute, 2021). This includes several major cities with minimum wages at $15 per hour or more, such as New York City ($15), San Francisco ($16.07), and Seattle ($16.69).) Evidence from Seattle, the first major city to pass a $15 minimum wage, suggests that the higher wage caused overall employment to dip slightly, but experienced low-earning workers saw increased hourly earnings and no job loss (Jardim et al., 2020).

Unemployment and Underemployment

Inequality also results from disparities in access to jobs. When the economy is in a recession, as it was in the Great Recession of 2007 to 2009, and is again in the Pandemic Recession of 2020, overall employment drops and many workers lose jobs. Even during periods of economic growth, unemployment and underemployment continue to structure labor markets.

Rates of unemployment and underemployment vary with age, race, and level of education, with less-advantaged workers generally seeing higher unemployment rates. As of the end of 2019, overall unemployment stood at 3.5%—the lowest rate in 60 years (Edwards & Smith, 2020). Although overall employment was low after a decade of economic growth, unemployment rates were greater for Black workers (5.6%), workers age 16 to 24 years (12.3%), and workers without high school degrees (5.3%) (Edwards & Smith, 2020). Economic effects of the COVID-19 pandemic increased both overall unemployment to 6.7% by the end of 2020, with (again) higher rates for Black workers, younger workers, and less-educated workers (US Bureau of Labor Statistics, 2021).

Underemployment occurs when skilled workers are employed at low-skilled jobs or when employees who would prefer to work full time are only able to find part-time employment (i.e., involuntarily part-time workers) (Economic Policy Institute, 2015; McKee-Ryan & Harvey, 2011). About a quarter of part-time workers report that they work part time because they cannot find full-time work or business conditions do not support full-time hours (US Bureau of Labor Statistics, 2021). Underemployment follows the same racialized patterns that mark other parts of the labor market, with rates for Blacks and Hispanics higher than that for whites (Economic Policy Institute, 2017b). Education also affects underemployment rates. In 2017, 19.3% of individuals older than age 16 years who had completed 1 to 3 years of high school were underemployed compared to 4.9% of individuals with a bachelor's degree or higher (Economic Policy Institute, 2017a).

Hours, Working Conditions, and Benefits

Job quality is about wages, but it is also about hours, working conditions, and nonpecuniary workplace benefits. Wages and hours together determine earnings for jobs paid by the hour. If wages are low, employees must work long hours for adequate take-home pay. Yet, part-time work has become increasingly commonplace. In January 2021, about 25 million US workers were employed on a part-time basis (less than 35 hours per week). Part-time workers not only work fewer hours, but also they face a significant hourly wage penalty

(Golden, 2020; Kalleberg, 2011). Taking into account demographic and educational differences between part- and full-time workers, the hourly wage of part-time workers is 29% lower than their full-time counterparts (Golden, 2020). Moreover, involuntary part-time workers are a growing share of all part-time workers (Kalleberg, 2011).

Thus, part time work—especially involuntary part-time work—is an important dimension of job quality that increasingly defines the labor market experiences of low-income individuals. Part-time hours are the result of employers adopting hiring and scheduling practices aimed at minimizing labor costs by keeping both wages and hours strategically low. For example, employers in low-wage workplaces tend to keep a relatively large pool of staff on payroll to maintain a flexible labor force to fill just-in-time labor needs and reduce reliance on more costly full-time employees (Lambert, 2008; Lambert et al., 2012).

The hiring and scheduling practices common in today's low-wage workplaces not only result in bloated staffing rolls and underemployment, but also they produce employees who are hungry for hours and ready to work with limited advance notice and at variable times (McCrate, Lambert, & Henly, 2019). National data indicate that 40% of employees in hourly jobs are made aware of their work schedule with 1 week or less advance notice, and almost two thirds are given no input into the timing of their work hours (Lambert, Henly, & Kim, 2019). Unpredictable, erratic work schedules are most common among workers paid by the hour, and they affect disproportionately workers of color, workers in low-wage occupations, and low-income parents (Lambert et al., 2019; Lambert, Fugiel, & Henly, 2014). In addition, nonstandard work hours—work outside of the standard daytime, weekday workweek—have become the norm in today's economy, and are more common among less-educated and lower income individuals, and more common among mothers than fathers (Enchautegui, Johnson, & Gelatt, 2015; Presser, 2003; Presser & Cox, 1997). Although some employees prefer these hours, 72% of low-income mothers with nonstandard work schedules report working nonstandard hours involuntarily (Enchautegui et al., 2015). Precarious scheduling practices sometimes go hand-in-hand with more nefarious cost-containment practices that constitute employer violations of employment and labor laws, such as uncompensated work hours, denial of breaks, and payment below the minimum wage (Bernhardt, Spiller, & Theodore 2013; Henly et al., 2021).

Last, workers in low-level jobs seldom receive employer-sponsored workplace benefits, another critical dimension of job quality (Kalleberg, 2011). Higher wages, when coupled with sufficient and stable hours, not only allow workers to earn sufficient, predictable earnings, but also these jobs—especially when they are salaried—are also more likely to include other forms of compensation that help support and stabilize workers' financial and personal well-being. For example, paid sick leave and paid family leave protect earnings and jobs when a worker or family member becomes ill or needs to take time off for medical care. However, low-wage hourly jobs seldom include access to benefits such as paid sick days, family and medical leave, or even paid vacation days. Among civilian workers, 52% of workers in the lowest quartile and 94% of workers in the highest quartile have access to at least some paid sick leave benefits tied to their employment (US Bureau of Labor Statistics, 2020c). Similar differences between higher and lower earning workers apply with paid vacations, personal leave, and jury duty leave, indicating that higher status workers have more access to rest, wellness, and even civic participation. These disparities affect workers in later life as well. Less than one third of the lowest decile of workers have access to (32%) and participate in (16%) employer-sponsored retirement plans, whereas more than 80% of earners in the top quartile take advantage of retirement benefits (US Bureau of Labor Statistics, 2020b). Thus, the work conditions and benefits associated with higher paid jobs protect and stabilize income and provide nonpecuniary benefits as well, whereas the more precarious work conditions and lack of benefits characteristic of jobs held by workers at the lower end of the labor market too often diminish and destabilize income.

Consequences of Employment Inequality

Declining job quality at the low end of the labor market can destabilize families and leave parents torn between their responsibilities to their families and their responsibilities to their employers. The precarious scheduling practices described earlier are related to income insecurity (Finnegan, 2018; Lambert et al., 2019); are associated negatively with employee well-being such as stress, fatigue, and sleep disruptions (Ananat & Gassman-Pines, 2021; Schneider & Harknett, 2019; Henly & Lambert, 2014); and can interfere with personal and family responsibilities (Clawson & Gerstel, 2014; Henly & Lambert, 2014). As employers cut and add hours at the last minute to track demand, employees scramble to accommodate employer requests by securing just-in-time child-care arrangements and rescheduling appointments—at a cost to family time, community engagement, and their own health and well-being (Harknett, Schneider, & Luhr, 2020; Henly, Shaefer, & Waxman, 2006). Moreover, maternal nonstandard work schedules, which seldom align with child-care center and preschool hours, are related to disproportionate rates of informal care use and multiple arrangements (Enchautegui et al., 2015; Han, 2004), and show negative associations with children's cognitive and behavioral outcomes (Gassman-Pines, 2011; Han, 2005, 2008).

Because some government programs establish a minimum number of work hours as a condition of program eligibility, part-time employees with scarce hours or hours that fluctuate have difficulties qualifying for important public benefits, such as those mandated by the Family and Medical Leave Act, unemployment insurance, and some state child-care subsidy programs (Lambert & Henly, 2013; Nicholson & Needles, 2006). Moreover, nonstandard work arrangements and precarious work schedules can lead to increased program instability, and make the process of securing and maintaining benefits more onerous as programs sometimes require additional employer verification when schedules are erratic or earnings are not verifiable through paycheck stubs or other standard means (Henly, Sandstrom, & Pilarz, 2017). Last, the limited access that low-wage jobs provide to employer-sponsored paid sick days and family and medical leave further affect both child development and employee performance (Berger, Hill, & Waldfogel, 2005; Ybarra, 2013).

Low wages can require parents to work multiple jobs—both in and outside of the regular economy—to supplement earnings; but, multiple job-holding exacerbates child-care difficulties and reduces the time available for parenting (Abraham, Haltiwanger, Sandusky, & Spletzer, 2017; Yoshikawa, Weisner, & Lowe, 2006). Although earned income is distinct from the accumulation of assets (wealth), low-wage employment restricts opportunities for investment in a variety of ways. In addition to limiting opportunities for asset accumulation through home ownership, low-wage employment complicates the ability of workers to save for future expenditures, such as their children's college expenses and their own retirement. For these workers, low levels of disposable income are often exacerbated by the lack of employer-sponsored retirement plans (Callahan, 2013).

Approximately 11 million children live in families with incomes below the federal poverty threshold (Haider, 2021). During most of the past 30 years, the child poverty rate in the United States has remained 1.7 times higher than the adult rate. With rates of child poverty decreasing somewhat in the years prior to the pandemic, the child poverty rate dropped to about 1.5 times the adult rate and two times the elderly poverty rate in 2018. However, as families face considerable economic hardship as a result of the COVID-19 recession, we can expect child poverty rates to rise again. On average, among Organization for Economic Co-operation and Development member countries, more than 13% of children experience income poverty. In 11 nations, including Germany, Denmark, Sweden, and Finland, less than 10% of children live in poverty. The United States, however, is in a group of five nations in which approximately 20% of children experience income poverty (Organization for Economic Co-operation and Development, 2016). This number had declined between 2016 and the onset of the pandemic, but the pandemic is expected to change these numbers.

A majority of low-income children in the United States have parents who work, but low wages and unstable employment leave their families struggling to make ends meet. Poverty has a negative impact on children, which can interfere with children's learning and contributes to social, emotional, and behavioral difficulties. A disturbing characteristic of the growth in income inequality is the corresponding inequality in access to high-quality child care, schools, and other enrichment resources it portends (Kalil, 2016). This resource–access gap contributes to a learning and achievement gap between economically better- and worse-off children that continues into adulthood.

DIMENSIONS OF INEQUALITY IN ASSETS

Wealth is the stock of economic resources in place as opposed to the flow of resources that comes via income to meet immediate needs. It is typically defined as net worth, or the total value of all assets owned by a household minus any debt or liabilities, including cash/monetary equivalents; vehicles; home equity; other property; stocks, bonds, and financial securities; and business equity (Nam, Huang, & Sherraden, 2008; Sherraden, 1991). Wealth is distinct from income not only in how it is defined and measured, but also in that it is not linked as closely to employment and is built over time, typically across generations. Some definitions refer primarily to liquid assets or nonhome wealth (Wolff, 2021), only to include assets that can be sold quickly and easily in times of need.

Levels of Wealth: Differences across the Economic Spectrum and by Race and Gender

Wealth inequality has increased dramatically during the past 40 years. Between 1983 and 2010, high-wealth families in the top 20% of the wealth distribution experienced an average growth in net worth of nearly 120%. In contrast, families in the middle of the wealth distribution saw an average increase of 13%, whereas families in the bottom 20% of the wealth distribution had, on average, a net worth of zero—meaning, their average debt was greater than their assets (McKernan, Ratcliffe, Steuerle, & Zhang, 2013). Similarly, between 1989 and 2019, the wealthiest 1% of families in the United States increased from an aggregate share of 30% to 37%, whereas the bottom 90% of families saw their aggregate share decline (Bricker, Goodman, Moore, Henriques Volz, & Ruh, 2020).

Racial disparities in wealth are much greater than racial disparities in income and have been widening in recent years. In 2019, non-Hispanic Black households and Latino households received a median income 58% and 64%, respectively, of the median income received by non-Hispanic white households (Wolff, 2021). By contrast, in 2019, non-Hispanic Black and Latino households had only 13 and 19 cents, respectively, for every dollar of median wealth held by non-Hispanic white households. After the Great Recession of 2007 to

2009, the net worth of both Black and Hispanic households plummeted, and although wealth levels have begun to increase, Black households still have not returned to what they held in 2007 (Wolff, 2021). The total median wealth for non-Hispanic white families in 2019 was approximately $188,200, compared to that of Latinos at approximately $36,200 and that of non-Hispanic Blacks at approximately $24,100 (Bhutta et al., 2020).

There are also major gender disparities in wealth. In 2013, single women had only 32 cents in median wealth for every dollar of wealth held by single men (Chang, 2015). Married couples tend to be wealthier. However, for Black women, neither marriage nor a college education reduces the racial wealth gap with white women (Zaw, Bhattacharya, Price, Hamilton, & Darity, 2017). For parents, having children seems to reduce wealth holdings. Single mothers (regardless of race) have virtually no wealth to draw upon in case of a financial emergency (Zaw et al., 2017).

Home Ownership

Home ownership is the largest contributor to net worth for families in the United States, particularly for those of low to moderate income (Wolff, 2021). When the overall housing rate was at its highest in 2004, 76.2% of non-Hispanic white households, 49.1% of non-Hispanic Black households, and 48.9% of Latino households owned their homes (US Census Bureau, 2016). Homeownership rates dropped across the board with the housing crisis and Great Recession of 2007 to 2009. Homeownership rates had just started to rebound at the end of 2019 going into 2020, but with the COVID-19 pandemic and the economic uncertainty it brings, homeownership again declined. The most recent statistics from 2020 show that homeownership rates are 74.5% for non-Hispanic white households, 44.1% for non-Hispanic Black households, 49.1% for Latino households, and 59.5% for Asian, Native Hawaiian, and Pacific Islander households (US Census Bureau, 2021). Equally important, Blacks and Latinos who did own homes saw less return in wealth from homeownership. For every dollar in wealth that median Black households gained through homeownership, the rate of return for median white households was $1.34. For every dollar in wealth gained by median Latino households through homeownership, median white households received $1.54 (Sullivan, Dietrich, Traub, & Ruetschlin, 2015).

Finding affordable housing is an issue whether one owns or rents. There is currently no housing market in the country where a minimum wage job will pay for a two-bedroom apartment at a fair market rate, as defined by the federal government as a rental that costs no more than one third of gross monthly income. And in only one state (North Dakota) can even the average renter earn enough to pay for a fair market rate two-bedroom apartment

(National Low Income Housing Coalition, 2020). In some housing markets, such as San Francisco, rents are too high for even middle-income families. With the COVID-19 pandemic leading to higher unemployment rates and risk of eviction, the need for affordable housing and emergency assistance are even more necessary than ever (National Low Income Housing Coalition, 2020).

Consequences of Wealth Inequality

The United States' extreme wealth inequality has critical consequences. The most immediate consequence is the inability of low-resourced households to meet emergency expenses. In 2018, 4 of 10 Americans did not have enough cash to cover a $400 emergency expense (Federal Reserve, 2019). There is no official definition of asset poverty, but, consistently, approximately one fifth of US households have zero or negative net worth (Wolff, 2021). A more formal asset–poverty measure is insufficient wealth resources to maintain a family at the poverty line for 3 months (Caner & Wolff, 2004; Nam et al., 2008). Based on data from 2016, 58% of Black and Latino households lack the liquid assets necessary to subsist at the poverty level for 3 months in the event of an unexpected income disruption. In contrast, half of white households (29%) are in a similar financial position (Prosperity Now, 2020). Thus, if these households face a job loss, medical emergency, or major unexpected expense, they do not have a sufficient cushion to cover such emergencies.

In the longer term, wealth inequality means that the majority never experience what Tom Shapiro terms "transformative assets," wealth or inheritance that lifts families beyond where their own achievements would lead, which might include investing in opportunities for mobility such as buying a home, starting a business, or paying for a child's education (Shapiro, 2004; Shapiro, Oliver, & Meschede, 2009). Black, Latino, and Native American children are more likely to be born into less-advantaged households with modest income and little wealth (Shanks, 2011). Thus, disparities in wealth also have consequences for the next generation. For example, the lack of down payment assistance means that, on average, Blacks take 8 years longer than whites to build home equity; similarly, the lack of assistance with college costs depresses college graduation rates (Asante-Mohammed et al., 2016).

Wealth inequality leads to an inability for many to achieve a secure retirement. As employer-provided pensions are disappearing, older Americans are becoming more dependent on Social Security and personal savings in retirement. This reality just exacerbates racial disparities in earnings, family composition, and employment benefits (Johnson, 2020). Among families between the ages of 31 and 62 years in 2016, 41% of Blacks and 35% of Hispanics had a retirement savings account compared to 68% among white families (Morrissey, 2019). Nearly half of families have no retirement savings at all.

However, families in the top-income quintile are almost seven times more likely to have retirement savings than those in the bottom quintile: 88% versus 13% (Morrissey, 2019). The actual amounts in these accounts are inadequate to replace working income, but also differ greatly by race and education level. In 2016, the median savings in families with retirement accounts was $79,500 for whites, $29,000 for Blacks, and $23,000 for Hispanics. Similarly, college-educated or higher families had median retirement savings balances of $107,000, whereas the median balance for all other education levels ranged between $30,000 and $40,000 (Morrissey, 2019). There are a range of approaches that could help reduce such racial inequities among older Americans, from increasing savings among low-wage workers and increasing preretirement income and assets, to making progressive changes in Social Security and expanding Supplemental Security Income (Johnson, 2020; Williams Shanks & Leigh, 2015).

SPECIFIC POLICY RESPONSES

A range of policy initiatives alone or in concert can begin to address the entrenched economic inequities that mark the United States. These initiatives aim at both income and assets inequality. To reduce economic inequality significantly, a multiprong approach is necessary. The policies described here are important foci for further work, but this is by no means an exhaustive list. Policies ranging from an increased minimum wage to broader healthcare supports, although not discussed here in detail, are also important avenues for change. Social workers are needed to concentrate on many of the avenues for reducing economic inequality. Such policy responses are urgently needed.

Policies Addressing Income Inequality

Among the significant policies that can be developed and strengthened to address the large and growing inequalities in earned income are the ones discussed in the following sections.

Tax Credits

Social workers can work with agencies and policymakers to extend tax credits and to increase their usefulness to clients. Refundable tax credits serve as the largest mechanism redistributing income to poor and near-poor Americans. Their planned expansion is a central feature of President Biden's *Build Back*

Better proposal with important implications for poverty reduction (Acs & Werner, 2021). Together, the Earned Income Tax Credit (EITC) and Child Tax Credit (CTC) transfer approximately $145 billion per year to working families in addition to offsetting income taxes owed (Congressional Budget Office, 2017). Most EITC benefits flow to low- and moderate-earning families with children, although childless workers can claim small benefits. In 2018, more than 26 million households received EITCs. For 2020, maximum amounts range from $538 for childless workers to $6,660 for workers with three or more qualifying children (Internal Revenue Service, 2021). The 2017 tax reform bill increased the value of the CTC to $2,000 per child, the value of which was largely offset by eliminating personal exemptions for many households (Maag, 2019). Unlike the EITC, which focuses on lower income earners, the CTC reaches 90% of families and provides most benefits to households in the top three income quintiles.

The design and administration of tax credits provide several practical and political advantages. Most notably, the EITC is a highly effective antipoverty program, in part because it targets its benefits to households just below the poverty line. Administered by the Internal Revenue Service as part of the annual income tax filing process, the EITC and CTC have high take-up rates and very low operating costs. Unlike other programs for the poor, tax credits do not require annual appropriation, and Congress and the president can only remove them via tax legislation, making them less vulnerable to attack.

These same features create drawbacks as well. The economic benefits that the EITC and the CTC provide to low-income families with children are predicated on employment. Neither program helps the unemployed poor nor those kept out of the labor force by disability or family health or caregiving circumstances. Childless workers do not become eligible for the EITC until age 25 years, and the credit amounts that they receive do not offset payroll taxes so that, after taxes, their net income is often below the poverty line (Marr, Hung, Murray, & Sherman, 2016). Noncustodial parents, including those who actively support their children through caregiving and financial support, receive no benefits beyond the small amounts available to childless workers, although reforms could address this (Maag & Airi, 2020). Last, many EITC claimants rely on paid tax preparers to file their returns, meaning some portion of the refund typically benefits financial services. Importantly, many of these drawbacks are addressed in current federal policy reform proposals.

Universal Child Allowance

A universal child allowance would address some of the weaknesses in family support exacerbated in this time of pandemic, climate-related disasters, and calls for social justice. The safety net for families with children has continued to erode as the number of families living in poverty and deep poverty has increased, and income in these families has become increasingly volatile (Edin & Shaefer, 2016). Most US safety net programs require employment as a condition of eligibility or are designed to move low-income individuals into employment. Families in which the parents are unemployed or sporadically employed have few options for obtaining assistance (Moffitt, 2015). The Supplemental Nutrition Assistance Program benefits provide food but cannot be used for expenses such as rent and utilities. The Temporary Assistance for Needy Families program provides cash assistance, but enrollment has been declining during the past two decades. When the Temporary Assistance for Needy Families program was initially enacted, 68 families received assistance for every 100 families in poverty; that number has since fallen to 23 families receiving assistance for every 100 families in poverty (Center on Budget and Poverty Priorities, 2016).

To address these issues, the child tax allowance and the child tax exemption could be replaced with a monthly universal child tax credit. The amount of the credit could vary with the child's age to reflect the higher costs and demonstrated benefits of providing cash support to very young children (Duncan, Magnuson, & Votruba-Drzal, 2014). Even such income as provided by a tax credit system could be available more generally to children in the poorest families through a universal child allowance (Vervalin, 2018).

This allowance system promises an increased level of basic income support to families in poverty. Furthermore, it is relatively straightforward to administer and to understand, and it provides dependable resources to families who are supporting children. This program could provide family stability for families that currently experience irregular employment, underemployment, as well as unemployment. Regular basic income benefits children's health, school achievement, and overall well-being (Dahl & Lochner, 2012; Marr et al., 2016; Milligan & Stabile, 2011; Strully, Rehkopf, & Xuan, 2010). As noted above, such a universal approach is central to Professor Biden's reform agenda and is being discussed at the time of this writing.

Although clearly of significant benefit to families, the costs of a child allowance system are considerable and not entirely offset by the concurrent proposed elimination of tax credits and exemptions (Harris & Shaefer, 2017). These costs, and the politics of introducing a new and universal program, may make this a difficult program to implement, although current discussions of an expanded CTC move toward a universal child allowance. During the past 5 years, social workers have joined scholars in other fields to develop models of universal child allowances and explore the ways in which these might be implemented (Shaefer et al., 2018). Although the costs could be substantial, evidence indicates that the long-term social and financial value could be great.

Public Employment Programs

Public employment programs, sometimes referred to as *active employment policy*, hire people directly on government projects, and the United States has a history of such programs. Public employment has the potential to reduce unemployment, provide income for families, and build experience and skills for future employment in the private sector (Sherraden, 2014). The Works Progress Administration (WPA) and the Civilian Conservation Corps (CCC) are classic examples of public employment from the 1930s Depression era. At any one time, the WPA employed several millions of people, peaking in 1936 at 40% of all those who were unemployed (Levine, 2010, p. 4). Harry Hopkins, a social worker and advisor to President Franklin D. Roosevelt, led the vision and implementation of the WPA to produce public goods and create jobs. Social workers need to understand and explore the benefits of job support and creation.

The CCC was created in 1933 by an executive order of President Roosevelt to undertake conservation work and employ younger workers. The CCC enrolled a total of 3 million young people, mostly men, between 1933 and 1942, in "essential, imperative" conservation work. During a divisive political period, the CCC enjoyed broad bipartisan support, and CCC alumni continued to express positive views of their CCC experience and its impact on their lives many decades later (Sherraden, 1979; Sherraden & Eberly, 1982).

As demonstrated by these Depression-era policies, public employment, with a little imagination, can become much more than "make work" or "jobs of last resort." With daunting environmental and social tasks facing the United States and other countries in the 21st century, public employment can become a vital response to major issues that are not addressed in the private market, including resource conservation, the transition to nonfossil fuel use, work with disadvantaged children, and support for a growing elderly population. Indeed, such essential tasks are better conceived as "jobs of first resort." Compared to the size of the current US labor force, a CCC for the 21st century would create 1 million new jobs, and a new WPA would create 10 million. Such programs are expensive, but they can also support the infrastructure needs of our changing society. As President Roosevelt and Harry Hopkins believed in the 1930s, when the challenge is great, we should not think small.

Fortunately, calls for a new employment related to infrastructure and the environment are growing. Regarding infrastructure, for example, a call for a Works Progress Administration 2.0, points out that America needs to invest $4.5 trillion by 2025 to repair bridges, roads, and other infrastructure deficiencies. These jobs would also be a platform for apprenticeships and "re-skilling" for 21st-century technology and production (Rosenbaum, 2020). Regarding the environment, a call to employ 7.7 million young people in a new "Tree Army" (as the CCC was sometimes called) came from the president of the National Wildlife

Association (O'Mara, 2020). Both of these job creation themes are also embodied in the Green New Deal proposal, which is gradually finding more footing in the US Congress, and President Biden has recently proposed a new Climate Conservation Corps—not accidentally with the same CCC initials (Editorial Board, 2021). Other current themes in public employment include a greatly expanded Health Corps to fight pandemics, and a Social Service Corps to support aging in place, reduce loneliness among older adults, and strengthen intergenerational bonds. All of these are important jobs, but will not be created by the market economy. They would be excellent national investments.

Employment and Work—Family Policies

To address extreme economic inequality and its consequences comprehensively, policies must also deal with job quality and the numerous aspects of work and family life affecting the quality of life of low-income individuals and families, in addition to increased wages.

Workplace Benefits

The majority of low-level employees, especially those working part time, are not eligible for benefits such as paid parental leave, short-term disability, and even paid sick days. Moreover, employee earnings are a function of wages and hours; hence, the benefit of wage increases such as those discussed earlier can be offset by corresponding reductions in work hours. Thus, policies that encourage employers to hire full-time workers in jobs that provide employer-sponsored benefits are critical.

At the federal level, the 1938 Fair Labor Standards Act (FLSA) includes basic minimum employment standards related to child labor, long work hours, and wage floors. Beyond this, the FLSA provides few protections to workers at the low end of the labor market (Fortman, 2014; Lambert, 2020). For example, beyond minimum wage and overtime laws, the FLSA does not address minimum hours, on-call employment, or other measures related to work timing, and there are no federal paid sick leave laws that cover workers. Slightly more than half (56%) of workers are eligible for the Family and Medical Leave Act, which requires employers who hire more than 50 employees to provide 12 weeks of unpaid leave for specific medical and caregiving situations for employees with at least 1,250 work hours over a 12-month period (Brown, Herr, Roy, & Klerman, 2020). Not surprisingly, low-earning workers report needing but not taking a caregiving or medical leave to a much greater extent than their higher-earning counterparts (Brown et al., 2020). The COVID-19 pandemic has elevated the need for covering sick leave; indeed pandemic-related laws have included requirements that employers pay for absences related to COVID-19 sickness and caregiving for COVID-19-related family members.

Although there were efforts to update federal standards and expand federal work–family supports during the Obama administration, efforts stalled during the Trump administration. Even so, state and local governments have been actively pursuing measures related to employer hiring and scheduling practices, minimum wage increases, mandatory sick days, and paid family leave. For example, in addition to several local and state minimum and living wage successes (Economic Policy Institute, 2021), at this writing, one state and six municipalities have passed comprehensive scheduling laws aimed at improving the predictability of work hours and providing workers greater input into work schedules (Lambert, 2020); 12 states and the District of Columbia, and more than 20 municipalities require employers to provide some paid sick days (Kaiser Family Foundation, 2020); and nine states and the District of Columbia have enacted paid family and medical leave laws or use state disability insurance to address parental leave supports (Kaiser Family Foundation, 2020).

The effects of the plethora of local initiatives are currently unknown. However, there are several studies in the field or completed recently related to implementation and outcomes of various laws. Although it is outside of the scope of this chapter to review these studies individually, early findings suggest the power of both employers and worker voice in shaping the content of local laws, several challenges to implementation and the importance of enforcement, and evidence of some early benefits for workers, especially regarding the use of earned sick time and paid family leave to support health and caregiving (Marotta & Greene, 2019; Romich, 2017; Schneider, 2020; Ybarra, Stanczyk, & Ha, 2019). Moreover, a randomized experiment in a US retail chain showed promising results in terms of increased productivity and sales from adoption of scheduling practices that improve work schedule stability, predictability, and employee input into work timing (Lambert, 2020; Williams, Lambert, & Kesavan, 2017).

Child Care and Early Education Supports

Three fourths of young children spend time in nonparental child care and early education settings while their parents work (Laughlin, 2013). The landscape of care ranges widely from preschool and center-based programs to home-based arrangements with licensed child-care providers and informal caregivers. These care settings provide essential caregiving support to working parents and to parents in higher education and training; they also serve as critical developmental contexts for children, who typically spend more than 30 hours per week in nonparental care (Laughlin, 2013). Thus, the developmental well-being of children and the economic livelihood of families are threatened without access to stable, high-quality, safe, and affordable care (Chaudry, Morrissey, Weiland, & Yoshikawa, 2017).

However, despite the almost universal demand for child care and early education services among working families, families face significant barriers finding and maintaining child care that meets their needs in terms of cost, quality, scheduling, and convenience. These caregiving challenges are exacerbated by geographic inequities in child-care access and by nonstandard and variable work schedules that do not match the schedules of most formal child-care and early education programs (Henly & Adams, 2018). These challenges are likely to increase given the serious financial losses and public health concerns that child-care programs have endured during the COVID-19 pandemic.

The considerable public resources that support the caregiving needs of families are insufficient to meet demand. The federal Child Care Development Block Grant (CCDBG) subsidizes the cost of child care across a range of settings for eligible low-income families, with the goal of improving the education, training, and employment outcomes of parents and the developmental well-being of their children in care. However, CCDBG program funding covers only 15% of eligible families (Chien, 2015), and subsidy spells are brief—median spells are 4 to 8 months across states (Swenson, 2014)—as a result of a range of factors, including complex program rules, administrative hassles, and instability in families' employment, housing, and other life domains (Ha & Meyer, 2010; Henly et al., 2017; Sandstrom & Chaudry, 2012). The 2014 reauthorization of the CCDBG made important changes to the law designed to improve parent access, program quality, and provider supports, but the reauthorization did not reverse revenue shortfalls that have kept the program from meeting its key objectives for program improvement and increased coverage. Fortunately, states have received additional federal dollars of late – especially as part of pandemic-related stimulus spending. Other government programs, such as the federal Head Start and state preschool programs (some funded with a combination of federal and state dollars), focus directly on expanding children's early education opportunities, with less attention to the needs of working parents. The return on investment of high-quality preschool and Head Start programs is clear (Chaudry et al., 2017; Heckman, 2011; Magnuson & Duncan, 2016). However, preschool remains underfunded, program availability and quality vary, many programs do not serve infants and toddlers, and many preschool programs are part time and provide only daytime weekday care. There are currently ongoing national, as well as more local, discussions about further support for child care (Smialek, 2021).

Social workers can support state and federal expansion of supports for child care to ensure they are available for all families, regardless of their ability to pay or their work schedules. Policies should promote access to all types of safe, legal, quality care (care in centers and preschools, licensed family child care, and informal home-based care) to address the diverse caregiving needs and preferences of families. It is critical that policies operate to reduce families' out-of-pocket expenses (e.g., refundable tax credits and child-care subsidies) and increase child-care supply (e.g., direct investments in early care and education). Families need high-quality and affordable arrangements that are proximate to home and/or work, and available during their work, school, and training hours. In addition, explicit attention to the training, technical support, and infrastructure needs of providers, as well as their salary and benefit opportunities, is critical to improving both provider job quality and program quality.

Policies for Lifelong Inclusive Asset-building

There are many possible approaches to help families build wealth. This section discusses several ideas, but it ends with the primary recommendation for a lifelong asset-building policy that is inclusive and progressive (Sherraden, 1991). One possibility is to focus on emergency savings. Offering low- to moderate-income households access to safe accounts and/or financial instruments with incentives for maintaining short-term savings is a promising strategy. Many programs incorporate this concept, especially with refunds received at tax time (Azurdia & Freedman, 2016).

Another approach is to capitalize business startups, including microenterprise and other individual entrepreneurship ventures, as well as cooperatives and community-initiated ventures. Such investment could spark employment and generate pride in producing quality local products and services. Federal loan programs administered by the Small Business Administration and the US Treasury Department's Community Development Financial Institution Fund are limited, and new funding pathways are necessary. In addition, startups could require protection from unfair competition by large firms (Cramer, 2014). Cooperatives combine social and economic development, and historically have been a source of economic independence in the Black community (Gordon Nembhard, 2014).

About $634 billion in tax benefits in 2019 went to subsidize retirement, housing, and other financial investments. However, almost 80% of these dollars go to the top quintile of income earners, whereas the bottom 40% of income earners see almost none of this money (Nieves, Ain, & Newville, 2020). These funds could be redeployed to ensure everyone has retirement savings, access to affordable housing, and secure pathways to homeownership. The tax code would be more equitable, and the country would be in better shape economically. In the past, many argued that the country could not afford to be so generous in tax subsidies and redistribution. In response to the COVID-19 pandemic, Congress passed the Coronavirus, Aid, Relief, and Economic Security Act at a cost of $1.7 trillion, and has both considered and passed other emergency relief bills. Although meeting immediate needs is important in the short run, investment in greater economic security over the long run to make asset-building more inclusive can also be prioritized.

Last, we have proposed child development accounts as a national platform for universal and progressive asset-building (Huang, Sherraden, Clancy, Sherraden, & Shanks, 2017; Sherraden, 1991). By enrolling all newborns automatically in existing financial platforms and providing additional financial incentives to financially vulnerable groups, everyone has access to asset-building mechanisms and saving. These are recommended key design elements (Clancy & Beverly, 2017), and seven states have passed a universal version of this idea, which was first piloted in a rigorous randomized experiment (Sherraden et al., 2015). A generous version of child development accounts called *baby bonds* has been proposed by Hamilton and Darity (2010), and was introduced in a bill by Cory Booker (Kijakazi & Carther, 2020). Such investments would reduce wealth inequality by ensuring that no individual begins life without assets.

SOCIAL WORK POLICY, ADVOCACY, AND PRACTICE

In the context of increasing extreme inequality, and the enormous challenges of 2020 and 2021, social workers can work with a renewed focus on economic justice. Our future efforts require strong coalitions with like-minded professional allies, the integration of economic inequality issues with social work education, and evaluation of our progress with both process and outcome measurements. For instance, social workers and allies should recognize and work to bring to fruition the possibilities and promise of, as well as increase the value of, refundable tax credits. In practice, social workers should educate families about the EITC, and about the costs and benefits of using paid preparers to file (Beverly, 2002). Social workers should advocate expanded access for childless workers and noncustodial parents, and either increased benefits or integration with other supports such as a universal child credit. Last, social workers should advocate for the development of low-cost or nonprofit tax preparation services and should educate consumers about their advantages.

Social workers can work with unions, employers, and agencies to obtain more humane and regular working conditions, wages, and benefits. They can support programs that provide families with regular schedules and income. They can help develop and support a full range of child-care options for low-income working parents.

Social workers can advocate at both the local level and the federal level for emergency savings programs, a more equitable distribution of tax benefits for retirement and housing, and greater economic support for college access initiatives and for child care. Ideally, the passage of a lifelong asset-building policy that is progressive and inclusive could help achieve all these goals.

The extreme and growing income and wealth inequality that exists in the United States is troubling on many levels. When power and economic resources are concentrated in the hands of a few, it threatens our democratic institutions and leads to undue suffering for families and children. Social work research, teaching, and practice working in concert can generate and advocate for practical solutions to reducing these inequalities. It is a grand challenge worthy of our focused effort and engagement. The issues and policy directions described in this chapter align with requirements of the profession's educational credentialing agency: the Council on Social Work Education. For instance, advancing "human rights and social and economic justice" is a core competency, and educational programs training bachelor's- or master's-level social workers should develop this competency. As a grand challenge working group, we seek to understand more fully and support how social work educational programs serve these aims. This work may lead to developing new learning materials or strategies to help student social workers learn practice skills for combatting modern economic inequality.

Substantial and inclusive economic change requires political, economic, and policy intervention at federal, state, and local levels. Social workers can develop detailed evidence and metrics for success in these arenas, and also design, propose, and assess innovations in services, programs, and policies. Progress requires specification of measurable goals for reducing extreme economic inequality, and also careful assessment of efforts to reach those goals. During the coming years, workgroups within this grand challenge will continue to design and test strategies, and apply informative metrics for evaluating these efforts.

REFERENCES

Abraham, K., Haltiwanger, J., Sandusky, K., & Spletzer, J. (2017). Measuring and accounting for innovation in the twenty-first century. Cambridge, Ma.: National Bureau of Economic Research.

Acs, G. & Werner, K (2021). How a permanent expansion of the child tax credit could affect poverty. Washington D.C.: The Urban Institute. Retrieved from https://www.urban.org/research/publication/how-permanent-expansion-child-tax-credit-could-affect-poverty

Akee, R., Jones, M. R., & Porter, S. R. (2019). Race matters: Income shares, income inequality, and income mobility for all U.S. races. *Demography, 56*, 999–1021.

Ananat, E. O., & Gassman-Pines, A. (2021). Work schedule unpredictability: Daily occurrence and effects on workers and families. *Journal of Marriage and Family, 83*, 10–26.

Asante-Mohammed, D., Collins, C., Hoxie, J., & Nieves, E. (2016). The ever-growing racial wealth gap. Washington, DC: Institute for Policy Studies. Retrieved from http://www.ips-dc.org/wp-content/uploads/2016/08/The-Ever-Growing-Gap-CFED_IPS-Final-2.pdf

Autor, D. (2010). The polarization of job opportunities in the U.S. labor market: Implications for employment and earnings. *Community Investments, 23*, 11–41.

Azurdia, G., & Freedman, S. (2016). Encouraging nonretirement savings at tax time: Final impact findings from the SaveUSA evaluation. Retrieved from https://www.mdrc.org/sites/default/files/SaveUSA_FinalReport_ExecSummary.pdf

Berger, L. M., Hill, J., & Waldfogel, J. (2005). Maternity leave, early maternal employment and child health and development in the US. *The Economic Journal, 115,* F29–F47.

Bernhardt, A., Spiller, M. W., & Theodore, N. (2013). Employers gone Rogue: Explaining industry variation in violations of workplace laws. *ILR Review, 66*(4), 808–832. Retrievedfromhttps://journals.sagepub.com/doi/10.1177/001979391306600404

Beverly, S. G. (2002). What social workers need to know about the Earned Income Tax Credit. *Social Work, 47,* 259–266.

Bhutta, N., Bricker, J., Chang, A. C., Dettling, L. J., Goodman, S., Hsu, J. W., . . . Windle, R. (2020). Changes in US family finances from 2016 to 2019: Evidence from the survey of consumer finances. *Federal Reserve Bulletin, 106*(5), 1–42.

Bricker, J., Goodman, S., Moore, K. B., Henriques Volz, A., & Ruh, D. (2020). Wealth and income concentration in the SCF: 1989–2019. FEDS Notes (2020-9-28-1.

Brown, S., Herr, J., Roy, R., & Klerman, J. A. (2020). *Employee and worksite perspectives of the Family and Medical Leave Act: Results from the 2018 surveys.* Rockville, MD: Abt Associates. Retrieved from https://www.abtassociates.com/files/Projects/PDFs/2020/whd_fmla2018surveyresults_finalreport_aug2020.pdf

Callahan, D. (2013, August 20). Low-wage work and the coming retirement crisis. Demos Policyshop. Retrieved from http://www.demos.org/blog/8/20/13/low-wage-work-and-coming-retirement-crisis

Caner, A., & Wolff, E. N. (2004). Asset poverty in the United States, 1984–99: Evidence from the Panel Study of Income Dynamics. *Review of Income and Wealth, 50,* 493–518.

Center on Budget and Poverty Priorities. (2016). Chart book: TANF at 20. Retrieved from https://www.cbpp.org/research/family-income-support/chart-book-tanf-at-20

Chang, M. (2015). *Women and wealth.* Evanston, IL: Asset Funders Network.

Chaudry, A., Morrissey, T., Weiland, C., & Yoshikawa, H. (2017). *Cradle to kindergarten: A new plan to combat inequality.* New York, NY: Russell Sage Foundation.

Chien, N. (2015). *Estimates of child care eligibility and receipt for fiscal year 2012.* ASPE issue brief. Washington, DC: Office of the Assistant Secretary for Planning and Evaluation, Office of Human Services Policy, US Department of Health and Human Services. Retrieved from https://aspe.hhs.gov/sites/default/files/pdf/153591/ChildEligibility.pdf

Clancy, M. M., & Beverly, S. G. (2017). *Statewide child development account policies: Key design elements.* CSD policy report no. 17–30. St. Louis, MO: Washington University, Center for Social Development. Retrieved from https://openscholarship.wustl.edu/csd_research/43/

Clawson, D., & Gerstel, N. (2014). *Unequal time: Gender, class and family in employment schedules.* New York, NY: Russell Sage Foundation.

Congressional Budget Office. 2017. Spending projections (supplemental data file): The budget and economic outlook: 2017 to 2027. Retrieved from www.cbo.gov/publication/52370

Cramer, R. (2014). Foundations of an asset-based social policy agenda. In R. Cramer & T. R. Williams Shanks (Eds.), *The assets perspective: The rise of asset building and its impact on social policy* (pp. 245–261). New York, NY: Palgrave Macmillan.

Dahl, G. B., & Lochner, L. (2012). The impact of family income on child achievement: Evidence from the Earned Income Tax Credit. *American Economic Review, 102,* 1927–1956.

Duncan, G. J., Magnuson, K., & Votruba-Drzal, E. (2014). Boosting family income to promote child development. *Future of Children, 24,* 99–120.

Economic Policy Institute. (2015, June 15). A more comprehensive measure of slack in the labor market. Retrieved from http://stateofworkingamerica.org/charts/number-of-underemployed

Economic Policy Institute. (2017a). State of working America: All races and ethnicities hurt by recession, racial and ethnic disparities persist. Retrieved from http://www.stateofworkingamerica.org/charts/underemployment-by-race-and-ethnicity

Economic Policy Institute. (2017b). State of working America: Underemployment highest for those with least education. Retrieved from http://www.stateofworkingamerica.org/charts/underemployment-education

Economic Policy Institute. (2019). The productivity-pay gap. Retrieved from https://www.epi.org/productivity-pay-gap/

Economic Policy Institute. (2021). Minimum wage tracker. Retrieved from https://www.epi.org/minimum-wage-tracker/.

Edin, K., & Shaefer, H. L. (2016). *$2.00 a day: Living on almost nothing in America*. New York, NY: Houghton Mifflin.

Editorial Board. (2021, February 19). Biden's Climate Conservation Corps could be an old answer for new problems. *Los Angeles Times*. Retrieved from https://www.latimes.com/opinion/story/2021-02-18/biden-climate-conservation-corps-global-warming-jobs

Edwards, R., & Smith, S. M. (2020). *Job market remains tight in 2019, as the unemployment rate falls to its lowest level since 1969*. Washington, D.C.: Monthly labor review. US Bureau of Labor Statistics.

Elsby, M., Hobijn, B., & Şahin, A. (2013). The decline of the U.S. labor share. *Brookings Papers on Economic Activity, Fall*, 1–63.

Enchautegui, M. E., Johnson, M., & Gelatt, J. (2015). *Who minds the kids when mom works a nonstandard schedule?* Urban Institute Report. Retrieved from http://www.urban.org/sites/default/files/publication/64696/2000307-Who-Minds-the-Kids-When-Mom-Works-a-Nonstandard-Schedule.pdf

Federal Reserve. (2019). Report on the economic well-being of U.S. households in 2018: May 2019. Federal Reserve. Retrieved from https://www.federalreserve.gov/publications/2019-economic-well-being-of-us-households-in-2018-dealing-with-unexpected-expenses.htm

Finnigan, R. (2018). Varying weekly work hours and earnings instability in the Great Recession. *Social Science Research, 74*, 96–107.

Fortman, L. (2014). A paper series commemorating the 75th anniversary of the Fair Labor Standards Act. US Department of Labor and Institute for Research on Labor and Employment at the University of California, Berkeley. Retrieved from https://www.dol.gov/sites/dolgov/files/OASP/legacy/files/FLSAPaperSeries.pdf

Gassman-Pines, A. (2011). Low-income mothers' nighttime and weekend work: Daily associations with child behavior, mother–child interactions and mood. *Family Relations, 60*, 15–29.

Golden, L. (2016). Still falling short on hours and pay: Part-time work becoming new normal. Economic Policy Institute. Retrieved from https://www.epi.org/publication/still-falling-short-on-hours-and-pay-part-time-work-becoming-new-normal/

Golden, L. (2020). *Part-time workers pay a big-time penalty*. Washington, DC: Economic Policy Institute. Retrieved from https://www.epi.org/publication/part-time-pay-penalty/

Gordon Nembhard, J. (2014). *Collective courage: A history of African American cooperative economic thought and practice*. University Park, PA: Pennsylvania State University Press.

Gould, E. (2016). Wage inequality continued its 35-year rise in 2015. Washington, DC: Economic Policy Institute. Retrieved from http://www.epi.org/publication/wage-inequality-continued-its-35-year-rise-in-2015

Grusky, D. B., Mattingly, M. J., & Varner, C. E. (2016). The poverty and inequality report. *Pathways* [special issue]. Retrieved from http://inequality.stanford.edu/sites/default/files/Pathways-SOTU-2016.pdf

Ha, Y., & Meyer, D. R. (2010). Child care subsidy patterns: Are exits related to economic setbacks or economic successes? *Children and Youth Services Review, 32*, 346–355.

Hacker, J. S. (2006). *Universal Insurance: Enhancing economic security to promote opportunity*. Washington, D. C.: The Hamilton Project. Retrieved from https://www.hamiltonproject.org/assets/legacy/files/downloads_and_links/Universal_Insurance_Enhancing_Economic_Security_to_Promote_Opportunity.pdf

Haider, A. (2021). The basic facts about children in poverty. Center for American Progress. Retrieved from https://www.americanprogress.org/issues/poverty/reports/2021/01/12/494506/basic-facts-children-poverty/

Hamilton, D., & Darity, W. (2010). Can "baby bonds" eliminate the racial wealth gap in putative post-racial America? *The Review of Black Political Economy, 37*, 207–216.

Hamilton, D., Darity, W., Price, A. E., Sridharan, V., & Tippett, R. (2015). Umbrellas don't make it rain: Why studying and working hard isn't enough for Black Americans. A joint publication of The New School, Duke Center for Social Equity, and INSIGHT Center for Community Economic Development. Retrieved from https://gallery.mailchimp.com/bf2b9b3cf3fdd8861943fca2f/files/Umbrellas_Dont_Make_It_Rain8.pdf

Han, W.-J. (2004). Nonstandard work schedules and child care decisions: Evidence from the NICHD study of early child care. *Early Childhood Research Quarterly, 19*, 231–256.

Han, W.-J. (2005). Maternal nonstandard work schedules and child cognitive outcomes. *Child Development, 76*, 137–154.

Han, W.-J. (2008). Shift work and child behavioral outcomes. *Work, Employment and Society, 22*, 67–87.

Harknett, K., Schneider, D., & Luhr, S. (2020). Who cares if parents have unpredictable work schedules? Just-in-time work schedules and child care arrangements. *Social Problems*.

Harris, D., & Shaefer, H. L. (2017, April 19). Fighting child poverty with a universal child allowance. *The American Prospect*. Retrieved from http://prospect.org/article/fighting-child-poverty-universal-child-allowance

Heckman, J. (2011). The economics of inequality: The value of early childhood education. *American Educator, 35*, 31–35.

Henly, J. R., & Adams, G. (2018). Increasing access to quality child care for four priority populations: Challenges and opportunities with CCDBG reauthorization. The Urban Institute. Retrieved from https://www.urban.org/research/publication/increasing-access-quality-child-care-four-priority-populations

Henly, J. R., & Lambert, S. J. (2014). Unpredictable work timing in retail jobs: Implications for employee work–life conflict. *Industrial and Labor Relations Review, 67*, 986–1016.

Henly, J. R., Lambert, S. J., & Dresser, L. J. (2021). The New Realities of Working-Class Jobs Since the Great Recession: Innovations in Employment Regulation, Social Policy, and Worker Organization. What has happened to the American Working Class since the Great Recession? (2009–2019). *ANNALS of The American Academy of Political and Social Science, 695*(1), 208–224.

Henly, J. R., Sandstrom, H., & Pilarz, A. (2017). Child care assistance as work–family support: Meeting the economic and caregiving needs of low-income working families in the US. In M. las Heras, N. Chinchilla, & M. Grau (Eds.), *Work–family balance in light of globalization and technology* (pp. 241–265). Newcastle-upon-Tyne, UK: Cambridge Scholars Publishing.

Henly, J. R., Shaefer, H. L., & Waxman, R. E. (2006). Nonstandard work schedules: Employer- and employee-driven flexibility in retail jobs. *Social Service Review, 80*, 609–634.

Holzer, H. J. (2015). *Job market polarization and U.S. worker skills: A tale of two middles*. Washington DC: Brookings. Retrieved from https://www.brookings.edu/research/job-market-polarization-and-u-s-worker-skills-a-tale-of-two-middles

Howell, D. R., & Kalleberg, A. L. (2019). Declining job quality in the United States: Explanations and evidence. *RSF: The Russell Sage Foundation Journal of the Social Sciences, 5*, 1–53.

Huang, J., Sherraden, M. S., Clancy, M., Sherraden, M., & Shanks, T. (2017). Start lifelong asset building with universal and progressive child development accounts. Grand Challenges for Social Work policy action statement. Retrieved from http://aaswsw.org/wp-content/uploads/2017/03/PAS.11.1-v2.pdf.

Internal Revenue Service. (2021). Earned Income and Earned Income Tax Credit (EITC) tables. Retrieved from https://www.irs.gov/credits-deductions/individuals/earned-income-tax-credit/earned-income-and-earned-income-tax-credit-eitc-tables

Jardim, E., Long, M. C., Plotnick, R., van Inwegen, E., Vigdor, J., & Wething, H. (2020). *Minimum wage increases and low-wage employment: Evidence from Seattle*. Seattle, WA: University of Washington.

Johnson, R. W. (2020). How can policymakers close the racial gap in retirement security? Urban Institute. Retrieved from https://www.urban.org/sites/default/files/publication/103045/how-can-policymakers-close-the-racial-gap-in-retirement-security_0.pdf

Kalil, A. (2016). *How economic inequality affects children's outcomes*. Washington, DC: Washington Center for Equitable Growth. Retrieved from http://equitablegrowth.org/human-capital/how-economic-inequality-affects-childrens-outcomes

Kalleberg, A. L. (2011). *Good jobs, bad jobs: The rise of polarized and precarious employment systems in the United States, 1970s–2000s*. American Sociological Association Rose Series in Sociology. New York, NY: Russell Sage Foundation.

Kaiser Family Foundation. (2020). Paid family and sick leave in the U.S. Retrieved from https://www.kff.org/womens-health-policy/fact-sheet/paid-family-leave-and-sick-days-in-the-u-s/

Karabarbounis, L., & Neiman, B. (2013). The global decline of the labor share. NBER working paper no. 19136. Retrieved from http://www.nber.org/papers/w19136

Kijakazi, K., & Carther, A. (2020). How baby bonds could help Americans start adulthood strong and narrow the racial wealth gap. Urban Institute. Retrieved from https://www.urban.org/urban-wire/how-baby-bonds-couldhelp-americans-start-adulthood-strong-and-narrow-racial-wealth-gap.

Lambert, S. J. (2008). Passing the buck: Labor flexibility practices that transfer risk onto hourly workers. *Human Relations, 61*, 1203–1227.

Lambert, S. (2020). Fair work schedules for the U.S. economy and society: What's reasonable, feasible, and effective. Washington Center for Equitable Growth. Retrieved from https://equitablegrowth.org/fair-work-schedules-for-the-u-s-economy-and-society-whats-reasonable-feasible-and-effective/

Lambert, S. J., Fugiel, P. J., & Henly, J. R. (2014). Precarious work schedules among early-career employees in the US: A national snapshot. EINet: Employment Instability, Family Well-Being, and Social Policy Network research brief. Retrieved from https://ssa.uchicago.edu/sites/default/files/uploads/lambert.fugiel.henly_.precarious_work_schedules.august2014_0.pdf

Lambert, S. J., Haley-Lock, A., & Henly, J. R. (2012). Schedule flexibility in hourly jobs: Unanticipated consequences and promising directions. *Community, Work and Family*, *15*, 293–315.

Lambert, S. J., & Henly, J. R. (2012). Frontline managers matter: Labour flexibility practices and sustained employment in US retail jobs. In C. Warhurst, F. Carré, P. Findlay, & C. Tilly (Eds.), *Are bad jobs inevitable? Trends, determinants and responses to job quality in the twenty-first century* (pp. 143–159). Basingstoke, UK: Palgrave Macmillan.

Lambert, S. J., & Henly, J. R. (2013). Double jeopardy: The misfit between welfare-to-work requirements and job realities. In E. Brodkin & G. Marston (Eds.), *Work and the welfare state: The politics and management of policy change* (pp. 69–84). Washington, DC: Georgetown University Press.

Lambert, S. J., Henly, J. R., & Kim, J. (2019). Precarious work schedules as a source of economic insecurity and institutional distrust. *RSF: The Russell Sage Foundation Journal of the Social Sciences*, *5*, 218–257.

Laughlin, L. (2013). *Who's minding the kids? Child care arrangements: Spring, 2011*. Washington, DC: US Census Bureau. Retrieved from https://www.census.gov/prod/2013pubs/p70-135.pdf

Levine, L. (2010). Job creation programs of the Great Depression: The WPA and CCC. Retrieved from https://ecommons.cornell.edu/xmlui/handle/1813/77652.

Lui, M., Robles, B., Leondar-Wright, B., Brewer, R., & Adamson, R. (2006). *The color of wealth: The story behind the U.S. racial wealth divide*. New York, NY: The New Press.

Maag, E. (2019). *Shifting child tax benefits in the TCJA left most families about the same*. Washington, DC: Tax Policy Center.

Maag, E., & Airi, N. (2020). Moving forward with the Earned Income Tax Credit and Child Tax Credit: Analysis of proposals to expand refundable tax credits. *National Tax Journal*, *73*, 1163–1186.

Magnuson, K., & Duncan, G. (2016). Can early childhood interventions decrease inequality of economic opportunity? *Russell Sage Foundation Journal of the Social Sciences*, *2*, 123–141. Retrieved from https://muse.jhu.edu/article/616923/pdf

Marotta, J., & Greene, S. (2019). *Paid sick days: What does the research tell us about the effectiveness of local action?* Washington, DC: Urban Institute.

Marr, C., Hung, C.-C., Murray, C., & Sherman, A. (2016). *Strengthening the EITC for childless workers would reward work and reduce poverty*. Washington, DC: Center on Budget and Policy Priorities. Retrieved from https://www.cbpp.org/research/federal-tax/strengthening-the-eitc-for-childless-workers-would-promote-work-and-reduce

McCrate, E., Lambert, S. J., & Henly, J. R. (2019). Competing for hours: Unstable work schedules and underemployment among hourly workers in Canada. *Cambridge Journal of Economics*, *43*(5), 1287–1314.

McKee-Ryan, F. M., & Harvey, J. (2011). "I have a job, but . . .": A review of underemployment. *Journal of Management*, *37*, 962–996.

McKernan, S. M., Ratcliffe, C., Steuerle, E., & Zhang, S. (2013). *Less than equal: Racial disparities in wealth accumulation*. Washington, DC: Urban Institute.

Miller, J. (2020). COVID-19 and the most vulnerable. *Harvard Medical School News & Research*. Retrieved from https://hms.harvard.edu/news/covid-19-most-vulnerable

Milligan, K., & Stabile, M. (2011). Do child tax benefits affect the well-being of children? Evidence from Canadian child benefit expansions. *American Economic Journal: Economic Policy, 3*, 175–205.

Moffitt, R. A. (2015). The deserving poor, the family, and the U.S. welfare system. *Demography, 52*, 729–749.

Morrissey, M. (2019). *The state of American retirement savings*. Washington, DC: Economic Policy Institute. Retrieved from https://www.epi.org/publication/the-state-of-american-retirement-savings/

Nadeau, C. (2020). New living wage data available for now available on the tool. Retrieved from https://livingwage.mit.edu/articles/61-new-living-wage-data-for-now-available-on-the-tool

Nam, Y., Huang, J., & Sherraden, M. (2008). Asset definitions. In S.-M. McKernan & M. Sherraden (Eds.), *Asset building and low-income families* (pp. 1–31). Washington, DC: Urban Institute.

National Conference of State Legislatures. (2021). State minimum wages. Retrieved from https://www.ncsl.org/research/labor-and-employment/state-minimum-wage-chart.aspx

National Low Income Housing Coalition. (2020). Out of reach: The high cost of housing. Retrieved from https://reports.nlihc.org/sites/default/files/oor/OOR_2020_Mini-Book.pdf

Nicholson, W., & Needles, K. (2006). Unemployment insurance: Strengthening the relationship between theory and policy. *The Journal of Economic Perspectives 20*, 47–70.

Nieves, E., Ain, J., & Newville, D. (2020). *From upside down to right-side up: Turning the tax code into an engine for economic and racial equity*. Washington, DC: Prosperity Now. Retrieved from https://prosperitynow.org/sites/default/files/resources/RSU_2020_Full_Report-7.13.2020.pdf

Nunn, R., & Shambaugh, J. (2020).*Whose wages are rising and why? Policy 2020*. Washington, D.C.: The Brookings Institution. Retrieved from https://www.brookings.edu/policy2020/votervital/whose-wages-are-rising-and-why/

O'Mara, C. (2020, May 18). 7.7 Million young people are unemployed: We need a new "Tree Army." *New York Times*. Retrieved from https://www.nytimes.com/2020/05/18/opinion/coronavirus-unemployment-youth.html

Organization for Economic Co-operation and Development. (2014). OECD employment outlook 2014. Retrieved from http://www.oecd-ilibrary.org/employment/oecd-employment-outlook-2014/summary/english_45c7c585-en?isSummaryOf=/content/book/empl_outlook-2014-en

Organization for Economic Co-operation and Development. (2016). Family database. Retrieved from http://www.oecd.org/els/CO_2_2_Child_Poverty.pdf

Presser, H. B. (2003). *Working in a 24/7 economy: Challenges for American families*. New York, NY: Russell Sage Foundation.

Presser, H. B., & Cox, A. G. (1997). The work schedules of low-educated American women and welfare reform. *Monthly Labor Review, April*, 25–34.

Prosperity Now. (2020). Prosperity Now scorecard. Retrieved from https://scorecard.prosperitynow.org/main-findings#takeaways

Romich J. (2017). Local mandate improves equity of paid sick leave coverage: Seattle's experience. *BMC Public Health, 17*, 60. Retrieved from https://bmcpublichealth.biomedcentral.com/articles/10.1186/s12889-016-3925-9#citeas

Rosenbaum, M. (2020). To solve America's unemployment crisis, we need to follow a plan from the Great Depression. *Business Insider*. Retrieved from https://www.businessinsider.com/covid-19-jobs-crisis-unemployment-new-deal-wpa-2020-9

Sandstrom, H., & Chaudry, A. (2012). You have to choose your childcare to fit your work: Childcare decision-making among low-income working families. *Journal of Children and Poverty, 18*, 89–119.

Schmitt, J., Shierholz, H., & Mishel, L. (2013). Don't blame the robots: Assessing the job polarization explanation of growing wage inequality. Economic Policy Institute. Retrieved from https://www.epi.org/publication/technology-inequality-dont-blame-the-robots/

Schneider, D. (2020). Paid sick leave in Washington state: Evidence on employee outcomes, 2016–2018. *American Journal of Public Health, 110*, 499–504. Retrieved from https://ajph.aphapublications.org/doi/full/10.2105/AJPH.2019.305481

Schneider, D., & Harknett, K. (2019). Consequences of routine work-schedule instability for worker health and well-being. *American Sociological Review, 84*, 82–114.

Shaefer, H. L., Collyer, S., Duncan, G., Edin, K., Garfinkel, I, Harris, D., . . . Yoshikawa, H. (2018). A universal child allowance: A plan to reduce poverty and income instability among children in the United States. *The Russell Sage Foundation Journal of the Social Sciences, 4*(2). Retrieved from https://muse.jhu.edu/article/687574

Shanks, T. (2011). *Diverging pathways: How wealth shapes opportunity for children*. Oakland, CA: INSIGHT Center for Community Involvement. Retrieved from http://ww1.insightcced.org/uploads/CRWG/DivergingPathways.pdf

Shapiro, T. (2004). *The hidden cost of being African American: How wealth perpetuates inequality*. New York, NY: Oxford University Press.

Shapiro, T., Oliver, M. L., & Meschede, T. (2009). *The asset security and opportunity index*. Waltham, MA: Institute on Assets and Social Policy.

Sherraden, M. (1979). *The Civilian Conservation Corps: Effectiveness of the camps*. (Doctoral dissertation). University of Michigan, Ann Arbor, MI.

Sherraden, M. (1991). *Assets and the poor: A new American welfare policy*. Armonk, NY: Sharpe.

Sherraden, M. (2014). Asset building research and policy: Pathways, progress, and potential of a social innovation. In R. Cramer & T. R. Williams Shanks (Eds.), *The assets perspective: The rise of asset building and its impact on social policy* (pp. 263–284). London, UK: Palgrave Macmillan.

Sherraden, M., Clancy, M., Nam, Y., Huang, J., Kim, Y., Beverly, S. G., . . . Purnell, J. Q. (2015). Testing universal accounts at birth: Early results from the SEED for Oklahoma Kids experiment. *Journal of the Society for Social Work and Research, 6*, 541–564.

Sherraden, M., & Eberly, D. J. (Eds.). (1982). *National service: Social, economic, and military impacts*. New York, NY: Pergamon.

Smeeding, T. M. (2005). Public policy, economic inequality, and poverty: The United States in comparative perspective. *Social Science Quarterly, 86*, 955–983.

Smialek, J. (2021). Powell says better child care policies might lift women in work force. *New York Times*. Retrieved from https://www.nytimes.com/2021/02/24/business/economy/fed-powell-child-care.html

Strully, K. W., Rehkopf, D. H., & Xuan, Z. (2010). Effects of prenatal poverty on infant health. *American Sociological Review, 74*(4), 534–562.

Sullivan, M., Dietrich, S., Traub, A., & Ruetschlin, C. (2015). *The racial wealth gap: Why policy matters*. Washington, DC: Demos. Retrieved from http://www.demos.org/publication/racial-wealth-gap-why-policy-matters

Swenson, K. (2014). *Child care subsidy duration and caseload dynamics*. Washington, DC: US Department of Health and Human Services. Retrieved from https://aspe.hhs.gov/report/child-care-subsidy-duration-and-caseload-dynamics-multi-state-examination

US Bureau of Labor Statistics. (2020a). Characteristics of minimum wage workers, 2019. BLS Reports, report 1085. Retrieved from https://www.bls.gov/opub/reports/minimum-wage/2019/home.htm

US Bureau of Labor Statistics. (2020b). Employee benefits in the United States, March 2020. News release, Bureau of Labor Statistics, US Department of Labor. USDL-20-1792. Retrieved from https://www.bls.gov/news.release/pdf/ebs2.pdf

US Bureau of Labor Statistics. (2020c). Selected paid leave benefits. Retrieved from https://www.bls.gov/news.release/ebs2.t06.htm

US Bureau of Labor Statistics. (2021). The employment situation: January 2021. US Department of Labor press release. Retrieved from https://www.bls.gov/news.release/pdf/empsit.pdf

US Census Bureau. (2016). Housing vacancies and homeownership (CPS/HVS): Historical table 16. Retrieved from https://www.census.gov/housing/hvs/data/histtabs.html

US Census Bureau. (2017). Quarterly residential vacancies and homeownership, fourth quarter 2016. Retrieved from https://www.census.gov/housing/hvs/files/currenthvspress.pdf

U.S. Census Bureau. (2021). Quarterly residential vacancies and homeownership fourth quarter 2020. Retrieved from https://www.census.gov/housing/hvs/files/currenthvspress.pdf

Valletta, R. G., Bengali, L., & van der List, C. (2020). Cyclical and market determinants of involuntary part-time employment. *Journal of Labor Economics, 38*(1), 67–93.

Vervalin, J. (2018). The case for a universal child allowance in the United States. *Cornell Policy Review*. Retrieved from http://www.cornellpolicyreview.com/universal-child-allowance/

Weil, D. (2019). Understanding the present and future of work in the fissured workplace context. *RSF: The Russell Sage Foundation Journal of the Social Sciences, 5*, 147–165.

Williams, J. C., Lambert, S. J., & Kesavan, S. (2017). How the Gap used an app to give workers more control over their schedules. *Harvard Business Review, December*, 2–6.

Williams Shanks, T. R., & Leigh, W. A. (2015). Assets and older African Americans. In N. Morrow-Howell & M. S. Sherraden (Eds.), *Financial capability and asset holding in later life: A life course perspective* (pp. 49–68). New York, NY: Oxford University Press.

Wilson, V. (2020). Racial disparities in income and poverty remain largely unchanged amid strong income growth in 2019. Economic Policy Institute. Retrieved from https://www.epi.org/blog/racial-disparities-in-income-and-poverty-remain-largely-unchanged-amid-strong-income-growth-in-2019/

Wolff, E. N. (2021). Household wealth trends in the United States, 1962 to 2019: Median wealth rebounds . . . but not enough. (No. w28383). Cambridge, MA: National Bureau of Economic Research.

Ybarra, M. A. (2013). Implications of paid family leave for welfare participants. *Social Work Research, 37*, 375–387.

Ybarra, M., Stanczyk, A., & Ha, Y. (2019). Paid leave, welfare, and material hardship after a birth. *Family Relations, 68*, 85–103.

Yoshikawa, H., Weisner, T. S., & Lowe, E. D. (Eds.). (2006). *Making it work: Low-wage employment, family life, and child development*. New York, NY: Russell Sage Foundation.

Zaw, K., Bhattacharya, J., Price, A., Hamilton, D., & Darity Jr, W. (2017). Women, race and wealth. *Research Brief Series, 1*. Oakland, CA: Samuel DuBois Cook Center on Social Equity and Insight Center for Community Economic Development. Retrieved from: https://www.insightcced.org/wp-content/uploads/2017/01/January2017_ResearchBriefSeries_WomenRaceWealth-Volume1-Pages-1.pdf

CHAPTER 12

Building Financial Capability and Assets for All

JIN HUANG, MARGARET S. SHERRADEN,
ELIZABETH JOHNSON, JULIE BIRKENMAIER,
DAVID ROTHWELL, MATHIEU R. DESPARD,
JENNY L. JONES, CHRISTINE CALLAHAN,
JOANNA DORAN, JODI J. FREY, GENA G. MCCLENDON,
TERRI FRIEDLINE, AND ROBIN MCKINNEY

People require financial capability and assets to satisfy basic needs, enhance financial stability and security, reach their potential, and achieve financial well-being (Sherraden, 1991, 2013, 2014). Therefore, building financial capability and assets for all, but particularly for minoritized racial, ethnic, and sexual and gender groups; people with low and moderate incomes, ill health, and disabilities; and victims of discrimination, oppression, and violence, is a grand challenge for social work.

During the Progressive Era, social workers assisted families with household financial management and saving in banks (Cruce, 2002; Stuart, 2013, 2016). Social workers were key players in the creation of the New Deal social policies that promoted financial stability, especially among the unemployed, women and children, people with disabilities, and older adults. Social workers provided a key inspiration for the War on Poverty, and engaged actively in the civil rights movement for economic justice (National Association of Social Workers, n.d.).

Today, in the face of rising income and wealth inequality, especially in low-income and minoritized households, and a pandemic that is magnifying people's financial troubles, social work is renewing its focus on financial well-being (Council on Social Work Education, 2017; National Association of Social Workers, 2021). There is growing recognition that social work's core constituents are among the most financially vulnerable members of society and that social work should play a key role in improving financial capability and asset-building (FCAB) (Birkenmaier, Sherraden, & Curley, 2013b). In 2015, the American Academy of Social Work and Social Welfare embraced the importance of financial well-being in selecting "FCAB For All" as one of social work's Grand Challenges, creating new opportunities for social work to improve people's financial well-being (Sherraden et al., 2015).

THE RISE OF FINANCIAL INSTABILITY AND INSECURITY IN US FAMILIES

Advancing FCAB For All is a strategic response by social work to trends that have placed growing numbers of households at risk, especially the most vulnerable. Three trends in particular—growing income inequality, increasing wealth inequality, and intensifying financialization and greater individual responsibility for addressing financial risk—seriously threaten the economic well-being of minoritized and low-income populations in US households. Along with a pandemic, these trends are leaving millions of households economically insecure.

Growing Income Inequality

Low- and moderate-income (LMI) households can no longer count on labor income to meet their financial needs because their real wages are stagnating or falling. Since the turn of the century, income from work declined 5% (in real wages) in low-income households and stagnated in middle-class households. Meanwhile, income increased 41% in high-income households (Mishel, Gould, & Rivens, 2015). The gap in income has increased over time, especially by race. Black men in America earned only 70% of what white men earned in 2019; this represents a decline since 1979, when Black men earned 80% of what white men earned (Daly, Hobijn, & Pedtke, 2017). The situation has improved for women, but they still only earned 82 cents on the dollar earned by men in 2019 (Fins, 2020). The gender wage gap in 2019 translates into a loss of $10,194 in annual median earnings for women (Fins, 2020).

Reasons for income inequality include the growing influence of technologies and skills (e.g., Autor, 2014), trade and globalization (e.g., Alderson & Nielsen, 2002), and diminishing power of organized labor (Kollmeyer & Peters, 2019). Low-income individuals lack education and job training opportunities to gain the skills required by high technology and high-paying jobs. Increased globalization also led to job losses in developed countries. US government policies also play an important role, creating an institutional structure for increasing income inequality [e.g., tax and monetary policies, deunionization, deregulation (Fortin & Lemieux, 1997)]. Income inequality plunged rapidly in the years following the New Deal, suggesting that redistribution policies can be effective strategies to reduce inequality. Growing income inequality calls for policy changes on the minimum wage, employment support, and education and training (Lein, Romich, & Sherridan, 2016).

Increasing Wealth Inequality

The second trend is that income from labor is declining overall while the proportion of household income from capital (assets) is rising (Cynamon & Fazzari, 2015). Unfortunately, assets are highly concentrated in upper income households, whereas low-income households hold few (or negative) assets (Eggleston, Hays, Munk, & Sullivan, 2020). Two thirds (63%) of US children live in families without sufficient wealth to maintain consumption at the income poverty line for 3 months (Rothwell, Ottusch, & Finders, 2019).

The result is wealth inequality—the gap between assets held by rich and poor—which is far larger than the income gap (Killewald, Pfeffer, & Schachner, 2017). In particular, racial wealth inequality is extreme. White families have approximately eight times the median wealth of Black families and nearly five times that of Latinx families (Kent & Ricketts, 2020). The most common source of wealth—homeownership—is much greater in white households. Less than half of Black (44%) and Latinx (45%) families own a home compared to more than 70% of white families (Kent & Rickets, 2020; Wolff, 2016). The racial wealth gap is persistent regardless of socioeconomic characteristics, and it creates intergenerational cycles of economic struggle (Hanks, Solomon, & Weller, 2018).

The wealth divide by gender is also dramatic. Single women have median wealth of $3,210 compared to $10,150 for single men (Chang, 2015). The gender wealth gap persists as a result of women's higher student debt levels, lower average earnings, employment segregation, caregiving burdens, longer life expectancy, and less retirement benefits compared to men (Bond, Saad-Lessler, & Weller, 2020; Chang, 2015; Wedderburn & Biddle Andres, 2020). Women of color hold even less wealth. Single Black and Latinx women have median wealth of $200 and $100, respectively, "less than a penny for every dollar owned by single white non-Hispanic men" (Chang, 2015, p. 6).

Asset-building policies favor families of means (Sherraden, 1991, 2014; Steuerle, 2016). Tax benefits for home ownership, investments, retirement savings, college savings, health savings, and medical savings build wealth in upper income households (Levin, Greer, & Rademacher, 2014). Low-income households receive almost none of these benefits. In 2018, less than 20% of households with incomes less than $25,000 had retirement savings accounts, compared to 87% for those with incomes more than $75,000 (Financial Industry Regulation Authority Investor Education Foundation, 2019). In 2013, only 41% of Black families and 26% of Latinx families owned retirement savings accounts—percentages substantively lower than that of white families (61%). The mean assets in retirement savings accounts for whites ($73,000) were approximately 330% more than those of Blacks and Latinxs ($22,000) (Morrissey, 2016).

Lack of assets means that LMI households, and particularly Black and Latinx households, do not have an economic cushion in a crisis nor a source of investment in future development and well-being (Sherraden, 1991). Insufficient assets limit minoritized and low-income groups' access to higher education, homeownership, and entrepreneurship (Hanks et al., 2018).

Intensifying Financialization and Greater Individual Responsibility for Addressing Financial Risk

The third trend is the growing role of finance in everyone's lives, even those with low incomes. This "financialization of everyday life" means that millions of families regularly face complex and difficult financial decisions (Aalbers, 2008; Pellandini-Simányi, 2020; van der Zwan, 2014), often with too little knowledge, guidance, and resources. Today, families must use a range of financial products and services, often requiring complex financial management skills. Online shopping, payment systems, consumer credit, home mortgages, educational loans, insurances, investments, retirement plans, and other mass-marketed financial products are a few of the financial services that everyone uses. Without them, households live on the margins of the mainstream economy, enduring its transformations and unable to reap its benefits (Baradaran, 2015; Servon, 2017). When they run into financial trouble, there is only a patchwork of places to turn for unbiased financial counseling and advice (Lander, 2018).

More than 7 million households (5.4%) lack a checking or saving account in a bank or credit union, and are considered "unbanked," including one quarter of households (23%) with incomes of less than $15,000 (Federal Deposit Insurance Corporation, 2020). Unbanked rates of Black and Latinx households are more than four times higher than rates in white households (Federal Deposit Insurance Corporation, 2020). In addition, 25% of low-income households are "underbanked," which means they have an account but also use non-banks for cashing checks, paying bills, borrowing, and other financial services (Federal Deposit Insurance Corporation, 2016a).

Reported barriers to using financial products and services include lack of money, distrust of financial institutions, high and unpredictable fees, and privacy concerns (Federal Deposit Insurance Corporation, 2016a, 2020). Some issues concern specific demographic groups such as immigrants, who report language barriers, unreceptive financial institutions, and lack of familiarity with the US financial system (Osili & Paulson, 2005). A history of racial and gender discrimination, victimization, and inequitable policies (Shanks, 2005) contributes to distrust and avoidance of mainstream financial services (Baradaran, 2017; Stein & Yannelis, 2020).

Among those living in low-income neighborhoods, nearly 30% lack a credit record, and an additional 15% have unscored credit records, indicating difficulty in obtaining safe and affordable credit (Consumer Financial Protection Bureau, 2016). Across all income levels, Black and Latinx households are less likely than whites to use bank credit (Federal Deposit Insurance Corporation, 2020). For example, among those with household incomes less than $15,000, white households (45%) are about 21% more likely to use bank credit than Black households (24%) (Federal Deposit Insurance Corporation, 2020).

Lacking access to safe and affordable banking and credit services, LMI families often turn to high-cost (and frequently risky) alternative financial services, such as auto title loans, subprime loans, remittance services, and payday loans (Federal Deposit Insurance Corporation, 2016a, 2020). Youths, racial minorities, noncitizen immigrants, and incarcerated and LMI men and women have a greater probability of using alternative financial services (Brown & Glidden, 2020; Federal Deposit Insurance Corporation, 2020). Half of Black and nearly 40% of Latinx respondents borrow from payday lenders, auto title lenders, pawnshops, and rent-to-own stores (Financial Industry Regulation Authority Investor Education Foundation, 2019).

Low financial literacy compounds these challenges. In a 2018 survey, approximately two thirds of Americans have a financial literacy score less than 80% (i.e., answered four or less of five basic financial questions correctly)—the lowest score of four surveys from 2009 to 2018 (Financial Industry Regulation Authority Investor Education Foundation, 2019). Women, Black, and Latinx individuals are less likely to answer financial knowledge questions correctly (Financial Industry Regulation Authority Investor Education Foundation, 2019). The gender gap has persisted, although there are increasing levels of financial knowledge and confidence among younger women (Mottola, 2018).

The Pandemic Intensifies Financial Vulnerability

The COVID-19 pandemic has magnified these trends, with severe financial hardship, particularly imposed on older adults, women, Blacks, Latinxs, Native peoples, people with disabilities, and other financially vulnerable populations.

Despite federal and state assistance, tens of millions of Americans remain unemployed and cannot afford basic household expenses (Center on Budget and Policy Priorities, 2021). Black and Latinx households are more likely to suffer from food insecurity during the COVID-19 pandemic than white households (Center on Budget and Policy Priorities, 2021), and often cannot protect their jobs by teleworking. Moreover, the impacts of the COVID-19 recession are not gender-neutral. Working women, especially those of color, have experienced the worst unemployment outcomes (Derbigny, 2020; National Women's Law Center, 2020). For example, out of 1.1 million jobs lost in December 2020, about 860,000 were women (Connley, 2020; Ewing-Nelson, 2021). These setbacks are likely to dampen future job prospects for women and contribute to the gender wage gap.

Financial hardships resulting from the pandemic further underscore the importance of financial equity. For example, it took several months for households that are unbanked or underbanked to receive the emergency income payment from the Internal Revenue Service (Cheung, 2020). As a result, public assistance funds often did not reach households when they needed them (Ordonez & Winn, 2020).

Growing financial instability and insecurity also lead to psychological stress, and sometimes lead to "toxic stress," which interferes with healthy human development (American Psychological Association, 2015; Brown, 2012; Shonkoff & Garner, 2012). Evidence is growing that persistent financial hardship and economic inequality contribute to poor physical and mental health (Deaton, 2011; Jones-Sanpei & Nance, 2020; Kahn & Pearlin, 2006; Purnell, 2015).

As the evidence demonstrates, the financial well-being of millions of households is at stake. The following sections discuss theoretical frameworks, the role of social work, and recent developments in financial capability and asset building.

FCAB: CONCEPTS

Everyone needs financial capability and assets to build financial well-being, and to hedge against the risk of financial instability and insecurity. We conceptualize financial capability using a capabilities approach (Nussbaum, 2000; Sen, 1985, 1993). Financial capability is a combination of financial knowledge and skills, and financial inclusion and equity. Together, they lead to financial well-being (Figure 12.1) (Johnson & Sherraden, 2007; Sherraden, 2013).

From the perspective of the financial capability framework, financial inclusion and equity are broad concepts that take into account all financial opportunities, including financial products and services (e.g., banks, credit unions, and alternative financial services), social policies (e.g., tax benefits,

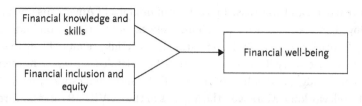

Figure 12.1 A conceptual framework of financial capability and asset building (FCAB)

income assistance and asset-building social welfare programs), and financial guidance (e.g., education, counseling, and coaching). Financial services, social policies, and financial guidance services together create an inclusive and equitable financial environment that allows individuals to apply their financial knowledge and skills toward their well-being. Financial inclusion and equity are necessary conditions and are the foundation of financial capability.

Financial capability is a developmental idea that expands people's life chances (Weber, 1978). It is the vision of the FCAB For All grand challenge to create equal and universal financial inclusion opportunities. For example, household assets are one of the most important financial resources to support family financial security and development. Asset-building for individuals and families, particularly for minoritized and LMI groups, requires more than individual saving. It requires an institutional approach to include everyone through asset-based social policies (Sherraden, 1991).

The Role of Social Work in FCAB

Social workers assist millions of LMI, minoritized, and financially marginalized people. Social work has adopted financial capability of vulnerable populations as a core professional goal of social work (Grand Challenges for Social Work, 2021; National Association of Social Workers, 2021). In addition, unlike other disciplines, social work encompasses strategies for individual and systems change as a core principle (Kondrat, 2013).

- At the micro level, social workers engage in financial education, financial coaching, financial counseling and therapy, and financial planning and advising with individuals and families to improve financial knowledge and skills, and to promote effective financial behaviors.
- At the mezzo level, social workers design, implement, and evaluate financial capability programs—such as consumer credit and savings programs—and integrate them into health and mental health, family services, housing, and employment organizations. They also organize grassroots coalitions and manage organizations that deliver financial capability services.

- At the macro level, social workers build coalitions and advocate for and develop financial and social policies—such as child development accounts (CDAs), fair access to banking, and consumer protections—that enhance individuals' and families' financial inclusion and promote equity.

At all levels of practice, social workers conduct applied research to provide an evidence base for these strategies.

> MAINSTREAMING GENDER
>
> *Inclusive Strategies for Building Financial Capability and Assets For All*
>
> TINA JIWATRAM-NEGRÓN
>
> Dominant financial systems and institutions center white men and reify male dominance. In the absence of accessibility and equity, gender mainstreaming is a strategy that mandates women-centric or focused programs and policies to transform systems and bring women into the "mainstream." This insert showcases how applying an intersectional gender mainstreaming approach to Building Financial Capability and Assets For All reveals the complexities of the work ahead and offers tangible solutions. True financial inclusion requires significant shifts to existing social structures while simultaneously strengthening financial knowledge and skills at the individual and relational levels through programs and policies.
>
> Many women and subpopulations, especially those relegated to the margins (e.g., women of color, Indigenous populations, immigrant and migrant women, sexual and gender minorities, people who use drugs and/or engage in sex work), do not enjoy the same access to financial services and ownership opportunities compared to their counterparts. Furthermore, one in three women experience intimate partner violence in their lifetime—a figure that is often magnified among multiply marginalized populations. Interpersonal violence often overlaps with financial or economic abuse, threatening progress in achieving Financial Capability and Asset Building (FCAB) For All and highlighting the fundamental need to adopt specific strategies for *centering safety* across planned financial initiatives. These include the following:
>
> 1. Considering personal agency within particular individual, social, cultural, and global contexts, such as violent relationships and subversive political environments;
> 2. Enacting safety procedures and policies to ensure those who are intended to benefit from a financial or asset-building resource benefit from and maintain the rights to those resources;
>
> *continued*

3. Offering options to support individual agency, such as emergency use options, that go beyond postsecondary education, home ownership, business investment, and retirement; and
4. Attending to stigmatizing and discriminatory practices that lead to financial exclusion among marginalized populations.

Embedded in longstanding patriarchy and kyriarchy, significant segments of the population lag when it comes to access to education, equitable employment, and wealth-building. Child Development Accounts (CDAs), which offer a pathway to universal financial inclusion, education, and assets, provide one example for the importance of centering safety. The ability to maximize the benefit of a CDA depends on varied multilevel policy and institutional factors and social norms, whereby ownership of property or education may or may not be permitted or supported for women and girls. Furthermore, particularly for women, asset ownership could present an opportunity for coercive financial control by family members, partners, or others, even if an account is held in one's name. Gendered or violent economic and financial control diminishes or eliminates the intended benefit of a CDA. To center safety, implementing bodies could identify mechanisms to safeguard the access and maintenance of assets, for example by training financial institutions to screen for coercive financial control. Simultaneously, researchers and policymakers should take concerted steps to understand the short- and long-term benefits of CDAs, or any other strategy to improve financial inclusion, such as universal or single banking platforms, through analyses disaggregated by gender and other axes of power to evaluate their success and modify implementation as needed.

Developing and implementing *gender- and community-specific strategies* that encourage and support the participation of all members of society in spaces designed to provide improved financial knowledge, skills, and resources are essential. Inclusive spaces consider where financial education, coaching, counseling, and other interventions occur, as well as the time of day programming is offered and the resources needed to participate (such as child care). It is also critical to create gender-inclusive and specific literacy programming, community-wide training, and flexible financial products that offer opportunities for growth. Such strategies must be considered alongside global location and cultural contexts, particularly as they relate to the rights and status of women and other marginalized groups. Indeed, *a gender-progressive, multilevel and multisectoral approach to policymaking, research, and programming provides an opportunity to enhance gender equity.* Feminist policy analyses or gender auditing that accounts for the underpayment and precarious financial positions held by marginalized groups may suggest the need for specialized financial packages or matched savings programs that are differentially, rather than uniformly, implemented based on an individual's social status and access to resources.

continued

> The need to reexamine existing policies and structures has become most apparent in the context of COVID-19. The amplification of existing structural-level problems underscores the need for progressive policies to safeguard all people, especially those at the margins. An exorbitant number of women have lost employment and/or seen significant shifts in their household and child-care burdens, demonstrating the need to reexamine family and sick leave policies. Current policies prioritize those employed in formal sectors or with legal status and have left behind undocumented workers and those who work in informal or hidden sectors of society, often placing them in difficult or impossible situations that jeopardize their families' health and livelihoods. In global terms, ensuring the success of FCAB For All requires the inclusion of marginalized and vulnerable populations at the decision-making table and at every stage, from gender analyses to gender budgeting, program and policy development, and implementation. Considerations along axes of race, culture, ableism, and global location must also be centered to mitigate existing problems and to work toward achieving FCAB For All.

DEVELOPMENTS IN FCAB

Since the early 1990s, social work has been an innovator in research, policy, education, and practice for FCAB. In diverse settings, social work practitioners apply professional interventions to enable families to generate income, build assets, and manage economic resources.

Reaching Underserved Households with Appropriate Financial Products and Services

Social workers and others promote progressive and universal measures to reach minoritized and LMI families. They strengthen policies and public institutions to advance financial inclusion and equity, including removing barriers and expanding pathways to banking services, affordable credit, asset-building, financial guidance, and financial protection (Birkenmaier, Despard, & Friedline, 2018a; Despard, Friedline, & Birkenmaier, 2018; Friedline, Despard, & Birkenmaier, 2018). The FCAB network envisions a strong role for the federal government in regulating the financial marketplace and expanding access to beneficial financial products and services. For example, the Consumer Financial Protection Bureau, created under the Dodd-Frank Wall Street Reform and Consumer Protection Act of 2010, is a landmark development to eliminate "unfair, deceptive, or abusive acts or practices" in the financial services industry (Consumer Financial Protection Bureau, n.d.). It provides supports for consumers and social service practitioners (Consumer Financial Protection Bureau, 2015).

The field is leading the way in innovations. Calling financial inclusion "the civil rights issue of our time," the chair of the National Credit Union Administration announced an initiative in 2020 to bring consumers of vulnerable and marginalized communities into the financial mainstream (Inclusiv, 2020; National Credit Union Administration, n.d.; Passman, 2020). The Cities for Financial Empowerment Fund—a national organization that promotes Bank On National Account Standards and supports local coalitions working for wider access to banking by unbanked and underbanked individuals—is a leader in reaching vulnerable households (Cities for Financial Empowerment Fund, n.d.). The standards identify bank account features that are appropriate for unbanked populations (e.g., minimum opening deposit, low or waived monthly maintenance fees). In 2017, Bank On–certified accounts were available in more than 27,000 bank branches across the country (Cities for Financial Empowerment Fund, 2019). Bank On has encouraged unbanked individuals to open certified bank accounts online so their stimulus checks and unemployment benefits can be deposited directly into their accounts.

Others endorse public options for banking, borrowing, and investing through the US Postal Service and the Federal Reserve Bank (Baradaran, 2015; Flitter, 2021; US Postal Service, Office of the Inspector General, 2014). Social workers propose that finance be a public good (Huang, Sherraden, & Sherraden, 2021b). Others call for expanding small-dollar lending with strict consumer protections and credit-builder loans that are not based on credit scores, but rather on borrowers' ability to make installment payments (National Federation of Community Development Credit Unions and Filene, 2015).

Advancing Fair Financial Technology

Financial technology, such as online and mobile banking, cryptocurrency, robo-advisors, online lending, and insurtech, offers ways to reach LMI populations with accessible products at low cost (The Pew Charitable Trusts, 2016b). Digital financial services have gained new prominence during the COVID-19 pandemic, and may be able to reduce racial and gender gaps in financial access (International Monetary Fund, 2020). Recent innovations and adoption of financial technology has the potential to bolster financial inclusion and equity through reducing transaction costs and reaching unbanked and underbanked populations (nLift, 2018), although some scholars challenge the potential of financial technologies to change fundamental inequalities in financial services (Friedline, 2020).

The FCAB network is examining how new financial technologies can improve families' finances and household decision-making. One possibility is the creation of a web-based financial capability service platform (Sherraden et al., 2015). As a public platform, it would reach everyone as a comprehensive and universal infrastructure for expanded integration of public services and financial services. The financial capability platform would synthesize an individual's financial records in one place, and provide education and support for FCAB. Users could organize, track, understand, and manage their financial transactions, including their use of public and financial services. They would receive customized and client-oriented financial education. The platform would also aggregate feedback from users that would inform product development, and consumer protection and policy.

Reaching Disadvantaged Households with Financial Guidance

Families with resources can pay for financial advice; but, overall, LMI households cannot afford to pay for help. To reach these families, organizations are integrating guidance into existing public and private services (Sherraden, Huang, Johnson, et al., 2019a). For example, at the federal level the Internal Revenue Service, in collaboration with local nonprofits, provide free tax preparation assistance through the Volunteer Income Tax Assistance program to ensure qualifying taxpayers receive tax benefits and save money while avoiding predatory tax-preparation companies (Lim, Dejohn, & Murray, 2012). A Refund-to-Savings initiative integrates guidance for saving by low-income families in tax services by creating a default allocation of tax refunds to savings in free online tax-filing services (Grinstein-Weiss et al., 2015).

At state and municipal levels, youth in employment programs open bank accounts, save, and gain financial knowledge and skills through programs such as MyPath (Loke, Choi, & Libby, 2015). The Cities for Financial Empowerment Fund promotes the integration of financial counseling into municipal services, such as housing, homeless services, and workforce development (Cities for Financial Empowerment Fund, n.d.; Mintz, 2014). The Local Initiatives Support Corporation, a community development organization, sponsors financial empowerment centers that help families solve financial problems and reach financial goals related to employment, public benefits, income supports, debt counseling, debt negotiation, credit building, and saving (Rankin, 2015; Roder, 2016). In 2015, the US Administration for Children and Families and Prosperity Now (2015) created a guide to support the integration of financial capability services into existing social services.

Change Machine is a financial technology platform that assists social service organizations and public social welfare agencies to embed financial guidance into their work, and provides financial products that serve low-income households (Watson Grote, 2020a). It integrates clients and practitioner feedback to assess its usefulness, to improve services, and to create new products and services that expand financial capability. Moreover, Change Machine uses data from its service delivery to develop and advocate for "pro-poor" policy change that "intentionally champions the aspirations of Black and Brown women who navigate financial insecurity" (Watson Grote, 2020b).

Many social work researchers have documented approaches that integrate FCAB into the nonprofit sector. Examples include community development and financial empowerment programs with minoritized and LMI families (Doran, 2020; Padua & Doran, 2016; Swanstrom, Winter, Sherraden, & Lake, 2013), domestic violence programs (De Marco et al., 2015; Hetling, Postmus, & Kaltz, 2016; Sanders, 2013), programs serving youth and older adults (Loke, Libby, & Choi, 2013; McCallion, Ferretti, & Park, 2013; Peters, Sherraden, & Kuchinski, 2016), health services (Parthasarathy, Dailey, Young, Lam, & Pies, 2014), disability services (Morris & Goodman, 2015), and disaster relief programs (Hudner & Kurtz, 2015).

Creating Policies for Financial Capability and Asset-building for All

The FCAB network of scholars advocates on behalf of minoritized and LMI populations for better representation in policies, including writing policy briefs on asset-building, emergency savings, banking services, cultural competency, social work in financial practice, and others. This section summarizes a few of these proposals.

Promote Lifelong Asset-building with Universal and Progressive CDAs

To address rising insecurity and instability, all families must have assets (savings and investments). Social workers propose universal CDAs as a feasible way to ensure that everyone owns assets (Sherraden, 1991). CDAs are lifelong investment accounts for long-term developmental purposes, such as education, homeownership, business investment, and retirement. Automatic enrollment and initial deposits, target investment options with growth potential, low administrative costs, and progressive features are key attributes (Beverly et al., 2016; Clancy & Beverly, 2017). CDAs can achieve goals of full inclusion, reduced asset inequality early in life, and improved children's early development (Huang, Sherraden, Kim, & Clancy, 2014a; Huang, Sherraden, & Purnell, 2014b; Kim, Sherraden, Huang, & Clancy, 2015), and have the potential to connect with other asset-building policies (e.g., retirement savings accounts) throughout the life cycle.

More than 70 CDA programs were operating in 2018, including nearly half a million children beneficiaries (Clancy, Sherraden, & Beverly, 2015; Huang, Sherraden, Clancy, et al., 2021a). Seven states have statewide, automatic, and universal CDAs, and around 500,000 newborns will be enrolled automatically into CDAs in 2021 (Huang, Sherraden, Clancy, et al., 2021a).

Integrating CDAs into a nationwide policy platform would maximize the policy's effects and efficiency. One option is to integrate CDAs into an existing nationwide asset-building policy platform, such as 529 college savings plans and the proposed Dependent Care Savings Accounts. These plans could automatically enroll all newborns and provide financial incentives to LMI families, and minoritized and other marginalized groups (Huang, Sherraden, Clancy, Sherraden, & Shanks, 2017). The US Senate and US Congress have considered options such as the America Saving for Personal Investment, Retirement, and Education Act of 2010, and USAccounts of 2015.

Social workers also have been instrumental in designing and testing savings and asset-building innovations for young people and vulnerable populations in the global context, including Azerbaijan, Canada, Israel, Korea, mainland China, Singapore, sub-Saharan Africa, and Taiwan (Huang et al., 2020).

Eliminate Asset Limits for Public Assistance Programs

Eliminating asset limits permits beneficiaries of public assistance to build assets. Means-tested public assistance programs such as the Supplemental Nutrition Assistance Program, Temporary Assistance for Needy Families, and Medicaid, often place limits on the maximum allowable assets (including vehicle ownership) for eligibility, requiring families to spend-down their assets to qualify.

Eliminating asset limits makes sense for several reasons. There is no evidence of an association between higher asset limits and welfare uptake (Hamilton, Alexander-Eitzman, & Royal, 2015; Rice & Bansak, 2014; The Pew Charitable Trusts, 2016a). Eliminating asset limits would encourage saving, and may reduce the likelihood that recipients cycle on and off benefit programs (Gehr, 2018; Ratcliffe, McKernan, Wheaton, & Kalish, 2016). In addition, eliminating asset limits lowers administrative costs, because workers are not required to investigate the assets of applicants (Corporation for Enterprise Development, 2011; The Pew Charitable Trusts, 2016a).

There have been developments. Some states have eliminated asset limits for Temporary Assistance for Needy Families and the Supplemental Nutrition Assistance Program (Corporation for Enterprise Development, 2011; Gehr, 2018; Hamilton et al., 2015; Hamilton, Rothwell, Huang, Nam, & Dollar, 2019). A complete elimination of asset limits from public assistance programs would expand asset-building opportunities for low-income families and would save public-sector funds.

Improving Financial Knowledge and Skills

Since former Federal Reserve Chairman Ben Bernanke proclaimed in 2006 that financial education "leads to better outcomes for individual consumers and for our economy generally," federal efforts to improve financial knowledge and skills have intensified (Bernanke, 2006). The US Financial Literacy and Education Commission (2006) created a national strategy and website for financial education (http://www.MyMoney.gov). Each year, public and private sectors spend nearly $700 million on financial education (Consumer Financial Protection Bureau, 2013), and the federal government spends an estimated $273 million (Mnuchin & Carranza 2019). The US Department of the Treasury (2019) reviewed federal financial education activities and suggested improving the delivery of financial education through better coordination, prioritization, and partnerships with local governments and private stakeholders.

The 2020 US National Strategy for Financial Literacy articulates the role of the federal government in promoting financial education (Financial Literacy and Education Commission, 2020). In addition to policies, research, and resource development, the Financial Literacy and Education Committee promotes best practices in financial education, including five principles of effective financial education: (a) know the target populations, (b) provide actionable and relevant information, (c) enhance financial skills, (d) build on individual motivation, and (e) facilitate good decisions (Consumer Financial Protection Bureau, 2017). Three additional best practices of financial education are recommended to develop professional standards for educators, provide them support, and evaluate for impact (Financial Literacy and Education Commission, 2020).

Many organizations provide financial education resources for various audiences. For example, the Consumer Financial Protection Bureau (2015) created a tool kit—Your Money, Your Goals—for social service providers, which is available in three languages. The Federal Deposit Insurance Corporation's Money Smart program uses a game format to teach key financial concepts to individuals across the life cycle, as well as to small business owners (Federal Deposit Insurance Corporation, 2016b). Other entities—such as the Federal Reserve, financial institutions, nonprofits, municipalities, the armed forces, colleges and universities, and employers—also offer financial education in seminars, workshops, and courses in various formats. Specialized financial education also is available for groups such as college students (National Financial Educators Council, 2013a), immigrants (Lutheran Immigration and Refugee Service, 2012), low-income consumers (Collins, 2010), adults planning for retirement (US Department of Veterans Affairs, 2016), prospective homeowners (NeighborWorks America, 2017), and service members and their families (National Financial Educators Council, 2013b).

Educating Social Workers in FCAB

Social workers must have the ability and tools to enable clients to understand and use financial services and asset-building opportunities. They also must be prepared to develop and implement programs and policies that expand financial inclusion, education, and guidance to minoritized and low-income populations.

In fact, social work faculty and students acknowledge the need for curricular content on FCAB (Huang et al., 2020; Loke, Birkenmaier, & Hageman, 2016). Faculty in minority-serving institutions underscore the importance of addressing race and discrimination in financial capability (Rochelle, et al., 2017). Faculty also report that financial issues frequently arise in classes and practicums (Hageman, Sherraden, Birkenmaier, & Loke, 2019). Although there is wide variation in knowledge and understanding of financial issues (Hageman et al., 2019), overall, faculty acknowledge a lack of education and lack of confidence in integrating financial content (Huang et al., 2020; see also Despard & Chowa, 2010; Fenge, 2012).

Teams of educators have generated FCAB curricula designed for social work students. In 2015, an FCAB curriculum was developed and evaluated with 28 faculty in 16 minority-serving institutions, and later with faculty mainstream colleges/universities (Rochelle, et al., 2017; Sherraden, Birkenmaier, McClendon, & Rochelle, 2017). A continuing education curriculum was also developed and evaluated (Frey, Hopkins, Osteen, et al., 2017a), along with other social work curricular models (Birkenmaier, Sherraden, Frey, et al., 2018b ; Horwitz & Briar-Lawson, 2017; Sherraden, Laux, & Kaufman, 2007). In 2017, the Council on Social Work Education published an FCAB curricular guide with support from FCAB network members.

Built on this work, the FCAB network has produced three books for educators and practitioners, including an edited volume for practice (Callahan, Frey, & Imboden, 2019), a textbook for financial capability in human services (Sherraden, Birkenmaier, & Collins, 2018), and an edited volume on FCAB practice with diverse populations (Birkenmaier, Sherraden, Frey, et al., 2018b). Faculty have introduced FCAB content into new and existing courses, field education, and extracurricular and continuing education (Birkenmaier, Kennedy, Kunz, et al., 2013a; Birkenmaier, Lane, Callahan, & Hageman, 2021; Frey, Sherraden, Birkenmaier, & Callahan, 2017b; Doran & Avery, 2016; Doran & Bagdasaryan, 2018; Frey et al., 2017a; Sherraden et al., 2007). Online curricular resources currently under development will provide videos and online curricular materials. Nonprofits and commercial organizations also offer certification in financial practice, including an academic certificate (Callahan, Frey, & Imboden, Under Review).

The Grand Challenge to Build Financial Capability and Assets For All is influencing development of financial capability education in social work in the global context. Singapore, mainland China, Taiwan, and Korea are incorporating financial capability training in professional social work education (Ghoh & Sherraden, 2020; Sherraden, Kuo, Fang, et al., 2019b). The China Council on Social Work Education and China National Association of Social Workers have established financial social work commissions and provided education and trainings to social work students and frontline social workers. In Africa, a network of African researchers, human service practitioners, and policymakers have joined forces with social work departments and the Alliance of African Institutes of Bankers to encourage financial education in social work.

FCAB RESEARCH

The FCAB network has been actively supporting social work research. It has convened five FCAB conferences since 2014, and organized five special issues on FCAB for leading social work and consumer science journals based on research presented at these convenings. The latest 2019–2020 convening includes more than 30 research presentations on a variety of FCAB topics, many of which will be published in two special journal issues. The FCAB network also has coordinated more than 200 research presentations, convened interest groups, and held activities at the annual conferences of the Council on Social Work Education and the Society for Social Work and Research.

In accordance with the FCAB framework, we propose measuring progress on FCAB research by outputs, outcomes, and impacts of financial inclusion, and financial knowledge and skills (Boxes 12.1 and 12.2).

COLLABORATION AND CROSS-SECTOR INVOLVEMENT FOR FCAB

The goals of the FCAB For All Grand Challenge intersect with other social work Grand Challenges, creating opportunities for collaboration. For example, racism is a root cause of financial vulnerability. The initiatives for FCAB education, policy, and practice will support the Grand Challenge to Eliminate Racism to promote antiracist social work education, foster systemic policy changes against racism, and improve the financial capability and well-being of minoritized racial and ethnic groups (Jones, Birkenmaier, Johnson, et al.,

Box 12.1 MEASUREMENT METRICS: OUTPUTS, OUTCOMES, AND IMPACTS

Outputs refer to financial capability and asset-building (FCAB) activities and services provided by the social work profession and other sectors. They may include, but are not limited to, policy development, financial education, financial coaching, financial and credit counseling, credit building, tax preparation, and asset-building programs. We can measure output in several ways: by the number of FCAB policies and programs, by the total number of professionals in these programs, by total program expenditures, and by the population receiving services.

Outcomes are improved financial inclusion and equity, and increased financial knowledge and skills at the individual level. Ideally, financial inclusion should include access to basic banking services, asset-building programs, credit, insurance, public assistance programs, financial education, and counseling. For example, we can measure improved access to lifelong asset-building policies (e.g., child development accounts) and basic financial services (e.g., banking services).

Impacts are the combined effects of financial inclusion, knowledge, and skills on desirable financial management and well-being. Impact measures could be categorized into main elements of FCAB on income generation, consumption and credit management, insurance and protection, and asset-building. For example, the rate of asset account holding and the amount of assets accumulated are two indicators of asset-building.

The design and development of FCAB research and measurement should consider principles for FCAB research and measurement carefully. Specifically, three principles aid in making such determinations (Box 12.2).

---

forthcoming). Both the FCAB For All and the Grand Challenge to Reduce Extreme Economic Inequality propose lifelong asset-building as a policy for narrowing economic inequality. Together, the two grand challenge groups developed a joint policy action statement for universal and progressive CDAs (Huang, Sherraden, Clancy, Sherraden, & Shanks, 2017). Multiple FCAB programs aim to improve financial well-being for children and youth (Beverly et al., 2016; Huang, Sherraden, Kim, et al., 2014a). Such programs have impacts on nonfinancial outcomes on children's attitudes and behaviors, and may be important prevention strategies for the Grand Challenge to Ensure Healthy Development for Youth. In addition, new financial technology has

> *Box 12.2* THREE PRINCIPLES OF FINANCIAL CAPABILITY AND ASSET-BUILDING RESEARCH AND MEASUREMENT
>
> - *Engage the people who are the focus of financial capability and asset-building (FCAB) efforts.* Racial, ethnic, gender, and social identities matter in the assessment of financial outcomes. Therefore, the FCAB network must ensure minority and low-income groups are engaged in the research process. Research should include input from community members, stakeholders, and marginalized groups.
> - *Frame the context clearly.* Researchers should frame the context of research questions and metrics clearly. The framing of questions and measurement should reflect a clear specification of contexts and conditions, and should not be limited to dichotomized terms (Small & Feldman, 2012). In these ways, FCAB research makes explicit efforts to identify how context shapes opportunities to act and individual financial capability.
> - *Implement comprehensive methods to test the research questions.* By leveraging a variety of methodological techniques, researchers can evaluate FCAB progress comprehensively and with different points of view. Mixed methods permit researchers to examine issues from different perspectives and build on the strengths of each approach (Chaumba, 2013). For example, the Mapping Financial Opportunity project triangulates data from several sources, including geographic information systems data; linked administrative, community, and household data; and original data collection (Friedline & Despard, 2017a, 2017b). Child development account research uses qualitative interviews, administrative data, longitudinal and secondary survey findings, and randomized experiments (Beverly, Clancy, & Sherraden, 2016).

become a powerful tool to promote FCAB, and may be an example that intersects with the Grand Challenge to Harness Technology for Social Good.

Other strategic partnerships with people and organizations across sectors and disciplines also are essential. Through such partnerships, the FCAB group amplifies its impact by drawing on the expertise, skills, and networks of other disciplines and organizations. Potential collaborators include scholars, practitioners, and policy leaders from a number of disciplines (e.g., family and consumer sciences, economics, psychology, business, finance, law, public policy, education) who work in a variety of contexts (e.g., community, human service, advocacy, business, financial, government organizations). Efforts to promote FCAB-related policy for vulnerable families bring social workers together with local, state, and federal policy actors, such as public officials, policy experts, lawyers, activists, and others (Weiss-Gal, 2013).

CONCLUSION

In the next 5 years, the FCAB network will study the financial well-being effects of financial capability policies, programs, and practices on minoritized and LMI populations; test social policy and intervention innovations to promote FCAB; and prepare social workers and human service practitioners in the United States and other countries with basic financial capability knowledge and practice skills.

Since its founding as a profession, social work has played an important and unique role in ensuring that everyone has access to societal benefits and an ability to achieve social and economic well-being. As key elements of well-being, financial capability and assets are among social work's Grand Challenges. Today, social workers are breaking ground and are leaders in shaping social institutions to promote FCAB For All. This grand challenge provides a rare opportunity to synthesize and institutionalize FCAB systematically as a core social good.

REFERENCES

Aalbers, M. B. (2008). The financialization of home and the mortgage market crisis. *Competition & Change, 12*, 148–166.

Alderson, A. S., & Nielsen, F. (2002). Globalization and the great U-turn: Income inequality trends in 16 OECD countries. *American Journal of Sociology, 107*, 1244–1299.

American Psychological Association. (2015). Stress in America: Paying with our health. Retrieved from https://www.apa.org/news/press/releases/stress/2014/stress-report.pdf

Autor, D. H. (2014). Skills, education, and the rise of earnings inequality among the "other 99 percent." *Science, 344*, 843–851.

Baradaran, M. (2015). *How the other half banks: Exclusion, exploitation, and the threat to democracy*. Cambridge, MA: Harvard University Press.

Baradaran, M. (2017). *The color of money: Black banks and the racial wealth gap*. Cambridge, MA: Harvard University Press.

Bernanke, B. (2006, May 23). Financial literacy: Testimony before the Committee on Banking, Housing, and Urban Affairs of the United States Senate. Retrieved from https://www.federalreserve.gov/newsevents/testimony/Bernanke20060523a.htm

Beverly, S. G., Clancy, M. M., & Sherraden, M. (2016). *Universal accounts at birth: Results from SEED for Oklahoma Kids*. St. Louis, MO: Washington University, Center for Social Development. Retrieved from http://csd.wustl.edu/Publications/Documents/RS16-07.pdf

Birkenmaier, J., Despard, M. R., & Friedline, T. (2018a). *Policy recommendations for financial capability and asset building by increasing access to safe, affordable credit.* Grand Challenges for Social Work initiative policy brief no. 11-2. American Academy of Social Work & Social Welfare.

Birkenmaier, J. M., Kennedy, T., Kunz, J., Sander, R., & Horwitz, S. (2013a). The role of social work in financial capability: Shaping curricular approaches. In J. M. Birkenmaier, M. S. Sherraden, & J. Curley (Eds.), *Financial capability and asset development: Research, education, policy, and practice* (pp. 278–301). New York, NY: Oxford University Press.

Birkenmaier, J. M., Lane, L. B., Callahan, C., & Hageman, S. (2021). Course models for increased competency for practice integrated with financial capability and asset building. *Journal of Social Work Education*, 57, 604–611..

Birkenmaier, J. M., Sherraden, M. S., & Curley, J. (2013b). *Financial capability and asset development: Research, education, policy, and practice.* New York, NY: Oxford University Press.

Birkenmaier, J., Sherraden, M. S., Frey, J. J., Callahan, C., & Santiago, A. M. (Eds.). (2018b). Financial capability and asset building with diverse populations: Improving financial well-being in families and communities. London, UK: Routledge.

Bond, T., Saad-Lessler, J., & Weller, C. (2020, May). Still shortchanged: An update on women's retirement preparedness. National Institute on Retirement Security. Retrieved from https://www.nirsonline.org/wp-content/uploads/2020/04/Still-Shortchanged-Final.pdf

Brown, A. (2012, October 30). With poverty comes depression, more than other illnesses. Gallup. Retrieved from http://www.gallup.com/poll/158417/poverty-comesdepression-illness.aspx?utm_source=alert&utm_medium=email&utm_campaign=syndication&utm_content=morelink&utm_term=All%20Gallup%20Headlines

Brown, T., & Glidden, M. D. (2020, July). Gender and financial capability from behind bars. Insights. FINRA Investor Education Foundation. Retrieved from https://www.usfinancialcapability.org/downloads/Gender-and-Financial-Capability-from-Behind-Bars.pdf

Callahan, C., Frey, J. J., & Imboden, R. (2019). *The Routledge handbook on financial social work: Direct practice with vulnerable populations.* New York, NY: Routledge.

Callahan, C., & Frey, J. J., & Imboden, R. (Under Review). *Developing a financial social work certificate program to meet the needs of community practitioners.*

Center on Budget and Policy Priorities. (2021, January 15). Tracking the COVID-19 recession's effects on food, housing, and employment hardships. Retrieved from https://www.cbpp.org/research/poverty-and-inequality/tracking-the-covid-19-recessions-effects-on-food-housing-and

Chang, M. L. (2015). *Women and wealth: Insights for grantmakers.* Asset Funders Network. Retrieved from https://assetfunders.org/wp-content/uploads/Women_Wealth_-Insights_Grantmakers_brief_15.pdf

Chaumba, J. (2013). The use and value of mixed methods research in social work. *Advances in Social Work*, 14, 307–333.

Cheung, B. (2020, May 9). Millions of unbanked Americans face longer wait for CARES Act checks. Yahoo Finance. Retrieved from https://finance.yahoo.com/news/millions-of-americans-face-longerwait-for-cares-act-checks-115915131.html

Cities for Financial Empowerment Fund. (n.d.). Bank On National Account Standards (2021–2022). Retrieved from https://2wvkof1mfraz2etgea1p8kiy-wpengine.

netdna-ssl.com/wp-content/uploads/2020/10/Bank-On-National-Account-Standards-2021-2022.pdf

Cities for Financial Empowerment Fund. (2019). The present and future of Bank On account data: Pilot results and prospective data collection. Retrieved from https://cfefund.org/the-present-and-future-of-bank-on-account-data-pilot-results-and-prospective-data-collection/

Clancy, M. M., & Beverly, S. G. (2017). *Statewide child development account programs: Key design features*. Unpublished manuscript. St. Louis, MO: Washington University, Center for Social Development.

Clancy, M. M., Sherraden, M., & Beverly, S. G. (2015). *College savings plans: A platform for inclusive and progressive child development accounts*. CSD policy brief no. 15-07. St. Louis, MO: Washington University, Center for Social Development. Retrieved from https://csd.wustl.edu/Publications/Documents/PB15-07.pdf

Collins, M. (2010). Effects of mandatory financial education on low-income clients. *Focus, 27*, 13–18.

Connley, C. (2020, October 2). More than 860,000 women dropped out of the labor force in September, according to new report. CNBC: Make It. Retrieved from https://www.cnbc.com/2020/10/02/865000-women-dropped-out-of-the-labor-force-in-september-2020.html

Consumer Financial Protection Bureau. (n.d.). The Bureau. Retrieved from https://www.consumerfinance.gov/about-us/the-bureau

Consumer Financial Protection Bureau. (2013, November). Navigating the market: A comparison of spending on financial education and financial marketing. Retrieved from https://files.consumerfinance.gov/f/201311_cfpb_navigating-the-market-final.pdf

Consumer Financial Protection Bureau. (2015, April). Your money, your goals: A financial empowerment toolkit for social services programs. Retrieved from http://files.consumerfinance.gov/f/201407_cfpb_your-money-your-goals_toolkit_english.pdf

Consumer Financial Protection Bureau. (2016). Who are the credit invisibles? How to help people with limited credit histories. Retrieved from http://files.consumerfinance.gov/f/documents/201612_cfpb_credit_invisible_policy_report.pdf

Consumer Financial Protection Bureau. (2017). Effective financial education: Five principles and how to use them. Retrieved from https://files.consumerfinance.gov/f/documents/201706_cfpb_five-principles-financial-well-being.pdf

Corporation for Enterprise Development. (2011). Resource guide: Lifting asset limits in public benefit programs. Retrieved from https://cfed.org/assets/scorecard/2011_2012/rg_AssetLimits.pdf

Council on Social Work Education. (2017). *Curricular guide for economic well-being practice*. Alexandria, VA: Council on Social Work Education. Retrieved from https://www.cswe.org/CMSPages/GetFile.aspx?guid=77de3a0d-8f9d-45e5-b48e-7a57f241945f

Cruce, A. (2002). *School-based savings programs, 1930–2002*. St. Louis, MO: Washington University, Center for Social Development. Retrieved from https://csd.wustl.edu/Publications/Documents/wp02-7.pdf

Cynamon, B. Z., & Fazzari, S. M. (2015). Household income, demand, and saving: Deriving macro data with micro data concepts. *Review of Income and Wealth, 63*, 53–69.

Daly, M., Hobijn, B., & Pedtke, J. H. (2017). Disappointing facts about the black-white wage gap. *FRBSF Economic Letter, 26*, 1–5.

Deaton, A. S. (2011). *The financial crisis and the well-being of Americans*. Cambridge, MA: National Bureau of Economic Research. Retrieved from http://www.nber.org/papers/w17128

De Marco, A., De Marco, H., Biggers, A., West, M., Young, J., & Levy, R. (2015). Can people experiencing homelessness acquire financial assets? *Journal of Sociology and Social Welfare, 42*, 55–78.

Derbigny, D. (2020, April). On the margins: Economic security for women of color through the coronavirus crisis and beyond. Closing the Women's Wealth Gap. Retrieved from https://womenswealthgap.org/wp-content/uploads/2020/04/OnTheMargins_April2020_CWWG.pdf

Despard, M. R., & Chowa, G. A. N. (2010). Social workers' interest in building individuals' financial capabilities. *Journal of Financial Therapy, 1*, 23–41.

Despard, M. R., Friedline, T., & Birkenmaier, J. (2018). *Policy recommendations for helping U.S. households build emergency savings*. Grand Challenges for Social Work initiative policy brief no. 11-3. Cleveland, OH: American Academy of Social Work & Social Welfare.

Doran, J. K. (2020, September 24). *The next big thing? Los Angeles county anti-poverty policy evolution towards FCAB orientation*. Poster presented at Financial Capability and Asset Building: Achievements, Challenges and Next Steps (2020–2025). [online conference]. Retrieved from https://www.youtube.com/watch?v=Ik3Nwww89cs&list=PLqpn7uAs8MJXcBxi3WYFupgGfYcNtaXbT&index=3&t=4s.

Doran, J. K., & Avery, P. (2016, October 14). *Financial empowerment through social work*. Paper presented at the National Association of Social Workers conference, Burbank, CA.

Doran, J. K., & Bagdasaryan, G. (2018). Testing infusion of financial capability and asset building content in social work courses. *Journal of Social Work Education, 54*, 122–134.

Eggleston, J., Hays, D., Munk, R., & Sullivan, B. (2020). The wealth of households: 2017. Current population reports. Washington, DC: US Census Bureau. Retrieved from https://www.census.gov/content/dam/Census/library/publications/2020/demo/p70br-170.pdf

Ewing-Nelson, C. (2021, January). All of the jobs lost in December were women's jobs. National Women's Law Center. Retrieved from https://nwlc.org/resources/all-of-the-jobs-lost-in-december-were-womens-jobs/

Federal Deposit Insurance Corporation. (2016a). 2015 FDIC national survey of unbanked and underbanked households. Retrieved from https://www.fdic.gov/householdsurvey

Federal Deposit Insurance Corporation. (2016b). Money Smart: A financial education program. Retrieved from https://www.fdic.gov/consumers/consumer/moneysmart

Federal Deposit Insurance Corporation. (2020). How America banks: Household use of banking and financial services (2019 FDIC Survey). Retrieved from https://www.fdic.gov/analysis/household-survey/2019report.pdf

Fenge, L. A. (2012). Economic well-being and ageing: The need for financial education for social workers. *Social Work Education, 31*, 498–511.

Financial Industry Regulation Authority Investor Education Foundation. (2019). *The state of US financial capability: The 2018 national financial capability study*. Washington, DC: Author. Retrieved from https://www.usfinancialcapability.org/downloads/NFCS_2018_Report_Natl_Findings.pdf

Financial Literacy and Education Commission. (2020). U.S. National Strategy for Financial Literacy 2020. Retrieved from https://home.treasury.gov/system/files/136/US-National-Strategy-Financial-Literacy-2020.pdf

Fins, A. (2020, March). Women and the lifetime wage gap: How many woman years does it take to equal 40 man years? National women's Law Center. Retrieved from https://nwlc.org/wp-content/uploads/2019/03/Women-and-the-Lifetime-Wage-Gap-v2.pdf

Flitter, E. (2021, January 12). Next Senate banking chairman sets low-income and climate priorities. *New York Times*. Retrieved from https://www.nytimes.com/2021/01/12/business/banking-environment-housing-democrats-sherrod-brown.html

Fortin, N. M., & Lemieux, T. (1997). Institutional changes and rising wage inequality: Is there a linkage?. *Journal of Economic Perspectives*, 11, 75–96.

Frey, J. J., Hopkins, K., Osteen, P., Callahan, C., Hageman, S., & Ko, J. (2017a). Training social workers and human service professionals to address the complex financial needs of clients. *Journal of Social Work Education*, 53, 118–131.

Frey, J. J., Sherraden, M. S., Birkenmaier, J., & Callahan, C. (2017b). Financial capability and asset building in social work education. *Journal of Social Work Education*, 53, 79–83.

Friedline, T. (2020). *Banking on a revolution: Why financial technology won't save a broken system*. New York, NY: Oxford University Press.

Friedline, T., & Despard, M. (2017a). *How do the features of banks' entry-level checking accounts compare to Bank On National Account Standards?* Lawrence, KS: University of Kansas, Center on Assets, Education, and Inclusion.

Friedline, T., & Despard, M. (2017b). *Mapping financial opportunity*. Washington, DC: New America. Retrieved from https://www.newamerica.org/in-depth/mapping-financial-opportunity

Friedline, T., Despard, M. R., & Birkenmaier, J. (2018, May). *Policy recommendations for expanding access to banking and financial services*. Grand Challenges for Social Work initiative policy brief no. 11-4. Cleveland, OH: American Academy of Social Work & Social Welfare.

Gehr, J. (2018, April). Eliminating asset limits: Creating savings for families and state government. CLASP. Retrieved from https://www.clasp.org/sites/default/files/publications/2018/04/2018_eliminatingassetlimits.pdf

Ghoh, C., & Sherraden, M. S. (2020). *Moving beyond "fire-fighting:" Social worker perspectives on achieving financial well-being in Singapore*. Washington, DC: Society for Social Work and Research.

Grand Challenges for Social Work. (2021). Building financial capability and assets for all. Retrieved from https://grandchallengesforsocialwork.org/build-financial-capability-for-all/

Grinstein-Weiss, M., Perantie, D. C., Russell, B. D., Comer, K., Taylor, S. H., Luo, L., . . . Ariely, D. (2015). *Refund to Savings 2013: Comprehensive report on a large-scale tax-time saving program*. St. Louis, MO: Center for Social Development, Washington University in St. Louis.

Hageman, S. A., Sherraden, M. S., Birkenmaier, J. M., & Loke, V. (2019). Economic and financial well-being in the social work curriculum: Faculty perspectives. *Journal of Social Work Education*, 57, 251–263.

Hamilton, L., Alexander-Eitzman, B., & Royal, W. (2015). Shelter from the storm: TANF, assets and the Great Recession. *SAGE Open*, 5, 1–6.

Hamilton, L., Rothwell, D. W., Huang, J., Nam, Y., & Dollar, T. (2019). Guarding public coffers or trapping the poor? The role of public assistance asset limits in program efficacy and family economic well-being. *Poverty and Public Policy*, 11, 12–30.

Hanks, A., Solomon, D., & Weller, C. (2018). Systematic inequality: How America's structural racism helped create the Black-White wealth gap. Washington,

DC: Center for American Progress. Retrieved from https://www.americanprogress.org/issues/race/reports/2018/02/21/447051/systematic-inequality/
Hetling, A., Postmus, J. L., & Kaltz, C. (2016). A randomized controlled trial of a financial literacy curriculum for survivors of intimate partner violence. *Journal of Family and Economic Issues, 37*, 672–685.
Horwitz, S., & Briar-Lawson, K. (2017). A multi-university economic capability-building collaboration. *Journal of Social Work Education, 53*, 149–158.
Huang, J., Sherraden, M., Clancy, M. M., Beverly, S. G., Shanks, T. R., & Kim, Y. (2021a). Asset building and child development: A policy model for inclusive child development accounts. *The Russell Sage Foundation Journal of the Social Sciences, 7*, 176–195.
Huang, J., Sherraden, M., Clancy, M. M., Sherraden, M., & Shanks, T. R. (2017). *Start lifelong asset building with universal and progressive child development accounts.* Grand Challenges for Social Work initiative policy action no. 11.1. Cleveland, OH: American Academy of Social Work & Social Welfare.
Huang, J., Sherraden, M., Johnson, L., Birkenmaier, J. M., Loke, V., & Hageman, S. (2020). Preparing social work students to improve family financial well-being: Where we stand. *Journal of Social Work Education.*
Huang, J., Sherraden, M., Kim, Y., & Clancy, M. (2014a). An experimental test of child development accounts on early social–emotional development. *JAMA Pediatrics, 168*, 265–271.
Huang, J., Sherraden, M., & Purnell, J. (2014b). Impacts of child development accounts on maternal depression: Evidence from a randomized statewide policy experiment. *Social Science & Medicine, 112*, 30–38.
Huang, J., Sherraden, M. S., & Sherraden, M. (2021b). *Toward finance as a public good.* CSD working paper no. 21-03. St. Louis, MO: Washington University, Center for Social Development. Retrieved from https://openscholarship.wustl.edu/csd_research/917/
Hudner, D., & Kurtz, J. (2015). *Do financial services build disaster resilience? Examining the determinants of recovery from Typhoon Yolanda in the Philippines.* Retrieved from https://www.mercycorps.org/sites/default/files/Philippines%20Resilience%20ToC%20Testing%20Report_Final_03.06.15.cm_.pdf
Inclusiv. (2020). *2020 Inclusive finance report.* Retrieved from https://www.inclusiv.org/2020-inclusive-finance-report/
International Monetary Fund. (2020). *The promise of fintech: Financial inclusion in the post Covid-19 era.* Retrieved from https://www.imf.org/-/media/Files/Publications/DP/2020/English/PFFIEA.ashx
Johnson, E., & Sherraden, M. S. (2007). From financial literacy to financial capability among youth. *Journal of Sociology and Social Welfare, 34*, 119–145.
Jones, J. L., Birkenmaier, Johnson, E., Nam, Y, Huang, J., & Onifade, E.. (forthcoming). Racism as a barrier to achieving financial capability and asset building for all. In M. Spencer & M. Teasley (Eds.), *Eliminate racism.* Grand Challenges for Social Work.
Jones-Sanpei, H. A., & Nance, R. J. (2020). Financial capability in addiction research and clinical practice. *Substance Use & Misuse, 56*, 214–223.
Kahn, J. R., & Pearlin, L. I. (2006). Financial strain over the life course and health among older adults. *Journal of Health and Social Behavior, 47*, 17–31.
Kent, A. H., & Ricketts, L. R. (2020, December 2). Has wealth inequality in America changed over time? Here are key statistics. *Open Vault Blog.* Federal Reserve of St. Louis. Retrieved from https://www.stlouisfed.org/open-vault/2020/december/has-wealth-inequality-changed-over-time-key-statistics

Killewald, A., Pfeffer, F. T., & Schachner, J. N. (2017). Wealth inequality and accumulation. *Annual Review of Sociology*, *43*, 379–404.

Kim, Y., Sherraden, M., Huang, J., & Clancy, M. (2015). Impacts of child development accounts on change in parental educational expectations: Evidence from a statewide social experiment. *Social Service Review*, *89*, 99–137.

Kollmeyer, C., & Peters, J. (2019). Financialization and the decline of organized labor: A study of 18 advanced capitalist countries, 1970–2012. *Social Forces*, *98*, 1–30.

Kondrat, M. E. (2013). *Person-in-environment.* Encyclopedia of social work. New York, NY: Oxford University Press.

Lander, D. (2018). The financial counseling industry: Past, present, and policy recommendations. *Journal of Financial Counseling and Planning*, *29*, 163–174.

Lein, L., Romich, J. L., & Sherraden, M. (2016). *Reversing extreme inequality.* Grand Challenges for Social Work initiative working paper no. 16. Cleveland, OH: American Academy of Social Work and Social Welfare. Retrieved from https://grandchallengesforsocialwork.org/wp-content/uploads/2016/01/WP16-with-cover-2.pdf

Levin, E., Greer, J., & Rademacher, I. (2014). *From upside down to right-side up: Redeploying $540 billion in federal spending to help all families save, invest, and build wealth.* Washington, DC: Corporation for Entreprise Development.

Lim, Y., DeJohn, T., & Murray, D. (2012). Free tax assistance and the earned income tax credit: Vital resources for social workers and low-income families. *Social Work*, *57*, 175–184.

Loke, V., Birkenmaier, J., & Hageman, S. A. (2016). Financial capability and asset building in the curricula: Student perceptions. *Journal of Social Work Education*, *53*, 84–98.

Loke, V., Choi, L., & Libby, M. (2015). Increasing youth financial capability: An evaluation of the MyPath Savings Initiative. *Journal of Consumer Affairs*, *49*, 97–126.

Loke, V., Libby, M., & Choi, L. (2013). *Increasing financial capability among economically vulnerable youth: MY Path.* San Francisco, CA: Federal Reserve Bank of San Francisco, Community Development Investment Center. Retrieved from http://www.frbsf.org/community-development/publications/working-papers/2013/march/financial-capability-economically-vulnerable-youth-my-path

Lutheran Immigration and Refugee Service. (2012). Financial literacy for newcomers: Weaving immigrant needs into financial education. Retrieved from http://www.higheradvantage.org/wp-content/uploads/2012/05/rw_financial_literacy.pdf

McCallion, P., Ferretti, L. A., & Park, I. (2013). Financial issues and an aging population: Responding to an increased potential for financial abuse and exploitation. In J. Birkenmaier, M. S. Sherraden, & J. Curley (Eds.), *Financial education and capability: Research, education, policy, and practice* (pp. 129–155). New York, NY: Oxford University Press.

Mintz, J. (2014). Local government solutions to household financial instability: The supervitamin effect. *Federal Reserve Bank of San Francisco Community Investment*, *26*, 16–19, 40–41.

Mishel, L., Gould, E., & Rivens, J. (2015). *Wage stagnation in nine charts.* Washington, DC: Economic Policy Institute. Retrieved from http://www.epi.org/publication/charting-wage-stagnation

Mnuchin, S. T., & Carranza, J. (2019, July). Federal financial literacy reform: Coordinating and improving financial literacy efforts. US Department of the Treasury. Retrieved from https://home.treasury.gov/system/files/136/FFLRCoordinatingImprovingFinancialLiteracyEfforts.pdf

Morris, M., & Goodman, N. (2015, July). *Integrating financial capability and asset building strategies into the Public Workforce Development System*. Washington, DC: National Center on Leadership for the Employment and Economic Advancement of People with Disabilities. Retrieved from http://www.leadcenter.org/system/files/resource/downloadable_version/integrating_fin_cap_asset_dev.pdf

Morrissey, M. (2016). The state of American retirement. *Economic Policy Institute, Washington, DC*. https://files.epi.org/2016/state-of-american-retirement-final.pdf

Mottola, G. (2018). Gender, generation and financial knowledge: a six-year perspective. *Insights: Financial Capability*. Washington, D.C.: FINRA Investor Education Foundation. Retrieved from https://www.usfinancialcapability.org/downloads/Issue-Brief-Gender-Generation-and-Financial-Knowledge-A-Six-Year-Perspective.pdf

National Association of Social Workers. (n.d.). Social work history. Retrieved from https://www.socialworkers.org/News/Facts/Social-Work-History

National Association of Social Workers. (2021). 2021 Blueprint of federal social policy priorities: Recommendations to the Biden-Harris administration and congress. Retrieved from https://www.socialworkers.org/LinkClick.aspx?fileticket=KPdZqqY60t4%3d&portalid=0

National Credit Union Administration. (n.d.). ACCESS: Advancing communities through credit, education, stability and support. Retrieved from https://www.ncua.gov/access

National Federation of Community Development Credit Unions and Filene. (2015). Borrow and save feasibility study report. Retrieved from http://www.cdcu.coop/wp-content/uploads/2016/03/BorrowandSave_FeasibiltyStudy_FINAL.pdf

National Financial Educators Council. (2013a). College student financial literacy curriculum. Retrieved from https://www.financialeducatorscouncil.org/college-student-financial-literacy

National Financial Educators Council. (2013b). The military financial literacy American dream movement campaign. Retrieved from https://www.financialeducatorscouncil.org/military-financial-literacy

National Women's Law Center. (2020, March 30). The wage gap has made things worse for women of color on the front lines of COVID-19. Retrieved from https://nwlc.org/blog/the-wage-gap-has-made-things-worse-for-women-on-the-frontlines-of-covid19/?campaign_id=10&emc=edit_gn_20200331&instance_id=17223&nl=in-herwords&regi_id=84041823&segment_id=23427&te=1&user_id=094da7a317185cfd0ea81f5e881599b2

NeighborWorks America. (2017). National industry standards for homeownership education and counseling. Retrieved from http://www.neighborworks.org/Training-Services/Resources-for-Counselors-Educators/National-Industry-Standards

nLift. (2018, Autumn). Fulfilling the promise of fintech: The case for a nonprofit vision and leadership. Aspen Institute. Retrieved from https://www.aspeninstitute.org/wp-content/uploads/2018/09/nLIFT-Manifesto-FINAL-1.pdf

Nussbaum, M. C. (2000). *Women and human development: The capabilities approach*. Cambridge, MA: Cambridge University Press.

Ordonez, V., & Winn, L. (2020, May 21). US seeing the cost of late unemployment benefits. *ABC News*. Retrieved from https://abcnews.go.com/Business/us-cost-late-unemploymentbenefits/story?id=70776627.

Osili, U. O., & Paulson, A. (2005). *Individuals and institutions: Evidence from international migrants in the U.S.* Chicago, IL: Federal Reserve Bank of Chicago.

Padua, L. A., & Doran, J. K. (2016). From being unbanked to becoming unbanked or unbankable: Community experts describe financial practices of Latinos in East Los Angeles. *Journal of Community Practice, 24,* 428–444.

Parthasarathy, P., Dailey, D. E., Young, M. E. D., Lam, C., & Pies, C. (2014). Building economic security today: Making the health-wealth connection in Contra Costa County's Maternal and Child Health Program. *Maternal and Child Health Journal, 18,* 396–404.

Passman, A. (2020, October 19). NCUA chief unveils plan to tackle 'the civil rights issue of our time.' *American Banker.* Retrieved from https://www.americanbanker.com/creditunions/news/ncua-chief-unveils-plan-to-tackle-the-civil-rights-issue-of-our-time

Pellandini-Simányi, L. (2020). The financialization of everyday life. In C. Borch & R. Wosnitzer (Eds.), *The Routledge handbook of critical financial studies* (pp. 278–299). New York, NY: Routledge.

Peters, C. M., Sherraden, M., & Kuchinski, A. M. (2016). Growing financial assets for foster youths: Expanded child welfare responsibilities, policy conflict, and caseworker role tension. *Social Work, 61,* 340–348.

Purnell, J. (2015). Financial health is public health. In Federal Reserve Bank of San Francisco & Corporation for Enterprise Development (Ed.), *What it's worth: Strengthening the financial future of families, communities and the nation* (pp. 163–172). San Francisco, CA: Federal Reserve Bank of San Francisco & Corporation for Enterprise Development.

Rankin, S. (2015). *Building sustainable communities: Integrated services and improved financial outcomes for low-income households.* New York: Local Initiatives Support Corporation. Retrieved from https://www.lisc.org/media/filer_public/e5/5e/e55ec07e-61c1-40df-9940-d2add976d774/110317_sranking_foc_report_april_2015.pdf

Ratcliffe, C., McKernan, S.-M., Wheaton, L., & Kalish, E. C. (2016). *The unintended consequences of SNAP asset limits.* Washington, DC: Urban Institute. Retrieved from http://www.urban.org/research/publication/unintended-consequences-snap-asset-limits

Rice, L., & Bansak, C. (2014). The effect of welfare asset rules on auto ownership, employment, and welfare participation: A longitudinal analysis. *Contemporary Economic Policy, 32,* 306–333.

Rochelle, M., McClendon, G., Sherraden, M. S., Brackett, M., Wright, M., Jordan, T., . . . Birkenmaier, J. (2017). Adopting a financial capability and asset-building curriculum at historically Black colleges and universities. *Journal of Human Behavior in the Social Environment, 27,* 367–384.

Roder, A. (2016). *First steps on the road to financial well-being: Final report from the evaluation of LISC's Financial Opportunity Centers.* New York, NY: Economic Mobility Corporation. Retrieved from http://www.lisc.org/our-resources/resource/liscs-financial-opportunity-centers-surpass-other-programs

Rothwell, D. W., Ottusch, T., & Finders, J. K. (2019). Asset poverty among children: A cross-national study of poverty risk. *Children and Youth Services Review, 96,* 409–419.

Sanders, C. K. (2013). Financial capability among survivors of domestic violence. In J. Birkenmaier, M. S. Sherraden, & J. Curley (Eds.), *Financial capability and asset development: Research, education, policy, and practice* (pp. 85–107). New York, NY: Oxford University Press.

Sen, A. (1985). *Commodities and capabilities.* Oxford, UK: Elsevier.

Sen, A. (1993). Capability and well-being. In M. Nussbaum & A. Sen (Eds.), *The quality of life* (pp. 30–53). New York, NY: Oxford University Press.

Servon, L. J. (2017). *The unbanking of America: How the new middle class survives.* New York, NY: Harcourt Brace.

Shanks, T. W. (2005). The Homestead Act: A major asset-building policy in American history. In M. Sherraden (Ed.), *Inclusion in the American dream: Assets, poverty, and public policy* (pp. 20–41). New York, NY: Oxford University Press.

Sherraden, M. (1991). *Assets and the poor: A new American welfare policy.* New York, NY: Sharpe.

Sherraden, M. S. (2013). Building blocks of financial capability. In J. Birkenmaier, M. S. Sherraden, & J. Curley (Eds.), *Financial education and capability: Research, education, policy, and practice* (pp. 3–43). New York, NY: Oxford University Press.

Sherraden, M. (2014). Asset building research and policy: Pathways, progress, and potential of a social innovation. In R. Cramer & T. Shanks (Eds.), *The assets perspective: The rise of asset building and its impact of social policy* (pp. 263–284). New York, NY: Palgrave Macmillan.

Sherraden, M. S., Birkenmaier, J. M., & Collins, J. M. (2018). *Financial capability and asset building in vulnerable households: Theory and practice.* New York, NY: Oxford University Press.

Sherraden, M. S., Birkenmaier, J., McClendon, G. G., & Rochelle, M. (2017). Financial capability and asset building in social work education: Is it "the big piece missing?" *Journal of Social Work Education, 53,* 132–148.

Sherraden, M. S., Huang, J., Frey, J. J., Birkenmaier, J., Callahan, C., Clancy, M. M., & Sherraden, M. (2015). *Financial capability and asset building for all.* Grand Challenges for Social Work initiative working paper no. 13. Cleveland, OH: American Academy of Social Work and Social Welfare.

Sherraden, M. S., Huang, J., Johnson, L., & Bernacchi, J. (2019a). *Delivering financial guidance: Models for reaching financially vulnerable households.* San Francisco, CA: Society for Social Work and Research.

Sherraden, M. S., Kuo, T., Fang, S., Liu, F., Huang, J., & Zhou, L. (2019b). *Financial social work in international perspective: Mainland China and Taiwan.* Presented at the 65th CSWE annual program meeting, October 24–27, Denver, CO.

Sherraden, M. S., Laux, S., & Kaufman, C. (2007). Financial education for social workers. *Journal of Community Practice, 15,* 9–36.

Shonkoff, J. P., & Garner, A. S. (2012). The lifelong effects of early childhood adversity and toxic stress. *Pediatrics, 129,* e232–e246.

Small, M., & Feldman, J. (2012). Ethnographic evidence, heterogeneity, and neighbourhood effects after Moving to Opportunity. In M. van Ham, D. Manley, N. Bailey, L. Simpson, & D. Maclennan (Eds.), *Neighbourhood effects research: New perspectives* (pp. 55–77). Dordrecht, The Netherlands: Springer.

Stein, L. C. D., & Yannelis, C. (2020). Financial inclusion, human capital, and wealth accumulation: Evidence from the Freedman's Savings Bank. *The Review of Financial Studies, 33,* 5333–5377.

Steuerle, C. E. (2016). *Prioritizing opportunity for all in the federal budget: A key to both growth in and greater equality of earnings and wealth.* Urban Institute. Retrieved from https://www.urban.org/sites/default/files/publication/80041/

2000758-Prioritizing-Opportunity-for-All-in-the-Federal-Budget-A-Key-to-Both-Growth-in-and-Greater-Equality-of-Earnings-and-Wealth.pdf

Stuart, P. H. (2013). Social workers and financial capability in the profession's first half-century. In J. Birkenmaier, M. S. Sherraden, & J. Curley (Eds.), *Financial education and capability: Research, education, policy, and practice* (pp. 44–62). New York, NY: Oxford University Press.

Stuart, P. H. (2016). Financial capability in early social work practice: Lessons for today. *Social Work, 61*, 297–304.

Swanstrom, T., Winter, W., Sherraden, M S., & Lake, J. (2013). Civic capacity and school/community partnerships in a fragmented suburban setting: The case of 24:1. *Journal of Urban Affairs, 35*, 25–42.

The Pew Charitable Trusts. (2016a). Do limits on family assets affect participation in, costs of TANF? Philadelphia, PA: The Pew Charitable Trusts. Retrieved from http://pew.org/29n0ICJ

The Pew Charitable Trusts. (2016b). Is this the future of banking? Focus group views on mobile payments. Issue brief. Philadelphia, PA: The Pew Charitable Trusts. Retrieved from http://www.pewtrusts.org/~/media/assets/2016/01/cb_futurebankingissuebrief.pdf

US Administration for Children and Families & Prosperity Now. (2015). Building financial capability: A planning guide for integrated services. US Department of Health and Human Services. Retrieved from https://www.acf.hhs.gov/sites/default/files/documents/ocs/afi_resource_guide_building_financial_capability.pdf

US Department of the Treasury. (2019). Federal financial literacy reform: Coordinating and improving financial literacy efforts. Retrieved from https://home.treasury.gov/system/files/136/FFLRCoordinatingImprovingFinancialLiteracyEfforts.pdf

US Department of Veterans Affairs. (2016). Retirement and Financial Literacy Education Program. Retrieved from https://www.va.gov/ohrm/worklifebenefits/rflep.asp

US Financial Literacy and Education Commission. (2006). Taking ownership of the future. Retrieved from https://www.treasury.gov/about/organizational-structure/offices/Domestic-Finance/Documents/Strategyeng.pdf

US Financial Literacy and Education Commission. (2020). U.S. national strategy for financial literacy: 2020. Retrieved from https://home.treasury.gov/system/files/136/US-National-Strategy-Financial-Literacy-2020.pdf

US Postal Service, Office of the Inspector General. (2014). Providing non-bank financial services for the underserved. Retrieved from https://www.uspsoig.gov/document/providing-non-bank-financial-services-underserved

van der Zwan, N. (2014). Making sense of financialization. *Socio-Economic Review, 12*, 99–129.

Watson Grote, M. (2020a). From inclusion to equity: Making fintech work for low-income consumers. Change Machine. Retrieved from https://change-machine.org/from-inclusion-to-equity-making-fintech-work-for-low-income-consumers

Watson Grote, M. (2020b). What does an equitable economy look like. Change Machine. Retrieved from https://change-machine.org/what-does-an-equitable-economy-look-like/

Weber, M. (1978). *Economy and society*. Berkeley, CA: University of California Press.

Wedderburn, R., & Biddle Andres, K. (2020). Majoring in debt: Why student loan debt is growing the racial wealth gap and how philanthropy can help. Aspen Institute Financial Security Program. Retrieved from https://assetfunders.org/wp-content/uploads/AFN-Majoring-in-Debt-10.12.20.pdf

Weiss-Gal, I. (2013). Social workers affecting social policy: An international perspective on policy practice. In J. Gal & I. Weiss-Gal (Eds.), *Social workers affecting social policy: An international perspective on policy practice* (pp. 59–78). Chicago, IL: Policy Press.

Wolff, E. N. (2016). Household wealth trends in the United States, 1962 to 2013: What happened over the Great Recession? *RSF: The Russell Sage Foundation Journal of the Social Sciences, 2*, 24–43.

CHAPTER 13

Achieving Equal Opportunity and Justice

ROCÍO CALVO, JORGE DELVA, SANDY MAGAÑA, AND LUCIANA GIORGIO COSENZO

We launched the Grand Challenge to Achieve Equal Opportunity and Justice with a tall order to fill: creating a society in which everyone has the same opportunities for advancement. Five years later, few countries have been as affected by the COVID-19 pandemic as the United States. With 4% of the world's population but a quarter of its confirmed cases, the United States leads the mortality rankings worldwide, especially among Blacks and Latinxs (Andrew, 2020). These disparities are not the result of individual behavior, but of entrenched systemic inequities that prevent racialized communities from accessing quality healthcare and education, fair wages, and affordable housing.

The systematic denial of opportunity to entire segments of the population not only stifles the well-being of these communities, but weakens the social fabric of the entire country. As we stated in the first edition of this chapter, pervasive injustice

> is the foundation of many of the social problems addressed by the other grand challenges, including incarceration, poverty, and the extent to which communities are affected by the changing environment. Lack of opportunity and justice results in lack of resources affecting healthy youth development, a nurturing family life, a productive and fulfilling life into old age, social engagement, and access to housing. As it is true with all the twelve grand challenges for social work, the challenge to achieve equal opportunity and justice is intrinsically intertwined with all the others. (Calvo et al., 2018, p. 249)

Although one the most complex challenges, achieving equal opportunity and justice for all is also an "exciting opportunity for our society. An opportunity that social work, from its interdisciplinary, asset-based, and translational approach from research to practice is well positioned to lead" (Calvo et al., 2018, p. 249). In this chapter, we look at the progress this challenge has made during the past 5 years and then propose an agenda for the remaining of the decade that helps dismantle the systemic dynamics that underlie inequality across policies, institutions, and programs.

PROGRESS REPORT: THE PAST 5 YEARS

To achieve equal opportunity and justice for all, we focused on four areas containing flagrant inequalities: access to quality healthcare, quality education, affordable housing, and gainful employment. We dedicated the first 5 years to build our network in these key areas. Countless collaborations led to a number of publications on how to address social stigma, integrate Latinx immigrants, support Black children, build inclusive communities, and reduce disparities in juvenile justice. These publications include specific, evidence-based recommendations for micro-, mezzo-, and macro-level interventions, and call upon social workers to act as advocates and agents of change in response to these inequalities. Unsurprisingly, the recommendations across publications describe efforts to eliminate barriers set by discriminatory policies and to increase well-being by intentionally investing in stigmatized communities. For example, work describing efforts to address the inequalities experienced by Black children and youth center on a reduction of stigmatization and discrimination in schools, investments of time and funding in developing restorative justice and behavioral health programs, and, if youth become involved in the juvenile justice system, a reduction in barriers to continued education, family involvement, employment opportunities, and affordable housing and healthcare (Calvo et al., 2016; Goldbach, Amaro, Vega, & Walter, 2015; Kim, McCarter, & Logan-Greene, 2020; Metzger & Khare, 2017; Teasley et al., 2017). In addition to publications, we spoke against the anti-immigrant policies of the Trump administration and advocated for the reauthorization of the Higher Education Act to ensure the affordability of higher education. We launched the School Success Project dedicated to reducing the disproportionate suspension of school-age youth, and established the Latinx Leadership Initiative to increase the number the Latinx social workers (Grand Challenges for Social Work, 2021). We also seized the opportunity to share the research and recommendations gathered during the past 5 years on this grand challenge with the Biden administration and underscore the importance of an equitable approach to the COVID-19 recovery plan to ensure stigmatized and marginalized communities are at the center of these efforts (National Association of Social Workers, 2021).

We now turn to examine the progress toward achieving equal opportunities and justice among the Latinx population. As mentioned previously, the Latinx population has been among the hardest hit by the COVID-19 global pandemic. This hardship follows years of heightened inflammatory anti-immigration and anti-Latinx rhetoric perpetuated by the Trump administration. Despite these challenges, the Latinx population continues to grow and strengthen, thus presenting the social work profession with a unique opportunity to accelerate progress toward equality and justice in this population.

It is promising to see the growth of the Latinx presence in the social work profession. The increase in number of master's degree in social work (MSW) and bachelor's degree in social work (BSW) programs between 2009 and 2019 (50% in MSW programs and 15% in BSW programs) and in enrolled students (34.9% MSW students and 12.6% BSW students) has brought a concomitant increase in the percent of Latinx students in social work programs (Council on Social Work Education, 2010, 2020). In 2009, the percentage of BSW and MSW Latinx students was considerably less than their representation in the general population: 16.6% (Pew Research Center, 2020). However, the percentages of BSW and MSW Latinx students in 2019 reflect more closely the 2019 Latinx population (~18.3%) (Pew Research Center, 2020). It is indeed encouraging to see the increased numbers of Latinx students pursuing BSW and MSW programs, because these individuals are more likely to work with Latinx individuals, families, and communities. It is also promising to see the growth of Latinx students in BSW and MSW programs because these changes occur against an overall context that reflects a lower percentage of Latinx youth who enroll and complete college compared to youth of other racial and ethnic backgrounds. For example, only 36% of Latinx enrolled in college in 2018—a disproportionately lower rate than among Asian Americans (59%), whites (42%), and Blacks (37%). Among first-time, full-time undergraduate 4-year college-attending youth, Latinx students have a 54% 6-year graduation rate, which is less than the rate for Asian American (74%) and white students (64%), but greater than that of Black students (40%) (National Center for Education Statistics, 2018).

In fact, there is a growing list of social work programs that aim to increase the number of Latinx students. Some exceptional examples include Loyola University Chicago's online bilingual (in Spanish) MSW program, the Latinx Leadership Initiative offered at Boston College School of Social Work, and Boston University's Building Refugee and Immigrant Degrees for Graduate Education Program. The University of Houston Graduate College of Social Work offers a specialization called "Social Work Practice with Latinos," with courses specific to working with Latinxs.

In addition to increases in the percentages of Latinx students who attend BSW and MSW programs, there has also been considerable progress attracting Latinxs to doctoral programs. Increasing the number of Latinx students in doctoral programs will result in the growth of research that is likely to be centered around the experience of Latinx communities, which may also serve to increase the number of Latinx faculty in schools and programs of social work. In 2009, 5.6% of Latinx students were enrolled in a doctoral program—a significantly lower percent than non-Hispanic whites (56.7%) and Blacks (14.8%). The percentage of enrolled students was only slightly less than the 6.2% Latinx individuals who applied to doctoral programs in 2009. These data seem to suggest that the low percentage of enrolled students of Latinx backgrounds in 2009 might have been the result of the overall low percentage of Latinx individuals who applied to these programs. Before we compare the 2009 and 2019 data, it is important to mention that the 2009 data on doctoral programs are mainly about research doctorates, which are different from the practice doctorates that have grown in numbers in the past decade. With this caveat in mind, in 2019, the percentage of Latinx students in research doctorate programs was 11.6%, a fairly large increase from the percentage a decade ago, but still much less than the percent of non-Hispanic white (46.0%) and Black (22.1%) students, which is a cause for concern. In 2019, Latinx students made up approximately 10.5% of practice doctorates, which is also considerably less than the percentages for non-Hispanic white (36.0%) and Black (35.8%) students (Council on Social Work Education, 2020).

Other concerns are the widespread economic and health disparities within the Latinx communities. Exacerbated by existing health disparities, the Latinx community has been one of the hardest hit groups in the global pandemic. They faced job loss rates of 18.5% at the peak of the pandemic compared to 12.8% among non-Latinx whites in the same time frame (Couch, Fairlie, & Xu, 2020; Krogstad & Noe-Bustamante, 2020). In addition, Latinx are more likely to be essential workers and less likely to receive medical care when infected with the virus (Laurencin & McClinton, 2020). In an analysis of COVID-19 deaths in the state of Texas, demographer Rogelio Saenz found that Latinx individuals had the highest number of years lost to COVID-19 than white or Black individuals (Kuchment, Hacker, & Solis, 2020). This is because a greater percentage of Latinx who died from COVID-19 were in the age range of 30 to 64; thus, collectively, the number of years that otherwise would have been dedicated to parenting and economic productivity have been lost, which will have a long-term impact on the economy in general and Latinx families in particular. Similarly, data from the Centers for Disease Control and Prevention (2021) as of February 2021 show that after adjusting for age, 38% of COVID-19 deaths nationwide are Latinx, whereas Latinxs represent 19% of the population.

The disproportionate impact of the COVID-19 on Latinxs stems from entrenched inequities established well before the beginning of the pandemic. Latinx adults have significant health disparities in chronic health conditions, and in health and mental health services. To summarize some of the disparities in chronic conditions, although Latinxs are less likely to die from heart disease than whites, they are 50% more likely to die from diabetes, and 50% of Latinxs will develop diabetes during their lifetime (Hostetter & Klein, 2018). Furthermore, Latinxs have a greater prevalence of chronic kidney disease and cirrhosis (Hostetter & Klein, 2018), and obesity than whites (Baskin, Art, Franklin, & Allison, 2005; Dubay & Lebrun, 2012). Latinxs are often considered to be a homogeneous group, which is erroneous in many ways. Recent research has examined differences in health outcomes between Latinxs with different national origins (Aviles-Santa et al., 2017). An important study that examined differences between self-identified Latinxs of Central American, Cuban, Dominican, Mexican, Puerto Rican, and South American heritage in cardiovascular risk found significant differences as well as similarities (Daviglus et al., 2012). For example, diabetes was more prevalent among those of Dominican, Mexican, and Puerto Rican descent compared to those of South American descent (Schneiderman et al., 2014). Research shows that health behaviors among Latinxs are worse for US-born versus foreign-born Latinxs (Hostetter & Klein, 2018), demonstrating variation associated with acculturation. Latinxs have consistently received lower healthcare coverage and worse healthcare quality than whites. One of the aims of the Affordable Care Act (ACA) was to reduce healthcare disparities in insurance and healthcare. A post-ACA study examined the impact of the ACA on receipt of health insurance and found that although uninsured rates dropped for all ethnic groups, Latinxs still showed the highest rates compared to Blacks and whites (Gonzales & Sommers, 2018). This study also examined differences within the Latinx sample based on heritage, and found that those of Mexican and Central American descent had higher rates of being uninsured compared to other groups (Gonzales & Sommers, 2018). Another analysis conducted post-ACA found that Latinxs were more likely to report receiving fair or poor healthcare compared to whites, demonstrating that many gaps remain post-ACA (Sommers, McMurtry, Blendon, Benson, & Sayde, 2017).

Research on Latinx children and health also shows disparities. Most notably, they have higher rates of being overweight and obese than non-Latinx white children (Parra-Medina, Liang, Yin, Esparza, & Lopez, 2015; White House Task Force on Childhood Obesity, 2010). Research shows that about 22% of Latinx children younger than 19 are obese compared to about 14% of white children (Ogden, Carroll, Kit, & Flegal, 2014). Latinx children also suffer from high rates of asthma and poor mental health functioning (Isasi et al., 2016). It is important to keep in mind that these disparities exist in all specialized areas of healthcare practice for children, in addition to practice with the broader population. Examining disparities among children with autism and developmental disabilities provides an example of this. Children with autism spectrum disorder (ASD) and other developmental disabilities require early intervention and treatment to ensure they develop successfully to function in society as adults. ASD can be diagnosed as early as 18 months, yet studies show Latinx children are diagnosed between 4 and 8 years old (Liptak et al, 2008; Magaña, Lopez, Aguinaga, & Morton, 2013). Furthermore, Latinx children are underdiagnosed with ASD compared to white children (Centers for Disease Control and Prevention, 2018). Once diagnosed, Latinx children receive fewer early-intervention and specialty services (Magaña et al., 2013; Son, Magaña, Martinez, Pedraza, & Parish, 2020).

Looking back, much has been accomplished to achieve equal opportunity for all. However, much more needs to be done in the next 5 years to close the opportunity gap for minoritized populations, especially for Latinxs.

MAINSTREAMING GENDER

Addressing Gender Inequity by Mainstreaming Intersectionality
IJEOMA NWABUZOR OGBONNAYA

Researchers studying gender-based violence (GBV), including myself, have worked to identify—and, in some cases, dismantle—gender inequities. GBV, a term that identifies and names the pervasive physical, sexual, and psychological violence against women and girls both nationally and internationally, is one of the few areas of social work research and practice that is thoroughly gendered. Women and girls are victims; men and boys are perpetrators. Women and girls are passive; men and boys are aggressive. Women and girls are powerless; men and boys are powerful. The focus on binary gender fails to consider that not all people are treated equally, and it ignores the ways that people's experiences are shaped by their positionality in terms of race, gender outside of the binary, sexuality, religion, immigration status, and (dis)ability.

Focusing our definition of GBV on the gender binary prevents us from helping those most in need of GBV intervention. The focus on GBV as a "woman problem" centers a white, cis-gender, heterosexual, able-bodied version of womanhood that marginalizes the suffering of those who do not adhere to this narrow conceptualization of what it means to look like, act like, and, indeed, be a victim. Expanding our view of "woman" may allow for more person-centered research questions or client assessments. For instance, although I have studied Black and Latinx women's experiences with intimate partner violence and intimate partner violence services, how

continued

can my work speak to women who identify with these minoritized racial/ethnic backgrounds and are newly immigrated? Single mothers? Suffering from life-threatening illnesses? Experiencing discrimination because of their sexual orientation or gender identity? Although the recognition of intersectionality has pushed the field in new directions, it is not clear that our approaches to GBV research account for the confluence of survivors' marginalized identities. Inclusivity in social work practice must begin with nuanced approaches to social work research and education.

Social work research and education are driven by those within the academy. Social work faculty representing marginalized populations model inclusivity and serve as important mentors, advisors, and supports for social work students, which better equips students to engage in culturally appropriate practice (Bowie, Cherry, & Wooding, 2005). As more marginalized groups are being recruited to social work, they must be provided with the mentorship and support needed to succeed as social workers while simultaneously dealing with systematic inequalities related to their identities. In a recent qualitative study with lesbian, gay, bisexual, transgender, and queer (LGBTQ) faculty at schools of social work, researchers found that faculty who disclosed their sexual orientation expressed fear of their personal and professional safety; concerns about being the "token" representative for the LGBTQ community; exclusion from and lack of support for research and teaching opportunities; and the need to prove their worth and justify their actions, research, and teaching (Prock, Berlin, Harold, & Groden, 2019). Such challenges are likely familiar to many faculty with marginalized identities who experience gender and other social inequalities. These challenges also have consequences for social work students who later become social work practitioners, as well as for the clients that they serve.

As social workers, we should ensure that our work challenges and addresses gender inequalities from all intersections. Let's not only compare Black women to white women, assuming that white women are the "standard" from which women of other racial/ethnic groups deviate. Instead, let's work to understand how the multitude of identities intersecting with gender influence overall well-being. We must step outside our comfort zone, no longer maintaining the status quo. Mainstreaming gender is not enough; it is only by mainstreaming intersectionality that we can progress within the social work field.

References

Bowie, S. L., Cherry, D. J., & Wooding, L. H. (2005). African American MSW students: Personal influences on social work careers and factors in graduate school selection. *Social Work Education*, 24(2), 169–184.

Prock, K., Berlin, S., Harold, R., & Groden, S. (2019). Stories from LGBTQ social work faculty: What is the impact of being "out" in academia? *Journal of Gay & Lesbian Social Services*, 31(2), 182–201.

THE NEXT 5 YEARS: THE (MISSED?) LATINX OPPORTUNITY

More than 40 million individuals, or almost 14% of the current US population, were born in a different country. The US-born children of these immigrants, or the second generation, represent another 12% of the population. The largest proportion of these immigrants, more than 50%, trace their origins to Latin America (Budiman, Tamir, Mora, & Noe-Bustamante, 2020; Waters & Pineau, 2015). The United States is at a brink of a demographic transformation. If current trends continue, by 2060, one of every three people in the United States will be of Latinx descent (Stepler & Brown, 2015). The successful integration of these immigrants and their descendants is one of the most under recognized opportunities of American society (Calvo, 2018, p. 250; Calvo et al., 2016).

Let's begin by clarifying frequently asked questions about who the Latinxs in the United States *are* and what are the main characteristics of this diverse population. *Who* are the Latinxs is a question without a unique response. The short answer is: anybody that self-identifies as such (Lopez, Krogstad, & Passel, 2020). The term *Hispanic* was created in 1976 by the US Congress by passing the only law in the history of the country that mandates the collection of data for a specific ethnic group: "Americans of Spanish origin or descent." Since then, Hispanics, or Latinos—a term introduced in the 2000 Census—are defined as members of an ethnic group that, regardless of race, trace their origins to more than 20 Spanish-speaking nations from Latin America and Spain (Flores-Hughes, 2006). Although this definition is used by the US Census Bureau to gather information about Latinxs, the identity of millions of individuals that fall into this description is much more complex and fluid than what any definition can muster. The pan-ethnic Latinxs qualifier clusters together people from a variety of countries who speak diverse languages, identify with multiple races, and trace their presence in the United States for centuries. Latinxs presence in the country is, in fact, the second longest, after Native Americans (Rumbaut, 2006).

Latinxs, however, are portrayed as new arrivals because of the Immigration and Naturalization Act of 1965, which effectively opened up an unparalleled increase in immigration from Latin America, and the arrival of immigrants to nontraditional destinations within the United States (Rumbaut, 2006). Most Latinxs (54%) live in three southern states that are considered traditional destinations: California, Texas, and Florida (Noe-Bustamante, 2019). Although these traditional destinations have the largest share of Latinxs in the United States, other states, such as Washington, New Jersey, South Carolina, Delaware, and Kentucky, have become new destinations for Latinx immigrants who arrived in the past decade (Batalova, Hanna, & Levesque, 2021).

Concerning heritage, almost 7 of 10 Latinxs trace their origins to Mexico. Mexicans constitute not only the largest group of Latinxs, but also the largest immigrant group in the United States (Budiman et al., 2020; Noe-Bustamante,

2019). Other predominant countries of origin are Puerto Rico, Cuba, El Salvador, the Dominican Republic, and Guatemala (Noe-Bustamante, 2019). Since 2000, both a decline in immigration and high birth rates among Latina immigrants have led to a nativity shift in the composition of the Latinx community. Nearly two thirds of US Latinxs are born in the United States, and 80% are US citizens (Noe-Bustamante, 2019).

These Latinxs are engaged in a dynamic process of integration. By integration, we mean the process that immigrants and their descendants undergo to reach parity with the native-born population concerning critical opportunities for advancement (Brown & Bean, 2006; Calvo et al., 2016; Waters & Pineau, 2015). Integration is a two-way process that depends on the participation of immigrants, but also of the acceptance of Americans (Alba & Nee, 2012, Waters & Pinau, 2015). Unfortunately, through indicators of immigration, colorism, and language, US Latinxs have been racialized—especially during the past 5 years—as individuals unfit to become part of the American social fabric. Racialization in this context "signals the processes by which ideas about race are constructed, come to be regarded as meaningful, and are acted upon" (Murji & Solomos, 2005, p. 1). Discrimination and racism impact the health and economic opportunities of Latinxs negatively, particularly Black Latinxs, who experience racialization and its detrimental effects differently than white Latinxs (Cuevas, Dawson, & Williams, 2016; Figuereo & Calvo, 2021).

Despite these systemic barriers, Latinxs have the untapped potential to become the pillar on which the future of the United States is built. With the right institutional supports, the political and economic power of the growing Latinx population could trigger lasting, systemic changes that advance equity and justice for all. A key opportunity is the growing eligible Latinx voting population (Igielnik & Budiman, 2020). Eligible Latinx voters increased by 80% in the past decade as a result of a) US-born Latinxs turning 18 years old and b) an increase in naturalizations (Igielnik & Budiman, 2020). Latinxs comprised 13% of the electorate in the 2020 presidential election—the largest minority segment of the voting population (Krogstad & Noe-Bustamante, 2020). Latinx youth represent 25% of children and young adults in the United States—the largest of all groups (US Census Bureau, 2019)—suggesting that the voting power of the Latinx population will only continue to increase as more youth become eligible to vote. By electing government representatives who prioritize issues important to the Latinx population, Latinxs can begin to dismantle decades of discriminatory policies and institutionalize lasting, inclusive agendas that promote Latinx integration and advance economic, health, and social well-being.

Although severely affected by the COVID-19 global pandemic, the second opportunity in the integration of Latinxs stems from the significant labor force and economic participation of this growing population. Given the size of this population, the contribution of Latinxs in taxes is significant, amounting to

$250 billion in 2017 alone (New American Economy Research Fund, 2020). In addition, Latinxs make up an important percentage of the workforce, particularly in the agriculture, construction, and healthcare industries, which consistently experience workforce shortages (New American Economy Research Fund, 2020). Compared to the overall labor participation in the United States (63.2%), US-born Latinx workforce participation was 67.4% in 2019, and was 68.7% for foreign-born Latinxs. Despite having a relatively high poverty rate (15.7% compared to 7.3% among non-Latinx whites), Latinxs have notable consumer spending power—approximately $780 billion in 2017 (Creamer, 2020; New American Economy Research Fund, 2020). Through labor force participation and cumulative spending power, Latinxs are critical to the sustainability of the US economy.

OUR AGENDA

Latinxs must be at the center of federal and local government pandemic recovery policies, not only to advance equity and justice in this group, but also to support the US economy. How do we do this? A way to start is to capitalize on the growing Latinx voting population. Studies show that social connection within Latinx communities predicts voting behavior significantly, even among Spanish monolingual Latinxs, which represent about 31% of the Latinx population in the United States (Johnson, Stein, & Wrinkle, 2003; Population Reference Bureau, 2010). Initiatives to establish strong social connections and disseminate civic information in Latinx communities are needed. Social workers are well positioned to partner with community agencies before, during, and after election cycles to increase civic participation. Organizations such as Voting Is Social Work have laid the groundwork for this initiative (Dubuque-gallo, 2020).

To vote, foreign-born Latinxs need to naturalize, including undocumented immigrants. The legalization of US undocumented will not only benefit immigrants, but also the larger American society, particularly in the area of economic growth (Dixon & Rimmer, 2009; Gonzales Baker, 1997). An example of the benefits of legalization can be seen in the Immigration Reform and Control Act (IRCA) of 1986. The IRCA provided amnesty to approximately 3 million undocumented immigrants by creating a pathway to legal status (Cornelius, 1981; Dixon & Rimmer, 2009). With the IRCA, immigrants could choose their place of employment, lowering the chances of exploitation by employers who took advantage of the precarious situation (Gonzales Baker, 1997). In addition, temporary work status decreased fear of deportation, encouraging immigrants to settle down. Legalization also allowed immigrants to strengthen their social and economic ties in their countries of origin (Gonzales Baker, 1997; Hagan & Gonzales Baker, 1993) . Immigrants visited their countries of origin to see family and to invest in developments that improved the infrastructure of their hometowns and the well-being of their families (Hagan & Gonzales Baker, 1993). Last, legalization of undocumented immigrants, along with sanctions placed on employers who hired undocumented immigrants, increased wages for undocumented immigrants (Cobb-Clark, Shiells, & Lowell, 1995).

The legalization of undocumented immigrant workers through the IRCA also benefited the larger US population. This policy supported the US economy by providing a continuous flow of stable workers in agriculture, an industry that chronically experiences workforce gaps, as well as other industries (Gonzales Baker, 1997; Hinojosa-Azaola et al., 2018) . A large workforce translates to increased gross domestic product, which strengthens the economy (Dixon & Rimmer, 2009; Hinojosa-Azaola et al., 2018). Legalization increases workers' compensation, which in turn increases income taxes and other tax revenue for the US government to fund social programs that benefit the country as a whole (Cornelius, 1981; Gonzales Baker, 1997; Hinojosa-Azaola et al., 2018). In addition, as immigrants earn higher wages and experience upward social mobility, they are able to spend more money in the local economy and invest in their communities (Hinojosa-Azaola et al., 2018). Last, reducing the percentage of labor from undocumented immigrants through the legalization of these workers increases the base wages for all workers in the United States, because undocumented immigrants working for lower-than-average wages create a wage depression as companies compete to reduce their operating costs by hiring undocumented immigrants not protected by labor rights laws (Phillips & Massey, 1999). Enacting immigration reforms that increase the stability and spending power of immigrants benefits all who live in the United States in the long term.

Besides a pathway to citizenship, access to healthcare and increasing the presence of Latinx in the profession are key to seize the Latinx opportunity. Prior to the enactment of the ACA in 2014, Latinxs were less likely to have health coverage, and more likely to delay care and use the emergency department as a source of primary care than non-Latinx whites (Alcalá, Chen, Langellier, Roby, & Ortega, 2017). The ACA increased the coverage of some Latinxs, such as Puerto Ricans, Latinxs who were naturalized citizens, and those with adequate English language proficiency (Alcalá et al., 2017). The ACA also increased accessibility and use of behavioral healthcare among Latinxs (Rosales, Takeuchi, & Calvo, 2020). However, major barriers to reduce the discrimination that Latinxs experience in the healthcare context, including a lack of ethnic- and language-concordant providers of services, continue to exist (Calvo, Jablonka-Bayro, & Waters, 2017).

As mentioned, we have advanced in the presence of Latinxs in the profession, but there is considerable room for improvement, given the underrepresentation when compared to their population numbers in the United States and when compared to whites and Blacks. Just as is the case with doctoral enrollment, the percent of Latinx faculty remains considerably underrepresented in schools of social work. In 2009, they represented only 6% of all full-time faculty compared to white (69.5%) and Black (14.0%) faculty. In 2019, only 8.2% of faculty were of Latinx backgrounds, a significantly lower percentage than the corresponding 58.3% and 16.9% non-Hispanic white and Black faculty, respectively. Interestingly, between 2009 and 2019, both the Latinx and Black faculty increased by about 2%, whereas the percent of white faculty was 11.2% lower (Council on Social Work Education, 2010, 2020).

Given the significantly lower percentages of Latinx doctoral students and faculty, it is not surprising that the number of deans and directors is also quite low. At the time of this writing, no formal data exist that document the racial and ethnic backgrounds of faculty in these roles. An informal poll of deans and directors of schools of social work who are members of the National Association of Schools of Social Work and members of the Association of Latina and Latino Social Work Educators identified approximately a dozen deans and directors of schools of social work nationally. It also appears that only six of these deans are at research-intensive institutions. The poll, however, revealed a considerably larger number of faculty of Latinx backgrounds who are in various associate dean or directorship positions, which may provide a pool of qualified individuals to consider serving as deans and directors of schools of social work. To improve representation across the social work academic pipeline, structural and programmatic obstacles that hinder Latinx applications and enrollment to schools and programs of social work need to be identified at all levels, but particularly with regard to doctoral education. Increasing the number of Latinx who pursue doctoral education will increase the pool of individuals who will become faculty, who in turn will be more likely to develop innovative programs that meet the needs of Latinx students such as those highlighted earlier. We are not suggesting that only Latinx faculty can or is interested in helping strengthen the Latinx pipeline. To the contrary, the support of non-Latinx administrators and faculty has been incredible and critical in helping to increase the number of BSW, MSW, and doctoral students as well as faculty who are of Latinx backgrounds. However, because of the severe underrepresentation, and the growing needs of the more than 60 million Latinxs—a number that will continue to grow—we posit that by increasing the number of faculty and academic leaders who are Latinx, more intentional attention to Latinx recruitment and experiences will be in existence to prepare the workforce of the 22nd century. In addition to the development of more Latinx-centered programs such as those describe here, more financial assistance and scholarships need to be made available to Latinx students. Increasing the quality of mentorship and involvement in research projects is paramount to ensuring higher graduation rates and to encourage more Latinx to pursue a doctoral education. As these numbers increase, schools will have larger pools of Latinx to hire for faculty positions.

To succeed in recruiting more Latinx students, it is imperative that more programs increase their commitment to addressing the needs of Latinx students through such offerings as certificates, specializations, minors, and bilingual programs, among others. As highlighted by Calvo, Ortiz, Villa, and Baek (2018), schools of social work will need a "high degree of intentionality" (p. 267) to increase the representation of Latinxs. Informed by critical race theory (Yosso, 2005) and the Council on Social Work Education's 2016 Educational Policy and Accreditation Standards (Council on Social Work Education, 2015), Calvo et al. (2018) proposed a theoretical model that includes not only continuing to increase the profession's efforts at recruiting more Latinx students, but also making meaningful changes to the curricula, research agenda, and faculty.

REFERENCES

Alcalá, H. E., Chen, J., Langellier, B. A., Roby, D. H., & Ortega, A. N. (2017). Impact of the Affordable Care Act on health care access and utilization among Latinos. *The Journal of the American Board of Family Medicine*, 30, 52–62.

Andrew, S. (2020). The U.S. has 4% of the world's population but 25% of its coronavirus cases. CNN Health. Retrieved from https://www.cnn.com/2020/06/30/health/us-coronavirus-toll-in-numbers-june-trnd/index.html

Aviles-Santa, M. L., Heintzman, J., Lindberg, N. M., Guerro-Preston, R., Ramos, K., Abraido-Lanza, A. L., . . . Vaszuez, M. A. (2017). Personalized medicine and Hispanic health: Improving health outcomes and reducing health disparities: A National Heart, Lung, and Blood Institute workshop report. *BMC Proceedings*, 11, 1–12.

Baskin, M. L., Art, J., Franklin, F., & Allison, D. B. (2005). Prevalence of obesity in the United States. *Obesity Reviews*, 6, 5–7.

Batalova, J., Hanna, M., & Levesque, C. (2021). *Frequently requested statistics on immigrants and immigration in the United States*. Migration Policy Institute.

Brown, S. K., & Bean, F. D. (2006). Assimilations models, old and new: Explaining a long-term process. *Migration Information Source*, 3–41.

Budiman, A., Tamir, C., Mora, L., & Noe-Bustamante, L. (2020). Facts on U.S. immigrants, 2018: Statistical portrait of the foreign-born population in the United States. Pew Research Center. Retrieved from https://www.pewresearch.org/hispanic/2020/08/20/facts-on-u-s-immigrants-trend-data/

Calvo, R. (2018). Introduction: The Latinx opportunity, *Journal of Teaching in Social Work*, 38, 246–250.

Calvo, R., Jablonka-Bayro, J. M., & Waters, M. C. (2017). Obamacare in action: How access to the health care system contributes to immigrants' sense of belonging. *Journal of Ethnic and Migration Studies*.

Calvo, R., et al. (2016). *Achieving equal opportunity and justice: The integration of Latina/o immigrants into American society*. Grand Challenges for Social Work initiative working paper. American Academy of Social Work & Social Welfare.

Calvo, R., Ortiz, L., Villa, P., & Baek, K. (2018). A call for action: Latinxs in social work education. *Journal of Teaching in Social Work, 38*(3), 263–276. https://doi.org/10.1080/08841233.2018.1466587

Centers for Disease Control and Prevention. (2018). *Spotlight on: Racial and ethnic differences in children identified with autism spectrum disorder (ASD)*. AADM Network.

Centers for Disease Control and Prevention. (2021, February 3). Health disparities: Race and Hispanic origin. Retrieved from https://www.cdc.gov/nchs/nvss/vsrr/covid19/health_disparities.htm

Cobb-Clark, D. A., Shiells, C. R., & Lowell, B. L. (1995). Immigration reform: The effects of employer sanctions and legalization on wages. *Journal of Labor Economics, 13*, 472–498.

Cornelius, W. A. (1981). The Reagan Administration's proposals for a new U.S. immigration policy: An assessment of potential effects. *The International Migration Review, 15*, 769–778.

Couch, K. A., Fairlie, R. W., & Xu, H. (2020). Early evidence of the impacts of COVID-19 on minority unemployment. *Journal of Public Economics, 192*, 104287.

Council on Social Work Education. (2010). 2009 Statistics on social work education in the United States: A summary. Unpublished manuscript. Retrieved from https://www.cswe.org/CMSPages/GetFile.aspx?guid=42983f18-d35d-4700-97fd-2e2ee07dd391

Council of Social Work Education. (2015). *Educational policy and accreditation standards for Baccalaureate and Master's Social Work Programs*. Alexandria, VA: Author.

Council on Social Work Education. (2020). 2019 Statistics on social work education in the United States. Unpublished manuscript. Retrieved from https://cswe.org/getattachment/Research-Statistics/2019-Annual-Statistics-on-Social-Work-Education-in-the-United-States-Final-(1).pdf.aspx

Creamer, J. (2020). Poverty rates for Blacks and Hispanics reached historic lows in 2019: American counts: Stories behind the numbers. Retrieved form https://www.census.gov/library/stories/2020/09/poverty-rates-for-blacks-and-hispanics-reached-historic-lows-in-2019.html

Cuevas, A. G., Dawson, B. A., & Williams, D. R. (2016). Race and skin color in Latino health: An analytic review. *American Journal of Public Health, 106*, 2131–2136,

Daviglus, M. L., Talavera, G. A., Aviles-Santa, M. L, Allison, M., Cai, J., Criqui, M. H., ... Stamler, J. (2012). Prevalence of major cardiovascular risk factors and cardiovascular disease among Hispanic/Latinx individuals of diverse backgrounds in the United States. *Journal of the American Medical Association, 308*, 1775–1784.

Dixon, P. B., & Rimmer, M. T. (2009). Restriction or legalization? Measuring the economic benefits of immigration reform.

Dubay, L. C., & Lebrun, L. A. (2012). Health, behavior, and health care disparities: Disentangling the effects of income and race in the United States. *International Journal of Health Services, 42*, 607–625.

Dubuque-gallo, C. (2020, July 27). Welcome: Voting is social work. Retrieved from https://votingissocialwork.org/

Figuereo, V., & Calvo, R. (2021). Racialization and psychological distress among U.S. Latinxs. *Journal of Racial and Ethnic Health Disparities* (in press).

Flores-Hughes, G. (2006). The origin of the term "Hispanic." *Harvard Journal of Hispanic Policy, 18*, 81–84.

Goldbach, J. T., Amaro, H., Vega W., & Walter M. D. (2015). *The grand challenge of promoting equality by addressing social stigma*. Grand Challenges for Social Work initiative working paper no. 18. Cleveland, OH: American Academy of Social Work and Social Welfare.

Gonzales, S., & Sommers, B. D. (2018). Intra-ethnic coverage disparities among Latinxs and the effects of health reform. *Health Services, 53,* 1373–1386.

Gonzales Baker, S. (1997). The "amnesty" aftermath: Current policy issues stemming from the legalization programs of the 1986 Immigration Reform and Control Act. *31,* 5–27.

González-Barrera, A., & López, M. H. (2015). Is being Hispanic a matter of race, ethnicity or both? Pew Research Center. Retrieved from https://www.pewresearch.org/fact-tank/2015/06/15/is-being-hispanic-a-matter-of-race-ethnicity-or-both/

Grand Challenges for Social Work. (2021). *Progress and plans for the Grand Challenges: An impact report at year 5 of the 10-year initiative.*

Hostetter, M., & Klein, S. (2018). In focus: Identifying and addressing health disparities among Hispanics. The Commonwealth Fund. Retrieved from https://www.commonwealthfund.org/publications/2018/dec/focus-identifying-and-addressing-health-disparities-among-hispanics

Igielnik, R., & Budiman, A. (2020). The changing racial and ethnic composition of the U.S. electorate. Retrieved from https://www.pewresearch.org/2020/09/23/the-changing-racial-and-ethnic-composition-of-the-u-s-electorate/

Johnson, M., Stein, R. M., & Wrinkle, R. (2003). Language choice, residential stability, and voting among Latino Americans. *Social Science Quarterly, 84,* 412–424.

Kim, B. E, McCarter, S., & Logan-Greene, P. (2020). *Achieving equal opportunity and justice in juvenile justice.* Grand Challenges for Social Work initiative working paper no. 25. Baltimore, MD: Grand Challenges for Social Work.

Krogstad, J. M., & Noe-Bustamante, L. (2020). Key facts about U.S. Latinos for National Hispanic Heritage Month. Pew Research Center. Retrieved from https://www.pewresearch.org/fact-tank/2020/09/10/key-facts-about-u-s-latinos-for-national-hispanic-heritage-month/

Kuchment, A., Hacker, H. K., & Solis, D. (2020, December 20). The color of COVID. *The Dallas Morning News.*

Laurencin, C. T., & McClinton, A. (2020). The COVID-19 pandemic: A call to action to identify and address racial and ethnic disparities. *Journal of Racial and Ethnic Health Disparities,* 1–5.

Liptak, G. S., Benzoni, L. B., Mruzek, D. W., Nolan, K. W., Thingvoll, M. A., Wade, C. M., . . . et al. (2008). Disparities in diagnosis and access to health services for children with autism: Data from the National Survey of Children's Health. *Journal of Developmental and Behavioral Pediatrics, 29,* 152–160.

Magaña, S., Lopez, K., Aguinaga, A., & Morton, H. (2013) Access to diagnosis and treatment services among Latino children with autism spectrum disorders. *Intellectual and Developmental Disabilities, 51,* 141–153.

Metzger, M. W., & Khare, A. T. (2017). *Fair housing and inclusive communities.* Grand Challenges for Social Work initiative working paper no. 24). Cleveland, OH: American Academy of Social Work & Social Welfare.

Murji, K., & Solomos, J. (Eds.)/ (2005). *Racialization: Studies in theory and practice.* New York, NY: Oxford University Press.

National Association of Social Workers. (2021). 2021 Blueprint of federal social policy priorities: Recommendations to the Biden-Harris administration and Congress. Retrieved from https://www.socialworkers.org/LinkClick.aspx?fileticket=KPdZqqY60t4%3D&portalid=0

National Center for Education Statistics. (2018). Digest of education statistics. Retrieved from https://nces.ed.gov/programs/digest/d18/foreword.asp

New American Economy Research Fund. (2020). Power of the purse: The contributions of Hispanic Americans. New American Economy Research Fund. Retrieved from https://research.newamericaneconomy.org/report/hispanic-americans-2019/

Noe-Bustamante (2019). Key facts about U.S. Hispanics and their diverse heritage. Pew Research Center.

Ogden, C. L., Carroll, M. D., Kit, B. K., & Flegal, K. M. (2014). Prevalence of childhood and adult obesity in the United States, 2011–2012. *Journal of American Medical Association, 311*, 806–814.

Parra-Medina, D., Liang, Y., Yin, Z., Esparza, L., & Lopez, L. (2015). Weight outcomes of Latinx adults and children participating in the Y Living Program, a family-focused lifestyle intervention, San Antonio, 2012–2013. *Preventing Chronic Disease, 12*, e219.

Pew Research Center. (2020). U.S. Hispanic population surpassed 60 million in 2019, but growth has slowed. Retrieved from https://www.pewresearch.org/fact-tank/2020/07/07/u-s-hispanic-population-surpassed-60-million-in-2019-but-growth-has-slowed/

Phillips, J. A., & Massey, D. S. (1999). The new labor market: Immigrants and wages after IRCA. *Demography, 36*, 233–246.

Population Reference Bureau. (2010). Population bulletin update: Latinos in the United States 2010. Retrieved from https://www.prb.org/latinosupdate2/

Rosales, R., Takeuchi, D., & Calvo, R. (2020). After the Affordable Care Act: The effects of the health safety net and the Medicaid expansion on Latinxs' use of behavioral healthcare in the US. *The Journal of Behavioral Health Services & Research*.

Rumbaut, R. (2006). Hispanics and the future of America. In *The making of a people*. Washington, DC: National Academies Press.

Rumbaut, R. (2011). Pigments of our imagination: The racialization of the Hispanic-Latino category. Migration information source. Migration Policy Institute.

Schneiderman, N., Llabre, M., Cowie, C.C., Barnhart, J., Carnethon, M., Gallo, L. C., . . . Aviles Santa, M. L. (2014). Prevalence of diabetes among Hispanics/Latinxs from diverse backgrounds: The Hispanic Community Health Study/Study of Latinxs (HCHS/SOL). *Diabetes Care, 4*, 2233–2239.

Sommers, B. D., McMurtry, C. L., Blendon, R. J., Benson, J. M., & Sayde, J. M. (2017). Beyond health insurance: Remaining disparities in US health care in the post-ACA era. *The Milbank Quarterly, 95*, 43–69.

Son, E., Magaña S., Martinez, Pedraza, F., & Parish, E. (2020). Providers' guidance to parents and service use for Latino children with developmental disabilities. *American Journal on Intellectual and Developmental Disabilities, 125*, 64–75.

Teasley, M. L., McRoy, R. G., Joyner, M., Armour, M., Gourdine, R. M., Crewe, S. E., . . . Fong, R. (2017). *Increasing success for African American children and youth*. (Grand Challenges for Social Work initiative working paper no. 21. Cleveland, OH: American Academy of Social Work and Social Welfare.

US Census Bureau. (2019). Population estimates show aging across race groups differs. Retrieved from https://www.census.gov/newsroom/press-releases/2019/estimates-characteristics.html

Velasco-Mondagron, E., Jimenez, A., Palladino-Davis, A. G., Davis, D., & Escamilla-Cejudo, J. A. (2016). Hispanic health in the USA: A scoping review of the literature. *Public Health Reviews, 37*, 31.

Waters, M.C., & Pineau, M.G. (Eds.). (2015). *The integration of immigrants into American society*. Washington, DC: The National Academies Press.

White House Task Force on Childhood Obesity. (2010, May). Solving the problem of childhood obesity within a generation. Retrieved from https://letsmove.obamawhitehouse.archives.gov/sites/letsmove.gov/files/TaskForce_on_Childhood_Obesity_May2010_FullReport.pdf

Wegar, K. (2000). Adoption, family ideology, and social stigma: Bias in community attitudes, adoption research, and practice. *Family Relations, 49*, 363–369.

Weiss, M. G., Ramakrishna, J., & Somma, D. (2006). Health-related stigma: Rethinking concepts and interventions. *Psychology, Health & Medicine, 11*, 277–287.

Yosso, T. J. (2005). Whose culture has capital? A critical race theory discussion on community cultural wealth. *Race, Ethnicity & Education, 8*, 69–91.

CHAPTER 14
Eliminating Racism

MARTELL TEASLEY, SUSAN MCCARTER, BONGKI WOO, LANESHIA R. CONNER, MICHAEL S. SPENCER, AND TATYANA GREEN

OVERVIEW OF THE GRAND CHALLENGE TO ELIMINATE RACISM

The Grand Challenges for Social Work (GCSW) have galvanized the profession, serving as a catalyst for change by bridging collaborative scholarly and public initiatives with innovative approaches that are backed by science to tackle long-standing and seemingly intractable social welfare problems. In 2013, the American Academy of Social Work and Social Welfare identified problems that were important, compelling to the broader public, and represented areas that were amenable to meaningful and measurable change within 10 years. From more than 80 concepts, the Academy identified 12 Grand Challenges for the profession under the three domains of *individual and family well-being*, *stronger social fabric*, and *just society*. "Ending racism" was proposed initially but not selected (Lubben et al., 2018).

Arguments against addressing racism in the Grand Challenges initially included that it is pertinacious, insoluble, and cannot be ameliorated in 10 years. The amount of empirical evidence backed by science was also discussed. Last, the supposition was made that racism intersects all other Grand Challenges and would thus be addressed within each of the selected GCSW and a stand-alone grand challenge was not necessary. Published in 2019, *The Grand Challenges for Social Work: Vision, Mission, Domain, Guiding Principles* and *Guideposts to Action* suggest that "the commitment to ending racism and other injustices is fundamental throughout the Grand Challenges for Social Work."

The Grand Challenge to Eliminate Racism calls for the social work profession to focus on the centrality of racism and white supremacy, both within

Martell Teasley, Susan McCarter, Bongki Woo, Laneshia R. Conner, Michael S. Spencer, and Tatyana Green, *Eliminating Racism* In: *Grand Challenges for Social Work and Society*. Second Edition. Edited by: Richard P. Barth, Jill T. Messing, Trina R. Shanks, and James Herbert Williams, Oxford University Press. © Oxford University Press 2022. DOI: 10.1093/oso/9780197608043.003.0014 society and within the profession. This chapter first reviews the history of race and racism in the United States to contextualize this work. We then reflect on the profession's racist history, and current positionality and commitment to racial justice. The claim that the topics of race and racism are infused across the Grand Challenges is then examined systematically. Last, insomuch as this Grand Challenge will provide both support and accountability to the profession to move forward and innovate to eliminate racism, the chapter concludes with specific strategies for moving forward at micro, mezzo, and macro levels of individual awareness and reflection, workforce development, social work education, and policy agendas.

A VERY BRIEF HISTORY OF RACE IN THE UNITED STATES

It is estimated that no less than 10 million people with hundreds of different Indigenous cultures and speaking almost 2,000 different languages lived on the North American continent prior to the contact of Columbus and others (Mann, 2005). Representing Spain, Columbus traveled to the Americas for exploitation and conquest. For more than two centuries after the start of European colonialization and genocide, the Indigenous populations were reduced to fewer than one million. Many of the Native Americans who survived had their land stolen and parental rights terminated and were forced to relocate to reservations with limited rights for self-government (The Indian Removal Act of 1830). Today, Native Americans comprise 1.7% of the US population, and 22% of them live on reservations (Office of Minority Health, 2021). James Loewen (2007, p. 53) describes how Columbus transformed the modern world and revolutionized race relations by the "taking of land, wealth, and labor from Indigenous people in the Western hemisphere, leading to their near extermination, and the transatlantic slave trade, which created a racial underclass."

The Dutch brought the first kidnapped and enslaved individuals from the West Indies to the colony of Jamestown, VA, in 1619 (Rawley & Behrendt, 2005). In the early 17th century, kidnapped Africans were sold as indentured servants, with a limited servitude after which they would live free. This soon changed, however, as Africans were differentiated from English indentured servants and enslaved for life, including their unborn children and the children born from white enslavers' rape of Black women (Daniels-Rauterkus, 2019; Farley, 2000). Africans were conferred a subhuman status, and the concept of whiteness took on a newly contrived superior social status as those with white skin subordinated those with dark skin legally and socially (Gregory, 2021). Antebellum American society and later Social Darwinism then reified the so-called/thought-to-be "scientific" discoveries of the time that built the rationale for white supremacy and continues to foster anti-Blackness.

Although chattel slavery ended after the Emancipation Proclamation and the ratification of the 13th Amendment to the US Constitution in 1865, segregation and discrimination continued to be practiced throughout the United States (Lyons, 2007).

The appropriation of Mexican and Indigenous land continued into the 18th century as whites redefined Native North Americans as "foreigners." The Naturalization Act (H.R. 40), passed in 1790, reads:

> Be it enacted by the Senate and the House of Representatives of the United States of America in Congress assembled, that any alien, being a free white person, who shall have resided within the limits and under the jurisdiction of the United States for the term of two years, may be admitted to become a citizen.

First-generation immigrants from Asia, the Caribbean, Central and South America, and Mexico were thus expressly denied citizenship rights, including the right to vote, own property, file lawsuits, and testify in court; and this Act was not eliminated until the McCarran Walter Act of 1952 (H.R. 5678).

Exploitation continued with the recruitment and abuse of Chinese, Japanese, and Filipino tradesmen commissioned to build the US railroads and work in the mines (Takaki, 1993). Then, in 1942, President Roosevelt signed Executive Order 9066 requiring Japanese Americans living near the Pacific coast, two thirds of whom were US citizens and three fourths of whom were younger than the age of 25 years, to relocate to 10 internment camps (Kashima, 2003). More than 120,000 Japanese Americans were forcibly evacuated to military internment camps during World War II, and their homes and property seized and sold to whites at reduced costs (Hosokawa, 1969; Park, 2020).

In 1977, the federal Office of Management and Budget attempted to standardize the federal government's race and ethnicity categories for the first time, but the categories were still rather inconsistent (Office of Management and Budget, 1997). "Black" was considered a "racial group" whereas "White" was not. "Hispanic" reflected Spanish colonization but excluded non-Spanish parts of Central and South America, whereas "American Indian or Alaskan Native" required "cultural identification through tribal affiliation or community recognition," which is not necessary for any other classification (Dismantling Racism Works - History, n.d., p. 4). The categories were amended in 1996, to add "Native Hawaiian and Other Pacific Islander." And in 2000, the US Census added the category "Two or More Races" to the Census (Jones & Smith, 2001). In 2010, 9 million people, or 3% of the US population, identified this way, and those selecting two or more races grew by 32% from 2000 to 2010 (US Census Bureau, 2012).

Meanwhile, immigration policy continues to reflect concerning times in US history. After September 11, 2002, the US Patriot Act (H.R. 3162) allows government officials to detain suspected "terrorists" without legal representation and for indeterminate periods of time (The USA Patriot Act, H.R. 3162). Although only 1.1% of the US population is Muslim (Mohamed, 2018), Muslims account for 25% of the discrimination complaints against employers (Durrani, 2012). In 2010, Arizona passed Senate Bill 1070, which requires all "aliens" older than 14 years to register with the US government after 30 days and to carry ID documents at all times, and includes penalties for anyone who shelters, hires, and transports unregistered "aliens." In 2012, the US Supreme Court upheld required immigration checks while striking down the other provisions. In 2016, Donald J. Trump won his bid for the presidency, campaigning on building a wall between the United States and Mexico; signed Executive Order 13769, also known as the Muslim Ban (in 2017); referred to Haiti and Africa as "shithole" countries (in 2018); consistently elected not to condemn the behavior of white supremacists (with incidents involving David Duke in 2016, Charlottesville in 2017, and Proud Boys in 2020), and went as far as to incite a riot on the US Capitol on January 6, 2021. During his administration, the Federal Bureau of Investigation reported an upsurge in hate crimes and attacks against American Muslims, immigrants, Black citizens, Jews, and transgender people (Edwards & Rushin, 2018).

On February 26, 2012, George Zimmerman shot and killed 17-year-old Trayvon Martin as he returned home from a convenience store in Sanford, FL. Zimmerman was acquitted. In 2014, police officer Daniel Pantaleo choked Eric Garner to death on a sidewalk in New York and is not indicted. Less than a month later, officer Darren Wilson shot and killed Michael Brown in Ferguson, MO, and was also not indicted. In June 2015, nine people were massacred during bible study at Mother Emanuel AME church in Charleston, SC, by Dylann Roof, a self-identified white supremacist, who was not arrested until the following day. Breonna Taylor was shot and killed by police on March 13, 2020, while sleeping in her apartment. None of the officers involved were charged with her death. In May 2020, George Floyd was killed after police officer Derek Chauvin, pressed his knee into Mr. Floyd's neck for a recorded 8 minutes 46 seconds. Many credit this as an international tipping point leading to widespread protest and condemnation of police tactics and the lack of social redress for racial justice (Deliso, 2021). Police killings of Black people are considered racialized terror and are being referred to as the second pandemic of the 2020s. Camera phones, social media, and #BlackLivesMatter continue to shed light on this national injustice and has raised public awareness for some Americans (https://blacklivesmatter.com/) (Davis, 2016; Dixon & Dundes, 2020; Dismantling Racism Works - History, n.d.), but we must move beyond raising awareness to addressing the oppression, brutality, and deaths.

During the COVID-19 pandemic, there has been spike in anti-Asian racism, including everything from verbal slurs to physical attacks, including mass murder. As of February 2021, Stop AAPI Hate (Asian Americans and Pacific

Islanders) received more than 3,795 reports of discrimination associated with the coronavirus (Jeoung, Horse, Popovic, & Lim, 2021). On March 16, 2021, a series of mass shootings by a sole assailant occurred in Atlanta, GA, leaving eight people—including six Asian women—dead. Amid this documented increase in anti-Asian racism and attacks, reports of depression and anxiety symptoms among Asians have also increased significantly compared to the figures in 2019 (National Center for Health Statistics, 2020). Elevated anti-Asian prejudice and racism calls for additional antiracism awareness, research, intervention, advocacy, and policy.

RACE AND RACIAL IDENTITY AS SOCIAL CONSTRUCTS

According to racial formation theory, race is a socially constructed identity and is situated in social structure (Omi & Winant, 2015). Racial formation is "a sociohistorical process by which racial categories are created, inhibited, transformed and destroyed. Those in power define groups of people in a certain way that depends on a racist social structure" (Schaefer, 2008, p. 15). An example of racial formation is the federal American Indian policy that combined previously distinct tribes into a single racial group and forced the relocation of most Indigenous people onto reservations (e.g., the Indian Removal Act of 1830, the Indian Appropriations Act of 1851). In the southern states, an example of racial formation is the *one-drop rule*, stipulating that if individuals had just one drop of "Black blood" or racial lineage, that person would be considered Black (Khanna, 2016). Marsiglia and Kulis (2016, p. 12) argue that the sole reason for racial formation is to establish a hierarchy used to discriminate against target groups.

Individual DNA can be analyzed through genetic similarities and differences to others living around the world and can then be matched to global migration patterns. Humans, however, cannot be distinguished genetically from one another by race or ethnicity (Marsiglia & Kulis, 2016, p. 11). Instead, race is a sociopolitical construct that was created and is reinforced by social and institutional norms and practices, and by individual attitudes and behaviors (Funk, Varghese & Zúñiga, 2018, p. 66). Delgado and Stefancic (2017) operationalize race as a group of individuals with observed or attributed common characteristics, and ethnicity as a group of individuals with common characteristics such as cultures, traditions, and/or national origins. They further contend that these classifications have been manipulated and embedded at the macro level to influence unjustly access to resources that benefits some while obstructing others (Delgado & Stefancic, 2017). In sum, Smithsonian scholars define race as, "a human-invented, shorthand term used to describe and categorize people into various social groups based on characteristics like skin color, physical features, and genetic heredity. Race, while not a valid biological concept, is a real social construction that gives or denies benefits and privileges" (National Museum of African American History and Culture, n.d.).

RACISM AND WHITE SUPREMACY

Racism can be defined as a system of advantage based on race (Wellman, 2012). It is also recognized as the subordination of individuals or groups based on a common characteristic and has been a central element in the historical and current social, political, cultural, and economic facets of America (Feagin, Johnson, & Rush, 2000). Thus, it is important to differentiate individual acts of bigotry and prejudice from racism. Dismantling Racism Works – Racism Defined (n.d.) suggests:

> Racism is different from racial prejudice, hatred, or discrimination. Racism involves one group having the power to carry out systematic discrimination through the institutional policies and practices of the society and by shaping the cultural beliefs and values that support those racist policies and practices. (p. 2)

Many associate the term *white supremacy* with *white supremacist/white nationalist*, *racist skinhead*, and *neo-Nazi*, but the term *white supremacy* actually refers to a hierarchy of any sort that prioritizes whites and whiteness over all other. Derald Wing Sue has written extensively on the topic and begins this differentiation with the term *ethnocentric monoculturalism*, with *ethnocentric* meaning focusing on one ethnic/cultural group as central or the best and *monoculturalism* meaning the belief in one "right" culture. Taylor (2006, p. 1) defines ethnocentric monoculturalism as "an unconscious or conscious overvaluation of one's own cultural beliefs and practices, and simultaneous invalidation of other cultural worldviews." Sue adds that ethnocentric monoculturalism has five dangerous components: belief in superiority (your group), belief in inferiority (other groups), power to impose standards, manifestation in institutions, and the invisible veil (Sue, Rasheed, & Rasheed, 2016, pp. 96–99). Sue (2006) contends that white supremacy involves viewing whiteness as normative and ideal, and concludes:

> Whiteness, White supremacy, and White privilege are three interlocking forces that disguise racism so it may allow White people to oppress and harm persons of color while maintaining their individual and collective advantage and innocence. If we are to overcome, or at least minimize the forces of racism, we must make Whiteness visible. As long as Whiteness remains invisible and is equated with normality and superiority, People of Color will continue to suffer from its oppressive qualities. (p. 53)

MAINSTREAMING GENDER

Centering Intersectionality in the Challenge to Eliminate Racism: Learning from Indigenous Feminisms
KATIE SCHULTZ

There is no such thing as a single issue struggle, because we do not live single-issue lives.
—Audre Lorde

We cannot eliminate racism without also addressing gender. Work by Black feminists on intersectionality and gender(ed) racism has shown how racism and sexism intersect readily and reliably to support systems of hierarchy, pointing to the inadequacy of using a single-axis framework for understanding disparities. This work established that the effects of racism are fundamentally distinct, based on gender identities. Moreover, multiple scholars have demonstrated how race and gender are constructed physically, socially, legally, and historically to co-create, legitimize, and maintain systems of oppression.

The Grand Challenge to Eliminate Racism calls on us to identify evidence and interventions to end racism, whereas gender mainstreaming challenges us to center gender in our research, policies, and practices. However, gender is racialized and racism is gendered; one cannot be addressed without affecting the other. Efforts to eliminate racism should not ignore the context of gender, nor should gender mainstreaming proceed without interrogating the shortsightedness and potential harm of this process when devoid of a racial equity lens. This grand challenge was added during a year when anti-Black violence renewed attention to racial injustice, compelling us to examine dominant frameworks within our profession.

Intersectional Indigenous feminist frameworks provide a foundation for understanding and addressing connecting axes of oppression. Indigenous feminists start from the premise that systems of oppression—settler colonialism, racism, and heteropatriarchy—rely on each other to persist. Indigenous feminists have detailed clear critiques of white feminism as centering gender above racial identities and sovereignty, and for assuming shared experiences of patriarchy. They offer a unique illustration of the complex intersectionality of race, Indigeneity, and gender in their analyses of the United States as a settler colonial nation-state and settler colonialism as a racialized, gendered process. Within this context, they describe how the needs of Indigenous women go beyond gender parity, and include decolonization and sovereignty for all Indigenous peoples.

Settler colonialism is a continuous social and political formation that erects and maintains a settler society on Indigenous land where colonizers come to stay. This ongoing process relies on the elimination of Indigenous populations to justify the taking of land. Settler colonialism is rooted in

continued

extraction—of land (in the case of Native nations) and labor (in the case of Black and Brown bodies). Settler power is exercised through the creation of racist narratives (e.g., savages) wherein settlers are situated as racially superior. Through this process, constructions of race are used to develop the nation-state and accumulate wealth. Moreover, this process is hyper- and heterosexualized as a tactic for taking land and bodies.

Indigenous feminists make clear the link between settler colonialism and heteropatriarchy, the latter of which naturalizes heterosexuality, gender binaries, and gender dominance. In attempting to eliminate complex systems of kinship and governance to weaken Native nations in the quest for land, settler colonialism also introduced binary gender roles and heteronormative dyadic relationships to create new settler citizens by dismantling gender balance and reciprocity. This racialized, gendered process can be seen in this country's history of forced sterilization of Black and Native women, persistent poverty, and historical and contemporary rates of violence against female-identified Black, Indigenous, People of Color.

Like this nation, dominant social work approaches are rooted in settler colonialism, heteropatriarchy, and white supremacy. We must challenge the assumptions and values embedded in our professional policies, the practices that uphold these ways of thinking, our positions within these hierarchies, and our complicity in maintaining them. Indigenous feminists urge us to move toward knowledge and governance rooted in reciprocity and relationships. Approaches to social work research, policy, and practice that emphasize care and responsibility toward each other, encourage collaboration, and promote equity are a starting place for reimagining our profession. These Indigenous activists and scholars also encourage us to look beyond existing nation-states and structures as sites of liberation, reminding us that inclusion in existing structures alone is not enough. The decision to include implies hierarchy. A parallel call for social work asks: What new systems must we create to lead us toward eradicating both racism and sexism in our profession and society as a whole? In what areas might we follow the lead of Indigenous feminists and transform our profession by considering liberated paths outside of existing systems?

In developing this path forward, social work scholarship, policy, and practice should draw from key principles of Indigenous feminisms and activism. Principle among these is positioning gender, race, and Indigeneity of equal value in efforts to destabilize hierarchical systems. Our profession must also decenter Western scholarly frames of reference, and related assumptions and values embedded in our policies and practice. Moreover, Indigenous feminists have been quick to acknowledge diversity among Indigenous populations. Likewise, an intersectional approach to social work requires us to be explicit in our attention to diverse intersections of racism and patriarchy in our education, research, and practice to dismantle policies and principles that sustain inequities, and to address intersecting injustices in our profession and society as a whole.

SOCIAL WORK'S POSITIONALITY WITH RACISM AND WHITE SUPREMACY: HISTORICAL AND CURRENT

The history, development, and current state of social work are interdependent. Thus, white supremacy not only undergirds US history, it is also at the foundation of social work practice, education, research, and advocacy (Almeida, Werkmeister Rozas, Cross-Denny, Kyeunghae Lee, & Yamada, 2019). During the early days of social work in the United States, the distribution of social welfare was predicated on beliefs of "deservingness," with non-whites deemed less deserving. Charity organization societies and settlement houses in the 19th century were segregated by race and were created largely by and for white individuals. Neither movement addressed or challenged systemic racism and white hegemonic norms directly (Gregory, 2021). Ironically, Jane Addams began her charity work with Blacks, but started Hull House excluding them (Carle, 2013). Bonilla-Silva and Zuberi (2008) suggest that social work is rooted in "white logic and white methods."

All professions are situated within their larger societal context, but social work has a unique and specific obligation to challenge social injustice.

> Social workers pursue social change, particularly with and on behalf of vulnerable and oppressed individuals and groups of people. Social workers' social change efforts are focused primarily on issues of poverty, unemployment, discrimination, and other forms of social injustice. These activities seek to promote sensitivity to and knowledge about oppression and cultural and ethnic diversity. Social workers strive to ensure access to needed information, services, and resources; equality of opportunity; and meaningful participation in decision making for all people. (National Association of Social Workers - Code of Ethics. Ethical Principles, Value: Social Justice, p. 1.)

The majority of social workers have historically and continue to identify as white, whereas the majority of those they serve (described earlier), typically identify as Black, Latinx, Indigenous, and other people of color (See Table 14.1). Social work has both historically perpetuated and been complicit in practices that embody the injustice and oppression that it claims to stand against (Cherry, 2018; Park, 2020). Gregory (2021, p. 33) argues that there is both a "historical and contemporary symbiosis between whiteness and social work."

In 1992, McMahon and Allen-Meares asked, "Is social work racist?" They conducted a content analysis to review social work publications between 1980 and 1989 and found that only 5.95% of the 1,965 articles analyzed addressed working with racially minoritized communities (McMahon & Allen-Meares, 1992). This analysis led them to conclude that the profession is "naive and

Table 14.1. ACTIVE SOCIAL WORKERS IN 2015 BY EDUCATION TYPE

Race	Non-SW Bachelor's	Bachelor's in SW	Master's in SW	Total
American Indian or Alaska Native	0.9%	1.2%	0.5%	0.8%
Asian	4.5%	1.8%	3.2%	3.6%
Black or African American	23.2%	25.7%	19.1%	21.6%
Native Hawaiian or Other Pacific Islander	0.3%	0%	0.1%	0.2%
Some other race	3.0%	1.9%	2.0%	2.4%
Two or more races	3.0%	2.1%	2.5%	2.7%
White	65.3%	67.4%	72.6%	68.8%
Ethnicity				
Not Spanish, Hispanic, Latino	87.4%	89.3%	90.5%	89.0%
Spanish, Hispanic, Latino	12.6%	10.7%	9.5%	11.0%

SW = social work.
Source: US Census Bureau (2016).

superficial in its antiracist practice" (p. 537). Twenty-five years later, Corley and Young (2018) replicated McMahon and Allen-Meares' content analysis, reviewing articles published from 2005 through 2015. Of the 1,690 articles they reviewed, only 7.28% addressed content related to racially and ethnically minoritized communities. Both studies suggest that despite social work's articulated stance on racism, the profession is failing to address racism and white supremacy, and the experiences of racially minoritized populations, and is failing to build racial equity. Corley and Young call for a transformation of the way research is framed, defined, and interpreted, and for a decolonization of social work's knowledge base.

Walter et al. (2017) suggest that social work's services and organizations continue to perpetuate ethnocentric monoculturalism. Many prominent social work organizations were established with and still have predominantly white leadership and membership—namely, the American Academy of Social Work and Social Welfare, the Council on Social Work Education (CSWE), the National Association of Deans and Directors, and the Society for Social Work and Research. Disproportionate representation in leadership ensures that the voices and experiences of people of color are not centered, and that the profession continues white supremacy culture. Despite its establishment as a helping profession dedicated to social justice, social work, at times, has struggled with and, at other times, has created pathways to be a profession that ameliorates racism and white hegemony. Gregory (2021, p. 33) argues that social work "has not taken an honest, rigorous, critical account of its own whiteness . . . [and] it is imperative that the profession begin to do so." The Grand Challenge to Eliminate Racism is an excellent place for the social work profession to examine and reflect on how it has been complicit in and has even perpetuated white supremacy, racism, and oppressive policies and practices.

EMPIRICAL/NONEMPIRICAL EVIDENCE OF RACE AND RACISM ACROSS THE OTHER GRAND CHALLENGES

We conducted a systematic review of the lead concept papers for each of the GCSW in February 2021 (n = 22 concept papers) to examine the claim that the topics of race/ethnicity and racism are addressed within each of the Grand Challenges. [Rao et al. (2021) conducted a similar review of the GCSW with the 21 concept papers available at the time with similar findings.] Also, within each of the Grand Challenge substantive topics, we provide a statistical glimpse into some of the most current and salient touchpoints with racism. Despite the supposition that white supremacy and racism can be addressed within each extant grand challenge without having a stand-alone initiative, the findings of our analyses suggest this has not yet been done. This evidence, then, sets the stage for innovation and strategies to eliminate racism.

Individual and Family Well-Being

Ensure Healthy Development for Youth

Prevention of Schizophrenia and Severe Mental Illness is a 15-page concept paper without a single reference to race or racism. *Unleashing the Power of Prevention* is a 23-page concept paper with six references to race and/or racism (pp. 4, 5, 10, 11, 14), including the recognition that behavioral health problems reflect and perpetuate social inequities and that "young people exposed to the highest levels of risk, children and adolescents who are often disproportionately low-income and/or youth of color, often benefit most from preventive interventions" (p. 11).

Close the Health Gap

Preventing and Reducing Alcohol Misuse and Its Consequences is a 15-page concept paper with three references to race or racism, perhaps most importantly noting that "tremendous disparities exist among and between demographic groups, communities, and nations in terms of rates for incidence and prevalence of alcohol problems, diagnosis and treatment, and prevention outcomes" (pp. 9–10). The authors recommend that practitioners apply a "social determinants of health" lens in integration across multiple levels of science, policy, and intervention. Understandably, *Health Equity: Eradicating Health Inequalities for Future Generations*, provides 21 pages replete with references to race and racism—far more than any of the other Grand Challenges. *Strengthening Health Care Systems: Better Health across America* is a 15-page concept paper with eight references to race and racism, including the suggestion that "social workers [can] use their skills to prevent adverse health conditions by intervening in community settings (e.g., schools, criminal justice) and by advocating for racial and environmental justice" (p. 4).

The COVID-19 pandemic has shone a light on the long-standing racial health gaps, and some practitioners have referred to COVID-19 as a "racialized disease" (Kumashiro, 2020; Walters, 2020). Compared to non-Hispanic whites, Native Americans/Alaskan Natives had 3.7 times greater COVID-19-associated hospitalization rates, and the rate was 3.2 for Latinxs, 2.9 for Blacks, and 1.1 for Asians (Centers for Disease Control and Prevention, 2021). Moreover, compared to whites, thus far, the US COVID-19 mortality rate is higher for Native Americans/Alaskan Natives (2.4), Latinxs (2.3), and Blacks (1.9).

Build Healthy Relationships to End Violence

Ending Gender-based Violence is a nine-page concept paper with two references to race or racism, including that Native American and Alaska Native girls and women are more likely to be victims of gender-based violence than girls/women from any other racial or ethnic group in the United States, and that Black women are twice as likely as white women to be killed by an intimate partner (p. 5). *Safe Children: Reducing Severe and Fatal Maltreatment* does not mention race or racism once in its 13 pages.

Advance Long and Productive Lives

Increasing Productive Engagement in Later Life is a nine-page concept paper with three references to race or racism, including the authors' comment that, given society's history of discrimination in the educational and employment sectors, solutions that address gender, ethnic, and racial diversity directly are essential (p. 9). *Productive Engagement Early in Life: Civic and Volunteer Service as a Pathway to Development* is 11 pages long with three references to race/racism, including the conclusion that rates of volunteering are particularly low among racial and ethnic minorities, first-generation immigrants, and people with low income (p. 7), but that the social and psychological benefits of volunteering are greater for these groups (p. 5).

Stronger Social Fabric

Eradicate Social Isolation

Social Isolation Presents a Grand Challenge for Social Work provides 12 pages without noting race or racism.

End Homelessness

End Homelessness offers 15 pages with the following single comment: "Homelessness has a disproportionate impact on certain historically marginalized or stigmatized groups, including African Americans and individuals with mental illnesses and other disabilities" (p. 5). According to the *Annual Homeless Assessment Report to Congress, Part 1* (US Department of Housing and Urban Development, 2021), those with the largest rate of homelessness in 2019 were Native Hawaiian and Pacific Islanders, at a rate of 159.8 per 10,000. In descending order, the remaining rates were Native American/Alaska Native at a rate of 66.6, Black at 55.2, Latinx at 21.7, white at 11.5, and Asian at a rate of 4.1 per 10,000.

Create Social Responses to a Changing Environment

Strengthening the Social Response to the Human Impacts of Environmental Change presents 20 pages with four references to race or racism, including this from page 4:

> There is robust evidence of socioeconomic and cultural differentials in both the impacts of and responses to disasters and disaster-related interventions; therefore, adapting interventions that are responsive to both structured inequities and cultural and ethnic differences will be an important cross-cutting dimension in these efforts.

Harness Technology for Social Good

Neither of the two concepts papers focused on harnessing technology for social good (29 pages total)—*Practice Innovation through Technology in the Digital Age* and *Harnessing Big Data for Social Good*—mention race or racism. This is surprising, given the research documenting both the "digital divide" and the "racial tech gap." For 2015, the US Census Bureau reports that Asian households have the greatest access (83%) to the Internet at home, followed by

72% for white households, 72% for Native American/Alaska Natives, 70% for Hispanics, and 68% for Black households (US Census Bureau, 2016). These figures absolutely contribute to what's being called the *racial tech gap* (Turner, 2016). In October 2019, a survey of leading technology companies found that combined, Black, Hispanic, and Indigenous technology company employees accounted for less than 5% of Silicon Valley firms, which certainly threatens the ability of members of these underrepresented groups to gain employment in the growing global technology field and digitized economy (Harrison, 2019; Walia & Ravindran, 2020).

Just Society

Promote Smart Decarceration

Despite significant overrepresentation of individuals of color in US justice systems, the 12 pages of *From Mass Incarceration to Smart Decarceration* devoted to promote smart decarceration only reference race or racism twice, including the statement that smart decarceration requires an amelioration of racial and social disparities.

Build Financial Capability and Assets for All

Financial Capability and Asset Building for All is 16 pages with one reference about the burden of student loans on low- and moderate-income and minority youth (p. 6).

Reduce Extreme Economic Inequality

Reversing Extreme Inequality is 14 pages but also has only one reference to race/racism, reporting that the median net worth of white households is 10 to 20 times greater than the median net worth of Black and Hispanic households (p. 5).

The Federal Reserve reports that in 2019, Black families' median net worth was $24,100, Hispanic families' was $36,100, and white families' was $188,200 (Bhutta, Chang, Dettling, & Hsu, 2020). The "Other" families' (those identifying as Alaska Native, Native American, Asian, Native Hawaiian, Pacific Islander, any other race, and all those reporting more than one racial identification) had a lower median net worth than white families, but more wealth than Black and Hispanic families (Bhutta, Chang, Dettling, & Hsu, 2020).

Achieve Equal Opportunity and Justice

The final Grand Challenge to Achieve Equal Opportunity and Justice has five concept papers. *Promoting Equality by Addressing Social Stigma* is a 29-page concept paper with five references to race or racism. *The Integration of Latina/o Immigrants into American Society* has one explanation of how Latinas/os are diverse in terms of race (p. 2) in its 19 pages. *Increasing Success for African American Children and Youth* is 18 pages long with four references to race or racism, whereas *Fair Housing and Inclusive Communities: How Can Social Work Move Us Forward?* is 20 pages long with four such references. Last, *Juvenile Justice* offers 39 pages with seven references to race or racism.

There were 1,380,427 individuals in US state and federal prisons in 2019. This means that, despite only comprising 5% of the world's population, the United States has 25% of all those incarcerated around the world (Carson, 2020). Meanwhile, per the goals of the Grand Challenge to Promote Smart Decarceration, the number of incarcerated individuals has been declining since 2009, but the racial and ethnic disparities in the US criminal justice system remain significant and largely unaddressed. Black adults are 5.12 times (at a rate of 1,096 per 100,000) more likely to be imprisoned compared to whites (214 per 100,000), and the rate is 2.45 times more likely for Latinx adults (525 per 100,000 compared to whites) (Carson, 2020). (Note: These are the only racial/ethnic categories provided by the Bureau of Justice Statistics for incarceration rates.)

INNOVATIONS/STRATEGIES TO ELIMINATE RACISM

Any effort to eliminate racism must begin at the individual level. How do you identify? What are your intersectional identities? How were you socialized? What were your family values and beliefs? Were these values and beliefs confirmed (at either conscious or subconscious levels) by your school, community, culture, the media? How might you have internalized these beliefs and experiences? Do they cause you any cognitive dissonance? The Grand Challenge to Eliminate Racism acknowledges that the United States was built on a legacy of racism and white supremacy that continues to affect—consistently and significantly—the daily lives of all its residents, and the work to dismantle both should begin at the micro level.

For those who recognize their role in perpetuating racism and white supremacy, either consciously or subconsciously, and then make a commitment to eliminate racism and foster racial equity, the next step is to commit to life-long learning and growth. Educate yourself and others. Empower your community. Begin to coalesce like-minded individuals and identify allies/co-conspirators in community. This is the eliminate racism national network that will continue existing and begin new transdisciplinary collaboration at the mezzo and macro levels to jettison a hierarchy of human value and instead build racial equity.

As social workers, we are obliged to promote social justice and racial equity through antiracism practice, research, policies, and education. The profession's code of ethics suggests that social workers strive to ensure access to needed information, services, and resources; equality of opportunity; and meaningful participation in decision making for all people (National Association of Social Workers, 2008). This commitment should begin with a focus on and critical analysis of the profession itself (Gregory, 2021). Andrews and Reisch (2002, p. 26) contend that "radical social work would require a transformation—of theory, status, educational models, and professional goals—in which most social workers are unwilling or unable to engage." The addition of the Grand Challenge to Eliminate Racism could signal the formalized start to that professional transformation.

The eliminate racism network acknowledges that racist policies, bias, and discriminatory practices continue to promote racial inequity in a myriad of ways. In response, the network will identify empirical evidence and practices that take on discrimination in all its forms and redress racism's most dangerous and negative side effects on the health and well-being of our country by joining national efforts to build and organize antiracism policies, systems, and communities. Specifically, the efforts of the Grand Challenge to Eliminate Racism focus on evidence- and practice-based research that cultivates innovation to improve the conditions of daily life for all. Because all are affected by racism and white supremacy. This Grand Challenge facilitates change at the individual, organizational, community, professional, and societal levels; and includes the following priorities:

- Eliminate racism and white supremacy and facilitate racial equity at the individual level.
- Develop an antiracism social work workforce that promotes access to resources, opportunities, and transdisciplinary collaboration, and advances community empowerment to build racial equity.
- Examine the social work profession to root out racist policies and practices, and revise social work education to address structural inequities and white privilege and their impact on individual and group outcomes.
- Develop a policy agenda for eliminating racism and white supremacy from institutions and organizations that includes continuous evaluation and accountability.

Eliminate Racism and White Supremacy and Facilitate Racial Equity at the Individual Level

The facilitation of racial equity starts with accurate information and includes self-reflection and an examination of internalized superiority/inferiority and power/oppression. This learning can then be applied to personal, professional, and advocacy roles. The bases for knowledge, conceptualization, science, and ways of living in the United States are rooted in white priority, white domination, white importance, and white supremacy. During Jim Crow, K–12 teachers who were non-white were not allowed to teach white children, further lessening the interaction of diversity in learning and robbing all students as well as the education profession of outstanding teachers (Noguera, 2008). Carter G. Woodson wrote that schools were educating all students that Black people were of lesser value, and taught white students to believe they were of greater value and were superior (Kohli, 2008; Woodson, 1933). In short, education as an institution in the United States is inherently racist and oppressive. As a result of bias in and censorship of textbooks, individuals must seek information from a variety of perspectives and sources to gain a more accurate and holistic view of the past when it comes to racial justice (Feagin, 2020).

The second step to facilitate racial equity is self-awareness. Engagement in continuous critical self-reflection and racial consciousness can help social workers assess their biases, worldviews, and values that influence their work (Harris et al., under review; Sakamoto, 2007). Sue et al. (2016) suggest that social workers begin with the question "Who am I?" and provide identity development models to guide that exploration. Adams et al. (2018) pose the same question, adding "Who are my people?," with considerations of the intersectionality of our identities and how we are socialized. King, Gulick, and Avery (2010) offer that once individuals obtain accurate information, they must reflect on how this information aligns with or challenges their values and beliefs.

Social workers who identify as white can recognize their potential power and privilege to center the voices and experiences of individuals of color. They are often in the best position to challenge white supremacy and should consistently use their energies to promote racial equity (National Association of Social Workers, 2007). Ideally, social workers who belong to underrepresented groups would have the bandwidth to overcome internalized oppression and domination, strive toward critical consciousness, collaborate in support of one another, and advocate for change. The reality is that, historically, voices of underrepresented groups have neither been welcomed nor encouraged, and that invitations or encouragements to them "overcoming" may be beyond their capacity (Sue et al., 2016). They may not have the energy or the resources to develop in ways for this type of change to actualize fully. If oppression leads to suppression of voice, feelings, and action, it can be premature to think that because a pathway is created, one will merely take it. Because of internalized racism, those being suppressed may not be able to recognize and acknowledge their situation, and those who see it and can, need to speak power to it, including the marginalized themselves, as well as allies and accomplices.

Social workers can promote racial equity in their multiple personal roles (Harris et al., under review). For example, all social workers commit to a lifelong learning process of understanding the oppression that minoritized communities have lived with and to become advocates, allies, or co-conspirators in the fight to dismantle racism and white supremacy and foster racial equity. Based on the understanding of racism and racial consciousness, social workers can initiate and maintain conversations about racism in both personal and professional contexts (National Association of Social Workers, 2007). Social workers have unique training to facilitate informal and formal discussions regarding specific social issues, practices, and policies that are related to racism and antiracism (e.g., Black Lives Matter, rallies against anti-Asian attacks, the Grand Challenge to Eliminate Racism) with their colleagues or members of their organizations. In doing so, it is essential that social workers discuss race and racism explicitly, instead of using concepts such as diversity or differences, which can dilute direct conversations on racism (Davis, 2016).

Social workers must not only understand the issues and root causes, but also they must name them and make them visible as oppressive ideologies (Sleeter & Zavala, 2020). "True justice demands the voices of those who are often unheard and silenced. . . . To effect racial justice, the principles espoused by the GCSW need to be explicit in naming racist and other forms of oppression" (Rao et al., 2021, p. 14).

Although it is rarely conceptualized as such, social work research is central to antiracism and racial equity work. Before we can address the effects of racism and white supremacy, we must be able to document and assess these effects and their outcomes. Consider in what order demographic data are collected and/or reported. Asking if individuals identify as white first is certainly not supported by an alphabetical order, but can serve to reinforce a conscious or subconscious hierarchy that considers white first/best and non-white after/less than. For a plethora of reasons, racial and ethnic communities are significantly underrepresented in all types of research (Konkel, 2015) and the Grand Challenge to Eliminate Racism can support and foster our profession's leadership role in addressing this disparity.

Develop an Antiracism Social Work Workforce that Promotes Access to Resources, Opportunities, and Transdisciplinary Collaboration, and Advances Community Empowerment to Build Racial Equity

As described at the individual level, the profession must take similar steps to develop an antiracism workforce. First, obtain accurate information and evidence-supported training, then reflect on the code of ethics and social work values, examine power/oppression, and, then, prioritize transforming organizational actions to address systemic racism and structural inequities in order to achieve equitable outcomes. Social work will have to address the racism in the room before meaningful change can happen. The prioritization will dictate the level of commitment and resources necessary to address the intrinsic natures of whiteness and white supremacy as default positions in policies and practices (Corley & Young, 2018). As a profession with core values that include recognizing and challenging social injustice, the social work organizational culture is well-positioned with evidence-based training practices, professionalism, priorities, and a posture of cultural humility to address these previously harmful default positions (National Association of Social Workers, 2008; Spencer, Lewis, & Guitierrez, 2000).

Social workers must be equipped with tools to dismantle racism and white supremacy, and build racial equity. Thus, social work organizations should promote continued learning and growth by providing regular supervision and training related to racial equity. As racism and white supremacy continue to exist in many forms and continuously remake themselves, social workers must commit to the lifelong journey of self-reflection and critical consciousness, instead of merely relying on the social justice courses they took in their degree programs in the past (Davis & Fields, 2021). The National Association of Social Workers, for example, provides racial justice training as continuing education (National Association of Social Workers, 2020). Social work organizations can share and promote such opportunities for training or conferences to their practitioners and can advance the organizational cultures in which the discussion on racial equity can take place consistently.

Importantly, evidence-based training is a mechanism that professionals can use to gain current and best practice information quickly and cost-effectively (Devine, Forscher, Austin, & Cox, 2012). Social work can make a radical change in this direction, but the effectiveness of this change is centered on competence, which must be strengthened with knowledge, awareness/reflection, and skill development. To this end, despite the rife adoption of diversity training and implicit bias workshops, there is little evidence regarding the efficacy of such programming (Dobbin & Kalev, 2018; Ngounou & Gutierrez, 2017). Much of what we do know about these types of training, however, is from the scholarly contributions of social workers (Abramovitz & Blitz, 2015; Hamilton-Mason & Schneider, 2018; James, Green, Rodriguez, & Fong, 2008; Johnson, Antle, & Barbee, 2009; McCarter & Granberry, 2020; McCarter, Wilson, & Anderson, under review), and many of these contributions were informed by critical race theory (CRT).

The central goal of CRT is to transform the relationship among race, racism, and power positively (Delgado & Stefancic, 2017). Although approaches to CRT differ, there are eight basic tenets specific to the social work profession identified by Canadian scholars Razack and Jeffery (2002) that can be used to facilitate necessary changes to influence the workforce directly: (a) racism as the norm, (b) the value of storytelling, (c) critique of liberalism, (d) recognizing power and privilege, (e) critique of whiteness, (f) integrating antiracist discourse, (g) legitimizing race scholarship, and (h) globalized understandings of race (Razack & Jeffery, 2002). And there are a myriad of applications of CRT for social work policy and practice (Kolivoski, Weaver, & Constance-Huggins, 2014).

Once accurate information is obtained through training, a workforce must be assembled. This requires building a representative team to co-develop racial equity goals (policy and practice change) and tools. And minoritized groups should not be charged with leading the efforts to promote antiracism in the workplace. For those who are willing and capable, their roles are crucial. Alliances are extremely important to create, sustain, and position the organization to tackle these difficult issues and promote substantial reform (McCarter et al., 2017).

Professional reflection must then occur. Given the profession's commitment to professional standards, there should be some review of the role of bias in how those standards are defined, operationalized, and enforced. For example, when applicants dress for mock interviews or for other professional events, Western standards of dress and hairstyle, speech, accent, word choice, and communication styles are often evaluated against the narrative of white supremacy that supports "professionalism" as we know it today (Gray, 2019; Gutiérrez y Muhs, Flores Niemann, González, & Harris, 2012). As organizations work to challenge and change their work culture, they must examine this bias and ethnocentric monoculturalism. Social workers can initiate these discussions on antiracism organizational reform with their colleagues and members of their organizations (National Association of Social Workers, 2007).

Furthermore, social work must examine power and oppression within the profession and prioritize and address any imbalances. Consider the role that national organizations and conferences play. Their membership and attendance afford social work practitioners, scholars, and educators with opportunities to interface with leaders in the field, to present themselves as experts in their specialty, and to continue their professional development through formal and informal presentation, workshop, and networking options. This type of exposure occurs through the dynamic and collaborative efforts of bringing institutions and organizations together—something that programs, independently, are unable to do. Contributing to and being recognized in the field are key components to establishing a successful and long-standing career in the profession. Anecdotally, and importantly, conference attendance is unaffordable; yet, interactions that occur at poster presentations, during dinners, and after workshops are where some of the best ideas emanate and fruitful connections are forged. The demographics at professional conferences are largely white. This makes it difficult to disentangle the effects of race from the effects of income (Hong, 2018). If attendance is an investment in one's career, financial provisions should be made for pretenure track faculty and doctoral students who are presenting or attending for professional development and institutional exposure.

Social work researchers also play an important role. They can continue to accumulate evidence, including data disaggregated by race and ethnicity, that expands our knowledge of the interventions that can address structural racism and its detrimental effects. More social work research needs to center race, racism, and white supremacy as core constructs in their investigations, and discuss racial and ethnic disparities explicitly (Corley & Young, 2018; McMahon & Allen-Meares, 1992; Woo, Figuereo, Rosales, Wang, & Sabur, 2018). In addition, given that race/ethnicity is constructed socially, explaining how race and racism are conceptualized in the studies will be an important step to initiate dialogues on race in social work research (Woo et al., 2018).

As gatekeepers to the profession, social work faculty and staff should adopt models of cultural humility to teach, model, and effectively evaluate the practice of antiracism across the profession. Cultural humility requires stepping outside the individual identity to honor the unique experience of others (McGee-Avila, 2018). It can, thus, address issues of power, social injustice, discrimination, and bias at all system levels (Hook, Davis, Owen, Worthington, & Utsey, 2013; Tervalon & Murray-Garcia, 1998). In sum, cultural humility serves to recognize power imbalances inherent in institutions and assumes institutional accountability to mitigate them.

Social workers recognize the importance of community engagement and empowerment and will thus center the community in the profession's efforts toward antiracism practice and building racial equity. Social workers should promote antiracism civic and community engagement (e.g., participating in the Black Lives Matter movement and in rallies against anti-Asian hate), helping voices in minoritized communities to be heard in program and policy decision-making processes. In so doing, social workers work side-by-side with local communities to understand more fully the needs of specific local racial/ethnic populations; to assess the effectiveness of programs, practices, and policies in communities of color; and to inspire and facilitate community-informed antiracism civic action. Social workers must collaborate with communities in reciprocal and participatory ways to generate new knowledge and problem-solving solutions.

Examine the Social Work Profession to Root Out Racist Policies and Practices, and Revise Social Work Education to Address Structural Inequities and White Privilege, and Their Impact on Individual and Group Outcomes

Schools of social work should regularly assess the extent to which their curricula and education teach content related to antiracism and racial equity. In addition to curricular revision, social work education must examine the demographics of its students and teachers and implement efforts to assess racial equity in educational outcomes. Although there have been commitments to increasing diversity in educational tools, there is a paucity of knowledge about how these commitments address the main vein of inequity and inequality: racism. CSWE Educational Policy and Accreditation Standards require that schools of social work prepare their students to understand the mechanisms of oppression and to develop strategies to eliminate structural barriers (Council on Social Work Education, 2016). Whereas schools of social work have largely promoted diversity and difference in their curricula, their efforts to facilitate racial equity can be strengthened by allocating greater attention to disparities and inclusion that create explicit dialogues on racism and white supremacy (Woo, Cano, & Pitt-Catsouphes, 2021).

Students want their educational content to be more expansive, addressing the imbalance of long-standing educational practices that sustain racism in education as compared to cultural humility in education (Arvanitakis & Hornsby, 2016). Admittedly, for a profession that is social justice oriented, there are shortcomings. Social work clinicians, educators, and researchers have failed historically to understand differences in social identity and privilege, and have often maintained a misguided focus on colorblindness, outdated concepts of cultural competence, and the white-centered history of liberal arts programs (Abrams & Moio, 2009; Davis, 2016).

Using storytelling and narratives with social work students can integrate antiracism into curricular content and the missions of departments, schools, and colleges of social work. Storytelling allows students to personalize experiences, take responsibility for them, and engage in critical reflection by acknowledging their own racism (Delgado & Stefancic, 2017; Hamilton-Mason & Schneider, 2018). This requires that faculty revisit course learning materials (e.g., textbooks, media, open access resources) and determine the best sources from which to draw. Adams et al. (2018) were able to use varied sources in their *Readings for Diversity and Social Justice* (4th ed.), many of which center diverse voices. In addition, field education activities that involve applied social action projects to learn about antiracism can be another important tool for antiracism pedagogy (Hamilton-Mason & Schneider, 2018).

Reflection on grading in social work programs should also take place. Social work educators need to address paternalistic behavior, such as the straight B syndrome, underestimating the academic abilities of students of color—especially Black students—and teacher bias. Often, no matter how much or how little effort the student makes, the student is being judged not as a student but as a race and is deemed at a "disadvantage." Is there a cumulative disadvantage experienced by some? Absolutely. Following models of adult learning, where life experience is recognized, celebrated, and integrated into the classroom (Knowles, Holton, & Swanson, 2005), is a way that social work educators can address these types of concerns directly and foster more racially equitable outcomes.

Social work educators have typically been white, but trends indicate a steady increase in the number of diversity social work program staff and faculty (US Census Bureau, 2016). That said, structural racism within units of social work is evident in the admission criteria for programs. Faculty and staff continue to support guidelines, admission rubrics and benchmarks, and unit policies from an Eurocentric perspective without regard to racial, ethnic, and cultural implications for underrepresented students (Crutchfield, Phillippo, & Frey, 2020). A closer review of contingent admissions (e.g., identifying resources that students will need related to writing skills or learning abilities) that fall among Black students and other underrepresented students compared to white students is warranted. It is likely that white students have the same needs yet are identified and supported in different ways and at different times (later in the program vs. having a stigma from the beginning of "needing assistance"). A review of grievances, as forms of punitive or corrective actions, have been linked historically to Black populations in the educational system disproportionate to whites (Gutiérrez y Muhs, Flores Niemann, González, & Harris, 2012), and is another manifestation of structural racism in social work education. Of particular note are grievances students file against underrepresented faculty. To address structural racism is long overdue, yet we can acknowledge its existence in our programs and develop interventions to respond to racism, white supremacy, and oppressive practices.

There is an assumption that because "equal opportunity" guides conversations related to aspiring for racial equality, that equal opportunity exists. Milner (2012) posed four questions around gaps in education practice, that dictate instructional content and methods. The third point is salient to developing an antiracism social work curriculum, as it asks, "[W]ho decides what it means to achieve, why, and how do we know?" (p. 695). Social positioning is a place that social work education can begin to address structural inequities that occur in educational settings (Longres, 1972). Identifying structural inequities for some curricula may require a backward design, and research that begins with the outcomes and tracks back to root causes. This should happen in social work classrooms, field placements, practice settings, communities, and institutions.

Develop a Policy Agenda for Eliminating Racism and White Supremacy from Institutions and Organizations that Includes Continuous Evaluation and Accountability

All social work institutions and organizations can develop policies and practices that transform organizational actions to address systemic racism and structural inequities, and to achieve equitable outcomes. This requires that the organization first understand the issues with root causes, which includes data collection, analysis, and dissemination. Second, and just as steps required at the micro and mezzo levels, institutions must reflect on their articulated values and beliefs, mission, vision, and so on. Third, institutions and organizations must assemble a representative team to co-develop and implement policy and practice change, and commit to continuous evaluation and accountability (Annie E. Casey Foundation, 2014).

Understanding the issues and their root causes includes training across all levels, from the front line to upper management. Having representation across all levels of employment is an important demonstration of accountability and organizational change. Needs analyses are then implemented to make organizational changes, with a goal of creating antiracism initiatives. These analyses and initiatives should always include the client and/or affected populations at every decision-making point. The findings should be accessible, transparent, and shared with all stakeholders (Annie E. Casey Foundation, 2014).

Because racism manifests within all that social workers engage and operate, a thoughtful self-assessment of social work organizations is necessary to facilitate racial equity. Does the organization articulate any goals regarding antiracism and racial equity? Why or why not? Directors can communicate their commitment to racial equity through the institutional processes inclusive of co-developing antiracism goals and programs (Cano, 2020; McCarter et al., 2017). More social work institutions and organizations have started recognizing the detrimental effects of racism and making a commitment to promote racial equity. The National Association of Social Workers, CSWE, and the National Association of Deans and Directors have identified racism as a key social issue that the social work profession needs to address (Council on Social Work Education, 2020; National Association of Social Workers, 2007; Teasley, 2020). These organizations can continue playing key leadership roles to challenge racism and white supremacy, and build racial equity.

Organizations must also build a representative team to co-develop and implement research, practice, and policy change. The first step is to hire social workers from diverse racial backgrounds who demonstrate a strong commitment to antiracism and racial equity. Understanding the challenges that such individuals many have inside many mainstream organizations, it is important that such individuals be supported by all levels of management and administration. Organizations can also provide these employees at all levels with training and supervision to mentor a diverse workforce (Cano, 2020).

When the organization's articulated mission/vision includes aspirations of antiracism and equity, evaluate its outcomes compared to its stated goals. Again, data should be disaggregated by race and ethnicity, and these analyses should be transparent and commonplace. Making difficult assessments more common and mainstream will help normalize this type of evaluation. These steps are necessary to increase accountability and are key to achieving long-standing change. Disparate outcomes need to be addressed at a bureaucratic level, holding officials among national social work organizations accountable if they fail to uphold antiracism research, practices, and policies. At the state level, officials and representatives should be evaluated annually on their efforts to create and meet racial equity goals by members, clients, and stakeholders. As McMahon and Allen Meares noted there is no neutral position:

> Social workers, therefore, must be more than sensitive or aware; they must be antiracist if there is not going to be a breach between their ideals and reality. Being antiracist implies transformative action to remove the conditions that oppress people. There is no neutral position. (McMahon & Allen Meares, 1992, p. 537)

CONCLUSION

As a critical social and political institution within US society, the profession of social work is built upon the values of social justice. A world free of racism and white supremacy is central to our professional vision. Our history as a profession, however, demonstrates that we have also served as perpetrators and/or complicit bystanders to racism and white supremacy. Therefore, it is imperative that social work take specific steps to eliminate racism, promote an antiracism perspective, and foster racial equity.

The first step must occur as individuals. Social workers are committed to continuous learning, and this learning should include critical self-examination and race consciousness. All individuals are at different place along a continuum of racial understanding, and we must deepen our knowledge, consider our values and beliefs, and build new skills to become effective antiracists. The second step builds upon the first to organize a collective that promotes equitable access to resources and opportunities. As a national network, eliminate racism uses transdisciplinary, antiracism collaboration and research to center and empower marginalized communities and build racial equity.

The third step requires that, as a profession, we conduct critical self-reflection to address our own racist research, practices, and policies, and revise social work education to address structural inequities and white privilege, and their impact on individual and group outcomes. Social workers must be taught the skills to generate and advocate for innovative research, practices, and policies that can eliminate racism and white supremacy. Working with communities and promoting their capacity and power, social work is arguably in the best position among institutions that serve society to be a leader in eliminating racism.

In sum, eliminating racism and white supremacy from institutions and organizations requires continuous evaluation and accountability. An antiracist perspective goes beyond understanding the conditions that oppress—to understanding specifically how racism and white supremacy continue to remake themselves and flourish, and how we as a profession can change systems to become antiracist, sustainable, and just.

REFERENCES

Abramovitz, M., & Blitz, L. (2015). Moving toward racial equity: The Undoing Racism Workshop and organizational change. *Race and Social Problems, 7*, 97–110.

Abrams, L. S., & Moio, J. A. (2009). Critical race theory and the cultural competence dilemma in social work education. *Journal of Social Work Education, 45*, 245–261.

Adams, M., Blumenfeld, W. J., Catalano, D. C. J., Dejong, K., Hackman, H. W., Hopkins, L. E., . . . Zúñiga, X. (Eds.). (2018). *Readings for diversity and social justice* (4th ed.). New York, NY: Routledge.

Almeida, R. V., Werkmeister Rozas, L. M., Cross-Denny, B., Lee, K., & Yamada, A. (2019). Coloniality and intersectionality in social work education and practice. *Journal of Progressive Human Services, 30*, 148–164.

Andrews, J., & Reisch, M. (2002). The radical voices of social workers: Some lessons for the future. *Journal of Progressive Human Services, 13*, 5–30.

Annie E. Casey Foundation. (2014). Race equity and inclusion guide: 7 Steps to advance and embed race equity and inclusion within your organization. Retrieved from https://www.aecf.org/m/resourcedoc/AECF_EmbracingEquity7Steps-2014.pdf

Arvanitakis, J., & Hornsby, D. J. (2016). *Universities, the citizen scholar, and the future of higher education*. New York, NY: Palgrave MacMillan.

Bhutta, N., Chang, A. C., Dettling, L. J., & Hsu, J. W. (2020). *Disparities in wealth by race and ethnicity in the 2019 Survey of Consumer Finances*. FEDS Notes. Washington, DC: Board of Governors of the Federal Reserve System. https://doi.org/10.17016/2380-7172.2797

Bonilla-Silva, E., & Zuberi, T. (2008). *White logic, white methods: Racism and methodology*. Washington, DC: Rowman and Littlefield Publishers.

Cano, M. (2020). Diversity and inclusion in social service organizations: Implications for community partnerships and social work education. *Journal of Social Work Education, 56*, 105–114.

Carle, S. D. (2013). *Defining the struggle: National organizing for racial justice, 1880–1915*. New York, NY: Oxford University Press.

Carson, A. (2020). Prisoners in 2019. Office of Justice Programs NCJ publication no. NCJ 255115. Retrieved from https://www.bjs.gov/content/pub/pdf/p19.pdf

Centers for Disease Control and Prevention. (2021). COVID-19 hospitalization and death by race/ethnicity. Retrieved from https://www.cdc.gov/coronavirus/

2019-ncov/covid-data/investigations-discovery/hospitalization-death-by-race-ethnicity.html

Cherry, K. (2018). Critical thoughts on American social work and the crisis of modernity: Lessons from theory and current events. *Journal of Progressive Human Services, 29*, 40–60.

Corley, N. A., & Young, S. M. (2018). Is social work still racist? A content analysis of recent literature. *Social Work, 63*, 317–326.

Council on Social Work Education. (2016). *EPAS handbook*. Alexandria, VA: Author.

Council on Social Work Education. (2020). We "have a way to go" to achieve racial equity in social work. Alexandria, VA: Council on Social Work Education.

Crutchfield, J., Phillippo, K., & Frey, A. (2020). Structural racism in schools: A view through the lens of the national school social work practice model. *Children & School, 42*, 187–193.

Daniels-Rauterkus, M. (2019). Civil resistance and procreative agency in Harriet Jacobs's incidents in the life of a slave girl. *Women's Studies, 48*, 498–509.

Davis, L. E. (2016). Race: America's grand challenge. *Journal of the Society for Social Work and Research, 7*, 395–403.

Davis, M., & Fields, L. (2021, January 7). Perspective: Are you a social worker guilty of performative allyship for Black Lives Matter? *The New Social Worker*. Retrieved from https://www.socialworker.com/feature-articles/practice/social-worker-guilty-performative-allyship-black-lives-matter/

Delgado, R., & Stefancic, J. (2017). *Critical race theory: An introduction* (3rd ed.). New York, NY: New York University Press.

Deliso, M. (2021). Timeline: The impact of George Floyd's death in Minneapolis and beyond. ABC News. Retrieved from https://abcnews.go.com/US/timeline-impact-george-floyds-death-minneapolis/story?id=70999322

Devine, P. G., Forscher, P. S., Austin, A. J., & Cox, W. T. (2012). Long-term reduction in implicit race bias: A prejudice habit-breaking intervention. *Journal of Experimental Social Psychology, 48*(6), 1267–1278.

Dismantling Racism Works – History. (n.d.) https://www.dismantlingracism.org/history.html

Dismantling Racism Works – Racism Defined. (n.d.) https://www.dismantlingracism.org/racism-defined.html

Dixon, P. J., & Dundes, L. (2020). Exceptional injustice: Facebook as a reflection of race- and gender-based narratives following the death of George Floyd. *Social Sciences, 9* (12), 231–248.

Dobbin, F., & Kalev, A. (2018). Why doesn't diversity training work? The challenge for industry and academia. *Anthropology Now, 10*, 48–55.

Durrani, A. (2012). Working while Muslim: Religious discrimination in the workplace. *Plaintiff*. Retrieved from https://www.plaintiffmagazine.com/recent-issues/item/working-while-muslim-religious-discrimination-in-the-workplace

Edwards, G. S. & Rushin, S. (2018). The effect of President Trump's election on hate crimes. *SSRN Electronic Journal*, 1–24. http://dx.doi.org/10.2139/ssrn.3102652

Farley, J. E. (2000). *Majority-minority relations* (4th ed.). New York NY: Prentice Hall.

Feagin, J. R. (2020). *The White racial frame: Centuries of racial framing and counter-framing*. New York, NY: Routledge.

Feagin, J., Johnson, J., & Rush, S. (2000). Doing anti-racism toward an egalitarian American society. *Contemporary Sociology, 29*, 95–100.

Funk, M., Varghese, R., & Zúñiga, X. (2018). Racism. In M. Adams, W. J. Blumenfeld, D. C. J. Catalano, K. Dejong, H. W. Hackman, L. E. Hopkins, . . . X. Zúñiga

(Eds.), *Readings for diversity and social justice* (4th ed., pp. 65–74). New York, NY: Routledge.

Gray, A. (2019). The bias of "professionalism" standards. *Stanford Social Innovation Review*. Retrieved from https://ssir.org/articles/entry/the_bias_of_professionalism_standards#

Gregory, J. R. (2021). Social work as a product and project of whiteness, 1607–1900. *Journal of Progressive Human Services, 32*, 17–36.

Gutiérrez y Muhs, G., Flores Niemann, Y., González, C. G., & Harris, A. P. (2012). *Presumed incompetent: The intersections of race and class for women in academia*. Boulder, CO: University Press of Colorado.

Hamilton-Mason, J., & Schneider, S. (2018). Antiracism expanding social work education: A qualitative analysis of the Undoing Racism workshop experience. *Journal of Social Work Education, 54*(2), 337–348.

Harris, A., Maglalang, D. D., Cano, M., Woo, B., Tucker, T. B., Rao, S., & Bartholomew, M. W. (in press). Eradicating racism: Social work's most pressing grand challenge. In M. Teasley & M. Spencer (Eds.), *Racism and the grand challenges for the social work profession*. New York, NY: Oxford University Press.

Harrison, S. (2019). Five years of tech diversity reports-and little progress. *Wired*. Retrieved from https://www.wired.com/story/five-years-tech-diversity-reports-little-progress/

Hong, J. (2018). The high cost of opportunity: Paying for academic conferences. Retrieved from https://diverseeducation.com/article/108234/

Hook, J., Davis, D., Owen, J., Worthington, E., & Utsey, S. (2013). Cultural humility: Measuring openness to culturally diverse clients. *Journal of Counseling Psychology, 60*, 353–366.

Hosokawa, B. (1969). *Nisei: The quiet Americans*. New York, NY: Morrow.

James, J., Green, D., Rodriguez, C., & Fong, R. (2008). Addressing disproportionality through undoing racism, leadership development, and community engagement. *Child Welfare, 87*, 279–296.

Jeoung, R., Horse, A. Y., Popovic, T., & Lim, R. (2021). Stop AAPI Hate national report. Stop AAPI Hate. Retrieved from https://secureservercdn.net/104.238.69.231/a1w.90d.myftpupload.com/wp-content/uploads/2021/03/210312-Stop-AAPI-Hate-National-Report-.pdf

Johnson, L., Antle, B., & Barbee, A. (2009). Addressing disproportionality and disparity in child welfare: Evaluation of an anti-racism training for community service providers. *Children and Youth Services Review, 31*, 688–696.

Jones, N. A., & Smith, A. S. (2001). *The two or more races population: 2000*. Census 2000 brief. Retrieved from https://www.census.gov/prod/2001pubs/c2kbr01-6.pdf

Kashima, T. (2003). *Judgement without trial: Japanese Americans imprisonment during World War II*. Seattle WA: University of Washington Press.

Khanna, N. (2016). If you're half Black, you're just Black: Reflected appraisals and the persistence of the one-drop rule. *The Sociological Quarterly, 51*, 96–121.

King, E., Gulick, L., & Avery, D. (2010). The divide between diversity training and diversity education: Integrating best practices. *Journal of Management Education, 34*, 891–906.

Knowles, M. S., Holton, E., & Swanson, R. (2005). *The adult learner: The definitive classic in adult education and human resource development* (6th ed.). Amsterdam NL: Elsevier.

Kohli, R. (2008). Breaking the cycle of racism in the classroom: Critical race reflections from future teachers of color. *Teacher Education Quarterly, 35*, 177–188.

Kolivoski, K. M., Weaver, A., & Constance-Huggins, M. (2014). Critical race theory: Opportunities for application in social work practice and policy. *Families in Society, 95*, 269–276.

Konkel, L. (2015). Racial and ethnic disparities in research studies: The challenge of creating more diverse cohorts. *Environmental Health Perspectives, 123*, A297–A302.

Kumashiro, K. (2020). COVID-19, racialized disease, and the yellow peril. Insight into Diversity. Retrieved from https://www.insightintodiversity.com/covid-19-racialized-disease-and-the-yellow-peril/

Loewen, J. W. (2007). *Lies my teacher told me: Everything your American history textbook got wrong*. New York, NY: Touchstone.

Longres, J. (1972). The impact of racism. *The Journal of Education for Social Work, 8*, 31–41.

Lubben, J. E., Barth, R. P., Fong, R., Flynn, M. L., Sherraden, M., & Uehara, E. (2018). Grand challenges for social work and society. In R. Fong, J. E. Lubben, & R. P. Barth (Eds.), *Grand challenges for social work and society* (pp. 1–17). New York, NY: Oxford University Press.

Lyons, D. (2007). Racial injustices in U.S. history and their legacy. In M. T. Martin & M. Yaquinto (Eds.), *Redress for historical injustices in the United States: On reparations for slavery, Jim Crow, and their legacies* (pp. 33–54). Durham, NC: Duke University Press.

Mann, C. C. (2005). *1491: New revelations of the Americas before Columbus*. New York, NY: Knopf.

Marsiglia, F., & Kulis, S. (2016). *Diversity, oppression and change: Culturally grounded social work* (2nd ed.). New York, NY: Oxford University Press.

McCarter, S. A., Chinn-Gary, E., Trosch, L. A., Jr., Toure, A., Alsaeedi, A., & Harrington, J. (2017). Bringing racial justice to the courtroom and community: Race matters for juvenile justice and the Charlotte model. *Washington and Lee Law Review, 73*, 641–686.

McCarter, S. A. & Granberry, J. (2020, January 16). *Using diversity trainings to reduce racial inequity: Are they effective or just a CYA technique?* Poster presented at the 24th annual conference of the Society for Social Work and Research, Washington, DC.

McCarter, S. A., Wilson, M. L., & Anderson, D. (under review). Evidence-based strategies to improve the effectiveness of diversity, equity, and inclusion training.

McGee-Avila, J. (2018, June 23). Practicing cultural humility to transform healthcare. Retrieved from https://www.rwjf.org/en/blog/2018/06/practicing-cultural-humility-to-transform-healthcare.html

McMahon, A., & Allen-Meares, P. (1992). Is social work racist? A content analysis of recent literature. *Social Work, 37*, 533–539.

Milner, R. H. (2012). Beyond a test score: Explaining opportunity gaps in educational practice. *Journal of Black Studies, 43*, 693–718.

Mohamed, B. (2018, January 3). New estimates show U.S. Muslim population continues to grow. The Pew Research Center. Retrieved from https://www.pewresearch.org/fact-tank/2018/01/03/new-estimates-show-u-s-muslim-population-continues-to-grow/

National Association of Social Workers. (2007). Institutional racism and the social work profession: A call to action. NASW President's Initiative: Weaving the Fabrics of Diversity. Retrieved from https://www.socialworkers.org/LinkClick.aspx?fileticket=SWK1aR53FAk%3D&portalid=0

National Association of Social Workers. (2008). *NASW code of ethics: Guide to the everyday professional conduct of social workers*. Washington, DC: Author. https://www.socialworkers.org/About/Ethics/Code-of-Ethics/Code-of-Ethics-English

National Association of Social Workers. (2020). Racial justice training. Retrieved from https://www.socialworkers.org/Practice/Ethnicity-Race/Racial-Justice/Training

National Center for Health Statistics. (2020). Percentages of selected mental health indicators for adults aged 18 and over, by race and Hispanic origin: United States, January–June 2019. Retrieved from https://www.cdc.gov/nchs/data/nhis/earlyrelease/ERmentalhealthbyrace-508.pdf

National Museum of African American History and Culture. (n.d.). Historical Foundations of Race. Retrieved from https://nmaahc.si.edu/learn/talking-about-race/topics/historical-foundations-race

Ngounou, G., & Gutierrez, N. (2017). Learning to lead for racial equity. *Phi Delta Kappa*, 99, 37–41.

Noguera, P. A. (2008). *The trouble with Black boys . . . and other reflection on race, equity, and the future of public education*. San Franciscom CA: Jossey-Bass.

Office of Management and Budget. (1997, July). Review of the racial and ethnic standards to the OMB concerning changes. Retrieved from https://obamawhitehouse.archives.gov/omb/fedreg_directive_15/

Office of Minority Health. (2021, January). Profile: American Indian/Alaska Native. Retrieved from https://minorityhealth.hhs.gov/omh/browse.aspx?lvl=3&lvlid=62

Omi, M., & Winant, H. (2015). *Racial formation in the United States* (3rd ed.). New York, NY: Routledge.

Park, Y. (2020). *Facilitating injustice: The complicity of social workers in the forced removal and incarceration of Japanese Americans, 1942–1946*. New York, NY: Oxford University Press.

Rao, S., Woo, B., Maglalang, D. D., Bartholomew, M., Cano, M., Harris, A. & Tucker, T. B. (2021). Race and ethnicity in the social work grand challenges. *Social Work*. 66(1), 9–17.

Rawley, J. A., & Behrendt, S. D. (2005). *The transatlantic slave trade: A history*. Lincoln, NE: The University of Nebraska Press.

Razack, N., & Jeffery, D. (2002). Critical race discourse and tenets for social work. *Canadian Social Work Review*, 19, 257–271.

Sakamoto, I. (2007). An anti-oppressive approach to cultural competence. *Canadian Social Work Review*, 24, 105–114.

Schaefer, R. T. (2008). *Racial and ethnic groups* (11th ed.). Hoboken, NJ: Prentice Hall.

Sleeter, C. E., & Zavala, M. (2020). *Transformative ethnic studies and schools: Curriculum, pedagogy, and research*. New York, NY: Teachers College Press.

Spencer, M., Lewis, E., & Guitierrez, L. (2000). Multicultural perspectives on direct practice in social work. In P. Allen-Meares & C. D. Garvin (Eds.), *The handbook of social work direct practice* (pp. 131–150). Thousand Oaks, CA: SAGE Publications.

Sue, D. W. (2006). The invisible Whiteness of being: Whiteness, White supremacy, White privilege, and racism. In M. G. Constantine & D. W. Sue (Eds.), *Addressing racism: Facilitating cultural competence in mental health and educational settings* (pp. 15–30). Hoboken NJ: Wiley.

Sue, D. W., Rasheed, M. N., & Rasheed, J. M. (2016). *Multicultural social work practice: A competency-based approach to diversity and social justice*. (2nd ed.). Hoboken NJ: Wiley.

Takaki, R. (1993). *A different mirror: A history of multicultural America.* New York, NY: Little, Brown.

Tatum, B. T. (1997). *Why are all the black kids sitting together in the cafeteria: And other conversations about race.* New York, NY: Basic Books.

Taylor, J. (2006). Ethnocentric monoculturalism. In Y. Jackson (Ed.), *Encyclopedia of multicultural psychology* (pp. 204–204). Thousand Oaks, CA: SAGE Publications.

Teasley (2020, September 1). NADD anti-racism statement. National Association of Deans and Directors Schools of Social Work. Retrieved from http://www.naddssw.org/pages/wp-content/uploads/2020/09/NADD-Antiracism-Statement.pdf

Tervalon, M., & Murray-Garcia, J. (1998). Cultural humility versus cultural competence: A critical distinction in defining physician training outcomes in multicultural education. *Journal of Health Care for the Poor and Underserved, 9*, 117–125.

Turner, D. S. (2016). Digital denied: The impact of systemic racial discrimination on home-internet adoption. Freepress. Retrieved from https://www.freepress.net/sites/default/files/legacy-policy/digital_denied_free_press_report_december_2016.pdf

US Census Bureau. (2012, September). 2010 Census shows multiple-race population grew faster than single-race population. Newsroom Archive. Retrieved from https://www.census.gov/newsroom/releases/archives/race/cb12-182.html

US Census Bureau. (2016). American Community Survey. Retrieved from https://www.census.gov/programs-surveys/acs/data/pums.html

US Department of Housing and Urban Development. (2021). The 2020 Annual Homeless Assessment Report (AHAR) to Congress: Part 1: Point-in-time estimates of homelessness. https://www.huduser.gov/portal/sites/default/files/pdf/2020-AHAR-Part-1.pdf

Walia, A., & Ravindran, S. (2020). *America's racial gap and big tech's closing window.* Deutsche Bank Research. https://www.dbresearch.com/PROD/RPS_EN-PROD/PROD0000000000511664/America%27s_Racial_Gap_%26_Big_Tech%27s_Closing_Window.pdf?undefined&realload=ernfyB3Oc1zaE7ronii2kpSlvOqMfl u190JlevGhl1G~AGoY06cPGISKWsn0/tjo

Walter, A. W., Ruiz, Y., Tourse, R. W. C., Kress, H., Morningstar, B., MacArthur, B., & Daniels, A. (2017). Leadership matters: How hidden biases perpetuate institutional racism in organizations. *Human Service Organizations, Management, Leadership & Governance, 41*, 213–221.

Walters, A. S. (2020). COVID-19 and racism: A mental health crisis. *The Brown University Child and Adolescent Behavior Letter, 36*, 8–8.

Wellman, D. (1993). *Portraits of White racism.* New York, NY: Cambridge University Press.

Woo, B., Cano, M., & Pitt-Catsouphes, M. (2021). Equity and justice in social work explicit curriculum. *Journal of Social Work Education.*

Woo, B., Figuereo, V., Rosales, R., Wang, K., & Sabur, K. (2018). Where is race and ethnicity in social work? A content analysis. *Social Work Research, 42*, 180–186.

Woodson, C. (1933). History is a weapon: The mis-education of the Negro. Retrieved from http://www.historyisaweapon.com/defcon1/misedne.html

CHAPTER 15
Conclusions and Looking Forward

RICHARD P. BARTH, KIRA SILK,
MARILYN L. FLYNN, EDDIE UEHARA,
JILL T. MESSING, TRINA R. SHANKS,
MICHAEL SHERRADEN, AND
JAMES HERBERT WILLIAMS

The Grand Challenges for Social Work (GCSW) is an innovation that aims to solve large, compelling problems and achieve social progress powered by science. When first developed and launched in 2016, the Grand Challenges emerged in the context of a pro-science federal government expressly committed to evidence-based practices and policies. Now, a half decade of anti-science sentiments, social media "disinformation" campaigns, and a pandemic with devastating effects that were greatly exacerbated by ignoring science and proven public health strategies have set the stage for a scientific resurgence. This book taps the intensity of the commitment to end the pandemics of chronic, systemic racism and coronavirus disease 2019 (COVID-19) to find new opportunities for addressing each of the 13 Grand Challenges. Efforts like the GCSW, which offer tools for scientific and social advancement, can accelerate these change efforts. The progress documented in this volume in advancing measurable outcomes, building networks, creating implementation plans, determining metrics to monitor outcomes, and drafting policy recommendations can lead to profound influences on society's major social problems. Lessons learned from activities can influence the future directions for GCSW and, we assert, the future of the profession and society. The framing and process of the Grand Challenges can also serve to inform other social and academic movements, which are described next.

BUILDING COALITIONS TO SOLVE MAJOR SOCIAL PROBLEMS

Each Grand Challenge focuses on solving significant social problems faced by people in communities across the United States. The complexity of these challenges calls for innovative and collaborative solutions, many of which are already areas of great interest to students and faculty across campuses and throughout the nation. Creating coalitions can maximize work efforts, urge the development of creative solutions, and break down academic and practice siloes; as such, some of the Grand Challenges have been joining forces with allies and other disciplines. For example, the co-leads for the Grand Challenge to Eradicate Social Isolation are working with the American Association of Retired Persons Foundation who, together with the National Academy of Science, Engineering and Medicine, are considering a consensus study on social isolation among older adults. Preventing problems such as anxiety, depression, and alcohol and drug use has been the driving vision of the Grand Challenge to Ensure Healthy Development for Youth (Chapter 2). The importance of healthy development for children and youth has united social workers, researchers, informaticians, and primary medical care practitioners in examining behavioral health problems in childhood and adolescence, and has engendered the creation of 40-member Coalition for the Advancement of Behavioral Health (https://www.coalitionforbehavioralhealth.org/publications). The Mainstreaming Gender Insert in Chapter 2 identifies gender transformative approaches as an example of centering gender with other identities and social locations to promote the healthy development of all young people.

Creative ventures, such as those discussed in Chapter 9 on the Grand Challenge to Harness Technology for Social Good, also create—and benefit from—the importance of coalition building. This Grand Challenge has been advanced through a joint venture between social work and engineering through the University of Southern California (USC) Center for Artificial Intelligence in Society, a by-product of faculty collaborative scholarship work in the Viterbi School of Engineering and the Suzanne Dworak-Peck School of Social Work. This collaboration fosters the application of technology and artificial intelligence to problems related to HIV and homelessness among youth (see, e.g., Rice et al., 2018).

Many more examples of building coalitions through strong community involvement and partnerships are emerging. Hazards related to a changing global environment and natural disasters require a societal response, as indicated in Chapter 8. Strengthening community resiliency and having an "urban community adaptation" is another example of starting with community priorities. The Grand Challenge to Close the Health Gap is using community-based and place-based approaches along with setting-based interventions to solve problems that affect population health, such as alcohol misuse. The importance of funding shifts, research, policy, and practice toward intersectional, relational, and nonbinary conceptualizations of health and healthcare to address inequities is underscored by work across this Grand Challenge. Joining forces with communities, particularly marginalized communities, represents a more urgent call for action in solving the major and compelling societal problems mentioned previously.

DEVELOPING POSITIVE APPROACHES

To minimize the continual negative stereotyping of many communities and marginalized populations, several of the Grand Challenges were innovative in developing transformative missions to reframe their focus for positive outcomes. The titles of each of the Grand Challenges are framed for a positive outcome. The Grand Challenge to Achieve Equal Opportunity and Justice is just one example of this transformation. The original working paper for this Grand Challenge was titled *Increasing Success for African American Children and Youth* (Teasley et al., 2017). This working paper confronts the frequently negative stereotype of Black youth and reframes the goal, as indicated by its title. This positive approach adapts the restorative justice model used in school systems to support the US Department of Education's Rethink Discipline campaign. The Positive Behavioral Intervention and Supports model is an evidence-based, three-tiered approach that uses environmental supports, specialized services, and clinical interventions—all of which reinforce the restorative justice model to reduce disciplinary disproportionality in schools (McIntosh, et al., 2021). Some programs to reduce the preschool-to-prison pipeline, although attentive to the impact of complex trauma, discuss healing circles and healing schools as part of their restorative practice models.

The Grand Challenge to Build Healthy Relationships to End Violence places strengthening relationships at the center of broad efforts to resolve conflict in nonviolent ways. The importance of disrupting the school-to-prison pipeline for Black girls, as well as the myriad ways that gendered social control is reproduced within the juvenile and criminal justice systems, are also addressed in the Mainstreaming Gender Insert in Chapter 4.

Chapter 10 and its Insert for the Grand Challenge to Promote Smart Decarceration address the often harsh and gendered stereotypes faced by people who are or have been incarcerated. To change society's view of persons in prisons, stop mass incarceration, and promote smart decarceration are major challenges, but co-leads of this Grand Challenge have been very successful in reframing and promoting strategies to build social capital by encouraging social and financial investments in communities most affected by incarceration. The importance of social capital is very much evident in the aging sector, and the Grand Challenge to Advance Long and Productive Lives perceives and promotes the ongoing engagement of elders through employment, volunteering, and education. The Mainstreaming Gender Insert in this chapter (Chapter 5) uses the example of transportation, which facilitates elders' engagement in caregiving, volunteering, and work activities, as an important social space where an intersectional gendered framework is necessary to ensure that practices and policies are equitable in their advancement of long and productive lives.

COMMITTING TO AN OPEN AND FLEXIBLE FRAMEWORK

Since its formal launch in 2016, the Grand Challenge initiative has adopted an open, flexible, but strategically articulated organizational structure. This has provided the Grand Challenges' many leaders with considerable autonomy in setting direction and focus for their efforts while allowing for the exchange of information, communication, and initiative coordination. We believe this innovative form of organization and distributed leadership has been key to the initiative's successful evolution. One of the largest offerings from the Grand Challenges open framework is the support from the initiative's communications partners: SCP Communications. Through e-newsletters, webinar support, and publication production, SCP Communications has helped disseminate the work throughout the country, as well as the accomplishments of the initiative itself, of all those involved in the Grand Challenges.

We suggest that the morphology of the challenges themselves—in other words, the level at which they are pitched, their collective scope and substantive foci—succeeded in galvanizing widespread interest across social work scholars, schools, and national organizations. From the outset, the Grand Challenges Executive Committee understood the importance of developing a suite of challenges that captured the substantive concerns of the field. At the same time, the committee followed guidance from previous grand challenge initiatives advising the creation of a delimited set (typically between 12 and 17) of very high-level goals or aspirations reflecting broad, integrative problems with deeply important societal implications, and solutions that are "right over the horizon"—that is, the science, technology, and know-how needed to address the challenges are imaginable, but the path to solution is not yet clear.

Previous initiative developers have stressed the importance that grand challenges be crafted in this mold—as widely applicable challenges for which scientifically sound solutions are imaginable but not quite at hand (which makes it a "challenge"), with deep societal importance (which makes the challenge "grand"). As Winter and Butler (2011) suggest, how we construct grand challenges matters, because it is through well-constructed statements that stakeholders are motivated and galvanized. They suggest that grand challenges, structured as broad, integrative problem statements, can play a pivotal role in managing tensions that naturally arise when diverse stakeholders are involved in cooperative scientific activities. Otherwise, the risk is creating challenges that replay a familiar litany of lower-level problems on the one hand, or abstract problem statements that are not practical to address, on the other. The developers of the GCSW sought "right-size" challenges that comprise a relatively small handful of challenges that lift a profession's collective problem-solving sights, galvanize its imaginations, and focus its scientific and practical efforts over the span of a decade or longer.

The original 12 Grand Challenges selected were viewed as insufficient by not including gender equity and systemic racism—two extremely important social problems impacting all aspects of the profession. We remained committed to Winter and Butler's (2011; p. 105) argument that grand challenges must be compelling and aspirational so that they are "perceived by a range of parties to be worth solving, with the expectation that the solution would have a significant impact on both academic fields and national or international concerns such as competitiveness, security, economy, or well-being." After the launch of the initial 12 Grand Challenges, it became apparent that excluding achieving gender equity and eliminating racism limited the aspirations of the Grand Challenges. The Executive Steering Committee decided that race and gender were linked inextricably to each of the 12 Grand Challenges and that each network should be examined and should address the intersections of gender equity and systematic racism within the other challenges. In 2019, the Committee issued the *Grand Challenges for Social Work: Vision, Mission, Domain, Guiding Principles, & Guideposts to Action*, a document that detailed the Grand Challenges' commitment to social justice, diversity, equity, and inclusiveness (see Appendix 4) (Grand Challenges of Social Work, 2019). Over time, it became apparent that gender equity and systematic racism were challenges for social work and society that are so compelling they needed greater prominence in the Grand Challenges Initiative. This was achieved by adding the Grand Challenge to Eliminate Racism in 2020 and the Mainstreaming Gender Inserts throughout the Grand Challenges, both in this volume and in a special issue in *Social Work* (Messing, 2020).

RELYING ON THE STRENGTH OF NETWORKS AND COLLABORATION

Dense networks and innovative forms of collaboration were indeed developed rapidly after the formal launch of the Grand Challenges. We suggest that the variability of these forms—and the ways in which they have been "lightly" rather than "tightly" coupled—have contributed to the initiative's success to date.

The Grand Challenges were selected, and have operated, as a suite of challenges based on the principle that multiple Grand Challenges reduce the risks associated with failure of any particular effort. Furthermore, this tactic increases the likelihood of forming dense networks within a diverse collection of stakeholders, and does so without requiring individuals, either within or outside the field, to reach consensus on all matters of methodology or motivation (Winter & Butler, 2011).

This approach has succeeded—as witnessed by the five-year impact report that documents the work of each Grand Challenge, and this volume (Grand Challenges for Social Work, 2021). Although some have done more than others, none of the Grand Challenges has been lost along the way. Thirteen faculty-driven, challenge-specific networks have developed, spanning schools, universities, and regions, and scholars at every stage of their careers. The networks are led by 49 senior and junior scholars from more than 25 universities across the country. The activities taken up by these networks include collaborative publishing and developing long-term strategies to inform relevant policy, research, education, and practice—all of which are clearly crucial to advancing the Grand Challenges. Some networks include interdisciplinary members—faculty and practitioners from nursing, public health, psychology, pediatrics, and psychiatry—whereas others hold plans to expand membership in this way.

In contrast to Grand Challenge networks, which span the nation, the regional consortium (thus far, only one in the West) is organized consciously by geography. This organizational mechanism is intended to provide the opportunity for small and large social work academic programs and their community/practitioner partners to "explore ideas for curriculum development, campus activities, use of internships and community service initiatives, [practice-based] research networks, [practice innovations,] and other mechanisms for implementation of work on the Grand Challenges" (E. Uehara, L. Nissen, M. Flynn, personal communication, October 11, 2017). Thus far, the Western Consortium has demonstrated that innovation, broad collaboration, Grand Challenge leadership on campus, and commitment to complex societal challenges can flourish among social work programs of all sizes, scales, and contexts.

Broad university support is also being cultivated. There are now subcommittees in the National Association of Deans and Directors of Schools of Social Work and St. Louis Group for Excellence in Social Work Research and Education (Saint Louis Group) focused on the Grand Challenges, led by identified representatives in each organization. The Chair of the Grand Challenges Executive Committee is now a member of the influential Social Work Leadership Roundtable convened by the Council on Social Work Education (CSWE). A mechanism for universities to support the Grand Challenges financially has been established and we now have sustaining, premier, and annual sponsorship levels and commitments.

In addition to traditional operational support functions (e.g., strategic planning, communications, fund-raising), the GCSW's national leadership organization is designed expressly to link the interests and needs of the Grand Challenge networks to the organizational strengths and personal expertise of Committee members. Thus, for example, national leaders in social work education co-chair the GCSW Education & Learning Subcommittee, whereas national policy and practice expertise is represented on the Practice & Policy Subcommittee. As the Grand Challenge networks move their strategies forward, the subcommittees are poised to play a critical role, linking Grand Challenge networks with important national organizations and actors beyond the scholar-led networks themselves.

The GCSW has required and benefited from an organic organization and implementation structure. We sometimes say that we are using Mao's Zedong's "let a hundred flowers blossom and a hundred schools of thought contend" (Short, 2000) approach to organizing the Grand Challenges. Indeed, the 13 Grand Challenges are an organizing framework for research, practice, and policy that is quite decentralized. The Grand Challenges are organized around *networks*, not the more common organizing construct of *centers*. Networks of partnerships have the capacity to obviate the common shortcoming of centers, which is that they generate siloed activities and may stunt innovation that is not generated from the core of a center. Just as social networks allow everyone to communicate with vast audiences—as in the case of "going viral"—the Grand Challenge networks are intended to allow for exponential growth of communications to help innovations arise and go to scale. Although each network has two or more leaders, the network itself is not intended to be managed; the intent is that the Grand Challenges are able to flow to follow the best opportunities for success.

Strong network collaborations allow interdisciplinary teams to identify research questions that are mutually beneficial; to implement, test, and modify rapidly research-informed interventions in community-based settings; to establish a common set of data points for collection; to support multisite data collection and sharing; and to analyze and disseminate results collectively (Kelly et al., 2015). The Grand Challenge networks have the potential to continue to expand leadership, accelerate the development of 13 national implementation networks, onboard sister social work organizations, facilitate an ever-growing interest from students, and contribute to a budding awareness from the public.

One example of a network structure that would facilitate success in one or more of the Grand Challenges is a practice-based research network (PBRN). PBRNs are an innovation arising largely out of the disciplines of medicine and primary care that are being adapted for social work. In their most basic form,

PBRNs represent networks composed of academic researchers and practitioners who are committed to ongoing and productive collaboration with the purpose of advancing both a research and a practice agenda. Network organization ranges from informal to formal, with the most sophisticated networks having prescribed components including strong infrastructures and criteria that include a mission and statement of purpose, staff, an organizational structure, and communication processes (Gehlert, Walters, Uehara, & Lawlor, 2015). One example of a successful PBRN that is facilitating the implementation of a Grand Challenge is the pioneering effort illustrated in the development of the Recovery-Oriented Care Collaborative (ROCC) in Los Angeles. ROCC is designed to improve services for people with serious mental illness and is led by a team that includes USC professor John Brekke (Kelly et al., 2015). The ROCC PBRN has infrastructure, defined roles, expectations of partners, and shared goals; key replicable components of ROCC's development and activities have been published (Kelly et al., 2015). The establishment of ROCC represents a new frontier that has the potential to be transformative for social work research, practice, and education, and, at the same time, improve outcomes for clients.

A formalized PBRN concept has been suggested to address the Grand Challenge to Close the Health Gap in the health equity working paper (Gehlert et al., 2015). The proposed National Health Social Work PBRN proposed by Gehlert et al. would represent an opportunity to collect high-quality data on populations of interest. A key stated benefit would be to increase research participant sample sizes for subpopulations with which social work is typically concerned. In this example, a national network could yield data sets with larger samples, facilitate multisite participation, and allow social work researchers to test interventions rigorously on subpopulations. Thus, Grand Challenge networks and their adaptations of PBRNs are a promising vehicle to foster transdisciplinary team science, bringing evidenced-based interventions to scale and aiding in the translation of research findings to practice and policy.

EVOLVING GRAND CHALLENGES LEADERSHIP STRUCTURE CONTINUOUSLY

An expanded leadership substructure is emerging for the GCSW. In January 2017, the Grand Challenges Executive Committee expanded from being composed of fellows and deans of the American Academy of Social Work and Social Welfare to include more deeply engaged national social work and non-social work leaders. Under the leadership of the original Steering Committee (Marilyn Flynn, Michael Sherraden, and Edwina Uehara), the Grand Challenge Executive Committee developed a 20-member Leadership Board. This board includes major social work organizations for education (the CSWE) and practice [the National Association of Social Workers (NASW)], key policy partners (the Congressional Research Institute for Social Work and Policy and the Fund for Social Policy), and other critical stakeholders. This shift was a step toward institutionalizing the Grand Challenges across the profession and to accomplish the transition from the academics who identified the challenges to a renewed group that will work to achieve the goals of the initiative, cultivate new partnerships, and determine how to measure progress over a decade and beyond. With this shift, and the intent to replicate more closely typical nongovernmental organizational structures, the original Executive Committee structure was replaced by the Leadership Board, and the Steering Committee was replaced by a renewed Executive Committee.

In January 2021, eight new Leadership Board members were brought on to expand the initiative's impact on the field of social work and on society as a whole. These members represent large state and national philanthropic leaders, federal government research leaders, county agency administrators, and social work deans. The newly formed governance committee of the Grand Challenges has also committed to continuing to broaden participation and has confirmed an electoral process and rotation of Leadership Board and Executive Committee members. The current Leadership Board at the time of this volume is listed in Appendix 1.

Educational change is following, and sometimes stimulating, this leadership commitment, aligning strongly with the guidance and strategies outlined for campus engagement and advancement of the Grand Challenges (Flynn, 2017). In 2018, the Leadership Board Committee on Education surveyed social work programs to assess the extent Grand Challenges had been adopted into course content in accredited social work programs. Education committee chairs Darla Spence Coffey and Ron Manderscheid, supported by Miguel Vieyra, found that half the responding institutions were integrating knowledge about the GCSW into their curriculum. In 2021, the committee repeated the survey and found that 60% of 118 respondents were including programming, particularly in bachelor of social work (BSW) programs (76%). Many (nearly half) of the programs responding to the survey (n = 112) also indicated they had been working on Grand Challenges with campus units other than social work.

Faculty around the country have incorporated aspects of the Grand Challenges into their curricula. The University of South Alabama uses a course in problem-based learning to examine the Grand Challenges. Many new courses have been developed to address the Grand Challenges, including courses on promoting smart decarceration at the University of Chicago Crown Family School of Social Work and the University of Maryland School of Social Work. At the University of Utah College of Social Work, a master of social work (MSW) class explored research studies that fell under the various GCSW.

Student poster events focused on the Grand Challenges have been held at Azusa Pacific University (MSW and BSW) and Seton Hall University Dr. Paul Shane Annual Policy Symposium, which reached 13 BSW programs in New Jersey. Several Grand Challenge networks have developed curricular guides with the CSWE. An end homelessness curricular guide was developed in concert with the National Center for Excellence in Homeless Services. Co-lead Lisa Reyes Masons for the Grand Challenge to Create Social Responses to a Changing Environment sat on the National Taskforce Steering Committee, which developed the *Environmental Justice Curriculum Guide*. The Build Financial Capability and Assets for All (FCAB) network had a significant role in developing the *Curricular Guide for Economic Well-Being Practice*, and the promote smart decarceration network developed the curriculum guide *Smart Decarceration Practice Behaviors for Social Work Competencies* for teachers and students of social work. The document presents smart decarceration practices within the framework of the nine core competencies of the CSWE.

The USC Suzanne Dworak-Peck School of Social Work developed its doctorate of social work program focused entirely on addressing the Grand Challenges. Participants in the program select one of the challenges, design an innovative approach to solve the challenge, and are prepared to implement their solution by the time they complete the program. Equally far-reaching was a 10-year initiative announced by Wayne State University School of Social Work in 2017 with their publication *Rising to the Challenge*. The school committed to exploring how the Grand Challenges will raise social well-being in Greater Detroit through innovative roles for faculty, staff, and students over the next decade. At the University of Maryland School of Social Work, an entire certificate program has been developed around the goals of the Grand Challenge to Build Financial Capability and Assets for All.

There have been numerous publications by the Grand Challenge networks through the first 5 years of the initiative. The FCAB network published the textbook *Financial Capability and Asset Building in Vulnerable Households* (Sherraden, Birkenmaier, & Collins, 2018) and a *Handbook on Financial Social Work with Vulnerable Populations* (Callahan, Frey, & Imboden, 2020). The Promote Smart Decarceration network created a number of "tools for the field," including guidance for administrators, educators, prosecutors, and students. Leaders of the Grand Challenge to End Homelessness published a volume on ending homelessness and transforming systems of care (Padgett, Henwood & Tsemberis, 2016).

Universities and colleges have also hosted events and seminar series that highlight the Grand Challenges, including Wichita State University's 2020 Power Conference themed around the GCSW, the Science for Action Series hosted by the Graduate School of Social Work at the University of Denver, and an ongoing lecture series at the University of Illinois at Urbana-Champaign School of Social Work that focused on harnessing technology for social good.

Equally exciting was a student-led competition at New York University's Silver School of Social Work where contestants applied innovative approaches and social work values to identify solutions to the Grand Challenges.

RESPONDING TO CHANGING CONTEXT AND CONTINUOUSLY ENGAGING INPUT

The original Steering Committee imagined and completed a rigorous process—from 2012 to 2016—to select 12 grand challenges. This was arduous, in part, because many ideas that could have generated additional challenges were put aside. This is not stress free for a profession that prides itself on inclusivity. Yet, the Steering Committee also recognized that we would benefit from having challenges that were manageable in scope and focused on achievable goals. Within those challenges, all other issues that were barriers to achievement would be articulated, and relevant variations proposed.

This raised considerable concerns that the broader Grand Challenges—especially eliminating racism and achieving gender equity—been ignored, or worse, that the Grand Challenges and social work as a profession were complicit in their perpetuation. As mentioned earlier, a statement of guiding principles (see Appendix 4) was developed to articulate the commitment of the Grand Challenges to racial and gender equity. As the COVID-19 and systematic racism pandemics shone a more prominent focus on gender and race inequities, the opportunities for the GCSW strengthen the initiative by adding a focus on ending racism and achieving gender equity. Given the pandemics and current political climate, it became clearer and the urgency became ever more obvious that, in addition to integrating systematic racism and gender equity into the 12 original challenges, a more specific focus was required.

The different approaches to addressing systematic racism and gender inequities in the Grand Challenges demonstrate both the flexibility of the organization and the importance of varying approaches to solving difficult social problems. Adding the Grand Challenge to Eliminate Racism as a separate challenge demonstrates a strong commitment within the profession to ending systematic racism and the attendant harms that centuries of racist behavior and policies have generated. The Gender Mainstreaming approach does not seek its own grand challenge, but rather asks that gender be placed at the forefront of practices, policies, and research within each of the Grand Challenges. The authors of the Gender Mainstreaming Inserts in this book intentionally took an intersectional and nonbinary approach to gender mainstreaming. As Schultz (this volume) eloquently writes in the Mainstreaming Gender Insert in Chapter 14 on eliminating racism, "Efforts to eliminate racism should not ignore the context of gender, nor should gender mainstreaming proceed without interrogating the shortsightedness and potential harm of this process when devoid of a racial equity lens."

Although the Grand Challenge Initiative made a critical course correction by adding the Grand Challenge to Eliminate Racism and by implementing a plan to mainstream gender across the 13 Grand Challenges, it is clear that foregrounding the intersections of race, gender, ability, sexuality, and other social identities is necessary to be successful in ameliorating the social problems being addressed by the Grand Challenge Initiative. We are confident that this volume has clarified ways that critical, intersectional feminist perspectives are needed to develop solutions that work for the most oppressed populations and have the capacity to benefit everyone. Reification of the gender binary, and attendant racialized and cis-/heteronormative oppression, are consistently identified in the Inserts as a call for social workers to commit to helping those most in need, including people who are homeless (end homelessness), incarcerated (promote smart decarceration), and survivors of gender-based violence (achieve equal opportunity and justice). The Inserts each focus on *how* we can create and implement interventions that lead to gender and race equity; solutions spanned primary prevention (build healthy relationships to end violence) and gender transformative interventions (ensure healthy development for youth) to macro-level structural and global solutions (eradicate social isolation). For example, in the financial sphere, centering safety on an individual intervention level could help to ensure that women and girls, particularly those who face multiple marginalized identities, have the same access and opportunity to assets and ownership as men (build financial capability and assets for all). On a structural level, it is imperative to shift blame for poverty from individuals to the racist and patriarchal systems that have generated the high rates of poverty among women of color (reduce extreme economic inequality). Throughout the Mainstreaming Gender Inserts, social work scholars embrace our professional values of human dignity and social justice, and assert that social workers can change systems to eliminate patriarchal and white supremacist value systems (harness technology for social good).

One of the most unique aspects of the Grand Challenge initiative is that it allows social work scholars and practitioners to make deep progress across major areas of inequity by looking at them through the lens of each specific Grand Challenge. The demands of an initiative such as the GCSW are many, and accomplishment is not at all guaranteed. As our commentators attest, we have made a considerable mark, but whether the imprint of the Grand Challenges will be lasting is not given. This depends on whether we are able to draw on the structures of the Grand Challenges to build science that leads to demonstrable social progress. As we work toward this goal, learning from stories of strength and resilience, and honoring those who have harnessed the power of social work to survive or thrive within these oppressive systems can provide hope for creating lasting change (see the Gender Mainstreaming Insert in Chapter 4).

Because the Grand Challenges are organized, most prominently, around networks to work on specific, social, health, environmental, and economic problems, progress can be assessed most logically by indicators of success in addressing those problems. Yet, we have observed several other kinds of outcomes that are connected logically to greater societal impact. We have seen an impact on the profession, and by the profession in higher education. Several social work academic leaders have been asked to take leadership roles on campus initiatives that align with the Grand Challenges. This may give social work more influence and access to other disciplinary partners with new tools and skills.

The work that university faculty do on the Grand Challenges is also aligned with the general effort to redirect the activities—and incentives—of the academy to be more "community engaged." Social work has long been so engaged and, in so doing, has sometimes found it difficult to compete for resources with fields that have more controlled research environments (and can often do scores of experiments in one year while a social work faculty member is still organizing an intervention trial). We now have several examples of positive influence on tenure decisions that cited Grand Challenges-related activities and demonstrate that this form of applied scholarship is valued.

- We see that the GCSW are also generating opportunities for social work leadership in creating different methods of problem solving and collaboration. Problem-focused learning programs, Grand Challenges competitions, and PhD dissertation awards are just a few examples. The doctoral social work program at USC, with its focus on the Grand Challenges, is generating an engaged professional practice community in this large-scale thinking and interdisciplinary work.
- "Social progress through science" continues to be a clarion call of the Grand Challenges—and one that is not often heard elsewhere. Although there is broad (unfortunately not yet universal) recognition that medical science, energy science, and genetics are heralded for their importance to the world's future, social factors are just as great. The COVID-19 pandemic that swept the world in 2020 brought this to light even further. Vaccinations, testing, and mask wearing have had social dimensions almost as large as social distancing. Yet, the social research on how to leverage ways most effectively to interrupt a pandemic was not as advanced as it needed to be—resulting in untold millions of infections, in the United States alone.

At the same time, we see that the calls for economic and racial equity are relying on the emerging science about the success of strategies to provide children's allowances (see Chapter 11 for a discussion) and direct cash payments to low-income people (Amy Baker and Stacia West's research, which is discussed in Chapter 12). Furthering these ideas, the FCAB Grand Challenge assert that (a) financial capability depends not only on individual knowledge and behavior, but also on what is possible in the environment; and (b) a broad array of practitioners and practices can help build assets in low-income households, beyond simply stabilizing income (Sherraden et al., 2018). Achieving this goal is part of the next era of Grand Challenge work.

As the United States struggled with decisions about whether to make nearly universal cash payments—rather than giving money only to those who were officially "unemployed"—social work's research on the positive benefits of direct cash payments were already in place to guide decision makers. The importance of social science and intervention development to the Grand Challenges can serve as a critical indicator of what society needs and the possible alleviators of those needs. We have long envisioned that the Grand Challenges would represent a social agenda that could be taken up, more comprehensively, in future policymaking. The work on universal basic income, child development accounts, and social factors in climate change may be a harbinger of these developments.

The first signs of a positive outcome for an initiative are institutionalization and incorporation of the agenda, practices, and philosophy of the initiative. The extent to which stakeholders do not actually adopt the philosophy and purpose of the agenda, the more it may depart from its original intent. Conversely, if there is buy-in, the more likely its impact will be sustained. Although those who sought a Grand Challenge on race equity and gender equity, respectively, did not accept the initial strategy (and selection of the 12 challenges), they have been continuously engaged in the process of the Grand Challenges. This is a sign of organizational health. So far, the original intent of the Grand Challenges has been maintained quite significantly, with all original challenges still engaged and making progress—as witnessed by the 15 chapters in this volume. Growth and change are demonstrated by explicit commitment to antiracism and gender equity. And the transition of the original Grand Challenge to Stop Family Violence to the Grand Challenge to Build Health Relationships to End Violence has broadened, refocused, and reinvented this Grand Challenge in a very stimulating way.

CONCLUSION

The GCSW are galvanized in energy and foster sustainable determination when there is a concerted effort to solve societal problems by joining with community-driven initiatives. Positive reframing to the approaches used with stereotyped populations have garnered enthusiasm and innovative thinking. Innovation is very important to engage future social workers and to keep the pipeline of the profession doing significant and transformative work to solve the major and challenging problems facing the clients they choose to impact through cross-disciplinary practice, policy, and research activities.

The Grand Challenge framework is also a mechanism for advocacy beyond values and one that has a scientific basis to support social justice aims. We see the emergence of efforts—in combination with the NASW and the Congressional Research Institute for Social Policy, which are calling on the leadership of Grand Challenge networks to help shape their own policy advocacy. This has included multiple congressional briefings and shaped the NASW's *Blueprint for Social Policy* for the incoming Biden/Harris administration—around the pillars of the 13 Grand Challenges (National Association of Social Workers, 2021).

The further development of cross-cutting efforts to strengthen the social work intervention and research strategies to achieve greater impact on the Grand Challenges is likely to be a part of this quest. We also need to pursue new ways to capture the public's imagination about the possibilities of transformational social change with science as a key contributor of lasting and fruitful social innovation.

Future steps most likely will involve deeper engagement of practitioners, engagement of scholars in more universities and more disciplines throughout the country (influencing the pipeline and recruitment of new social work students at the elementary and high school levels), better information dissemination to the public, more robust communications, and focused efforts to influence public policy. We will expose new barriers to success and innovations to achieve more. This is social work's history. The Grand Challenges have now become a key living chapter of our story and aim to add new chapters to a story of a more robust and equitable society.

REFERENCES

Callahan, C., Frey, J. J., & Imboden, R. (2020). *The Routledge handbook on financial social work: Direct practice with vulnerable populations*. New York, NY: Routledge, Taylor & Francis Group.

Flynn, M. (2017). The grand challenges concept: Campus strategies for implementation. *Journal of the Society for Social Work and Research, 8*, 87–98.

Gehlert, S., Walters, K., Uehara, E., & Lawlor, E. (2015). The case for a national health social work practice-based research network in addressing health equity. *Health & Social Work, 40*, 253–255.

Grand Challenges of Social Work. (2019). Grand Challenges for Social Work: Vision, mission, domain, guiding principles, & guideposts to action. Retrieved from https://grandchallengesforsocialwork.org/resources/gcsw-guiding-principles/.

Grand Challenges for Social Work. (2021). *Progress and Plans for the Grand Challenges: An impact report at year 5 of the 10-year initiative*. https://grandchallengesforsocialwork.org/grand-challenges-for-social-work/impact-report/

Kelly, E. L., Kiger, H., Gaba, R., Pancake, L., Pilon, D., Murch, L., . . . Brekke, J. S. (2015). The Recovery-Oriented Care Collaborative: A practice-based research network to improve care for people with serious mental illnesses. *Psychiatric Services, 66*, 1132–1134.

McIntosh, K., Girvan, E. J., McDaniel, S. C., Santiago-Rosario, M. R., St. Joseph, S., Fairbanks Falcon, S., Izzard, S., & Bastable, E. (2021). Effects of an equity-focused PBIS approach to school improvement on exclusionary discipline and school climate. *Preventing School Failure, 65*(4), 354–361. https://doi.org/10.1080/1045988X.2021.1937027

Messing, J. T. (2020). Mainstreaming Gender: An Intersectional Feminist Approach to the Grand Challenges for Social Work [Review]. *Social Work (United States), 65*(4), 313–315. https://doi.org/10.1093/sw/swaa042.

National Association of Social Workers. (2021). NASW releases its 2021 blueprint of federal social policy priorities. Retrieved from https://www.socialworkers.org/News/News-Releases/ID/2276/NASW-releases-its-2021-Blueprint-of-Federal-Social-Policy-Priorities

Padgett, D., Henwood, B., & Tsemberis, S. (2016). *Ending homelessness, transforming systems, and changing lives.* New York, NY: Oxford University Press.

Rice, E., Yoshioka-Maxwell, A., Petering, R., Onasch-Vera, L., Craddock, J., Tambe, M., . . . Wilson, N. (2018). Piloting the use of artificial intelligence to enhance HIV prevention interventions for youth experiencing homelessness. *Journal of the Society for Social Work and Research, 9*, 551–573. doi:10.1086/701439

Sherraden, M. S., Birkenmaier, J., & Collins, J. M. (2018). *Financial capability and asset building in vulnerable households: Theory and practice.* New York, NY: Oxford University Press.

Short, P. (2000). *Mao: A life.* New York: MacMillan.

Teasley, M. L., McRoy, R. G., Joyner, M., Armour, M., Gourdine, R. M., Crewe, S. E., . . . Fong, R. (2017). Increasing success for African American children and youth (Grand Challenges for Social Work initiative Working Paper No. 21). Cleveland, OH: American Academy of Social Work and Social Welfare.

Wayne State University School of Social Work (2017). *Rising to the Challenge.* Retrieved from wsu-ssw_rising_challenge_2017_digital_version_07_24_17.pdf (wayne.edu)

Winter, S., & Butler, B. (2011). Creating bigger problems: Grand challenges as boundary objects and the legitimacy of the information systems field. *Journal of Information Technology, 26*, 99–108. doi: 10.1057/jit.2011.6

Commentaries

LISSA JOHNSON, SARAH CHRISTA BUTTS,
RON MANDERSCHEID, MICHAEL SHERRADEN,
AND CHARLES E. LEWIS, JR.

We, as a country, have blazed unimagined trails technologically and industrially. We have not yet begun to pioneer in those things that are human and social. Social work is uniquely equipped to play a major role in the social renaissance of our society.
—Whitney M. Young, Jr.

Grand Challenges for Social Work (GCSW), which was launched in 2016, provides a broad framework and partnership to increase the influence of social work research in federal, state, county, and municipal policy and practice. Research results can take 20 or more years to percolate into practice. This lag is especially problematic when research knowledge can improve the life conditions of vulnerable persons, groups, and communities (Gehlert, Manderscheid, Teasley, McClain, & Butts, 2020).

GCSW has specified a research-informed social policy agenda led by networks of social work experts. Our goal is to inform social innovations that change lives for the better. As social worker Whitney Young said during the civil rights era, "Social work is uniquely equipped to play a major role in the social renaissance of our society" ("Society Needs to Care," as cited in Mahaffey, 1972). He was at the table in the White House with President Lyndon Johnson and Reverend Martin Luther King, hammering out the Civil Rights Act of 1964 and Voting Rights Act of 1965.

FROM RESEARCH KNOWLEDGE TO POLICY ACTION

One of the first actions of the GCSW was to organize a policy conference. In September 2016, stakeholders of each of the networks gathered to strategize on research and policy for the next 10 years, and to develop specific policy proposals for a new federal administration.

The following years saw a rise in political polarization, environmental disasters, economic inequality, and racial tension, the latter fueled primarily by national outrage at the unjust mistreatment of Black and Brown people by police officers. During this time, GCSW leadership responded with policy action—organizing congressional briefings on policing reform and expungement of prison records, providing expert testimony on homelessness and healthy youth development, participating on a government committee related to social isolation and to the aging workforce, and speaking out against the Trump administration's immigration policies and lack of attention to climate change. For example, research from the leadership of the Grand Challenge to Promote Smart Decarceration informed passage of federal prison reform: the First Step Act of 2018.

At the state level, the financial capability and asset-building network has provided significant leadership in the passage of child development account (CDA) legislation in four states: Pennsylvania, Nebraska, Illinois, and California (Clancy, Sherraden, & Beverly, 2019). Policy initiatives of the ending homeless network contributed to passage of Maryland's Ending Youth Homelessness Act.

In 2020, the United States faced a global pandemic (COVID-19), crippling businesses, overwhelming healthcare organizations, and creating high unemployment, economic distress, social isolation, and mental illness and substance use sequelae. The health impact was worse on Black and Brown people, magnifying the already wide socioeconomic and health status racial gap. The GCSW responded by approving a 13th Grand Challenge—the Grand Challenge to Eliminate Racism—with a network well-positioned to formulate and manifest strong policy to eliminate racism.

EMPHASIS ON POLICY IMPACTS

In its first five years, the GCSW has made substantial progress in forwarding policy innovations at all levels of government. Working with national partners, they are setting domestic policy agenda, forwarding innovative policy solutions, and scaling interventions based on rigorous research (Grand Challenges for Social Work, 2021).

Roadmap for Social Policy

In 2021, social work's leading professional association, the National Association of Social Workers (NASW), included all 13 Grand Challenges as part of its *NASW 2021 Blueprint of Federal Social Policy Priorities* (Mangum et. al., 2021). This policy agenda provides a unique opportunity for the GCSW, its partners, and social workers across the country to coalesce in addressing these Grand Challenges through policy action at the local, county, state, and federal levels. Although each Grand Challenge has identified policy recommendations, we call for all social workers to take on a greater role in policy action to ensure that the social work profession has a voice at the policy table. GCSW will design and promote a purposeful policy and practice agenda. The following are examples and recent achievements.

The *Blueprint* articulates meaningful actions the Biden-Harris administration and the US Congress can take to address the COVID-19 pandemic, promote mental and behavioral health, eliminate systemic racism, and ensure civil and human rights for all (Mangum et al., 2021). The *Blueprint*'s 21 issue areas are organized according to the GCSW and include actionable recommendations. The *Blueprint* is a roadmap for progress over the next 4 years that reflects social work's best thinking on the pathway to a more just and equitable society. We offer some examples in the following subsections.

Bringing Social Work Expertise to Complex Problems: Reimagining Policing

In the 116th Congress, Rep. Karen Bass (D-CA-37), a social worker, and Sen. Chris Van Hollen (D-MD), introduced the Community-Based Response Act. This bill would create a new community-based emergency and nonemergency response grant program through the US Department of Health and Human Services that would establish services to make available an additional option beyond law enforcement for community-based emergency response. NASW staff and policy experts were invited to review and provide input to the bill's development. NASW Chief Executive Officer Angelo McClain was quoted in the press release, and both the NASW and the American Academy of Social Work and Social Welfare endorsed the bill upon introduction (Bass & Van Hollen, 2020).). In a step toward this goal, the 2021 American Rescue Plan offers states 85% federal matching funds to provide community-based mobile crisis intervention services, including social workers as part of the multidisciplinary mobile crisis response teams. This is an example of the potential and possibilities when social workers are engaged at multiple points in federal policy formulation.

Bringing Interventions to Scale: CDAs as an Exemplar

CDAs, an intervention under the Grand Challenge to Build Financial Capability and Assets For All, have been proposed as a nationwide policy solution using the 529 College Savings Plan as the financial platform. A similar federal proposal with similar characteristics is baby bonds (Fields, 2021; Nova & Schoen, 2019). The vision for CDAs, the subject of applied research for two decades, has been for a universal and progressive policy aimed at lifelong asset-building for *all* children. CDAs are savings or investment accounts that begin as early as birth. In many cases, public and private matching funds are deposited into these accounts to supplement savings for the child. They are a mechanism that can address economic inequality, the racial wealth gap, and access to education. CDAs have already been implemented or enacted in several states (Maine, Rhode Island, Nevada, Connecticut, Pennsylvania, Illinois, Nebraska, and California). Model legislation with design elements to enact statewide CDA policy are available (Clancy et al., 2019). If CDAs are implemented and scaled nationally, all newborns would be "banked" immediately and building assets for their future. CDAs could be the policy foundation for universal, progressive, lifelong asset building (Sherraden, 1991).

Organized Policy Action

With leadership from national social work organizations, policy action is increasing. Consider some examples:

> *Presenting at White House executive briefing cohosted by NASW.* On July 7, 2021, the National Association of Social Workers (NASW) cohosted "Social Work is Essential," a virtual White House executive briefing on priorities of the Grand Challenges for Social Work. The event brought together key Biden-Harris Administration officials and social work leaders. Panelists, which included leaders from NASW and the Grand Challenges, "urged the administration to tackle issues important to the profession and the people we serve." Remarks centered on action in the following areas: suicide rates, especially among Black youth; mental and behavioral health access; relief of high student loan debt for social workers; national and universal Child Development Account policy to promote asset building for all; universal housing vouchers for homeless persons; immigration reform; public health and safety innovation; interrupting the school to prison pipeline, and ending systemic racism (National Association of Social Workers, n.d.).

Hosting congressional briefings to translate research into policy. Examples of congressional briefings are as follows:
- Undoing Racism: Eliminating Debilitating Criminal Penalties (Congressional Research Institute for Social Work and Policy, 2020)
- Bringing the Power of Social Work to Schools (Congressional Research Institute for Social Policy & National Association of Social Workers, 2020)
- Black Lives Matter: Social Work and the Future of Policing (Congressional Research Institute for Social Policy, Center for Social Development at Washington University in St. Louis, & National Association of Social Workers, 2020)*Participating in public comment, statements, and sign-on letters.* The Council on Social Work Education (CSWE) and NASW work across government and nonprofit agencies, and educational institutions to identify key issues and solutions, and promote policy reform. Examples include the following:
- Letters to the transition teams of each of the newly elected presidents
- Joint testimony of the NASW and CSWE to the Subcommittee on Labor, Health and Human Services, and Education; and a CSWE letter to the Department of Education supporting a Higher Education Act reauthorization (Council on Social Work Education, 2019; National Association of Social Workers, 2020; Council on Social Work Education & National Association of Social Workers, 2020).

Educating on informing policy through research and practice. Examples include presentations and webinars such as the following:
- Making Research Useful to Policymakers (Zlotnik & Harris Rome, 2018)
- Advocacy and Public Policy Formation during the COVID-19 Pandemic (Butts, Coffey, Manderscheid, Singer, & Walters, 2021)
- Making Change: Messaging Your Work For Policy Audiences (Johnson, Beilenson, Manderscheid, & Silk, 2020).

Supporting social workers being considered for government leadership positions. Social work organizations have collaborated in writing letters of support for social work experts who are being considered for career leadership roles in government and appointments within the Biden-Harris Administration.

MOVING FORWARD

According to the US Bureau of Labor Statistics (2019), well over 700,000 social workers actively work in the United States to improve family and community well-being. Moreover, the expected growth in social work employment is

13% over the next 10 years (US Bureau of Labor Statistics, 2019). This vast and growing social labor force is very much *among the people*, day in and day out, addressing family and community problems.

Social workers provide direct expertise and support to individuals and families, in community development, and in policy innovation at local, county, state, and national levels. The work is highly social, fundamental, and consequential. Consider the potential of this social labor force. Social worker Whitney Young was thinking about it; social work has the potential to be a transformational force.

Social work's history of active policy engagement guides us. Social workers have played leading roles in positive, transformational social policies that include child support and protection, civil rights, social insurance, employment protections, housing and community development, and civic engagement (Sherraden et al., 2014). Social workers have organized coalitions, provided expert testimony, and organized press briefings. They have used evidence and organized to wrangle political support. This journey is never completed, and the road is never easy. As social worker Grace Abbott, founder of the US Children's Bureau, wryly commented, this work is "uphill all the way" (Jabour, 2016, p. 561)

The GCSW is reinvigorating social work's professional infrastructure and professional identity through collective participation in research for policy action. We work at all levels—micro, mezzo, macro—to achieve positive change. Everyone's work matters, and social workers know how to work together. We encourage partnerships across sectors and disciplines to build a more decent society, with more equitable prosperity and human development into the future.

Social work's policy strategy over the next 5 to 10 years builds on our long history of effective engagement, and our training and commitment to work for social justice and investment in people and communities to achieve the best possible lives and well-being for all.

The GCSW and the American Academy of Social Work and Social Welfare represent an organized cadre of experts prepared to inform policy reform and innovations. Because social work practitioners are *among the people*, they bring evidence and rich stories to the policy process.

The CSWE and the NASW encourage and facilitate involvement with federal, state, county, and local coalitions to share expertise and evidence. To emphasize the importance of such involvement and ensure time for such participation, social work academic leadership can also support faculty, staff, and student participation in the social policy process.

Social workers know this terrain. For example, the social determinants of health, currently gaining currency in policy circles, are nothing more than social issues that social workers and allies have been working to understand

and overcome for decades. We know very well that social and economic conditions are determinants of not just health, but also housing, education, jobs, migration, stable families, strong communities, and a great deal more. Social determinants are what we aim to understand in research, and aim to improve in policy and practice.

For example, there was no need to inform social worker Frances Perkins of the social determinants of shortened lives in the Triangle Fire; she knew the women garment workers who jumped to their deaths from the burning building. Perkins took that experience and knowledge to become the first Secretary of Labor under President Franklin Roosevelt; she was America's first female cabinet member. "Madam Secretary," as Roosevelt called her, went right to work. She was a key author of the National Fair Labor Standards Act and the Social Security Act of 1935—arguably the two most important pieces of social legislation in US history.

Social workers welcome deep collaboration across disciplines to address social challenges. For example, the COVID-19 pandemic and other disasters highlight dramatically the wide gaps in access to fundamental resources such as healthcare, education, and banking by race, income, and geography. Technology has the capacity to expand access to vulnerable families and communities, but reaching this goal will first require a policy intervention that guarantees universal Internet access. Working across disciplines will be necessary to reach this goal.

Last, reinforcing social work's policy potential will require a bustling workforce pipeline. Field education departments at schools of social work across the nation can facilitate access to internships in policy settings, including federal, state, county, and city agencies; the US Congress and state legislatures; and national policy research settings, such as the Urban Institute, Children's Defense Fund, Brookings Institution, and others. Such placements can provide students with an understanding of the policy process, and networking that creates policy opportunities.

Fellowships, such as the Robert Wood Johnson Foundation (RWJF) Health Policy Fellows, are another avenue for cultivating policy engagement. GCSW partners on Capitol Hill, such as the Congressional Research Institute for Social Work and Policy and the NASW, can work together with the GCSW, the American Academy of Social Work and Social Welfare, the CSWE, Influencing Social Policy, and the MACRO SW Commission to share information about the availability of policy fellowships and to facilitate applications.

Strong policy emphasis is, in some respects, a regrounding for the profession. Although much of our work in the past 50 years has been clinically focused, the profession was founded on a person-in-environment perspective, with social workers leading the efforts in policy during the Progressive Era, the New Deal, and the Civil Rights era—always working toward policy solutions to protect the most vulnerable and to develop the whole society. In our time, when racial, economic, and environmental justice are at the forefront, the GCSW is renewing the social work emphasis on policy to ensure that freedom, justice, security, and positive development are indeed for everyone.

REFERENCES

Bass, K., & Van Hollen, C. (2020, October 1). Bass, Van Hollen, introduce new community-based crisis response legislation. [press release]. Retrieved from https://bass.house.gov/media-center/press-releases/bass-van-hollen-introduce-new- /

Butts, S., Coffey, D., Manderscheid, R., Singer, J., & Walters, K. (2021, January 19–22). Advocacy and public policy formation during the COVID-19 pandemic. Virtual conference presentation for the Society for Social Work and Research. Retrieved from https://sswr.confex.com/sswr/2021/webprogram/Session11784.html

Clancy, M. M., Sherraden, M., & Beverly, S. G. (2019). *Child development accounts at scale: Sample state legislation.* CSD policy summary no. 19–46. St. Louis, MO: Washington University, Center for Social Development.

Congressional Research Institute for Social Work and Policy (2020, December 2). Undoing racism: Eliminating debilitating criminal penalties. [virtual congressional briefing]. Retrieved from https://www.crispinc.org/12-2-congressional-briefing/

Congressional Research Institute for Social Work and Policy, Center for Social Development at Washington University in St. Louis, & National Association of Social Workers. (2020, June 30). Black Lives Matter: Social work and the future of policing. [virtual congressional briefing]. Retrieved from https://csd.wustl.edu/congressional-briefing-black-lives-matter-social-work-and-the-future-of-policing/

Congressional Research Institute on Social Work and Policy & National Association of Social Workers. (2020, September 23). Bringing the power of social work to schools. [virtual congressional briefing]. Retrieved from https://schoolsocialwork.net/bringing-the-power-of-social-work-to-schools-our-9-23-congressional-briefing/

Council on Social Work Education. (2019). Ensuring quality and accessibility: CSWE principles for a Higher Education Act reauthorization. Retrieved from https://www.cswe.org/CSWE/media/Public-Policy/CSWE-HEA-Principles116thCongress.pdf

Council on Social Work Education & National Association of Social Workers. (2020). Council on Social Work Education and National Association of Social Work testimony prepared for the Subcommittee on Labor, Health and Human Services, and Education, and Related Agencies. Retrieved from https://www.socialworkers.org/LinkClick.aspx?fileticket=8hbt94cBKQU%3d&portalid=0

Fields, S. (2021). How baby bonds could help close the racial wealth gap. Retrieved from https://www.marketplace.org/2021/01/13/how-baby-bonds-could-help-close-racial-wealth-gap/

Gehlert, S., Manderscheid, R., Teasley, M., McClain, A., & Butts, S. (2020, January 15–19) Leveraging social work research expertise to influence public policy to improve American's wellbeing. Virtual conference presentation for the Society for Social Work and Research. Retrieved from https://sswr.confex.com/sswr/2020/webprogram/Session10940.html

Grand Challenges for Social Work. (2021). *Grand Challenges 5 year impact report.* Baltimore, MD: University of Maryland-Baltimore. Retrieved from https://grandchallengesforsocialwork.org/grand-challenges-for-social-work/impact-report/

Jabour, A. (2016). "Uphill all the way": Grace Abbott and women's work in building the welfare state. *Social Service Review, 90*(3), 550–561.

Johnson, L., Beilenson, J. Manderscheid, R., & Silk, K. (2020). *Making change: Messaging your work for policy audiences.* [video]. Grand Challenges for Social Work & Brown School at Washington University. Retrieved from https://www.youtube.com/watch?v=OjQjicsB9JA

Mahaffey, M. (1972). Lobbying in social work. *Social Work, 17*(1), 3–11. https://doi.org/10.1093/sw/17.1.3

Mangum, A., Butts, S., Coleman, M., Dorn, C., Herman, C., Kastner, D., & Richardson, T. (2021). NASW 2021 blueprint of federal social policy priorities: Recommendations to the Biden-Harris Administration and Congress. Retrieved from https://www.socialworkers.org/LinkClick.aspx?fileticket=KPdZqqY60t4%3d&portalid=0

National Association of Social Workers. (2020, November). NASW letter to Biden and Harris presidential transition team. Retrieved from https://www.socialworkers.org/LinkClick.aspx?fileticket=xMxmMZi6mc4%3d&portalid=0

National Association of Social Workers (n.d.). *NASW joined Biden official July 7 for White House policy briefing.* Retrieved from http://www.socialworkblog.org/advocacy/2021/07/nasw-co-hosts-policy-briefing-with-white-house/

Nova, A., & Schoen, J. (2019, April 25). Cory Booker wants to give "BABY BONDS" to EVERY newborn: Here's how that would work. Retrieved from https://www.cnbc.com/2019/04/24/cory-booker-wants-to-give-baby-bonds-to-every-newborn.html

Sherraden, M. (1991). *Assets and the Poor.* New York: ME Sharpe.

Sherraden, M., Stuart, P., Barth, R. P., Kemp, S., Lubben, J., Hawkins, J. D., . . . Catalano, R. (2014). *Grand accomplishments in social work.* Grand Challenges for Social Work initiative, working paper no. 2. Baltimore, MD: American Academy of Social Work and Social Welfare. Retrieved from https://grandchallengesforsocialwork.org/wp-content/uploads/2015/10/AASWSW-GC-Accomplishments4-2-2015.pdf

US Bureau of Labor Statistics. (2019). Occupational outlook handbook: Social workers. Retrieved from https://www.bls.gov/ooh/community-and-social-service/social-workers.htm

Zlotnik, J., & Harris Rome, S. (2018). Making research useful to policy makers. [video]. National Association of Social Workers, Influencing Social Policy, and Grand Challenges for Social Work. Retrieved from https://naswinstitute.inreachce.com/Details/ProductPreview?groupId=12c93e1b-5fca-44fb-b40a-573c69c53652

MARY M. McKAY

Five years ago, the Grand Challenge initiative set forth a bold goal: eliminate seemingly intractable and highly burdensome social problems. The Grand Challenges were unique in that, first, they were led exclusively by social work scholars. Visible leadership by stewards of the profession was welcome and immediately credible, given social work's scope of expertise. The leveraging of fellows recognized by the American Academy of Social Work & Social Welfare as Grand Challenge leaders ensured that scholarly expertise would guide the development of goals and activities associated with each area.

Furthermore, what was also unique about the Grand Challenges was the research-informed foundation laid by network leaders. Specifically, beginning immediately, network leads highlighted the existing science-backed solutions available to end burdensome challenges affecting far too many across the nation. Social work research as a tool for social change and improvement of social circumstances was an important visible step forward. Combining the significant investment made to enhance the scientific capacity of social work with the core value of social work—the elimination of suffering—set the Grand Challenge Initiative apart.

The organizational strategy underlying the Grand Challenges also made this effort distinct. More specifically, organizing networks of scholarly experts for each challenge area across institutions and geographic area increased the visibility and viability of products and collaborations. Forward movement would not only belong to a single entity, but also could be shared and characterized by exponential commitment and energy. Each Grand Challenge network was active, and elevated centrally the issues and scientific solutions via conferences, webinars, policy briefs, scholarly articles, and presentations across time. This organizational strategy of collaborative network leadership made the initiative more robust and a quickly raised a "large tent" for important activities.

In addition, the Grand Challenges Executive Committee was able to listen to feedback and course-correct. From the launch of the Grand Challenges, there was an important critique from many in the field, including myself, regarding the absence of visible recognition that identity—particularly racial and ethnic identity—played a disproportionate influence on many, if not all, of the grand challenge areas. The addition of the call to eliminate racism as a grand challenge pillar was a critically important response to this critique. The Grand Challenge to Eliminate Racism, although added to the complement of challenge areas several years into the effort, was seen as an important advancement and became extremely relevant again as our nation protested the senseless deaths of Black and Brown people as a result of interactions with the police. The Grand Challenge to Eliminate Racism is clearly aligned with the national call to end racial injustice. Identified leadership for this grand challenge visibly elevated the need to focus exclusively and discretely on using science to dismantle structures that oppressed people of color systematically and disproportionately. However, simultaneously, network leaders articulated the need to understand how racism in particular, and identity more broadly, operated within each one of the grand challenge areas.

Thus, the ambitious science-based, visible approach to the elimination of serious challenge areas was an important step that helped to mobilize social work leadership and spark collaboration across the profession. Commitment, coordinated efforts, and a willingness to grapple with feedback also made the Grand Challenges have 5 years of staying power, where less-organized efforts might not have continued as robustly.

During the next 5 years, there are serious barriers to fulfilling the promises of the Grand Challenges—namely, creating robust partnerships and support for these shared goals of the social work profession. Incentives for policymakers, advocates, funders, and the academy of scholars need to align to take the Grand Challenges forward. Where are the easy "wins" for the Grand Challenges? First, contributions to a Grand Challenge network could be framed as service to the profession of the highest order. Applications to join a network with recommendations could help network leaders and contributors articulate more clearly the commitment to the elimination of a grand challenge area, and an articulation of recommendations for exponential growth and new paths forward. Exceptional service as part of the initiative then becomes a highly recognized and sought-after opportunity, rewarded by universities via the faculty evaluation process.

More difficult to mobilize are the Grand Challenges Leadership Board and network leaders to dedicate time and attention to building coalitions outside the profession. Eliminating the most intractable social problems of the current day is not a volunteer effort. The capacity for grand challenge leadership to elevate the work of the networks and collaborate with government officials to align resources to mount serious interventions in these key areas remains limited. Without significant influencers—government, foundations, and individuals—accepting the Grand Challenges as an urgent mandate or roadmap for investment, the promise of the Grand Challenges will remain only partially fulfilled. To mount an effort to address this barrier is not easy; the profession has struggled with being part of the policy agenda-setting table. However, there are examples from select Grand Challenge networks that, with sustained effort, policy partnership is possible.

For example, two of the Grand Challenge networks, to build financial capability and assets for all and to reduce extreme economic inequality, summarized policy recommendation in 2016 that are part of the current policy debate across the nation. More specifically, child development accounts (CDAs) as a tool to alter the trajectory of children and their poverty-impacted families is part of the current policy debate nationally. Local community and state governments have partnered with grand challenge leadership to examine the impact of CDAs to address serious structural obstacles out of poverty for children and families. Inserting CDAs as a policy option has taken a strong commitment by grand challenge leaders and leveraging resources of the Center for Social Development (led by Michael Sherraden at the Brown School, Washington University in St. Louis). Without these resources, it is challenging to see how the network would be able to organize conferences and policy briefings in Washington, DC; travel to meet with local, state, and federal government officials; and collaborate over and over again with advocacy groups, including the Congressional Research Institute for Social Work and Policy.

Certainly, grand challenge leaders have the capacity to amass resources and champions of these ambitious plans and actions. However, to prioritize these next steps, careful consideration needs to be given with regard to how to align the needs of faculty to carry out their own research, as well as elevate and fund Grand Challenge areas. I have no doubt, given the leadership and contributing members of the Grand Challenges, tackling barriers and elevating this work is completely possible and likely to make a substantial difference for many.

ANGELO McCLAIN

When the Grand Challenges for Social Work launched in January 2016 after 5 years of collaboration and planning under the leadership of the American Association of Social Work and Social Welfare, I was so excited to be invited to make a few comments to help commemorate the world premiere of the Grand Challenges.

As I thought about what I might say that was worthy of this important moment, I thought back to my early days in the profession as a student, as a young professional just entering the field, and as an emerging leader. My thoughts quickly went to a question that we all ask ourselves: Why social work? Deep down, I knew the answer. Like most colleagues, social work was my profession of choice because I wanted to help people and make a difference in the world.

Like most of our colleagues, as we matured as professionals and transitioned those initial desires (to make a difference in the world) into a professional discipline, we began to understand that helping meant strengthening the social safety net, fortifying the social fabric, pursuing racial and social justice relentlessly, and advancing social progress and social development.

As I prepared my remarks, I had a deep-down belief that the Grand Challenges were a great vehicle for facilitating what we have dedicated our professional careers to achieving: individual and family well-being (for all people), a stronger social fabric, and a more just society.

Since 2016, I have enjoyed the privilege of serving on the Grand Challenges Leadership Board, which has provided an ongoing forum for me as Chief Executive Officer of the National Association of Social Workers (NASW) to stay connected intimately and unwaveringly to the work of the initiative.

The halfway point in the Grand Challenges decade-long journey provides a natural opportunity to look back and reflect, and to look ahead with vision and renewed commitment and determination. We have a grand opportunity (no pun intended) to advance our nation's social progress agenda and build on the work to advance, protect, and promote the profession through the Grand Challenges.

The Grand Challenges' public education work has provided a solid foundation for a more common understanding of the "grand value" that social work brings to society. In the coming years, we need to conduct public education continually to garner ongoing public support and understanding of social workers' contributions to society. Through the NASW Foundation's Public Education Program, the NASW will continue to play an important role in this endeavor.

The Grand Challenges' consistent organizing principle, "powered by science," helps fuel the growth in scientific proof of social work solutions, thereby improving the profession's capacity to document and disseminate empirically its contributions to society. With the initiative's reinvigorated emphasis on the importance of social work science, we can expect accelerated growth in social work knowledge, and faster identification and application of social work solutions. The resulting implications for social work practice are exciting. Imagine a better "two-way bridge" that connects and shortens the distance between research, education, practice, and policy.

At its core, the work of the Grand Challenges is essentially about highlighting the patterns of excellence of the profession—recognizing it, anchoring it, refining it, and recreating it to achieve better societal outcomes and advance the profession. Thus, much of the work of the Grand Challenges is about identifying and evaluating excellence, finding the many pockets of excellence where social workers have performed extraordinarily well. Ultimately, the success of the Grand Challenges will be measured by our collective ability to go above and beyond envisioning to evaluating, replicating, and energizing the very best of evidence-informed social work practice.

In the coming half decade, to grow and elevate the profession, social work must commit to being intentional and deliberate about leveraging the Grand Challenges for transformational societal change. The transformational change we seek does not happen by chance. It is measured, intentional, and deliberate. The Grand Challenges give the profession the framework and forums for triangulating knowledge from different social work perspectives (education, practice, research) to build a better understanding of the clients and communities with whom we work, and of how we can leverage better solutions for better results. Research academic findings and expertise; practice knowledge, skills, and wisdom; and lived experiences and the views of people accessing services (individuals, families, caregivers) are important sources and viewpoints for triangulation analysis that, in due course, will result in increased validity and credibility for social work solutions.

Through the Grand Challenges, we are gaining a greater appreciation of the importance of collective impact, learning strategies for establishing new allies and partnerships, and enlarging our collective understanding that acting alone will not get it done. Hopefully, these lessons will be galvanized within the profession and serve to energize the profession for greater transformative social change in the coming decades. It is truly admirable that so many social work organizations have come together for the greater good. It is inspiring to see social work leaders sacrifice and make a collective commitment to the Grand Challenges, which better enables social work to be the engine that powers victories against our nation's biggest social challenges.

Consider the pivotal work of the Grand Challenges' practice, policy, education, and research networks in advancing social work competencies for addressing societies biggest challenges. Through the Grand Challenges networks, the profession is better positioned to achieve greater collective impact. Through the networks, we established extraordinary partnerships and robust cross-organizational teams, champions, and ambassadors; we developed an enhanced collaboration model wherein uncommon mutual respect has flourished. The networks provide a forum for bridging the worlds of social work education, research, practice, policy, and advocacy wherein collective contributions are made related to strategy, implementation, support, and accountability, which are essential to sustaining the Grand Challenges' efforts during the next half decade.

As our Grand Challenges work advances over the coming years, we have an opportunity to develop and strengthen further the two-way bridge that connects and shortens the distance between research and practice. Imagine how exciting our collaborative work will be when we better connect the day-to-day, week-to-week social work practice world with social work research, policy, and education. The two-way bridge becomes the conduit for transferring and translating case to cause, case to evidence, case to education, and clients to cause, resulting in research initiatives that are centered more truly on clients and communities. Through the increased engagement of practitioners and clients in the identification and evaluation of the most effective social work interventions and solutions, the potential for improved practice effectiveness and outcomes is enormous.

The importance of elevating social work science in the coming years for accelerated identification and application of social work solutions cannot be overstated. The social progress and development challenges society faces now, and in the years to come, demand quicker identification and application of evidence-informed solutions. As we have experienced recently with COVID-19, our nation's racial reckoning, and the increase in natural disasters resulting from climate change, the need for planning, response, and recovery solutions requires pivoting not only quickly, but also with precision. As the profession develops greater capacity to deploy and use social work solutions in this manner, we will garner broader community acknowledgment and recognition of the true value and impact of social work.

As the Grand Challenges advance in the coming years, we need to leverage partnerships with even more allies and partners outside the profession. We need the benefit of other perspectives, experience, and expertise. We need to leverage the common ground between our commitments and those of other disciplines and sectors. By leveraging today's critical issues (e.g., COVID-19, racial justice, climate change), we can build a broader constituency base that includes new partners, clients, communities, and practitioners from all fields of social work practice.

The NASW looks forward to continuing our role as a major contributor to advancing the Grand Challenges. We appreciate the opportunity extended to us by the Academy to help facilitate grand challenge thinking for its most important strategic initiatives. We look forward to making additional contributions, through our 110,000 members, our 55 chapters, hundreds of volunteer leaders, our professional development education and training center, our online CE Institute and Leadership Academy, the NASW Foundation and NASW Press, our social media platforms (tweeter, Facebook, LinkedIn, Instagram, Clubhouse, MyNASW Community), our social justice and policy work, and our specialty practice sections as the profession collectively pursues more evidence-informed practice solutions and proof of social work concepts.

It's been said that "social work is the special sauce" for addressing societies grandest challenges. Perhaps, the Grand Challenges are the special ingredient that bridges, solidifies, galvanizes, and powers social work to contribute grandly to creating a more just society that ensures a vibrant social fabric, a more compassionate social safety net, and truly centers individual and family well-being at the forefront of all policy and social development decisions.

DARLA SPENCE COFFEY

Grand Challenges for Social Work captured my attention the first time I heard of the initiative in 2012, and I love that the title of this book, *Grand Challenges for Social Work and Society*, clearly articulates that this is an initiative that is good for the profession *and* for our world. Modeled after other professional grand challenge initiatives (such as engineering), the Grand Challenge initiative communicates the breadth and depth of the science and impact that social workers have on big societal issues. In this way, it is a fantastic way to recruit action-oriented visionaries to the profession. And we need more of them! The Grand Challenges also remind us of our deep roots in the case-to-cause conceptualization—that ours is a profession that, in the words of Mary Richmond, "doesn't simply [sic] go on helping people out of a ditch. Pretty soon, we [sic] begin to find out what ought to be done to get rid of the ditch." We need to eschew the false dichotomy that categorizes social workers as either micro or macro. True social workers hold both perspectives simultaneously, regardless of the target of our attention. When we preserve this dialectic, there is no end to ways in which social work practitioners and scholars can contribute to improving society.

It is exciting to observe where the Grand Challenges for Social Work have been embraced by schools and programs of social work in both curricula and research. Claiming one or more of the Grand Challenges lends cohesiveness to curricula, facilitates connections with like-minded peers across the country, and lifts the profession as a leading actor for societal impact.

YANNIS YORTSOS

In its 2003 seminal report, *A Century of Innovation*, the National Academy of Engineering (Constable, G. & Somerville, B., 2003) singled out 20 engineering achievements in the 20th century that transformed our lives. Ranging from electricity to television to the automobile to the computer, they reflected human ingenuity and the almost exponential growth and power of science, technology, and engineering. Such growth is inherent to knowledge-based innovation. Many of us are familiar with exponential growth through its association with Moore's law, the demonstration of the growth of innovation on an electronic device. I would argue, however, that, in fact, Moore's law is much more than that manifestation. Indeed, if we were to assume that the rate of generation of innovation (and/or knowledge) is itself proportional to the state of innovation (and/or knowledge), then, another form of exponential growth arises, this time applicable to innovation at-large.

This extraordinary attribute of innovation prompted the NAE to ask in a subsequent study: What are the important technological challenges we can anticipate in the 21st century? The resulting 2008 report on the NAE grand challenges (National Academy of Sciences, 2008) identified 14 grand challenges that can be generally categorized in four bins: sustainability, health, security, and life enrichment, paralleling a Maslow hierarchy. Crucially, and for the first time in our history, we have realized that we now possess the fundamental technological innovation ability to confront and solve grand challenge–like problems, never thought possible before. Reflecting the quintessence of innovation, that the more advanced the state of innovation and knowledge, the higher their rates for their further growth, addressing grand challenges then becomes a fundamentally ethical decision. Soon after the NAE report was published, a number of initiatives were launched, including the Grand Challenges Scholars Program, which creates the generation of students that will solve these grand challenges.

Parallel moonshot efforts, such as the 2015 United Nations Sustainable Development Goals (SDGs), reaffirmed this understanding of humans' power for innovation. Importantly, however, the SDGs also introduced novel issues of a strong societal dimension, largely unstated in the NAE grand challenges. A year later, in 2016, the Grand Challenges for Social Work were announced. If the NAE grand challenges addressed the technological end of the spectrum of grand challenge–like problems, the Grand Challenges for Social Work boldly addressed the other part of the spectrum—focusing squarely on tough human- and societal-centric problems. Having participated to some extent in the initial launch of the Grand Challenges for Social Work project, I have always thought of the strong parallelism in the connection between engineering and natural sciences, with the connection between social work and social sciences. In many ways, work implies transformation and the ability to change, concepts that are fundamental to any process, and certainly to engineering processes.

At the same time, there are exist key fundamental differences, with social work addressing fundamental societal issues, where conventional engineering has largely not been part of that conversation. There arise two key questions: Can grand challenge–like problems in social work be solved within the social work community alone, specifically without the participation and mind-sets from the engineering community and the associated exponential rate of innovation? And can engineering grand challenge–like problems be addressed without the consideration of societal consciousness? In neither of these two questions the answer is affirmative. Indeed, I think that the ability for exponential solutions in technological innovation can impart an adjacent effect in innovation for the solution of human-centric problems. How strong this effect will be remains to be discovered, remains to be seen. The University of Southern California's Center for Artificial Intelligence in Society, or CAIS, is one space where computer science and social work coexist for the solution of social work grand challenges. How fast and how enabling this synergy will be is currently being discovered. Although societal consciousness is widely acknowledged, and it is already, a component of the NAE Grand Challenges Scholars Program, we have only just begun its exploration.

The two speeds by which solutions are developed in these two respective areas were demonstrated most emphatically in 2020. On the one hand, we witnessed the extraordinary speed by which COVID vaccines were developed and, more generally, the seamless adaptability of technology to circumvent COVID-induced constraints and enable a more-or-less smooth function of a shocked world during the pandemic. And on the other hand, we also saw the extraordinary societal response to racial reckoning, spread quickly in time and widely across the world, aided in large part by technology.

But there is a larger convergence between the two realms. I view engineering and technology as leveraging phenomena (possibly also including social phenomena) for useful purposes, with accelerating innovation, including discovering new phenomena, new artifacts and devices, and new, powerful methods (from artificial intelligence to machine learning). The vision is to *engineer a better world for all humanity*, which is realistic, timely, urgent, and the *right thing* to do. In fact, the increasing ability to address more complex problems, perhaps even "wicked"-type problems, dominated by human and societal complexity, endows the engineering grand challenges with an important societal and *human-centric* component.

At the same time, powerful, exponential technologies have strong *unintended consequences*. Our world being complex, with many nonlinear interactions and degrees of freedom, cause does not always lead to the desired effect. Unintended consequences in the past, where the rate of change was small, or the technologies not as powerful, could have been managed passively. This is not the case today, however, where the rate of change and disruption continue to grow larger and one cannot, and should not, expect that things will be sorted out by themselves. The need for an active intervention, then, brings to the fore issues of *ethical decision-making*, which is becoming increasingly vital in choosing how we develop or apply technologies. That empowerment means that today, more than ever before, *character* must be developed in addition to *competence*, which is the skill many professional disciplines provide. This attribute of *technology ethics*, ultimately one of *trustworthiness*, with new examples provided every day in the news, will be an integral part of the near future, if not indeed today.

Creating *trustworthy professionals* (with superb competence and outstanding character, whether in engineering or social work) should be an important goal of our endeavors. Such trustworthiness is, therefore, the ultimate connecting thread between engineering and social work mind-sets and grand challenges. And it should be demanded of all our future professionals, who will be counted on to develop powerful technologies and innovative solutions to solve the grand challenges of our times, whether in engineering, the United Nations SDGs, or in social work.

REFERENCE

Constable, G., & Somerville, B. (2003). *A Century of Innovation: Twenty Engineering Achievements that Transformed our Lives*. Washington, DC: Joseph Henry Press. https://doi.org/10.17226/10726National Academy of Sciences. (2008). *NAE Grand Challenges for Engineering*. http://www.engineeringchallenges.org/File.aspx?id=11574&v=34765dff

APPENDIX 1
Grand Challenges Leadership Board

July 2021

Grand Challenges Leadership Board

Richard Barth, PhD, MSW (Chair, Executive Committee)
Past President, AASWSW
Professor and Past Dean
University of Maryland, School of Social Work
rbarth@ssw.umaryland.edu

Melissa Begg, ScD (Executive Committee)
Dean and Professor
Columbia University, School of Social Work
cssw-dean@columbia.edu

Marilyn Flynn, PhD (Executive Committee)
Dean and Professor (retired)
University of Southern California, Suzanne Dworak-Peck School of Social Work
mflynn@usc.edu

Ron Manderscheid, PhD (Executive Committee)
Executive Director, National Association of County Behavioral Health & Developmental Disability Directors
National Association of County Behavioral Health & Developmental Disability Directors
rmanderscheid@nacbhd.org

Michael S. Spencer, PhD (Executive Committee)
Presidential Term Professor
Director, Native Hawaiian, Pacific Islander & Oceanic Affairs
University of Washington, School of Social Work
mspenc@uw.edu

James Herbert Williams, PhD (Executive Committee)
Director and Arizona Centennial Professor
Arizona State University, School of Social Work
james.herbert1@asu.edu

Steve Anderson, MSW, PhD
Dean and Professor
University of Illinois at Champaign-Urbana, School of Social Work
sandersn@illinois.edu

Darla Spence Coffey, PhD
President and Chief Executive Officer
Council on Social Work Education
dcoffey@cswe.org

Catherine Gayle, PhD
Department Chair of Social Work, Associate Professor
Savannah State University, College of Liberal Arts and Social Sciences
gaylec@savannahstate.edu

Neil B. Guterman, MSW, PhD
Dean and Paulette Goddard Professor
New York University, Silver School of Social Work
nguterman@nyu.edu

Benjamin Henwood, LCSW, PhD
Associate Professor & Director
University of Southern California,
Suzanne Dworak-Peck School of Social
Work, Center for Homelessness,
Housing and Health Equity Research
bhenwood@usc.edu

Robert Sheehan, MSW, MBA
Chief Executive Officer
Community Mental Health Association
of Michigan
rsheehan@cmham.org

Percy Howard, LCSW
President and CEO
California Institute for Behavioral
Health Solutions
phoward@cibhs.org

Michael Sherraden, PhD (Ex-Officio Executive Committee Member)
George Warren Brown Distinguished University Professor
Washington University in St. Louis,
Brown School
sherrad@wustl.edu

Charles Lewis, PhD
President
Congressional Research Institute for
Social Work and Policy
celewisjr@crispinc.org

Audrey Shillington, MPE, MSW, PhD
Dean
San José State University, College of
Health and Human Services
Audrey.Shillington@sjsu.edu

Angelo McClain, PhD
Chief Executive Officer
National Association of Social Workers
naswceo@naswdc.org

Nancy Smyth, MSW, PhD
Dean and Professor
University at Buffalo, School of Social
Work
swdean@buffalo.edu

Mary McKay, PhD
Niedorff Family and Centene Corporation Dean of the Brown School
Washington University in St. Louis,
Brown School
mary.mckay@wustl.edu

Marvin Southard, LCSW, DSW
Past Director & DSW Chair
LA County Department of Mental
Health & University of Southern
California, Suzanne Dworak-Peck
School of Social Work
casasouthard@aol.com

Trina R. Shanks, PhD
Harold R. Johnson Collegiate Professor; Director, School of Social Work Community Engagement
University of Michigan, School of Social
Work
Faculty Associate,
Survey Research Center,
Institute for Social Research
trwilli@umich.edu

Martell Teasley, PhD
Dean and Professor
University of Utah, College of Social
Work
martell.teasley@utah.edu

Gautam Yadama, MSSA, PhD
Dean and Professor
Boston College, School of Social Work
gautam.yadama@bc.edu

Emeritus Members

King Davis, PhD
Robert Lee Sutherland Chair in Mental Health and Social Policy
University of Texas at Austin, Steve Hicks School of Social Work
king.davis@austin.utexas.edu

Diana M. DiNitto, Ph.D.
Cullen Trust Centennial Professor in Alcohol Studies and Education and Distinguished Teaching Professor
University of Texas at Austin, Steve Hicks School of Social Work
ddinitto@mail.utexas.edu

Rowena Fong, EdD
Ruby Lee Piester Centennial Professor in Services to Children and Families
University of Texas at Austin, Steve Hicks School of Social Work
rfong@austin.utexas.edu

Sarah Gehlert, PhD
Past President, AASWSW
Dean, University of Southern California College of Social Work
gehlert@usc.edu

J. David Hawkins, PhD
Social Work Endowed Professor in Prevention
University of Washington Social Development Research Group
jdh@uw.edu

James Lubben, DSW
Professor Emeritus
Boston College, School of Social Work
james.lubben@bc.edu

Edwina Uehara, PhD (Chair Emeritus)
Professor and Ballmer Endowed Dean in Social Work
University of Washington, School of Social Work
sswdean@uw.edu

Karina Walters, PhD
Professor, Katherine Hall Chambers Scholar Co-director, IWRI
University of Washington, School of Social Work
kw5@uw.edu

Patricia White, MSW
Executive Director, Fund for Social Policy Education and Practice
Silberman School of Social Work at Hunter College
pw182@hunter.cuny.edu

Luis H. Zayas, PhD
Dean and Robert Lee Sutherland Chair in Mental Health and Social Policy
University of Texas at Austin, Steve Hicks School of Social Work
dean-ssw@austin.utexas.edu

Appendix 1: Grand Challenges Leadership Board [431]

APPENDIX 2
Grand Challenge Network Co-Leads

Ensure Healthy Development for Youth
Kimberly Bender, PhD
Professor, Associate Dean for Doctoral Education, and Interim Associate Provost for Research
University of Denver, Graduate School of Social Work
kimberly.bender@du.edu

Melissa Lippold, PhD
Associate Professor, Prudence and Peter Meehan Early Career Distinguished Scholar
University of North Carolina at Chapel Hill, School of Social Work
mlippold@unc.edu

Valerie Shapiro, PhD
Associate Professor, Director of PhD Program, and Co-Director of the Center for Prevention Research in Social Welfare
University of California Berkeley, School of Social Welfare
vshapiro@berkeley.edu

Close the Health Gap
Michael S. Spencer, PhD
Presidential Term Professor; Director, Native Hawaiian, Pacific Islander & Oceanic Affairs
University of Washington, School of Social Work
mspenc@uw.edu

Karina L. Walters, PhD
William P. and Ruth Gerberding Endowed University Professor and Associate Dean for Research, Co-Director of the Indigenous Wellness Research Institute
University of Washington, School of Social Work
kw5@uw.edu

Build Healthy Relationships to End Violence
Samuel R. Aymer, PhD
Associate Professor
Hunter College, Silberman School of Social Work
saymer@hunter.cuny.edu

Richard P. Barth, PhD
Professor and Past Dean
University of Maryland, School of Social Work
rbarth@ssw.umaryland.edu

Todd I. Herrenkohl, PhD
Marion Elizabeth Blue Professor of Children and Families; Editor, *Journal of the Society for Social Work and Research*
University of Michigan, School of Social Work
tih@umich.edu

Megan R. Holmes, PhD
Associate Professor, Director, Center on Trauma and Adversity
Case Western Reserve University, Jack, Joseph and Morton Mandel, School of Applied Social Sciences
mxh540@case.edu

Patricia Kohl, PhD
Associate Professor and Associate Dean for Social Work
Washington University in St. Louis, Brown School
pkohl@wustl.edu

Shanti J. Kulkarni, PhD
Professor of Social Work
University of North Carolina at Charlotte, College of Health & Human Services
skulkar4@uncc.edu

Jill T. Messing, PhD
Professor
Arizona State University, School of Social Work
Jill.Messing@asu.edu

Dexter R. Voisin, PhD
Dean and Professor, Sandra Rotman Chair in Social Work
University of Toronto, School of Social Work
dexter.voisin@utoronto.ca

Advance Long and Productive Lives

Guillermo Ernest Gonzales, PhD
Associate Professor
New York University, Silver School of Social Work
geg2000@nyu.edu

Jacqueline James, PhD
Co-Director of the Boston College Center on Aging & Work, Research Professor in the Boston College Lynch School of Education
Boston College, School of Social Work
jacquelyn.james@bc.edu

Christina Matz-Costa, PhD
Professor
Boston College, School of Social Work
matzch@bc.edu

Nancy Morrow-Howell, PhD
Bettie Bofinger Brown Distinguished Professor of Social Policy and Director, Harvey A. Friedman Center for Aging
Washington University in St. Louis, Brown School
morrow-howell@wustl.edu

Michelle Putnam, PhD
Professor and Associate Dean for Research
Simmons College, School of Social Work
michelle.putnam@simmons.edu

Eradicate Social Isolation

Suzanne Brown, PhD
Professor
Wayne State University, School of Social Work
fb7139@wayne.edu

Robert L. Cosby, Jr., PhD, MSW, MPhil
Assistant Dean for Administration
Howard University, School of Social Work
robert.cosby@Howard.edu

Sandra E. Crewe, PhD
Professor and Dean
Howard University, School of Social Work
secrewe@howard.edu

Michelle R. Munson, PhD, LMSW
Professor and Associate Dean of Faculty Affairs
New York University, Silver School of Social Work
michelle.munson@nyu.edu

Erika Sabbath, ScD
Associate Professor
Boston College, School of Social Work
erika.sabbath@bc.edu

End Homelessness

Benjamin F. Henwood, PhD
Associate Professor
University of Southern California, Suzanne Dworak-Peck School of Social Work
bhenwood@usc.edu

Deborah K. Padgett, PhD
Professor and McSilver Faculty Fellow
New York University, Silver School of Social Work
Professor of Psychiatry
NYU School of Medicine
deborah.padgett@nyu.edu

Create Social Responses to a Changing Environment
Susan P. Kemp, PhD
Charles O. Cressey Endowed Professor
University of Washington, School of Social Work
spk@uw.edu

Lisa Reyes Mason, PhD
Associate Professor
University of Denver, Graduate School of Social Work
LisaReyes.Mason@du.edu

Lawrence A. Palinkas, PhD
Albert G. and Frances Lomas Feldman Professor of Social Policy and Health; Director, Behavior, Health and Society Research Cluster
University of Southern California, Suzanne Dworak-Peck School of Social Work
palinkas@usc.edu

Harness Technology for Social Good
Brendan Beal, PhD
Assistant Professor
University of Montevallo, Department of Behavioral and Social Sciences
bbeal@montevallo.edu

Stephanie Cosner Berzin, PhD
Dean
Simmons University, College of Social Sciences, Policy & Practice
berzin@simmons.edu

Claudia J. Coulton, PhD
Distinguished University Professor and Lillian F. Harris Professor of Urban Social Research
Case Western Reserve University; Jack, Joseph and Morton Mandel School of Applied Social Sciences
claudia.coulton@case.edu

Shari Miller, PhD
Dean and Professor
Stony Brook University School of Social Welfare
Shari.Miller@stonybrook.edu

Melanie Sage, PhD
Assistant Professor
University at Buffalo, School of Social Work
msage@buffalo.edu

Jonathan Singer, PhD
Associate Professor
Loyola University Chicago, School of Social Work
jsinger1@luc.edu

Eliminate Racism
Michael S. Spencer, PhD
Presidential Term Professor; Director, Native Hawaiian, Pacific Islander & Oceanic Affairs
University of Washington, School of Social Work
mspenc@uw.edu

Martell Teasley, PhD
Dean and Associate Provost
The University of Utah, College of Social Work
martell.teasley@utah.edu

Promote Smart Decarceration
Pajarita Charles, PhD
Assistant Professor
University of Wisconsin-Madison, Sandra Rosenbaum School of Social Work
paja.charles@wisc.edu

Matthew W. Epperson, PhD
Associate Professor
University of Chicago, Crown Family School of Social Work
mepperson@uchicago.edu

Ashley N. Jackson, MSW
PhD Candidate Washington University in St. Louis, George Warren Brown School of Social Work
ashley.jackson@wustl.edu

Charles Lea, PhD
Assistant Professor
University of Houston Graduate, College of Social Work
chlea@central.uh.edu

Carrie Pettus-Davis, PhD
Associate Professor
Director, Institute for Justice Research and Development
Florida State University, College of Social Work
cpettusdavis@fsu.edu

Durrell M. Washington, MSW
PhD Candidate University of Chicago, Crown Family School of Social Work
dwashington5@uchicago.edu

Reduce Extreme Economic Inequality
Laura Lein, PhD
Katherine Reebel Collegiate Professor Emerita of Social Work, Professor Emerita of Social Work, Former Dean
University of Michigan, School of Social Work
Professor Emerita of Anthropology
University of Michigan, College of Literature, Science, and the Arts
leinl@umich.edu

Jennifer L. Romich, PhD
Professor; Director of the West Coast Poverty Center
University of Washington, School of Social Work
romich@uw.edu

Trina R. Shanks, PhD
Harold R. Johnson Collegiate Professor; Director, School of Social Work Community Engagement

University of Michigan, School of Social Work
Faculty Associate, Survey Research Center, Institute for Social Research
trwilli@umich.edu

Build Financial Capability and Assets for All
Julie Birkenmaier, PhD
Professor of Social Work
Saint Louis University, College for Public Health & Social Justice
birkenjm@slu.edu

Jin Huang, PhD
Professor of Social Work
Saint Louis University, College for Public Health & Social Justice
jhuang5@slu.edu

Margaret S. Sherraden, PhD
Professor Emerita
University of Missouri–St. Louis, School of Social Work
sherraden@umsl.edu
Research Professor
Washington University in St. Louis, Brown School
msherraden@wustl.edu

Achieve Equal Opportunity and Justice
Rocío Calvo, PhD
Associate Professor; Director, Latinx Leadership Initiative (LLI)
Boston College, School of Social Work
Rocio.calvo@bc.edu

Martell Teasley, PhD
Dean and Associate Provost
The University of Utah, College of Social Work
martell.teasley@utah.edu

Jorge Delva, PhD
Dean
Director and Paul Farmer Professor, Center for Innovation in Social Work and Health
Boston University, School of Social Work
jdelva@bu.edu

APPENDIX 3
Sponsors of the Grand Challenges for Social Work

Academic Sponsors
Arizona State University (Premier)*
Boston College*
Boston University*
Case Western Reserve University*
Colorado State University*
Columbia University*
Fordham University*
Indiana University
Loma Linda University
Loyola University Chicago
Michigan State University
New York University (Premier)*
Rutgers University
Smith College
The Ohio State University*
University of Alabama*
University at Buffalo*
University of California Berkeley*
University of California Los Angeles*
University of Chicago*
University of Connecticut
University of Denver*
University of Georgia*
University of Houston
University of Illinois at Urbana-Champaign*

University of Kansas
University of Louisville
University of Maryland (Premier)*
University of Michigan*
University of Missouri
University of Nebraska at Omaha
University of North Carolina
University of Pennsylvania*
University of Pittsburgh*
University of Southern California (Premier)
University of Tennessee
University of Texas at Austin
University of Utah
University of Washington
University of Wisconsin-Madison
Washington University in St. Louis

Individual Sponsors
Richard Barth*
Bratberg Torstein Dahl
Nancy Dickinson
Marilyn Flynn
Erika and Raheem Lay

*Repeat Donor

APPENDIX 4

Grand Challenges for Social Work: Vision, Mission, Domain, Guiding Principles, & Guideposts to Action

This statement is a guide for the Grand Challenges for Social Work as a national initiative to address each of the 12 Grand Challenges. The commitment to ending racism and other injustices is fundamental throughout the Grand Challenges for Social Work.

OUR VISION

The Grand Challenges for Social Work (GCSW) will shape a more positive future for our society by promoting culturally relevant, attainable, generative, multidisciplinary, scientifically sound, and sustainable efforts to address the 12 Grand Challenges. The GCSW is open and welcoming to all who wish to participate. The GCSW focuses on innovations to solve social problems, especially those that disproportionately affect the most vulnerable in our society. Foremost in this vision is complete elimination of injustices and inequities due to race, ethnicity, religion, sexual and gender identity and expression, abilities, custom, class, and all other human differences.

OUR MISSION

The mission of the Grand Challenges for Social Work is expressed in five priorities:

- To identify major social challenges for the nation
- To gather evidence based on rigorous science

- To design imaginative, effective, and culturally relevant solutions
- To promote policies and professional practices that lead to positive change
- To advance sustainable initiatives that achieve the positive impacts for *all* families and communities, tribal nations, and society as a whole

OUR DOMAIN

The domain of social work, and the domain for efforts to address the 12 Grand Challenges for Social Work, can be summarized by the words *social, scientific,* and *application*.

Social is fundamental. Humans are highly social, and social interactions are the most influential force on our planet. Social relationships in families, communities, organizations, education, and governance are basic to human growth, problem solving, and achievements of all kinds. Social relationships ultimately account for the most important advances in health, daily functioning, political stability, and world peace. The Grand Challenges for Social Work is committed to strengthening our capacity to engage in productive relationships that enhance well-being, reduce conflict, and bridge across the many factors that divide us. We support the design and implementation of positive social interventions that increase human efficacy and freedom, not coercive measures for problem solving and social control. We support delivery of programs and services that arise from and strengthen positive, healthful social relationships and institutions.

Scientific in this context means that knowledge and understanding are achieved through the development of theory and the collection and analysis of evidence. To be sure, social work operates with commitment, but that commitment is guided by science. We engage in and draw upon rigorous, high-quality research. The selection and use of research methods must always be consonant with the values and principles embodied in the initiative. The Grand Challenges for Social Work aims for research that informs and provides direction for design, implementation, and improvement of practices, programs, and policies to address the 12 Grand Challenges.

Grand Challenges for Social Work: Vision, Mission, Domain, Guiding Principles, & Guideposts to Action February 2019

Application refers to the use of knowledge for positive impact. Social work is an applied profession. We are not content just to know; we aim to know and do. The simple word *do* has profound ramifications. In knowledge building, social work must be as scientific as any academic discipline, but *the knowledge must also inform meaningful and consequential action*. This is a very high bar. It requires careful selection of issues and research questions; testing solutions that are efficient, scalable, and sustainable; and then making those solutions real and relevant in the world.

OUR GUIDING PRINCIPLES

The Grand Challenges for Social Work is grounded in a set of core principles that reflect the deepest commitments of the profession. These universal guiding principles are what social workers hold to be most worthwhile. They provide the aspirational conditions that shape our science and our professional practice. They guide us in our unwavering commitment to reduce human suffering, promote human development, and enhance human potential. Moreover, these principles shepherd inquiry and create pathways toward collaborative solutions; they direct choices in interdisciplinary and professional collaborations, and inform tests of outcomes.

The national endeavor to address the Grand Challenges for Social Work embraces social justice, inclusiveness, diversity, and equity. These principles are far more than guidelines and even more than intended outcomes. For social work, these principles are the pillars of outlook and action. These four pillars provide the foundation, form, and substance of all GCSW decisions and actions.

Social Justice

We strive to create a more socially just and equitable society through the science and solutions of the Grand Challenges for Social Work. We support diversity, community, intergenerational collaboration, and empowerment through the networks and coalitions formed to address the 12 Grand Challenges. The initiative promotes research on social, racial, tribal, gender, sexuality, abilities, and economic justice (among others), and social justice principles imbue the GCSW's choices and efforts.

Inclusiveness

In the GCSW, everyone is in. We build a society of full inclusion. We embrace diverse ways of knowing and methodologies to procure culturally and scientifically rich approaches that can produce meaningful, culturally relevant, and impactful solutions. The research and potential solutions for the Grand Challenges are strengthened when communities most affected have genuine voice and collaborative power—in other words, when they authentically join and contribute to this work.

Diversity

In the GCSW, we value the unique historical and cultural legacies and experiences of diverse populations, the contributions of those populations to society and community, and their partnership in the science and solutions for all undertakings. We value, respect, and support the cultural dignity and worth of all individuals, communities, and populations, including all genders, races, ethnicities, LGBT and two-spirit populations, abilities, religions, and nationalities.

Equity

Economic systems and strata of power can confer extravagant privileges to some while prohibiting equal access for all, thereby begetting injustice and inequity. Achieving equity requires continually challenging exclusive and unfair systems, including challenging them through action in economic and political arenas, where problems are produced and sustained, and also through the applied science that examines societal challenges. The concept of equity embodies values, worldviews, practices, and policies to ensure that all people—including but not limited to those who have been historically underrepresented because of their race, ethnicity, tribal status, age, ability, sexual orientation, gender, gender identity, socioeconomic status, geography, citizenship status, and religion—are represented in the design and implementation of actions to address the Grand Challenges, and particularly population-specific challenges. The pursuit of equity embraces diverse areas of knowledge, diverse ways of knowing, collaborative scientific and community based partnerships, and evidence-based solutions.

Challenging inequities and working in robust partnerships are the vehicles by which the Grand Challenges for Social Work initiative takes hold of large issues and promotes social change. All communities and populations deserve access to a full and healthful life, as well as voice and efficacy in how this is achieved. This access and voice are essential to a democratic, engaged, and renewing society.

Social justice, inclusion, diversity, and equity are the four pillars of outlook and action in the Grand Challenges for Social Work. Together these pillars point to an active, ongoing process requiring critical, deep, and continual engagement by everyone to promote effective social solutions in our own time and for future generations.

HOW EFFORTS TO ADDRESS THE GRAND CHALLENGES EMBRACE THE FOUR PRINCIPLES

Imagination, Discovery, and Innovation

The GCSW initiative embraces imagination, inquiry, and discovery, bringing to light improvements in research practices, new knowledge, and innovations to achieve meaningful and culturally relevant social solutions regarding each of the Grand Challenges.

Excellence

Excellence is advanced through design and practice of the highest-quality, culturally relevant research, and through the use of knowledge to shape social practices, social services, and social policies to achieve the objectives of the Grand Challenges for Social Work.

Integrity

All activities to address the Grand Challenges for Social Work are carried out with high standards of quality and protections against harm, and with accountability to professional bodies as well as to the communities and constituents we collaborate with and serve.

Service

Through beneficial research and effective innovations in practice and policy, efforts to address the 12 Grand Challenges respond to issues and priorities of the communities we collaborate with and serve. At the end of the day, the GCSW and all of social work are evaluated foremost on service to people and society.

Impact

Through all of the above principles, strategies, and efforts, the GCSW seeks meaningful impacts. As described above, social work is applied science, with strong emphasis on applied. In the GCSW, *impact* refers to *applications leading to major and lasting social change affecting large numbers of people.*

OUR GUIDEPOSTS FOR ACTION

The guiding principles of the Grand Challenges for Social Work are embodied in and realized by the following eight guideposts:

Recognizing contexts. We recognize contexts by acknowledging the reality and impacts of historical and contemporary occupations, thefts, repressions, exploitations, and genocides. These include settler colonialism, slavery, sexual and gender exploitations, and other political, economic, and social injustices. We seek to be honest about harms that have happened and harms that are still happening. This perspective supports research and innovations toward remedies that bring about positive development—for example, empowering tribal nations' restoration of sovereignty, eradication of deleterious intergenerational impacts of chattel slavery, and ending a long history of racialized mass incarceration. Recognizing the underlying roots of the Grand Challenges includes examining the historical and bio-socio-political contexts in which social problems take root, grow, and reproduce. Such examinations are necessary if efforts to address the Grand Challenges are to mitigate or eradicate the deleterious impacts of oppressive policies and practices.

Embracing resistance, resilience, and resurgence. Our efforts to address the Grand Challenges recognize and respect the power of communities and their strengths, including resistance, resilience, and resurgence of healthful practices that generate community and familial well-being and survival. In other words, the work of the GCSW is not all about problems—it is about the potential for positive development of all people and society as a whole.

Welcoming process. The GCSW initiative nurtures a culture of open-mindedness, compassion, and inclusiveness among all stakeholders and groups.

Broadening inclusion. Efforts of the Grand Challenges for Social Work are actively designed to bring in everyone and, in the process, to incorporate a broad and diverse range of scientific, professional, disciplinary, and communal voices representing people of diverse cultures, life experiences, and backgrounds.

Opening up to all perspectives. The Grand Challenges for Social Work initiative embraces diverse worldviews, methodologies, and scientific approaches to ensure that our efforts are culturally relevant and the proposed solutions are culturally respectful, safe, meaningful, effective, and sustainable.

Creating opportunities. The GCSW creates opportunities for critical engagement, discourse, and education relevant to each of the 12 Grand Challenges, with steady attention to social justice, inclusion, diversity, and equity across and within the networks organized to address the Challenges.

Engaging purposefully. The GCSW is dynamically engaging in community, tribal, agency, and transdisciplinary collaborations and partnerships within each Grand Challenge and across the initiative as a whole.

Evaluating accountability. The Grand Challenges for Social Work is committed to and building the process for analysis of whether and how research, education, and professional practice results in measurable population- and systems-level changes.

AUTHORS

The authors are members of the Committee on Values and Principles of the Grand Challenges for Social Work and are listed in alphabetical order:

Richard P. Barth, *University of Maryland* (rbarth@ssw.umaryland.edu)
Sarah Gehlert, *University of South Carolina* (sgehlert@mailbox.sc.edu)
Sean Joe, *Washington University in St. Louis* (sjoe@wustl.edu)
Charles E. Lewis Jr., *Congressional Research Institute for Social Work and Policy* (celewisjr@crispinc.org)
Angelo McClain, *National Association of Social Workers* (naswceo@naswdc.org)
Trina R. Shanks, *University of Michigan* (trwilli@umich.edu)
Michael Sherraden, *Washington University in St. Louis* (sherrad@wustl.edu)
Edwina Uehara, *University of Washington* (sswdean@uw.edu)
Karina L. Walters (Chair of committee), *University of Washington* (kw5@uw.edu)

ABOUT THE GRAND CHALLENGES FOR SOCIAL WORK

The 12 Grand Challenges for Social Work are the targets of a groundbreaking effort to champion social progress powered by science. Initiated by the American Academy of Social Work & Social Welfare, this effort seeks to address society's toughest social problems through the concerted work of many. Additional information on the Grand Challenges may be found at GrandChallengesforSocialWork.org or by emailing gcsocialwork@ssw.umaryland.edu.

APPENDIX 5

Progress and Plans for the Grand Challenges

Every day for more than a century, social workers have been on the front lines finding innovative ways to address our nation's toughest social problems. In 2016, the American Academy of Social Work & Social Welfare launched the Grand Challenges for Social Work (GCSW) to harness the ingenuity, expertise, dedication, and creativity of individuals and organizations within the field of social work and beyond to champion social progress powered by science.

This ambitious effort actually began several years earlier with the creation of a strong, evidence-based foundation for the initiative. A founding Executive Committee—which included some of the nation's leading scientists, educators, and policy experts—reached out across the profession and developed strategic partnerships with social work's national organizations, interest groups, and academic entities. The committee then issued a broad call for ideas for large-scale challenges to tackle, then ultimately distilled a list of more than 80 submitted concepts down to the 12 GCSW. Their criteria: that a grand challenge must be important, compelling to the broader public, and have a science base connected to interventions that could lead to meaningful and measurable change. These challenges were announced at the 2016 annual Society for Social Work and Research conference "Grand Challenges for Social Work: Setting a Research Agenda for the Future," in Washington, DC. Multidisciplinary networks were formed to support work on each of the grand challenges.

In 2020, as the nation and the world's attention focused on racial injustice and ending systemic violence against and oppression of Black people and people of color, an additional grand challenge was announced: the Grand Challenge to Eliminate Racism. Although the initiative had understood racism as linked inextricably to each of the first 12 grand challenges, the establishment of the Grand Challenge to Eliminate Racism brought greater attention to promoting culturally grounded, upstream interventions and prevention efforts designed to eradicate racist policies, bias, and discriminatory practices.

The 13 grand challenges are grouped under three broad categories:

Individual and Family Well-being

- Ensure healthy development for youth
- Close the health gap
- Build healthy relationships to end violence
- Advance long and productive lives

Stronger Social Fabric

- Eradicate social isolation
- End homelessness
- Create social responses to a changing environment
- Harness technology for social good

Just Society

- Eliminate racism
- Promote smart decarceration
- Build financial capability and assets for all
- Reduce extreme economic inequality
- Achieve equal opportunity and justice

RESEARCH

Building on the existing, robust bodies of research in each of the grand challenge areas is a critical component of the GCSW. Scholars from across the country have engaged in myriad research efforts and have published their findings in journals too numerous to list here. Some research highlights include the following:

- From the Grand Challenge to Advance Long and Productive Lives, network co-lead Ernest Gonzales, PhD, is conducting a study of best practices for intergenerational programs. He was also invited to present his work to help shape a research agenda on work, aging, and health at the National

Academies of Sciences funded by the National Institute on Aging. Nancy Morrow-Howell, PhD, network co-lead, is leading a research project to assess the effects of tutoring on the well-being of older adults.
- Related to the Grand Challenge to Create Social Responses to a Changing Environment, two studies provided insights and practical recommendations for the local communities of Flint, MI (Amy Krings, PhD, Dana Kornberg, PhD(c), and Shawna Lee, PhD) and North St. Louis, MO (Joonmo Kang, PhD, Vanessa D. Fabbre, PhD, and Christine C. Ekenga, PhD, MPH). Also, Praveen Kumar, PhD, Assistant Professor at Boston College, is conducting intervention research on the use of solar lamps to improve study time for children, reduce air pollution, and provide access to electricity in rural India.
- Special issues have been developed on many of the grand challenge topics, including social isolation, productive aging, smart decarceration, and mainstreaming gender.
- Rocío Calvo, PhD, co-lead of the Grand Challenge to Achieve Equal Opportunity and Justice, received a grant from the Russell Sage Foundation to conduct a study on how older Latinx immigrants navigate community resources. The findings and implications of the study How Social Protection Policies and Institutions Contribute to Older Immigrants' Well-being and Sense of Belonging in America will be especially critical in light of the coronavirus disease 2019 (COVID-19) pandemic.
- University of Washington School of Social Work Associate Professor Megan Moore, PhD, and a university team received more than $1 million from the National Institute of Justice to study intimate partner violence among youth.
- The University of Maryland and the University of Washington have created competitive research awards for PhD students. One recipient of the University of Maryland award went on to receive the 2021 Society for Social Work and Research Outstanding Social Work Doctoral Dissertation Award.
- the end homelessness network co-lead Benjamin F. Henwood, PhD, and his colleagues at the University of Southern California have been awarded a large-scale Patient-Centered Outcomes Research Institute grant on homelessness and COVID.
- Research from the Grand Challenge to Ensure Healthy Development for Youth and the Social Development Research Group at the University of Washington School of Social Work evaluated elementary-school interventions that helped children form healthy attachments to family and school, which led to positive relationships and responsible decision-making in adulthood.

- The study Family-Centered Treatment, Juvenile Justice, and the Grand Challenge of Smart Decarceration conducted by a team at the University of Maryland School of Social Work found that family-centered treatment shows more favorable adult criminal justice outcomes than group care, making it a potentially effective community-based service to support smart decarceration for court-involved youth.

EDUCATION

The engagement of universities and colleges, as well as professional organizations, has been central to the success of the GCSW efforts to educate the next generation of social workers to develop evidence-based interventions and policy proposals. Organizations and schools of social work across the country are weaving the grand challenges into their programs in a number of significant ways, from curriculum enhancements to core programming. Consider the following examples:

- An entire doctoral social work program at the University of Southern California, a postmaster's fellowship at Florida State University, and a dual-degree program at the Colorado State University School of Social Work and the Colorado School of Public Health all have been organized around the grand challenges.
- The New York University Silver School of Social Work conducted #NYUSilverUp4theChallenge—a student competition grounded in the principles of the grand challenges that reflect the unique and powerful ways that social workers are positioned to address the challenges. Topics ranged from the development of programs to eradicate social isolation, to examining food insecurity and instability in a changing environment, to ending homelessness by taking an antiracist stance in efforts toward eviction prevention.
- The University of Denver featured the grand challenges in their Science for Action series, and the University of Illinois at Urbana-Champaign School of Social Work held a Harness Technology for Social Good yearlong lecture series.
- Many of the grand challenges, including ensure healthy development for youth, reduce extreme economic inequality, build financial capability and assets for all, and harness technology for social good, have developed textbooks, education modules, and webinars to train students, professionals, and the public.
- Faculty around the country, including Azusa Pacific University and Fresno State University, have incorporated aspects of the grand challenges into

their curricula. The University of South Alabama uses a course in problem-based learning to examine the grand challenges. New courses have been developed to address the challenges, including courses on smart decarceration at the University of Chicago and University of Maryland School of Social Work.
- Countless books, book chapters, journal articles, and other publications have been written by network members and leadership team members about individual grand challenges and the Grand Challenge Initiative as a whole.
- More than 60 departments and schools of social work have formed the Western Consortium for the grand challenges to identify, highlight, and implement initiatives such as teaching innovations, new practices in field education, learning networks for scholarly professionals, and fresh concepts of community service.
- The GCSW has shared access to a variety of educational events, ranging from our own webinar COVID-19: Learning from History about Disaster and Economic Inequality, to The Art of Policy Practice: Navigating the Legislative Process, co-branded with Influencing Social Policy, a nonprofit organization for social work educators, students, and practitioners, and the National Association of Social Workers.
- The GCSW has partnered with Prof2Prof to serve as an intellectual hub for connecting network members and their contributions to the grand challenges. Prof2Prof is a platform that allows scholars, higher education faculty, doctoral students, and academic staff to share their best teaching, research, and management materials across disciplines and on a global scale. This partnership is intended to advance grand challenge goals related to education, shed light on the contributions of social work professionals, inspire collaboration and partnerships with other disciplines, and create a working space for the Grand Challenge networks.
- Grand challenges leaders and members have continued to be highly visible at national and regional conferences, participating in roundtable discussions, presentations, and special interest groups, as well as staffing booths and seeking networking opportunities at conferences held by organizations including the National Association of Social Workers, the Council on Social Work Education, the Society for Social Work and Research, the American Council for School Social Work, Wichita State University School of Social Work's POWER Conference, the Kentucky Association of Social Work Educators, and others.
- Wayne State University has committed faculty, staff, funding, and other resources to advance the grand challenges, particularly in Greater Detroit, and documented these efforts in *Rising to the Challenge 2017*.

POLICY

Advances in the grand challenges have come not only by educating students, social work practitioners, and our interdisciplinary colleagues, but by working toward policy changes at the local, state, and national levels. There has been a variety of activity on the policy front during the past 5ive years, including the following:

- The annual Social Work Day on the Hill brings together students and practitioners to Washington, DC, to discuss current social work-related policy issues and learn skills to become better advocates. The GCSW has also co-sponsored several legislative briefings.
- Members of the Grand Challenge to Build Financial Capability and Assets for All are leading a statewide policy experiment testing universal child development accounts, and findings have informed design and implementation of child development accounts policies in several states.
- In advance of the 2020 election, the Grand Challenge to End Homelessness released a comprehensive policy brief to educate state and federal officials on the issue.
- Members of Grand Challenge networks have contributed to several reports from the National Academies of Sciences, Engineering, and Medicine.
- Members of the Grand Challenge to Ensure Healthy Development for Youth have participated in creating the Colorado Statewide Strategic Plan for Primary Prevention and have worked to promote the infrastructure necessary to increase the use of tested and effective preventive interventions in Colorado, Utah, Massachusetts, and Delaware.
- Research by members of the Grand Challenge to Promote Smart Decarceration contributed to passage of the First Step Act (2018) prison reform bill.
- Members of Grand Challenge networks have provided congressional testimony related to several of the grand challenges.

PRACTICE

Hand-in-hand with education and policy work, involving social work practitioners in the grand challenges is imperative to achieving "social progress through science." During the first 5 years of the GCSW, there have been a variety of innovative and far-reaching efforts geared toward and involving the practice community, including the following:

- Skills webinars on policy and practice have been offered regularly to help social workers become more effective advocates. Topics have ranged from Stay Home? Housing Inequities, COVID-19, and Social Welfare Policy Responses to Making Change: Messaging Your Issue for Policy Audiences.

- Several of the grand challenges have been featured in podcasts conducted by social workers, including the Grand Challenge to Create Social Responses to a Changing Environment and the Grand Challenge to Promote Smart Decarceration.
- A PhD candidate at the University of Utah College of Social Work developed a state-of-the-art virtual reality photography-based simulation tool to help social workers assess in-home risks and protective factors for child abuse.
- The Grand Challenge to Harness Technology for Social Good led a webinar series on several ways technology has been incorporated into social work practice.
- Leaders of Grand Challenge networks have been instrumental in implementing programs and tools such as SurvivorLink, MyPlan, SWVirtualPal, and GenPRIDE Center that help social work practitioners and the people with whom they work.
- The Coalition for the Promotion of Behavioral Health has developed four training modules for students, practitioners, and the public on prevention practice, policy, and research.

THE CREATION OF INFRASTRUCTURE AND SUSTAINABILITY

The GCSW has also strengthened its organizational and leadership structure, and sought to create a sustainable funding strategy. It has invested in bolstering communications across the initiative and advancing a wide range of academic and other opportunities to share knowledge and ideas.

Growing momentum and increasing participation in the initiative during its first 4 years led to a reorganization in October 2019. A new, more traditional structure now includes an interdisciplinary Leadership Board with external partners and a five-member Executive Committee. These changes have strengthened leadership's ability to facilitate the work of the 13 Grand Challenge networks, address diversity issues, and position the initiative more effectively to secure external support and funding.

Other organizational highlights during the first 5 years include the following:

- **Developing a comprehensive statement to guide all the work of the grand challenges**. Adopted in February 2019, this includes *Vision, Mission, Domain, Guiding Principles, & Guideposts to Action*.
- **Creating sponsorship opportunities**. Sponsorships fund further development of research, interuniversity collaboration, and a wider public understanding of the broad aims and tools of social work. Funds also support infrastructure, including administration, the 13 Grand Challenge networks, webinars, website updates, coordination across networks, communications, and vital connections with other social work organizations

and partners. There have been six premier sponsors and 30 sustaining sponsors, as well as several contributing and individual sponsors since 2017. (Contributing sponsorships are $1,000, sustaining sponsorships are $2,500 per school/organization, and premier sponsorships are $7,500 per school/organization.)

THE CREATION OF COLLABORATIVE COMMUNICATIONS TOOLS

During its first 5 years, the GCSW built a collection of powerful communications vehicles to engage more fully those already involved in the initiative and inspire even more people to take up this important work and enter into and support the social work profession. These vehicles provide consistent messaging and are designed to help those involved in all the Grand Challenge networks spread the word about their crucial work more effectively.

Key communications vehicles include

- A Communications Collaborative made up of communications staff at universities and partner organizations that meets several times per year to share resources and ideas related to the work and promotion of the grand challenges;
- the *Up!* e-newsletter, which came out quarterly when it debuted in December 2017, and moved to monthly production in 2020 because the newsletter needed more space to share all the exciting news from across the grand challenges;
- an engaging website with everything one needs to know about the grand challenges—from information on each of the challenges and links to their websites, to valuable resources, including a COVID-19 Resources page with information specific to social workers and the grand challenges;
- an active social media presence with the Grand Challenges Facebook page, Facebook group, Twitter account @GCSocialWork, hashtag #Up4theChallenge, and LinkedIn page;
- a lively and informative YouTube page featuring original videos and archived webinars;
- colorful and compelling graphics, from logos to infographics, that illustrate the initiative or show how to get involved;
- a themed calendar for 2020 that focuses on one grand challenge each month, and uses social media to highlight work to advance the field and address some of society's greatest challenges; and
- the development of materials in 2020 to orient students to the grand challenges, including a video and other resources designed to help social work and other students find ways to join in the work.

INDEX

529 College Savings Plan, 409

AARP (American Association of Retired Persons), 155, 167
ACA. *See* Affordable Care Act
Accelerated Study in Associate Programs (ASAP), 32–33
accountability, 382
accountable care organizations (ACOs), 58
active employment policy, 295
Addams, Jane, 3, 63, 366
Adelphi University School of Social Work, 219, 221
adolescents. *See* youth
Adoption and Safe Families Act, 86
advanced data analytics, 242–243
advocacy, 57, 190, 221, 300, 403
Affordable Care Act (ACA), 48, 49, 50, 60, 54, 165, 345
affordable housing, 130, 191, 192, 299
Africans, enslavement, 359
Age-Friendly Cities and Communities movement, 131, 161
ageism, 113
 calls for innovation on, 132
 charge to social work profession on, 133-134
 ending of, 131–132
aging in place, 187
aging populations, 111–112. *See also* older adults; productive aging
air pollution, 208
alcohol misuse
 collaborations on problem of, 62–63
 consequences of, 61–62
 problem of, 61
 race and, 368

research development in, 60–61
workforce development to address, 63
algorithms, 239, 242, 243
Allen-Meares, P., 382
Amazon, 236
America Saving for Personal Investment, Retirement, and Education Act, 323
American Academy of Social Work and Social Welfare, 1, 4, 13, 311
American Association of Retired Persons (AARP), 155, 167
American Civil Liberties Union, 191
American Journal of Epidemiology, 156
American Rescue Plan Act of 2021, 60
AmeriCorps, 123, 128
applied ecological theory, 57
artificial intelligence, 239
ASAP (Accelerated Study in Associate Programs), 32
Asian people, 6. *See also* race
 family violence and, 90
 racism against, 361–362
 volunteer rates among, 122, 122f
asset building. *See* financial capability and asset building
asset inequalities
 consequences of 291
 emergency expenses and, 291, 322
 gender and, 289–290, 312
 in home ownership, 290–291
 net worth measure, 289, 290, 291, 371
 policy responses to, 299–300
 race and, 291–292, 312, 313, 371
 retirement and, 292
 transformative assets and, 291–292
 wealth accumulation opportunities, 298
 wealth gap, 279–280, 312–313
autism spectrum disorder, 152, 346

baby bonds, 300
bachelor's programs, 14–15, 343
Baltimore, violence, 87
Bank On National Account Standards, 321–322
banking services, 313, 314, 321
BASICS (Brief Alcohol Screening and Intervention for College Students), 32
Bass, Karen, 408
batterer's intervention programs (BIPs), 89–90, 96
benefit-cost analyses, 23
Berkman–Syme Social Network Index (SNI), 156
bias, 33, 38, 269, 377. *See also* ageism; racism
Biden administration, 192, 292, 410
big data, 234–235, 241–242
BIPs. *See* batterer's intervention programs (BIPs)
birth rates, 111
Black, Indigenous, and People of Color (BIPOC), 8, 76, 235, 235–36
Black Coalition Against COVID-19, 156
Black Lives Matter, 6, 231, 361, 413
Black people. *See also* race; racism
    criminal legal system disparities of, 260, 261, 264, 372
    economic inequalities, 280, 282, 289, 292, 311, 313
    family violence and, 90
    maternal mortality among, 54
    mortality rate from COVID-19, 341
    occupational status of, 119f
    police violence against, 236, 361
    volunteer rates among, 122, 122f
Blueprint of Federal Social Policy Priorities, 221, 403, 408
Blueprints for Healthy Youth Development, 24, 25, 32, 34
bottom-up approaches, 209
Botvin, Gil, 22
Brekke, John, 3
Brief Alcohol Screening and Intervention for College Students (BASICS), 32
Brown, Megan, 10
Build Back Better proposal, 292
building healthy relationships. *See* healthy relationships
bullying, 33, 75, 88, 146, 152, 162

business startups, 299, 299
Butler, Robert, 114

California Policy Lab, 189
Calvo, Rocío, 342
Carebanks, 128
caregiving
    COVID-19 pandemic and, 125
    current realities of, 124–126
    data on, 116, 124–125
    demand for, 112
    economic value of, 116
    financial support for, 126–127
    by LGBTQ persons, 125
    outcomes of, 115, 116
    psychoeducational support for, 125
    social support for, 150, 151
    transitions among working, volunteering and, 130
Caregiving Counseling and Support Intervention, 125
Cash and Counseling study, 127
CDAs. *See* child development accounts
Center for Artificial Intelligence in Society (at USC), 390, 426
Center for Homelessness, Housing, and Health Equity Research, 187
Center for Housing and Homelessness Research, 187
Center for Social Development, 417
Centers for Disease Control and Prevention, 48
Centers for Medicare and Medicaid Services, 58
A Century of Innovation (National Academy of Engineering), 425
Change Machine, 321
Chicago's CeaseFire, 87
Child Abuse Prevention and Treatment Act, 85
child care, 288, 298
Child Care Development Block Grant (CCDBG), 298
child development accounts (CDAs), 300, 317, 322–323, 318, 409, 417
Child Tax Credit, 293
child welfare systems, 23, 95, 100, 153, 244
childhood trauma, 163
children
    with developmental disabilities, 346

early education support, 297–398
health disparities of Latinxs, 345–346
maltreatment, 6, 73, 85, 91, 95–96, 100
poverty rates, 288–289
social isolation in, 151–154, 162–163
Children's Health Insurance Program, 23
Cities for Financial Empowerment Fund, 320, 322
civic service, 116, 122–23
civil rights era, 406
Civilian Conservation Corps (CCC), 295, 296
climate change, 10, 202, 213, 217, 218. *See also* social response to changing environment
Climate Conservation Corps, 296
coaching/ mentoring programs, 122
coalition building, 390–391, 416
Coalition for the Advancement of Behavioral Health, 1401
Coalition for the Promotion of Behavioral Health, 19, 21
code of ethics, 366, 373
Coffey, Darla Spence, 423
Cognitive-Behavioral Intervention for Trauma in Schools, 203
cognitive behavioral therapy, 96
collaborations. *See* interdisciplinary collaboration
collaborative modeling, 62
Collaborative on Healthy Parenting in Primary Care, 22, 24
collective violence, 73
College Savings Plan (529s), 409
Colorado, youth development initiatives in, 26
Columbia University, 249
commentaries, 406–407, 415–427
Commission on Social Determinants of Health, 55
Communities That Care, 23
community-based interventions, 391–392
for alcohol misuse, 62
in criminal legal system, 268
health equity and, 55
to strengthen relationships, 86–88
community-based research, 165
Community-Based Response Act, 408
Community Development Financial Institution Fund, 299

community empowerment, 55, 375
community engagement, 209, 378
Community Mediation Centers, 87
community-oriented research, 55
community resilience, 209
community revitalization work, 242–243
community safety, 270–271
community violence, 73
Comprehensive Child Welfare Information System, 100
concept papers, 368–372
congressional briefings, 24, 410
Congressional Research Institute for Social Work and Policy, 417
+ Connect, 166
Connect2Affect, 155
Connecting-the-Dots Framework, 78, 100
Consumer Financial Protection Bureau, 324, 331
Coronavirus Aid, Relief, and Economic Security Act, 191, 192, 299
Corporation for National and Community Service, 128
Council on Social Work Education, 62, 185, 219, 248, 394
couples' interventions, 93
COVID-19 pandemic
access to healthcare during, 58, 131, 231, 232
ageism and, 113
anti-Asian racism due to, 361–362
caregiving during, 125–126
disproportionately impacted groups, 314, 315, 341, 344–345, 369
economic effects of, 120, 285, 290
employment during, 120, 315
environmental change and, 202
financial hardship and, 314–315
gender and effects of, 315, 319
homelessness and, 191, 192, 184
legislation involving, 131, 191, 192, 299
mortality rate disparities, 48, 341, 344, 369
parental social support, 151
as racialized disease, 369
social dimensions of, 401
social isolation and, 147, 156–157
volunteer roles during, 123–124
CPBH. *See* Coalition for the Promotion of Behavioral Health

crime statistics, 75
criminal legal system. *See also* incarceration; smart decarceration
- community supervision in, 259, 268, 269, 263
- deinstitutionalization and, 268
- disparities in, 259–264, 270, 261, 372
- exit points from, 268
- family violence and, 89
- front-end changes to, 258, 265
- gender mainstreaming in, 261–262
- innovations in, 267–268
- overview of, 259
- poverty and experiences in, 260
- redressing existing social disparities in, 270
- reform accomplishments in, 271
- systemic bias in, 270

critical race theory, 89, 119, 376–377
Critical Time Intervention, 182
crosscutting issues, 10–11
CTC (Communities That Care), 23, 24
cultural competence, 379
cultural humility, 378, 379
curriculum guides, 398
cycle of violence, 91

data
- analytics, 232, 233–234, 242–243
- big data, 234–235, 242–242
- open access to, 234
- privacy issues, 234
- surveillance systems, 26, 100–101, 244

data science, 233, 248, 249
decarceration. *See* smart decarceration
decriminalization policies, 101
dementia, 147, 154
Department of Veterans Affairs, 186
Depression-era policies, 295
digital divide, 370
disabilities, people with, 147
disaster risk reduction, 203–204, 216
discrimination. *See also* racism
- COVID-19 related, 361–362
- in employment settings, 120, 132
- health and, 51, 56
- older adults, against, 113, 131–134

Distinguished Advisory Board, 13
doctoral programs, 14–15, 344

Dodd-Frank Wall Street Reform and Consumer Protection Act, 324
domestic violence. *See* intimate partner violence
Domestic Violence Prevention Enhancement, 86
domestic violence shelters, 148
Duluth-oriented (BIP) programs, 96

early-career scholars, 215–216
early education support, 298–300
earned income tax credit (EITC), 85, 292
Ecohealth Model, 57
ecological knowledge, 213
economic inequalities. *See also* asset inequalities; income inequalities
- concept paper on grand challenge, 371
- educational level and, 283, 285, 292
- in employment, 282–289
- gender inequities driving, 18, 289–290, 281–282
- government program eligibility and, 287, 293
- impact on children, 287–289
- labor market forces and, 280, 282
- nature of problem, 229–282
- policy responses to, 292–299, 401–402, 417
- race and ethnicity and, 280, 284–285, 289–290, 291–92, 371
- social work's role in, 299–300

economic insecurity, 120, 311
economic recessions, 280, 284, 290
economic sexism, 9
education, as racist institution, 374
Education & Learning Subcommittee, 395
educational curricula. *See* social work education
educational level
- active social workers by race and, 367t
- economic inequality and, 283, 285, 292

Educational Policies and Accreditation Standards, 248, 379
elder abuse, 73, 154, 161
elder mistreatment, 154, 155
eldercare, 124. *See also* caregiving
Eliciting Change in At-Risk Elders (or ECARE), 161

Emancipation Proclamation, 360
employee volunteer programs, 130
employment. *See also* workforce development
  benefits, 285–286, 296–298
  consequences of inequalities in, 286–289
  COVID-19 pandemic impact on, 120, 315
  discrimination, 120, 131
  educational level and, 283, 285
  employee volunteer programs, 130
  family policies in, 126, 296–290
  flexible work options, 120–121, 129
  gender inclusion in, 184
  government program eligibility and, 287, 292, 293
  hours of, 120–121, 285–286
  inequalities in, backward view of, 282–283
  job quality, 285, 286, 296, 299
  labor market conditions and, 280, 282, 283
  legislation, 126, 130, 287, 297
  multiple job-holding, 287
  nonstandard arrangements, 282, 286
  occupational status by gender, race and ethnicity, 120f
  of older adults, 112, 113, 116–121, 119f, 129–130
  outcomes of, 115
  policy response to inequalities in, 292–298
  public employment programs, 295–296
  retirement and, 112, 113, 116, 118, 120
  scheduling practices, 121, 285–286, 287, 297
  social relationships in, 157
  in social work, 410–411
  in technology field, 371
  transitions to and from, 130
  wages, 283–284
  working conditions, 285–286
engineering grand challenges, 425–427
environmental change. *See* social response to changing environment
environmental disadvantages, 52, 55–57, 63
environmental justice, 202, 209, 221, 204
Environmental Justice Curricular Guide, 219
environmentally displaced populations, 204–209
Equal Access Rule, 184
equal opportunity and justice, achieving. *See also* Latinx people
  agenda for Latinxs, 350–353
  concept papers on, 372
  intersectional analysis in, 8
  key areas of focus, 342
  next 5 years, 348–350
  overview, 341–342
  progress report, 342–348
  racial equality and, 380
equity. *See also* gender equity; racial equity
  financial, 315, 316
  intersections with race and gender, 212–214, 243–244, 393, 400
  in preventive interventions, 25
  youth behavioral health problems and, 36–37
Equity Task Force, 25
ethics
  in decision-making, 427
  social work profession's code of, 366, 375, 376
  technology and, 231, 249, 427
ethnic groups, racialization of, 349
ethnicity. *See* racial/ethnic disparities
ethnocentric monoculturalism, 363, 367, 377
evictions, 192
evidence-based training, 376
Executive Committee, 12, 396, 397, 415
extreme economic inequality. *See* economic inequalities
extreme weather events, 203

Facebook depression, 146
facial recognition software, 243, 235
Fair Employment Protection Act of 2014, 130, 132
Fair Labor Standards Act (FLSA), 297
families
  child care support, 287, 298–299
  economic inequalities of, 295
  living wages to support, 283
  in poverty, 229, 280, 293
  social support from, 157
  workplace benefits and, 296–298
FAMILY Act of 2020, 126

Family and Medical Leave Act, 126, 287, 297
Family First Prevention Services Act (2018), 23
family-focused interventions, 24, 33
family therapy, 88
family violence. *See* violence
family well-being, grand challenges for, 7
FCAB. *See* financial capability and asset building
federal legislation. *See* legislation
Fedock, Gina, 11
feminist approach. *See* intersectional feminist perspectives
feminization of poverty, 9
financial capability and asset building (FCAB)
  banking, use of, 314, 314, 324–325
  centering safety and, 317
  collaboration for, 326–327
  community-specific strategies, 318
  concept paper on, 371
  conceptual framework for, 315–316, 316f
  credit issues, 314, 325
  developments in, 324–326
  educating social workers in, 331–326
  emergency savings and, 299
  financial guidance for, 321–322
  future work on, 402
  gender-specific strategies, 318–319
  inclusive strategies for, 317–319
  knowledge building, 330–331
  measurement metrics on, 327b
  overview of, 310–311, 358–359
  policies for, 322–330, 417
  policies supporting, 299–299, 313–314
  principles of research and measurement on, 328b
  reaching underserved and disadvantaged, 324–325, 321–322
  research on, 326, 358
  role of social work in, 316–324
  technology in, 325–321
financial exploitation, 154
financial inclusion, 315, 316, 324
financial insecurity, 311–315, 326
financial literacy, 314, 330–331
financial products and services, 314–314, 324–325
financial risk, 314
financial technology, 325–321
financialization, trend of, 314–314
First Step Act, 12, 259
food insecurity, 216, 315
Forum on Promoting Children's Cognitive, Affective, and Behavioral Health. Activities (NASEM), 24
foster care, 22, 85
Foster Grandparents, 122, 128
Framework for Research Transfer, 57
friendly visitor programs, 122

gamification, 239–240
gaming, 239–240
gender advocacy, 207
gender analysis, 205
gender-based violence, 6, 7, 14, 76, 78, 99, 346, 369, 400
gender budgeting, 207
gender differences
  COVID-19 impact, 315
  financial literacy rates, 314
  homelessness and, 187–188
  impact of environmental change, 212–214
  incarceration rates, 264–265, 261
  income levels, 311
  loneliness, experience of, 154
  in net worth, 289–290
  occupational status of older adults, 116, 118–120, 118f
  transportation-related, 117
  violence and, 6, 9, 31–32, 78, 76–78
  volunteering rates by, 121–122, 121f
  wealth divide, 313
  youth development and, 31–33, 28–30
gender equity
  addressing in grand challenges, 393, 399–400, 402
  as goal of gender mainstreaming, 16, 16, 8, 11
  intersections with race and, 212–214, 243–244, 393, 400
gender exclusion, 10
gender identity, 9, 31, 76
gender inequity, 16, 17
gender mainstreaming
  aim of, 8–9, 11
  approach overview, 7, 16–17, 399–400

binarisms, rethinking, 9
connecting crosscutting issues, 11
in criminal legal system, 261–264
economic inequality and, 281–282
environmental change and, 204–207, 205f
financial capability and asset building strategies, 317–319
global connections, making, 10
health equity and, 53–54
of homelessness interventions, 183–185
Indigenous feminist framework for eliminating racism, 364–366
intersectionalities and, 9, 346–347, 400
linking research, policy, and practice, 11
mainstreaming intersectionality and, 346–347
power structures, disentangling gender from, 9–10
prioritizing transformation, 11–12
situating contexts and, 10
social isolation, eradicating, 147–149
technology, harnessing, 235–237
transportation equity for older adults, 11, 117–118
violence and, 76–78, 346
youth development and, 28–30
gender norms, 77, 184
gender parity, 11
gender response, 205, 207
gender-role stress, 33
gender sensitivity, 207
gender transformative (GT) approach, 29–30
gendered social control, 261–268
Generation Z, 154
GenerationPMTO, 35
genetics, 164–165, 362
Geneva Convention, 209
geographic information systems (GISs), 240
geospatial technology, 240–242, 235
geriatric assessment, 160
Global Agenda for Social Work and Social Development, 202
global connections, gender mainstreaming and, 10
globalization, income inequality and, 311, 313

global–local (glocal) eco-social justice, 242
Graham, Laurie, 9
"Grand Accomplishments of Social Work and the Grand Context of Social Work" (Sherraden), 5
Grand Challenges for Social Work, 358, 393
Grand Challenges in Social Work, 7–8
advocacy, mechanism for, 403
background, 1
barriers to, 416
changing context and input, responding to, 399–402
coalition building, 390–391
commentaries on, 406–413, 415–427
concept papers on, 368–372
continuous engagement in, 402
creation of, 4–7, 389
defined, 1–2
domains of, 358
educational initiatives, 13–15
engineering grand challenges and, 425–427
future steps, 403
history of, 3–4
journals featured in, 12
key papers on, 5
leadership, 392, 395, 396–399
list of 13 challenges, 7–8
networks for, 15–16, 393–396, 415
open and flexible frameworks for, 392–393
organizational structures, 392–393, 395, 415
pervasive injustice and, 341
positive approaches to, 391–392
publications, 7, 358, 393, 398
racism, addressing within original 12 challenges, 368–372
rationale for, 2
research-informed foundation, 406, 415
selection criteria, 5–6
stakeholders, identifying and motivating, 12–13
structures for, 13
subcommittees, 395
university support, 394–395
working committee members, 4
Great Depression, 3

Great Recession, 280, 284, 290
Green-EcoSocial Work Network listserve, 220
Green New Deal, 296
growth-fostering connections, 84

Hartford Center of Excellence at Boston College, 161
hate crimes, 361
Hawkins, J. David, 22
Head Start, 299
health
  alcohol misuse and, 61
  environmental change and, 202, 212
  population level, 51, 53, 55–58
  racial/ethnic disparities, 50, 53, 52, 54, 344–345, 368–369
  social determinants of, 49, 50, 52, 53–55, 411–412
  social isolation and, 145, 146, 147–148, 151, 158–159
  technology for monitoring, 238–239
  of US population, 50–51
Health and Retirement Study, 118
health apps, 166
Health Corps, 296
health determinants, 52, 53–55
health gap, closing, 47
  action priorities for achieving, 51–52
  behavioral interventions and, 51
  characterization of, 53
  community empowerment and, 55
  concept papers on, 368, 369
  gender mainstreaming and, 10, 53–54
  'leveling up' strategy, 57
  maternal mortality example, 10, 53–54
  models of, 57
  multisectoral advocacy to promote, 57–58
  research on social determinants of, 55–57
  settings-based approach to, 52, 55
  social determinants and, 53–55
  social work efforts on, 49–50
  social work's leadership role in, 62–64
health inequalities, 53
health insurance, 51, 53, 59, 60, 345, 351
healthcare
  access to, 51, 53, 58, 59–60, 130, 351
  addressing social isolation in, 160–161
  costs, 59–60, 62
  enrollment in, 55
  expenditures, 161
  family-focused interventions for youth, 24
  individual *versus* population focus of, 51, 55–58
  innovation in primary care, 58–59
  mental health services, 160–161
  representation in governance in, 55
  social needs and, 50
  telehealth visits in, 130–131
  workforce development in, 51, 60–61
healthy development for youth
  access to prevention programs and, 26
  accomplishments toward, 21
  action steps for, 21–27
  approach to, 20–21
  barriers to, 27–28
  community assessment and capacity building, 23–24
  concept papers on, 368
  funding for, 23
  future directions for, 20, 36–39
  gender and, 30–33, 28–30
  goal of, 19
  infrastructure, increasing, 25–26
  interdisciplinary leadership in, 28
  interpersonal identities and power structures in, 9–10
  public awareness of preventive interventions, 21–22
  publications on, 27, 368
  race and, 30, 33–36, 368
  science, completeness of, 30
  social work engagement in, 28–30
  summary on, 39–40
  workforce development strategies for practitioners on, 26–27
Healthy Kids Act (2017), 23
Healthy People 2020, 50, 51, 52, 75
healthy relationships to end violence, 72
  community interventions, 86–88
  concept papers on, 369
  conceptual framework for, 78–80, 79f, 80f, 81f
  core efforts, 99
  federal policies supporting, 86
  5-year strategic plan for, 98–99

[462] Index

individual skills, improving, 96–97
interdisciplinary work on, 97–98
interpersonal skills, strengthening, 91–93
mediation and, 87, 94
needs gap, 80
policy direction to relationship-building, 99–101
restorative practices and, 94–96
revision of grand challenge, 6–7, 72, 78
social work interventions, 88–91
societal strategies, 85–86
values approach to, 80, 84–85
higher education. *See* social work education
Higher Education Act, 342
Hispanics, 260, 264, 348. *See also* Latinx people
home equity, 292
home ownership, 290–291, 313
home visitations, 87, 91
homeless shelters, 9, 187, 184
homelessness
    accomplishments on, 182, 185–191
    approach to, 182–185
    concept papers on, 370
    COVID-19 pandemic and, 191, 192, 184–185
    current problem of, 181–182
    demographics on, 187, 370
    expanded research on, 186–190
    future directions, 191–194
    gender and, 9, 187–188, 183–185
    housing transitions for, 192–193
    key reports on, 186
    original call to action on, 181
    overview of grand challenge on, 181–182, 194
    policy advocacy for, 190–191
    race, rates by, 370
    racism and, 190
    upstream efforts, 189–190
    of veterans, 188–189
    workforce development and, 185–186
    of youth, 22, 188
Homelessness Policy Research Institute, 187
homicides, 75
Hopkins, Harry, 3, 295
household income. *See* asset inequalities; income inequalities

Housing First, 181, 182, 189, 190
housing initiatives, 192–193
housing markets, 291
Hull House, 366
human rights, 204
human service systems, 233, 244

IDSs. *See* integrated data systems
immigrants
    environmentally displaced, 204–209, 206
    healthcare access of, 60
    legalization of, 350
    naturalization of, 360
    social isolation among children, 152
    transportation services and, 11, 117–118
Immigration and Naturalization Act, 349
immigration policies, 342, 350, 360–361
Immigration Reform and Control Act (IRCA), 350
implicit bias, 33, 38
incarceration
    alternatives to, 101, 266, 268
    changing narrative on, 266–267
    gendered social control through, 262–268
    goal to reduce prison population, 269–270
    histories of, 258, 269
    public safety and, 266
    rates of, 257–258, 259, 372
    recidivism, 267
    school-to-prison pipeline, 391
income inequalities
    consequences of, 286–289
    current trends in, 282, 283–284, 311
    gender and, 311
    policies addressing, 292–299
    race and, 311
    reasons for, 311–313
income insecurity, 286
income support policies, 85
Indigenous feminist framework, 9, 364
Indigenous peoples, 49
    environmental threats to, 213, 217
    maternal mortality among, 54
    technology benefits to, 235–237
    in US history, 359, 360, 362

individual well-being, grand challenges for, 7
information and communication technology (ICT). *See* technologies
infrastructure, 25, 296
injustice, 341
innovation, 425
inSocialWork podcast, 218
Instiue on Aging at Boston College, 161
Institute for Social and Environmental Justice, 220
institutional racism, 52, 54, 98, 381
integrated care models, 64
integrated data systems (IDSs), 237, 242–243, 243
Intel's Encore Fellows program, 130
interdisciplinary collaboration, 412
  on environmental change issue, 212
  for financial capability and asset building, 326–327
  on problem of alcohol misuse, 61–62
  on social isolation, 164–166
  technology, harnessing for social good, 244–248, 245–247t
interdisciplinary leadership, 28, 64
intergenerational disadvantages, 52, 55, 58, 313
Internal Revenue Service, 292, 321
International Federation of Social Workers, 219
Internet, 237–238
Internet of Things, 239
interpersonal identities, 9–10
interpersonal skills, strengthening, 91–93
interpersonal violence, 73, 75
intersectional feminist perspectives, 7, 17, 11, 147, 204, 235, 364, 400
intersectional frameworks, 17, 9
interventions, scaling, 409
intimate partner violence (IPV), 73, 75, 85, 88–91, 91–96, 76, 346. *See also* violence

Jiwatram-Negrón, Tina, 10
job creation programs, 295–296
job loss, 344
job quality, 285, 286, 296, 299
Joint Venture Model of Knowledge Utilization, 57

Journal of Social Work Education, 185
Journal of the Society for Social Work and Research, 22
just society, grand challenges for, 8
justice. *See* equal opportunity and justice, achieving
juvenile justice system, 342

Kennedy, Edward, 128
Kids' Club, 96
Knowledge Brokering Framework, 57

labeling, social isolation and, 146–147
labor market, 280, 282. *See also* employment
Latinx
  consumer spending power, 350
  criminal legal system involvement of, 260, 264
  discrimination of, 120, 342
  economic inequalities, 290, 313, 314
  health disparities of, 344–345
  healthcare access, 345, 351
  integration process, 349
  legalization of immigrants, 350
  mortality rate from COVID-19, 341
  poverty rate, 350
  progress on equal opportunity for, 342–348
  racialization of, 349
  in social work profession, 343–344, 351–353
  terminology for, 348
  US population demographics, 348–349
  volunteering rates of, 121, 121f
  voting population of, 349–350, 350
  workforce participation, 118f, 120, 350
  youth, 35, 345–348, 350
Latinx Leadership Initiative, 342
law enforcement, 6
  facial recognition software, use of, 243, 235
  lethal force by, 260
  mandatory arrest policies for violence against women, 101
  police violence in, 235, 361
  racial profiling by, 260
  reform for, 268, 408

Law Enforcement Assisted Diversion (LEAD), 266
leadership, 4, 28, 62, 392, 395, 396–399
Leadership Board, 9, 396–397
Leadership Council for Healthy Communities, 156
Leadership Through Alliances program, 86
legislation. *See also* policies
  age discrimination protection, 121, 131–132
  COVID-19 related, 130, 191, 192, 299
  employment laws, 126, 130, 287, 297
  healthcare (*See* Affordable Care Act)
  on immigration, 342, 349, 350, 360–361
  on prison reform, 16
  on violence, 86, 101
  youth initiatives, 23, 26
lesbian, gay, bisexual, transgender, questioning, intersex, and asexual (LGBTQIA+)
  homelessness among, 188
  incarceration of, 264
  social isolation of, 152–153
  in social work, 347
  youth, 33, 77, 124, 152
life course perspective, 132
life expectancy, 111
life transitions, 130
LifeSkills Training, 26, 33
Littleton, MA, 129
living wages, 283, 284
loans, 193, 299, 314, 325, 371
local advocacy, 193
Local Initiatives Support Corporation, 321
loneliness, 146, 147, 148, 151, 153–154, 158, 162. *See also* social isolation
long and productive lives
  barriers to, 113–114
  challenge of, 111–112
  concept papers on, 369
  current realities of, 116–124
  discrimination and, 131–134
  environments to promote, 130–131
  metrics on, 116
  next steps for, 124–126
  opportunities for improvement of, 113–114
  outcomes of, 112, 114–116, 115*b*

  supportive interventions for, 126–130
longevity, 111
Lubben Social Network Scale, 157

machine learning, 239, 243
Macro Encyclopedia of Social Work, 219
mainstreaming gender. *See* gender mainstreaming
Maori, 49
Marshmallow Experiment, 38
masculinity, 33
mass incarceration, 259, 269–270
mass violence, 151
Maternal, Infant, and Early Childhood Home Visiting Program, 87
maternal mortality, 10, 53–54
Mauldin, Rebecca, 11
McCarran Walter Act of 1952, 360
McClain, Angelo, 419–422
McKay, Mary, 415–417
McMahon, A., 382
mediation, 87, 94
Medicaid, 60, 54, 126
Medicare, 130
Medicare Shared Savings Program, 58
mental health
  of children exposed to violence, 96
  healthcare for, 160–161
  incarceration rates and, 260–264
  of older adults, 115
  social isolation and, 145, 148, 156, 160
  technology for monitoring, 238, 239
mentoring programs, 122
Messing, Jill, 7, 8
microaggressions, 52
microsimulation models, 243
midlife, social isolation in, 153–154
migrants, 204
Millennials, 154
MindGeek, 235
minimum wage, 283, 284
misogyny, 10
mobile technologies, 166, 238
Model of Knowledge Translation and Exchange with Northern Aboriginal Communities, 57
model programs, 35
Money Smart program, 331

monitoring systems, 26
Montpelier, VT, 129
mortality, 10, 52, 53–54, 147–148
motivational interviewing, 96
Moving On initiatives (MOIs), 189
Murdered and Missing Indigenous Women, 6
Muslims, 361
myPlan app, 237

NASW 2021 Blueprint of Federal Social Policy Priorities, 408
National Academies of Sciences, Engineering, and Medicine, 24, 27, 50
National Academy of Engineering, 425
National Alliance to End Homelessness (NAEH), 186, 190
National Association of Deans and Directors of Schools of Social Work, 394
National Association of Social Workers (NASW), 366, 403, 408
National Center for Excellence in Homeless Services (NCEHS), 182, 185
National Conference of Social Work, 62
National Health Social Work PBRN, 396
National Institute of Minority Health and Health Disparities, 37
National Institutes of Health, 63, 167
National Intimate Partner and Sexual Violence Survey, 75
National Low Income Housing Coalition, 190
National Prevention Science Coalition to Improve Lives (NPSC), 22
National Research Council, 147
National Vital Records Program, 100
Native American populations, 6, 50, 349, 359, 360, 362, 370
natural disasters, 203
Naturalization Act, 360
Neighborhood Justice Centers, 87
net worth measures, 289, 290, 291, 371
networks, 15–16, 393–396
neuroscience, 162–164, 165
New Deal, 310
New York City, 130
nonbinary people, 17, 9, 188, 183–184. *See also* gender mainstreaming

OASIS Intergenerational Tutoring program, 122
obesity, 147, 151
occupational trends, 60–61
Office of Violence Against Women, 101
Ogbonnaya, Ijeoma, 9
older adults. *See also* productive aging
　ageism toward, 113, 131–134
　aging as problem, 112
　career development for, 121
　as caregivers, 122–124, 126–128
　challenge of advancing long and productive lives, 111–112
　current realities of, 116–124
　dementia in, 147, 154
　employer support for, 129–130
　environmental change, impact on, 216
　financial exploitation of, 154
　financial support for, 126–130
　gender mainstreaming for transportation equity, 11, 117–118
　homelessness among, 187
　life transitions of, 130
　maltreatment of, 154
　occupational status by gender, race and ethnicity, 118f
　problem analysis, 112–114
　retirement and, 112, 113, 116, 118, 120
　social isolation of, 156
　transportation equity and, 11, 117–118
　as volunteers, 121–122, 121f, 128–129
　workforce participation, 112, 113, 116–121
Older American's Act, 121
Olweus Bullying Prevention program, 88
online support groups, 166
online technologies. *See* Internet; social media
online training, 62, 161, 230
op-eds, 22, 191
open data, 234
open-source online training, 62
oppression, forms of, 17
Organization for Economic Co-operation and Development, 161, 280, 289

Paid Sick Leave Law, 130
Pandemic Recession, 284

[466]　Index

Parekh, Rupal, 11
parent–child relationships, 87, 88, 91, 151
parenting interventions, 24, 95
part-time employment, 118, 283, 284, 285, 287
participatory research, 38
Patient-Centered Outcomes Research Institute, 165
Patient Protection and Affordable Care Act (ACA), 50, 51, 52, 60, 54, 165, 345
patriarchy, 8, 400
Pearce, Diana, 281
Perkins, Frances, 412
person-centered research, 165
person-environment fit perspective, 134
person-in-environment perspective, 57, 158
personal ties, 147
Pew-MacArthur Results First initiative, 25
physiological tracking, 239
police violence, 235, 361
policies, 16. *See also* legislation
  advocacy on, 57, 190, 206, 300, 403
  antiracism, 381–382
  for asset building, 299–299
  emphasis on impacts, 407–408
  employment inequalities, addressing, 292–299
  examples of organized action, 409–410
  family economic supports, 296–299, 401, 417
  on homelessness problem, 190–191
  investing in human capital, 130
  research knowledge to action, 407
  roadmap for, 408
  social work's engagement in, 411–412
  violence, addressing, 86, 99–101
Policy Options for Improving Children's Wellbeing, 24
pollution, 209, 209, 212
population health, 50–51, 53
Positive Behavioral Intervention and Supports model, 391
posttraumatic stress, 204
poverty
  children in, 287–289
  criminal legal system disparities due to, 260
  feminization of, 10, 281
  Latinx, rate among, 350

older adults and, 120
rates in United States, 229, 280
of transgender and nonbinary people, 184
war on, 310
power structures
  gendered identities and, 9–10
  technology and, 235
  violence and, 88
Practice & Policy Subcommittee, 395
practice-based research networks (PBRNs), 395–396
predictive analytics, 243
preschool programs, 299
prevention science, equity and, 37–39
primary care settings, 58–59
primary social groups, 157
prison reform. *See* smart decarceration
productive aging, term, 114
Productive Aging Interest Group, 134
professional conference attendance, 377–378
professional development, 377–378
professional journals, 12
professional organizations, 12, 367, 377, 381
professional standards, 377
Progress and Plans for the Grand Challenges, 13
Progressive Era, 49, 310
Project Towards No Drug Abuse, 33
Promote Smart Decarceration Network, 16, 271, 272, 261
PROmoting School-Community-University Partnerships to Enhance Resilience (PROSPER), 23, 24
Protect Older Workers Against Discrimination Act, 131
Protecting Access to Post-COVID-19 Telehealth Act of 2020, 130
Psychological First Aid, 204
psychopathology, 63
public assistance programs, asset limits, 330
public awareness, 21–22
public dissemination, 218, 234
public employment programs, 295–296
public relations, 12
public safety, 101, 266, 270–271
public support, 21

Putting Prevention Science to Work
(Colorado), 26

quality of life, 112

race
   active social workers by education
      and, 367t
   defined, 362–363
   federal categories, 360
   one-drop rule of, 362
   as social construct, 362–363
   in US history, 359–362
race formation theory, 362
racial equity
   facilitation at individual level,
      374–375
   priorities to eliminate racism, 375
   in social work profession, 365, 372–
      378, 379, 381
   training in, 376–377
   violence, perspective on, 98
racial/ethnic disparities. *See also* Latinx
     people
   criminal legal system interactions,
      259–260, 261
   economic inequalities, 280, 284–285,
      289–290, 292, 313–314
   environmental change and, 212–214
   family violence and, 90
   in health and healthcare, 50, 53, 52,
      54, 344–345, 368–369
   in higher education, 343–344
   incarceration rates, 259, 260
   income levels, 311
   minorities in research, 63–64
   occupational status of older adults,
      118, 118f, 369
   social isolation and, 147
   technology and, 231, 243–244
   volunteering rates, 121–122, 121f, 369
   youth development and, 30, 33–34
racial tech gap, 370, 371
racism
   defined, 37
   financial vulnerability and, 326
   health and, 52, 60
   homelessness and, 190
   institutional, 381–382
   intersection with sexism, 6, 9, 364
   interventions for healthy youth
      development, 33–34
   references to across the GCSW,
      368–372
   social work's positionality with, 366–368,
      367t
   white supremacy and, 363
racism, elimination of
   grand challenge overview, 358–359,
      393, 399–400, 416
   Indigenous feminist framework for,
      364–366
   individual-level efforts, 374–375
   institutional and organizational
      policies, 381–382
   social work education curricula
      revisions, 379–380
   in social work profession, 379–380
   strategies to eliminate, 372–382
   workforce development and, 375–378
randomized controlled trials, 243
RE-AIM (reach, efficacy, adoption,
     implementation, and
     maintenance), 211
REACH, 124
Recovery-Oriented Care Collaborative
     (ROCC), 396
Reducing and Preventing Alcohol Misuse
     and Its Consequences workgroup, 61
refugees
   definition of, 205
   environmentally displaced, 204–209,
      205
   social isolation of, 10, 148
   youth in, 22
Refund-to-Savings initiative, 321
relational-cultural theory, 84
reproductive justice, 54
research
   on alcohol misuse, 61–62
   convening at conferences and
      symposia, 217–218
   on financial capability and asset
      building, 326, 358
   knowledge to policy action, 407–410
   practice-based, 58
   racism, addressing, 378
   results into practice, 406, 421
   on social determinants of health, 55–56
   on socioenvironmental issues, 212

underrepresentation of
  investigators, 63
Research Council of the National Alliance
  to End Homelessness (NAEH), 186
restorative practices, 89, 94–96, 272, 391
Rethink Discipline, 391
Retired and Senior Volunteer Program
  (RSVP), 122, 128
retirement, 112, 113, 116, 118, 120, 286
retirement savings, 292, 313, 314
risk assessment, 23–24, 92, 95
robotics, 239
Roosevelt, Franklin D., 295

SafeDates, 77
SBIRT (screening, brief intervention,
  and referral to treatment), 58, 62
school-based programs, 26, 161–162
School Success Project, 342
Schultz, Katie, 9
science, geography of, 52
Science for Action, 22
scientific development, 2–3, 30
SCP Communications, 12, 392
screening, brief intervention, and referral
  to treatment (SBIRT), 58, 62
Seattle, 266, 284
secondary social groups, 157
self-awareness, 374
self-control, 38
self-directed violence, 73
Senate Bill 1070, 267
Senior Community Service Employment
  Program, 130
Senior Companion Program, 122, 128
Senior Entrepreneurship Works, 121
SeniorCorps, 128
sensors, 238–239
Sequential Intercept Model, 266
Serve America Act of 2009, 122, 128
settler colonialism, 50, 52, 213, 364
sexism
  economic inequality and, 281, 282
  intersection with racism, 6, 9, 364
sexual assault, 78, 94, 187
sexual harassment, 32, 187
Sharma, Bonita, 11
Shelton, Jama, 9
Sherraden, Michael, 5
Skills for Psychological Recovery, 204

Skills2Care, 124
slavery, 359–360
Small Business Administration, 299
smart decarceration. *See also* criminal
  legal system
  accomplishments toward, 271–272
  community-based interventions, 268,
    271, 272
  concept paper on, 371
  defined, 258
  evidence-driven strategies in, 268–269
  family systems approach to, 272
  future directions on, 272–272
  gender and, 11, 261–264
  goals of, 269–271
  guiding concepts of, 266–269
  metrics for goals, 269
  overview of challenge, 257–259
  policymaking and, 267
  public safety and, 266, 270–271
  social capacity and, 265–266
smartphones, 166, 238
SMS text-messaging intervention, 148
SOAR (SSI/SSDI, Outreach, Access, and
  Recovery), 186
social capacity, 265–266, 267
social capital, 391
social control, 261
social determinants of health, 52, 53–55,
  55–56
Social-Ecological Model of Violence, 79f
social fabric, strengthening, 7
social health expenditures, 161
"Social is Fundamental" (Sherraden), 5
social isolation
  biological effects of, 151, 162
  in children and youth, 148–153, 161–162
  collaboration on challenge of,
    164–166
  concept paper on, 370
  COVID-19 pandemic and, 147, 156
  critical feminist perspectives on, 10,
    147–149
  current problem of, 145–146
  evidence on reducing, 147–148
  future progress on, 161–164
  health and, 145, 146, 147–148, 151,
    158–160
  historical progress of research on,
    156–158

Index [469]

social isolation (cont.)
  innovation to overcome, 165–166
  interventions for, 148, 153, 155
  in midlife, 153–154
  in older adults, 154–156
  overview of issue, 145–147, 167
  personal network size and, 145–146
  in practice settings, 160–161
  psychometric measures on, 156, 157
  of refugees, 10, 148
  research efforts to overcome, 158–160
  research priority areas, 166
  risk factors for, 155
  role of social work for, 165–166
  social problems related to, 146
  stigmatization and, 146–147, 166
  violence and, 151, 162, 164
social justice, 62, 84
  environmental change and, 201, 204, 206
  social isolation and, 166
  social workers' obligation toward, 366, 375
  technology and, 249, 235
social media, 146, 154, 166, 237–238
social network analysis, 157
Social Network Index (SNI), 156
social norms, 38, 77
social progress, 401
social response to changing environment
  approach to, 215
  assessment of progress, 211–212
  community engagement on local impacts, 209
  concept papers on, 370
  convening of research sessions on, 217–218
  curriculum development on, 209, 212
  demonstrable progress on, 212
  disaster risk reduction efforts, 203–204, 216
  displaced populations and, 204–209
  effects of, 201–202, 217
  food and water insecurity and, 216
  future directions on, 219–220
  gender and, 212–214, 204–207, 205f
  goals of grand challenge on, 203
  health risks and, 202, 212
  impacted groups of, 206–202, 212–214, 216–217
  importance of challenge, 209–211
  innovation on problem of, 212
  interdisciplinary collaboration, 212
  organization of grand challenge group on, 215–216
  overview of challenge, 206–203, 220–222
  productive aging and, 130–131
  public dissemination of information on, 218
  race and, 212–214, 370
  research projects and initiatives on, 216–217
  as social justice issue, 201
  urban adaptation and resilience practices for, 209
  youth engagement on, 217
Social Security, 120, 130, 186, 292
Social Security Caregiver Credit Act, 130
Social Service Corps, 296
social stratification, 53, 120
social structures, oppressive, 38
social support networks, 145–146, 151, 156–157, 158, 160, 161
Social Work, 393
social work education
  addressing racism in, 379–380
  campus initiatives, 13–15, 397–399
  certificate programs, 13, 211, 219, 398
  curricula on grand challenge topics, 27, 134, 185, 202, 204, 212, 219, 325, 397–398
  curriculum guides, 325, 398
  data science in, 248
  degree programs, 14–15, 343, 344
  student admissions criteria in, 380
  student demographics, 343–344, 351–353
  technology in, 248
social work educators
  bias, 380
  grading practices, 379
  Latinx faculty, 343–344, 351–353
  leadership role, 401
  sexual orientation of, 347
Social Work Leadership Roundtable, 394
social work profession
  advocacy work in, 299–300
  ageism, charge on, 132–134
  awakening to Grand Challenges of, 3–4

dichotomy of micro and macro in, 423
employment growth in, 410–411
engagement of, 28–30
healthy equity efforts in, 49–50, 51–52, 62–64
historical mission, 62
interdisciplinary efforts in, 49, 64
obligation to challenge social injustice, 366, 375
occupational trends, 60–61
organizational leadership in, 367
outreach, 220
policy engagement, 411–412
positionality with racism and white supremacy, 366–368, 367t
professional standards in, 377
racism in, 379–380, 382
relationship-strengthening interventions of, 88–91
role in financial capability and asset building, 316–324, 331–326
role in social isolation, 165–166
role on economic inequality, 299–300
scientific development in, 2–3
technologies, adoption of, 230–231, 232
value to society, 420
visibility, 220
workforce development, 26–27, 60–61, 62, 185–186
social work science, 3, 420, 421
Society for Human Resource Management, 126
Society of Social Work and Research, 12, 217
Spencer, Michael, 6
SSI/SSDI, Outreach, Access, and Recovery (SOAR), 186
St. Louis Group, 394
stakeholders, 12–13, 402
State Office of Behavioral Health (Colorado), 26
Steering Committee, 396
stereotypes
 of Black youth, 391
 gender, 268, 391
 of older adults, 113, 131, 134
stigmatization, 146–147, 164, 166, 318, 342

Stop Asian Hate, 6, 361
Storer, Heather, 9
Strengthening the Social Response to the Human Impacts of Environmental Change, 370
strengths-based approach, 98
structural inequality, 9
structural racism, 60, 54, 378, 380
student loans, 371
subcommittees, 395
Substance Abuse and Mental Health Services Administration, 58, 62, 186
substance use disorders, 160, 260–264. *See also* alcohol misuse
suicide, 147, 151, 240
Supplemental Nutrition Assistance Program, 85, 293, 330
Supplemental Security Income, 292
sustainable development, 209
Sustainable Development, Urbanization, and Environmental Justice, 217

Tane, 49
tax benefits, 299, 313–314
tax credits, 292–293
tax refunds, 321
Teasley, Martell, 6
tech ethics, 231, 427
technologies
 accessibility, 231, 237, 238, 370–371
 adoption by social workers, 230–231
 benefits and harms to society, 232, 243, 235
 development of, 234
 employment in tech companies, 371
 ethical use of, 231, 249, 427
 failure to incorporate into social work, 232
 financial, 325–321
 geospatial, 240–242
 interventions using, 148, 155, 166–166, 234, 249
 limitations to use of, 234
 racial disparities related to, 231, 370–371
 in social work education, 248
 unintended consequences of, 427
 wearable, 238–239

Index [471]

technology for social good
  accomplishments on, 244
  approach to, 244
  concept papers on, 370
  future directions on, 248–249
  gender and, 11, 243–244, 235–237
  innovations, 237–243
  interdisciplinary collaboration opportunities, 244–248, 245–247t
  leadership on, 231
  opportunities for improvement, 232–237
  overview of challenge, 230–232
  race and, 243–244, 370–371
teen dating violence, 97
telehealth, 58, 130, 166, 230, 231
telomeres, 162
Temporary Assistance to Needy Families, 85, 293, 330
text-messaging intervention, 148
text mining, 243
Thomas, Margaret, 10
time banks, 129
Title V of the Older American's Act, 121
toxic stress, 315
tracking technologies, 238–239, 240–242, 235
training curriculum. *See* social work education
transgender persons, 9, 31, 183–184. *See also* lesbian, gay, bisexual, transgender, questioning, intersex, and asexual (LGBTQIA+)
Translational Research Framework to Address Health Disparities, 57
transportation equity, 11, 117–118
trauma exposure, 63
trauma-informed practices, 97, 98, 204
Treatment Foster Care Oregon (TFCO), 32
Trump, Donald J., 361
trustworthy professionals, 427
tutoring programs, 122

Uehara, Edwina, 3, 4
underemployment, 284–285
unemployment, 284–285, 292, 315, 344
unemployment insurance, 287
United Nations
  1951 Convention Relating to the Status of Refugee, 205
  Sustainable Development Goals, 209, 425

United States
  ethnic group demographics, 348–349
  health of population, 50–51
  history of race in, 359–362
  immigrant integration, 348, 349
  older adult population in, 111
  poverty rates in, 229, 280
universal child allowance, 293–295
University of Chicago Poverty Lab, 189
University of Denver, 187, 219
University of Southern California, 187, 219, 390, 398
university programs, 14–15, 398
Unleashing the Power of Prevention (Hawkins), 19, 21
urbanization, climate and, 209, 217
US Administration for Children and Families and Prosperity Now, 321
US Census, 360, 370
US Council on Social Work Education, 202
US Department of Education, 391
US Department of Health and Human Services, 408
US Department of Housing and Urban Development (HUD), 189
US Financial Literacy and Education Commission, 330
US Interagency Council on Homelessness, 190
US Office of Management and Budget, 360
US Patriot Act, 360
USAccounts, 322
Utah, youth development initiatives in, 26

Van Hollen, Chris, 408
veterans
  homeless, 188–189
  suicide risk in, 240
Veterans Affairs Supportive Housing Program, 189
VetoViolence, 78
video games, 239–240
Village models, 161
violence
  bystanders of, 88, 77
  community risk factors for, 86
  cycle of, 91

defining, 73, 75–78
future violence interruption against children, 100
gender and, 9, 30–32, 33, 76–78, 262, 317
legislation on, 86, 101
mandatory arrest policies for, 101
police-related, 235, 361
psychopathology and exposure to, 63
race and, 90, 369
risk and protective factors for, 99, 317
Social-Ecological Model of, 79f
social isolation and, 151, 162, 164
social relationships and, 72–73
societal response to, 72, 90
statistics on, 75–78
in teen dating, 97
typology of, 74f
victims of, 91
Violence Against Women Act (VAWA), 86, 101
violence interrupters, 87
virtual reality, 240
virtual volunteerism, 122–122
Volunteer Income Tax Assistance, 321
volunteering
  creating opportunities for, 113
  current realities, 121–122
  economic value of, 116
  employee programs, 130
  federal recognition for, 128–129
  informal acts of, 122
  local support for, 129
  metrics on, 121–121
  positive outcomes of, 115
  rates by gender, race and ethnicity, 121f
  roles during COVID-19 pandemic, 122–122
  transitions among working, caregiving and, 130
Voting is Social Work, 350

Wachter, Karin, 10
wage growth, 280
wage inequality. *See* income inequalities
War on Poverty, 310
Washington State Institute for Public Policy, 25
water insecurity, 213, 216
water pollution, 209
wealth gap, 229–280, 313–314. *See also* asset inequalities
wearable technology, 238–239
weather-related events, 203
Western Consortium, 394
White privilege, 363, 379
White supremacy, 7, 52, 89, 235, 363, 366–368, 374–375, 381–382. *See also* racism
Whiteness, 363
women. *See also* gender differences
  criminal legal system involvement of, 264–265, 261–285
  labor force participation rates, age 55 and older, 116, 118–120, 118f
  transportation services and, 11, 117–118
  volunteering rates, age 55 and older, 121f
women's health, 53
workforce development
  on addressing alcohol misuse, 522
  to eliminate racism, 375–378
  for employed older adults, 121
  in healthcare, 60–61
  homelessness, training on, 185–186
  for roles in youth development and prevention, 26–27
workplace. *See* employment
Works Progress Administration (WPA), 295, 296
World Health Organization, 50, 57, 73, 161

Yortsos, Yannis, 425–427
Young, Whitney, 406
Your Money, Your Goals, 331
youth
  behavioral health problems of, 20
  bullying and, 33, 75, 146, 152, 162
  dating violence, 97
  engagement in environmental issues, 217
  gender differences, 30–33
  homeless, 188
  lesbian, gay, bisexual, transgender, questioning, intersex, and asexual (LGBTQIA+), 33, 77, 124, 152
  mentoring, 162

youth (*cont.*)
    overweight, 151, 152, 345
    parenting interventions, 24
    peer support, 164
    protective factors, 23–24
    race factors, 30, 33–36
    risk assessment, 23–24
    self-esteem, 146
    social isolation in, 146, 147, 148–153, 161–162, 166
    technology-based interventions for, 166
Youth Relationships Project, 97